Compiled by Graham Capel and R M Clarke

ISBN 1 85520 5556

BROOKLANDS BOOKS LTD.
P.O. BOX 146, COBHAM,
SURREY, KT11 1LG. UK
sales@brooklands-books.com

ACKNOWLEDGEMENTS

Eight years ago Fred Vogel, a long standing Australian friend and Lotus enthusiast, suggested that we publish a book on the early Lotus sports racers. The outcome was a 172 page Gold Portfolio covering the front engined cars only and which went out of print late last year. It was our intention to reissue the book adding a further 40 pages that had been uncovered in our library. That was before we were introduced to Graham Capel.

Graham, a long time Lotus afficionado and historian, came to our aid in a number of ways. Firstly, he located and kindly loaned us further valuable material including rare sales brochures, photographs, technical articles, and other fascinating literature that we never knew existed. Secondly, he agreed to write introductions to each of the sports racing models produced between 1951 and 1965. These introductions help to bring each marque into focus and to understand Colin Chapman's motivation during these formative Lotus years.

Our sincere thanks go to Graham for his generous help and for turning this book into a much more complete work of reference for Lotus enthusiasts. Our thanks also go to Fred Vogel who kindly supplied all our cover photographs from his extensive picture library.

Regular readers of Brooklands Books know that we rely on the generosity and understanding of the world's leading magazine publishers to produce books like this one. So we are pleased to express our grateful thanks on this occasion to the proprietors of *Australian Motor Sports, Autocar, Autocourse, Autosport, Canada Track & Traffic, Car and Driver, Car South Africa, Classic Cars, Classic and Sports Car, Lotus Engineering Co. Ltd., Motor, Motor Clubman and Special Builder, Motor Racing, Motor Sport, Motor Trend, Road & Track, Small Car, Sporting Motorist, Sportscar Quarterly, Sports Car, Sports Car & Lotus Owner, Sports Car Graphic, Sports Car World, Sports Cars Illustrated, Trade Magazine, Victory Lane* and *Wheels*.

R.M. Clarke

INTRODUCTION

The Front Engined Lotus Sports Racing Cars 1951-1959

Between 1951 and 1959 Lotus produced eight front engined sports racing cars each of which contained innovative engineering design developments. From humble beginnings using converted Austin Seven based specials, Colin Chapman developed his own chassis and produced his own sports car. Over the following eight years with a new Lotus model virtually each year, with each model distinctively different from its predecessor, Lotus rose from the ranks of a special builder to a race winning constructor of sports racing cars which included countless race victories at circuits throughout the world, plus success at world renowned international races at Le Mans and Sebring.

The Lotus Mark III of 1951 set the trend for Lotus lightweight sports racing cars, although the Austin Seven chassis formed the basis of the car with much Lotus modification, and an even more modified Austin engine.

The Lotus Mark VI of 1952 saw the beginning of the Chapman designed space frame chassis, and torsional strength with riveted body panels. The use of modified standard production components saw the Lotus developed independent suspension by divided Ford front axle which lasted throughout the first five models until 1957. Over three years of production Lotus sold some 110 Mark VI cars.

The Lotus Mark VIII of 1954 was a radical aerodynamic design for international sports car racing, and featured a fully triangulated space frame chassis on the prototype which proved effective, but impractical. Only seven Mark VIIIs were built. The remaining cars used modified Mark VI chassis and Lotus gained some impressive race victories to establish their reputation in British motor racing.

The Lotus Mark IX of 1955 saw the move to Lotus designed standardisation of specialised parts, plus modified aerodynamics on the body shape. About 25 Mark IX cars were sold, with a substantial number to the USA where Lotus's reputation was developing.

The Lotus Mark X, also of 1955, was a customer inspired move into larger capacity sports racing cars which caused Lotus some problems and included detachable chassis tubes, disc brakes, etc. Only 6 cars were produced.

The Lotus Eleven of 1956 was the major step forward which established Lotus as a winning sports racing constructor. It also set the trend for Lotus models beginning with the letter E. The Lotus Eleven was an exercise in style and shape. Component accessibility was superb and the car was offered in a choice of three options, and with a variety of body styles. The big innovation was the use of rack and pinion steering and later, with the Series 2 of 1957, wishbone front suspension that was to be the mainstay of Lotus design for the next three years and was used on five models. A total of 270 were built in three years of production, and were sold all over the world.

The Lotus Fifteen of 1958 was a larger capacity sports racing car aimed at international competition. When it worked, it worked very well and achieved some major international success for Lotus. However, it was hampered by the rear mounted Lotus 'queerbox' sequential gearbox on the earlier models. Twenty eight were produced and were driven at major international races to build on Lotus's reputation.

The Lotus Seventeen of 1959, was not a success. Chapman was too busy on a multitude of developments, and the innovative strut front suspension did not work adequately. A total of 20 cars were built.

The Rear Engined Lotus Sports Racing Cars 1960-1965

Lotus were slow to move into the rear engined innovation of the late 1950's, but when they did with their rear engined Lotus 18 in 1959, the supremacy was soon established. Stirling Moss in Rob Walker's Lotus 18 F1 scored the first Grand Prix victory in a Lotus at Monaco in May 1960, and Innes Ireland won at Watkins Glen late in 1961 to score the first Grand Prix victory for Team Lotus. In the meantime Lotus sports racers also became rear engined.

The Lotus Nineteen of 1960 was designed to continue Lotus prestige in large capacity sports car racing, and although only 12 cars were built, they were very fast. Most success was achieved in USA.

The Lotus Twenty Three of 1962 was a return to small capacity sports racing cars on which Lotus had built their reputation in the mid-1950's. This was as successful as its predecessors, and won races all over the world. It is still winning in historic racing today. Some 131 cars were built with engines from 1100cc-1800cc.

The Lotus 30 was a great idea, and a superb looking car when it was introduced in 1964, but it failed to deliver the goods. The problem was the lack of torsional stiffness in the uprated Elan type backbone chassis which just could not cope with the V8 power. A total of 33 cars were built.

The Lotus 40 of 1965 was the last sports racing car to be built by Lotus. It was a dismal failure and only 3 were built. It was a sad finale for Lotus to relinquish their construction of sports racing cars in which they had made such a name for themselves over the past 15 years.

Graham Capel - Lotus Historian August 2000

CONTENTS

Page	Title	Source	Date		Year
6	The Lotus Story - Part 1	Motor Racing	Nov		1954
8	The Lotus Story - Part 2	Motor Racing	Dec		1954
11	The Lotus Story - Part 3	Motor Racing	Jan		1955
15	The Lotus Story - Part 4	Motor Racing	Feb		1955
18	The **Lotus Mark III** Introduction	Graham Capel			
18	Emphasis on Sports Cars - The Lotus-Austin Mk III	Motor Sport	Sept		1951
20	First Born Mk III	Autocar	Dec	7	1988
24	The **Lotus Mark VI** Introduction	Graham Capel			
26	Lotus VI Brochure	Lotus Engineering Co. Ltd.			
28	The Lotus Chassis - Mk VI	Road & Track	June		1953
30	The Lotus Project - Mk VI	Autocar	Sept	25	1953
32	The Lotus - Mk VI Road Test	Autosport	Oct	2	1953
34	Lotus Salad - Mk VI	Motor Sport	Sept		1956
36	Build your own Sports Car	Wheels	Nov		1957
40	Lotus Maintenance - The Mark Six	Sports Car & Lotus Owner	Feb		1959
41	Two Days to Sunshine - Mk VI Part 1	Motor	Feb	11	1959
44	Two Days to Sunshine - Mk VI Part 2	Motor	Feb	18	1959
47	Any Old Iron... - Mk VI	Classic Cars	May		1984
51	The **Lotus Mark VIII** Introduction	Graham Capel			
53	A New Lotus-MG - Mk VIII	Autosport	Apr	9	1954
54	The Lotus Mk VIII Track Test	Autosport	Nov	19	1954
56	SIF at 134 mph	Trade Magazine			1956
58	White Spirit	Classic Cars	Oct		1997
63	The **Lotus Mark IX** Introduction	Graham Capel			
64	Lotus IX Brochure	Lotus Engineering Co. Ltd.			
66	The New Lotus	Autosport	Mar	18	1955
67	Pit Patter	Motor Racing	Apr		1955
68	Ninth Mark for Lotus	Autocar	Apr	1	1955
73	The Lotus-Eaters, to Cornwall and Back - Mk IX	Autocar	Dec	2	1955
78	Lotus Mk IX	Road & Track	June		1955
80	It's Easy to Build a Fast Lotus 9	Sports Car			1955
82	With the Lotus at Sebring - Mk IX	Sports Cars Illustrated	July		1955
87	Lotus, a Range of Build-it-Yourself Competition Models	Motor	Oct	12	1955
88	The Lotus Blossoms	Autocourse	Oct		1955
93	Lotus Mark IX - MG & Coventry Climax Power Units	Autosport	Nov	18	1955
95	Road Impressions of the Works Mk IX	Motor Sport	Jan		1956
97	49 Miles per Gallon at a Mile a Minute! - Mk IX	Motor	Feb	1	1956
101	Mark Nine as a Road Car	Sports Car & Lotus Owner	May		1957
102	SCI Visits Colin Chapman	Sports Cars Illustrated	Mar		1956
105	Lotus Maintenance - The Mark Nine	Sports Car & Lotus Owner	Mar		1959
106	The Most for the Least - Mk IX Technical Report	Sports Car Illustrated	Aug		1956
113	Nine in Line	Classic Sportscar	Jan		1993
118	Lotus Mark IX	Classic Cars	Jan		1984
120	Lotus Mk IX - State of the Art from '55	Classic Cars	Jan		1993
126	The **Lotus Mark X** Introduction	Graham Capel			
127	The 2-litre Lotus	Autosport	Apr	15	1955
128	Cars & Drivers - The James Dean Lotus	Victory Lane	Nov		1988
130	The **Lotus Mark XI** Introduction	Graham Capel			
132	Lotus XI Brochure	Lotus Engineering Co. Ltd.			
134	The New Lotus-Climax "Eleven"	Autosport	Feb	10	1956
136	Product of Genius	Autocar	Feb	10	1956
138	Lighter, Lower Lotus - Mk XI Le Mans	Motor	Apr	4	1956
140	The Mark Eleven Lotus	Autocourse	Apr		1956
142	The Lotus Mk XI "Le Mans"	Autosport	June	22	1956
144	Club Sports Lotus Road Test	Autosport	Nov	23	1956
146	Lotus for 1957	Sports Car & Lotus Owner	Nov		1956
148	Lotus 11 Le Mans Model Road Test	Autocar	Nov	30	1956
152	The Mark XI "Le Mans"	Road & Track	June		1956
153	Bare Maximum - An Open Verdict on the Basic Issues	Motor	Jan	9	1957
155	Lotus 11 Road Test	Road & Track	Mar		1957
158	Test Report on the Lotus Eleven Sports	Motor Sport	Feb		1957
160	Lotus for 1958	Sports Car & Lotus Owner	Oct		1957
162	Lotus Sports	Road & Track	Sept		1957
165	Lotus "Training"	Sports Car & Lotus Owner	Nov		1958
166	The Lotus XI Le Mans "85" Road Test	Motor	Dec	18	1957
170	The Lotus Club - Slight Screamer	Motor Trend	Dec		1958
172	Lotus Special - Powered by Nardi	Sportscar Quarterly	Dec		1958
174	Colin Chapman Explains why Lightweight Cars are Safer	Motor Racing	Oct		1958

174	Colin Chapman Explains why Lightweight Cars are Safer	Motor Racing	Oct		1958
176	Lotus Maintenance - The Eleven (Series One and Two)	Sports Car & Lotus Owner	Apr		1959
178	Lotus XI Series 1 & 2 Track Test	Motor Clubman and Special Builder	May		1961
180	Life with the Lotus-Eaters	Sports Car World	June		1963
186	Adrien's Masterpiece	Sports Car World	May		1977
190	Slippery Customer	Classic and Sports Car	June		1988
196	The **Lotus Fifteen** Introduction	Graham Capel			
197	Lotus Fifteen	Autosport	Apr	4	1958
198	Lotus Fifteen Brochure	Lotus Engineering Co. Ltd.			
200	The Lotus Fifteen	Motor	Apr	2	1958
202	Lotus Fifteen	Sports Car & Lotus Owner	Apr		1958
204	New Lotus Fifteen	Motor Racing	May		1958
206	And now the Fifteen	Autocar	Apr	4	1958
209	A Series Two Lotus Fifteen	Sports Car & Lotus Owner	Sept		1958
210	Lotus is the Word for Go! - Mk 15	Sportscar Quarterly	Sept		1958
212	Lotus - a New 1100cc Model and an Improved "Fifteen"	Motor	Jan	21	1959
215	Further Thoughts on the 2-Litre Fifteen	Sports Car & Lotus Owner	May		1959
216	Common Factors Lotus vs. Cooper	Motor	Apr	8	1959
220	Fertus? Lorari? Who Knows; It Goes!	Sports Car Illustrated	Dec		1959
222	Lotus-Alfa XV	Car South Africa	Apr		1961
226	Dizzy Addicott's Lotus-Buick Track Test	Motor Racing	Aug		1962
228	Lotus 15	Classic Cars	Nov		1975
232	Fine Fifteen	Sports Car World	May		1979
238	The **Lotus Seventeen** Introduction	Graham Capel			
239	Lotus Developments	Autocar	Jan	16	1959
241	New Lotus Seventeen	Motor Racing	Mar		1959
242	Lotus for 1959	Autosport	Jan	16	1959
244	New Lotus Models	Autocourse	Feb		1959
246	Lotus for 1959 - New Model Seventeen, Improved Model Fifteen	Sports Cars Illustrated	Mar		1959
248	Lotus Seventeen - Road Impressions	Sports Car & Lotus Owner	Aug		1959
250	New Lotus Lower Still - Seventeen	Sports Car World	May		1959
252	The Many Faces of Lotus	Sports Car Graphic	Sept		1959
258	Modified Suspension for a Lotus Seventeen	Sports Car & Lotus Owner	Aug		1961
259	Sorting out the Seventeen	Sports Car & Lotus Owner	July		1959
261	The **Lotus Nineteen** Introduction	Graham Capel			
262	Lotus Nineteen Sports Racing Car	Motor Racing	Nov		1960
263	Lotus Monte Carlo	Sporting Motorist	Dec		1960
266	The Lotus Nineteen	Autosport	Mar	31	1961
268	The Winner They Don't Want to Build - Tech. Report	Sports Car Graphic	May		1961
274	A New Lotus and a Mended Moss...	Motor	Aug	3	1960
275	Road Test Lotus XIX	Car and Driver	June		1961
279	Lotus Nineteen Monte Carlo	Road & Track	Apr		1961
282	The **Lotus Twenty Three** Introduction	Graham Capel			
283	The Lotus XXIII Sports Car	Autosport	Feb	9	1962
284	The Lotus Twenty Three	Autosport	Jan	5	1962
286	The Lotus Twenty Three - Monte Carlo in Miniature	Sports Car Graphic	May		1962
292	How Green is my Ear-'Ole	Small Car	Dec		1962
296	Track Test of Mike Beckwith's Lotus 23	Autosport	Dec	21	1962
298	Lotus 23 Driver's Report	Road & Track	Jan		1963
301	A Force to be Reckoned with - Lotus 23	Australian Motor Sports	Mar		1962
302	Riding the 23	Sports Car World	Aug		1963
306	The Normand Lotus 23B Track Test	Motor Racing	Dec		1963
308	Lotus 23 & Elva Mk 7 Track Test	Road & Track	Oct		1963
315	New Sound on the Circuits	Autosport	Feb	5	1965
316	Up-Dating the Lotus 23	Sports Car Graphic	June		1965
320	Lotus 23B Track Test	Canada Track & Traffic	Nov		1964
321	Hindsight	Autocar	Oct	27	1993
322	Lotus 23B Built to Win	Classic Cars	Apr		1985
324	The **Lotus Thirty** Introduction	Graham Capel			
325	Power-Packed Lotus	Sporting Motorist	Mar		1964
326	Biggest Yet	Autocar	Jan	22	1964
328	Lotus Thirty	Road & Track	Apr		1964
330	Lotus 30	Car and Driver	Apr		1964
332	JCB Lotus 30 Track Test	Motor Racing	Oct		1965
334	Nightmare come True	Classic Cars	Sept		1985
337	The **Lotus Forty** Introduction	Graham Capel			
337	Lotus 40	Motor Racing	Oct		1965
338	Forgotten Forty	Classic and Sports Car	July		1992
344	Lotus 40 Technical Report	Sports Car Graphic	Nov		1965

The Lotus story

By COLIN CHAPMAN

The first Lotus climbs a trials hill in 1947. Below the 1954 Mark VIII streamline Lotus winning the international sports-car race at Silverstone in July this year. Colin Chapman is driving both cars.

This is the story behind the development of Lotus cars, told by the man whose ingenuity has made the name famous in motor racing.

It was in 1951 that a Lotus car hit British sports car racing with sudden impact, but it was in 1948 that experiments first started with Austin Sevens.

I BUILT my first car when I was seven. I didn't realise it at the time but that car had independent front wheel suspension. I had cut a pram axle in half and that alone seemed to give my soap-box quite an advantage over the other competitors.

My interest in motor racing seemed to wane after that early experience, and although I was always interested in building mechanical things, and derived great pleasure out of a finished self-made product, I left cars alone.

At seventeen I went to London University, and during the following three years, between studies, I learned to fly in the University Air Squadron. This helped me when in 1948 I went into the RAF and continued my training on Harvards, because by then I had made up my mind to be a fighter pilot. This was probably the turning point in my career, because I began to read motoring publications in the Mess, and I was to learn subsequently that the RAF had no real flying opportunities to offer. I got more and more interested in motoring as a sport, particularly in the accounts of trials, which I thought was the one branch which perhaps I could afford and for which I could build a suitable car. It was in my endeavour to build a suitable car for trials that the Lotus series was started.

The first car was basically an Austin 7 chassis and engine, it was called a Lotus too but I am not going to tell you why. I have been asked many times the origin of the name of my cars but that cannot be divulged for several years. It is one of those things, rather like the chap who will never tell you why his friends call him "Stinker."

DETACHABLE BODY

To get back to the Austin 7, which was originally a fabric-body saloon I had found rotting in a garden. The first job was to get the car home and the second was to remove the body, but in fact it was one simple operation since the driver's door fell off when I first got in and the rest of the body detached itself as we towed it home. Then the interesting pro-

COLIN CHAPMAN

Colin Chapman, creator of the Lotus series sports cars is a structural engineer employed by British Aluminium Co. Ltd. With that company he is engaged on the development of light-alloys for commercial vehicles. Colin, aged 26, unmarried until October 16, 1954, is a BSc(Eng), and holds diplomas in Geology, and Hygiene Sanitation.

cess of building started. Apart from what I had read in books I had nobody else's personal experience to go on. There was nobody in my area that I knew of who had built a special, so I just had to think it all out myself—between 36-hour passes from the Air Force.

After stripping it all down, one of the first things I did was to box the chassis and modify the brakes. There was one thing which had stuck in my mind and that was that other Austin 7 Specials used to lose their tails, they just dropped off. To overcome this I built up a body framework with three bulkheads and stressed the whole on aircraft principles with double-ply skin on battens of ash. These battens formed a frame which I extended aft beyond the back axle to carry a rear extension to the body which held two spare wheels. The Austin 7 habitually over-steered so I turned the back-axle upside-down, which brought the links to the top, and without any sacrifice in ground clearance, obtained the understeer I required.

Apart from that the only alterations were obvious ones, but it was on that car that I did most of my early chassis developments. The obvious things were making special linkage and actuating cams for the brakes, putting up the compression ratio and fitting double valve springs. An inlet manifold was made for a down-draught carburetter. Then, of course, there was the usual tuning which everybody did to their specials.

MARK II

We had a lot of fun rebuilding that car during which I learnt a lot about car construction and the unforeseen snags that crop up, so I was highly delighted when I gained two class awards with it. About that time the RAF indicated that as I had served three years in the University Air Squadron and that short service commissions were not to be offered, I had the option of leaving, and so I left.

I had by now become engrossed in competition work and I must admit that the events themselves and the repair work which followed them had made life increasingly hectic in the limited time that short leaves had made available. I therefore welcomed the opportunity of devoting more time to this hobby which had by then become an obsession with me. I did regret having to drop my flying career but I have carried on club flying and still manage to do a little between racing commitments, although I really have little spare time.

After that brief but instructive experience with the first Austin 7, I decided that the next step should be an improved trials car. Again I used an Austin 7 frame but chose the popular 1172-cc Ford engine as a power unit. This was to be the Mark II Lotus. It went so well that although I had built it for trials, I began to think about racing it.

I eventually decided to enter for the 1950 Eight Clubs meeting at Silverstone. To my intense delight I won the 1½-litre sports-car race over the old Club Circuit after a tremendous "dice" with Dudley Gahagan on his elderly but potent Type 37 Bugatti. At the same meeting the first-ever 750 Formula race was held and won by Holland-Birkett in the "Orange TT Car"—a very famous Austin 7 which was running with a mildly tuned standard engine and not the potent power-unit which had originally propelled the car in the 1930 TT. I also had some success at speed trials with that car.

In next month's MOTOR RACING, Colin Chapman tells of the birth of his fantastic 750 Formula car—the Mark III Lotus.

Mark II Lotus—Ford 10 engine in Austin 7 frame—storms a trials hill at some time in 1950. Passenger is Rodney Nuckey, later also to become a successful racing driver.

The Mark II comes off the banking at Great Auclum Speed Trials. The behind-grille headlamps swivelled with the steering. Originally conceived for trials, the Mark II was later raced.

The Lotus story

By COLIN CHAPMAN—Part 2

Prescott international hill-climb 1951. Colin Chapman in his Mark III Lotus accelerates away from the start. This was after he had fitted a carburetter "schnorkel" which is described in this article and can be seen on the near-side of the car.

Lotus triangulated tubular structure, which in conjunction with boxed Austin Seven chassis members provided a stiff frame for coping with the power of the Mark III engine. The large-size double-choke carburetter and jubilee clip holding "schnorkel" can just be seen. Water is returned to the header tank from the light-alloy cylinder head by means of a specially made three-branch pipe. This was the first 750 Formula car to have hydraulic brakes. Note the powerful throttle pull-off spring and the Newton shock absorbers.

Since his earliest experience with a road vehicle Colin Chapman has aimed at improving the handling qualities of his cars. Alongside chassis development he has conducted unusual experiments to improve engine power output. This month the writer describes how he achieved success in early trials and early races with the Mark II and Mark III Lotus, and other developments in the Lotus series of cars.

IN the last issue of *MOTOR RACING* I told you a bit about the first Lotus, but before going on to describe Lotus Mk II I should explain the reasoning behind some of the earlier "mods," it was not quite as simple as perhaps it seemed.

My very first vehicle had been a three-wheeler of a make which happily is no longer produced. I kept it for slightly less than 29 hours, because in driving home after buying it I was so appalled at the way it handled, that the next day I decided on a re-sale. This came off, some one who was perhaps less critical than I took it away and left me £10 the richer. It seemed such easy money that I bought and sold a few more semi-derelict machines after that. As motor cars they were all right but they were all found wanting as far as I was concerned, I wanted to enjoy my motoring so gradually the idea of a Chapman "special" grew and grew.

A car is but a structure, as amenable as a building to stress calculation—if only one knows what stresses it must sustain and what safety factors are required. There was the "rub," because nowhere could I find the "open sesame." As I mentioned last month, there was nobody to ask, so I haunted the Institute of Mechanical Engineers library and read everything from the most learned papers to the non-technical articles in the motoring press. None clearly stated the answer, but they did suggest that there were such things as under-steer and oversteer, and that if you can spin the wheels you won't break the transmission.

Then I joined the 750 Club and talked to the chaps about this and that. If they didn't know exactly how and why, there were a lot of things about which they could and did tell me. When you plan a bridge or put up a building it is never exactly like any other one and a whole set of individual requirements must be evaluated and the best solution chosen. It's just the same with a motor-car.

INVERTED AXLE

Sometimes the requirements for a production car change but the design goes on because the manufacturers have a lot of money tied up in it, or for some other reason. Take the case of Austin Seven and oversteer. That may have been all right when the original "Chummy" staggered up to 45 mph, but it wasn't all right for me who wanted a snappy "special."

The reason for oversteer was obvious. The back springs sloped downwards so that as the car rolled on a corner the outside spring flattened and moved the back-axle backwards, whereas the inside one did the opposite, which together helped steer the car into a corner. The sports models got over it by having straight springs, but that lessened ground clearance and as the Mk I was for trials I wanted plenty of ground clearance. The obvious solution was to turn the axle upside down.

I shall never forget the first trial run with the Mk I. I was convinced that it would take another fortnight to finish the car, but Ray Wooton arrived on the scene and declared, "Nonsense, we'll have it going to-day." We did get it going but only as a two-man effort. Because there was no throttle pedal Ray sat on the bonnet and worked the throttle while I steered. As he chose to sit on the bonnet facing me at the wheel, yes, there was a steering wheel, his ideas and mine on cornering and the consequent desired throttle opening was difficult to co-ordinate. It was one of those experiences that becomes more amusing as times goes on and your memory gets hazier, and the more "cold sweat making" moments are forgotten.

At that time the trials car "vogue" was swinging away from large V8-engines to small, manoeuvrable Ford 10 powered cars, usually with Austin-Seven chassis. This chassis was becoming a great favourite with successful trials drivers because of its flexibility, the "whippiness" of the frame enabled the cars to traverse the most undulating country because the wheels were free, to a large extent, to follow the "ups and downs."

JELLY-JOINT

In deciding to race with the Mark II, I was confronted with an immediate chassis problem. As a fast road car it would need a stiff frame, but if I was to continue with any trials success I needed to retain the inherent "whippiness." I eventually hit upon an idea which turned out to be most effective.

The "top-hat" section members were boxed by welding steel strips along the bottom, as I had done on the Mark I. The structure was braced with a series of light steel tubes, and those "mods" gave me what I wanted, a light, stiff frame. Next I made what I have always referred to as my "jelly-joint," a device which was decided upon after spending some time studying tractor front "suspension" systems. They usually consist of a springless beam axle, pivoted in the centre to allow the front wheels great freedom of movement. Tractor front wheels will "pick their way" over the roughest going, but high speed on the road is out of the question.

My "jelly-joint" gave "tractor" advantages for cross-country motoring and rigidity for high-speed road work. The whole thing could be locked solid by the simple expedient of tightening two bolts with welded-on tommy-bars in the centre of the transverse leaf spring. The gadget was hidden from prying eyes behind a hinged aluminium plate, and it was my practice on arrival at an observed section after a high-speed run, to lift the plate, slacken the bolts and storm through with a really flexible chassis—it was highly satisfactory. As soon as the observed section was finished I would tighten up the "jelly-joint" and drive off to the next one with a perfectly good road car possessing excellent handling qualities. Naturally, I had to be a bit careful where I carried out my "tightening" and "slackening" because I wanted to keep the secret of my "jelly-joint" to myself.

It was a simple affair which consisted of a front-spring bracket modified to carry a pin which hung in a bracket attached to the chassis. This allowed the front axle to swing from a pivot. Two bolts, tapped into the bracket, were screwed down to make the whole assembly rigid. The arrangement can be seen in the sketch.

For the greater part of the car's life the engine of the Mark II was a perfectly standard Ford Ten unit, which I "came by" in a rather unconventional manner. I was still serving in the RAF and running the Mark I in trials during week-end leaves. Although I was having a fair measure of success with the car, my mind was already turning to thoughts of a Ford-engined machine, a type which was becoming increasingly popular amongst trials drivers because of its excellent power-output, low cost and first-class spares availability. Although the initial cost of one was comparatively low, it was that item alone which was stopping me from getting one—I had no money. However, when you want something badly enough there is usually some way of getting it—but luck has to be on your side.

It so happened, one morning, that I noticed a burned-out Ford-Ten saloon in a local garage, the car looked a dreadful mess but the main mechanical parts were intact. An enquiry to the proprietor confirmed my deduction that the car was an insurance "write-off." A few more enquiries and I located the owner who assured me that nobody had made him an offer for the "wreck." This was interesting, but what was more so was the fact that the engine was a reconditioned unit which had done only about a thousand miles. It was just what I wanted, so I got in touch with the insurance company and asked the price of the remains—thirty-five pounds. That was reasonable enough, but to a chap with no money at all they might as well have said thirty-five thousand pounds.

CHEAP ENGINE

Now, at that time I knew that a certain car constructor was buying all the Ford Eight and Ten parts he could lay his hands on. He was paying reasonable prices for all components, but particularly chassis frames if a log book was included. I called him up and offered the Ford Ten chassis complete with axles, running gear and log book at forty pounds which was accepted, so the first part of my plan had worked out all right. The next step was to tempt a car breaker with an "easy fiver." As I had no money I had to have a middle-man, so I made a deal. My breaker bought the burned-out car from the insurance company for thirty-five pounds. I removed the engine and gearbox at his premises and the

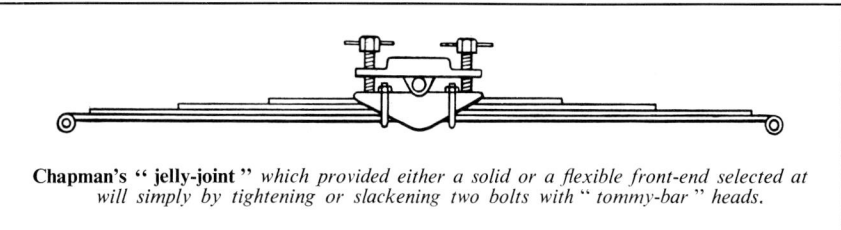

Chapman's "jelly-joint" which provided either a solid or a flexible front-end selected at will simply by tightening or slackening two bolts with "tommy-bar" heads.

Start of the 750 Formula race at the Eight Club's Silverstone meeting 1951. Mark III Lotus, No. 12, had only three pistons and was throwing up a smoke-screen. Although left on the line it later caught up and led by half a lap until the crankshaft broke.

chassis was passed on for forty pounds—clear profit of five pounds for him, and I was left with a 1000-mile Ford-Ten engine and gearbox. Most satisfactory.

As it turned out, I used an Austin-Seven gearbox and was thus able to sell the Ford gearbox for five pounds. So I made a profit of five pounds as well. That engine was used for trials and races in perfectly standard form. The car was light and steered well which accounted largely for its performance. The engine was still in standard form when I beat Dudley Gahagan's Bugatti at Silverstone. Later I fitted stronger valve springs, raised the compression and fitted a different carburetter which improved the performance a bit more.

750 FORMULA

Encouraged by the racing success of the Mark II Lotus, and having several ideas on ways of enhancing the power-output of the Austin-Seven engine, I decided that racing in general and the 750 Formula in particular was the thing for me. Accordingly I sold the Mark II to Mike Lawson who notched up a large number of trials and rally successes with it.

I had enjoyed my trials experience and successes, but I had taken up competitive motoring largely to prove that I could build a motor-car better than the next man, and I was finding out rapidly that trials were not the best proving ground. Luck enters so much into the results—you may have a "dry" climb whereas the next competitor goes up after a shower of rain. To go on improving the design of your vehicle under such conditions is a bit frustrating at times whereas racing seemed to offer just about every opportunity for "improvement of the breed," so I decided to concentrate wholeheartedly on that aspect of the sport.

I built the Mark III during the winter of 1950-51 and as the car was built to comply with the 750 Formula, an Austin-Seven frame was used again. In body design the frontal area was kept to the minimum, but it was the engine on which I lavished the most care and attention.

The Mark III went very well in its trials and its first racing appearance was at a Bristol MC and LCC's meeting at Castle Combe early in 1951. We had some trouble during practice period—fuel drops from the Ford V8 downdraught carburetter were being swept back into my face making it difficult to see at speed. This large carburetter was mounted outside the bonnet to preserve the low body-line and also to ensure a good flow of air to the intake. The carburetter was fitted with an accelerator pump which was causing an excess of fuel under large throttle openings and that was blowing back.

THREE-CYLINDER RACER

Obviously I had to cure the trouble somehow, but I didn't want to cut down rate of delivery at the pump. A visit to a garage in Chippenham produced a piece of "right-angle" radiator hose and in a matter of moments the air-intake was equipped with a facing-forward "schnorkel." It did the trick, no more fuel bothers. In the race we romped home the winner and lapped every competitor except the second man—a promising start, and the success of the car was no mere flash in the pan. In ten 750 Formula events entered, we won eight, blew up in one and failed to start in another.

Of these last two, the first one was at Gamston and on the way up I had trouble with valve guides on numbers two and three cylinders which worked loose and broke up.

Memorable "dice" between Chapman with his Mark II, and Gahagan with his Type 37 Bugatti at the 1950 Eight Club's meeting. The photograph was taken at Stowe Corner on the old " long " Silverstone club circuit. It was a contest between a racing car of a past era and the prototype of a future sports racing car, which the " modern " won.

Variations on a theme. Start of a recent 1172-cc Formula race which demonstrates Lotus progress and influence. Desoutter is in No. 118 Lotus Mark VI with exposed rear wheels and headlamps, Adam Currie is in No. 25 Mark IIIb with Ford Engine, whilst Nigel Allen is driving a Mark VI with enclosed rear wheels and headlamps. Car in foreground is not a Lotus but a definite Lotus influence can be detected.

As I had fitted a double-choke carburetter and a "de-siamesed" inlet manifold (of which more later), I was able to block up one carburetter choke, by cutting on suitably shaped gasket, and continue on numbers one and four cylinders only. The performance of the car on two cylinders amazed me, but nevertheless I decided to be a spectator at Gamston. On the way home I found I could work up to about 65 mph—not bad for a 375-cc side-valve "twin."

The other race in which the Mark III didn't finish was at the Eight Clubs meeting at Silverstone. A big-end bearing broke up during the practice period, so we withdrew the piston and rod and went racing on three cylinders. The car responded well, but unfortunately after working up a considerable lead the crankshaft broke and that was the end of that. Undoubtedly the greatest single factor towards the car's speed was the de-siamesed inlet ports. At the time of racing the Mark III this feature was a carefully guarded secret. The 750 Club subsequently forebade modifications of such a nature in the 750 Formula, but it may be of interest to explain the principles employed.

> *Next month* COLIN CHAPMAN *describes his ingenious engine modifications which were later to be disallowed in 750 Formula racing, and other developments in the Lotus series of sports cars.*

The Lotus story

By COLIN CHAPMAN—Part 3

Colin Chapman divulges some of the tuning secrets which have made Lotus cars so formidable.

THE Austin Seven, like most production four-cylinder side-valve engines, has inlet ports "siamesed" on cylinders one and two and again on three and four. The idea is to keep down production costs —and for touring conditions that form of porting is entirely satisfactory. "Siamesing" is the joining together of two cylinder inlets so that both are fed from one port.

Under racing conditions that system is not efficient, because the ingoing charge of fuel/air mixture to the inner cylinders (2 and 3) of each pair is robbed by its neighbour as each induction stroke takes place. The valve on No. 4 opens before the inlet on No. 3 is shut and likewise No. 2 inlet is shutting as No. 1 is opening on a 1, 3, 4, 2 firing order. This is an important factor at high engine speeds because it prevents complete filling of the inner pair of cylinders.

Racing engines which are designed as such from the start invariably use a separate port and carburetter for each inlet valve, with consequent efficiency because there is no direct connection between one inlet port and the next.

Modern racing engines are invariably of the overhead-valve type, which gives more power than side-valves due to better head shape, but nevertheless good results can be obtained with the "L-head" (side-valve) type of engine if its limitations are appreciated and allowed for.

FILLING THE CYLINDERS

Side-valve engine tuning is an art in itself. Although a lot of useful information can be gleaned from tuning ohv engines, before applying it considerable care must be taken to ensure that it applies equally well to the side-valve case.

For example, consider the case of breathing. In an ohv engine everything is concentrated on reducing the restrictions offered by manifold shape, by the carburetter, and by the shape of the valve head and seat, it being assumed that those are the limiting factors in breathing capacity. It is even worthwhile accepting some penalties in distribution and atomisation with four separate instruments, in the interests of better cylinder filling.

In the case of the side-valve, however, the ultimate limit on cylinder filling will be the restriction caused by the closeness of the cylinder head to the edge of the cylinder bore. For this reason it is generally futile to keep on increasing the

Colin Chapman *racing a 1172-cc Ford-engined Lotus Mark VI. In two years this type has become almost invincible in 1172 Formula racing.*

Mrs. Colin Chapman, *in 1952 as Hazel Williams, racing the Lotus Mark VI prototype with Ford Consul engine. Over sixty Mark VI models have been built.*

Handling characteristics *of Lotus cars depend largely upon the extremely stiff frame composed of round- and square-section steel tubing. Complex in appearance the structure is actually very light. It also serves as a body framework, the "stressed" aluminium panels of which further strengthen the frame. Mounting points for suspension and steering parts can be seen.*

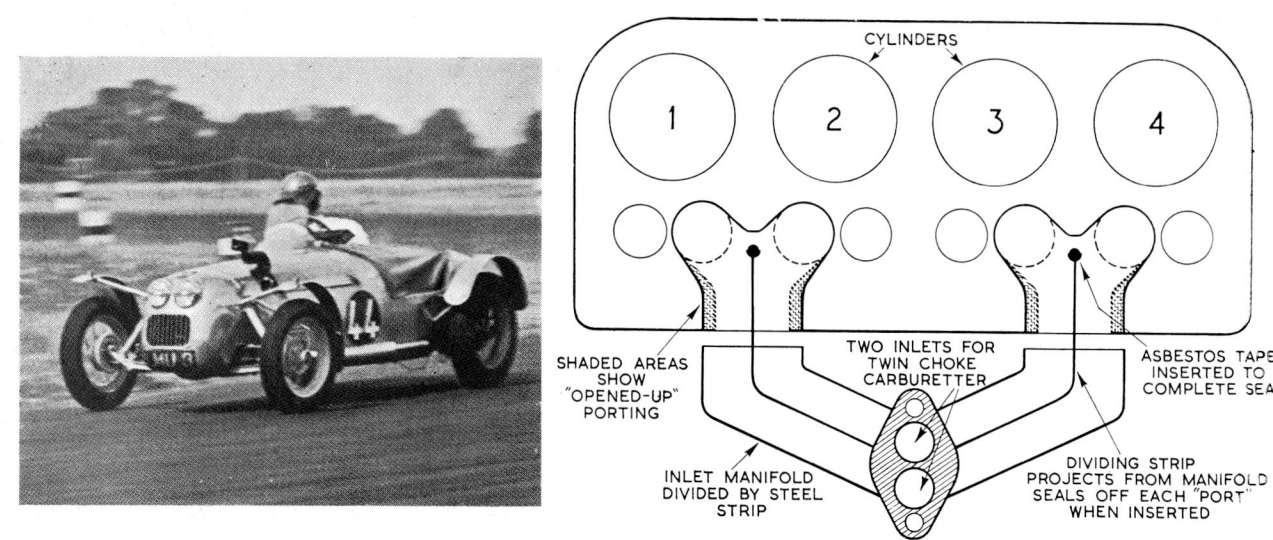

Chapman winning a 750 Formula race in the Lotus Mk III. (Right) Diagram of the Mark III's induction modification which played such a large part in the car's racing successes in the 750 Formula. Chapman hopes one day to build a 100 mph Austin Seven-engined sports car.

compression ratio because each increase brings with it a consequent reduction in breathing capacity, which is all right for "poke" low down but no good for more speed.

With the ultimate limit on breathing, set by internal considerations, it is better to try and improve the quality and quantity of mixture distribution by external modifications. For instance, more even mixture strength can be obtained from one carburetter of the fixed choke variety than from four separate units, and better atomisation can be obtained from using a slightly smaller choke size. Again, distribution can be improved by "centrifuging off" all the heavy globules of petrol round a sharp right-angle bend straight into a very hot hot-spot. Hence the use of the 30-hp V8 Stromberg downdraught carburetter, and the exhaust hot-spot for more "poke" on a side-valve engine. All these factors, although in ohv theory reduce the breathing, in actual fact give a very worthwhile increase in power and smoothness over the SU.

CARBURETTER TOO SMALL

Unfortunately this system could not be applied to the Mark VI Lotus as I have not yet found a sufficiently large Stromberg carburetter for the purpose, but I am sure that if one could get a suitable carburetter and was prepared for a very unsightly bump in the bonnet, then more power would be available from this set-up than the conventional twin SUs commonly employed to-day.

It was obvious that if I was to have more power from a "2-port block" than anyone else in 750 Formula racing, a modification which gave as near as possible the advantages of a "four-port head" was the thing to go after. No other competitor seemed to be paying much attention to this subject but I gave it a great deal of thought. It wasn't until I was enjoying a Christmas party in 1950 that the solution to this problem suddenly struck me. I seem to get my best design ideas after Christmas parties, probably because I have time to sit back and think. Anyway, the idea was to "de-siamese" the inlet ports. The 750 Formula requires that standard pre-war Austin Seven cylinder blocks only may be used, but some "mods" had to be made somewhere to achieve the end.

INDUCTION MODIFICATION

The first step was to open up the inlet port areas by grinding away the cast-iron on each side of the passages. A special inlet manifold was then built-up from sheet steel welded together, with a vertical steel strip division down the centre of the manifold which divided each pair of cylinders. This dividing strip, which as the sketch shows virtually made two manifolds from one, was arranged to project out of each manifold so as to divide also the inlet port passages in the block, thus each valve had its own separate port. A piece of asbestos tape acted as a seal where each end of the strip butted against the inside of the casting.

As mentioned already, a twin-choke downdraught Ford V8 carburetter was used. Each of the chokes mated with its corresponding port in the top flange of the manifold, providing in effect a twin carburetter induction system. The modification permitted a clean alternate "pull" on each induction stroke which reduced the "changes of direction" inevitable with an ordinary 2-port system with only one carburetter. This resulted in a worthwhile power increase and for the season that I raced the car, no other 750 Formula car could beat it.

The 750 Club subsequently incorporated in its Formula the clause, "Inlet and exhaust ports must not be reversed in function, nor must the siamesed inlet ports be divided." I think it was a pity to make such a restriction on development because I am sure the Austin engine has a potential which has not been exploited to the full, and that was one modification which really made the car go fast. I have reached "96" by rev-counter calculations on the slightly uphill straight of the old Silverstone Club Circuit and I am quite sure that 100 mph with an unblown Austin 7-engined sports car is possible. One of these days I am going to build a car like that. By that I mean a proper road sports/racing car with decent suspension and brakes as against those rather basic-looking vehicles that were reputed to have reached 100 mph "coming off the banking" at Brooklands before the war. I would have made one long ago, but with my racing commitments, the Company and my job, I have little spare time.

COMPANY FORMED

With the end of the 1951 season, I was completely "sold" on racing, not only for enjoyment but because of the lessons I was learning about development. Lotus Mark III had performed so well that people were asking me to build Lotus cars for them too and it was that demand which prompted me to form Lotus Engineering Company Limited.

My associate in Lotus Engineering was Michael Allen, whose brother Nigel has since become well known in competition with Lotus cars. We two shared the financial responsibilities of the company and there has not been any other financial backing.

Up to then all Lotus cars had had modified Austin Seven frames, the early ones because they were simple, easily obtainable, and excellent for starting with in competition motoring. The Mark III had to have Austin Seven main chassis side-members because the 750 Formula required it.

My ultimate idea was to build lightweight cars with rigid frames but as mentioned already the Austin Seven chassis is too flexible. My training as an engineer gave me a knowledge of stressing and I have always tried to apply that knowledge to the design and construction of all "production" Lotus cars. In the case of the Mark III I decided that the Austin Seven side-members were not nearly rigid enough so, as on the Mark II, I welded a steel strip along the bottom of each frame member.

BUILD IT YOURSELF

This modification, which resulted in the side-members becoming box-section pattern, increased the rigidity a little, but not enough, so in addition I built up a multi-tubular structure which was bolted to the chassis frame. This stiffened the chassis. A few more tubes were added to carry the body panelling, which again contributed to the stiffness of the complete structure. These "mods" added weight but the consequent rigidity was worth it. It meant that I could use really soft suspension and achieve good directional control—it worked out very well.

When Lotus Engineering came into existence we set out to design a car which could be bought "in sections" and assembled by any enthusiast who was

Mike Lawson *storms a trials hill with the first " production " Lotus. This three-year-old car is still performing regularly, and recently won the Roy Fedden Trial.*

Club Racing. *Dave Kelsey talking to owner-driver Nigel Allen (in cap) while a quick transmission change-over is made between Silverstone races.*

competent with spanner and drill. We were not tied to the Austin Seven chassis for that so I set out to design a multi-tubular frame of great strength and low weight.

I do not believe in the "two-tube" chassis principle, the type of frame which has two large-diameter steel tubes as the main frame members. Mathematically it is not as rigid as the multi-tube "space frame." The "two-tube" frame seems to me to be a waste of time because the body framework has to be built on to it, and that could so well be employed as part of the frame proper, as in a "space-frame."

My idea was to build a robust multi-tubular "body-frame" which would be rigid enough to take the suspension parts, the drive and the engine. The suspension, engine, transmission and so on could be bolted to this basic frame. The whole should be light and made so that with easily assembled "accessories" it would provide a fast car for the none-too-rich enthusiast for racing and/or touring.

It was essential that the engine, suspension and transmission parts should be of the, let us say, "popular" variety in order to make the supply position reasonable—and that problem didn't take long to solve. I had used Ford components on both the Mark II and part of the Mark III with complete satisfaction, so it was decided that modified Ford front axle, brakes, rear axle, torque tube, radius arms, gearbox, wheels and so on would be used.

Oddly enough, the first car we built to order was another Lotus for Mike Lawson—Lotus Mark IV with Austin Seven frame! The reason was that although the Mark II had given him every satisfaction, trials cars were becoming more and more extreme in design and it was necessary to

go a lot further to build a car capable of achieving success. The new car was built, Mike collected it and that was the last Austin-based car that Lotus Engineering made.

We decided to call our first tubular-framed car the Mark VI, Mark V was reserved for the 100-mph unblown Austin Seven-engined project which is still to be perpetrated.

The Mark VI was designed and built as a 1500-cc car and the prototype was very similar to the "production" cars which bear the same mark number to-day. That car was fitted with a Ford Consul engine considerably hotted up. A special cylinder head and camshaft was developed. We intended from the start that almost any engine up to 1500-cc capacity could be accommodated in the Lotus frame and we made sure that the "first" one had bags of power. It was just that. We were very pleased with the performance when the car was finished, but the cost of the Consul engine was in the region of £120 as against the Ford " 10 " at £50.

RACING CONSUL

Although the Consul-engined car did have bags of power, it was good torque rather than power at high revs and although the acceleration was impressive, the top speed was disappointing. I still think that the Consul would make a good competition 1½-litre engine if someone would design and sell a cylinder-head with good head shape for it—that is where I think improvement can be made. The bearings are large and I should think the engine is just about "unburstable." An oil-radiator is a necessary fitting if the Consul engine is to be raced.

We were a bit disappointed about top speed of the Mark VI but we were cer-

THE LOTUS STORY

tainly more than pleased with the road-holding and steering—it seemed that all the theories were working out. Then, as now, people ask me why I use divided-axle ifs. It was not arranged specifically to fit in with the use of Ford axle components, although it was very convenient. The reason for using a "swing-axle" is because I think that with a small, relatively low-powered car it is absolutely essential to keep your wheels as vertical as possible whilst cornering. As soon as your wheels start to lean out on a corner they develop camber thrust *away* from the direction in which you wish to travel. This camber thrust has to be resisted by an increase in cornering force and to provide this the wheel must run at a greater slip angle. Now as the slip angle is increased so does the drag, or rolling resistance, and this means that as a car with "leaning out wheels" goes through a corner it suffers a considerable retarding force which slows it down appreciably.

This effect is quite noticeable, and once or twice I have nearly been caught out when following one of these cars through a flat-out corner, as it gives the impression that the driver in front has applied his brakes although his stop lights have not come on at all. Also it must be borne in mind that a tyre under any given set of conditions can only generate a certain amount of cornering force and if some of this is being used up to offset camber thrust, then there is less available to counteract centripetal acceleration—so the cornering speed must suffer.

UPRIGHT WHEEL ANGLE

This wheel "lean out" is tolerable when there is tremendous power on tap to accelerate away from the corner but when the engine is of small capacity and relative low-power it is imperative that "way" is not lost through the fast corners. The finest way to achieve cornering with upright wheels is with a beam front axle, but this type of axle has several inherent defects in "shimmy" and "tramp" when used in conjunction with currently desirable soft suspension.

A "swing-axle" front end will give you an almost upright wheel angle if a low enough roll-centre is used and it will also provide the desirable soft ride in conjunction with ample suspension movement. This type of front suspension coupled with a "live" rear axle has gained Lotus cars the reputation for fast cornering. We found that the standard rod-operated Girling-Ford brakes gave excellent results as the car was light and maximum speed was not of the three-figure order.

Unfortunately soon after we had the "Consul-Lotus" built and running, we ran into financial difficulties and it was a problem for us to make up our minds on the next move. Our minds were made up for us. Nigel Allen, taking the car to Boreham where it was to be raced one Saturday in 1952, was involved in a pile-up which completely "wrote-off" the car. Nigel was unhurt, happily. It was heart-breaking to have the only Mark VI wrecked when it was just one month old. We had lavished so much thought and work on it but fortunately the other driver was convicted of "driving without due care" and the insurance money obtained just about put our finances straight again!

THE SECOND CHAPTER

As we were now financially in order, Michael decided to withdraw from the company, to which I agreed. I decided to carry on—enough had been learned from the Mark VI prototype in this short time to press on with the "production" models, I thought. Accordingly, Michael ceased to be a director of Lotus Engineering but Nigel continued to take a close interest and to race our products. Hazel Williams, my fiancee then and my wife now, took Michael's place as a director and we were all set to commence the "second chapter."

Eight "production" Lotus Mark VIs were built "straight off the drawing board" and I was so busy organising everything that I did not have the chance of driving one of them. They were all "cleaned-up" versions of the Mark VI prototype, and fitted with a variety of engines, MG J4, Ford 1100, MG TC, Consul and Ford 1172. The owners found there was no difficulty in assembling the cars with the Ford-based "bits" and they all reported high performance and good handling. This was very gratifying—I decided to build one for myself and see what they were really like.

Number nine was completed and a Ford "10" power-unit was chosen because it cost less. I raced the car with a fair amount of success and found that orders continued to come in at a fairly steady rate. Since the first Mark VI was sold, over seventy replicas have been built. Perhaps you are wondering where on earth I found the time to build so many cars.

Mine is a most unusual organisation. As I see it the only successful way the conflicting interests of production and racing can be reconciled is to keep the two entirely separate. I therefore have two separate organisations as it were, the Lotus Engineering Company which produces all the components under the very able management of R. L. "Nobby" Clarke, and Team Lotus which is an amateur staffed racing organisation which helps me design, build, and race, "next year's" model.

This band of enthusiasts are an indispensable part of the Lotus set-up and to name a few we have Mike Costin, who is number one, the "Uhlenhaut" of the crew, and is in charge of all engine and chassis maintenance and preparation. Mike's brother Frank Costin, who is a tame aerodynamicist employed by one of our leading aircraft companies, spends part of his time testing the car with a whole instrument panel full of pressure plotting instruments and a pressure probe, studying the high and low pressure regions. I have seen him strapped on to the car in most precarious positions at over 110 mph, "watching the air flow, old man!"

On the design side, and one who is with the same aircraft company, we have "Mac" Macintosh and Peter Ross who act as stressmen and produce reams and reams of "worse cases" which lead one to think that the chassis is going to break up any day!

The actual racing mechanics which help prepare the cars for and at the meetings are Tony "A.C." McKusker, Peter Mayes, and John Standen, with occasional intervention from Tony Holder and friends. Tony, by the way, is also our cameraman, full time he is employed by Kodaks but we have yet to see any of his films.

> *One of the most exciting designs of 1954 was Colin Chapman's Lotus Mk VIII aerodynamic car. It is that car which is described next month.*

WEST ESSEX CLUB

Nearly three hundred people sat down to dinner at the West Essex Car Club's annual function at the Park Lane Hotel on December 3. President of the Club, The Hon Gerald Lascelles, said in an after-dinner speech, that it had been a good year, membership was satisfactory and they had even enjoyed good weather for most of their events. He paid tribute to George Matthews who had been such an excellent competitions secretary for such a long time but who was resigning due to pressure of work with his own business. Thanks went also to Mrs. Matthews for her great help but the President believed neither was really lost to the Club. A presentation was made to them both. John Cooper of *The Autocar*, in replying for the guests, endorsed the tribute and remarked that George Matthews had set an example to other clubs. A large number of the awards were presented to Roy Salvadori, S. G. Greene, and Jim Russell for successes during the year.

Lotus Mark VIII, the streamlined car of 1954. The theories, the painstaking testing and development of this sports car are described in the final instalment of The Lotus Story. Colin Chapman also touches briefly on the necessary equipment for home assembly.

The Lotus story

By COLIN CHAPMAN—Part 4

AFTER three years in several classes of racing I started to think about a car for 1954. The new car would need to be as far ahead of other competition cars in its class as the Mark VI was when it emerged in 1951. That is the ever-present problem—always to keep one or two steps ahead of the competitors. People ask me why I don't give up racing and concentrate on design—the answer to that is that I must race the cars myself to find out design faults. Drivers are always a bit vague about handling and similar details so the only thing to do is to find out things yourself.

It seemed to me that an efficient aerodynamic body would be the thing to have for the 1954 season if some sort of a " march was to be stolen " on the others. Accordingly Frank Costin designed the now familiar Mark VIII body. I designed a new triangulated " space-frame " of 1¼-in, 20-gauge, steel tubing which would provide the utmost rigidity but would be without an ounce of superfluous weight. This car was for myself and to serve as a mobile test-bed to try out the various new features I had included.

The prototype was built during the winter of 1953-4 and weight was kept down to a minimum. Normally the main disadvantage of a streamlined body in racing was that of extra weight as compared with a " normal " body. We set out to produce an aerodynamic car which weighed less than most " conventional " sports/racing bodies—the never-ending problem of " keeping ahead."

A 1½-litre engine built-up of TC MG and Morris " 10 " components was chosen as the power-unit. This would give us a chance in the highly competitive 1½-litre class.

PROBLEMS OF STREAMLINING

A model was wind-tunnel tested and with a power-output of around 85 bhp, we estimated that the car could reach a maximum speed in excess of 125 mph. This coupled with the fact that the streamlined body was going to cause a fair amount of wheel and brake " masking," indicated that something different in the way of brakes would be required. Stopping a low-drag car from high speed, even if it is light, can be quite a problem and it is one that has yet to be solved on a production basis.

Another problem was the front suspension. I have already outlined my views on swing-axle " front-ends " and although

Frank Costin, *aerodynamics expert, made ten runs strapped in this position at various speeds up to 110 mph. He was studying air flow in the well behind the wheel by peering under the wheel arch. Wool tufts were attached inside the well and showed that air flow was virtually stationary up to 80 mph after which it flowed in the reverse direction.*

Chapman setting off *with Costin to record instrument readings. The pressure head with static and dynamic tubes was raised well above the disturbed air flow to avoid position error. Top three instruments on the panel are altimeters to measure the air pressure at various distances from the body surface. Bottom instruments are left, air speed indicator, and right, vertical-speed indicator which was used to measure static pressure variations through a roving probe. Drag caused by the instrument panel was of no consequence since tests were merely to measure frontal air flow.*

it has many excellent features the drawback of gyroscopic " kick " must be faced. On a small light car the wheels can be made sufficiently light to make this factor unimportant but naturally as the speed goes up the gyroscopic forces increase. I had previously assessed the limit to be about 120 mph, but decided to incorporate this suspension on the new model as I felt that its medium-speed advantages would far outweigh its disadvantages. I was subsequently pleased

Pick-up tubes *connected to altimeters on the instrument panel. By comparing pressure differences between pressure head and pick-up tubes, boundary layer behaviour and efficiency of body contours generally was studied. Valuable information was obtained from these practical tests.*

Colin Chapman *looks serious as he stands behind the car talking to Frank Costin in the helmet. In the driving seat is his brother Mike Costin. Useful assistance was also given by the other three in this photograph, "Fifi" Fifield in the hat, a Martin-Baker test pilot, Bruce White (yawning) and Tony Chalk both de Havilland aerodynamics experts.*

that I did so because the car handled perfectly, and it seems that the limit has not yet been reached, in fact 150 mph should be easily possible.

De Dion type of rear suspension was fitted with inboard brake drums, and the suspension medium was a transverse coil spring. This form of rear-suspension was chosen mainly to keep down wheelspin, and to reduce unsprung weight, a " live " axle tends to lift under wide throttle openings, as torque reaction tends to lift one rear wheel to induce wheelspin. This is obviated with the De Dion-type axle due to the " diff " housing being bolted up solidly to the frame, the drive was taken out to the rear wheels by two separate, short-drive shafts.

Among the many special features of the Mark VIII Lotus was a semi-*monocoque*-type of body panelling. Whilst this has quite a worthwhile advantage in weight saving I can now say that the snags which arise during routine servicing, repairs to accident damage and so on are such as to render it inadvisable for sports/racing cars. This year's car and all the production Mark VIIIs have much more easily accessible components and more easily removable body panelling.

Another snag with this car is that it poses special problems whilst being driven on the road. The good shape and lack of wind rush past the driver are factors which give a smooth ride and make speed very deceptive. In consequence it has been involved in three major shunts whilst being driven to and from race meetings by my mechanics, due possibly to misjudging just how fast the car was going.

WORKSHOP EQUIPMENT

Great trouble was experienced initially with valve gear at the high rpm required for maximum power but this was finally solved and then the car became remarkably reliable. During the whole of its 15,000 road miles, including driving to the Nurburgring and back twice, it has only let us down once, when a suspension link broke. And that, of course, had to be on that fated August weekend in the Eifel Mountains.

So much for the development of the Lotus sports car. Our aim has always been to improve the breed, which alone has given us a lot of fun, and at the same time to design a car so that replicas could be built privately. I believe that any amateur with enthusiasm can get an enormous amount of enjoyment out of building his own car in his own garage and subsequently using it on the road and competing in trials, rallies, and races.

I have often been asked about the tools and workshop accommodation required for competition work. There seem to be all too many who worry about assembling a car in a private garage without a vast quantity of equipment. I can assure them that I started with very little.

The first Austin was built in a lock-up garage adjacent to Hazel's house, that was because I was not allowed to use my father's garage at home. I had only the normal set of car spanners, rings, and open-ended, but no sockets or welding gear. I did have one important item which I think is absolutely necessary—an electric drill. I modified this so that it would drive a grindstone, wire brush, or anything else which had to revolve quickly. It was a most valuable asset.

We didn't have a jack in those days, but we just used bricks, and when the car had to go up on them everybody stood around and lifted. As a matter of fact, one of my first presents from Hazel was a hydraulic jack just after we had built the Mark II Lotus. We found that to change wheels during a trial was a bit of a problem because it was not always possible to find the bricks or enough people to do the lifting, so Hazel's present was gladly accepted. I did not have

A corner of the Lotus Engineering Company's workshop at Hornsey, with drawings in the foreground lying on parts of a body-building jig. On the bench is Mike Costin's Austin 7 engine and a Mark VIII Lotus differential casing.

Floor space is scarce as can be seen in this photograph. A Mark VI chassis is under construction and Mark VIII rear wing panels are stacked in the corner. A separate engine workshop and test house is under construction.

a lathe or any other machinery, and when any welding or brazing had to be done I co-opted the help of a local welder. I would assemble the pieces that had to fit together and dash down to the other chap's workshop and hold it while he got on with the job.

We did have a ten and sixpenny Vernier gauge which we could get down to "two thou.," and that was near enough; even the painting was done by hand, and I can remember many evenings when Hazel sat in the cold patiently painting each spoke separately.

As we have progressed so we have equipped our workshop, but the ordinary enthusiast taking it up needs only the bare necessities. I suggest that to assemble a car from bits and pieces you need a bench and vice, a complete set of spanners, a hammer, a screwdriver, and an electric drill.

I have been encouraged by the acceptance of the Lotus, of which already more than 100 Mark VI replicas have been or are being assembled privately. Now the chassis frames and bits and pieces for the Mark VIII are available for assembly in the same way. I hope that Lotus Engineering will go on developing better and faster cars for sale on the same system to provide enjoyable racing for those who cannot afford to buy expensive machinery. At the same time I do hope to branch out with another project. We intend to offer a complete sports car in open and in coupé form, giving a very high performance. This is my answer to the sporting motorist who has not the time or the inclination to "roll his own."

It is too early yet to say exactly what my plans are for next season, but my present ambition is to beat the Porsches, Borgwards and OSCAs on the Nurburgring. It's a pretty tall order, I know, but when that is done I may turn to other things. The biggest difficulty at the moment is the lack of a suitable engine, but I hope that this will soon be rectified and then we can really have a go!

I will finish this series with a plea for the sports car, because as a sports car manufacturer I am worried about the future of sports car racing. I believe that if we do not prevent this particular branch of the sport from becoming over specialised it will kill itself. By the term over specialised I mean, for example, the way in which British reliability trials have become so specialised that only about two dozen drivers compete successfully each week-end in cars which are so "special" that they are impractical road cars.

The same thing will happen to sports cars if they, too, become impractical for road use. I believe it would be fair for all concerned if a rigid set of international regulations, modelled on Le Mans regulations for example, was drawn up. This would permit manufacturers to compete with each other to the maximum limit as laid down, but the cars they used would still be a saleable proposition for the enthusiast wanting to buy a sports car with an ultra-high performance. As a start I would call for pump fuel, for drivers to sit on one side of a centre line and for the car to provide weather protection and adequate, sensible room for passengers.

The fastest 1½-litre sports car in the country. The Lotus Mark VIII with Connaught engine owned and driven by John Coombs. This car won the 1½-litre sports car race in the last meeting of the season at Brands Hatch on Boxing Day and on the same day very nearly won the unlimited class sports car race.

Mark III

When Colin Chapman teamed up with brothers Michael and Nigel Allen in 1950 he had already built his first two cars. The Lotus Mark I was a converted Austin 7 and was used for hillclimb and trial events. The Mark II was much the same and had introduced Colin Chapman to motor racing. The Mark III was their first combined, purpose built sports racing car. It still used the converted and modified Austin 7 chassis, engine and transmission, although all very much modified by Chapman and the Allen brothers in the Allen's family home in Wood Green in North London.

The intention was to build three cars, one for each of them to race. However, due to pressure of business and racing commitments only the first car was raced in 1951 and this mostly by Colin Chapman. A second car was completed later for a customer and the third car never progressed beyond chassis form.

The Austin 7 front Axle was replaced by a modified Ford 8 beam axle cut in half to give independent front suspension. This system, pioneered by Lotus, was used very effectively until 1956 and on five subsequent models. Bendix light alloy aircraft brakes were fitted and, to maintain chassis rigidity, the engine bay was braced with a multi-tube construction over and around the much modified Austin 7 engine. The Lotus modifications were such that, for future years, the 750 Motor Club banned much of the work which made the Lotus-Austin Mark III so quick during 1951.

During the 1951 racing season the Lotus-Austin Mark III achieved fourteen first places out of thirty-two events and was placed in a further thirteen. The success of the much modified, and highly innovative, Lotus-engineered Mark III set Colin Chapman on the road to his own sports racing car design for the following year.

Graham Capel

Emphasis On Sports Cars—
THE LOTUS-AUSTIN

AFTER building the successful Ford-engined Lotus trials car, now driven by Michael Lawson, Colin Chapman started to build another trials car. Then the 750 Club announced its revised Formula Racing for Austin Sevens and Colin, in syndicate with the Allens, Michael and Nigel, decided to start on a team of three of the new Austin Specials but modified for the dual role of "Formulae" racing in summer and trials in the winter. Last November a 1930 Austin Seven saloon was bought for £15 and this formed the basis of the first car, which was racing early the following season and which has proved to be something quite outstanding amongst amateur-built specials.

When we say that the car was completed in under six months, was rendered completely race-worthy during its first season, is driven to and from meetings and, handled by a variety of drivers including Chapman's friend, Hazel Williams, has set up the following lap-times—Silverstone Club Circuit 1 min. 58 sec., Boreham 2 min. 26 sec., Gamston 1 min. 83 sec., Ibsley 1 min. 58 sec., Castle Combe (early stages) 1 min. 43 sec.—readers will appreciate why we hastened the Plus Four to Alexandra Park to examine this car. To those not conversant with lap times, we have only to say that the Lotus is a scientifically-designed, very handsome unblown 750 c.c. road-equipped two-seater which has done a s.s. quarter mile in 17 sec., 0-50 m.p.h. in 6.6 sec.

Its builders claim that so far it has cost them less than £200. The principle on which Chapman worked was to put nothing into the Lotus which had not been carefully weighed first. "Simplicate and add lightness" was his motto, rather than drill everything full of holes afterwards.

The chassis is Austin Seven, of 6 ft. 9 in. wheelbase. The side-members are boxed in and two 14-gauge tubular cross-members replace the originals. An extension at the rear, in 20-gauge steel, serves as a mounting for the Newton shock-absorber struts and will carry the alternative trials back besides carrying a 1930 Austin Seven petrol tank, cut away to clear the axle casing. The rear springs, mounted normally within the side-members, are flat set and considerably softer than standard. The wide-track back-axle has the 4.9 to 1 ratio. The propeller-shaft is late-type Ruby.

Going to the front of the car you observe a tubular pyramid around the engine and thereby hangs a most interesting story. Originally the Lotus would take Beckett's Corner at 75 m.p.h. Its owners noticed that the crankcase studs of the rigidly-mounted two-bearing engine were pulling out, so rubber-mountings were substituted, using 3s. Ford rubbers. The cornering speed was now 5 m.p.h. down. Clearly, chassis flexion was to blame for both these short-comings, hence the aforesaid structure. It is properly-stressed and bolted together with h.t. bolts, so that it can be dismantled for complete engine removal, and has restored and improved on the original cruising speed. In addition to this elaborate bracing, a 15-gauge tube encircles the scuttle, acting as an anchorage for the steering column and enhancing the safety-factor. So rigid is this that the firewall further forward is merely a sheet of alloy attached to the sides of the body shell.

The front axle is a Ford Eight beam, divided in the middle for i.f.s. The spring is above it and Silentbloc bushes are liberally dispersed here and there about the rest of the chassis. The track is 4 ft., the axle 2½ lb. heavier than an Austin axle but more durable in its king-pins. Ford radius arms anchored on Silentblocs and Newton struts damp the soft transverse spring. The steering column is extended forward to an Austin Seven steering box laid on its side ahead of the axle so that its drop arm can operate a transverse drag link coupled to separate track rods. The column incorporates a fabric joint and is adjustable. The steering wheel, of sprung type, can be

THE ASTONISHING LOTUS, here seen at a "Club Silverstone" with Hazel Williams driving. The rubber-hose air-intake above the bonnet is to obviate a possible vacuum over the carburetter, but on one occasion it collected a passing bee.

adjusted for "spring" and is a beautiful thing, made by the Allens' and Chapman's girl-friends. The brakes have light alloy back-plates and are Lockheed hydraulic from a new Morris Minor, 2LS at the front, using the stiffer Girling drums.

The wire wheels were made up by the West London Repair Co. and feature special light centres which do not shroud the brake drums as Austin wheels would. They weigh 9 lb. 10 oz., against over 13 lb. for the Austin wheel, or 21 lb. complete with tyre and tube; 4.00-15 front and 4.50 or 5.00-15 rear tyres are used, depending on requirements.

Throughout, the builders of the Lotus have carried a tiny 25-lb. spring-balance, and any component that brings this to its full reading is regarded with very deep distaste indeed! So we find a front wing, complete with rigid 24-gauge struts and sidelamps, weighing a mere 10 oz., and the beautiful little polished aluminium body shell only 65 lb. complete with hoops.

Turning to the engine, from which such wonderful results have been obtained, originally a two-bearing unit was used. This was at times taken up to 6,500 r.p.m., but the standard Austin Seven rods bent into quite astonishing shapes. "Ulster" rods were substituted, retaining the $1\frac{5}{16}$-in. crankshaft, and then big-ends started to run. This explains why the Lotus started on three cylinders at the Eight Clubs Meeting. Chapman was criticised unfairly in some quarters for going flat-out on three pots; unfortunately the crank broke in shear nevertheless.

So, in spite of much prejudice against it, a three-bearing engine was installed. This had the advantage that a brand-new crankshaft and rods were obtainable, the latter for a mere 22s. 6d. each, and that the rods had thin-shell bearings, enabling rapid replacements to be made if bearing trouble intruded, and of course eliminated the inevitable whip of the two-bearing crank.

Chapman believed that three-bearing cranks broke only because, due to poor crankcase breathing, corrosion set in, causing wear in the rear main bearing and consequent flexing of the shaft about its centre bearing. To overcome this he decided to fit a Hoffman type 0 rear-main race and to incorporate a Fram filter in the lubrication system. This filter feeds oil back over the timing gears and a tap cuts it out during racing, in case a pipe should break.

The cylinder block is over-bored 0.050 in. and the inlet valves enlarged to $1\frac{3}{8}$ in., to accommodate which the exhaust valves have been reduced to $\frac{3}{32}$ in. less than standard. The bores are carefully radiused to assist gas flow and an alloy head has been modified to give the desired shape and the highest possible compression-ratio. The combustion spaces have been cleverly built-up by aluminium welding.

Up to the last Boreham Meeting the compression-ratio was 6.1 to 1, but it is now up to 7.2 to 1, which, with a new inlet system, gives an additional 500 r.p.m. in top gear. A normal C. and A. "Ruby" gasket is used. The engine will run on Pool, but now prefers 80 octane petrol.

The carburetter is a downdraught pump-type, twin-choke Stromberg from a 30-h.p. Ford V8, on a square-section V-manifold, asbestos-lagged to obviate heat conduction from the exhaust pipes. Fuel feed is by normal Austin Seven pump. The external exhaust system consists of square-section off-takes for Nos. 2 and 3 ports and ordinary small-bore pipes from Nos. 1 and 4, leading into a double Servais-type silencer, the whole planned to provide an extractor effect.

A "Nippy" camshaft is used with "Ulster" springs and the latter, being secondhand, have broken rather frequently due to fatigue, new springs being on order. So fine is the clearance between valves that a template was made to determine the optimum sizes that could be used, while so close do the pistons come to the head that crankcase whip as on the earlier engine would cause contact between these components!

The pistons are modified solid-skirt Covmo, with two $\frac{1}{16}$-in. compression and one $\frac{5}{32}$-in. scraper ring.

Cooling is looked after very thoroughly, a Stuart Turner water pump being driven from the front of the camshaft and a three-branch off-take taking water from the head. The radiator is modified Austin Seven, converted to film-type by the John Lancaster Radiator Co. It operates under pressure and is cowled by a featherweight shell incorporating two close-set Lucas pass-lamps as headlamps. The fan is retained but cut down. Oil (Shell) is contained in a "Nippy" sump.

Ignition is by a Scintilla Vertex magneto driven from the dynamo and inclined rearwards to clear the bonnet. The engine takes normal automatic advance (8 deg. at magneto, 16 deg. at engine), but a hand control is also fitted, and 14-mm.

plugs are used. The rev.-counter drive is taken from the magneto drive. No support has been found necessary for the magneto, but a cast-iron end casing is used on the dynamo.

The flywheel was lightened to reduce torsional loading on the crankshaft on the over-run rather than to humour pick-up. It now weighs $16\frac{1}{2}$ lb.

The standard clutch, with springs 1 gauge heavier and mechanical advantage in the pedal linkage, has given no trouble. It is lined with Mintex of the kind supplied for two purposes—racing, and to the Ministry of Works for their lady drivers! The gearbox is "Nippy," with remote control. A Morris Minor handbrake is fitted, with enclosed cable linkage to the rear brakes.

The very handsome two-seater body is nicely upholstered, has a lightweight hood, and a 22-gauge undershield runs the length of the car. A pleasing detail, typical of the care that has gone into the whole of the Lotus, is the use of tiny ball-bearings for the fold-flat windscreen!

The performance of this car is truly outstanding and far surpasses that of other 750 Formula contenders. Indeed, owners of the most potent Ford Ten specials, Meadows H.R.G.s, and even larger cars are apt to find the Lotus harrying them along the straights and as likely as not passing out of the corners! Very few "500s" can live with this astonishing Austin Seven in its present form, and it must be giving more b.h.p. than blown "Ulsters" of happy memory. 5,500 r.p.m. is adhered to in the lower gears and 5,900 r.p.m. has been held in top, equal to 88 m.p.h. Chapman puts the genuine maximum in road trim, with screen down, as 84-85 m.p.h. and the acceleration . . . ! The roadholding is entirely in keeping, making the Lotus a most formidable sports/racing car. And, to and from meetings, it does 50 m.p.g., indicating how freely it breathes. It is a great credit to its builders, of whom Michael Allen has done most of the engine work, Nigel that on the chassis, with Chapman responsible for the design, development and general construction.

That such a car has been built so economically in a small garage is an enormous tribute to this keen team, and to the tolerance of their parents and girl-friends! The Lotus is a fine example to would-be special-builders willing to approach such work scientifically and burn gallons of midnight oil.—

·W. B.

First born

The MkIII was the first racing Lotus, the very beginning of the legend. Mark Hughes investigates the car which revealed the first hints of Colin Chapman's design genius

THERE ARE NO BADGES, NOR EVEN a chassis plate, to reveal the identity of this odd little car, but upon its success a motoring legend was built. This is the first ever racing Lotus, a home-spun special built in 1951 around the chassis and drivetrain of a £15 1930 Austin Seven saloon and a hotch-potch of other secondhand parts. Cheap and amateurish though it was, LMU 3 contained enough ideas from Colin Chapman's innovative mind to give it a decisive advantage in the club-racing category for which it was built. It set Lotus on the path to dramatic success.

LMU 3 was the third Chapman special, and so was designated MkIII. His first two cars, also put together around ancient Austin Seven bits, were built in 1948 and 1949 for mud-plugging trials, a form of competition which Chapman, then a civil engineering student at University College, London, had discovered by chance when he stumbled across an event at Aldershot. All he had been planning to do with his first special was to turn an old Austin Seven, one which he had been unable to shift from his spare-time car dealing stock, into a more exciting road car. Seeing the fun to be had slithering up muddy hills, however, made him turn his half-finished creation into a trials car. He gave it the name Lotus to distinguish it from other Austin Seven specials. Nobody has ever known why.

His second car was an improved version for trials, but on 3 June 1950 he took it to Silverstone for a circuit race. Despite never having been to a race meeting, he was such a gifted driver that he managed to win his event. From then on his enthusiasm shifted away from trials to this more sophisticated world. He decided to build a third car for track work, specifically for the Austin Seven specials championship run by the 750 Motor Club. This car would be LMU 3

With two friends, Michael and Nigel Allen, Chapman put all his energy into wringing the best from the Austin Seven parts which 750 Formula rules obliged him to use. He wanted his MkIII to be as light, stiff and powerful as possible. With racing so new to him, he did his research thoroughly while he mulled over the MkIII's design, spending hours grilling 750MC president Holland Birkett to glean the knowledge needed for the ultimate Austin Seven special. Denis Jenkinson, the famous motor racing journalist, was in on some of these sessions, and remembers that both he and Birkett were impressed by this young man with curly hair and toothbrush moustache.

LMU 3 began with its donor Austin Seven stripped to a bare chassis, which was then given some clever Chapman treatment. Austin Seven chassis were notoriously flexible, so two new 14-gauge tubular cross-members were welded between the pair of longitudinal chassis legs. These legs, made of top-hat section steel, had their open faces boxed-in to form roughly square, rigid tubes. After the first few races, triangulated tubing was welded around the engine bay to give further stiffness — part of this tubing was bolted in place so that the engine could be removed.

On to this chassis was fitted an aluminium body made by a small local firm, F. L. Hine & Co, since neither Chapman nor the Allen brothers were skilled in panel-beating. The 750 Formula rules required that cars should be road equipped, so a pair of headlamps were placed half an inch apart on the front cowl and sidelamps (bicycle rear lamps with clear ▶

Streamlining looks rudimentary but underside was sealed with full-length aluminium undertray

◀ lenses) were mounted on the front cyclewings. The MkIII's streamlining looks rudimentary, but one Chapman novelty was to seal the underside with a full-length aluminium undertray. He considered lightness so important that every part was weighed on a 25lb spring balance and discarded or modified where possible. The complete car weighed around 800lb.

But Chapman's best trump card was his brilliant ideal for extracting more power from the humble 747cc Austin Seven sidevalve engine. Like most low-cost production engines, it had siamesed inlet ports to the cylinders, with two ports feeding fuel and air to four cylinders. With a 1-3-4-2 firing order, this meant that the cylinder at each end of the block fired first, taking most of the mixture — starved of their correct share, cylinders three and four could never work as hard. While other 750 Formula competitors seemed to accept this situation, Chapman resolved to get as near as the rules allowed to a four-port inlet for the sidevalve block.

He and the Allen brothers enlarged the openings in the block by grinding out as much metal as possible. They then welded together a special two-branch inlet manifold of sheet steel, externally identical to the standard manifold but with a central strip in each branch to divide the mixture along two channels. The end of this dividing strip formed a tongue which fitted into the centre of the enlarged ports, and asbestos tape was used to provide a gas-tight seal. It was simple but ingenious.

A huge twin-choke Stromberg carburettor from a Ford V8 engine perched on top of the manifold, poking through a hole in the bonnet. The engine was balanced, and the con rods were filed so that they all weighed exactly the same. In his quest to make the engine rev higher, Chapman also devised a pressure-fed crankshaft bearing lubrication system instead of the standard Austin Seven 'spit and hope' splash lubrication.

Since Chapman had no access to a dynamometer, the power advantage of his home-made four-port arrangement was never quantified, but when the car came to race it proved decisive. As the three young men had been careful to make the new manifold look just like a standard one, none of their competitors ever knew the trick. Birkett had a suspicion which led to a rider being added to the rules to exclude such modifications for the following season's racing, but he could never be quite certain. Everyone else just wondered in awe at the Lotus's speed.

Bits from all sorts of sources were used on the MkIII, many of them from North London breakers' yards. The water pump came off a Stuart Turner marine engine, the handbrake was from a Morris Minor and a Scintilla Vertex magneto was used for ignition. The independent front suspension was cunningly devised from an old Ford Eight beam axle cut in half to create two swinging arms, which actuated specially made slender leaf springs and Newton shock absorber struts. Lockheed hydraulic drum brakes and special lightweight spoked wheels were fitted all round.

The MkIII made its debut at Castle Combe on 12 May 1951, Chapman winning after lapping all but one of his rivals. The morning's practice, however, had raised a problem with fuel blowing back from that massive Stromberg into the driver's face. The novice team's answer, after a dash to nearby Chippenham, was to fit a large piece of right-angle lorry water hose projecting forwards from the top of the carburettor. At the next meeting, some of the Lotus's rivals appeared with similar hoses fitted, their drivers believing that ram effect accounted for the MkIII's mysterious power advantage . . .

A busy season followed, with LMU 3 being handled in every available race by four drivers; Chapman himself, the Allen brothers and Hazel Williams (Chapman's girlfriend from teenage days and eventually his wife). The car was fast but fragile, a characteristic of many subsequent Lotuses. Provided it held together it always won 750 Formula races, and it could even hold its own in classes up to 1500cc. It captured the imagination of everyone in this amateurish racing world, in which 'impecunious enthusiasts' (as they were always called) competed on a proverbial shoestring at the redundant war-time airfields where the sport was gradually being re-established through the period of post-war austerity.

By the end of the season, LMU 3 had taken part in 32 events, winning 14. Nine of the wins were in 750cc races, the others in higher capacity classes. By now, though, Chapman was looking to the future, thinking out his next car, the prototype MkVI. LMU 3 was advertised in the May 1952 *Motor Sport*, with offers invited over £475 — Chapman always looked for a handsome profit.

John Davidson bought the car and raced it for three more seasons before parting with it. After passing through several car dealers, it was eventually bought by Nigel Moores for a fabulous collection (he had six Jaguar D-types) which he built up before his death, in a road accident. For several years he kept LMU 3 on

Cramped interior features raided parts, chassis and suspension were stiffened and lightened

Jersey to use as a runabout. Although most of the Nigel Moores Collection has recently been sold, LMU 3 has been kept. It is now in the custody of ex-Team Elite driver Bill Allen and tended by Moores' long-time assistant, Paul Kelly. With the help of Mike Marsden of the Historic Lotus Register, I eventually traced Kelly to a Lancashire address and the car to the Lakeland Motor Museum at Holker Hall, Cumbria. As it is believed that the MkI and MkII no longer survive, LMU 3 is the oldest Lotus in existence.

The car is in remarkably original condition, its bare aluminium bodywork still etched with scuffs and dimples. The front cowl and bonnet are new parts made by Len Pritchard (of Williams & Pritchard, Lotus body manufacturers) because the old panels had corroded, but otherwise the post-Chapman changes have simply been minor ones to keep the car running, like fitting reinforcing plates where the cyclewings attach to the body.

Squeezing yourself into the MkIII is as much of a struggle as climbing into a modern single-seater racing car. You have to put your left foot on the cockpit floor, place your hands carefully on the edge of the aluminium bodywork behind the seat to support your weight and swing the other leg in. Then you can gradually slide your legs underneath the steering wheel and down into the footwell, dropping your backside onto the seat. As neither Chapman nor the Allen brothers were tall, I found it impossible to straighten my legs once I had folded myself into the seat.

The pedals, with clutch and brake drilled for lightness, are so close together in the narrow footwell that you need to wear slender shoes to avoid catching the edge of the brake pedal when you accelerate. The throttle, however, is so neatly angled that heeling and toeing is second nature. The gear-lever sits exactly where your left hand drops from the steering wheel; a simple shaft hinged at the base of the lever runs forward to form a remote-control linkage to the four-speed close-ratio Austin Seven gearbox. The 'box feels crisp and brisk, but selecting reverse requires both hands.

The cockpit is very bare, with a plywood floor resting on the two main chassis legs and single-skin aluminium forming the body sides. A simple wood rim steering wheel is fitted now as the original sprung steering wheel, a complex assembly of high-tensile aluminium made by Nigel Allen's girlfriend, is falling apart. There is an air of Lotus and even Caterham Seven in the simplicity of the seats, which are fashioned from a single backrest and a couple of flat cushions — they look as if they are still covered in their original vinyl — resting on the floor on either side of the folded aluminium sheet covering the propshaft. The only concessions to practicality are a flat 'parcel' tray (a place for Hazel to put her handbag?) and a passenger grab handle, the latter created simply by making a hand-sized cut-out where bodywork meets the tubular scuttle hoop.

An aluminium panel standing proud of the scuttle and shaped like an orange segment contains basic instrumentation. There are four Smiths and Lucas dials (all of different size and style, as if raided from several sources) looking after revs, water temperature, battery charge and oil pressure. Apart from an ignition switch, choke and pull-out starter knob, there are just four other unlabelled flick switches to control the lights. There is no fuel gauge, but Kelly has made a calibrated wooden 'dipstick' which lives in a recess behind the seat.

Unfortunately it was not possible to get LMU 3 started, so my hopes of an outing on the Holker Hall estate roads evaporated. It last ran three years ago when Bill Allen gave Hazel Chapman a demonstration ride around Brands Hatch, but now the fuel pump needs attention before the sidevalve 'four' will buzz again. All I could assess on the end of a tow rope is that the brakes have enough bite to lock up the front wheels easily and the steering has the lock of a London taxi.

Just after my visit, though, I made contact with Michael and Nigel Allen, both of whom drove LMU 3 regularly. They remember it mainly for its sheer speed. They calculated its top speed at 96mph, and the *Motor Sport* ad gave its standing-quarter mile time as 17secs — on a par with a Golf GTI, and this from just 747cc! It could reach its top speed very quickly on a straight, whereas its rival Austin Seven specials needed the whole length to wind up.

Contemporary photographs show LMU 3's front wheels at crazy camber angles when being hustled through a corner, but it always looks nicely balanced. The Allen brothers say that the chassis stiffness made it tremendously agile and faithful in its responses, especially after extra tubing was welded into the engine bay. They also remember that it could insult any of the faster cars it met in 1500cc races by outbraking them into corners, only to be passed on the way out.

It is good to know that this fascinating relic of Lotus history still exists, albeit in quiet retirement. You can see LMU 3 for yourself next year when the Lakeland Motor Museum reopens at Easter. ■

Mark VI

The Lotus Mark VI was conceived by Colin Chapman, and Michael and Nigel Allen, his two partners in Lotus Engineering Co in the early days of 1952 after they had had a very successful racing season with their Austin Seven based Lotus Mark III. The VI was the first *all Lotus* chassis designed by Colin Chapman using a number of small diameter tubes to create a rigid chassis onto which proprietary car components could be bolted to make a space frame sports or racing car, or a combination of both.

In 1952 only two Mark VIs were built due to pressure of work in the fledgling Lotus Engineering Co., where the only employee was Michael Allen, Colin and Nigel both having full daytime occupations. The first Lotus VI was XML 6 and was driven by Colin, Michael and Nigel. It caused a sensation when it first appeared at the MG Car Club race meeting at Silverstone on 5th July 1952. Unfortunately, on the way to their first international race meeting at Boreham on 2nd August 1952, Nigel, who was driving XML 6 to the event on the road, collided with a Cooperative Society bread van, and the car was written off. It nearly wrote off Lotus Engineering as well, as this was their main asset! However, the loss of their racing car gave them more time to get on with supplying customer orders for modified components, and other cars.

H. Sinclair Sweeny, known to most as 'Sweeny Todd', had ordered a Mark VI for trials and hillclimb events. His car, HEL 46, was completed by Lotus Engineering in November 1952, and although he entered it as a Lotus-Vicki, it was the second Lotus VI to be built. By the end of 1952, there were orders for more Lotus Mark VIs, and at the beginning of the 1953 season, Phil Desoutter, Fred Hill (Empire Lotus) and Dennis Wilkins were competing in Mark VIs. Nigel Allen had a replacement chassis built for the crashed XML 6, and this re-appeared in June 1953. Colin Chapman, with the help of Mike Costin, who had joined him 'after hours' from the de Havilland Aircraft Company, built a very lightweight Mark VI, 1611 H, which he began racing in July 1953. With Chapman's verve, and Mike Costin's hot engine, plus the lightweight chassis, this car was phenomenal. At the September 1953 Crystal Palace race meeting, Colin and 1611 H were so impressive in the 1500cc Sports Car event against an international field with their 1172cc Ford sidevalve engine, that *The Motor* magazine referred to Chapman's drive 'with the preposterously fast Lotus'. Other publicity soon followed with THE LOTUS PROJECT in *The Autocar* of 25th September 1953 which included a cutaway drawing of the Mark VI. John Bolster tested the Mark VI in *Autosport* of 2nd October 1953, and Lotus reprinted this article, and used it as their first brochure for potential customers. Over the winter of 1953/4 another 10-12 cars were ordered, and Lotus were on their way to success. Notable contenders in Lotus Mark VIs in 1954 included Peter Gammon, who had beaten Colin Chapman in 1953 with his very quick MG special and had won the Performance Cars 1500 Championship, Harlequins rugby football star Mike Anthony who went on to race the Lotus Mark X and 11's, Frank Nicholls who later became the founder of Elva Cars, Edward Lewis who raced the first Lotus Seven and founded Westover Driving Shoes, Rod Easterling who later jointly built REJO sports-racing cars in the 1960s and many others, most of whom made a name for themselves in racing in the mid 1950s.

The Lotus Mark VI was sold in kit form to avoid nearly 50% Purchase Tax on manufactured cars. The space frame chassis sold at £110.00 and was built for Lotus by The Progress Chassis Co. just around the corner in Hornsey, and set up by Colin Chapman's school chum, John Teychenne. Other suitably modified components for building a Mark VI were sold by Lotus as follows: independent front axle conversion £19.50; suspension units £5.00 each; alloy fuel tank £10.00; modified Morris Minor radiator £13.00; upholstery kit £22.00; light alloy windscreen £11.50; hood and frame £13.75, etc.

Orders continued to flood in, and Lotus Engineering became a Limited Company. They expanded rapidly, building a stores in the roof of the stables alongside the Railway Hotel in Tottenham Lane, Hornsey in North London where Colin's father, Stan, was the landlord. Colin was still working for the British Aluminium Company in the daytime, but other helpers joined him and Mike Costin in the evenings to try to keep up with the flow of orders. 'Nobby' Clark was their first full-time employee and was in charge of production of the customer Mark VIs. He was soon joined by John Standen as storekeeper now that they could afford to keep a range of spares, and Peter Ross and Mac MacIntosh from de Havilland helped out in the evenings.

In March 1954 Lotus received their first overseas order. This was for a Mark VI for Gunnard Rubini in Toledo, Ohio, USA who had read about the Lotus VI in a major publicity article in *Road & Track* magazine in June 1953 entitled THE LOTUS CHASSIS. He received chassis No 26, and this was followed by another American order from 'Bumpy' Bell of Tuscon, Arizona who received chassis No 30 in mid 1954. The price was $1989.00 which was then equal to about £500.

By the middle of 1954 Lotus Mark VI production had reached 50, although there was probably no time to celebrate this milestone. Lotus expanded further by taking on Ernie Unger as a mechanic. In November 1954 Alex Strachan of Waitara, Australia ordered a Lotus Mark VI with all the extras that Lotus were now developing for the car - Alfin aluminium finned brake drums, close ratio gears, de Dion rear axle, etc. Strachan asked if he could become agent for Lotus in Australia, which he did, but not until after a year's wait for his car. Chassis No 109 was eventually shipped to him in August 1955.

Lotus had moved on in 1954 to the aerodynamic Mark VIII, and this was followed by the Mark IX and X in 1955, but still orders for the Mark VI continued to arrive. The price for a complete car was now £400 minus engine. A variety of engines were being fitted to the Mark VI. The original Ford 1172 sidevalve was still popular for road use, and the BMC 'A' Series was also fitted. Racing versions were powered by the MG XPAG units of 1250 and 1500cc capacity, and the newly introduced lightweight Coventry Climax single overhead camshaft engine developed from the firepump was becoming a popular installation, and Bill Perkins even managed to squeeze a 2-litre BMW engine under the bonnet of his Mark VI.

Lotus Mark VI production continued until the end of 1955 with approximately 110 cars being sold by the time that Colin Chapman began production of his highly successful Lotus Eleven in 1956. The Mark VI was dated by Lotus standards. Colin Chapman was now into the age of aerodynamic cars with more sophisticated suspension and steering than the modified Ford Popular mechanics of the early 1950s. The Mark VI was obsolete in Lotus terms four years after it had been introduced. Colin Chapman was never noted for his nostalgia, and continued production of past technology would have been considered totally non-progressive in a forward thinking company that was about to win the class at Le Mans, and enter Grand Prix racing within two years.

However, the 'square cut' motoring image that the Mark VI created is still timeless today, and the Mark VI is very collectible.

Graham Capel

DUELLISTS.—Colin Chapman and Dargue, respectively in the Lotus and M.G. Special, at close quarters during the North Staffs M.C. Silverstone meeting.

LOTUS ENGINEERING Co. Ltd.,

MOUntview 8353

BUILD YOURSELF A LOTUS REPLICA ON A LOTUS CHASSIS FRAME

THERE IS STILL PLENTY OF TIME TO ASSEMBLE A CAR FOR RACING THIS SEASON AS THE LOTUS SPECIFICATION IS DESIGNED TO REQUIRE THE MINIMUM OF TIME AND TROUBLE

LOTUS MK. VI IN ACTION

THIS semi-monocoque chassis unit as shown above is being offered to help the enthusiast in his quest for a very high-performance but lightweight, economical and inexpensive sports car. It is designed so that the home constructor, without the use of welding plant or any extensive machinery, technical knowledge, or craftsmanship, can build for himself, by the addition of new or secondhand components, a " NEW " car at a fraction of the cost of a normal production unit. It is an original concept of integral chassis frame construction, comprising an inherently rigid system of triangulated 18 and 20 g. steel tubes, carrying stressed aluminium alloy panels as a means of combining the utmost strength with extremely light weight. These panels are an integral and permanent part of the chassis frame, which owes a large part of its great rigidity to the bracing thus provided. The design is based around the use of the relatively easily available and inexpensive Ford 8/10 Girling axle units but slightly modified to give outstanding roadholding and braking. Suspension is by coil springs and telescopic dampers all round. The engine compartment is fitted with lugs to accommodate either Ford 8/10, Ford Consul or T-type M.G. power units, to suit customers' performance requirements. This basic structure as shown and containing all mounting brackets and attachments for the engine unit, suspension systems, shock-absorbers, brake linkage, etc., forms the essential nucleus of a car, weighs only 90 lb. and costs **£110**

A comprehensive range of modifications, specialised components, etc., can be supplied to complete customer's requirements, and it is possible to complete the body as illustrated for approximately **£75**

WE are also able to supply a similar assembly to the above but expressly designed to the limits of the new R.A.C. formulae for trials cars. Although this will be a little more stark than the Sports-Racing unit, it will only weigh about 80 lb. and can use either normal, rigid, or swing axle front suspension system as preferred. Price **£110**

- ★ Other components to complete, such as upholstery, body panels, windscreens, steering-columns, shock-absorbers, etc., can be supplied from our large stock of spare parts if required.
- ★ Weight of complete car with Ford Ten engine — approx. 8½ cwt.
- ★ 85 m.p.h. by moderate tuning.
- ★ Swing axle independent front suspension.
- ★ Panhard rod rear axle location.
- ★ Race and go to work with the same car by competing in the 1,172 formula.
- ★ The most inexpensive high-performance car to run.

7, TOTTENHAM LANE, HORNSEY, LONDON, N.8

LOTUS

★ *Autosport, 2-10-53* ".... I feel that the Lotus is the best attempt yet to provide the enthusiast with a competition car at a price he can afford to pay. In essentials, it is just as sound an engineering job as the most expensive sports car, and the economy is only brought about by the clever adaptation of mass-produced components   J. V. Bolster.

FASTER THAN YOU THINK!

Technically . . . .

The Lotus System enables any enthusiast to build for himself a replica of a Lotus Sports Car, with the minimum of difficulty and expense. With this in mind all the separate elements are obtainable piece by piece and the actual assembly is a simple process needing little specialised knowledge or equipment.

The major unit is the chassis frame which is of semi-monocoque design and therefore extremely light and strong; it is supplied complete with all attachment points, including those for axles, suspension and steering components, engine and gear-box. The total weight of this structure is 63 lbs. The plan bracing of the frame comprises a sheet of high tensile light alloy rivetted to the underside which serves both as undertray and flooring. This has the advantage of giving a low centre of gravity with good ground clearance, effecting at the same time a great saving in weight.

Because of its integral construction the Mk. 6 body shape closely follows the lines of the chassis: so to assist the customer, and at the same time maintain the high standard of our products, a set of light alloy body panels including cowl, bonnet top and sides, all wings and stays, propshaft tunnel, boot door, etc., can be fabricated to separate order for approximately £60, plus £15 for materials.

JOHN BOLSTER HOLDS BASIC CHASSIS FRAME   PHOTO AUTOSPORT

With regard to the major mechanical components, firstly the customer should obtain either new or secondhand, a pair of Ford 8/10 post '39 Girling braked axle assemblies. From these it is necessary to supply us with certain components (see price list) for conversion to our specification. Secondly he should obtain an engine and gear-box unit of a type for which standard engine mountings are provided (e.g., Ford 8, 10 or Consul and M.G., T.C. or T.D., Coventry Climax). If a different power unit is contemplated he must fit his own mountings. It will be seen from the price list that various other specialised components and optional equipment are available from our Hornsey works to enable the customer to carry construction through to completion easily and quickly. To sum up we can do no better than to quote The Autocar "... the Lotus is a very attractive proposition to those desirous of possessing a lively, small sports car at low cost but with the desirable attributes of good weather protection, simplicity, reliability and readily available spares from the world-wide Ford organisation."

Aerodynamic bodies of Lotus Mk. 8 and Mk. 9 can also be built to special order.

★ *Autocar* "..... the handling qualities are of a very high order indeed ..... extremely well balanced and refused to roll ... wheel adhesion is quite outstanding .... few, if any, cars which are quicker through sharp 'S' bends."   J. A. Cooper.

Can I..?

1.—Build a LOTUS in my lock-up garage?

   Yes, even with normal hand tools and a bench; no welding or machining facilities are required.

2.—Buy axles, engine and gearbox easily?

   Yes, there are of course plenty of second-hand items available, but Ford and Austin main agents should be able to supply new components against special order as required.

3.—Fit a Riley 9 (or other engine) into a LOTUS chassis frame?

   Yes, but you will need to make your own mountings—we can only fit brackets for the five "standard" engines.

4.—Buy a LOTUS chassis with a door?

   Either one or two doors can be supplied in any Mk. as required.

5.—Get some information about paying purchase tax?

   Read the relevant articles in "Autocar" of 25.9.53 and "Autosport" of 2.10.53, which explain the position.

6.—Seat three abreast or have four seats in my chassis?

   No, the frame design will allow only a small third seat—transversely in the back, suitable for a child up to about 12 years old.

7.—Visit the LOTUS Works—what is the best time?

   Yes, anytime—please telephone first.

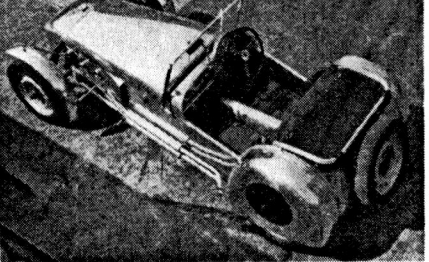

DESPITE THE CLEAN LINES AND EXTREMELY LOW BUILD OF THIS SPORTS CAR THERE IS AMPLE ROOM FOR DRIVER AND PASSENGER, HOWEVER TALL.

8.—Have a glass fibre body?

   No, the present LOTUS frame is designed as a semi-monocoque unit which utilises stressed aluminium panels for part of its stiffness.

★ *The Motor*
"... The preposterously fast Lotus!"

SHOWING ALL-WEATHER EQUIPMENT   OPEN TYPE REAR WINGS ARE OPTIONAL

LOTUS Engineering Co. Ltd.

7 TOTTENHAM LANE
HORNSEY LONDON N8

TELEPHONE: MOUNTVIEW 8353

...........Speaking

Most definitely recommended is our Mk. VI upholstery kit designed in conjunction with the frame for minimum weight and which, apart from the comfort, gives just that air of finish to complete the production car appearance.

Also on the price list are the Racing Components of which these items merit particular interest: (1) Lotus 15" Wheels which have three advantages: giving reduced unsprung weight, better gearing and allowing use to be made of the range of Dunlop racing tyres. (2) Special Close Ratio Gears for Ford 8/10 Gearboxes. (3) Special Crown Wheel and Pinion Sets of 4·7 (Ford 8/10) and 4·125 (1·5 Litre Engines) to fit Ford 8/10 back axles.

Competition Successes 1953: First Production Year

In one season only, the first four Mk. VI cars to start racing gained **forty-seven** awards in competitive events—circuit racing, sprints and hill climbs—including 19 Firsts taken at the following well known tracks: Silverstone, Goodwood, Snetterton, Castle Coombe and Thruxton. Colin Chapman's car—chassis No. 9 fitted with a linered down (1099 c.c.) unblown Ford 10 side valve engine—has raced in many events at 11 meetings, took **twenty** awards and was never beaten in its class. Since then the cars have been even more successful, and in the hands of private owners more than 120 awards were won during 1954 by over 40 different drivers. It can be seen from this that success in competition is not confined to a few "works" cars and drivers, but is available to all LOTUS owners.

Main Dimensions of Mk. VI:
Weight with Ford 10 approximately 8·5 cwts.
Wheelbase 7' 3·5"   Overall width 4' 3·5"
Track Front 4' 1·5"   Overall length 10' 1"
Track Rear 3' 9"   Scuttle height 2' 6·5"

PHOTO F. J. SMITH   LOTUS 1st, 2nd & 3rd AT SILVERSTONE

Performance Figures (approx.)

Engine		STANDARD	MEDIUM	HIGH
Ford 10	Degree of tuning	(Normal Prefect)	(Limits of 1172 Formula)	(Special Cam, etc.)
	Maximum Speed	75 m.p.h.	88	94
	Petrol Consumption	45 m.p.g.	48	40
	Standing ¼ mile	21 secs.	19	17·5
Ford Consul	Degree of Tuning	(Normal Consul)	(Twin Carbs., etc.)	(Special Cam, etc.)
	Maximum Speed	99 m.p.h.	106	113 Plus
	Petrol Consumption	40 m.p.g.	42·5	38
	Standing ¼ mile	18·8 secs.	17·4	16·5
M.G.	Degree of Tuning	(Normal 1250)	(Max. of 1250)	(1500, Special Cam, etc.)
	Maximum Speed	104 m.p.h.	113	120
	Petrol Consumption	40 m.p.g.	42·5	38
	Standing ¼ mile	17·8 secs.	16·5	15·8

★ *Autosport* "..... Very exceptional cornering powers .... uncanny, exemplary behaviour of the rear end ..... brakes may be applied at maximum speed without any deviation or patter ... frequently exceeded 90 m.p.h." J. V. Bolster.

The Lotus Chassis

The complete frame. Both square and round tubes are used for the truss type structure and the stressed body panels add to rigidity. This assembly costs $310 f.o.b. England.

Imagine an MG-powered machine which weighs exactly one-half that of a stock TD and you have a thumbnail sketch of the Lotus. The new Lotus kit chassis offers the competition-minded sports cars fan a chance to assemble his own sports car at moderate cost. Powered by a stock MG engine the top speed is about 104 mph, and the standing ¼ mile time is 17.8 secs. With a highly tuned (but unsupercharged) MG engine the top speed increases to 120 mph, and the ¼ mile time decreases to 15.8 seconds.

The Lotus chassis has been designed around the small Ford 8/10 chassis components. (The English Ford Anglia and Prefect model) The frame itself is the multi-tube type with aluminum panels riveted to the frame for the added stiffness of a stressed skin construction—literally a semi-monocoque design.

The front suspension is made up from Ford 8/10 components into a swinging axle type I.F.S. with coil springs enclosing tubular type shock absorbers. These same suspension units are used at the rear, where the Ford axle is supported by trailing links and carries a special gear ratio of 4.125 to 1.

Ford 8/10 wheels and the standard Girling mechanical brakes are normally supplied, but special magnesium wheels in either 15 or 16 inch size are available at extra cost. In this case the brakes are 9 x 1.25 Lockheed 2 L.S. type operating in drums cast integral with the wheels.

The builders offer a choice of frame brackets to accommodate any one of 3 powerplants. These are the 1172 cc Ford L-head; the 1250 cc MG (XPAG); or the 1508 cc Ford Consul. This latter engine can be reduced to just under 1500 cc by regrinding the crankpins .020 undersize on a .009 shorter crank throw radius. Any of these three engines may be used and, of course, their procurement (along with the mating clutch and transmission) is the responsibility of the "assembler".

The frame assembly, as illustrated, costs $310, including the stressed panels and floor, but not including crating, duty and shipping.

A set of body panels is available for an additional $210 f.o.b. This includes cowl, hood, hood sides, all fenders, floor tunnel and rear deck door.

The Lotus Company will undertake modification of the owner's suspension parts for a very nominal charge. Shortening the torque tube and drive shaft, for example, costs only $17.00, and a full set of four combined coil springs and shock absorbers costs only $56 f.o.b. However, for the American market a complete kit is to be available, priced at approximately $1540 f.o.b. This kit includes the frame, all body panels, axle converted to I.F.S., rear axle with 4.125 ratio, suspension units, pedals, steering, radiator, upholstery, fuel tank, instruments, Ford brakes, and wheels and tires.

All that remains to be done is to drop the engine-transmission in place, couple up the drive shaft, and complete the necessary wiring. The completed car in sports car trim, with battery, generator, starter, etc., weighs just over 1000 pounds. It gives a very potent 1500 cc class competition machine.—J.B.

Lotus Engineering Co., Ltd., 7, Tottenham Lane, Hornsey, London, N.8

The 1499 cc Consul powered Lotus Mark 6 in action at Silverstone. Driven by A.C.B. Chapman, the car's designer and builder. Note the small size compared to the TC MG.

NEW CARS DESCRIBED

The LOTUS Project

A SUCCESSFUL SMALL SPORTS CAR AVAILABLE FOR HOME CONSTRUCTION

SPECTATORS at sports car race meetings in recent months have by now become familiar with the appearance of several examples of a small, racy-looking sports car which has had a good deal of success in this type of event. This car is the Lotus, the product of the Lotus Engineering Company, Ltd., of North London, and the brainchild of Mr. A. C. B. Chapman, who has himself competed with one on many occasions.

The intention of the constructors is to enable any enthusiast to build for himself a replica of the original Lotus with the minimum of difficulty and expense. With this in mind, all the separate elements are obtainable piece by piece; the actual assembly is a simple process needing little specialized knowledge or equipment, but the way is open for the more skilled purchaser to reduce the cost still further by constructing or modifying some of the necessary components himself should he so desire.

The basic structure comprises the chassis frame, complete with all attachment points for the axles and suspension components, the engine and gear box. Many of these parts are of Ford manufacture, while the engine most usually employed is the well-tried Ford Ten unit; the Eight, the Consul, and M.G. TC and TD units can, however, be catered for if desired. The frame structure is of multi-tube construction, braced and strengthened by flat light-alloy panels riveted to the main tubes. The lower tubes are 1⅞in dia. by 18 s.w.g., while for the upper ones both 1in square and 1in round material, of the same thickness, is employed. The total weight of this structure is 63 lb. For bodywork, suitable light-alloy components comprising cowl, bonnet top and sides, all wings, tunnel, locker and so on, can be constructed to order by the firm of Williams and Pritchard, which has developed a special technique for this car.

It is then up to the customer to obtain, either new or second-hand, the engine and gear box unit of his choice and a set of Ford Eight or Ten front and rear axle assemblies. The Lotus concern will undertake the necessary modifications to the front axle beam, radius arms, track rod, torque tube and propeller-shaft, if desired, these being outside the scope of the majority of home constructors. The axle beam is divided in the centre, lugs being welded to the halves for attachment to the frame; the pivot point is deliberately kept low to reduce the height of the roll centre of the resulting swing-axle i.f.s. The track rod is also divided, the halves being attached to a bell crank back from which the drag link runs at an angle to the special steering box. The torque tube and propeller-shaft are shortened to a suitable length.

The Ford rear axle is used otherwise unaltered; but the suspension medium at both front and rear is by coil springs built up as units on to Woodhead-Monroe telescopic dampers. The rear axle is located laterally by a Panhard rod. The brakes are standard Ford-Girling components,

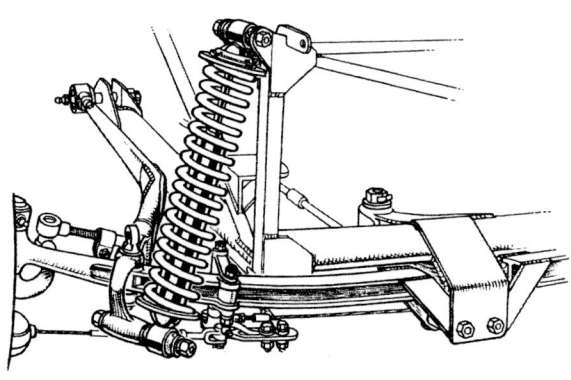

Front suspension details: the existing spring lugs are used to attach the combined coil spring and damper unit to the divided axle beam. The cable-operated and compensated brake mechanism is also visible.

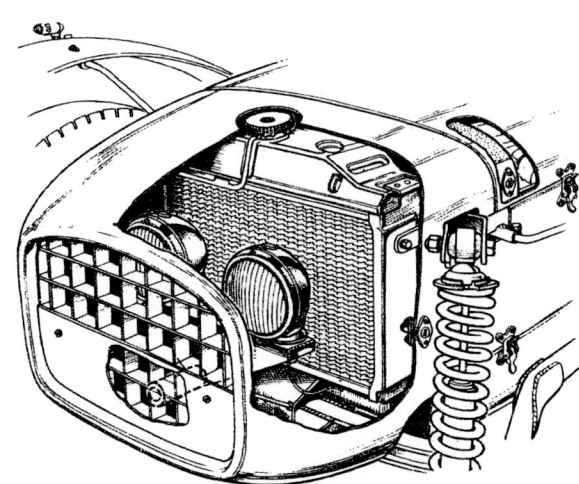

The front cowling, and all the body panels with the exception of the bonnet top and sides, are attached to the framework by quick-release Dzus fasteners. Two small-diameter head lamps may be mounted as shown.

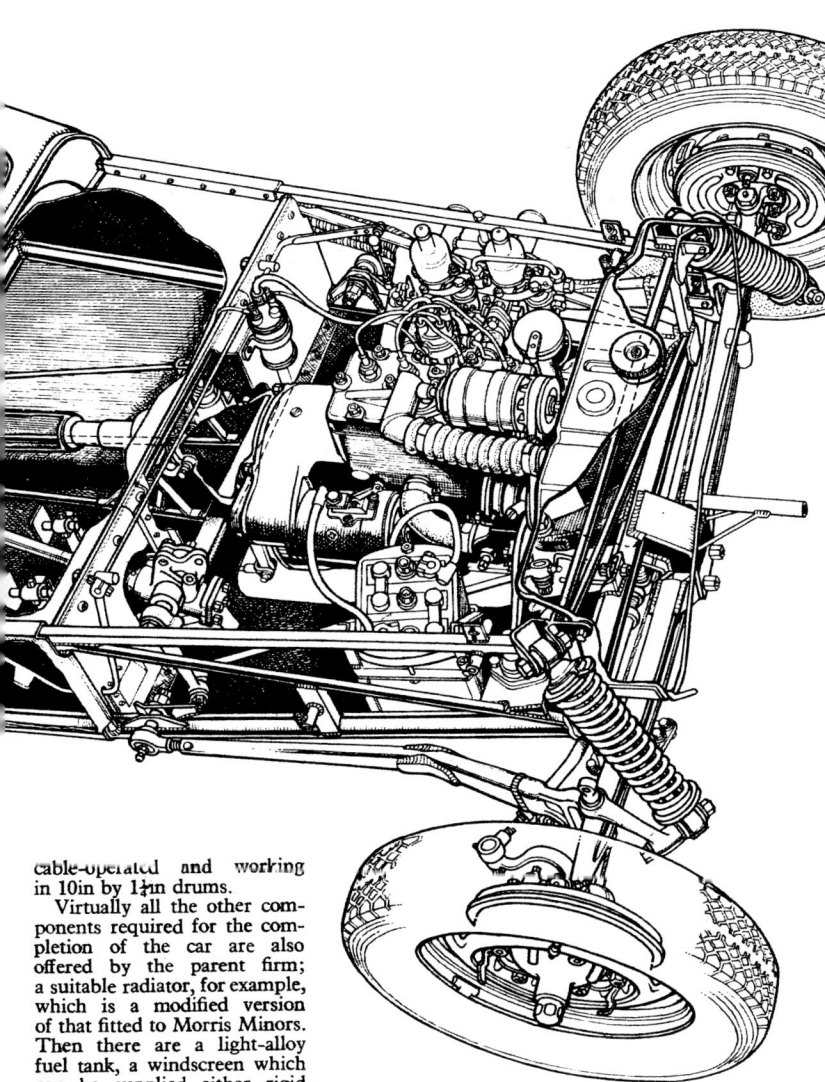

This skeleton view of a completed Lotus car (fitted, in this instance, with a modified Ford Ten power unit) shows the simplicity of the basic design. The multi-tube frame structure is rendered extremely stiff by the judicious use of flat riveted panels.

cable-operated and working in 10in by 1¼in drums.

Virtually all the other components required for the completion of the car are also offered by the parent firm; a suitable radiator, for example, which is a modified version of that fitted to Morris Minors. Then there are a light-alloy fuel tank, a windscreen which can be supplied either rigid or fold-flat, a complete upholstery and trimming kit (using Dunlopillo cushion and squab interiors, covered in real hide), a hood complete with frame, a tonneau cover, and so on. The complete pedal assembly, hand brake lever, ratchet and cable, remote-control gear change (of a simple and well-tried pattern)—all the parts can be supplied.

Alternative Schemes

The degree of tune applied to whichever power unit is employed, is, naturally, left entirely to the customer; there are, of course, many specialist firms who will undertake any modifications of this type which may be desired. Similarly, close-ratio gears for the gear box, and higher final drive ratios than standard, are on the market from different sources. Should any purchaser be interested in serious competitions with a lot of power available, he would probably be interested in an alternative specification offered by the Lotus firm and including such items as cast-Elektron wheels with integral brake drums, two-leading-shoe Lockheed brakes, and a special rear axle capable of transmitting much more power and with alternative ratios. These items, however, naturally increase the cost considerably.

Since production commenced in January of this year, orders have come steadily in, and the number of frames supplied is now well into the second dozen. As the question of power unit and degree of tune is so much a matter of individual choice, no performance figures can usefully be quoted; but a run by a member of *The Autocar* staff in Colin Chapman's own car (which has a Ford Ten engine with a raised compression and two S.U. carburettors, among other modifications) showed that the handling qualities of the car are of a very high order indeed. There is no oversteering tendency, the car being extremely well balanced, but if pressed to the limit the rear end will break away first; the car refuses to roll, and the wheel adhesion is quite outstanding in view of the relatively high proportion of unsprung weight—there can, in fact, be few, if any, cars which are quicker through sharp S-bends such as are encountered on roundabouts. This particular car, incidentally, has a genuine maximum speed not far short of 90 m.p.h. with very lively acceleration, the dry weight of 8½ cwt contributing largely both to this and to a very low fuel consumption. As a car home-built from components for personal use only is not liable to purchase tax, the overall cost is also low; it should not total more than £400 even if labour charges are incurred for everything but the most simple assembly work. All in all, the Lotus is a very attractive proposition to those desirous of possessing a lively small sports car at low cost, but with the desirable attributes of good weather protection, simplicity, reliability and readily available spares from the world-wide Ford organization.

SPECIFICATION AND PRICE LIST

Main Dimensions.—Wheelbase 7ft, track (front) 4ft 1in; (rear) 3ft 9in.

Tyre Sizes.—(recommended) 4.50-15in front, 5.25-15in rear.

Weight.—Dry weight 8½-9 cwt, depending on equipment, with Ford Eight or Ten engine and gear box.

Price List.—

	£	s	d
Basic frame structure	110	0	0
Conversion charge for front suspension components	15	10	0
Coil spring suspension and damper units (4) each	5	0	0
Steering column and box, with mounting strap	7	17	6
Foot and hand brake assemblies, with cables and conversion charge for front mechanism	12	4	6
Conversion charge for torque tube and propeller-shaft	6	0	0

Manufacturers.—The Lotus Engineering Company, Ltd., 7, Tottenham Lane, Hornsey, London, N.8.

Cost of body to original design: approximately £60 plus £15 for materials.

The complete car shows clean lines and extremely low build ; yet there is ample room inside for driver and passenger, however tall.

JOHN BOLSTER

TESTS

THE

LOTUS

HEY PRESTO!: "Magician" John Bolster demonstrates the lightness of the Lotus frame; weight is 55 lb. bare, 90 lb. with panels and brackets.

AT the Crystal Palace on 19th September, we beheld an astonishing sight. During a sports car race, in which some of the "hottest" 1½-litre machines in the country were engaged, a vehicle propelled by a *side-valve* Ford 10 engine, linered down to 1,100 c.c., proved itself capable of fighting it out with the best. This was what a contemporary described as, "the preposterously fast Lotus," and it was the talk of the paddock afterwards.

Naturally, I was duly impressed with these goings-on, as seen from my commentator's box, and so it came to pass that I arranged to borrow this little projectile for a week of varied motoring. I had observed that, in the very skilled hands of Colin Chapman, the Lotus appeared to possess the most phenomenal road-holding, braking and cornering power. What I wanted to know was whether it would do the same sort of thing for me, or if it were all much more difficult than it looked.

At this point, it might be as well to digress and give a brief explanation of the Lotus set-up. In the first place, it must be made clear that the Lotus Engineering Co., Ltd., of 7 Tottenham Lane, Hornsey, N.8, do not supply complete cars. Their main product is a space-type, multi-tube frame, to which you fit your own machinery. They will carry out certain modifications to your components for you, but it is up to you to acquire such things as engine, axles and wheels, either new or second-hand, in the open market. The thing has been found to work out more satisfactorily that way, from every point of view, and it avoids the interference with production and skyrocketing costs that the incorporation of customers' own ideas usually entails. In other words, Colin Chapman will sell you a chassis frame for £110 and tell you how to make the best use of it, but he won't complete your car for you or furnish a kit of parts.

The Lotus chassis is extremely rigid and very light, which are the main essentials of any sports car frame. It weighs 55 lb., bare, or 90 lb. complete with all mounting brackets and stressed panels. A standardized bonnet, mudguards and floor tunnel are available from a neighbouring coachbuilder, and when these are added the total weight is 120 lb. A Ford Eight or 10 rear axle is normally used, though the torque tube and propeller shaft must be shortened. Similarly, a Ford front axle is employed, and is converted to swing-axle i.f.s. by dividing the main beam and the track rod, and modifying the radius arms. Messrs. Lotus will do all this for £15 10*s*., and they will shorten your prop. shaft and torque tube for £2 10*s*. and £3 10*s*. respectively. I have no room to go into further details, but suffice it to say that all the necessary parts are easily available, and no welding or machining are called for in assembly.

Such proprietary power units as the M.G., the Ford Consul, or, of course, the ubiquitous Ford 10, will "drop straight in", so to speak. To give some idea of the expense involved, a Ford 10-powered car, complete with hood, screen and full equipment, could be built, with all new material, for about £425. Naturally, such things as engine tuning and close ratio gears would be added to choice.

"My" Lotus had a Ford 10 engine which had been warmed up as far as the "1,172 Formula" allows. It had an aluminium cylinder head, raised compression ratio, larger inlet valves than standard, and double valve springs. It had twin S.U. carburetters mounted on a flexible induction system, to avoid frothing of the fuel

★

WEATHERPROOF: With hood up, the Lotus occupants are well protected from the elements, while headroom is adequate.

★

from vibration. Two separate exhaust manifolds paired cylinders 1 and 4, 2 and 3, as is correct practice.

The three-speed Ford gearbox was converted to close ratios by the use of Buckler C-type gears. A remote control was mounted on top of the propeller shaft tunnel, which was of considerable height, due to the general low build. The rear axle had been fitted with a 4.7 to 1 final drive.

On the road, the performance just didn't make sense! I have driven many Ford 10-engined cars—in fact I own one myself—but this was an entirely different experience. At the very bottom end, it had not perhaps quite the "stepaway" of the standard job, and the tick-over was a little lumpy. Once on the move, however, the little thing screamed away at apparently unlimited revs. I would say that the unit peaked around 6,000 r.p.m., but the owner told me that I could exceed "seven thou." if I felt like it. As that would be equivalent to 84 m.p.h. in second gear, it will be realized that this is quite a car!

The total weight of only $8\frac{1}{2}$ cwts. gives the willing power unit every chance to show its paces. The acceleration is even better than the figures in the data panel indicate, for the very high bottom gear makes considerable slipping of the clutch essential on get-away. However, that component seemed to have no objection to such rough treatment, in spite of the many standing starts that are entailed when taking the average of a number of runs in both directions. The mean maximum speed was 88 m.p.h., and I frequently exceeded 90 m.p.h. under favourable conditions. After all that, I had to have another look under the bonnet and, yes, it really was a side-valve.

In close-ratio form, the Ford gearbox gave a very easy change between top and second, the synchromesh operating well. First speed was a little less easy to engage, and one had to judge the relative speeds fairly accurately if noiseless meshing of the pinions was to be secured. By pressing the lever to the right, the shift from bottom to second went through in one quick, clean movement.

The suspension was fairly firm without being in any way harsh, and the ride was level and free from pitching. The springing was by helical springs all round, with telescopic hydraulic dampers. At the rear, lateral location of the axle was by a Panhard rod, and alternative holes were provided in its brackets, so that the roll centre could be raised or lowered to choice. In front, the divided axle automatically gave a high roll centre, and certainly the machine remained on an even keel while cornering.

To begin with, the steering felt a little unusual. The Burman box gave light operation and a moderate degree of caster return action but, at low speeds only, one felt that there was a slight tendency to wander. As soon as one became used to the general "feel" of the car, that tendency entirely disappeared, and one was free to enjoy the very exceptional cornering powers provided. This car has just enough under-steer for stability, and no more. What is so uncanny is the exemplary behaviour of the rear end. Thus, although a corner may be taken with the back wheels definitely sliding, a complete breakaway does not occur. Once one has learned that the machine will not "swop ends", the curves may be swerved with a very great degree of abandon indeed.

The standard Ford brakes are comparatively enormous, having regard to the weight to be stopped. More elaborate equipment is available, but I would

POWER PACK: The Ford 10 engine in the car tested had an aluminium head, twin carburetters and other "mods".

regard the present arrangement as entirely adequate for any type of competition. The brakes may be applied at maximum speed without inducing any deviation or patter; that comes from the positive location of the axles.

The very low seating position was comfortable, and the steering wheel was ideally placed for "doing a Farina". At the outset, the pedal department seemed rather full of feet, but I soon became accustomed to the fairly narrow space. The weather protection, with hood and side flaps in position, was much better than one would expect, even though a slight defect in the body allowed some water to enter my right shoe during heavy rain.

As Mr. Chapman has no intention at present of invading the Rolls-Royce and Bristol market, he has given a little less attention than those two manufacturers to sound deadening and exhaust silencing. In consequence, particularly at peak revs. with the hood up, one can definitely hear the machinery at work, to put it mildly. Let us remember, though, that I took over the car exactly as it was raced at Crystal Palace, apart from the replacement of the hood and screen, and for touring purposes one could easily fit larger silencers.

I feel that the Lotus is the best attempt yet to provide the enthusiast with a competition car at a price he can afford to pay. In essentials, it is just as sound an engineering job as the most expensive sports car, and the economy is only brought about by the clever adaptation of mass-produced components. Its excellent handling qualities ensure not only that the driver has safe and enjoyable motoring, but that he will automatically receive the right sort of training, with nothing to unlearn if he graduates to big-time racing. It is a fine little road car, too, and lots of fun to drive.

SPECIFICATION AND PERFORMANCE DATA

Car Tested: Lotus Sports two-seater (for price, etc., see text).

Engine: Four cylinders, 61.5 x 92.5 mm. (1,099 c.c.). Side-valves. $8\frac{1}{4}$ to 1 compression ratio. Approx. 40 b.h.p. at 6,000 r.p.m. Twin horizontal $1\frac{1}{4}$-in. S.U. carburetters. Lucas coil and distributor.

Transmission: Single plate clutch. Three-speed gearbox with central remote control, ratios 4.7, 6.2 and 10.8 to 1. Torque tube transmission and spiral bevel final drive.

Chassis: Multi-tubular construction with stressed-skin panels. Swing axle i.f.s. and conventional beam rear axle. Helical springs front and rear surrounding Woodhead Monroe telescopic dampers. Front swing axles located by radius arms, and rear axle positioned by torque tube and Panhard rod. Cable operated Girling brakes, 10 x $1\frac{1}{4}$ in. 4.50 x 15 in. front tyres and 5.25 x 15 in. rear tyres on bolt-on disc wheels.

Equipment: 6-volt lighting and starting. Speedometer, revolution counter, ammeter, oil and water temperature and oil pressure gauges.

Dimensions: Wheelbase, 7 ft. $3\frac{1}{2}$ ins. Track, front, 4 ft. 1 in., rear, 3 ft. 9 ins. Weight, as tested, $8\frac{1}{2}$ cwts.

Performance: Maximum speed 88 m.p.h. Speeds in gears, 2nd 75 m.p.h., 1st 40 m.p.h. Acceleration, 0-50 m.p.h. $9\frac{4}{5}$ secs., 0-60 m.p.h. $12\frac{3}{5}$ secs., 0-70 m.p.h. $16\frac{3}{5}$ secs.

Fuel Consumption: 40 m.p.g.

LOTUS SALAD

by

David Scott-Moncrieff

AUTHOR IN LOTUS.—" Nowadays, when Bunty is on the starting-line, a still small voice murmurs in her ear ' you're not only an old man, you're a very silly old man to go on doing this sort of thing.' "—D.S.-M. This is the original 750 c.c. Lotus-Austin, now owned by David Scott-Moncrieff.

(*Photo by A. Hollister*)

MOST chaps very soon learn that, while any form of sporting motoring may be sanctioned during the courting period, it is definitely not compatible with married life. A family saloon for transport and that's it.

My wife, Averil, is the exception. She liked to drive Bugattis as fast as they would go, even if, sometimes, she went motoring the less usual way up. It is hardly necessary to add that this Bugattisme put us in the most apalling financial jams. The last one, caused by the disintegration of a roller-bearing crankshaft, involved a bill from Molsheim that put us out of motor racing for two years.

When at last we recovered, we drew up a short list of motor cars which would give the same fun for a lower maintenance cost. Finally, after the third bottle, we decided on a Lotus. At that time it was believed that a Mark VI could be built for an outlay of about £450 on bits and pieces. I did some costing, but gave up when the sum total exceeded £600 as we did not have that much money.

So we went to see Colin Chapman who had, I think, at that time, supplied the parts to build about a couple of dozen cars. I told him that I thought his chassis was technically superior to almost everything, but that, much as we would like a Lotus Mark VI, we could not afford to build one. Chapman reacted immediately and produced, with the same apparent ease that a conjuror produces a rabbit out of a hat, a charming young man called Robin Howard, who had built a very good one with a 1,172 c.c. Ford engine, and then didn't want it after all.

I drove it back to the Midlands from London and fell in love with it at once. I felt that it was, like the Mercedes 300SL I had driven in Germany (they were hardly in production at that time), a car that was with you the whole time, but I couldn't help feeling that if there had been a good deal more power the Lotus would have been rather tail happy on wet surfaces.

Next day when Averil went to go motoring the cylinders were full of water. The much vaunted aluminium cylinder head was found to have assumed the shape of a fairly steeply-curved rainbow. We had it milled flat and it promptly did it again. So we threw it away and fitted a Ford Eight head which cost two bob secondhand. The performance was no worse, and, if anything, slightly better.

We ran the Mk. VI with the 1,172 c.c. engine in about a dozen events and had relatively little trouble. At Rest and Be Thankful the Buckler high second gear kept jumping out in practice. So I spent half the night, with the help of a Polish welder, constructing the sort of appliance that might be made for a disabled driver for Averil to hook round her knee and hold the gear lever in second. I don't think she was quite bottom of her class but needless to say she did not make a very good time.

The only other serious trouble is that the back-end has twice chewed up. This seems a fairly common occupational disease in Loti. The reason is that the taper pin holding the tail shaft of the pinion to the prop.-shaft, shears. The splines are then free to " work " and eventually twist off. However, with a new crown and pinion costing £7 10s. this does not present a very serious financial hazard.

But there was one inescapable snag. Whatever you do to a 1,172 c.c. Ford engine, you can't get more than something slightly in excess of 40 h.p. out of it. Here again Chapman was wonderfully helpful. He told us exactly what to do and most religiously we did it. But, whatever we did we could not squeeze much above 80 m.p.h. on the flat.

Our final outing in 1955 was the Six Hour Relay Race. The other cars in the team all ran into trouble, but Averil's Lotus-Ford went round and round as reliably as any steam engine. She carried most of that race on her back. In spite of this fine effort, however, it was quite clear that we were getting nowhere at all with a 1,172 cc. Ford engine.

We considered an o.h.v. head, but this would take us out of the Formula into a class with cars infinitely more powerful than an o.h.v. 1,172 c.c. Ford could ever begin to be.

We did not have the three hundred quid plus necessary to install a Climax engine, so we bought an XPAG (1,250 cc.) M.G. engine. Ted Lund, who, after all these years, knows as much about M.G.s as anybody, was entrusted with its installation, and a very good job he made of it. We hoped to have it ready for events at the tail end of the season. *But we were unaware of the incredible fact that it is far, far easier to get spare parts for an obsolete 1927 G.P. Bugatti, than for a 1955 B.M.C. product.*

We had been unable to get a gearbox with our secondhand engine, so we ordered a new one (a T.F.) from the makers. It took months to come. Just think of that; B.M.C., the largest automobile building corporation in the country, unable to supply one gearbox for a current model; I can only hope that Sir Leonard Lord reads this, seeks out the man responsible, and kicks his backside till it resounds like a gong.

What with one thing and another of this ilk we did not get the Lotus back till the spring of this year, and, I must say, we were delighted with it. The only fly in the ointment was that the extra power given by the 1,250 c.c. M.G. engine made the tail distinctly tricky on wet surfaces. But, before we had a chance to tackle this, we had a fresh calamity. As you probably know, on most B.M.C. products the gudgeon-pin is nipped by a bolt located in the connecting rod. These bolts, unless specially treated, are apt to slack off or break, with pretty far-reaching results. We had barely finished running in and Averil was motoring modestly at 4,000 r.p.m. when it happened. We were lucky and got away with a bent con.-rod, a broken piston and a slightly damaged block.

As there are very few events nowadays which run a 1,250 c.c. class, almost always lumping everything together under 1,500 c.c., we decided to rebuild as a 1,446 c.c. T.F. So we darted down to Abingdon to see Eric Blower, who has been simply wonderfully helpful all through. He is a chap of encyclopaedic knowledge and acts as technical liaison between customers and works. This is similar to what Kling, the racing driver, now does at Stuttgart.

The TC head, we learned, does not fit the TF 1,446 c.c. block. This did not surprise us very much, but, what did was that *there was not a single head to fit this last year's model in the M.G. stores*; It really does not seem surprising that overseas buyers foam at the mouth at the mere mention of those three letters B.M.C. In the end they found us a Vaun cross-flow head that had been used for one or two tests only.

Now, we thought, we shall be motoring again soon. But it did not work out as easily as that. When we were at Abingdon we ordered a new crankshaft. There was not a lot of room left in the car so we arranged to have it sent on by passenger train. One whole week elapsed between the time it was ordered and paid for in advance, and the time it was despatched. Then, after this brilliant piece of stores efficiency British Railways promptly lost it !

It is not by any means the first time that British Railways have lost goods consigned to me, so I know the drill pretty well. It is not the very slightest use complaining at a low level. You simply get the stock reply : " We have sent a telegram about it." A B.R. telegram takes anything from 24 hours upwards to get answered, and, certainly as far as I have found, never produces results. If you want to see your bits and pieces inside a month or six weeks, you must get on to the head boy for parcels traffic for your district. You will find him invariably a person of the greatest helpfulness and charm. He is also a man of considerable importance within the structure of the railways. When he picks up his telephone things happen. I learned this long ago when a Type 51A Bugatti consigned to me in Scotland was irretrievably lost for three weeks. The underlings just said they didn't know where it was, I got on to the big shot and, within 14 hours the van containing the Bugatti was found (it had been shunted up a siding near Carlisle) and coupled on to the next passenger express, a privilege normally only available to Royalty. It was, I thought, a charming gesture.

As soon as British Railways had discovered and delivered our crankshaft, we ran into fresh trouble. But this time we had the B.M.C. stores system to reckon with, a much more difficult proposition. With the crankshaft, I ordered, naturally, a complete set of big-end bolts. A curt note was enclosed to say that the M.G. works had not got any. I made the rounds of half-a-dozen B.M.C. Main Dealers before I located any. I don't know what they do when they overhaul engines. I can only suppose that they replace the old ones. The big-end bolts, when we did eventually get them, pulled out like chewing gum long before the requisite tension was reached with the torque wrench. I must give the M.G. people full marks about faulty material, however. On those rare occasions when such material was supplied, they always, immediately on receipt of a 'phone call, have despatched the same day, without fuss or argument, replacements free of charge, by passenger train, always provided, of course, that they had them in the stores.

Anyway, after a few more troubles, we've got it together again and the 1,446 M.G.-Lotus bids fair to be a charming little sports car.

But in my chase after bits and pieces I sampled quite a good cross-section of the stores system of B.M.C. dealers. My local concessionaires, Peppers, I finally gave up as hopeless when they quoted me one week to get some standard ignition parts from Lucas at Birmingham, barely fifty miles away. The Stafford distributors have had a half-shaft and one floorboard for my 8-h.p. Morris van on order for seven weeks so far, and up to the time of writing " can't say when they will come." As there are literally thousands of 8-h.p. Morris vans on the road this could not be more disgraceful. The stock reply I have had on all occasions is " Other people have been waiting much longer than you." This seems to me no excuse at all, merely an additional irritant. I can't help contrasting it with Lloyds, the Stafford Ford agents, who (this was the first time I had ever dealt with them) telephoned every Ford dealer within a 60-mile radius till they found a bit I wanted. And, what's more, they didn't even charge me for the calls. . . .

I had a long chat with Oscar Stevenson, manager of Kennings, B.M.C. concessionaires. This is what he says " We are in this business to make money and it does not pay us to carry large stocks of spares just in case someone needs one in a hurry." My contention is that if, as a recent law case revealed, there is a differential of 200% on the cost of spare parts, B.M.C. can afford to maintain an efficient spares service. Alternatively, if, as Stevenson maintains, the distributors cut of 200% does not justify the holding of considerable stocks, the manufacturers should make it worth their while.

Then there is another debatable point. There is a very considerable

(Photo by Charles Dunn)

SPECIAL versus PRODUCTION MODEL.—" Averil, in her Lotus-M.G. had a terrific dice at the A.M.O.C. Silverstone Meeting with two M.G.-MGAs. She beat one and the other just put it across her. This is a most interesting picture, as it shows how the M.G. leans over and the Lotus does not."—D.S.-M.

profit on the sale of new cars. Are the concessionaires justified in regarding this as clear profit, or should a small portion be allocated towards the amortisation (i.e., writing down in the books) of existing stocks of spares so that they can remain on hand for the benefit of customers who like, or have, of necessity, to keep their cars for several years? I am but a lone voice crying in the wilderness and it is unlikely that Sir Leonard and his co-directors would take the slightest notice of my insignificant writings. But just take a look at the export figures, now that the gilt is off the gingerbread of the post-war boom. There is writing on the wall, for all to see.

Let's leave this rather disagreeable subject and get back to the Lotus, or rather Loti, for, last year I acquired Colin Chapman's original 750 c.c. Lotus. Since the time that Chapman sold it, this grand little car has had rather a hard life, and with all the bothers in connection with my wife's Lotus, not nearly enough work has been done on it. The first trouble that manifested itself was a tendency to break valves, but I think that we have got over that one. The two big headaches at present are the cooling—she boils like a tea kettle the whole time—and the designing of a new manifold. When the 750 Formula was brought in it outlawed siamesed-ports with tongues projecting into them. The problem now is to design a new manifolding which complies with the Formula and still maintains the same power. It looks as if I shall have to borrow Uhlenhaut's sodium-cooled slide rule for that one. At present the little car has to run with the 1,172 c.c. boys, and although I can, occasionally, catch one or two of the slower ones, we have little hope of doing any good. Apart from this the car generally is in a somewhat tatty condition and will need many, many hours spent on tidying oddments. It has the makings of the most fascinating seven-fifty I have ever known and promises several years of extremely cheap motor racing. It is also the most admirable road car and can be driven to meetings instead of being transported on a 12-m.p.g. truck. Being so small and light it does a very honest 50 miles to the gallon on the road. I think I shall keep it for a decade or so till Colin wants it for a place of honour in his Bond Street showrooms and offers me a Mark XXXIX Lotus in exchange.

To return to Averil's 1,446 c.c. Mark VI. I should like to conclude by recording two occurrences which may be of use to other Lotus owners. A week or two back both our stub-axles snapped off with finely crystallised fractures. When I told Colin he said that I had naughtily omitted to change them every two years. I didn't know this ; perhaps some other Lotus owners don't either. So if you didn't know count quickly up to two and if the age of your car exceeds this change 'em immediately. Being basically Ford they are both cheap and easily obtained.

The other thing is that we couldn't think why we couldn't get maximum revs. out of our engine and there was a flat-spot big enough to play billiards on. This turned out to be because we had bolted the carburetters direct on to the manifold and the engine vibration joggled the petrol in the float chambers around, thus upsetting carburation. We cured this with a thick neoprene joint. This should not be nipped too tight and is secured by bolts with Simmons or similar self-locking nuts.

Got £1700 to spare — all at once, or a few pounds at a time? If so, you can build one of these sleek, pacy sportsters in your own back yard.

LOTUS AVAILABLE HERE IN KITSET FORM

BUILD YOUR OWN SPORTS CAR

A sleek new sports/racing car . . . over 100 m.p.h. . . . 50 m.p.g. . . . shattering performance . . .
And now, here in Australia, you can build it yourself from a factory kitset for approximately £1700.

To the enthusiast there is probably no more interesting pastime than building a sports "special", yet the melancholy truth is that exceedingly few "specials" turn out to be honestly worthwhile. Some present so many involved technical problems that their owners lose heart before the job is completed. Others, again, run up such a costly budget that the task has perforce to be abandoned before the closing stages. Of those specials which eventually do take the road in more or less the form their builders envisaged, surprisingly few prove to be worth the time and painstaking effort required to build them.

That this is inevitably so is natural. Car design is a highly specialised field, and where a man has to make use of components intended to do one specific job in a totally different type of chassis, his task is made three times more difficult. Again, very few enthusiasts have sufficient technical knowledge to ensure accurate steering, sound road-holding and vice-free performance at high speed in the finished car.

Several years ago an English firm took this problem boldly by the horns and marketed a well-tried basic design of kit-set car—the Lotus—which could be assembled by an enthusiast, and modified to suit his own particular needs without provoking complicated headaches in suspension design or steering geometry.

In course of time the Lotus came to Australia. Its successes—first in the hands of Alex Strachan, and, later, Doug Chivas—were most impressive, and the future of the new-comer looked exceedingly bright.

Now the Lotus is available in kit form made in Australia, and to match it the enthusiast can choose between a fibreglass and two aluminium bodies, one aerodynamic, and all made in Sydney, N.S.W.

For a total outlay of £1,700, the home mechanic can build his own sports-racing car, knowing that the

Inset above: Instrumentation in the build-it-yourself Lotus is what you make it; can be austere or ornate, according to personal whim. Chivas has settled for king size tachometer (note position of telltale hand), oil and water thermometers, ammeter, and oil pressure gauge.

design is both sound and proven, and the finished car will be almost invincible in its class.

Background . . .

This kit-form Lotus is one of a line of cars which have behind them a fascinating story. Its designer, Colin Chapman, scored many notable successes in trial driving in England following the outbreak of peace in 1955. His car—basically an Austin 7—incorporated many interesting and advanced technicalities of Chapman's own design. Later, Chapman turned to racing the "Lotus", as he called his car, and once more achieved notable success in the 750 c.c. class.

As an aeronautical engineer, Chapman then turned his hand seriously to chassis design, and eventually produced a "space frame" composed of multiple small diameter steel tubes.

Before long, he had a specialist working out the lines of a low-drag aerodynamic body. The finished car was spectacular—and Colin Chapman was in business!

High performance, superlative road holding and remarkable fuel economy have characterised all his Lotus cars. accelerates from 0-60 m.p.h. in 7.9 seconds, clips along at 113 m.p.h., and seconds, clips along at 113 mp.h., and returns 55 m.p.g. at a constant 50 miles an hour.

Remarkable? Yes, but remember that the Lotus weighs 9½ cwt. and is less than knee-high to a Cadillac.

Climax Engine . . .

Unquestionably, the Lotus owes much of its performance to its 1098 c.c. Coventry Climax power plant, which punches out 75 b.h.p. at 6,250 r.p.m. Tuned to stage one, this unit costs £400 in Australia, and is available, together with the remainder of the Lotus kit, from Lotus Cars (Australia).

An alternative engine, with stage two tuning, has a high-lift camshaft, modified manifolds, and a few other detail alterations. Towards the end of next year the Formula II 1,500 c.c. Coventry Climax engines will be

Back end is conventional De Dion, has finned magnesium alloy inboard brakedrums. Lotus cars are proverbially sweet handling; have fantastic stopping power.

BUILD YOUR OWN SPORTS CAR

available also, alternatively.

Meanwhile, the 1300 c.c. and 1,460 c.c. engines are available on three months delivery.

The chassis frame is built from both round and square section tubing, and its unique design reflects Chapman's former occupation as a designer of light alloy structures. Priced at £160, the frame can be used to carry a variety of engines.

Lotus Cars (Australia) have arranged for local production of a number of the components included in the kit. These include the turbo-finned magnesium alloy brake drums (£24 each, complete with liners), and the magnesium backing plates (£3/10/- each). The complete set of brakes alone thus amounts to £110.

Kitset Components . . .

The Lotus rear end design follows the true de Dion pattern, and has the magnesium alloy differential housing bolted to the frame. The housing bolted to the frame This housing, complete with sump—finned for cooling—costs £35. The de Dion tube is made from 3 in. steel, has provision for de Dion-type hubs, and is located by long radius arms and a Panhard rod. Price, £36. Twin universal jointed axle shafts — from the inboard brake drums to the rear wheels—cost £56 a pair.

The de Dion hubs — made from magnesium alloy casing, cost £45/5/- each, and are fitted with splined shaft, bearings, oil seals, spacers and tapered sleeves. The differential drive shafts, taking the power from the diff. housing to the brakes, cost £36 a pair.

A rather surprising feature of the Lotus is its divided front axle, based on Ford Prefect components. It is basically a beam axle, but is divided in the centre and hinged to the chassis frame. Made up and ready to instal, it sells for £20.

The suspension system is all-Girling, with flexible coil springs encircling extremely firm telescopic dampers. Total cost, £30.

M.G. T.C. Gearbox

Several types of gearboxes are suitable for the power unit, but an M.G. TC box is recommended and costs roughly £100. Wire wheels, gleaned from either a TR3 or an M.G. TF, suit the car admirably, and, if bought new, add a further £54 to the assembly bill.

The Lotus-designed body is not generally available in Australia, but Lotus Cars (Australia) have an excellent Australian-designed all fibreglass envelope-type body in production. It is built for them by a Sydney garage which specialises in this type of work, and the Lotus shown in our illustrations (owned by Bill Reynolds) is fitted with the first fibreglass body to be produced locally specially for the Lotus.

Its designer claims that the body incorporates features "borrowed" from the D-type Jaguar, as well as the latest Ferrari and Maserati. Be that as it may, it is no secret that the fibreglass Lotus provoked a minor sensation when it made its debut at a recent race meeting.

Unpainted, but complete with mounting brackets, the body costs £220. Alternatively, it can be sprayed and mounted on a chassis for an all-in total of £370.

Again, the builder can choose between the "square rigger" sports type or fully areodynamic body, both made from aluminium by Stanley Brown, who built the first original bodies in England for Chapman. Brown is now resident in Sydney. In this case, prices are: £300 plus tax for the "Square rigger" complete with sptace frame and all mounting brackets; and £500 plus tax for the fully streamlined job.

Incidentally, the same bodies will also fit all types of M.G. "Midgets", the small Singers, the Morris Minor, and the VW. A range of trim, hoods, sidescreens, etc., can be supplied to meet the owner's requirements, and these cost on an average around £80.

Build-it-Yourself

Assembly instructions come with every kit, and the car can be put together by ordinary men working with limited tools and having no more than average mechanical ability

All parts are subject to sales tax.

Tailpiece

(For high-speed enthusiasts only.)

In racing trim, the 1,100 c.c. Lotus is an astonishingly potent car. British drivers report that in the Le Mans, they peaked at 7,800 r.p.m. down the straight—a speed which represents about 136 m.p.h. on the road. And in acceleration it will hold its own with a C-type Jaguar! ●

Above: Doug Chivas poses in his Lotus for "Wheels" cameraman. Clean lines, low frontal area, are apparent. (Chivas is the man on the left — his passenger has not yet been identified).

Below: Here's what makes the Lotus scamper; turn in upwards of 50 m.p.g., at 60 m.p.h. cruising speeds — the huge-hearted Coventry Climax 1100 c.c. engine, designed originally, believe it or not, to drive fire pumps!

Lotus Maintenance
The Mark Six

by Mike Costin

THE chassis of the Mark Six Lotus is a very robust structure which requires very little maintenance, but it is essential that it should be kept carefully painted and free from corrosion. The wheel base is 7 ft 3 in, with a front track of 3 ft 11 in and a rear track of 3 ft 9 in. There is one degree positive camber angle at normal ride position. Castor angle is 3 degrees and toe-in is $\frac{1}{8}$ in.

Suspension units fitted to the Mark Six are of the co-axial coil spring/telescopic damper type, manufactured by Woodhead Monroe. The front units, which have eye-type fixing top and bottom, measure $16\frac{1}{4}$ in between eye centres when fully extended. They have a 5 in stroke, 185 lb per inch springs and double action shock absorber incorporated. The rear units measure $18\frac{1}{2}$ in between the eye centres, with eyes top and bottom. The stroke is 7 in and 58 lb per inch springs are fitted.

The Mark Six braking system is of the single cable type, with one inner and one outer cable only. The inner runs between the actuating arms on the front and rear axles and is partially covered by an outer cable fitted between the cable stop on the rear axle torque tube flange and the cable abutment on the bottom of the footbrake pedal. Firstly the cable must be well lubricated, in order to secure correct compensation between front and rear. Secondly, the outer cable must not be fixed to anything at all, only constrained where it passes along the undertray, i.e. by a stirrup which allows the outer cable to move approximately $2\frac{1}{4}$ in when the footbrake pedal is depressed. There are three different positions for attaching the front cable to the actuating lever, two of these being provided by the lever extension as supplied by Lotus and the third being the normal position when the lever extension is removed. The two extensions are mainly for use when Consul or MG engines are fitted. Standard brake linings are quite suitable for racing when the side-valve Ford Ten engine is used, even in its most advanced form, but should an overhead valve conversion or a Coventry Climax engine be fitted, then a better type of brake lining, such as Ferodo VG95 or Mintex M14, will become necessary.

Later chassis were fitted with two engine anti-judder stays and these were picked up on brackets mounted on the front cross tube, whereas the early type had only one of these mountings, which was fitted on the offside.

The steering gear used on the Mark Six is of the Burman worm and nut type, similar to that used on the Ford Popular but specially built for Lotus. The wear on the steering gear is such that in the first few hundred miles there may be up to an inch of play at the rim of the wheel, but thereafter the wear rate is very slight. The track rod bell-crank on very early chassis was fitted with a pin, working through two plain bearings; later chassis had a modified bell-crank with the pin working in two taper roller bearings, which is infinitely preferable. The stub axles should be changed whenever contact is made with a bank or any other hard object outside the course of normal motoring, because the steering arms may fracture at the root. In any case this is a point to be watched.

Normal ride height of the Mark Six is $6\frac{1}{2}$ in to axle pivots at the front and six inches at the rear.

The engine normally used is the Ford Ten E93A unit and, for tuning this, either a proprietary aluminium high compression cylinder head or the Ford Eight head with spigot type dynamo mounting are to be recommended. Double valve springs are available for this engine and are supplied by Messrs. Herbert Terry and Son, the part number being VS 318. The gearbox is best suited for racing when fitted with Buckler C-type close ratio gears.

Failure of the two round section tubes on which the gearbox is mounted may be experienced on cars fitted with MG TC gearboxes in unit with either MG, Consul or Climax engines. This can be repaired by the substitution of 1 in square 16 gauge rectangular tube.

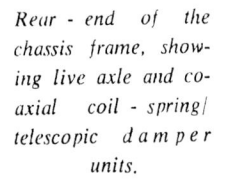

Fully-tuned Ford Ten engine installed in Mark Six frame. The Mark Six will still be eligible for 1172 Formula racing this season.

Rear-end of the chassis frame, showing live axle and co-axial coil-spring/telescopic damper units.

A Lotus Mk. VI, a Feminine Crew, and some Unexpected Snow in an Adventurous Journey into Spain in Search of Winter Warmth

Part I

"... a rather Spartan racing affair. It didn't run to such niceties as a heater, a demister or a fog lamp."

TWO DAYS to SUNSHINE

By
Renata Kenmore

HAVE leaden skies and bitter winds in a typical January ever made you long for a sunny southern climate? In January 1958, the longing became too much for us. Armed with a small car, plenty of sun-tan lotion and a heaven-sent invitation to stay at a villa near Gibraltar, we set off to motor through France and Spain to the Costa del Sol.

Of course, there'd been a lot of sinister warnings from our friends about the roads in Spain. We'd laughed them away, since they were obviously due to jealousy. After all, Spain has become one of the most popular holiday countries in recent years. In 1957 some fifty thousand British motorists took their cars to Spain. In 1958 there were even more. The roads simply couldn't be that bad! Inquiries at the Spanish State Tourist Office and the various motoring organizations reassured us even more. All we needed to do, it seemed, was to keep to those roads on the map which were marked International Throughways.

There'd been another reason for our inquiries. The car itself, a Lotus-Ford Mk. VI, was a rather Spartan racing affair. It didn't run to such niceties as a heater, a demister or a fog lamp. To a certain extent we'd converted it for touring. The extent got as far as full weather equipment, a luggage grid and traction-grip tyres. We were going to be very grateful for those tyres before the run ended.

In Paris the weather reports talked happily of snow in the Massif Central and that confirmed us in our original decision to go the shortest way, through Bordeaux to reach the Spanish frontier on the west. During the winter months the long range of the Pyrenees forms a formidable barrier, to be crossed only at its seaboard extremities. To the west N.1 takes one from Irun at the frontier to Madrid. It is known as the best road in Spain.

It rained heavily all the way through France. At Bayonne it was still pouring as we filled all our containers with oil and high-octane fuel. This is a necessary precaution before crossing the frontier, since good oils are obtainable only on the Black Market. High-octane petrol can be found only in the large towns and of them Spain has, when compared to England, relatively few. But we were confident that the rain couldn't last for ever. Surely at the frontier we could hope to get our nose above water. And even as our visas and papers were being stamped at Irun, the rain stopped. In a few moments we should be speeding along N.1 to Madrid in the glorious Spanish sunshine. Our delight at the prospect must have been showing on our faces, because every Spaniard was smiling back at us. Slowly it dawned on us that there was too large an element of amazement in their interest. They had eyes only for the Lotus, the like of which they had plainly never seen.

More Complex Than Their Cookery

I had at the back of my mind a phrase which I once read in a Spanish cookery book. The cooking in Spain, it said, follows the climate. In the north they stew, in the centre they roast and in the south they fry. But Spanish geography is much more complex than Spanish cookery and their weather follows their geography in its complexities. There are monstrous and sudden variations in climate for the traveller in Spain. In Castile it may be snowing, on the Atlantic coast there may be chilly rain, in Andalusia warm rain and in Malaga hot winter sunshine. We were to meet some of these variations quite quickly.

By the time we left San Sebastian it had started to snow, and we found ourselves alone on the road. Worse, a blizzard was coming down as we climbed the pass (2,460

"They had eyes only for the Lotus"

TWO DAYS to SUNSHINE

feet) which lay between us and Burgos. Our plan was to reach Burgos that night. It grew more and more dense as we climbed. Soon it was necessary to stop every hundred yards to remove a great carpet of snow from the windscreen. And talking of the carpets, the white one along which we were travelling wasn't at all like the dusting of snow which follows the first 10 minutes of a snowstorm in England. It looked smooth and white and crisp, but in fact it was already a foot deep. As for smoothness, it concealed within itself all kinds of rocks and small boulders. The knowledge that the car has a normal clearance of 7 in. explained the nasty scraping noises. Some of those hidden lumps were scraping dangerously against the sump.

In spite of the incessant stops for snow-clearing, we caught up with a large diesel. We couldn't overtake. By now the road was a narrow ribbon winding up one side of the gorge and the unfenced and precipitous descent was hardly inviting. In a way we almost felt comforted by having a companion in this battle through the elements. We were nearing the summit when, to our horror, we saw the road crumble into the gorge on the right immediately after the rear wheels of the lorry had passed over it. And not just the edge of the road. The road. We slithered to a stop in time. If you've never seen a road yawn like that into a precipice, I can assure you that it isn't comforting. There was indeed a shaky-looking width of 3 ft. left, but since the Lotus has a width of 4 ft. 4 in. and can't walk on one leg, we had obviously finished the journey for the time being. We rolled a cigarette and considered the situation. One can't spend the night on a crumbling hillside in a blizzard in a Lotus. But how far back had the nearest habitation been? Quite a long way, though come to think of it there'd been a notice up. That was it! Peones Camineros had said the legend. And Peones Camineros wasn't an advertisement for a soft drink. If it meant anything at all, it meant road-menders.

Luckily, the roads don't often vanish in England. But if they did I doubt whether the local council could respond the way those road-menders did. We found four of them, and gay and willing they came as soon as they grasped our problem. Dressed in rough brown cloaks and armed only with smallish picks they trudged up to the gap. I couldn't quite see how they could possibly rebuild the road which had crumbled, and, of course, they didn't. They'd got a simpler answer than that. They hacked away at the cliff light-heartedly, and by the time dusk came, several hours later, they'd produced a road wide enough for the Lotus to pass. As we waved them good-bye, I wondered just how much wider that gorge would ultimately be if that sort of thing continued.

Unexpected Excellence

There was now no hope of reaching Burgos that night, but we couldn't stay on top of the pass. Since darkness had now been added to the swirling snow, visibility was negligible, and we had to pin our faith on the lorry tracks. Some hours and several grey hairs later, we arrived at Vitoria. And with the unexpectedness of Spain, there was an excellent hotel. An excellent hotel is a delight under any circumstances, but after that first day of Spanish travel it seemed a positive miracle. The Basque country has a lot of famous dishes, and perhaps the one best known to tourists is the Bacalao a la Vizcaina based on dried hake, but after a journey like that we settled for the Cordero Asada . . . the roast lamb being very good indeed in this part of Spain.

It was dismaying to find that it was still snowing next day, but everyone assured us that we had left the worst behind us. From now to Burgos was flat. Not that it was likely to be without event, as we saw at once.

In manoeuvring the car out of the

"Seventy-three vehicles, most of them diesel lorries, were halted nose to tail. Some of them were already on their sides. Others just about to topple over."

of which they had plainly never seen."

garage a lad who was more interested in our headgear than the job in hand managed to bend a front wing. But there was hardly time to get it repaired, so after using the magic word *plomo*, which might only mean "lead," but which in this connection means high octane, we filled the tank and started off on the next leg of the journey.

In Vitoria itself, the snow was deep and crunchy, and in the town there were none of the hidden boulders which had proved a menace the day before. But outside on the open road we ran at once into solid ice. That in itself would have made progress slow and difficult, but there was another hazard. Lorry tracks were deep and the only way to move without grounding on account of our slight clearance was to drive with two wheels deep in a lorry track and the other two riding on the frozen hump between. After two hours of travelling at this undignified angle we were relieved to see that conditions were about to change. We were approaching an immense plain, treeless and white. It stretched as far as the eye could see. But it wasn't the immensity or the flatness which made it memorable. It was the impossibility of the scene a hundred yards away. At first glance it was as neat and static as a circus ring full of elephants. And just as improbable and dynamic. Seventy-three vehicles, most of them diesel lorries, were halted nose to tail. Some of them were already on their sides. Others just about to topple over.

Trouble in Pale Pink

We drew up behind a monster Pegaso on to the wheels of which the driver and his mate were attaching huge chains. Many of these diesels, by the way, have been imported from England. Leaving the car and battling on foot against a piercing wind we stumbled along to the front of the line to see what was going on. It turned out to be a matter of what had gone off. A pale pink Cadillac inhabited by four weeping South Americans was being dragged back to where the road was hoped to be by a number of burly Guardias Civiles. The operation completed, tears dried and shoulders braced, they started off again, braving destiny with some muttered if lurid imprecations. We watched their progress for a moment or two. It was spectacular if hardly progress, as they went sliding and slithering over that limitless ice rink.

We trudged back past the toppling lorries to where we had left the Lotus. It was still there, though neither of us would have been surprised if, left unattended, it had taken it into its head to go scurrying back to that English January from which we had been trying to escape. But delighted though we were to see it, it hardly qualified as a first-class hotel in which to spend the night in that sort of climate. The only answer was to jump the queue. The low weight of the car and the Firestone "Snow Tyres" on the rear wheels just about made it possible to cross that ice plateau. Even that included a succession of groundings. And not always did one of us heaving outside clear some of the wedgings. But, whenever that happened, black-coated figures emerged from the swirling snow and silently lent an arm in return for the right number of pesetas. By the time the skating rink gave way to a village, it was far too dark to hope to reach Burgos, still thirty kilometres away. At the end of our first two days of driving in Spain, we had failed to make our target for the first day, nor had we seen anything but snow. But we were cold and hungry and feeling like some unpaid and forgotten section of the Geophysical Year. Willing, indeed, to forgo the splendid hotels of Burgos for any kind of food and warmth. For a few seconds we pondered the odd collection of farmhouses . . . or were they bars? We chose the most brightly lit of the lot and nosed our way in.

(To be concluded)

". . . black coated figures emerged from the swirling snow and silently lent an arm in return for the right number of pesetas."

TWO

The Mk. VI Lotus crossing the great Vega, north-west of Madrid. Although straight and uncluttered, the roads were so badly surfaced that a comfortable maximum speed was no greater than 45 m.p.h.

IT cannot be gainsaid that the scene in the brightly-lit village bar was interesting and the decor vigorous. The floor was littered with straw and with bones and with manure. In one corner two or three goats nosed about in this delectable paradise. Against a massive wooden bar leaned half a dozen equally massive shepherds in cloaks. They were eating whole fish. It is undeniable that this corner of Spain is notable for its fish cookery, but we didn't stay to try it. The smell was overpowering, though whether it came from the fish, the shepherds, the goats or the decor we never discovered. We knew we were beaten and we retreated hastily. Luckily, the next bar was cleaner and evidently less popular. Furthermore they had a room. And to add to our delight, they also had a granary into which we could put the Lotus. To add to their delight, everyone in the bar came out to watch us slither the car through the slush into its shelter. The operation was both worth watching and worth listening to. With a sickening crunch the Lotus impaled its entrails on an unseen piece of iron projecting from the centre of the threshold. The shouts of encouragement from the peasants were heartening. The discovery that the impact had bent double the clutch arm wasn't. However, all misery is relative and temporary, and the food and the warmth and the wine convinced us that the Middle Ages, in which for the night we seemed to be living, had many virtues.

The morning, too, when it came seemed determined to make up for the first two days. The sun was shining and the snow was melting on the road and (thank God for craftsmen everywhere!) the village blacksmith straightened the clutch arm quite successfully. We were in Burgos in no time at all and had an excellent lunch almost next door to the famous Gothic cathedral which certainly deserves a longer visit than, because of our slow start, it got from us. And now of course we'd finished with the foothills of the Pyrenees. Before us stretched the great plain or Vega. When next we saw mountains it would be the Guadarrama, the great mountain barrier to the north-west of Madrid where the Madrilenos go for their skiing.

However, we couldn't just head for Madrid across the Guadarrama like that. For one thing the Somosierra Pass was closed at that time of the year. For another thing, the lower Guadarrama pass which was likely to be open, though it meant taking a longer way round, would lead us through Valladolid. And we wanted to see Valladolid, even apart from the fact that it would make a pleasant change from the Vega, situated as it is in the centre of that great plain. So we said goodbye to N.1.

A Continuing Process

When will one ever learn about roads? I suspect the answer is as soon as one learns about life, fully. It's a continuing process and never completed. The road we took across this great plain is as straight and uncluttered as a measuring tape, but its surface is far from good. We found very quickly that the maximum

"Rush hour in a Spanish village," or, "Will we catch those lights?"

44

DAYS to SUNSHINE
By Renata Kenmore

A Lotus Mk. VI, a Feminine Crew, and some Unexpected Snow in an Adventurous Journey into Spain in Search of Winter Warmth

Part II

Traffic in Spain always keeps to the right.

comfortable speed on it was in the region of forty miles per hour, with an occasional mad burst of forty-five. It's very frustrating for a sports car, used to crowded roads but freed at last from its inhibitions by a ten-mile straight to discover that though there mightn't be traffic lights and pedestrians and blind corners and radar traffic-checks, there are as many pot-holes as atoms in a pin-head and the tarmac is as rippled as an undulating snake. So down to forty.

Empty and Desolate

The landscape was empty apart from desolate groups of umbrella pines. Now and then we saw an occasional flock of sheep or goats, the shepherds wrapped in rough, woollen blankets and carrying crooks, unchanged in appearance from remote times. Now and then a team of mules and a driver dragged a primitive plough through the stony and half-frozen soil. In the distance a cordillera of grey, flat-topped hills was relieved by specks of white, the white-washed entrances to cliff dwellings. Now and then, high above us, soared an eagle. Now and then . . . indeed, it was almost all "then." Never have I seen a landscape so completely in the Middle Ages. The only note of "now" was the Lotus in which we drove.

And then into the monotony burst Valladolid. The crowded streets and the lively animation of a Spanish town are probably the most welcome sight in the world to the eyes of a weary traveller. At least, to a traveller on Spanish roads. For one must face the fact that the pot-holes and the ripples exist not only on the road from Burgos to Madrid but on practically all the roads in the country. Schemes for improvement are in hand but, like the delivery of a new road system in England, the actual performance seems to lag a little behind the promise. Yet, despite the roads, even a town like Valladolid has its cars, mostly Volkswagens and small Renaults produced in Spain and, of course, the Spanish Fiat . . . the S.E.A.T. Not everyone feels that craters and ripples are a blemish on the road, of course. Some pedestrians who look for variety after walking miles seem almost to welcome them. And if in Spain the roads are not really a motorist's paradise, perhaps it is because they were designed for pedestrians. For more than a thousand years they have served, and served well, the man and the mule, the goats and the oxen. And, of course, the beggar.

"Tio Pedro"

It was at Valladolid that Tio Pedro walked into a bar as we drank an aperitif. His face was as weathered as the bar itself and as polished. His bamboo staff was too thin to be a support and we couldn't work out why he wore two scallop shells, one on his fez and one on his cloak. We never found out about the little leather bag at the end of his staff, but it looked suspiciously as though with its help he could have collected money from the deeper ranks of a crowd had he ever decided to do a little busking. Not that he gave any sign of wanting to sing or dance, yet he was cheerful enough. Someone bought him a drink and then we bought him another and with his cheerful sun-blackened face and his gay scallop shells he looked as picturesque a ruffian as one could hope to meet on a bright morning. When we left the bar and Pedro behind, it suddenly was a bright morning. From that moment on we had fine weather. After that first two and a half days of snow and ice, we ran into the warmth and sunshine we'd come to find. We stayed in it all the way down through Madrid to Granada and way up again to

Fly-over system: road above, dry river-bed below.

A happy family of cliff dwellers, their cave in the background.

TWO DAYS to SUNSHINE

Barcelona. But that's a separate journey and perhaps some time we'll get that down on to paper too. For the moment let's get back to Tio Pedro, the man who brought the sunshine. At the very end of our trip, months later, we ran into him again, north of Barcelona, as we filled our tank with the last drop of Spanish high octane. There was no mistaking him, staff and leather bag and scallop shells and all. He didn't recognize us but with the instinctive gesture of a man who tramps forever the whole of the land, he waved to us and we to him.

"Who's that?" we asked the garageman as he replaced the filler cap. He looked up after the retreating Pedro.

"That one!" he said. "Who knows?"

"We met him first in Valladolid," we explained, "months ago and he brought us good travelling."

"Ah," said the garageman giving us a sly, sideways grin as if to see whether we were ready for a little joke . . . "You can always be sure of shell!"

We don't know to this day whether Pedro was a self-appointed advertisement or whether he was really some terrible kind of weather sprite in disguise. For just as he'd brought us good weather, he took it away again. Half an hour after he'd vanished down the road we were in the Pyreneees again.

Battling with another blizzard.

"Tio Pedro," or the "Representative" of the well-known firm, the man who brought the sunshine. We met him in Valladolid and again near Barcelona, months later, still with his staff and little leather bag.

ANY OLD IRON...

Dave Kelsey relates how he built the first Lotus Mark VI production chassis with a bare minimum of tools, using an old iron bedstead as a chassis jig

"BRAND new Lotus VI chassis frames for sale, rustproofed and painted, £30 each." Back in the early Fifties, £30 was indeed what we – the Progress Chassis Co – got for building a complex multi-tube frame, including all suspension mods and delivery, from the budding, struggling Lotus Engineering Co. Rustproofing meant wiping over with Jenolite, and painting was by brush using Valspar Light Battleship Grey, at least it was until we invested in a Burgess electric spray gun. This had the immediate advantage that, as it required water-thin paint to work at all, we could paint the whole chassis from one position, relying on drips to cover the lower parts.

Although John Teychenne and I had been working together building his 1172 Special and Clive Clairmonte's Chapman-designed Lea Francis special, my first sight of a Lotus MkVI was in 1952 when Nigel Allen and John turned up at my house in Hornsey with the very first of the breed, complete with parts-bin Consul engine. The car was immaculate in unpainted aluminium, gleaming in the Sunday morning sunshine, but I had no way of knowing that this was to be the forerunner of a whole new breed of car. Specials were thick on the ground in the Fifties, most of them so horrible as to defy description. It was revelatory, therefore, to see this shiny, neat two-seater – engine lost in a spacious and spotless engine compartment, exhaust burbling, twin SU carburettors rocking gently as Nigel blipped the throttle. I already knew Colin could make a car go, having watched the Lotus MkIII perform spectacularly at various meetings, and now he had produced one that looked right and almost professional.

Colin wanted to produce MkVIs and, as John had a little space in his father's back garden workshop and a few rudimentary tools, we were ideally placed to take on the contract. Today, of course, you need 100,000ft^2 of factory, 200 office staff and a team of designers to build a kart, but then we were ignorant of this and thought we could do it with just the two of us!

The ball was set rolling when Nigel crashed the MkVI on the way to compete at Boreham Wood on August Bank Holiday Monday 1952, producing a few hundred pounds (at the time, it was supposed to have been £600, but now it seems to have grown to £800) by way of insurance payout. Lotus Engineering had been formed on January 1, 1952 with Nigel Allen, his brother Michael, Colin Chapman and his father Stanley as directors. Colin commandeered a small workshop at his father's pub in Tottenham Lane, Hornsey, for minor assembly and customer entertainment, and John and I began the construction of the second MkVI in our workshop.

The first thing we did was to acquire an old bedstead made of four lengths of angle iron joined by castings at the corners. This was to be our main chassis jig, since we knew that high precision would be vital. The jig was actually a good deal flimsier than the chassis but a firm and positive kick at the legs of the worm-eaten wooden trestles the whole thing stood on, usually served to correct any errors in alignment. We already had a hacksaw, two hammers, a worn bastard file, an ancient (probably pre-First World War) hand-turned drill, a Wolf ¼in electric drill, one set of gas welding gear, and an old Keetona hand shear mounted on a railway sleeper. This was actually bolted on so that the sleeper stuck out behind the shears, instead of in front where you could stand on it to hold it down, so there was a powerful tendency for the sleeper to rise up and smite you in the face when cutting thick material. We also had a large and rusty vice mounted to a wooden bench by two ½in bolts in 1in holes.

Almost everything was in short supply in the Fifties, so if you wanted to make a car, recycling was the order of the day. Anything metal would be pressed into service, and old filing cabinets, water pipes, bits of cars and scrap of all kinds found their way into the MkVIs. We were completely skint, so there was no question of buying any tools, and as the profit margin on a chassis was around nine old pence (4p), there was not much prospect of it either.

The first MkVI took us six weeks of evenings and weekends to build, and the drawing, such as it was, got consumed by fire in the process, so all the rest were built from memory. I learned to weld on the job, so to speak, keeping the fact a secret from Chapman, in case he felt I wasn't up to it. Actually, by the time I started on his own chassis, (number five, I think) I was quite competent, but some of the earlier ones may have been a bit suspect in places.

Much to our surprise, we were asked to build another chassis, then another, until we had built five or six, by which time the world must surely have been full of Lotuses. At the time, IBM predicted that the total world market for computers was six machines, so we were in good company in our accuracy of foresight.

Nigel Allen racing the prototype Lotus MkVI at Silverstone in 1952. The twin carb Ford Consul engine was reduced to 1,499cc

ANY OLD IRON...

The cars won races right from the beginning, frequently against more powerful opposition, and pressure on us increased. We added a greenhouse to our extensive factory complex, and cleared the rubbish out of a lean-to so as to set up a production line of one car at a time. We had the time down to one a week now, mainly by working from 8am until 1am the next day, and we had two hacksaws and two vices. We also began to take on other kinds of work such as point-of-sale displays, to cushion the blow when Lotus could not raise the £30 for a chassis and we had to march it back to our works again.

I experimented with making the chassis lighter by using 20-gauge tube instead of 18 gauge, and 16-gauge sheet instead of 10 gauge for various brackets and components, and eventually got down to 36lb for a complete chassis. I can't remember who the lucky owner was who got that one. When I see today's kit car manufacturers boasting in their ads about using 10-gauge tube and ¼in plate for extra strength, I can only assume that they must take all their design staff from JCB.

Although we found the whole business of building cars one continuous laugh, we did really take it seriously in the engineering sense, and the cars were well and conscientiously built. The reputation that Lotus acquired for flimsiness was, in my view, quite unfair; such breakages as took place being mainly in the proprietary components like hubs, rather than in the Lotus parts *per se*. Of course, they were not intended to be driven like American speedway racers, and so if you did hit

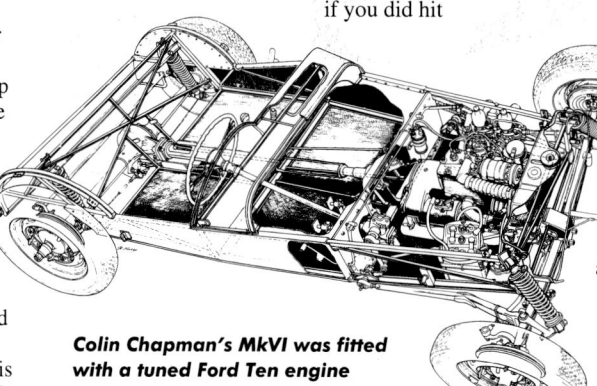

Colin Chapman's MkVI was fitted with a tuned Ford Ten engine

anything, the chances were something would break. I know from having repaired virtually every Lotus that crashed over a three-year period just how tough the chassis was – so tough in fact that we tended to reduce weld penetration in order that minor shunts would not transmit damage to every part of the frame.

As a pointer to the sheer practicality of the MkVI frame, it was used as the basis for the Marks VIII, IX, and X, and subsequently in essence for the Seven and the later spaceframe cars, in spite of experiments with 80-ton high-tensile tubing (it broke), eutectic bronze welding (it broke), swaged sheet metal bulkheads (they cracked), and various radical design departures by the De Havilland part-timers that Colin employed for practically no money. I believe the key to its strength was that being made of welded furniture tube with a maximum tensile strength of 28 tons, the frame yielded homogeneously to stress, rather than creating stress concentrations at the welds. By contrast, 80-ton tube necessarily has to put up with 20 tons or less tensile at the welds, whilst bronze welding is so rigid it simply does not yield at all but snaps catastrophically.

Progress Chassis Co began to gain a reputation in the esoteric field of racing car chassis construction, and rival designers approached us to build their cars. This gave some insight into the competition, and I am still amazed at the crudity of the chassis design of the day – basic ladder frames with no real torsional stiffness at all, bracing tubes bent into curves – in spite of Buckler and Chapman, who showed the way things should be done.

Around this time, I ventured into design myself, with a Special called the Kelsey GT 2/4, another for Sid Marler, and a 500cc Norton racer for Ken Smith. The latter won the championship for non-works cars that year in Ken's capable

G A Horton competing in his MkVI 1172 (chassis 104) at Brands Hatch in June 1957 at the 750 MC, 250 MRC and Club Lotus meeting

hands. He subsequently went on to drive a Lotus MkIX with great verve, particularly on the road, where he filled up three driving licences with endorsements in about three years, before his tragic death from kidney failure.

I had developed a yen for racing by this time and, having a steady income of £14 or £15 a week, I figured I could well afford it. Nowadays, I understand that you have to reckon on spending £25,000 a year to run a Formula Ford, but then – provided that you could scrounge a few free tyres from Dunlop and free petrol – about £12 would see you through a season's racing.

I had done a lot of work for Lotus directly, patching up and modifying the works cars, with no payment, and Colin Chapman let me have various components free of charge, which enabled me to build a MkVIII for £180 in total. I then arranged with Jabby Crombac, who had bought Colin's works MkVI, to have his engine and gearbox in exchange for fitting a Consul engine and flared front wings to his car. So I had Colin's superb and secretly tweaked 1100 engine, in a state-of-the-art car, with which to conquer the world. It didn't work out quite like that.

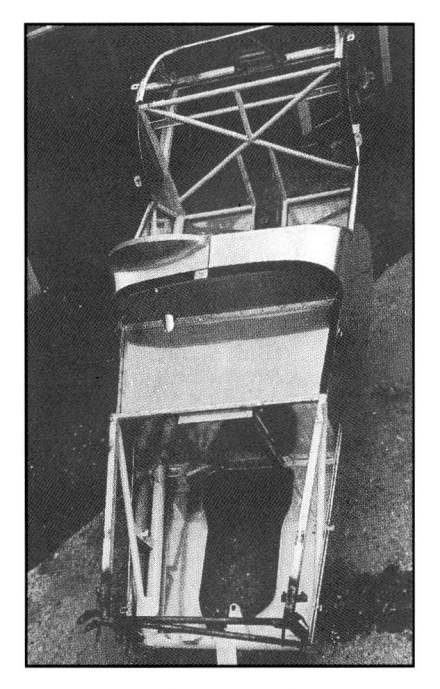

The tweaks, to which only Colin, Mike Costin, Jabby and I were privy, consisted of replacing the standard E93A non-adjustable tappets with special ones having a T-shaped crosspiece at the cam end to increase the dwell time. The simpler route – changing the cam profile – was not permitted in the 1172 Formula for which the car was primarily intended, so the legendary Chapman ingenuity was called into play, together with Mike Costin's stamina, to produce the tappet shapes by hand traversing on an old lathe bed. To prevent the tappet from rotating, a keyway was machined in it, and an Allen caphead screw installed in the valve chest as a key.

To borrow a portent-laden phrase from the late Gerard Hoffnung, 'unfortunately' en route to my first race in the car, one of the capheads came loose, permitting the tappet to rotate until it was crosswise to the cam, where it shaved no less than 0.16in from the cam peak. Not unreasonably, this reduced the performance and made a bit of a clatter, so I removed the spark plug in the hope of limiting the damage until I could do something about it. I am not sure what I thought this would achieve.

As a temporary measure, a new Ford tappet was procured and fitted in the paddock, and the car was raced in this condition. A most regrettable occurrence, since the tappet ate heavily into my racing budget for the year, and so far we had attended only one meeting. I soon had other problems, however, as I shunted a straw bale at Ibsley after mistaking a slow corner for a fast one, and Williams and Pritchard thought I should wait until the end of the season before repairing the bent tail fin.

At the end of the season, with 1,750 miles on the MkVIII's clock and the wing repaired, I put the car with Performance Cars on sale or return. Unfortunately, when the car was collected, they broke the crank (at my expense), so the net proceeds from the eventual sale were £400. I saw a MkVIII advertised for sale a few weeks back for £80,000.

One thing about MkVIs has intrigued me of late. As far as I can remember, I built 80 of them, yet I have seen cars advertised with chassis numbers 130 and 140. Perhaps I numbered them out of sequence, with MkVIIIs and Xs mixed in, but I suspect that some were the product of moonlighting by our workforce, whilst others may well be log-book restorations.

On this theme, a journalist rang me a few months ago to say that my Kelsey GT 2/4 Special had been "superbly restored", and looked absolutely beautiful, and it was hoped to do the same with the other five. As I am almost certain I only built one, and that took me five years from

Top, the MkVI's simple tubular spaceframe design used riveted-on flat panels for stiffness (photo: Historic Lotus Register Collection)
Above, Lotus derivatives dominate the grid of the 1172 Formula scratch race at the Eight Clubs Meeting at Silverstone in May 1954

Colin Chapman's own Lotus Mark VI in 1953. Dave Kelsey built the chassis

ANY OLD IRON...

1956 to 1961, I must have done the others in my sleep!

I have also heard of a MkVI once owned by my son, which he bought in the early Seventies for £180 and sold for £200, changing hands for £7,500. This particular car had been altered by an earlier owner to take a Vanguard 2-litre engine, and had fat tyres and radius arm location for the rear axle. Unfortunately (that word keeps cropping up) the radius arms had single forward pivots and ran back to two locations welded to the axle at the top and bottom each side, thus forming a gigantic anti-roll bar out of the axle. This and the tyres made the car hopeless, and I refused to drive it more than 50 yards.

Eventually, I changed the rear end to double radius arms each side, which helped a bit, but it was undoubtedly the worst MkVI that I had ever seen. Even the rear wings had been hammered crudely flat to clear the fat tyres, chipping the dreadful green paint job. I gather that now it is a heap of scrap, barely suitable for restoration, which is why it is so cheap! Still, I expect the log-book is in fairly good nick.

With all the interest there seems to be in early Lotuses at the moment, I wonder if there is room for a new MkVI, (and, indeed, MkVIIIs, IXs and Xs) using currently-available parts and a fabricated swing axle, but otherwise identical to the originals. At least, if I build them, they would be a touch more authentic than the average 'replica'. Is anyone interested? ▲

Above, Peter Gammon's MG-engined Lotus was one of the most successful MkVI racers. Here he is winning the sports car race at Brands Hatch on Whit Monday, 1954

Above, Dave Kelsey, racing at Ibsley in 1955, shunts a straw bale, damaging the tail of the Lotus MkVIII which he had built from the remains of Dick Steed's chassis

It took Dave Kelsey five years to build the only Kelsey GT 2/4, pictured here just after its completion in 1961

Mark VIII

The Lotus VI was fun, but it was not really a serious sports racing car. Although Colin Chapman did well with Mk VI, 1611 H, in the Crystal Palace race against international sports cars, his 'preposterously fast' little Lotus was more of a novelty than a serious long term competitor. Add to this the fact that, for 1954 international competition, cycle wings on sports cars were to be banned. So, for Colin Chapman to take his Lotus cars into more serious racing he needed a proper sports racing car.

All the serious sports racing cars of the time had streamlined enveloping bodies like Connaught, Jaguar, Osca, Maserati, etc. Over the winter of 1953/4 when they were still building Lotus VI chassis as fast as they could, Dave Kelsey of Progress Chassis Co, who built the chassis for Lotus, made a model of a streamlined sports-racing car with Colin Chapman's ideas in mind. Mike Costin introduced Colin to his brother Frank who was an aircraft design engineer with the de Havilland Aircraft Company. The model was sent to Frank Costin to slip into the de Havilland wind tunnel in a spare moment. Frank had no previous experience with car design, but he realised that with Chapman's specification of 125mph and 85bhp, in an overall weight of 1000lb, high speed straight line stability was needed. The model grew plasticine elongated tail fins, and a lower pointed nose for reduced wind penetration, much to Dave Kelsey's disgust! In addition to further aid aerodynamic efficiency, the passenger seat was enclosed with a solid tonneau to reduce cockpit air turbulence, and rear wheel spats covered the wheels to maintain unbroken side airflow. Finally, the design had a full length undertray to eliminate under car turbulence. Even Dave Kelsey had to admit that it did look impressive.

With such a futuristic body shape, Chapman set his mind to work on the chassis. The Mark VI chassis was too simple, so using pure theory as an exercise in structural strength by triangulation, based on his BSc (Eng) qualification from university, he designed the first, and probably the last, pure triangulated space frame chassis which was to be used in his new creation, the Lotus Mark VIII, the VII being held back for an updated Mark VI in due course.

The chassis consisted of two forward facing triangles connected to a vertical triangulated box section at the apex onto which the front suspension was mounted. Within the front triangles was the engine bay, and as in so many purely theoretical ideas, in practice they have limitations! In this case, getting the engine in and out, could only be achieved by half dismantling and reassembling each time, which was not an ideal situation with a racing car. The chassis design was put on paper, and shown to stress engineers 'Mac' MacIntosh and Peter Ross, also from de Havilland, and who also helped out at Lotus 'after hours'.

Progress Chassis Co. built the chassis. Colin Chapman specified 80 ton high tensile 20 swg tubing. The welding was in sif-bronze, but with the high tensile tubing, and the incredible rigidity of the triangulated chassis, there was absolutely no flexibility in the joints which led to tube cracking under racing stress.

The body was built by Williams and Pritchard, who had made the Lotus VI mudguards and nosecone. It was attached to the chassis by steel outrigger brackets, and when finished it looked so fantastic that workers at Lotus were allowed a few minutes respite to sit on an old ammunition chest which was dubbed 'the lusting box' and look at the car.

SAR 5 was registered on 27th March 1954, when the first of the 1954 Lotus Mark VIs were appearing from their winter building by enthusiastic owners. *Autosport* magazine was first with the publicity for the new car. Colin Chapman had invited them to the Lotus works, and a full page article entitled *A NEW LOTUS-MG* appeared in the 9th April 1954 edition.

The Lotus VIII was due to make its debut at Oulton Park on 10th April 1954 at the British Empire Trophy Race meeting. Colin Chapman and Mike Costin drove SAR 5 up on the roads. Unfortunately, they suffered the indignity of crashing the brand new car on the way. Mike Costin, who was driving, misjudged his braking distance and ran over a roundabout north of London, apparently after he was distracted when wind nearly blew his cap off whilst trying to outdistance a police car that they had spotted! The car was hastily pulled into a side road whilst the police went straight on. The following band of Lotus

CASTROL SERIES OF RACING CARS
No. 21. LOTUS

Motor racing is an expensive business and to compete in the top International class costs a mint of money. The problem of how to make racing possible to the average man has been brilliantly solved by Colin Chapman, driving force behind the Lotus Engineering Co. He supplies a cleverly designed chassis frame and, if need be, body, and the purchaser then fits in engine, axles and wheels according to choice or finance. The result has been most successful in achievement and also in the opportunity it has given to many drivers to race on a limited budget.

1955   With the compliments of Castrol

helpers in a tender car helped to straighten out SAR 5 beside the road. They eventually made it to Oulton Park too late, and had to practice out of session which meant starting from the back of the grid. There were several new Mark VIs making their debut at the same event, and although Colin Chapman had fought his way up to 4th place, and achieved joint fastest lap, the head gasket blew and the car retired. After Oulton Park, Frank Costin arranged some aerodynamic testing which took place at a disused airfield near Chester. One of the tests involved Frank being strapped to the bonnet of SAR 5 at 100mph to observe tufts of wool in the front wheel arches. Apparently at 100mph all the tufts were facing forward which led to some later wheel arch redesign on the Mark IX. A photo of Frank during the test appears in THE LOTUS STORY - PART 4, on page 15.

SAR 5 won its class at the Daily Express International race at Silverstone on 15th May 1954, finishing 15th overall. Colin Chapman took the new Lotus to Germany on 23rd May 1954 for the seventy one mile Eifelrennen race where German driver Erwin Bauer finished 4th in Lotus's first continental excursion. Another class win was secured at Goodwood on Whit Monday, 7th June 1954, but the first race win came at the most ideal event for Colin Chapman. The British Grand Prix 1500cc Sports Car race. Not only did Colin Chapman score his first race victory with his new car, but Lotus won the team prize with Lotus VI drivers, Peter Gammon and Mike Anthony.

Other drivers had seen the new Lotus VIII and they wanted one as well. However, the brittle nature of the chassis on SAR 5 and the problems of the inaccessible engine bay rendered it impractical to create more for general sale, plus Colin Chapman did not want his customers to have the same advantages. So, after a quick re-think, the Mark VI chassis was pressed into service with a few additional side tubes for extra rigidity. Williams and Pritchard made a new set of outrigger tubes, and clothed the Mark VI chassis with the Mark VIII streamlined body shape for customers.

John Coombs, who had previously raced Connaughts from his garage in Guildford ordered the first production Mark VIII. Instead of SAR 5's MG XPAG engine, Coombs used his tried and tested Connaught engine, and VPD 97 made its debut at Colin Chapman's victorious British Grand Prix Sports car event, where he finished 4th. Nigel Allen was one of the original partners at Lotus with Colin Chapman, He had raced the prototype Mark VI, XML 6, which he crashed and nearly destroyed the Lotus fortunes back in 1952. He later raced a rebuilt version of XML 6 in 1953. He decided that he had to have a new aerodynamic Mark VIII - he had sat on the 'lusting box' often enough! His car, 624 BMG, also made its debut at the British Grand Prix Sports Car race powered by an MG XPAG engine with his own design cylinder head, and new Solex side draught carburettors.

The fourth Lotus Mark VIII was bought by London car dealer, Dan Margulies. It was fitted with an MG XPAG engine, and was registered 867 BMX. It was finished in time for the first Team Lotus continental event at Nurburgring on 1st August 1954. Three cars were driven to Germany. Colin Chapman in SAR 5, Nigel Allen in 624 BMG, and Dan Margulies in 867 BMX. Unfortunately, none of the Lotus entries finished. Colin Chapman and Nigel Allen were entered at Brands Hatch the next day, so after hasty repairs they set out for the night Channel crossing home.

The next Mark VIII was completed in August 1954 for Dick Steed the son of a Fleet Street Newspaper editor. His car, HUD 139, was fitted with the 3rd Coventry Climax single overhead camshaft engine that Wally Hassan, at Coventry Climax, had been developing for racing from their production lightweight firepumps.

No more Mark VIIIs were built during 1954, but publicity continued with another article in Autosport on 19th November 1954 when John Bolster tested THE LOTUS Mk VIII. Brian Naylor a VW dealer from Stockport, bought the Margulies Mark VIII, 867 BMX, and raced it at the traditional Brands Hatch Boxing Day event, and registered it with his own number, JBN 1. Dave Kelsey, who had been so involved with the early planning, and subsequent construction of the Mark VIII, bought Dick Steed's HUD 139 when Steed ordered a new Lotus Mark IX for 1955. This was re-registered 918 EMK.

Early in 1955 when Lotus was announcing the next model, the Mark IX, Thomas 'Tip' Cunane of Wells registered his Lotus VIII, TYC 700. He painted it white and it became known as 'The White Lotus'. He raced it in sprints and hillclimbs as well as club events until 1958, and even took it touring in Europe one summer.

The 7th and last Mark VIII, was bought by Staffordshire garage owner George Nixon. It was registered 777 FRE, completed in April 1955, and was painted bright yellow. The car was fitted with the somewhat troublesome Turner $1^{1}/2$ litre fuel injected twin overhead cam engine reputedly producing 110bhp. The car made its debut at Hockenheim for the International Rhine Cup race on 7th May 1955 where it finished 8th. On 6th July 1955 George Nixon was entered in the Leinster Trophy race in Ireland. This was a handicap event based on practice times. The Lotus was one of the first to start and later in the race was involved in the accident that killed Don Beauman in a Connaught. The Lotus was repaired, and Nixon carried on racing it until 1956 when it was for sale less engine.

Although the Lotus Mark VIII undoubtedly established Lotus as an international sports car manufacturer, only seven cars were built in 1954 and early 1955. Progress at Lotus was never slow!

Graham Capel

The striking-looking aerodynamic sports-racing Lotus-M.G. which is due to appear in tomorow's British Empire Trophy race.

A NEW LOTUS-M.G.

Wind-Tunnel-Tested 1½-litre Car to Make Its Début at Oulton Park

LATEST creation of Lotus Engineering, Ltd., is an aerodynamic machine with a body developed in a wind-tunnel. Chassis frame is built up from 1¼ ins., 20-gauge steel tubes and the complete structure weighs only 35 lb. At the front, the well-known divided-axle front suspension is retained, controlled by helical springs and Woodhead-Monroe hydraulic dampers.

At the rear a de Dion type of axle is used, in conjunction with a transverse helical spring held in tension, and damped by Armstrong piston-type units. The Lockheed brakes are mounted inboard and to avoid excessive heat, generated by the final drive, being transmitted to the 9½ ins. by 1¼ ins. drums, Chapman has designed a clever lubrication system. A pressure-cum-scavenge pump is driven from the propeller shaft and picks up oil from the engine sump. Approximately every 10 secs. the axle casing is replenished with cooled lubricant from the engine.

Actual oil-cooling is effected in a light-alloy, fully ducted radiator which incorporates a heat-exchanger for the lubricant. The normal engine oil pump is retained.

Steering is by a combination of rack-and-pinion and Burman gearbox, and the steering column is universally jointed. Rear axle ratios are 4.1, or 3.67 to 1.

Bodywork, built by Williams & Richards of Tottenham Lane, associates of Lotus Engineering, is of semi-monocoque construction. The headlamps are fully retractable, being inspired by the design of the very fast Panhard raced by the Chancel brothers. A 12-gallon fuel tank is carried in the rear, whilst a further 10 gallons are contained in side tanks. The spare wheel is located in the rear boot.

Power is supplied by a modified M.G. TD, enlarged to 1,500 c.c. and supplied with a Laystall-Lucas light-alloy cylinder head and twin 1¾-in. SU carburetters. Transmission is via a Borg & Beck competition clutch and M.G. gearbox.

Total dry weight of this very interesting little machine is about 9 cwt., and with 3.7 to 1 rear axle, maximum speed should be in the region of 125 m.p.h.

The car is due to make its first appearance at Oulton Park tomorrow (Saturday) for the British Empire Trophy race, and is expected to run later in the year in the Rheims 12-Hours event. It has been built as a Lotus team car, and will be driven by designer Colin Chapman at Oulton.

(Above) Front suspension showing layout of helical springs, light-alloy radiator, air-intake and oil heat-exchanger.

(Left) Rear wings of the new Lotus also act as stabilizing fins. Twelve gallons of fuel are contained in a tank at the rear, and a further 10 gallons in bolster tanks between the wheels.

HAVING WONDERFUL TIME: The Lotus, writes the author, "obviously enjoyed some rapid laps of the Brands Hatch road circuit". One suspects Bolster found the experience enjoyable also.

JOHN BOLSTER TESTS THE LOTUS Mk. VIII

Low Weight and Efficient Aerodynamics Give Over 120 m.p.h. from 85 b.h.p. in Competition-Proved 1½-litre Sports Car

EVERYBODY who takes the slightest interest in motor racing knows Colin Chapman's streamlined Lotus. This phenomenally successful 1½-litre sports-racing car has had a most spectacular season, in which victories and record laps have abounded. Perhaps its defeat of a formidable German car at Silverstone was its greatest triumph, but even more valuable data was gained on those occasions when things did not go so well.

As a result of the concentrated experience that this car has provided, an improved version is now in steady production. It was the hard-worked prototype, however, that I took over recently for a busy week of varied motoring. It carried me to various social occasions in London's West End (perhaps you saw it parked outside the "Steering Wheel"?). It was used for long, fast journeys, it was put through its paces against the watch, and it obviously enjoyed some rapid laps of the Brands Hatch road circuit. Before discussing these activities, however, let us take a brief look at the design of the car.

The basis of the machine is a rigid, multi-tubular chassis. The front wheels pivot on swing axles, which are supported on helical springs embracing telescopic dampers. At the rear the final drive gear housing is solidly mounted on the frame, and carries the brakes, which obtain their cooling air from an aperture in the undershield. Behind this assembly is the de Dion tube, which has fore and aft location by parallel trailing arms, and is positioned laterally by a central sliding block. The axle is hung on bell cranks, which compress a single helical spring. This layout gives no roll stiffness, but in production cars a modified arrangement does provide some roll resistance. The front end geometry has also been slightly amended to correspond, and new tubular half shafts eradicate a previous weakness.

The body is one of the most important features. It is scientifically streamlined as a result of a mathematical design approach, followed by wind tunnel tests and the photography of woollen tufts during actual racing. It has a wide but shallow air entry and two large stabilizing fins above and behind the enclosed back wheels. There is ample room for the two occupants and some luggage space, but the passenger's seat is normally covered during racing. This body can also be fitted to the Mark VI chassis.

Various engines may be installed in the Lotus by the owner, including 2-litre Bristol, 1½-litre Connaught, Turner, and M.G., and the 1,100 c.c. Coventry Climax. The Climax-engined car is also sold complete for £1,150, though purchase tax must then be added to this figure. I hope to test the 1,100 c.c. car later on, but as the present test refers to the M.G. version, a short description of this power unit is indicated.

The block is a standard one, bored and fitted with cast iron liners for strength, with Cromard liners therein. In this slightly laborious fashion the 66.5 mm. bore is increased to 72 mm., and the ex-1¼-litre engine approaches 1½ litres. There are no water passages through the gasket, these being external. The head is a light alloy Laystall-Lucas, with special Lotus valve gear and a racing camshaft. It gives a compression ratio of 9 to 1 and its enlarged ports are mated with two 1¾ in. S.U. carburetters. The connecting rods are special, but the crankshaft is standard. This unit develops around 85 b.h.p. at 6,200 r.p.m.

It is not the maximum b.h.p. which first impresses the driver, however, but the astonishing torque of the engine in the middle ranges. Right from 1,800 r.p.m. upwards it pulls strongly, and top gear may be engaged at quite low speeds, the half-ton car accelerating strongly on this ratio. Any premium grade fuel may be used, without a sign of pinking, though running-on does sometimes occur when switching off. The engine revs. freely, and I went up to 6,000 r.p.m. on the gears during the performance tests. While timing the maximum speed, the rev. counter remained steady at about 6,500 r.p.m. so a slightly higher gear ratio might increase the already excellent figure.

The streamlining must be very efficient, for to exceed 120 m.p.h. on 85 b.h.p. is a phenomenal achievement. Another virtue of this body shape is its directional stability. In spite of the extremely light weight and short wheelbase, I have never driven any car which was steadier at two miles a minute. One simply sits back in comfort, well protected by the high body sides, and the machine rides absolutely level, ironing out the bumps in a most praiseworthy manner. At high speeds some engine vibration can be felt, which is probably "telephoned" down the propeller shaft to the chassis-mounted differential.

At lower speeds the "streamliner" is at

CLOSE CONFINES beneath the Lotus bonnet, showing the very low and forward-mounted radiator, the long helical springs of the front suspension, and the increased-bore, 1¼-litre-type M.G. engine of 1,467 c.c.

54

first less easy to handle than the earlier Lotus cars. I think that this is probably due to the unusually light steering, with very little caster return action. At all events, I soon became accustomed to the handling, and the initial tendency to wander disappeared. The controls are all well placed, the steering wheel is arranged for the modern straight-arm technique, and the aerodynamic body does not impede the driver's view.

The acceleration is tremendous, even in the upper speed ranges. The time of 15.5 secs. for the standing quarter-mile deserves special emphasis, and it was only made possible by the virtual absence of wheelspin. Not only does the de Dion axle confer its usual advantages, but the petrol tank, battery and spare wheel all lie behind the beam. This puts the weight where it is wanted for maximum traction.

From a racing point of view, such a getaway is very valuable, for a lead snatched on the starting grid may be decisive in a hard-fought race. It also pays dividends after sharp corners, for full throttle may be applied far earlier than with a conventional rear axle.

The well-known M.G. gearbox gives an easy change, and the ratios suit the Lotus very well. The clutch has a short pedal travel and is most positive in action, which makes it far more suitable for competition work than the usual M.G. article.

An interesting detail is the headlamp mounting. The lamps fold away beneath the bonnet during the day, and when they are erected at night they have the advantage of being higher than is normally the case with small streamlined cars. Although they are not large, they give a good light, and I exceeded 100 m.p.h. in the dark with their aid.

I found the Lotus quite tractable as a town and shopping car. The exhaust only became really noisy at full throttle, and I never had occasion to change a sparking plug. Nevertheless, it is as an extremely potent competition machine that most people will buy this car, and for this purpose it really has all the essentials. One does feel that this is a scientifically designed vehicle, and not the "lucky accident" that some sports cars really are.

Above all, I am completely converted to the fully aerodynamic type of body. It gives so much extra speed, and such improved stability that one would be foolish to ignore its advantages except on the very slowest circuits. It certainly gives the brakes a harder task, but these proved quite adequate on the car under review, though requiring fairly heavy pedal pressure. The new larger drums of the production cars should be a worthwhile improvement.

The Mark VIII Lotus is a sports-racing car that must be seriously considered by anybody who is in the market for a competition machine. Whatever engine he may choose, he can be certain that this chassis and body will give it every chance to distinguish itself. I shall remember its incredible steadiness at maximum speed, and the ease with which it can be taken round appreciable curves at over 100 m.p.h., for a long time.

ACCELERATION GRAPH OF THE 1½-LITRE LOTUS MK. VIII

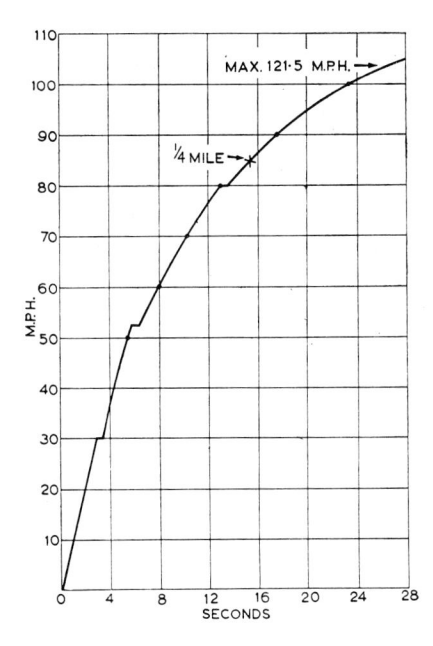

MAX. 121.5 M.P.H.
¼ MILE

SPECIFICATION AND PERFORMANCE DATA

Car Tested: Lotus Mark VIII Sports 2-seater. Price (component form, without engine), £800.

Engine: Four cylinders, 72 mm. x 90 mm. (1,467 c.c.). Pushrod-operated valves in light alloy head. 85 b.h.p. at 6,200 r.p.m. 9 to 1 compression ratio. Twin 1¼ in. SU carburetters. Lucas coil and distributor.

Transmission: Borg and Beck racing clutch. Four-speed gearbox with central remote control and synchromesh on upper three gears, ratios: 4.1, 5.5, 8.0, and 13.8 to 1. Open Hardy Spicer propeller shaft to chassis-mounted spiral bevel and differential unit. Articulated shafts to rear hubs.

Chassis: Multi-tubular space frame. Independent front suspension by swing axles, helical springs, and telescopic dampers. Rear suspension by de Dion axle, bell cranks, single helical spring, and piston-type dampers. Lockheed hydraulic brakes in Al-fin drums, 2LS in front, inboard mounted at rear, 9 ins. x 1¼ ins. (11 ins. x 2¼ ins. on production cars). 4.50-15 ins. front, 5.25-15 ins. rear tyres on bolt-on wire wheels (knock-on hubs for production cars).

Equipment: 12-volt lighting and starting, speedometer, revolution counter, oil pressure and temperature, water temperature, and fuel gauges.

Dimensions: Wheelbase, 7 ft. 3½ ins.; track, front, 4 ft. 0½ in., rear, 3 ft. 11½ ins. Overall length, 11 ft., weight, 10¼ cwt.

Performance: Maximum speed, 121.5 m.p.h. Speeds in gears, 3rd 80 m.p.h., 2nd 52 m.p.h., 1st 30 m.p.h. Standing quarter mile 15.5 secs. Acceleration: 0-50 m.p.h., 5.4 secs.; 0-60 m.p.h., 8 secs.; 0-70 m.p.h., 10.4 secs.; 0-80 m.p.h., 13 secs.; 0-90 m.p.h., 17.4 secs.; 0-100 m.p.h., 23.8 secs.

Fuel consumption: 30 m.p.g. (approx.).

RECIPE for fast cornering: "The controls are all well placed, the steering wheel is arranged for the modern straight-arm technique, and the aerodynamic body does not impede the driver's view".

★

RETRACTABLE: (Right) The small but adequately powerful headlights on the Lotus fold away beneath the bonnet when not in use.

SIF at 134 mph

BY T. J. PALMER

The Lotus, pictured while cornering at Silverstone.

1. Fabricating the base frame

2. At work attaching the prefabricated side frame

A RECENT visit to the Progress Chassis Co. of Hornsey revealed some interesting "behind the scenes" activities in the production of the Lotus Racing Car which has done much to stimulate interest in British motor car racing.

The Lotus Chassis is a classical example of all-welded construction, and there are no fewer than 140 welded joints all told. Good design, careful set-up, correct operational sequence, and S.I.F. materials have all combined in keeping distortion and other problems at an exceptionally low level.

Jigs are simple yet highly effective, and distortion is prevented by the use of heavy R.S.J.'s as a basis for the main frame jig, and by diagonal bracing of all unsupported sections of the superstructure.

In Fig. 1 a main joint in the $1\frac{7}{8}$" diameter steel tubular bottom frame is being welded, using a "Demon" light duty blowpipe, and Sifsteel No. 11 copper-coated mild steel filler rods. The method of setting-up with R.S.J.'s and the employment of clamps at various points may be especially noted, as careful alignment of the component members is highly important at this early stage.

Fig. 2 shows part of the prefabricated side frame being attached to the main frame. $1" \times 1\frac{1}{2}" \times 18$ swg rectangular steel section and $1" \times 18$ swg round section form the basis of most of this part of the structure, and its rigidity and strength is amply evident from a glance at Fig. 3, which shows the central area.

The welding itself is excellent, as may be seen from the special close-up of Fig. 4 which focusses upon the junction of tubes at the lower front corner of the main frame.

This particular joint is important, being one of the most highly-stressed parts of the vehicle, but it is only fair to say that a close examination of all other joints in the structure revealed a similar high standard of workmanship.

Fig. 5 shows the complete all-welded chassis, which has a weight of only 75 lb. The special streamlined aluminium-alloy body (which is wind-tunnel tested) is made elsewhere and fitted as a complete unit; and for this reason alone prefabricational accuracy is of paramount importance with the chassis — a limit of ⅛" being normally laid down at Hornsey.

The action photograph on page 10 shows the Lotus racing at Silverstone driven by its designer. This particular model has a 1½ litre M.G. engine, all-enveloping fully aerodynamic body, and de-dion rear suspension. It has a top speed of 134 miles per hour.

Progress Chassis Co also make "specials", (Fig. 6); in that work,

extensive use is made of Sifbronze welding in addition to many Sifsteel joints.

The design has been carefully worked out by aircraft designers who have long had a "soft spot" for Sifbronze welding, and this is hardly surprising in view of the hundreds of successful applications of Sifbronze in that field.

The illustration shows the central section of chassis only, with an operator making one of the side frame joints by Sifbronze welding.

3. Some idea of the frame-work's great strength and rigidity may be gained from this picture.

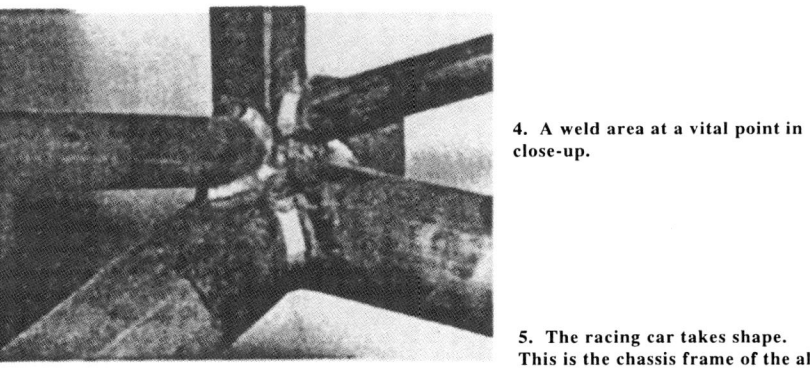

4. A weld area at a vital point in close-up.

5. The racing car takes shape. This is the chassis frame of the all welded Lotus.

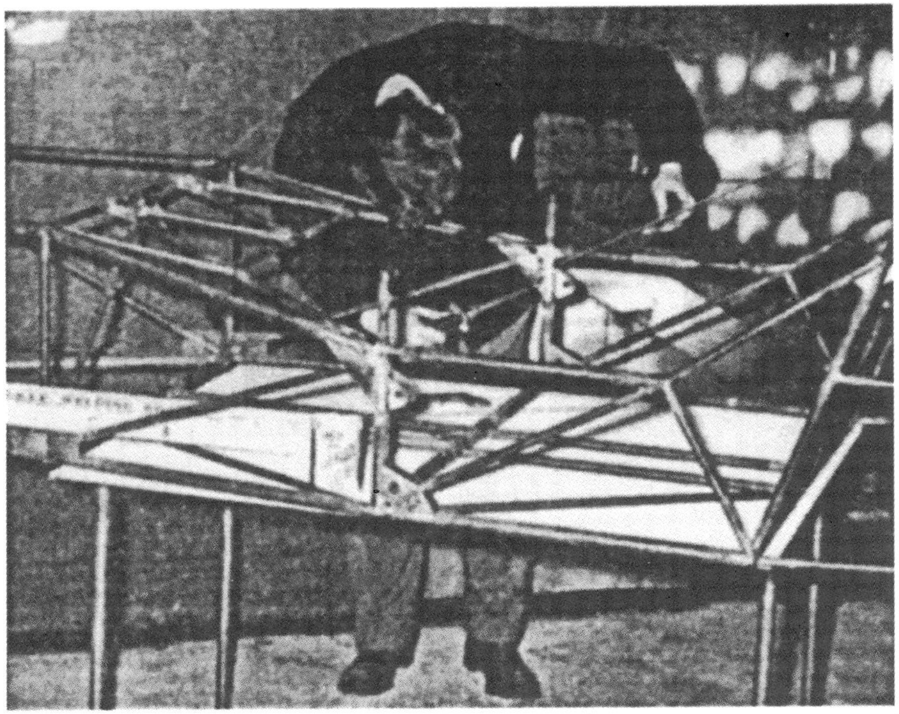

6. Sifbronze-welding the chassis frame of a racing "special".

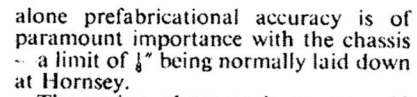

The most original Lotus MkVIII in the world has been found and restored after over 30 years out of action. **Tony Dron** experiences its magic on the track at Castle Combe

White Spirit

LOTUS REALLY STARTED TO MAKE ITSELF FELT BACK IN 1954 by fitting a streamlined body, designed by Frank Costin, to a new spaceframe chassis. In sports-car racing, the 1500cc class was then a closely contested hotspot with the Lotus MkVIII marking a turning point: the car was a sensation, capable of beating much larger sports machinery. Lotus' boss, Colin Chapman, appeared on the tracks with his first MkVIII, registered SAR 5, from April 1954 and very quickly T G 'Tip' Cunane, the manager of the paper mill at Wookey Hole, ordered one.

Although probably the very first to place an order, Mr Cunane was made to wait. Maybe others had more clout at the Lotus factory, or lived nearer, but after nearly ten months, when Chapman was already producing the MkIX, Cunane's car was the last of the six production MkVIIIs released. It was first registered as TYC 700 on April 4, 1955.

As the works car suffered chassis failures, and it was impossible to install or remove the engine in one piece, customers' MkVIIIs had their chassis based on the existing MkVI sports car, with body-bearing outriggers welded on which proved successful.

Oddly enough, this car has the earliest MkVIII chassis number (MK6/2-1, meaning 6+2=8, no 1). Experts guess that the chassis were stored in a batch and it was first in, last out. The number 1911 is stamped conspicuously on to the chassis — Cunane, who was born in 1911, did this when he couldn't find the well-hidden original number.

Cunane's car became known as 'the White Lotus' and it has survived incredibly well because, way back in 1963, the then owner 'Dick' Whittington dismantled it for restoration, but never got any further. It also helps that it has never crashed and its full ownership history is known.

In July 1987, the collection of parts was inspected by Graham Capel of the Historic Lotus Register. He was 'absolutely astounded' and ⇨

PHOTOGRAPHY BY TIM ANDREW

Last of six production MkVIIIs, the 'White Lotus' was registered as TYC 700 in April 1955

the car is now universally recognised as being easily the most original MkVIII in existence.

Restored under the supervision of its present owner, Olav Glasius, President of Lotus Club, the Netherlands, it is a car to marvel at. It was ready in time for static exhibition at this year's Goodwood hillclimb.

Two days later, I had the exclusive privilege of driving it at Castle Combe. As I drove slowly between the Caterham Sevens in the paddock, none of the drivers gave it a second glance. Did any of them have the slightest idea of the identical root of their chassis and that of the White Lotus? If the modern Seven racers were ignorant of this, one of the older circuit staff did a giant double-take, as if he'd seen a ghost car rolling out of the pack; then he grinned. He at least understood.

So did Eric Willmott, who was also present. Forty-one years ago, as Tip Cunane's friend and racing colleague, Eric achieved fastest time by a club member in the MG Car Club's 1956 Castle Combe sprint meeting, driving this very car. He still has the cup at home in nearby Wells. Tip Cunane himself gained many awards, especially in hillclimbs, but when he raced it at Combe in 1955 he spun twice, trying a bit too hard.

Sadly, Tip Cunane died several years ago but his sister and daughter turned out with other enthusiasts, including Rob Ford of Club Lotus Avon Area, who has done much of the research on this car and helped bring everybody together. It obviously meant a lot to them all to see the old car revived and running. They stood on the bank at Camp Corner as long as the car was out.

At the specified running-in speed of 4000rpm in top gear, it was just possible to take the corner without slowing down. All went well, this first proper trial producing only two minor faults: a sticky throttle cable and the need to adjust the front suspension slightly.

Sitting inside was incredible, with a strong, 'genuine article' feel about everything. The White Lotus has its original seats – green Rexine with white piping – and they don't even look worn. Olav was lucky to find a new piece of

Odd feature: the 'boot' area is really just a lid over the fuel tank, de Dion axle, inboard Alfin brakes and structural tubes

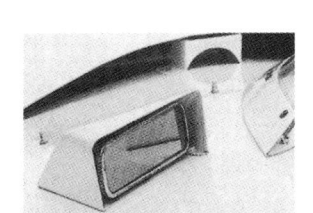

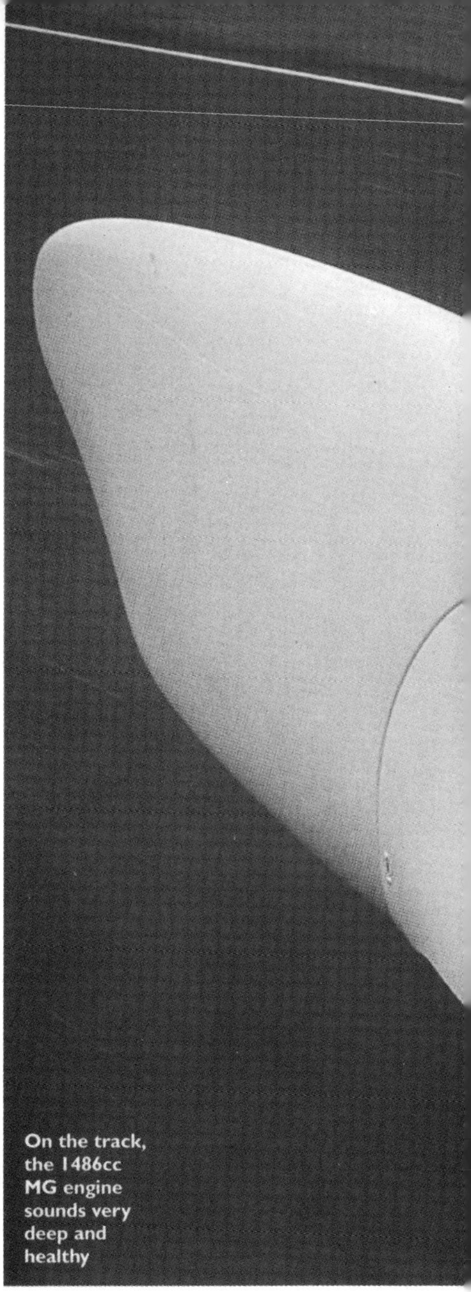

On the track, the 1486cc MG engine sounds very deep and healthy

Inside, there is a strong 'genuine article' feel about everything

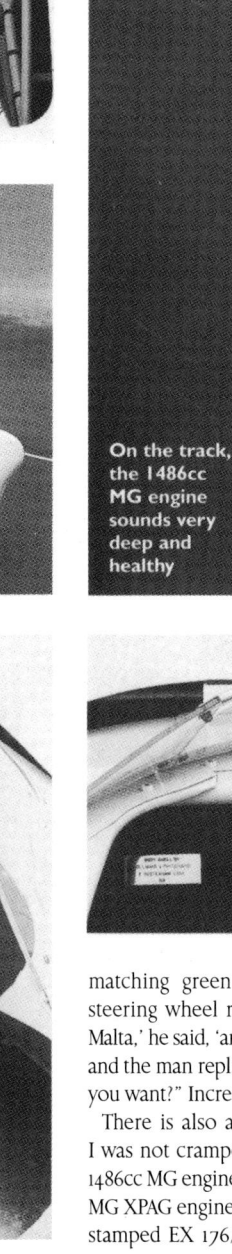

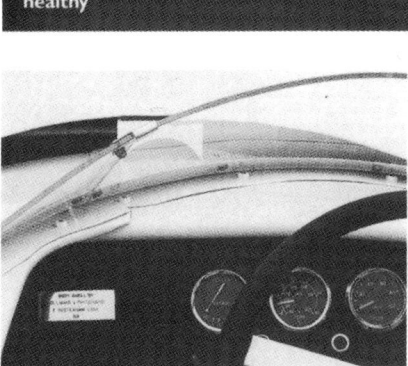

matching green material for the dash and steering wheel rim. 'I went into this shop in Malta,' he said, 'and asked if they had any Rexine, and the man replied, "Certainly, what colour do you want?" Incredible!'

There is also a surprising amount of room: I was not cramped in there. On the track, the 1486cc MG engine sounds very deep and healthy. MG XPAG engines are rare enough but this one, stamped EX 176/1, was extra-special, with an

'One of the older circuit staff did a giant double-take, as if he'd seen a ghost car'

At 4000rpm in top gear, it was just possible to take the corner without slowing down

external water flow between head and block minimising gasket trouble. It breathes through the original twin 1¾in SUs.

Back in 1954, XPAG racing engines were reckoned to produce over 85bhp. It's not known what this version turns out. Eric recalls that they would rev it to about 6000rpm, but adds: 'By the time we got the car, the Coventry Climax was into its stride and we were always a bit down on them.'

There is a bit of play in the standard Ford steering box, but once on the move the car is easy to control, well-balanced on corners, light and precise. As it is fitted upside-down, the box has LHD internals to make the car turn the right way.

The divided front axle betrays itself by a slight tendency to wander on surface imperfections, but that's really not a problem. What made these MkVIIIs so effective was that they could slip through the air, then their drivers could brake late and enter corners fast. Attention to detail was ahead of its time: this car has a fully flat floor and proper radiator ducting.

With minimal air resistance, Lotus VIIIs don't slow down much when you lift. The ultra-light magnesium Alfin drum brakes, inboard at the rear, work well, however, and pull the car up squarely. Other VIIIs did not have this arrangement and, although SAR 5 had a de Dion rear end, the production models had live axles, like the MkVI, and bolt-on wire wheels. Because this car was made so late, it had many MkIX parts in it, including de Dion rear suspension, Alfin brakes and knock-on wheels from new.

'We did not realise that then, when we built up the kit,' Eric told me. 'We just thought it was an VIII. It was very easy to assemble the kit, just a dodge to avoid Purchase Tax. Later, after a steering arm broke as I was driving it on the road, I was told by the Lotus factory that we should have had the special, forged arms. They sent them and we had no more trouble.'

Driving such a car on the road in the Fifties was incredible, according to Eric: 'We did a hell of a lot of road driving in it. Cunane also had an ⇨

Light and precise, it's easy to control and well-balanced on corners

XK140 and it just couldn't live with the Lotus once you got really going.'

Eric also explained why the car has two fold-down doors, while normal VIIIs had only one: 'Tip was going to do the 1957 Alpine, so the car was modified at the Lotus factory. It had a special high screen and a crude hood was then added. But the rally was cancelled because of the Suez crisis: probably just as well, because the high mileage on unmade roads would have been tough on the Lotus.'

Another couple of oddities on this car can be seen in the 'boot' area, which is really just a lid over the fuel tank, de Dion axle, Alfin brakes, structural tubes and the road. The chassis has been repaired there, and strengthened with extra tubes. Tip Cunane had a 16-gallon tank fitted for ultra-long-range driving, but it was so heavy when full that it broke the chassis. The repair and modification were both carried out at the time. During the restoration, the old 16-gallon tank was cut down and rebuilt neatly to hold a more sensible eight gallons.

Bolted inside at the very back are the rudimentary headlights. At lighting-up time, you could unbolt them and mount them on the front.

By this time, Fred Fairman had arrived. He is the distant cousin of Jack, the racing driver, and was responsible for restoring the entire body, chassis and piping. Virtually all of the Williams &

Tip Cunane's friend and racing colleague Eric Willmott

> 'The result is superb, exactly right and second to none in its craftsmanship'

Pritchard aluminium body remains original, which is what everybody wanted, but it was no easy task. First Fred removed all the old grime and paint, to discover that although it wasn't dented, it was riddled with hairline cracks and very brittle. He had to spend hours with a magnifying glass, finding all the tiny faults so that a perfect rebuild could be achieved. The result is superb: strong, exactly right and second to none in its craftsmanship.

MG XPAG engine features an external water flow between head and block and breathes through the original twin 1¼in SUs

This four-year restoration is a considerable achievement, masterminded by an owner who surely knows more now than anyone else about the sensational Lotus MkVIII. Although a racer himself, Olav wisely does not intend to risk competing in the White Lotus. He will save it for special demonstrations. ●

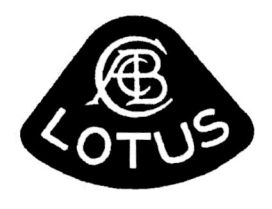

Mark IX

The Lotus Mark IX of 1955 was the natural successor to the Mark VIII of 1954. Colin Chapman had enjoyed a fantastically successful season with his Mark VIII-SAR 5 throughout 1954, and the production Mark VIIIs had also proved highly competitive in the up-to-1500cc Sports Racing class, both in British Club racing events as well as International competition.

Over the winter of 1954/5, Colin Chapman achieved two of his major ambitions. Firstly, he married Hazel Williams his childhood sweetheart, who had supported him so well in the early days of Lotus. Secondly, he resigned from his job with the British Aluminium Co, and became the full time Managing Director of Lotus Engineering Co Ltd, and professional car builder. Mike Costin also left the De Havilland Aircraft Company, and became a director of their associated company, Racing Engines Ltd. By dividing the production between Lotus Engineering Co Ltd who supplied the Lotus body/chassis units, and Racing Engines Ltd which supplied the engines and modified components, the punitive Purchase Tax legislation could be avoided.

SAR 5 had been sold to Austin Nurse, and with the sale of more Lotus Mark VIs, there was enough money to commission patterns for Lotus designed magnesium alloy differential housings, de Dion hub carriers, eleven inch turbo-finned brake drums, plus steel fabricated de Dion rear axle tubes. All of these parts, which were standard to the Mark IX, made production of the cars a lot easier. Some parts even found their way onto the Mark VIs still being built.

The chassis was still basically the Mark VI, but with certain specific modifications for the Mark IX. The specification of the new model from Lotus was announced in Autosport of 22nd October 1954 whilst Colin and Hazel were on honeymoon! At the time it was listed as a Mark 8F, and included the newly developed Coventry Climax single overhead camshaft engine giving 76bhp, a 4-speed gearbox and centre-lock wire wheels.

The chassis was built by Progress Chassis Co and weighed just 63lbs complete with brackets. Despite all the specially manufactured components, the 1950's Ford split axle and Ford Popular steering box were still used. Frank Costin reworked the Mark VIII body shape reducing the elongated rear wings, but making them stick up into the airstream in a 'cock-tailed' fashion. The nose was less pointed, and the lessons learned from the tufts of wool in the front wheel arches on the Mark VIII, now gave the Mark IX cutaway side pontoons to aid smoother exit flow.

In motor racing the 1500cc Sports Racing class still continued, but a new 1100cc class was added which suited the new 1098cc Coventry Climax engine. So, the Lotus Mark IX was offered with a choice of MG XPAG or Coventry Climax engines. The cost of a Mark IX in 1955 varied from a standard Ford torque-tube, rear axle car with Ford sidevalve engine and drum brakes at £590, to the de Dion, turbo-finned braked car with either MG or Coventry Climax engine at £850. Both prices were in self assembly form. For the first time Lotus now offered a completely assembled car at £1150 plus Purchase Tax, making a very expensive £1633. This compared to the Austin A30 saloon at £475, or the Jaguar Mark VII at £1616. In the USA a complete Lotus Mark IX sold at $3500. Racing a Lotus was never cheap!

The first two Mark IXs were built shortly after the new year of 1955. These two cars had been ordered by Frank Miller of New York, an official of the Sports Car Club of America, and Bobby Burns of Wichita, Texas for Norman Scott of Continental Motors in Houston to drive. Both cars were entered for the International 12 hour race at Sebring in Florida on 13th March 1955. Both cars were only just completed in time and the new turbo-finned brakes had not arrived, so the earlier nine inch ribbed Alfin type were fitted.

Both the Lotus cars were entered as Mark 8Fs for the Sebring 12 Hours race. Miller's co-driver was George Rabe, and Norman Scott's was 'Sad' Sam Samuelson. Colin Chapman flew out to attend the race and see the debut of his new cars. In the race which started at 11 am, both cars ran well leading Class G first and second, and also leading the Index of Performance. At dusk, Samuelson spun off when blinded by the setting sun and holed the sump ending his race. Less than an hour before the end of the race, and whilst leading Class G comfortably, Miller hit a straw bale knocked on to the track by a spinning car. The bent Lotus was hastily repaired, and Rabe took over for the final drive to the finish. With only one headlight, the race officials called the car into the pits. The light was repaired, but the Coventry Climax engine would not start due to overheating. To try and qualify as a finisher, the car was pushed to the finish line as the race ended, but they were disqualified. The race was won by Mike Hawthorn and Peter Walker in a D-Type Jaguar. A most unsatisfactory end to a promising debut for the new Lotus Mark IX.

Colin Chapman returned from Florida to the welcome discovery of a full page article on his NEW LOTUS in Autosport of 18th March. This was followed by a picture of the Miller/Rabe Mark IX on the front cover of Autosport a week later, 25th March. The Autocar produced an article entitled NINTH MARK FOR LOTUS in their publication on 1st April 1955 which included a cutaway drawing by Vic Berris. Road and Track magazine in the USA produced their introductory article headed LOTUS MK IX in their June 1955 edition. This was followed by Sports Cars Illustrated in July 1955 entitled WITH THE LOTUS AT SEBRING.

A third USA export Mark IX had been ordered by Len Bastrup, but this was not completed for Sebring, and was shipped in May 1955. Colin Chapman wanted to continue his racing success, and Lotus had built two very special Mark IXs for Team Lotus. As in the Mark VI, 1611 H with its lightweight chassis, and the Mark VIII, SAR 5 with its very special triangulated chassis, the works Mark IXs had a specially developed small diameter, multi-tube space frame chassis, lighter and stronger than the earlier or later customer models, plus newly developed disc brakes. 9 EHX was fitted with an MG XPAG 1500cc engine for the 1500 Sports Racing class, and XPE 6 was fitted with the 1100cc Coventry Climax engine for the small class racing.

The British debut of the Mark IX was at the traditional season opener, the British Empire Trophy race at Oulton Park on 2nd April 1955 where Colin Chapman drove 9 EHX. Just like the year before with his debut of the Mark VIII, SAR 5, the new car failed due to overheating when in 4th place. Peter Jopp had joined Colin Chapman as the second works driver, and these two cars took awards throughout 1955 in British and Continental events. The major continental excursion was to the Le Mans 24 Hour race on 11/12th June 1955 in XPE 6. Colin Chapman co-drove with works Jaguar driver Ron Flockhart. The new Lotus produced the fastest lap for 1100cc cars in practice at 98mph. This was the year of the terrible disaster involving Pierre Levegh's Mercedes Benz. Shortly after midnight, Chapman spun into the bank at Arnage, but in reversing back on to the track, the car was disqualified.

As the 1955 season progressed, more and more Lotus Mark IXs began to appear. By October 1955 a total of 18 cars had been produced. Mike McDowel won the 'Chapman Trophy for 1172cc Formula Cars' in his Ford sidevalve, drum braked Mark IX - PDD 76.

In October the annual Motor Show took place in Britain, and Lotus Engineering Co Ltd were in attendance. However, as they were not accredited members of the Society of Motor Manufacturers and Traders, their Mark IX, RYF 446 Chassis No 130, was displayed on the first floor gallery amongst the accessory suppliers stands. Nevertheless, it created somewhat of a sensation. Another specially prepared Mark IX chassis was displayed in the showroom of Coventry Climax in London's Piccadilly.

On 18th November 1955, John Bolster wrote a test report in the 18th November Autosport on THE LOTUS MARK IX, in which he sampled both the MG and the Coventry Climax engined works cars.

Over the Winter of 1955/56, whilst Colin Chapman was at his drawing board designing his new car for 1956, a further 6/7 Mark IXs were produced largely for American customers of Ken Miles of Hollywood, California, who was advertising as 'sole distributor' for Lotus cars in the Western USA.

Graham Capel

THE LOTUS SYSTEM

THE LOTUS SYSTEM enables anyone to build a replica of a Lotus sports car. Proven in competition motoring all over the world, Lotus precision components are designed for builders of sports and sports/racing cars seeking extremely high performance at minimum expense. Using these components in conjunction with one of a range of proprietary engines and gearboxes, the enthusiast can build an outstanding touring or competition car with a bare minimum of difficulty.

Fundamental to the success of the Lotus System, is the multi-tubular space frame of exceptional torsional rigidity. Like all Lotus components it is designed and tested according to strict engineering practice. Light in weight, this welded tubular mild steel structure is designed to accept five types of engine for which mounting brackets are provided. It weighs 63 lb. complete with these brackets.

Two basic types—the Mk. 6 and the Mk. 9—are produced. The Mk. 6 is designed to accept a simple, two-seat body of conventional form, and the basically similar Mk. 9 has additional frame members necessary for a more complex full aerodynamic two-seat body.

For use with the Lotus frame, a complete range of components is produced. These include the simple, swing axle, independent front suspension conversion, using combined shock absorber and coil spring units, a de Dion rear axle, using similar spring units, hydraulic or cable operated drum brakes with cast magnesium drums, or hydraulically operated disc brakes produced to Lotus specifications. A light alloy adaptor is produced to enable the Coventry Climax engine to be mated to the gearbox. Other items include controls, steering gear, a special radiator, special light weight wheels and exhaust silencers. All of these items may be employed in either the Mk. 6 or Mk. 9 frames.

From the range, the enthusiast can build a car with the precise degree of performance required, and with the assurance that handling, road holding, braking and steering will be of the highest standards. Lotus components are designed for use exclusively in combination with Lotus frames and are produced to assist builders of Lotus Mk. 6 and Mk. 9 replicas.

Some indications of the range of types which can be built up are give overleaf

From start to finish, Lotus components are designed to combine lightweight and low cost with race-winning efficiency and robustness

For the man who wants high speed at low cost, the Mk. 6 is especially suitable

1. BASIC. *This specification caters for the enthusiast seeking a car at minimum expense for normal touring purposes.*
Chassis Frame. Lotus Mk. 6 multi-tubular space frame fitted with Mk. 6 integral body panelling.
Front Suspension. Swing axle conversion embodying Lotus suspension units with coil springs around telescopic shock absorbers.
Rear Suspension. Modified Ford 10 back axle embodying Lotus suspension units, coil springs around telescopic shock absorbers with suspension unit adaptors. Final drive ratio of 5.5 to 1.

TYPICAL LOTUS

Brakes. 10" × 1¼" standard Ford brakes with Lotus brake linkage.
Power Unit. Ford 8 or Ford 10.
Instruments. 3" speedometer, oil pressure gauge, ammeter.
Fuel System. 7 gallon light alloy tank fitted at rear. A.C. mechanical pump.
Cooling. Lotus type 'B' radiator to suit power unit installed.
Wheels. Standard Ford 16" wheels. Standard tyres as required.

2. SPORTS. *For the enthusiast seeking an inexpensive everyday motor car, suitable for mild forms of competition.*
Chassis Frame. Lotus Mk. 6 multi-tubular space frame with Mk. 6 integral body panelling.
Front Suspension. Swing axle conversion embodying Lotus suspension units with coil springs around telescopic shock absorbers.
Rear Suspension. Modified Ford 10 back axle embodying Lotus suspension units, coil spring around telescopic shock absorbers with suspension unit adaptors. Final drive ratios of 4.125, 4.4 or 4.7 to 1 available.
Brakes. 10" × 1¼" standard Ford brakes with Lotus brake linkage.
Power Unit. Coventry Climax 1100 cc. with MG/TC gearbox and Lotus adaptor kit or alternatively Ford 10 or MG 'T' type engine and gearbox.
Instruments. Full set of racing instruments including tachometer 0-8000 r.p.m., oil pressure gauge, water temperature, ammeter.
Fuel System. 7 gallon light alloy tank fitted at rear. A.C. mechanical pump.
Cooling. Lotus type 'B' radiator to suit power unit installed.
Wheels. Lotus superlight bolt-on disc wheels 4.50 × 15 front and 5.25 × 15 rear. Fitted with Dunlop racing tyres.

LOTUS

TYPICAL PERFORMANCE FIGURES

Engine	Degree of Tuning	Maximum Speed	Standing ¼ mile	m.p.g.
Mk. 6	Standard	75 m.p.h.	21 secs	45
FORD 10	Medium (Limit of 1172 formula)	88	19	48
	High (Special cams, etc.)	94	17.5	40
MG T-type	Standard 1250 cc.	104	18.8	40
	Maximum 1250 cc.	113	16.5	42.5
	1500 cc. (Special cams, etc.)	120	15.8	38
Mk. 9 COVENTRY CLIMAX	Standard 1100 cc. FWA	130	16	42 (cruising) 22 (racing)

Functional in appearance, the Mk. 6 is an all-weather, all-purpose car

POWER/WEIGHT RATIOS

Mk. 6 with medium-tuned Ford engine
94 b.h.p. per ton

Mk. 9 with Coventry Climax 1100cc. engine
182 b.h.p. per ton

Basis of the Lotus is the multi-tubular space frame; the Mk. 9 has additional body hoops as shown

WHAT THEY SAY ABOUT LOTUS...

"THE PERFORMANCE of the 1100 cc. Lotus . . . was so good that. in our opinion, in so far as the relation between developed horsepower and both maximum and circuit speed is concerned, it can be described as the most efficient car in the race".
AUTO COURSE, report on le Mans 24-Hours, 1955

"AN EYE-OPENER was the sight of Chapman in his 1100 cc. Lotus Climax, leading all the 2-litre and 1½-litre cars . . ."
MOTOR SPORT, report on Tourist Trophy, 1955

"THE (LOTUS) Mk. 6 . . . has for the first time, made it possible for the man of moderate means to own a genuine sports/racer."
AUTOSPORT

"THE LOTUS is a very attractive proposition for all those desirous of possessing a lively small sports car at low cost."
AUTOCAR

"VERY EXCEPTIONAL cornering powers . . . uncanny, exemplary behaviour of the rear end, brakes may be applied at maximum speed without deviation or patter".
AUTOSPORT

SPECIFICATIONS

3. CLUB. *Suitable for less expensive forms of competition equivalent to club racing events in Great Britain.*

Chassis Frame. Lotus Mk. 9 multi-tubular space frame for aerodynamic bodywork.
Front Suspension. Swing axle conversion embodying Lotus suspension units with coil springs around telescopic shock absorbers.
Rear Suspension. Modified Ford 10 back axle embodying Lotus suspension units, coil springs around telescopic shock absorbers, with suspension unit adaptors. Final drive ratios of 4.125, 4.4 or 4.7 to 1 available.
Brakes. 10" × 1¼" standard Ford drum brakes with Lotus brake linkage.
Power Unit. Coventry Climax 1100 cc. with MG/TC gearbox and Lotus adaptor kit, or alternatively Ford 10 engine and gearbox.
Instruments. Full set of racing instruments including tachometer 0-8000 r.p.m., oil pressure gauge, water temperature gauge, ammeter.
Fuel System. 11 gallon side tank. SU electric pump, twin SU carburettors.
Cooling. Lotus cross-flow ducted radiator.
Wheels. Lotus ultra lightweight bolt-on disc wheels 4.50 × 15 front and 5.25 × 15 rear. Fitted with Dunlop racing tyres.

4. LE MANS—*for serious international sports car competition.*

Chassis Frame. Lotus Mk. 9 multi-tubular space frame designed for aerodynamic bodywork.
Power Unit. Coventry Climax 1100 cc. single overhead camshaft engine with MG/TC gearbox and Lotus adaptor kit.
Brakes. Ultra light 9½" disc brakes. Outboard front; inboard rear.
Front Suspension. Swing axle conversion embodying Lotus units with coil springs around telescopic shock absorbers.
Rear Suspension. De Dion with electron final drive unit. Ratios available: 3.9, 4.2, 4.5, 4.9 or 5.125 to 1.
Wheels. Lotus knock-on conversion with 4.50 × 15 front and 5.25 × 15 rear. Dunlop racing tyres.
Cooling. Lotus cross-flow ducted radiator.
Instruments. Full set of racing instruments including tachometer 0-8000 r.p.m., oil pressure gauge, water temperature gauge, ammeter.
Fuel System. 11-gallon side tank. SU electric pump, twin S.U.-carburettors.

Efficient aerodynamically and light in weight the Mk. 9 is an international class car

DETAILS of the Lotus, visible in these pictures, include the shallow, low-mounted radiator and the large brake drums, mounted inboard at the rear. The retracted headlamps lie facing upwards as in the 1954 car.

The new LOTUS...

THE first two examples of the new Mark IX Coventry Climax-engined Lotus have now been delivered to their American owners for Sebring. This model is being supplied as a complete 1,100 c.c. sports car for £1,150 (plus P.T.), though it can also be had in the form of a basic frame and suspension parts for the home builder, like the other Lotus models.

The frame is a triangulated multi-tubular structure, and some of the tubes are smaller in diameter than before, whereas others are larger. Experience has been the guide, and the result is a frame that is lighter and stronger than ever. The wheelbase is 7 ft. 3½ ins. as before, front track 4 ft. 0½ in., and rear track 3 ft. 11½ ins. Naturally, the well-known swing axles are retained in front, while the de Dion axle at the rear has been cleaned up in detail.

Helical springs embracing telescopic dampers are used all round. A much stronger form of rear hub and articulated

IMPROVED airflow around the nose and better cooling for the enlarged front brakes is achieved through modifications to the body shape.

NEW LINES in the aerodynamic body of the 1955 Mk. IX Lotus are shown in the pictures above. It is two feet shorter than the earlier model, and to compensate, the tail fins are higher. The Coventry Climax engine, being smaller than the M.G. used last year, enables a lower bonnet line to be used. The drop-hinged door is shown in the picture on the left, where the car is seen with its designer, Colin Chapman. The whole forward section of the aluminium bodywork is removable, giving complete access to power unit, front suspension and the back of the instrument panel.

PIT PATTER

half shaft has been evolved, the same tube forming the Rudge hub and live stub axle, with no changes of section. As before, the rear brakes are inboard mounted, and the spiral bevel final drive has a large ribbed sump on its light alloy housing.

The new brakes—not yet fitted to the two Sebring cars—are literally enormous for an 1,100 c.c. car. The size is 11 ins. by 2¼ ins., and the drums are Elektron with steel liners. Ingeniously, the turbo fins of the front drums use the wheel rims as shrouds, the brakes being well inside the wheels. Behind, normal light alloy shrouds will be used. The Lockheed cylinders are mounted on special light alloy back plates, and these big brakes are actually lighter than the previous 9-in. type.

The body is no less than 2 ft. shorter than last year's streamlined Lotus. This has been made possible by the smaller engine, which allows a lower bonnet and the rest of the car in proportion. As well as a shorter nose, the tail is abbreviated, higher fins avoiding loss of area. Detailed improvements in the body shape around the front wheels give lower drag and superior brake cooling.

The lighter power-unit calls for an imponderous rear end if the car is to be in balance. Accordingly, the petrol tank has been taken from the tail and lies along the nearside of the body. These light alloy tanks come in 19-, 12- or 7-gallon sizes, according to the race in view. The battery and spare wheel still occupy the rear locker. A new mounting for the retractable headlamps allows them to be erected more quickly.

The single overhead camshaft engine is mated with a TC type M.G. gearbox. It is cooled by a ducted light alloy crossflow radiator only eight inches deep. The redesigned frame allows easier entry to the driver's seat through the downwards-opening offside door.

Fully equipped and with some petrol and oil aboard, the Lotus Mark IX weighs 9¼ cwt. ready to go. It is a much sturdier machine than last year's car, but is actually a few pounds lighter in spite of that. It is certain to be a most formidable contender during the racing season which is now upon us.

I was glad to hear, when I was at the Lotus works, that large numbers of the earlier Mark VI car are still being assembled. This much cheaper model has, for the first time, made it possible for the man of moderate means to own a genuine "sports-racer" and is therefore just as important as the more glamorous versions of the *marque!*

JOHN BOLSTER.

Colin Chapman dwarfs one of the first two new production Lotus Mark IXs on the eve of shipment to Sebring. They will be driven by Americans Frank Miller and Bob Scott. Power-unit is the 1100-cc Coventry Climax and gearbox is MG. Knock-on wheels are now standard. The bi-metal brakes are as before but brakes on subsequent cars will be "turbo" finned and enlarged to 11 in. Frame and all-enveloping bodywork have been designed complementary to each other. Rear suspension is De Dion with half-shafts as before but with tubular 2¼-in diameter stub axles constant throughout their length. Although tube thickness is only .095 in Chapman claims them to be 12 times stronger and half as heavy as last year's solid stub axles which also reduces unsprung weight.

New Lotus body is smaller, and 5 in lower than last year's Mk IX. Frontal area is less, and although a little of the aerodynamic efficiency has been lost due to new panel shape behind front wheels, brake cooling is greatly improved.

The four Sebring cars awaiting despatch from the works.

Mark 8F

Engine: (Coventry Climax) 4-cyl., o.h.v., 72.39 x 66.6 mm. (1,097 c.c.); two SU carburetters; 76 b.h.p. at 6,400 r.p.m.
Transmission: 4-speed gearbox; ratios: 13.9, 8.04, 5.56 and 4.125 to 1; Borg & Beck clutch; spiral bevel final drive; alternative ratios: 3.67, 4.125, 4.56 or 5.15 to 1; Hardy-Spicer open propeller shaft.
Suspension: Independent front by swing axles and helical springs; de Dion rear axle with parallel radius arms and helical springs.
General: Centre-lock wire wheels, 450 x 15 ins. front tyres; 5.00 x 15 ins. rear; weight (dry), 9 cwt.; height, 2 ft. 3 ins.; length, 11 ft.; wheelbase, 7 ft. 3½ ins.; track (front), 4 ft. 0½ ins.; (rear), 3 ft. 11¾ ins.; Lockheed brakes, inboard at rear; fuel tank capacity, 18 galls.; aerodynamic body.
Top gear speed at 1,000 r.p.m.: 18 m.p.h.
Estimated maximum speed: 125 m.p.h.
Estimated fuel consumption (50 m.p.h.): 40 m.p.g.
Price: £1,150 + P.T.
N.B.: Alternative engines recommended: Bristol 2-litre, Lea-Francis 1½-litre, Connaught 1½-litre.
Makers: Lotus Engineering Co., Ltd., 7 Tottenham Lane, Hornsey, London, N.8.

LOTUS ENGINEERING COMPANY *congratulates* **LOTUS** *owners and drivers on winning their classes in every important sports car race entered so far this year.*

SEBRING 12-HOUR RACE
1100 cc Class - 1st & 3rd
(3rd on Index of Performance)

BRITISH EMPIRE TROPHY RACE
2 Litre Class - 1st, 2nd, 3rd, 4th
1100 cc Class - 1st, 2nd, 3rd, 4th, 5th, 6th, 7th

GOODWOOD INTERNATIONAL MEETING — EASTER MONDAY
2 Litre Class - 1st & 3rd
1500 cc Class - 1st, 2nd
1100 cc Class - 1st, 2nd, 3rd, 4th, 5th, 6th
1100 cc Series Prod. Class - 1st, 2nd, 3rd

MEXICAN G.P. of AVANDORA
1100 cc Class - 1st
General Classification - 4th

COUPE DE VITESSE-MONTLHERY
1100 cc Class - 1st
General Classification - 3rd

S.C.C.A. PALM SPRINGS MEETING   1100 cc Class - 1st & 2nd

All enquiries to:—

LOTUS ENGINEERING CO., LTD.
7 TOTTENHAM LANE, HORNSEY,
LONDON, N.8   Tel: MOUntview 8353

INTERESTING COMPETITION CARS

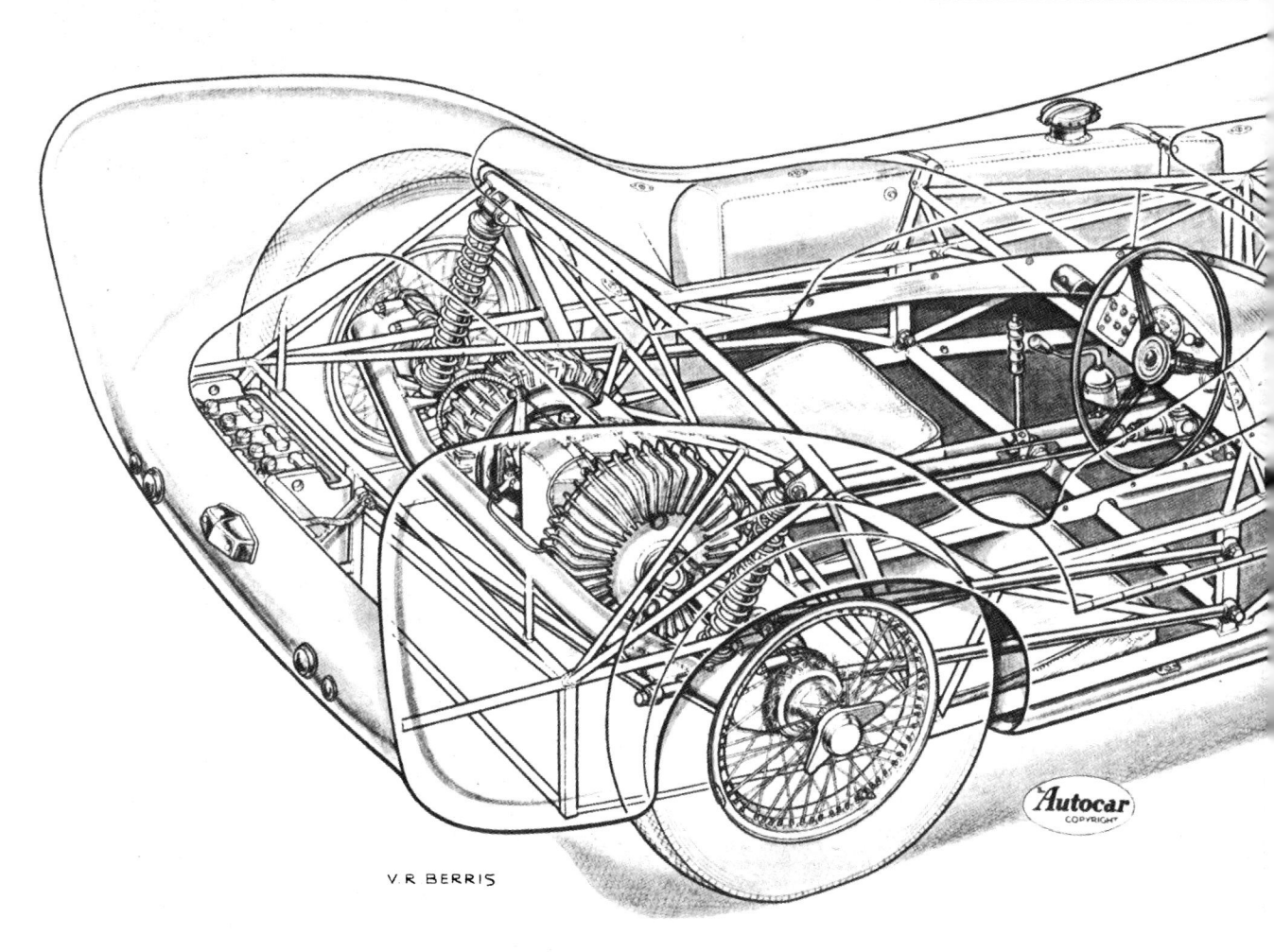

V.R. BERRIS

NINTH MARK fo

LATEST OF A SUCCESSFUL SERIES

IN the short space of three years the name of Lotus has established and distinguished itself in small sports car racing. Originally conceived so that the enthusiast could build a car at home with the minimum of difficulty and expense, the parts were obtainable as a number of units and sub-assemblies in much the same way as vehicles are sent to overseas assembly plants in a knocked-down condition. The first cars to be built in quantity were the Mark VI, available with engines by M.G. (types J4 and TC) and Ford (Consul and Prefect). To date over eighty of these models have been built, and particularly in 1,172 formula racing during the past two years, have proved to be almost invincible.

Last year saw the introduction of a streamlined car, with de Dion rear axle, designated Mark VIII; with its aerodynamic form and stabilizing fins over the rear wheels, this car struck a new note in sports car body design, and its influence was to become evident as the 1954 season progressed. This body form was evolved from models tested in a wind tunnel, and further testing of the complete car with scientific instruments under the guidance of aerodynamic experts resulted in a shape which reduced drag to a very low level. Furthermore, it was possible to fix precisely the areas of high and low pressure in order to locate the most efficient points required for air ducting.

A further stage in the development of the Lotus is the Mark IX car, to be available for the 1955 season. The original conception of availability in component form still applies, but in addition it can now also be bought as a complete vehicle ready for racing.

The Mark IX car is similar in appearance to its immediate predecessor, but to reduce drag and weight still further, the overall length is reduced by approximately two feet and the height by five inches. It was found also that the size of the two stabilizing fins over the rear wheels could be reduced without spoiling the handling properties. Initially the car will be equipped with the 1,098 c.c. four-cylinder Coventry Climax engine, but the chassis has been designed to accommodate alternative 1½-litre units at a later stage.

The chassis frame is of the space type, built up with round and square section tubes in mild steel, all the joints being acetylene welded. Racing experience has shown that mild steel is most satisfactory for this type of construction. In the past nickel steel tubing has been used but it tended to crack at the joints, presumably as a result of residual stresses set up during welding. The main constructional members of the frame consist of 1⅛in diameter tubes at the bottom and 1in square section tubes at the top, suitably braced with tubes of smaller diameter, the size of tube varying with the load. Attachment points for the final drive unit, engine, and suspension are welded to this main frame. A reference to the frame drawing will show that all the members making up the structure have been designed to avoid any cantilever loading.

Colin Chapman, head of the Lotus concern and designer of the cars, received his early engineering training as a structural engineer and considerable knowledge of this subject is reflected in his present field of activities. The result is an extremely rigid chassis frame weighing only 63 pounds complete with all its mounting brackets. It is interesting to record that

68

The disposition of the main components on the Lotus Mark IX. The gear box is mounted in unit with the four-cylinder single o.h.c. engine. Final drive unit and brakes are chassis-mounted and a de Dion rear suspension layout is employed. The low seating arrangements with ample passenger space, and fuel tank mounted on the left side of the chassis frame, are evident. The negative camber on the rear wheels can be discerned in the photograph, which also shows the shape of the rear fins

LOTUS

NOW AVAILABLE

after preparation of initial designs a scale model of the frame is made up in balsa wood to check its stiffness before proceeding with the manufacture of any prototype.

As in previous models the divided front axle and hubs of Ford manufacture are retained. The standard axle beam is cut in half, and plates are welded on each side for attachment to the chassis frame. To reduce the roll centre height on the resulting swing axle type of suspension, the pivot point has been kept low, and as a result of experimental work the roll centre at the front is now six inches above the ground.

Fore and aft location of each half axle is controlled by a Ford radius arm, modified to accommodate a standard Thompson steering ball joint at the chassis attachment end. The axles also carry a bolted bracket to which is attached the lower end of the suspension unit, comprising a Woodhead-Monroe telescopic damper surrounded by the coil spring. Each end of the damper is provided with a Silentbloc bush, the upper end being attached to forward and outward facing calliper-type brackets welded to the square-sectioned tubes of the chassis members. Alternative dampers of Girling manufacture are also being tried during the development stages.

There is a divided track rod, the two inner sections of which are attached to a bell crank lever mounted on the frame lower cross-tube. Running backwards at an angle from this lever the drag link connects to the drop arm of the steering box, which is a worm and nut type. Specially forged steering arms are bolted to each stub axle.

The rear wheels are supported by a de Dion tube and are, therefore, not fully independent. The axle tube is swept behind the final drive unit and is made from 3-inch-diameter 16 s.w.g. mild steel tube. Each end of the tube merges into a fabricated housing, provided with two opposed conical seatings. Into this fits an aluminium casting containing the hub and race assembly, which is held in position by four $\frac{5}{8}$-inch-diameter high-tensile bolts passing through each component. The hollow shafts are made from splined hubs welded to a Hardy-Spicer joint before final machining. Two ball-races are mounted on the outside diameter of the hubs and the assembly is locked up by the wheel nuts, which makes an ingenious and extremely light unit.

Driving and braking torque are taken through two $\frac{3}{4}$in-diameter 18 s.w.g. parallel arms, mounted on Silentbloc bushes at each side of the car. This method of location was pioneered by Ferrari and relieves the de Dion tubes of

With the designer, Colin Chapman, seated at the wheel, the sleek and functional body lines can be fully appreciated. There are exit ducts for cooling air from the front brakes, and stabilizing fins at the rear

NINTH MARK for LOTUS...
continued

The scuttle-mounted header tank for the cooling system, and brake twin master cylinders. The single, chassis-mounted float chamber fits snugly between the carburettors

The Coventry Climax FWA power curve shows the peak power of 75 b.h.p. produced at the comparatively low piston speed of 2,740ft per min. The b.m.e.p. of 130 lb per sq in at 2,000 r.p.m., rising to a peak of 158 at 4,800 r.p.m., is indicative of good breathing capacity

BORE 2.850
STROKE 2.625
COMPRESSION RATIO 9.75
FUEL ..... PREMIUM

The final drive unit consists of two major components. An Austin-Healey nosepiece with an aluminium casing contains the spiral bevel and crown wheel with the conventional bevel gear differential. This assembly is spigoted and bolted to the light-alloy main casing on which are mounted the back plates of the inboard brakes. Short stub shafts, provided with a single bearing on the outside and splined on their inner ends to the differential, terminate with a flange on which is mounted the brake drum. From this flange the drive is transmitted to the rear hub through short Hardy-Spicer universally jointed shafts. Each shaft carries a telescopic spline to allow for variation in length owing to wheel movement.

The underside of the main casing forms a well-ribbed shallow sump, which extends forward under the differential assembly and is provided with two widely spaced mounting lugs. A further lug is cast on top of the casing to provide three mounting points, which pick up with brackets welded to the main frame.

On the earlier Mark VIII streamlined cars, considerable trouble was experienced with overheating of the brakes, and the new car incorporates several features designed to overcome this problem. The brakes are provided with turbo-finned drums of magnesium alloy, into which is cast an iron liner for the braking surface. The outside diameter of the fins is arranged to fit snugly inside the wheel rims, providing for the front brakes an extractor effect for cooling air.

As a result of the fully instrumented tests carried out for airflow over the body shapes,

Three separate divisions make up the front aperture. In their raised position the head lamps provide adequate visibility for fast driving at night

any torsional strain should the car roll or one wheel rise. Lateral location of the axle is controlled by a Panhard rod attached to the frame on the left side, and anchored on the extreme right-side edge of the de Dion tube. As at the front, the suspension medium is coil springs built up as units with telescopic dampers and mounted on the axle tube via fabricated and welded brackets. The roll centre at the rear is $12\frac{7}{8}$ inches above the ground.

At static loading the rear wheels are provided with two degrees of negative camber and the front wheels with half to one degree of positive camber. Measured from the static position, rear-wheel deflection is $3\frac{1}{2}$in bump and rebound, and for the front wheels $2\frac{1}{2}$in bump and $3\frac{1}{4}$in rebound.

Contrary to modern practice, the periodicity of the front suspension is higher than that of the rear, being 85 and 75 cycles per minute respectively. Although other combinations have been tried, these frequencies have given the best overall results.

Taken with the front body section removed, this picture shows the depth of the chassis frame and front end cross-bracing. The mountings and inclination of the suspension units are shown

cooling ducts have been sited in the most efficient areas. At the front the low-positioned air duct is divided into three parts, the centre portion serving the radiator only and the outer ones directing the air over the brakes via panels swept inside the wheels. Although some small loss in aerodynamic efficiency has resulted at the front end the increase in braking efficiency is considerable.

At the rear end of the body an opening is provided below the locker lid at a high pressure point, resulting in a reverse flow of air over the final drive unit and brakes, with an exit at a low pressure area in the floor panelling.

Dual master cylinders are mounted on the scuttle rearwards of the pendant brake pedal, linked by an adjustable balance bar. This provides a means of varying the ratio of braking between front and rear wheels in four steps between 45-55 and 60-40 per cent.

Motive power is provided by the four-cylinder 1,098 c.c., single o.h.c. Coventry Climax engine, which was fully described in *The Autocar* of June 4, 1954. Since its introduction to the sports car world this engine has been developed to deliver 75 b.h.p. at 6,200 r.p.m. With a dry weight, less clutch, of 208 lb, this gives a figure of 2.78 lb per b.h.p., which is remarkably low for a standard production engine. Carburation is provided by two 1½in bore S.U. semi-downdraught carburettors, which are fed with fuel via flexible pipes from one large float chamber mounted on the chassis. To obtain good filling the induction pipes are quite long, and with an engine of such light mass the inherent vibrations of a four-cylinder engine at high speeds resulted in unsteady carburation with the float chambers mounted on the carburettors in the normal manner.

The front axle radius arm with its bc'l joint attachment on the frame. Inside the chassis can be seen the front engine mounting and inlet connection of the coolant pump

A detailed view of the frame indicates the method of using tubular construction to obtain a rigid structure with low weight

Cooling is provided by a belt-driven centrifugal water pump delivering 1,800 gallons per hour at maximum engine speed. From the outlet at the rear of the cylinder head water is fed into a separate scuttle-mounted header tank and routed from here through an aluminium pipe passing over the induction pipe to the radiator. The Winn radiator is of the cross-flow type with aluminium gilled tubes and side tanks which permit a large frontal area with a low overall height.

From the wet sump, which has a capacity of eight pints, oil is fed to a chassis-mounted full-flow filter. For long-distance races a Serck heat exchanger for oil cooling is fitted in series with the oil filter; in addition to providing a quick warm-up it maintains the oil and water at approximately the same temperature during running conditions.

A 7¼in Borg and Beck single dry-plate clutch is bolted to a light flywheel which also carries the shrunk-on starter ring. The four-speed M.G. TC type gear box is mounted to the rear engine plate by means of a light alloy adaptor casting. Gear selection is controlled by a short, cranked,

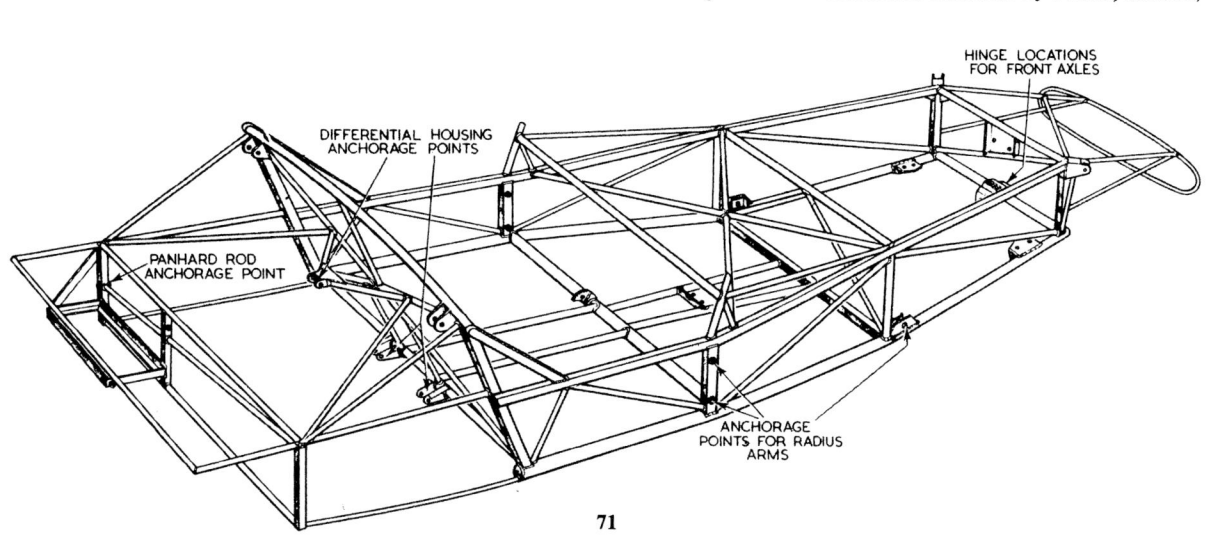

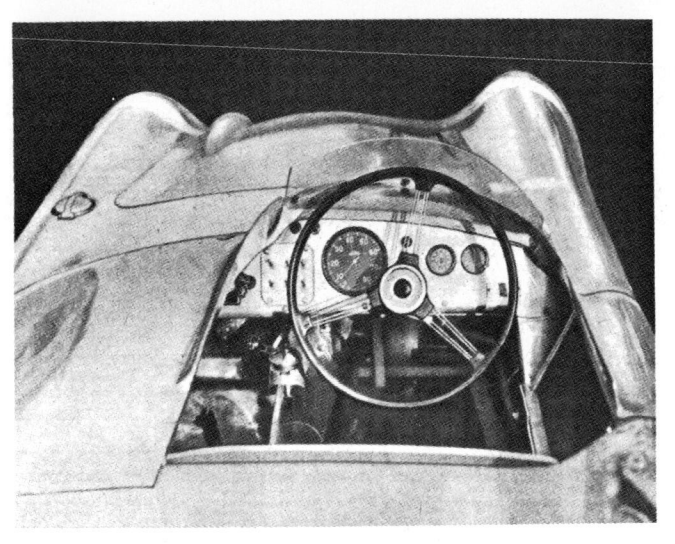

The driver's compartment is clearly functional; the change speed gear lever is well positioned

This drawing of the headlamp mountings indicates the method of retraction inside the bonnet when not in use

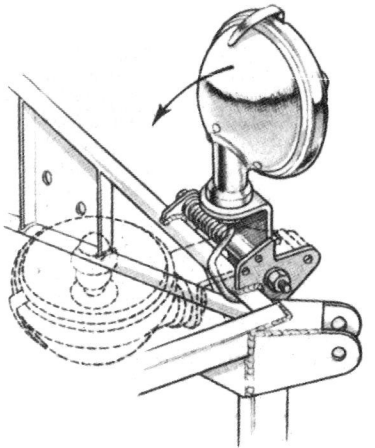

NINTH MARK for LOTUS... continued

remote control lever placed centrally. From the output flange of the gear box a Hardy-Spicer shaft continues the drive to the chassis-mounted final drive unit.

The body contains two seats placed slightly below and on either side of the transmission drive shaft. A full-width windscreen can be provided, but for competition purposes the passenger seat is enclosed by a metal tonneau cover fixed with Dzus fasteners. In this condition a swept-round windscreen is fitted to the driver's compartment. To comply with regulations and for ease of entry a dropdown door, hinged on its lower edge at about wheel centre height, is provided on the driver's side.

The front main section of the body is arranged for quick detachment, being mounted on the front aperture ring of the chassis frame and locked at the rear of each side with budget locks, which are operated by carriage key. Access to the top of the engine is provided by a detachable bonnet lid; again this is fastened by budget locks, as Dzus fasteners have caused difficulty during quick pit stops. A removable lid secured by Dzus fasteners provides access to the final drive unit, brakes and rear-mounted battery.

The head lamp mountings are another example of the detailed thought given to reduce drag. They are arranged on a spring-loaded hinge and can be swung down inside the bonnet when not in use.

The petrol tank is mounted amidships, outrigged from the chassis frame on the passenger's side. The tank is of light alloy, and the normal capacity is 12 gallons, but a sprint tank containing 6½ gallons is available for short races. For long distance work a tank with 18 gallons capacity can also be supplied. A quick-action filler protrudes through the front wing valance. Fuel is fed to the carburettors from an S.U. high-pressure electric pump mounted at the rear. Polythene petrol pipes are used throughout the fuel system, being extremely light, and resistant to fatigue; their transparency also allows the presence of vapour locks to be readily detected.

On the starting line with fuel and driver the car will weigh around 1,300 lb, giving a figure of approximately 130 b.h.p. per ton, which, combined with a low frontal area and good streamlined form, will make it a formidable contender for honours in 1,100 c.c. class races. Cars have been entered for Le Mans, the Mille Miglia and several other British and Continental major events, and this latest effort from the Lotus concern will be watched with great interest by all followers of the sport.

SPECIFICATION

Engine.—Coventry Climax 4-cyl, 72.39 × 66.6 mm (1,098 c.c.), single overhead camshaft, driven by gears and chain, operating the 20 deg inclined valves directly through inverted tappets. Three-bearing crankshaft. Compression ratio 9.75 to 1. Maximum b.h.p. 75 at 6,200 r.p.m.

Transmission.—Borg and Beck dry single-plate clutch, 7¼in diameter. M.G. type TC gear box, 4 forward speeds and reverse, synchromesh on second, third and top. Internal gear ratios: top 1, third 1.35, second 1.96, first and reverse 3.38 to 1. Optional rear axle ratios. Austin-Healey spiral bevel final drive, mounted in cast aluminium housing. Normal type differential.

Suspension.—Front, divided axle with radius arm. Rear, de Dion controlled by two parallel radius arms each side. Transverse location by Panhard rod. Combined coil spring and damper unit front and rear.

Brakes.—Lockheed hydraulic, two leading shoe front, leading and trailing shoe rear. Both drums 11in diameter 2¼in wide. Rear mounted inboard.

Steering.—Burman worm and nut. 1¾ turns from lock to lock.

Wheels and Tyres.—Dunlop wire wheels; tyre sizes 4.50 × 15in front and 5.25 × 15in rear.

Electrical Equipment.—12-volt, 31 ampère-hour battery, mounted at rear. Coil ignition.

Fuel System.—12-gallon light alloy tank as standard. Alternative capacities of 18 gallons and 6½ gallons available. S.U. electric fuel feed pump mounted at rear.

Main Dimensions.—Wheelbase, 7ft 3⅓in. Front track, 4ft 0½in; rear track, 3ft 11⅜in. Overall length, 11ft 7⅓in; width, 4ft 8in (plus ⅓in in each side for hub nuts); height, 2ft 3in (plus 6½in for windscreen). Ground clearance 6in. Dry weight, 9cwt.

Price.—In component form but less engine and gear box, £850.

The front suspension and steering layout; with the wheel removed details of the turbo fins which provide the maximum cooling area for the brake drums can be seen. Note the axle locating arm

The pendant brake pedal operates the scuttle-mounted twin master cylinders with an adjustable balance bar. Alternative mounting points for the balance bar are seen in the detailed view of the pedal

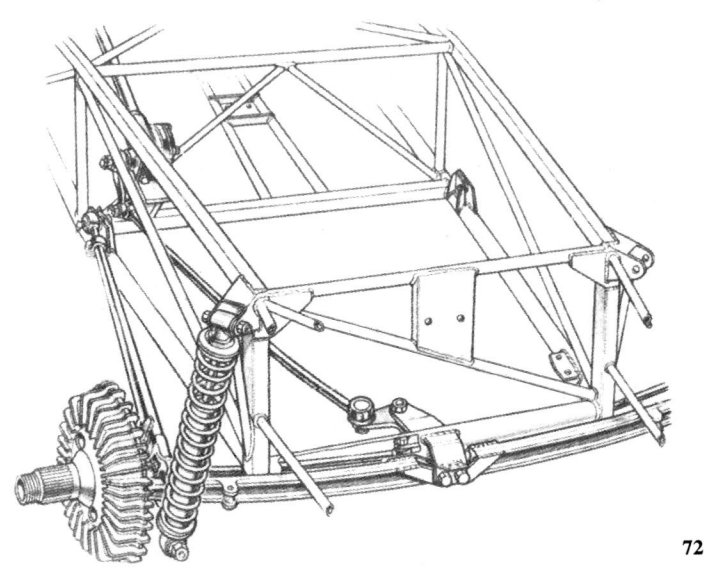

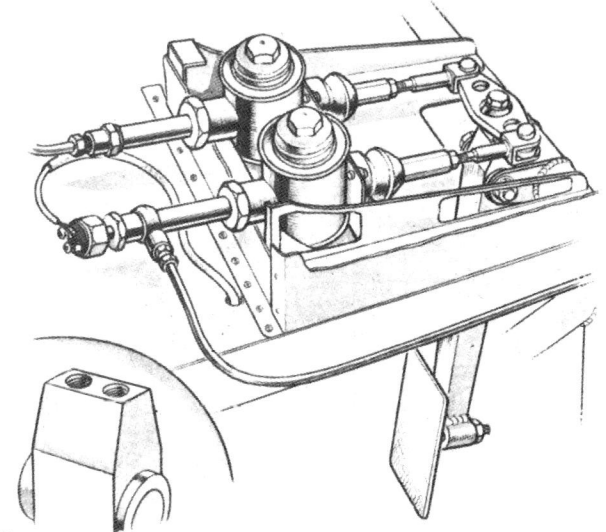

THE LOTUS-EATERS*

To Cornwall and Back in Colin Chapman's Masterpiece

By PETER GARNIER

NOT so very long ago a much hardier breed of British enthusiasts than exists today looked upon their rugged sports cars as a source of supreme pleasure. The cars were inclined to be temperamental; they required cajoling and nursing, and were uncomfortable, bumpy and draughty. But they could be well controlled, steered to a hair's breadth, were essentially safe and, above all things, gave pleasure from the moment they were driven proudly from their garages.

The demand for heaters, radio and other aids to comfort in passenger cars meant, inevitably, their adoption in production sports cars and, in my opinion, the cars have suffered for it. It is amazing, mind you, that the modern sports car can give the performance of a pre-war racing car and yet carry round with it veneered woodwork, luxurious leather seats, a radio, heater and what not; but these trimmings do not seem productive of the sustained concentration required for very fast travel.

There are still cars, however, mostly in the sports-racing field, which are rugged enough not to dull the senses with their warmth and comfort; which have high-geared, precise steering and handle impeccably, with leech-like adhesion; which have moved with the times and have powerful brakes and softer suspensions; cars which have perfect visibility and a pair of bucket seats comfortable only for those endowed with considerable inbuilt padding of their own. They please the eye—not necessarily of the man in the street, whose tastes are moulded by the popular stylists, but of the true believer—and look as though they were born and brought up on the road. And, finally, they are a joy to take out of their garages just for the pleasure of driving them fast. The Lotus is one of these cars.

The Mark IX is the current member of a line of cars which started with trials specials in the days when 1,172 c.c. cars were usurping the position held by the V8-engined specials. Sooner or later it was bound to happen—the cars began to appear on the circuits; Colin Chapman—the genius behind them—gave up trials and took to racing. The Mark III became supreme in the 750 formula class and was seldom, if ever, beaten.

In 1952 the Mark VI came along, using a tuned version of the Ford Consul engine; these cars, with their familiar exposed, inclined coil springs at the front, were sold as "build it yourself" kits. Peter Gammon, using an M.G. engine, entered 29 races in 1954 and won 17 of them. The aerodynamic Mark IX made its debut this year and its successes are too well known to enumerate. A list of Colin Chapman's wins and places in the Climax-engined car which I have just driven to Cornwall and back is given at the end of this article.

Switches to the left control the lights—side, tail, head, number illumination, facia and registration number—separately. The revolution counter is ideally placed and ammeter, water and oil temperature and oil pressure gauges are grouped round it. The cockpit is roomy, and warmer than many open cars; the full arms' length driving position is excellent

---

* Greek λωτός: Plant yielding the fruit eaten by the Lotophagi: represented by Homer as producing a state of dreamy forgetfulness and loss of all desire to return home (Oxford Dictionary).

73

THE LOTUS-EATERS...

Noon, Remembrance Sunday. The Lotus halts outside Penzance, with the smoke from what used to be the G.W.R. blowing across the town

When Chapman suggested that I should sample his own Lotus-Climax, it was in the middle of a hard season, the car racing almost every weekend—so the borrowing was postponed until the programme was quieter. Originally the intention had been to put it through its paces on one of the aerodrome circuits but it was decided eventually that the Lotus' circuit career was too well known to warrant further comment.

"Why not try it as a road car?" someone suggested. "Take it on a long journey and see how it compares with a more normal machine." So, in the early hours of a Saturday morning, following the B.A.R.C. dinner-dance at Grosvenor House, the Lotus thundered out of *The Autocar* park and headed westwards through empty London streets.

As a small concession to passenger comfort, a shallow, wrap-round Perspex screen had been added and, to comply with the law, two small pinpoints of light served as sidelights and a single, retractable driving light gave inadequate illumination of the road ahead. In contrast, at the rear there was almost a Christmas tree display of red and white lights. There were the stop and tail lights, reflectors, registration plate lights and two racing number lights, one each on the outsides of the fins, which gave traffic from both directions a good indication of the car's width. "Turn the lot on," Mike Costin, Chapman's chief mechanic, advised.

If the lighting arrangements complied with the law (which might be arguable), the exhaust note did not sound as if it did. Passage through towns—particularly London—was made as unobtrusive as possible by trickling along at the side of the road at about 1,500 r.p.m. in top—at 17.2 m.p.h. per 1,000 r.p.m. with the 4.5 to 1 rear axle, it was hoped that this would offend nobody; it seemed not to. Even so, progress through London was somewhat heart-in-mouth and it was with relief that the Great West Road was reached and the end of the limit.

In spite of this entirely unsuitable treatment for such a car, it seemed perfectly happy, the engine temperature keeping round 75 degrees; there was no tendency to oil plugs, the note picking up crisply at the end of the limit. Despite the 9.7 to 1 compression ratio the car is surprisingly tractable in top gear, pulling away happily from 1,000 r.p.m.

Whatever impressions of the suspension had been formed during the frustrating passage through London were quickly dispelled on the open road. At around 40-50 m.p.h. the ride levelled off and became very comfortable and steady, the bumpiness at low speeds being completely ironed out. The steering took some getting used to, being high-geared (1½ turns from lock to lock), very light indeed and with very little self centring. After daily use of a car with low-geared and much heavier steering, one found oneself holding the wheel too firmly and using too much helm. After a few miles it was found that the lightest possible wheel grip was enough, and that it was not necessary to do more than incline the body for the wider radius main road corners.

Amenities

The cockpit was comfortable and roomy enough for two, and the full-arms'-length driving position perfect; the response to the controls was quick and good and the Girling disc brakes—inboard at the rear—were very powerful indeed and completely smooth, requiring very light pedal pressures. Before long one realized that the car was free from the idiosyncrasies that make it wise to serve a tentative apprenticeship to driving one or two of the really fast sports cars. As the miles went by it was found that, despite the November night, the car was surprisingly warm, there being need for no more than a Burberry to be completely comfortable.

Night-time is ideal for a long run with such a car and the traffic that was about was quickly left behind—with an unaccustomed close-up view of wheels and hubs from the very low seating position, the occupants of the cars towering above.

Unfortunately, the period of growing accustomed to the car was cut short by fog, which closed in at Bagshot and continued as far as Honiton. Borrani wheels being rather fragile and costing some £16, kerbs were treated with the utmost regard and speed was kept down, though by looking over the screen it was possible to proceed considerably faster than other nocturnal travellers. The frustrating, foggy miles went by and, around 4 a.m. and Honiton, the stars became visible. Because the roads were wet and the undershield had been drilled and cut about in fitting long-range tanks and the like, the cockpit, by now, had shipped a fair amount of water and we were far from dry. The Lotus is not a touring car, so this was forgiven.

As confidence grew, and within the limitations of the somewhat inadequate single driving lamp, it was great fun to take the car through fast bends on the slippery, empty roads, steering with the throttle, sliding the rear wheels and

Borrani wheels, fragile and £16 a time but saving greatly in unsprung weight, dictated extreme caution during the foggy night run

using the high-geared steering to hold the car on the desired line through the corner. With the considerable power available (and the fact that one of the rear tyres was not over-endowed with tread) it was necessary to be discreet in the use of the accelerator, the rear wheels breaking away very easily in the wet. Though slides were easily started, however, they were equally easily stopped, and the Lotus gave the impression that a comparatively inexperienced driver could learn many of the tricks without getting into difficulties —provided that he used the necessary discretion.

It is this inbuilt ease of handling which, as has been frequently observed, results from racing and makes a good sports car far safer than anything else on the road *because of*—not despite—its high potential speed. In the hands of a complete novice such cars can be dangerous, and it is questionable whether they should be available to beginners— but that is another matter. In sound hands they are the safest things on wheels.

Journey's end—Newlyn—was reached in time for breakfast. Though the run had not been outstanding for its comfort, what with fog and wet roads, it had been warm, and enormous fun. We were not particularly tired and there had been no tendency towards the drowsiness that would have occurred on an all-night run in a closed car—though, in fact, the occupant of the passenger seat had slept for a considerable part of the journey.

The remainder of the day was occupied in showing the Lotus to enthusiastic friends in the district—and basking in the reflected glory of its passage through the West Country towns and villages. The pleasure it gave to those who were driven in it was outstanding, particularly those who enjoy motoring for its own sake. Though born and bred on the circuits, it was perfectly amenable to pottering round country lanes.

Unfortunately, the roads were wet for the return journey the following day, and there was a strong wind blowing. In daylight, however, it was possible to use much more of the performance, the car settling down to a comfortable cruising speed of 85-90 m.p.h. whenever the roads were clear enough. On the one occasion when it was possible to make use of a clear, straight road—the exposed Gossmoor, to the west of Bodmin—about 6,500 r.p.m. was seen—112 m.p.h. But the combination of the wet and a strong wind on the starboard bow made the car difficult to hold.

Possibly because of the fact that one front wheel was badly

Inboard-mounted Girling disc brakes, de Dion tube and Panhard rod running behind the final drive can be studied in this illustration. Driving and braking torque are controlled by twin parallel torque arms, with Silentbloc bushes

Bob Berry, noted Jaguar driver, tries the car. An XK140, undergoing road testing, can be seen beyond the Lotus with fifth wheel driving the generator for the electric speedometer attached

Good Lotus country—Bodmin Moor, bleak and free of traffic, provided some eight miles of fast travel

THE LOTUS-EATERS...

out of balance (one of the balance weights having fallen off), or because of the changing gyroscopic action of the front wheels caused by the familiar Lotus divided front axle, the car tended to make small darts from the straight, their amplitude to leeward being increased by the wind. With a weight of slightly over 8 cwt, the car is susceptible to winds.

The de Dion rear axle and slight negative camber on the rear wheels gave the Lotus cornering powers which were a constant source of surprise. With restrained use of the throttle through the curves themselves, I found I was taking corners towards the end of the journey at speeds which, at the beginning, would have seemed impossible, and yet apparently with plenty in hand. It would need a great deal more time to get accustomed to the car—and a closed circuit —to discover the limit.

There was no trace of roll or, as the roads dried, tyre scream. One thing that was particularly noticeable was that, because of the good shape of the body, the Lotus lost speed

The Coventry-Climax engine could not be much more accessible. The radiator header tank, connected to the cross-flow radiator, and the twin brake fluid reservoirs can be seen mounted on the bulkhead. The twin master cylinders are to the left and, to the right, the frame-mounted twin S.U. carburettors which are connected to the inlet manifold by flexible rubber pipes

The Lotus in its proper environment; Colin Chapman drives the car to victory in the 1,200 c.c. sports car race at Brands Hatch on October 9—breaking the lap record for sports cars of all classes.

THE LOTUS-EATERS...

very slowly when the throttle was closed. For slow, gradual speed reductions the brakes were needed when, in a less wind-cheating car, the air resistance would have done the job.

As it was Remembrance Sunday, the Lotus' progress through towns was contrived on little more than a tick-over. In Yeovil we were led through the streets by a military band, complete with a strong turn-out of the British Legion, Boy Scouts and so on. The reactions of the onlookers, who lined the pavements, at being provided with an unexpected close-up of a racing car ranged from enthusiastic appreciation of their good fortune to open hostility. The police appeared not to object to the thunderous accompaniment to the band, so all was well.

In a car of this sort, where one's progress between towns is so very quick, one finds oneself driving through them in a much more restrained manner than is usual. Aware that the public eye is on one, I suppose, and that anything one does wrong will be observed and commented upon, everything is treated with respect, particularly speed limits. After all, one can afford to be quixotic—the time so spent can easily be made up; roads which, in less exciting cars, seem fast and open appear suddenly to have become an unending succession of towns and villages.

The fuel consumption, on a rough check over the weekend, worked out at between 25 and 30 m.p.g.—for a 1,100 c.c. engine with a maximum of somewhere around 130 m.p.h. The same engine used in the Cooper-Climax for the record-breaking runs at Montlhéry, and running continuously at 7,000 r.p.m., maintained a figure of 35 m.p.g.—which goes to show that a racing engine is not an extravagant version of a touring engine, but merely an infinitely more efficient version. A standing quarter-mile, incidentally, was covered on a wet track in 15.2 sec.

Particularly pleasant was the way the Lotus, with its ample reserve of power, and maximum in third gear of comfortably over 90 m.p.h., overtook the Sunday afternoon traffic. There was none of the frustrating pottering behind cars whose drivers prefer to travel at 30 m.p.h. or less, nor any of the patient waiting for a stretch long enough for overtaking. With a quick change into third gear the car would accelerate from 60 m.p.h. to 90 in the length of road bounded by nine or ten telegraph poles, leaving the potterers well astern. In this respect the Lotus proved itself, once more, to be one of the safest cars on the road.

In its present state it is, of course, not a road car—the exhaust note alone sees to that—and the extremely light gauge body panels are too frail for everyday chores, denting easily if one leans too hard. Suitably modified, it could become one of the most enjoyable forms of long distance travel, not only for the younger generation but also for all who drive for the enjoyment of it.

During the 650-odd miles covered in the car over the weekend, it proved conclusively that, by sacrificing a few creature comforts, one gets from a car that has been developed through constant racing the most exhilarating, controllable and safe transport that can be found anywhere —and with surprising economy in the case of the Lotus.

THE LOTUS YEAR IN RETROSPECT

June
11-12.—Le Mans 24-hour race. Fastest 1,100 c.c. car. Delayed initially by slipping clutch, but regained lead in class by 11th hour. Was finally disqualified for a regulation infringement.

July
10.—Brands Hatch. 2nd in up to 1,200 c.c. sports car race.
30.—Crystal Palace. 4th in 1,100 c.c. class in sports car race.

September
17.—Tourist Trophy. 2nd in 1,100 c.c. class. Leading class and Index of Performance until 5th hour when delayed with oil pipe fracture. Pit stop of 11 minutes to rectify. Recovered position towards end of the race and was finally beaten by 5 seconds for class win.
24.—Goodwood. 1st in up to 1,250 c.c. race and 1st in up to 1,500 c.c. race.
25.—Snetterton. 1st in up to 1,500 c.c. race.

October
1.—Castle Combe. 2nd in both up to 2,000 c.c sports car races.
9.—Brands Hatch. 1st in up to 1,200 c.c. sports car race.
30.—Tarrant Rushton Speed Trials. 1st in up to 1,200 c.c. and 1,101-2,000 c.c. sports car classes.

Lap record for 1,100 c.c. sports cars held at the following circuits: Goodwood, Snetterton, Le Mans, Dundrod, Oulton Park, and Brands Hatch.

LOTUS MK IX

Article and photography: **Rolofson**

Substituting fork lifts for loading ramps at Houston airport cost car minor nose dents.

DESIGNED BY Colin Chapman, famous English competition driver and designer, the newest brainchild of the Lotus Engineering firm has been redesigned to meet competition experience. By substituting the single overhead camshaft 1,100 cc Coventry Climax engine in place of the previous modified MG engine, Mr. Chapman has come up with a very strong entry into the increasingly popular small displacement ranks. The new streamliner is being supplied as a complete sports car for about $3500, and, as with previous Lotus competition equipment, the basic frame and suspension system may be purchased in various stages of assembly for home builders. (See R&T for June, 1953)

The small engine drives through a TC type MG gearbox, and is cooled by a ducted light alloy cross-flow radiator only eight inches high. The smaller engine also made it possible for the designer to build a much lighter and stronger frame of triangulated multitubular construction, to lower the hood line, shorten the nose section, and abbreviate the tail fins. These modifications all work together, providing lower drag from nose section to tail, and greatly improving the flow of cool air through the brakes. The new aerodynamic body shell, developed from exhaustive wind tunnel testing, follows the latest trend in English competition machinery by using a semi-monocoque type of construction. Noteworthy is the fact that the stabilizing fins have been made larger (higher) than on the original MG-powered streamliner to competsate for the reduced rear-end overhang. The all-aluminum shells are being made by Williams & Richards of Tottenham Lane, London, associates of Lotus Engineering. The wheelbase of the 1954 streamlined Lotus has been retained at 87.5 ins., with a front tread of 48.5 in., and a rear tread of 47.5 inches. The previous competition-proved swing axles are retained in the front suspension, an improved de Dion axle with inboard brakes at the rear, and coil springs are damped by aircraft-type shock absorbers in the front and rear. The rear hub and articulated half shaft have been redesigned, utilizing the same tube to

To compensate for shorter body, tail fins are higher to avoid loss of area. The front end changes provide less drag, improve brake cooling.

Antennae-like headlights pop up for night work; whole front section is removable for maintenance.

form the Rudge hub and live stub axle.

To balance the shorter body, the fuel tanks have been moved from the tail to the midsection, and are removable. Tanks are provided in seven, twelve, and nineteen gallon sizes, furnishing a selection of weight saving combinations to suit the requirements of varied road racing circuits. The spare wheel and battery are carried in the streamlined tail section, just behind the deDion axle and inboard brakes. A set of new brakes (not fitted to the Sebring cars) are planned for installation in the Mark IX models now in production. They are 11 inches by 2¼ inches, and are magnesium with steel liners —huge for an 1,100 cc car! The turbo fins of the front drums use the wheel rims as shrouds, the brakes being well inside of the wheels. The brake wheel cylinders are mounted on special light alloy backing plates, and these big brakes are actually lighter than the previous nine-inch type! A stronger and lighter machine than its forebears, the 1955 Mark IX version of the streamlined Lotus provides a power-to-weight ratio which should make this little machine a giant in competition.

Developing 72 bhp at 6300 rpm, the four cylinder Coventry-Climax engine has a bore and stroke of 2.84″ x 2.62″ and is capable of turning at 7000 rpm without too much fuss. Both the cylinder block and head are cast aluminum and valves are in line, actuated by a single overhead camshaft. The weight of the Lotus is claimed to be 1035 lbs with oil, water and a gallon or two of gasoline. If true, this gives a power to weight ratio of 14.4 lbs/bhp and acceleration from zero to 60 mph (with driver added) should be in the order of 12 seconds.

One of two factory prototypes rushed to American owners in time for the Sebring races, the Mark IX shown in our illustration is the latest car to join the sports car stables owned by Bobby Burns of Wichita Falls, Texas. It will be serviced and raced in the United States by Norman J. Scott, Jr. of Continental Motors Ltd., Houston, Texas, a distributor for Lotus. ●

Strengthened frame allows easier entry to the driver's seat via the unique drop-down door.

The Coventry Climax, 1100 cc sohc engine looks tilted but is not. Note retracted lights.

Sparse, business-like cockpit has half canopy fused into the body shell for streamlining.

BRITISH RACING car enthusiasts can now build a replica of the Lotus Mark 9. Only normal hand tools and work bench are required and no part needs welding.

IT'S EASY TO BUILD A FAST LOTUS 9

From ROGER FULLER

HERE'S a new idea for the "hot rod" or sports racing car enthusiast: Buy your parts in kit form and build yourself an international class car.

It's called the Lotus system and it enables anyone to build a replica of a Lotus sports car, which, in no time at all, has risen from an enthusiast's backyard prototype to a car that has been proved in competition motoring all over the world.

This idea, previously connected with model aeroplane enthusiasts, must hark back to the time when a young London engineer, Colin Chapman, started making sports cars as a sideline from secondhand Ford and Austin parts. Today, at the age of 27, with his wife Hazel and more than 20 skilled mechanics, he is turning out at least three Mark IX racers powered by 1100-cc Coventry Climax engines (giving 130 mph) a week.

Now, he is adding to the range precision components designed for builders of sports and sports-racing cars seeking extremely high performance at minimum expense. Using these components in conjunction with one of a range of proprietary engines and gearboxes, the enthusiast can build an outstanding touring or competition car with little difficulty. Total cost can be less than £700.

Fundamental to the success of the Lotus system, is the multi-tubular space frame, — it's a delight to the eye because of its delicate tracery — of exceptional torsional rigidity. It is designed and practically tested according to strict engineering practice. Light in weight, this welded tubular mild steel structure is designed to accept no fewer than five types of engine for which mounting brackets are provided. It weighs only 63lb. complete.

Two basic types — the Mark 6 and the Mark 9 — are produced. The Mark 6 is designed to accept a simple, two-seat body of conven-

LONDON ENGINEER Colin Chapman has given sports-car builders a rare chance to assemble two Lotus basic types — Mark 6 and Mark 9 — at a minimum of expense.

tional form, and the basically similar Mark 9 has additional frame members necessary for a more complex fully aerodynamic two-seat body.

For use with the frame, a complete range of components is produced. These include the simple, swing-axle, independent front suspension conversion (using combined shock absorber and coil spring units) a de Dion rear axle using similar spring units, hydraulic or cable-operated drum brakes with cast magnesium drums, or hydraulically-operated disc brakes produced to the firm's specifications.

A light-alloy adaptor is produced to enable the remarkable Coventry Climax engine to be mated to the gearbox. Other items include controls, steering gear, a special radiator, special lightweight wheels and exhaust silencers. All these items may be employed in either the Mark 6 or Mark 9 frames.

From the range, the amateur can build a car with the precise degree of performance required, and with the assurance that handling, roadholding, braking and steering will be of the highest standards. Yet only normal hand tools and a bench are needed — no welding or machining facilities are required.

Power/weight ratios are remarkable; 94 bhp per ton with a medium-tuned Ford engine, and 182 bhp per ton with the old Coventry Climax 1100-cc firepump engine. ●

EASILY DETACHABLE body panels save precious seconds in pit stops and make maintenance simple

With the

Frank Miller tries out the new Lotus in practice at Sebring.

THERE have been very few cars that have made really impressive records in their first forms. Most of the world's outstanding automobiles have run the gamut from a meager beginning, through numerous stages of development, to the full blown article, but all of this usually takes a number of years. So many a prospective sports car builder abandons the entire project while it's still in the "gee, wouldn't it be wonderful if . . ." stage.

In this, the Lotus seems to be a real exception. It jumped into the winner's circle right from the drawing board of the talented Colin Chapman without so much as a pause to have the usual bugs, and has been going great guns ever since.

True, the car and design have gone through successive stages of development between the first trials special and the latest version but the basic design and thinking have paid off in uniformly successful models all down the line. In spite of the successes of these small beasts, however, they have been almost totally absent from the American competition scene, and, in fact, it was due to an American expatriate that the Mark was present at Sebring.

Actually the Lotus arrived at Sebring primarily by the good offices of an unofficial ambassador, and if his account is taken at face value, one that has very little reason to be a willing Lotus enthusiast.

A conversation between Bob Said and Frank Miller of New York can really be credited with bringing the Lotus Mark IX to Sebring. Bob was recounting his experiences at one of the British races to Frank. It seems that while he was barnstorming the OSCA in Europe he entered a scratch race against the Lotus cars. He found himself, by his own account, circulating around the bends at a reasonable speed when Colin in one of the Lotus cars passed him. Intent on catching this special and with a foot well down, everything was going well until Peter Gammon in another Lotus also passed the laboring OSCA. From there on, until the two impertinent MG powered machines passed him again a few laps later, Bob had to content himself with chasing the two flat little cars with exaggerated fins over the rear wheels.

This account wasn't intended as a sales talk, but it had that effect, and Frank Miller went out and bought a Lotus! Of course, it wasn't as simple as that in the long run. Lotus Engineering's greatest disadvantage is that its quarters are too small to allow full production of the cars already on order. With a capacity of only two cars a week and a backlog stretching toward three figures, there were a good many delays in the initial assembly. Then, too, the two cars on order (Scott's and Miller's) were to be semi-prototypes of the new Mark IX series and considerable individual thought and attention had to be given both of them. As an example, the new cars differ from the Mark VIII in that the Mark VIII chassis that

lotus at Sebring

The Lotus proved itself a true road car in the drive from New York and a potent racing machine.

appeared on the prototype cars last year has been abandoned in favor of the tried and proven Mark VI type. The body is some eighteen inches shorter, five inches lower at the instrument panel and one-and-one-half inches closer to the ground, occasioning the thicker tail fins at the rear fenders. These are not only necessary to maintain directional stability in the extremely light car, but the de Dion rear end (incidentally fitted now with coil springs at both sides rather than the single transverse one used on the Mark VIII) will allow the wheels to bounce well up into the fenders on a hard bump.

The Mark IXs have center-lock wire wheels too, and would have sported eleven inch brake drums had not the time element forced some last minute revisions in construction. Needless to say, these rather major changes over last year's cars required all of the two months to complete, and Frank's car arrived less than a week before Sebring. The only problem then was to unravel the red tape connected with an individual importation and get the car off the docks. There is hardly enough room here to cover the details of this operation, and it must suffice to quote Frank's "never again without an agent!"

All things come to an end though, good or bad, and eventually the gleaming aluminum beauty was released to the new owner, barely in time to leave for Sebring and its maiden race.

Colin suggested that the car be driven to the course to limber it up a bit and bed in the brakes and such, so with true enthusiasm the convoy consisting of two definitely non-weather-proof cars (the Lotus and C Jaguar) and a station wagon set off in a rain storm for the fourteen hundred mile trek to the Florida orange groves. After the first few minutes Frank, physically but not spiritually dampened, fell completely in love with the perfect handling little car, and was enjoying himself thoroughly, rain or no. The willing 1100 cc. Coventry Climax engine would kick it along at speeds equal to the bigger Jaguar, and the riding qualities were superb. Only one fly was present in the ointment. Apparently the car was built with the thought of a six-foot plus driver in mind and neither Frank nor George Rabe, his co-driver, filled the bill. After a bit of ingenuity was applied to a sleeping bag, however, the cockpit was padded to the owners' specifications and quite comfortable.

Arrival at Sebring and technical inspection over, work began on trying to prepare the car for the grueling 12 hours ahead. Here the usual bugs that seem to be present in most new cars began to make their presence known. The gear box needed reworking, and mechanics Ned Hudler

Gas and oil go into Miller's Lotus prior to the 12 hour run. The sleeping bag is non-standard.

Scott's car gets a last minute adjustment in the pit area. The pits are new at Sebring this year.

Frank Miller (79) overtaking Jim Pauley's Siata V-8

and Bud Powell tackled an all night job before the race. There was some trouble with a gasket, and a bit of adjustment on valve guides had to be made before the car was run flat out. Nothing serious, but all time-consuming, and since the course was only open during practice for testing the crew abandoned sleeping rather than practicing.

At last race day dawned and the Lotus was pushed into line to await the starting signal. When the bomb went off, drivers sprinted across the track and piled into the cars and were away, all except the Lotus. The sleeping bag, a necessity for both Miller and Rabe made itself difficult, and some precious seconds were lost in adjusting it. Fortunately the Porsche driven by O'Shea and Koster, the biggest threat to the Lotus, refused to start and the Mark IX began overtaking some of the class C cars with an aplomb that the 1100 cc. engine is not usually thought capable of.

By the end of the first hour a good many of the Ferraris had removed themselves from the race by pranging things, burning, and what have you, and the Lotus was firmly ensconced in the lead of class G. About this time it rocketed around one circuit at four minutes and eight seconds for an average speed of a bit over seventy-five miles per hour. This was enough to let it pace even the D type Jaguar for part of the course, but was a bit uncertain since the tachometer had decided that the effort wasn't worth it, and had given up during the first ten minutes.

About eleven-thirty the Lotus lapped the Abarth, and the next time around seemed well on the way to doing it again. An hour later though the Lotus and a Mercedes had the same ideas about the same corner at the same time and Frank lost seven minutes getting out of the sand and straightening a bit of bent aluminum. When the car came into the pits Frank ignored the cold drinks in favor

"Sad Sam" Samuelson in the 78 Lotus

of the ice and water they were packed in, and while George Rabe tore off in pursuit of the now leading Lotus driven by Norman Scott, Frank tried vainly to remove some of the grime left by the first three hours. This proved unsuccessful, so he climbed into the station wagon to try to make up for the lost night's sleep.

Rabe meanwhile ignored the seven-minute loss, and by one o'clock was back in the lead in class G and happily bushwhacking at the larger cars just to keep them on their toes. The Lotus was having no trouble lapping the production cars in class C and seemed quite willing and able to take on the Mercedes from time to time.

From here on until six o'clock the two Lotus cars had their own private dice, taking time out only to lap a few of their competitors every now and then. They were both ahead of the index of performance, and several laps ahead of the third place car in class G in spite of the usual

MILLER PASSING RUBIROSA'S
DEFUNCT FERRARI.

TOO MUCH SUN...

jack benson

racing ailments of slipping clutches and fading brakes. The latter are to be enlarged from nine to eleven-inch drums, and Frank and Norman Scott both feel that if they won't then work as well as disc types, they'll come near enough to it to keep well ahead in the future.

As the evening came on the cars continued to build up their class and index lead until Samuelson on his first lap away from the pits, after taking over from Scott, got the full effect of the setting sun right in the eyes, at the chicane. Unable to see ahead the Lotus went off course, through a couple of sandpiles and across an abandoned concrete foundation that had been left carelessly in the grass when the building was torn down. In spite of considerable bouncing over the concrete block walls of the foundation and a bit of cross-country travel, the car remained perfectly level and could have continued the race but for a holed sump.

This left Miller and Rabe in practically undisputed possession of the first place in their class. Their clutch, though slipping a bit, and holding the top speed down somewhat below maximum, still gave them enough in hand to maintain a three-lap lead over the Koster/O'Shea Porsche. This 'was when the race began to unravel a bit for the Tottenham Lane speedster.

Frank passed his pit and saw a go signal flying rather frantically, and since the crew had not kept lap charts all assumed that the Porsche was gaining. He opened up the Lotus and was drawing away (actually the Porsche was still several laps behind) when disaster struck, or rather was struck.

On positioning for the final bend, and in the process of passing a production Jaguar to boot, the two cars began their drifts. Suddenly there in the headlights was a hay bale, and nothing to do to avoid it! The Lotus smacked through the hay with only a slight shudder, and a crumpled front fender to continue to the pits for inspection.

Here it was looked over, and since no damage other than the bent aluminum could be found, George Rabe took the Lotus back into the melee. It also developed that the wayward haybale had been ooched out into the course by a car cornering with a bit more nerve than skill, and the marshal at that point, on seeing the Lotus and Jaguar bearing down on him had decided that that was no time to dash out and replace it. This was soothing news, indicating that the car hadn't been off course after all, and until George Rabe appeared around the same hairpin a sense of well being and joie de vivre pervaded the number 79 pit. They were still leading class G, still well up on the Index, and the bump had been "one of those things." Then the Lotus screamed around the bend, and

George Rabe cornering the Lotus ahead of the Bandini during morning practice on Saturday.

Frank Miller flashes past the pits after his encounter with a wandering haybale.

into the pit straight—with only one headlight!

Out came the course marshals and black flags, and the car was pulled in. Due to the black flag the engine had to be stopped while repairs were hurriedly made, with the Porsche gaining minutes each lap. Then, like the last year's plight of Gonzales at Le Mans, the engine wouldn't start. The wandering haybale had pushed a rubber hose against the block, and it had burned through, leaving the car without engine, and twenty-five minutes to go.

Here the technicality of longer races entered into consideration. The car had to cross the finish line under its own power, and be running under its own power when the race ended. It was a quarter of a mile from the finish, and the lightweight battery would hardly drive the starting motor that distance, so the car was pushed from the pits, the entire length of them, toward the checkered flag. All the while the crew tried their utmost not to think of he Koster/O'Shea Porsche gobbling up their lead, and when the bomb went off, they ran the car across the finish line. Difficulties about whether or not it had left the pit under its own power, and some indecision on the part of everyone as to just where the finish line was, however, resulted in the car being disqualified for a time, then re-qualified, and now even Frank Miller isn't positive as to its status.

The main thing, Frank points out, is that the car proved to be a veritable giant killer in the competition, and that never has he driven a car that was so responsive and docile under the demands of racing.

At present, he has the engine out for balancing, and a few minor modifications, such as relocating the fuel pump to give shorter lines, knurled pistons with nonchromed rings and the like. It will be ready for the fray again by the time the Cumberland race rolls around, and should be hard to beat, because it is truly a competition car.

Its greatest recommendation is that it is truly a sports car. In spite of its extreme design (so well-done, incidentally, that an extra two hundred rpms. could be had by just sliding lower into the cockpit during the Sebring race), the car is perfectly road-worthy, making no fuss at traffic driving and, according to Frank, its handling makes it ideal for a novice. The soft spring smooths out bumps like a Detroit creation, but it should be possible to carry a glass of water on the hood without spilling it, if the cornering at Sebring is any indication of normal dead-level ride.

All in all, the Lotus is a mechanized ambassador to this country that we predict will be more than well received, and if the number of admiring (and covetous) glances the two little cars received in Florida is any indication, we'll probably be up to our necks in Lotuses by the end of the season. Not a bad situation at that.

—☆—

DESIGNED to accommodate this streamlined two-seat body with its side-mounted light alloy fuel tank and twin tail fins, the Lotus chassis is here seen in the Mark IX form with Coventry Climax 1,100 c.c. engine which will be exhibited at Earls Court.

1956 CARS

LOTUS

A RANGE OF BUILD-IT-YOURSELF COMPETITION MODELS

FAMILIAR to all who follow racing, the name Lotus will be new to many Earls Court visitors. On a components stand immediately adjoining the ground floor car stands, the Lotus Engineering Co., Ltd., will be showing an 1,100 c.c. chassis with Coventry Climax engine to represent the varied types of 2-seater competition cars which may be built around chassis frames and other components designed and built by them. It is estimated that more than 100 Lotus cars have been built in three years, with such power units as Ford, M.G. and Bristol, while many more are under construction and chassis are being delivered at the rate of two per week.

Designed by Colin Chapman, the Mark VI and Mark IX Lotus chassis are both of exceptionally light multi-tubular construction, and have demonstrated outstanding qualities of road-holding. The full-width aluminium-panelled bodywork used for the latter model has had its streamlining developed by a great deal of full-scale testing with wool tufts.

Multiple small-diameter steel tubes welded up to form a deep and rigid space frame are used for every Lotus, as is a very simple and effective system of independent front wheel suspension by swinging half-axles, coil springs encircling telescopic shock absorbers being fitted at both front and rear. The suspension is very flexible, with 6-in. travel permitted at the front and 7-in. range of movement at the rear. According to requirements, cars can be built with Girling brakes of Ford pattern, with large-size hydraulic brakes operating in ribbed light-alloy drums, or with 9-inch disc brakes of Girling design.

Many examples of the Lotus use Ford rear axles and shortened torque tubes. When the price of higher performance is being paid, a rear axle of de Dion type gives improved road holding and acceleration, the final drive casing which is then mounted on the frame being a magnesium-alloy casting on which sprung rear brakes are mounted. Twin radius arms on each side of the car locate this rear axle, and exposed drive shafts incorporating Hardy Spicer universal joints are attached to tubular hubs running in lightweight bearing housings, a detail which typifies the Lotus policy of lightness through simplicity being use of the knock-off hub cap to locate (through the wheel and a distance piece) the hub ball-races laterally. Other interesting components which it will be possible to see at the Motor Show include the lightweight fuel tank, an oil-to-water heat exchanger, and a very low radiator, extreme care to save weight on every detail being a Lotus secret of success.

Initially founded to supply components to those building or modifying cars for racing, the Lotus Engineering Company is still mainly concerned with the sale of chassis (usually complete with body panels) and other components. Increasing export business has however led to an expansion of the works at Hornsey, London, enabling a small number of complete cars to be assembled there.

DETAILS to be noted here are the centre-lock wire wheel, Girling disc brake, and coil-type front spring enclosing a telescopic shock absorber.

The Lotus Blossoms

ACCORDING to the dictionary, the fruit of the Lotus tree is believed to cause a state of dreamy content and forgetfulness of home and friends, but this is the last state which could be associated with Colin Chapman – head of the Lotus Engineering Co – notable for his alert discontent. It is by his refusal to bow to convention in the few short years since 1947 that Lotus cars have become competitors to be feared, and not only in relatively minor national and pseudo-international events over short distances. During the earlier stages of Chapman's career he was employed by British Aluminium Co on the development of light alloys for commercial vehicles.

At first, Chapman's efforts were confined to building and modifying what can best be described as trials specials, but soon – as is inevitable – the lure of speed events and racing attracted him away from boyish things. The car on which the fame of Lotus was founded was the Mk. III, which swept to success under the 750 cc. Formula. During active racing, the Mk. III was never once beaten. Much of this car's success was due to Chapman's iconoclastic approach to the problems of carburation, which led him to a drastic, but simple, method of converting the siamesed ports of the Austin Seven cylinder head into four ports, which were fed from a double-choke Stromberg carburettor, of the type fitted to a Ford V8.

The unceasing demand, from both within and without the Lotus organization, led to the search for greater power when the prototype of the Mk. VI was built in 1952. Instead of a simple Ford Ten side-valve engine – costing around £50 – a very tuned-up edition of the Ford Consul – costing almost three times as much – was employed. On this model, many Ford components were used, in the interests of reducing cost to the purchaser and also of making easier the system of selling the car as a 'make-yourself' kit. An excellent example of the successes achieved with the Mk. VI Lotus – in this case fitted with a MG engine – by private owners is demonstrated by Gammon's record for 1954. He entered 29 races, and obtained 17 firsts, 7 seconds and 5

The Mk. VI Lotus

The Mk. IX Lotus

thirds. It should be remembered that six of these twenty-nine events were for cars larger than 1500 c.c., and in two cases were Formule Libre. All we have said so far is truly preamble, as the car that matters is the Mk. IX, under review.

Chapman's early studies as a structural engineer are traceable in the general construction of the current model. The chassis frame is of the space type, built up from round- and square-section mild steel tubes, a form of structure which has been proved in racing to be more suitable than the previously used nickel steel. In the interests of weight reduction, the size of the bracing tubes, joining the main upper and lower structural members, vary in proportion to the load. Study of the illustration will show that cantilever loading has been avoided throughout. The main members are $\frac{7}{8}$ in. at the bottom and 1 in. square section at the top. Points for attaching engine, final drive assembly and the suspension elements are welded on to the frame at suitable points. On the earliest Lotus the braking system was by courtesy of Austin Seven, while the many Mk. VIs used Ford brakes and wheels. The change to aerodynamic form brought with it the normal problems; the greatly reduced drag of the body demanded better braking, as the resistance of the air was of little assistance, while, despite careful ducting, there was still an appreciable masking of the brake drums.

On the Mk. IX the brake drums are turbo-finned and made of magnesium alloy, into which is cast an inner lining of iron. The outside diameter of the drum is such that it fits neatly inside the wheel rims, so giving an appreciable

The space frame of the Mk. IX

The wheel and braking mechanism are of Ford manufacture on the Mk. VI

The turbo-finned magnesium drum of the production Mk. IX

The Girling disc brake fitted to the factory development Mk. IX

The final drive assembly and the inboard disc brakes. The de Dion tube and the Panhard rod can be seen

The depth of the space frame can be assessed from the shallowness of the door, which complies with regulations

... The Lotu

extractor effect. The rear brakes, which incorporate similar drums, are fitted either side of the final drive assembly. On the factory-controlled cars – as run in both Les Vingt Quatre Heures du Mans and the Nine Hours of Goodwood – disc brakes were employed, which, while causing a weight penalty, guaranteed excellent braking. This was of particular importance at the end of the Mulsanne straight, where the Lotus – in spite of its limited power output – was travelling at over 130 m.p.h., a speed which was considered commendable for the unlimited sports/racing cars a few years ago. The braking is initiated by a pendant pedal which operates through two master cylinders, linked by an adjustable bar, which can be set to give four variations of front/rear braking, within the limits 45–55 and 60–40.

The front suspension is independent, by means of a divided front axle, of Ford manufacture; the actual suspensory mediums are helical springs, the volutions of which surround the Woodhead-Monroe hydraulic dampers. The roll centre at the front is six inches, as the pivot point of the swing axles has been kept low. The rear suspension is again by helical springs, controlled by a de Dion tube, while lateral positioning of the assembly is by a Panhard rod. Both driving and braking torque are absorbed by twin parallel arms, mounted on Silentbloc bushes. Much of the excellent reputation of the Lotus for high-speed cornering can be traced to the use of three degrees of negative camber on the rear wheels, while the front ones are provided with one degree of positive camber. Many small but clever features can be observed throughout the car. For example, the manner in which the aluminium casting holding the hub and race assembly is contained within two conical housings, and the whole assembly is held in position by four $\frac{5}{16}$ in. bolts, and locked by the wheel nuts themselves. The roll centre at the rear is $6\frac{3}{8}$ in. higher than at the front and, while the front wheels are provided with $2\frac{1}{2}$ in. bump and $3\frac{1}{2}$ in. rebound, the rear are given $3\frac{1}{2}$ in. bump and rebound.

The present Mk. IX is not as efficient aerodynamically as was the prototype, as the provision of air entries to cool the front brakes has increased the drag to some extent, but it can claim to have been the most efficient car at Le Mans, in achieving the highest maximum speed relative to its power. Chapman is fortunate in having several part-time 'boffins' available to assist him with aerodynamic matters, and

The divided air entry directs about half the air on to the front brakes

Immediately after passing through the radiator, the air is diverted down and away

lossoms . . .

the results achieved indicate that it is not essential to have a vast organization to obtain results. So meticulous is Chapman on the importance of reducing drag that a single excrescence from the bodywork — a screw head for example — causes him almost physical agony. One illustration shows the manner in which air is conducted through the cross-flow Winn radiator. From the central portion of the low air entry the air is passed through the radiator and immediately expelled beneath the car, without entering the engine compartment. The entire front section of the body can be removed for attention to engine or chassis parts, once the securing locks have been unfastened. While earlier models were partially monocoque, this method of construction has been discarded, owing to the difficulties caused in minor repairs, which are so often required during a racing season. At first glance, the Mk. IX Lotus looks rather *outré*, but it is worth recording that Chapman is among the strongest supporters of the suggestion to limit sports car racing to proper production cars, and he believes firmly that it is possible to produce a car which combines a low-drag body with adequate luggage accommodation, and a reasonable degree of protection against the weather. The lines of the Mk. IX give the impression of a longer-than-average car, so it is important to bear in mind that it is 24 ins. shorter than the previous model, and 5 in. lower.

The method of headlamp mounting is a good example of the trouble taken to reduce the frontal area. They are fitted on a spring-loaded hinge, so that when not in use they can be retracted beneath the engine cover. Three alternative fuel tanks are listed; a sprint one of 6½ gallons, a medium-sized one of 12 gallons, and one suitable for long-distance events holding 18 gallons. As can be appreciated, the largest tank is easily sufficient to comply with the Le Mans regulation, which demands a minimum of 32 laps between replenishment. Ready to race, the car, with driver and fuel, weighs 11·6 cwt., which gives a power/weight ratio of approximately 130 b.h.p./ton. While this guarantees adequate low-speed acceleration, the low frontal area and excellent form assist in producing a very high maximum. If, as has been suggested, the Mille Miglia in 1956 is emasculated by some form of capacity limit, the Lotus would be a most suitable car, as its excellent cornering, allied with high maximum speed, would make it equally at home on the twenty-mile long Adriatic straight and over the mountain passes.

Although the Mk. IX is designed to take alternative engines — among the alternatives already used are 1500 cc. MG and Connaught, and 2000 cc. Bristol — the most interesting, currently, is the 1100 cc. Coventry Climax, as used in the factory car at both Le Mans and the Nine Hours of Goodwood. When one recalls the performances achieved by 1100 cc. sports cars only a few years ago, the capabilities of the Lotus with the Coventry Climax engine become more startling. On the axle ratio used at Le Mans, the following speeds were obtained on the four gears without exceeding 7,000 r.p.m.: 49, 77, 104 and 130 m.p.h. The four-cylinder single overhead camshaft engine has dimensions of 72·4 × 66·6 mm., giving a capacity of 1097 cc., and from this is extracted 78 b.h.p. at 6,200 r.p.m. The speed at which maximum power is obtained is no indication of the engine's limit, as

The Coventry-Climax engine. The two master cylinders, the header tank and the chassis-mounted float chamber can be seen

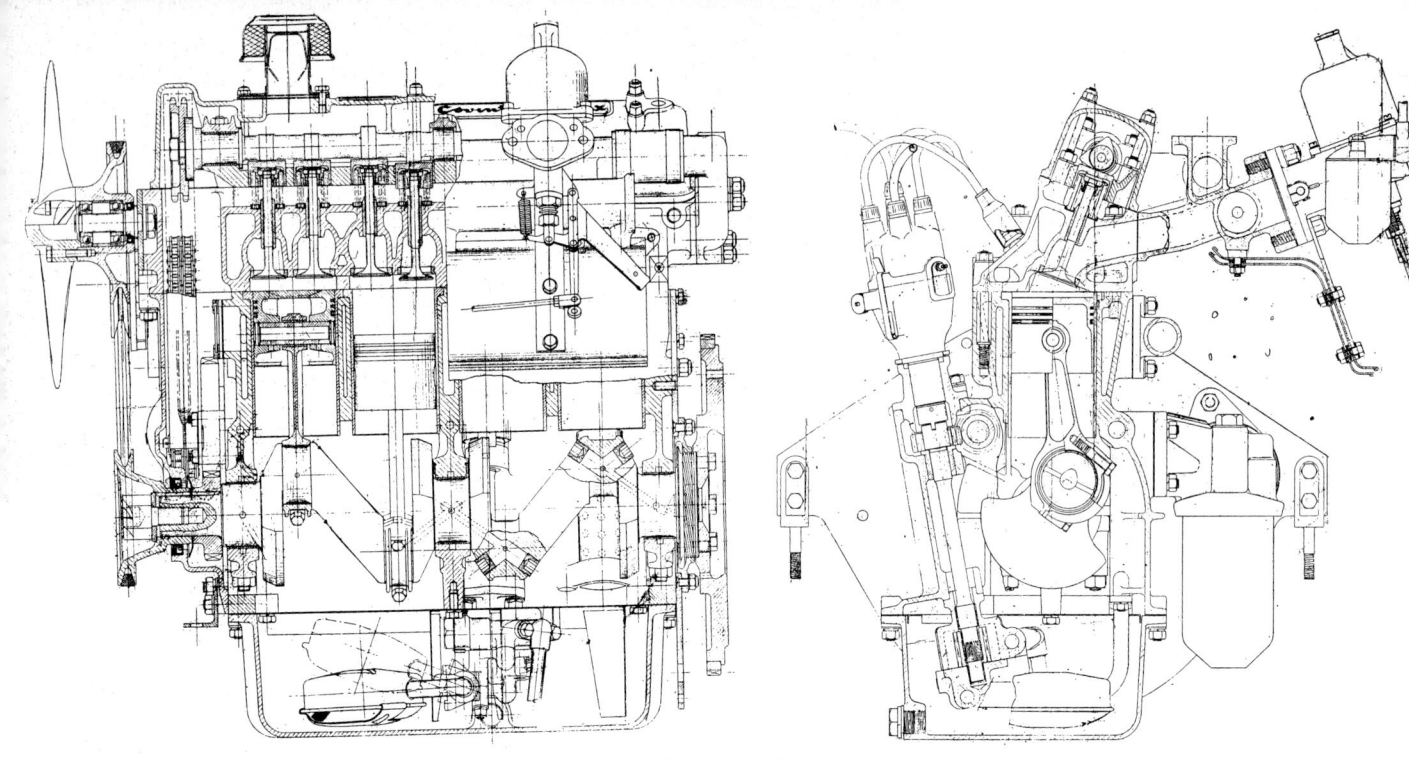

The 1100 cc. Coventry Climax Engine

... The Lotus Blossoms

engine speeds of over 7,200 r.p.m. have been repeatedly obtained. Less clutch, the engine weighs only 208 lb., which gives the remarkably low figure for a production engine of 2·66 lb./b.h.p. The drawings indicate more clearly than could words the massive dimensions of the crankshaft and the beautiful proportions of the connecting rods, which in alliance, should guarantee that bottom-end troubles will be unknown on this engine. On early examples some trouble was experienced because of the long induction pipe used to ensure proper filling. The separate float chambers attached to the carburettors caused variable carburation, owing to vibrations transmitted from the engine. This has been overcome by using a single large float chamber attached to the chassis and delivering the fuel by flexible pipes.

The power is transmitted through a $7\frac{1}{4}$-in. Borg and Beck dry-plate clutch to a four-speed MG gearbox, of TC type. A Hardy-Spicer shaft delivers the power onward to the chassis-mounted final drive unit, which uses an Austin-Healey nosepiece. Among the many cars which have been discussed in this series, the Lotus emanates from the smallest organization, but, in our opinion, it is none the worse for that. It has, of course, the great advantage, which a bigger firm would lack, of enjoying the co-ordinated efforts of director, designer, head tester and driver all in one man.   R. N.

Photographs: John Ross

Engineer Chapman baffled by the construction of a tripod

The line of the stabilizing fin blends satisfyingly with the rear wing

JOHN BOLSTER TESTS
THE LOTUS MARK IX

with both M.G. and Coventry Climax power units

A YEAR ago, I tested the then prototype aerodynamic Lotus. At that time, the machine had only been seen in the hands of its progenitor, Colin Chapman. Since then, the thing has been rationalized, finalized and delivered to quite a number of lucky customers. Having come in at the beginning, as it were, I was naturally agog to try the current version.

I was thus extremely elated when Colin offered me the loan of *both* the works cars. One of these has a highly tuned M.G. engine, in which respect it resembles the car I borrowed last year. This is the well-known 1¼-litre unit, "stretched" to nearly 1½-litres. The long stroke and pushrod valve operation limit the ultimate performance, but the exceptional torque in the middle range of revolutions is invaluable when maximum acceleration is required. About 85 b.h.p. is developed at 5,800 r.p.m.

The other car has the Coventry Climax engine, an "over-square" 1,100 c.c. light alloy job, with a single overhead camshaft. When Colin Chapman took the Brands Hatch sports car record, the engine was standard, but it now has a special camshaft giving additional overlap. In this form, it produces 81 b.h.p. at 6,700 r.p.m.

Apart from the difference in power units, the two cars are virtually identical. Both engines are attached to M.G. gearboxes of the early "J" series, without synchromesh. Customers' cars normally have the later type of box, but a few pounds of weight are saved if one is willing to forgo the alleged advantages of a simplified gear change. The final drive is a spiral bevel, for which various ratios are available. It transmits its power, through articulated half shafts, to the tubular hub assemblies that carry the knock-on wheels.

The real basis of the Lotus is a triangulated space frame of welded-up tubular construction. The independent front suspension is by swing axles, and at the rear there is a de Dion axle. Suspension is by helical springs and telescopic dampers all round. The brakes are Girling 9 ins. discs, inboard mounted at the rear. The Lotus aerodynamic body is too well known to need description.

On the road, the performance figures of the two cars were very similar, and yet the difference in handling was surprisingly large. Pulling a 3.66 to 1 gear, the M.G. version registered 128.6 m.p.h., whereas the Climax did 127.7 m.p.h. The latter unit had a 3.9 to 1 rear end and the rev. counter showed just about 6,500 r.p.m. continuously during the timed runs. There was a slight side wind blowing throughout the test period, and it is possible that under ideal weather conditions one could attain peak revs and "bust" 130 m.p.h.

It will be seen, from the graph, that the 1,100 c.c. car was fractionally quicker in the lower part of the acceleration range. Both machines are commendably free from wheelspin, having regard to their very high performance, but the smaller one is fractionally the better in this respect. It is lighter by some ¼ cwt. than the M.G.-powered model, and consequently there is better traction, because the weight is taken off the forward end of the chassis.

Once third gear has been engaged, cubic capacity tells. The high torque of the M.G. engine pays dividends, and the 1½-litre car takes the lead. That is not the whole story, however. The difference in weight distribution naturally affects the handling characteristics, and whereas the heavier car understeers, the lighter one is just about neutral in response.

The steering of the Lotus is a typical feature. It is very light and high-geared, with little caster action, and there is no lost motion at all. A driver who had only handled the "soggier" type of modern saloon would at first find himself putting on too much helm and swerving involuntarily. After a time, he would find that, left alone, the car tended to run straight, and then he would suddenly realize what he had been missing.

The Lotus, particularly in its Climax-engined form, has phenomenally high cornering power. I was extremely happy to take it very fast through the curves of a road circuit, and there are no peculiarities to learn. I would, however, require a good deal more practice before I was certain that the ultimate limit was being attained. The whole cornering process is so effortless, with no rolling, bouncing, or tyre scream to give an air of urgency to the proceedings, that only experience gives warning that one is going from the improbable to the impossible. I know a particular corner which I habitually negotiate at just on 100 m.p.h. in the better class of sports car. The Lotus Climax took it first try at better than 110 m.p.h. You see what I mean!

The Girling disc brakes are very

POTENT PACKAGE: The Coventry Climax unit is mounted well back in the tubular frame; the body is readily removable. In the heading picture the M.G.-engined car is on the right—but who could tell?

Specification and Performance Data

Cars Tested: Lotus Mark IX Sports-racing two-seaters. Price (component form without engine and gearbox), £850.

Lotus M.G.

Engine: Four cylinders, 72 mm. x 90 mm. (1,467 c.c.). Pushrod operated valves in light alloy head, 85 b.h.p. at 5,800 r.p.m. 9.5 to 1 compression ratio. Twin S.U. carburetters. Lucas coil and distributor.

Transmission: Borg and Beck racing clutch. Four-speed gearbox with central remote control, ratios 3.66, 4.87, 7.10 and 12.25 to 1. Open Hardy Spicer propeller shaft to chassis-mounted spiral bevel and differential unit. Articulated shafts to rear hubs.

Chassis: Multi-tubular space frame. Independent front suspension by swing axles. Rear suspension by de Dion axle. Helical springs and telescopic dampers all round. Girling 9 ins. disc brakes. Racing type wire wheels with knock-on hub caps, fitted 4.50 x 15 ins. front, 5.25 x 15 ins. rear tyres.

Equipment: 12-volt lighting and starting, ammeter, revolution counter, oil pressure and temperature and water temperature gauges.

Dimensions: Wheelbase, 7 ft. 3½ ins.; track, front 4 ft. 0¼ in., rear 3 ft. 11½ ins.; overall length, 11 ft. 8 ins.; weight, 9 cwt.

Performance: Maximum speed, 128.6 m.p.h. Speeds in gears: 3rd, 85 m.p.h.; 2nd, 53 m.p.h.; 1st, 32 m.p.h. Standing quarter mile, 15.4 secs. Acceleration: 0-30 m.p.h., 3.4 secs.; 0-50 m.p.h., 6.6 secs.; 0-60 m.p.h., 8.6 secs.; 0-80 m.p.h., 13.2 secs.; 0-100 m.p.h., 22.4 secs.

Fuel Consumption: Racing, 20 m.p.g.; Road, 30 m.p.g. (approx.).

Lotus Climax

Engine: Four cylinders 72.4 mm. x 66.6 mm. (1,097 c.c.). Single overhead camshaft operating valves in light alloy head. 81 b.h.p. at 6,700 r.p.m. 9.8 to 1 compression ratio. Twin S.U. carburetters. Lucas coil and distributor.

Transmission: As above, except ratios 3.9, 5.27, 7.64 and 13.07 to 1.

Chassis: As above.

Equipment: As above.

Dimensions: As above, except weight 8 cwt. 1 qr.

Performance: Maximum speed, 127.7 m.p.h. Speeds in gears: 3rd, 95 m.p.h.; 2nd, 60 m.p.h.; 1st, 36 m.p.h. Standing quarter mile, 15.8 secs. Acceleration: 0-30 m.p.h., 3.2 secs.; 0-50 m.p.h., 6.2 secs.; 0-60 m.p.h., 7.8 secs.; 0-80 m.p.h., 14.6 secs.; 0-100 m.p.h., 23.6 secs.

Fuel Consumption: As above.

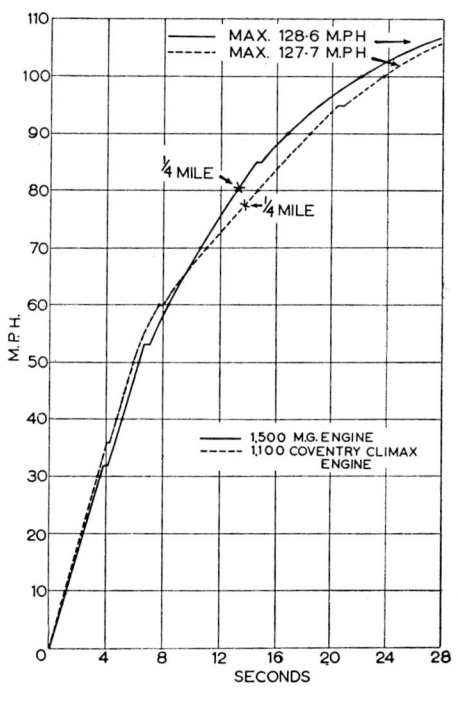

Acceleration Graph

powerful, but entirely smooth and constant in action. Some earlier discs were inclined to be fierce and noisy at low speeds, but the Lotus equipment has absolutely perfect manners. There is, in fact, no particular in which a drum brake would be superior and, of course, the complete elimination of fading is an advantage that needs no emphasis.

As already related, the two cars tested were fitted with "crash" boxes. I must say that, for this type of machine, the absence of synchromesh is, if anything, an advantage. All the half forgotten tricks of one's youth can again be employed, and the ratios can be snatched just as fast as hand can move the lever. The Borg and Beck racing clutches gripped instantly after every shift, but they were not too fierce for gentle use in traffic.

Speaking of traffic, I had occasion to drive both cars in London, though this is scarcely a normal procedure for sports-racing machines. I had no trouble with oiled plugs, though both engines were fairly "lumpy" at the lowest speeds. In standard trim, the Coventry Climax is a very flexible engine, but the special camshaft deletes all power below 2,500 r.p.m. On the open road, the phenomenal acceleration and powerful brakes render the Lotus a very safe car. One can frustrate the knavish tricks of even the British Sunday Driver, and 100 m.p.h. cruising is normal on the more deserted stretches.

Regarding the Lotus as a competition car, which is after all its *metier*, one cannot but be impressed by the excellent accessibility. A normal bonnet panel is removed for routine maintenance, but the rest of the body is secured by aircraft-type fasteners, and a virtually bare chassis can be achieved in a few minutes. There is no need to emphasize the advantage of being able to strip the car down in this way between races. It makes possible a thorough check-over under ideal conditions, and all chassis parts can be as carefully maintained as the engine.

Compared with last year's car, the body is greatly improved; the vibration of the panels at high engine revolutions has been noticeably reduced. The general sensation is that one is sitting in a solidly constructed vehicle, and there seems no reason why the body should not stand up well to a hectic competition career. Retractable headlamps of a simple but effective type remain a typical feature.

For the rest, there has been much cleaning up of details, and the knock-on racing wheels add greatly to the appearance as well as being stronger than the original bolt-on type. The rear suspension with zero roll resistance has been replaced by a more normal layout, and the front roll resistance has been increased to match. As a result, cornering is even more effortless than before.

The racing successes of the Lotus need no underlining from me. However, I now have a fuller understanding of how they have been achieved. Particularly in the case of the Climax-engined car, one finds a machine which is so well balanced that all the power can be used nearly all the time; and, on the rare occasions when this is not so, those Girling discs give straight-line braking as powerful as it is dependable.

ABINGDON PRODUCT: A 1,250 c.c. M.G. unit, bored out to nearly 1½ litres, is fitted to 9 EHX and develops some 85 b.h.p.

HEAT EXCHANGER (above) on the Climax car effects a balance between the temperatures of lubricating oil and cooling water.

EMPHASIS ON SPORTS CARS—
ROAD IMPRESSIONS OF THE WORKS Mk. IX LOTUS

DISTINCTIVE APPEARANCE characterises the aerodynamic Mk. IX Lotus, a 1,100-c.c. sports/racing car of outstanding performance and controlability.

THERE is no need to underline the excellent performance, one might write "circuit-performance," of Colin Chapman's Mk. IX aerodynamic Lotus, for its race successes at various club meetings and its splendid showing, while it was running, at Le Mans and in the T.T., speak nearly as loudly as the little car's exhaust note! Moreover, enthusiasts who went to last year's Earls Court Motor Show were able to examine the appetising components which Chapman offers to "specials"-builders on his stand in the main hall—such covetable fare as divided-axle i.f.s., de Dion back-end, a lightweight tubular space-frame with low-drag radiator and other factors enabling it to wear a two-seater sports body of reasonable aerodynamic form.

I write of this Lotus in the singular because this article is concerned with the actual Le Mans/T.T. car, Mk. IX/87, which is the property of Peter Jopp and is driven in races by its designer/creator, Colin Chapman. In fact, of course, the small firm of Lotus Engineering Ltd., at 7, Tottenham Lane, Hornsey, London, N.8, has been "mass-producing" these advanced little cars for some time—"mass-producing," that is, for a concern of this modest size, making what are essentially specialised sports/racing cars—Lotus supply the chassis frame and components in various combinations at prices which they will quote gladly if you apply to them.

This particular Lotus, when MOTOR SPORT had it for test in November, had led a particularly hard life. Apart from doing a very appreciable proportion of Le Mans and the T.T.—at Le Mans the car was disqualified and in the T.T. it was leading on Index of Performance until an oil-pipe broke, causing it to lose the 1,100-c.c. class to a Cooper-Climax by a mere five seconds—it had been driven in various lesser races and used by two other motor journals for assessment purposes, besides which, on November 16th, just before we went to Hornsey to take it over, XPE 6 had been tried out at Brands Hatch circuit by a dozen different drivers, who collectively drove it at racing speed for more than 240 laps (or over 300 miles), six of them unofficially approaching or equalling the absolute sports-car lap record for this course. Reg. Bicknell clocked 61.2 sec., Alan Brown 61.6, Ivor Bueb and Graham Hill both got round in 61.7, George Wicken recorded 62.8 and Dennis Taylor 62.9 sec., while Ken Tyrrell, D. Boshier-Jones, F. Hobart-Smith, John Brown and Chapman himself all "had a go," the last-named modestly refraining from quoting his lap times. And all this without a proper overhaul since it was registered early in June.

Not surprisingly, after such high-speed usage, the Lotus was becoming rather weary during our spell with it, and we experienced a few minor bothers, such as a "flat" battery due to a "shorting" electrical lead, a flat tyre, failure of the rev.-counter drive (which mystified us for a time by rotating its drive-gearbox until the latter chafed against the base of the distributor, cutting out the ignition), and breakage of a dynamo support bracket. It takes more than this to mar the joy of driving a Lotus and, anyway, the car wasn't built to run in a Mille Miglia and is probably more at home going to Silverstone or Brands Hatch in a van, accompanied by a plentiful supply of tools, than being put to work as a long-distance road-express.

Certainly this low, tail-finned two-seater places emphasis on "racing" rather than "sports" and is today's equivalent of the Grand Prix Bugatti or Amilcar Six of earlier times—so that lack of a spare wheel, an exhaust note more obvious than that of a Grand Prix car, and a driving position calling for helmet and goggles, are all part of the fun.

The battery is a small 12-volt affair, sharing the tail with a six-gallon fuel tank which would have to be removed to extract it, the snap-action filler of this tank had to be wired down, no speedometer graces the dash, and for the benefit of those who have never examined a Lotus I add that before the single headlamp could be used the bonnet panel had to be lifted and the lamp prised upwards into the night; obviously, there were no hood or sidescreens!

Yet if these remarks paint the T.T. Lotus as a stark sports/racing car, as you would doubtless expect it to be, the Coventry-Climax engine is happily devoid of temperament, whether poodling through towns or shooting the car up to 85 m.p.h. along the meanest straights, the Lodge HLNP plugs uncomplaining, consuming normal Esso Extra petrol, lubricating itself with Essolube 30 and, incidentally, remaining commendably free from oil leaks. Moreover, with the not-unduly-fierce camshaft which produces 81 b.h.p. at 6,700 r.p.m. on a compression ratio of 9.5 to 1, this clever little 72.4 by 66.6-mm. (1,097 c.c.) engine proved able to run up to 7,000 r.p.m. in the indirect gears in the normal course of business, Harry Mundy, who had a large hand in its design, telling us that something around 400 r.p.m. beyond this wouldn't really stress things too far. And 7,000 r.p.m. in third is equal to no less than 87½ m.p.h. on the low axle ratio!

On this "sprint" ratio of 4.5 to 1 the Lotus-Climax is well able to reach 85 m.p.h. between corners on the average rolling English road, and on our test circuit, under not very favourable conditions, achieved 100 m.p.h. at the end of a stretch where far larger-engined sports cars do not often exceed this figure. Given time to work right up to it the maximum should be approx. 108 m.p.h., while with a high axle ratio (3.9 to 1) installed, speeds in the region of 130 m.p.h. are encompassed.

The handling qualities of the car are interesting. The driving position suits persons of medium height, although even then the pedals seem rather distant and not amenable to easy heel-and-toe gear changes. The position is essentially arms-straight to the pleasing (if slippery) three-spoke, 15-in., leather-rimmed steering wheel, and, as has been hinted at, a gale of wind sweeps round the driver's head, although the flatter screen before the passenger gives him or her quite good protection.

On first acquaintance there are two surprises. First, the comparatively hard suspension; secondly, the high-geared steering. The former intrudes only over bad surfaces taken at modest speeds *i.e.*, up to 65/70 m.p.h.; above this speed the ride smooths out and bad roads have less effect on the car. The Lotus rack-and-pinion steering, however, is geared like that of a "chain-gang" Frazer-Nash, asking barely 1¾ turns lock-to-lock, with a reasonable turning circle. The result is that in cornering the wheel is scarcely moved and certainly it is impossible to steer into skids in the cus-

THE WORKS.—A very useful feature of the Lotus is the manner in which the various components are rendered accessible by removing the quickly-detachable body panels.

tomary enthusiastic manner — just a flick and the car is under control. It is fatal to grip the wheel tightly or the Lotus proceeds in a series of swerves, yet kick-back from the divided-axle i.f.s. precludes letting the wheel go free, the technique over bumps being to let the rim play through one's fingers. Incidentally, castor-action is virtually nil.

The cornering characteristics of the Lotus-Climax are of the kind that win races. There is a tendency to understeer which never becomes embarrassing; indeed, the action is virtually neutral, while the de Dion rear-end enables the power to be turned on early out of slippery corners, for both wheels spin together and the car keeps to the intended course. If it doesn't, the aforesaid flick of the taut yet light steering is all that is required.

Everyone who tried the Lotus was impressed with its excellent acceleration for a 1,100-c.c. machine, aided by reasonable spacing of the gear ratios in the M.G. J2 box—for want of a substitute, Chapman uses secondhand, but overhauled, M.G. J2 boxes, substituting for the cast-iron bell-housing a light-alloy one, drilled with lightening holes—what a tribute to the quality in pre-war M.G. cars! A standing-start ¼-mile, essayed two-up, without fireworks, and without practice, occupied a mere 16½ seconds. While driving over our measured ¼-mile we took pains to check the engine/road speed relationship, 1,000 r.p.m. being equal to 15.8 m.p.h. in top gear and 12.5 m.p.h. in third gear.

The enjoyment of this excellent and progressive acceleration is somewhat marred by the force required to change gear, the remote lever being set high up, so that the action is that of lifting rather than moving from one position to the next; using strength, the swapping of cogs is a rapid action, but how tiring in a long race . . . The central hand-brake lever is also too long and moves through too great an arc for convenience, and it cannot be dismissed as merely a parking adjunct, for on a car which likes the revs. maintained for a brisk get-away, it is useful to approach road junctions holding the car back temporarily by hand.

The Borg and Beck racing-type clutch is either in or out and heavy to operate, but showed no general tendency to overheat, save when changing rapidly into top after 7,000 r.p.m. had registered in third gear.

The brakes—9-in. Girling disc—deserve a paragraph to themselves, for in all ordinary circumstances of fast road motoring nothing more was called for than just resting the foot on the pedal; in an emergency they were of exceptional power, to wearing flats on the Dunlops on a dry road or converting the car into a toboggan in the wet! They gave a real sense of security and gain 100 per cent. full marks. Twin master-cylinders and fluid reservoirs are used, one for the front and one for the back brakes.

In appearance XPE 6 is exciting, for the well-known aerodynamic form was offset by racing number discs and night-racing recognition lamps. Of more practical interest is the extreme ease with which the body can be removed completely from the chassis. During our times of trouble we took off the one-piece bonnet, front wings and scuttle in a matter of minutes, when almost all the machinery is accessible. Genuine Dzus fasteners facilitate this useful operation. This body, which has ample accommodation laterally and fore-and-aft for two adults, is in a very thin-gauge light alloy and is the work of Williams and Pritchard.

The general specification of the Lotus-Climax Mk. IX is well known but for those who like details, let us run over the general layout and construction. The multi-tubular space-frame has swing-axle front suspension, formed from a divided Ford axle beam, liberally drilled, with long radius-arms, suspension being by coil-spring-cum-damper units. At the back similar suspension units are employed with the de Dion rear-end, where the disc brakes are mounted inboard. Centre-lock wire wheels are used, those on the car tested being shod with 4.50–15 Dunlop racing tyres at the front, 5.25–15 at the back.

Right in the nose of the car is the small ducted radiator, from which a long pipe on the near side runs to a tiny water-system header tank under the scuttle, the water return pipe leaving the back of the head on the off side, and a pump on the near-side front of the engine encouraging circulation. This pump is belt-driven in conjunction with the dynamo on the off side, which is a normal Lucas dynamo with an extension driving a Smith's 5-in. rev.-counter reading to 8,000 r.p.m. Normal Lucas coil ignition is used, the sparking plugs being inclined in the off side of the cylinder head.

Above the radiator is a water/lubricant heat-exchanger. Two 1½-in. H4 S.U. carburetters are used, which have ram-pipes projecting into an air-box on the near side of the car, and on the same side four separate exhaust pipes feed into a single larger-bore pipe which ends flush with the side of the car. The oil-filler is accessible on the off side of the engine and there is a breather in the camshaft cover adjacent to the interesting(!) Godiva emblem which forms the Coventry-Climax trademark. A Purolator oil-filter lives outside the frame behind the near-side front wheel and fuel is fed from the tail tank by a single electric petrol pump, also situated outside the engine compartment nearer the scuttle. The steering column incorporates a universal joint, voltage regulation is through the latest Lucas RB310 unit, and stop-lamps, as required for night racing, are actuated by the brake pedal.

The dash is pretty fully occupied with accommodating two fuse-boxes, aircraft-type switches for panel lighting, the triple rear lamps, the side lamps, the two retractable Lucas headlamps (only one being fitted when we had the car), the recognition lamps, ignition and fuel pump, the aforesaid rev.-counter, and three small Jaeger dials indicating water temperature (normally 65/70 deg. C.), dynamo charge, and oil pressure (normally 40 lb./sq. in.), the last-named being a combined oil pressure/water-temperature dial, with the latter function deleted. The steering-wheel spokes rather blank the essential dials. In addition, there are: a dynamo master-switch, a switch for cutting out the lamps circuit during daylight racing, a dipper for the non-existent headlamp, and a pull-out starter switch, as well as a Tapley performance meter, horn button and central mirror. Incidentally, no fuel gauge or reserve tap was fitted. The fuel range wasn't great, but for long-distance racing an auxiliary pannier tank is carried on the near side.

The interior of the cockpit is devoid of trimmings, but the shallow seats are not uncomfortable and the driver is kept nicely in place by the propeller-shaft tunnel, which is not upholstered. In the tail, under a Dzus-fastened panel, repose the tightly-packed fuel tank and lightweight battery, and when a spare wheel has to be carried this is somehow inserted in front of them and secured by a length

Continued on page 104

WHAT MAKES IT GO?—Perhaps the most impressive part of the Mk. IX Lotus which we tested was the Coventry-Climax single-o.h.c. engine. It would run happily down to 1,000 r.p.m. in top gear or rev. to 7,000 r.p.m. quite unconcernedly, as occasion demanded.

96

FLAT OUT on the Belgian motor road, the Lotus shows its paces in the quiet conditions early on a winter Sunday morning.

49 MILES PER GALLON AT A MILE A MINUTE!

JOSEPH LOWREY, B.Sc.(Eng.) Reports on Some Tests of the Low-drag 1,100 c.c. Lotus Mk IX Two-Seater

JUST about nine years ago, I was a fairly regular competitor in sprints and occasional races for 1,100 c.c. sports cars. Using the same H.R.G. which had been my business conveyance all through the war years, and with an honest maximum speed not far above 70 m.p.h. on a too-high axle ratio, I was quite often able to collect "place" awards. My! How times have changed!

Just how much standards of performance in races for small sports cars have advanced was clearly illustrated recently, when I was given the chance to drive an 1,100 c.c. Lotus, a car which has been very near to big successes repeatedly in a busy, but unlucky, summer of racing. It is a car which many people have driven in many different circumstances, but which has survived a lot of fast miles on most of Europe's racing circuits amazingly well. Despite winter conditions, a sparse set of instruments, and the realization that to try to fit a "fifth wheel" behind such a light and well-streamlined car would seriously reduce its performance, we decided to apply "Road Test Report" methods to finding out as much as possible about just what sort of performance a modern 1,100 c.c. sports racing car really has.

As handed over to us, the Lotus had the same Coventry Climax engine with which it had been raced in the Tourist Trophy (and led on handicap until an oil pipe broke), much used since but still sound in wind and limb except for an unidentified fault (probably a tired valve spring) which snuffed out the power rather suddenly at about 500 r.p.m. beyond the speed giving maximum power. The long-range tank on the left side had been removed, leaving some six gallons of fuel in a rear tank. Rear axle gears of 4.22/1 ratio were in use, alternatives also available and used on fast or slow courses being 3.89/1 and 4.55/1. The one big divergence from racing trim comprised a full-width windscreen giving protection for a passenger, whereas in racing the car has usually had only a small curved windscreen to protect the driver and has had the passenger-carrying half of the cockpit covered over.

Built in a very small works in North London from which an astonishing number of replicas are now being dispatched to America, the Lotus Mark IX is one of a line of cars which record a fascinating story. After scoring notable successes in Trials with a car of Austin 7 ancestry which incorporated some strictly personal ideas on wheel adhesion, Colin Chapman turned to racing under the "750 Formula" which, by compelling use of the side-valve Austin 7 cylinder block and other parts, was supposed to provide inexpensive racing. Having read Ricardo's classic textbook on The Internal Combustion Engine as an early edition (before the best parts

LOTUS MK. IX SPECIFICATION

Engine dimensions		
Cylinders		4
Bore		72.39 mm.
Stroke		66.6 mm.
Cubic capacity		1,098 c.c.
Piston area		25.4 sq. in.
Valves		Single o.h. camshaft
Compression ratio		9.75/1
Engine performance		
Max. power		72 b.h.p.
at		6,000 r.p.m.
B.H.P. per sq. in. piston area		2.83
Piston speed at max. power		2,620
Engine details		
Carburetters		2 S.U., 1¼ in.
Fuel pump		S.U. electric
Transmission		
Clutch		7¼ in. s.d.p. Borg and Beck
Gear ratios:		
Top (s/m)		4.22 (Optional 4.55 or 3.89)
3rd (s/m)		5.7
2nd (s/m)		8.24
1st		14.4
Rev.		14.4
Prop. shaft		Open
Final drive		9/38 (optional 9/41 or 9/35)

Chassis details		
Brakes		9-in. Girling disc
Suspension: Front		Coil springs and divided axle
Rear		Coil springs and de Dion axle tube
Shock absorbers		Girling telescopic
Wheel type		Centre-lock wire
Tyre size		5.25—15 rear / 4.50—15 front
Steering gear		Rack and pinion
Dimensions		
Wheelbase		7 ft. 3¼ in.
Track: Front		4 ft. 0¼ in.
Rear		3 ft. 11¼ in.
Overall length		11 ft. 7¼ in.
Overall width		4 ft. 8 in.
Overall height at scuttle		2 ft. 3 in.
Unladen kerb weight		9¼ cwt.
Front/rear weight distribution		51/49
Gearing		
Top gear m.p.h. per 1,000 r.p.m.		17.2
Top gear m.p.h. per 1,000 ft/min. piston speed		39.3

97

MECHANICS of the Lotus shown in the left-hand picture include the half-blanked aircraft pattern radiator, an oil cooler, front suspension by coil springs and a divided axle, disc brakes, multiple tube "fuselage," Coventry Climax engine and rear mounted coolant header tank. One headlamp is also shown folded back below the bonnet line.

PRACTICAL trials with wool tufts aided development of the Lotus body lines, seen (right) broken by a raised headlamp and a windscreen of full-width type. Dzus fasteners secure the front section of the body, which is quickly removable for major servicing jobs.

49 MILES PER GALLON

were deleted as out of date), Chapman found means of splitting siamesed inlet ports into two small but shapely halves, going on to evolve a car which, when a mechanical failure called for hurried removal of a piston and connecting rod, still lapped Silverstone on three cylinders faster than could most of its rivals on four.

Having proved himself as an engine tuner, Chapman (who was then employed on design of light alloy structures) concentrated for a while on chassis design, and evolved a "space frame" of multiple small-diameter steel tubes, incorporating Ford 10 components wherever possible but leaving room for any of several engines such as the M.G. Since then, the Lotus frame and the components to fit it have both developed steadily, but the next advance came with the evolution of an aerodynamic body, much of the design and practical testing being done by Frank Costin in his spare time from work as an aircraft aerodynamicist.

Ready-made Power

Whereas in Italy various engines are built almost purely for racing, and in Germany the Porsche engineers have developed so far beyond the Volkswagen design with which they started that no significant mechanical component of the VW is now used, in Britain the small teams which build super-sports cars for racing have not in the post-war years usually built their own engines from scratch. Almost always they have preferred to build lighter, more controllable and better streamlined cars around tuned versions of existing power units. Recently, however, their work was mightily encouraged when Coventry Climax Engines, Ltd., announced a lightweight engine designed for use in portable fire pumps, a single overhead camshaft engine but one which incorporated many lessons which Wally Hassan had learned while developing the XK120 Jaguar. Like their rivals in various classes, the designers of the Cooper and the Buckler, the Lotus team have made very good use of the Coventry Climax 1,098 c.c. power unit during the past season.

As loaned to us for test, the Lotus had this engine, fed by two S.U. carburetters on Y branch pipes, and with an abbreviated exhaust system unobstructed by any perceptible silencing. It had the usual divided-axle independent front suspension, a de Dion rear axle located by long radius arms and a Panhard rod, and four Girling suspension units comprising flexible coil springs encircling extremely firm telescopic dampers. Mated to the engine was an M.G. gearbox of TC type, and Girling disc brakes were mounted outboard on the front hubs, inboard on the sprung differential unit at the back. Lightweight knock-off wire wheels completed the picture.

Collecting the Lotus from Hornsey and heading into central London, the first impression was inevitably made by the exhaust note which, to say the least, makes other "audible warning of approach" superfluous! The next impression was of delight, however, at discovering that

LOTUS MK. IX PERFORMANCE

Fuel Consumption at Steady Speeds (with passenger)		Acceleration through Gears (Damp road, no passenger)	
			Driver "X" / Driver "Y"
65.0 m.p.g. at steady 30 m.p.h.			
61.0 m.p.g. at steady 40 m.p.h.			
55.5 m.p.g. at steady 50 m.p.h.		0-30 m.p.h.	3.2 sec. / 3.2 sec.
49.0 m.p.g. at steady 60 m.p.h.		0-40 m.p.h.	4.5 sec. / 4.5 sec.
43.5 m.p.g. at steady 70 m.p.h.		0-50 m.p.h.	6.1 sec. / 6.0 sec.
38.0 m.p.g. at steady 80 m.p.h.		0-60 m.p.h.	8.2 sec. / 7.9 sec.
33.0 m.p.g. at steady 90 m.p.h.		0-70 m.p.h	10.8 sec. / 10.2 sec.
Acceleration in Gears (no passenger)		0-80 m.p.h.	13.9 sec. / 13.3 sec.
	Top gear / Third Gear	0-90 m.p.h.	18.0 sec. / 17.6 sec.
30-50 m.p.h.	7.7 sec. / 4.7 sec.	0-100 m.p.h.	25.0 sec. / 25.8 sec.
40-60 m.p.h.	7.6 sec. / 4.8 sec.	Standing ¼ mile	16.6 sec. / 16.1 sec.
50-70 m.p.h.	7.6 sec. / 5.2 sec.	**Maximum Speed** (no passenger)	
60-80 m.p.h.	8.0 sec. / 6.1 sec.	See text—approx. 113 m.p.h. mean.	
70-90 m.p.h.	9.7 sec. / —		
80-100 m.p.h.	14.9 sec. / —		

dawdling through city traffic as un-noisily as possible at 1,000-2,000 r.p.m. (usually in top gear) did not provoke this well-worn racing engine into the slightest trace of overheating, plug oiling or other temperamental behaviour.

Our objective with the Lotus was not London, however, but the familiar Jabbeke motor road in Belgium where hard facts about the performance of this remarkable little car could be discovered. The objective was duly attained, after the negotiation of such hazards as rain, fog, pavé, and a Dover policeman who was unconvinced of the legality of far-inboard sidelamps or a much-sloped front number plate.

Obviously, alas, what everyone wants to know about this (or almost any other) car is the answer to the "What'll she do, Mister?" query. Ignoring fog delays, let it be put on record that driver X wearing a leather helmet recorded 111 m.p.h. upwind and 115 m.p.h. downwind, a mean of 113 m.p.h. at an indicated 6,200 r.p.m. Driver Y, with more height to project above the

AT A MILE A MINUTE! - - - .

windscreen and using a bulkier crash helmet to keep his ears warm, was approximately 2 m.p.h. and 100 r.p.m. slower each way. In both cases, the car was running solo, but with full-width screen and open cockpit, tyre pressures having been set cold to 28 and 35 lb., front and rear, the r.p.m. figure suggesting that Colin Chapman made a very accurate choice of rear axle ratio.

Magnificent as the Coventry Climax engine is in its combination of smoothness and economy with high performance, there are limits to the power which can be expected from a simple 1,100 c.c. unit which proved very un-fussy as to what (premium) brand of pump fuel was fed to it. High top speeds have to come from low wind production car Road Tested during the past two years have been 100 lb. for the M.G. "A" 2-seater with hard tyres and raised hood, 105 lb. for the Renault 750 saloon, 106 lb. for the Standard 10 saloon, 107 lb. for the Volkswagen and the Doretti 2-seater.

Alongside low wind resistance, the other big contribution to high performance on a limited amount of power is light weight. Exaggerated claims are sometimes made, but carrying a spare wheel and with its modest petrol tank full the Lotus scaled $9\frac{3}{4}$ cwt. at the L.C.C. Weights and Measures Office, so that with a low fuel level, but complete with its spare wheel and tyre, it would weigh $9\frac{1}{2}$ cwt. In this latter trim, the front/rear weight distribution would be 51/49, the driver's added weight coming towards the rear with the car in use. Whilst lower figures have been claimed, a kerb weight of $9\frac{1}{2}$ cwt. means a lot

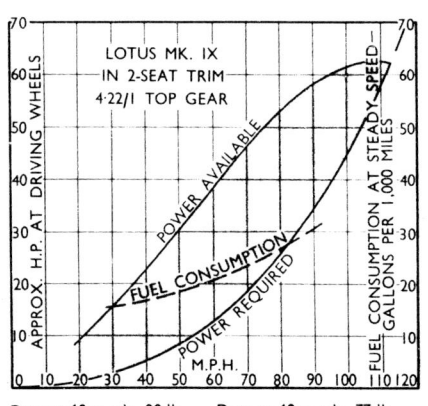

Drag at 10 m.p.h., 20 lb. Drag at 60 m.p.h., 77 lb.
Specific fuel consumption when cruising at 80% of maximum speed (i.e. 90 m.p.h.), based on power delivered to rear wheels, 0.63 pints/b.h.p./hr.

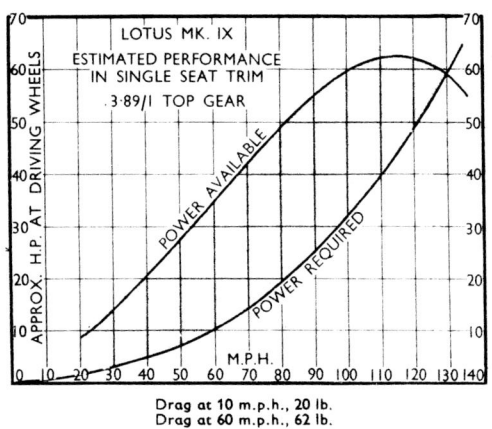

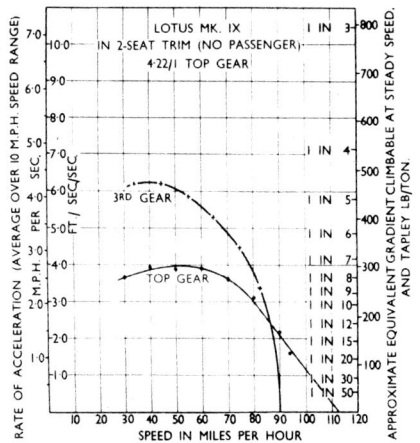

Drag at 10 m.p.h., 20 lb.
Drag at 60 m.p.h., 62 lb.

and rolling resistances, and despite the handicap of being unable to supplement sparse instrumentation without spoiling performance, curiosity impelled me to attempt some measurements of what the drag of the Lotus really is. I would make no claim of dead accuracy for my drag figures, but the averaged experimental points plot much more tidily on graphs than might have been expected (some of the timing had to be done from a second car holding close formation behind the Lotus), and no major inconsistencies are shown up by cross-checking results.

As the graph shows, then, my estimate of the power needed to propel the Lotus at 100 m.p.h. in touring trim is approximately 45 b.h.p. at the road wheels, corresponding to a drag figure of 168 lb., and the drag at 60 m.p.h. is only about 77 lb. In contrast, the lowest 60 m.p.h. drag figures which we have estimated for any of care over quite innumerable details as well as over fundamentals of the design.

How much faster will this 1,100 c.c. Lotus go in racing trim? One pointer is that when a single Lucas foglamp of $5\frac{1}{2}$-in. diameter was in position on top of the bonnet instead of retracted back out of sight on a hinged mounting there was an apparent top speed loss of at least 5 m.p.h. Set well forward, this lamp is no doubt in a "better" strategic position for spoiling the streamlining than is the windscreen, but the full-width screen and uncovered passenger space would account for a substantial loss of top speed. Drivers report that at Le Mans this car was reaching 6,800 r.p.m. down the straight, which with the 3.89/1 final drive gears then used and with 5.25-15 rear tyres would represent appreciably over 130 m.p.h. There seems to be no reason to doubt this speed, on the basis of which it is possible to re-draw power and

IMPERFECT weather is one of the worries of winter testing, fog thick enough to make ordinary traffic use headlamps in daylight providing the background for tests at up to 70 m.p.h. on double-carriageway road.

49 MILES PER GALLON AT A MILE A MINUTE! - - - -

drag curves for racing trim and the high-ratio axle. The 10 m.p.h. drag will not change appreciably from its "touring" figure of 20 lb., but the 60 m.p.h. drag seems likely to be roughly 62 lb. total instead of 77 lb., and the 100 m.p.h. drag approximately 118 lb. instead of 168 lb.!

One immediate product of these low drag figures is a most remarkable economy of fuel. The Coventry Climax engine was tuned for performance, with carburetter settings rich enough to permit starts from cold without choking. But, running the car two-up at steady cruising speeds, petrol almost refused to disappear from the glass burette of our test outfit, figures of note being 65 miles per gallon at a steady 30 m.p.h., 49 miles per gallon at a steady 60 m.p.h., and 33 miles per gallon at a steady 90 m.p.h. Shortly after I had recorded these figures, the body stylist of a leading British factory in conversation about his latest product, asked me: "Do you really think streamlining matters?" On the spur of the moment, a polite answer eluded me, but perhaps when the car concerned turns up for Road Test its fuel consumption at 60 m.p.h. will provide one!

As a car on the road, of course, the Lotus is impressive in the extreme. From rest to 70 m.p.h., without a passenger, driver X recorded 10.8 sec., and driver Y 10.2 sec., on a damp road in each case. For comparison, the 3½-litre Jaguar C-type took 10.1 sec. from rest to 70 m.p.h. (carrying a passenger) when tested in the autumn of 1952, and the 5½-litre Cadillac-Allard (also with passenger) took 10.2 sec. early in 1951. The proximity of the Lotus figures to those for much larger machines is, to say the least, striking!

Disc Braking

Doing without unwanted drag is all very well, but there come times when drag is needed aplenty. On the Lotus, 9-inch Girling disc brakes look after these occasions, and very well too. On a patchily wet road, the car could be braked from 100 m.p.h. to rest with the wheels just about locking throughout, with quite a moderate pedal pressure and without any fade or sideways pull—although there was an aroma of warmed brake lining in the air as the car came to rest! Wet never seemed to affect the braking system, the behaviour of which was a good omen for disc-braked production cars some day.

With high performance and ultra low weight, the roadworthiness of the Lotus could hardly be taken for granted —especially as earlier models, whilst outstandingly good on corners, were apt to hop about a bit on the straight. In actual fact, this Mk. IX Lotus was amazingly well behaved in very varied conditions, completely stable right up to its maximum speed on a smooth surface. Interestingly, being rather big for the cockpit of the test model, I found I could cruise down smooth sections of the Autostrade hands-off for as far as I liked, steering quite precisely with one knee pressed gently against the leather-over-rubber rim of the lightweight steering wheel.

Handling Technique

On bumpy surfaces, driving at high speeds is less easy. The simple swinging half-axles of the I.F.S. allow the steering to kick somewhat, a stranger's reaction being to hang on tight—but to do this with quick rack-and-pinion steering the sensitivity of which stops only just short of oversteer, produces snaking. On corners, the Lotus adheres to the road in magnificent style, and whilst use of too much throttle can make the tail move outwards pretty smartly, the response to corrective action is equally brisk. This is, after all, a racing machine, and whilst there are cars which give the unskilled driver more warning when he approaches the limit of adhesion on a corner, this chassis appears to let a skilled driver go that much nearer to the limit yet still does not suddenly fly right out of control when pressed too hard.

Comfort? Colin Chapman's ideas on suspension run to very soft coil springs indeed, in conjunction with telescopic dampers so abnormally firm that when you step into the car it sinks oh so slowly to the accompaniment of a long sigh from the rear shockers. The result is not exactly a "Boulevard Ride," but the objective of keeping the wheels on the road is seemingly achieved, and many more conventional suspensions can give a much jerkier ride. In detail, of course, the much-raced car which we drove let muddy water pour on to the driver from above, below, in front and behind, also neatly splitting a new pair of waterproof golf trousers before many entrances and exits had been made. But, on a fair day, with goggles and a helmet to provide protection above the low windscreen, there was quite a lot of comfort, a nice feature being the lateral support provided by lightly padded frame tubes. With fog freezing into black ice on the road, life was less comfortable, but the de Dion rear axle still permitted astonishingly rapid acceleration.

Produced by a huge amount of intelligent enthusiasm and sheer hard work, the Lotus is now a production car with a useful export market. Its performance, by showing up the unnecessary weight and air resistance of many recent cars, is undoubtedly helping to "improve the breed" of more ordinary vehicles. Incidentally, the all-round achievements of a team of young men who started work with very limited resources provide some answer to those who say that present-day conditions make it impossible for a young man to gain the varied experience which can lead eventually to a top-level job. Remembering the chief engineers around the industry who once built their own cars and ran them in competitions, before going on to produce such vehicles as the model T Ford, the Morris Minor or the Javelin, it would be dangerous to predict for the marque the long future it deserves.

MARK NINE AS A ROAD CAR

By KEN SMITH

At the request of the Lotus Editor the author of this article has recounted his reactions to using for normal motoring, a car which is basically designed for circuit racing. As a BRDC member and constructor of two " one-off " 500 cc racing cars, he is well qualified to make some interesting observations

AS a contrast to the frequent accounts of Lotus cars in competition I am pleased to be able to set down some of my reactions to driving my Mark 9 on the road. I use it practically every day for business and have just completed 15,000 miles in it under the most varying conditions.

Firstly let us take a look at the main components on my car. This is necessary so that it can be appreciated that I am in no way " hacking " a very much subdued Mark 9—in fact the opposite is the case. The chassis frame and body shell of EMK 972 are constructed of 20 gauge material. This follows the practice used in the 1955 factory cars and, I understand, saves approximately half a hundredweight over the production cars in which 18 gauge material was used.

During assembly I took great pains to reduce weight where possible. Axle beams and radius arms were ground and drilled before attachment. The De Dion tube was also to factory specification with 2½ in. diameter and 18 gauge material. I must confess to a certain uneasiness about this item as it appeared very fragile for the work it was to do. However, my fears proved groundless and the stressing is faultless.

Brakes are the impressive 11-in. turbo-finned sort with 2½-in. shoes, which I know caused many headaches during casting and machining. I was extravagant and purchased a set of Borrani alloy wheels of which, I am told, there are thousands in use daily in Italy.

The redoubtable Coventry Climax FWA 1100 cc engine provides the power. I have not improved performance by incorporating Stage II tuning but I have replaced the Lucas distributor with a Scintilla magneto. Praise becomes a habit when describing the performance of this engine. I drive the Lotus hard, but so far I have not had to touch the engine, not even for valve adjustment. The Lodge RL47 plugs have been changed once, and now and again I check the carburetters.

At 3,000 to 4,000 mile intervals I change, without fail, the engine oil adding the requisite amount of Bardahl additive.

An MG TC gearbox is used in my car as it has more desirable intermediate ratios than the later MG units. Although it is heavy by modern standards, I feel this is fully justified by its exceptional ruggedness. Really rough treatment results only in a willingness for more punishment.

The cast alloy back axle unit incorporates a pre-war Morris 8 nose-piece and differential with a special Regent cut crown wheel and pinion giving a final drive ratio of 4.2 to 1. Brakes are, of course, inboard at the rear and the drive is carried to the wheels through short, universally jointed, shafts.

On completion I weighed the car with spare wheel and one gallon of petrol and discovered the weight to be 9 cwt 27 lb.

The car is outstandingly tractable—due, in the main, to the Coventry Climax engine. With 5.60 × 15 in. rear tyres the gearing provides between 18 and 19 mph per 1,000 rpm in top gear. In traffic, 1,400 rpm can be held in top gear for long periods without snatch or oiled plugs.

Using the Mark 9 as everyday transport I have encountered every type of road and climatic condition. On a wet or greasy road, the car is tricky to handle and rather like a high spirited horse if you should relax your concentration too much. I am aware that all cars which have a useful power to weight ratio are similar but, in this case, I am referring mainly to the behaviour of the brakes which become " two edged swords " directly the heavens open. As anyone who has inspected these turbo-finned brakes will have noticed, there is no complete back-plate. This allows water to enter the drums and as a result one has fun and games guessing which wheel will lock first.

If there are bumps when you are travelling fast, the Mark 9 will tend to wander disconcertingly. The remedy is not to grip the wheel tightly but to let it play through your hands. I believe this is a fault of the Ford steering box when applied to the low pivot swing axle. The cure appears to have been found on the Eleven which has a rack and pinion system.

In the dry the car is a joy to drive and I revel in the wonderful performance, superb roadholding and braking efficiency. These have been ably demonstrated by Colin Chapman on the racing circuits and confirmed by Laurence Pomeroy who specifically mentioned the Lotus Mark 9 in a review of the world's leading sports cars. Under good conditions the fastest speed I have ever attained in my car is 118 mph. This is an indicated 6,400 rpm with my 4.2 axle ratio—achieved on such roads as the Newmarket to Thetford stretch and across Salisbury Plain, where such speeds are relatively safe. Overall fuel consumption is excellent between 30 and 32 mpg.

Public reaction to the Lotus is interesting. Small boys regard the driver in wonderment—despite the fact that the tachometer only reads up to 80 ! The adult population give you sympathetic glances ! Enthusiasts, bombard you with questions. The police treat both you and your car with hostility !

As explained, the Mark 9 has its faults as a road car. But judging from reports in the motoring press, so have other dream cars.

This Lotus, however, is the only fast car I have owned that has given me a combination of high performance, reliability, economy and fun, which makes it completely unique and exceptionally satisfying.

Author of this article, Ken Smith, with his car which has a standard Mark 9 body. FIA regulations and Lotus body re-shaping which reduced the size of rear fins, makes the modern " Eleven " even more suitable for road work

SCI visits Colin Chapman and his *Lotus*

By BOB ROLOFSON

Colin Chapman, engineer and designer of the Lotus.

THE man on the phone said that I would see the plant on my left, just after turning the corner. Tain't so, I passed the Lotus plant three times before finding it, and then only because I saw one of the stabilizing fins from a Mark IX projecting from the doorway of a small building.

Housed in a small, contemporary, concrete building (set *well* back from the road), is the most successful and industrious automobile factory for its size in the world. It is fairly bursting at the seams with beautiful, shiny, sculptured little racing cars. Every available inch of space is being used, and with an eye to the future, the adjoining property has been bought for expansion. Chassis are scattered all over the floor, leaving barely enough room for the craftsmen to walk around as they assemble the cars. Hanging from the ceiling are the finished aluminum bodies which are lowered onto the chassis units as they are completed, and fastened into place. I couldn't help thinking that Alexander Caulder would have felt right at home here, because the slightest breeze turns the workshop into a giant mobile with the odd-shaped, shiny aluminum shapes throwing reflections along the walls. Each unit has an address and buyer's name on it, and all but two of those being assembled were bearing addresses in the United

The Lotus at speed. Good aerodynamic qualities plus excellent cornering have made Colin Chapman's creation a giantkiller in spite of its small engine.

Well lit but cramped conditions do not affect workmanship of technicians.

Cramped for space in the tiny shop, employees suspend half-finished bodies from ceiling.

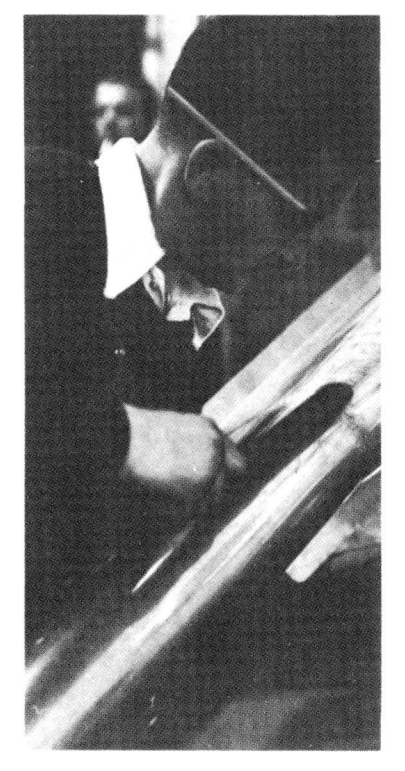

Metal body sections are formed by hand to provide a flawless finish on the alloy skin.

States — one of them was addressed to Ken Miles, North Hollywood, California, and will no doubt be fitted with a "going" MG engine!

My "guide" through the Lotus plant was a friendly young man named Colin Chapman, and as the tour progressed it developed that this unpretentious person was THE Colin Chapman who designs, produces, races, and IS the Lotus Engineering Company! His first car was an Austin based trials special, named the Lotus. As Hazel, Colin's wife would put it, "He used to spend his weekends and spare time building specials to go mud plucking". An English counterpart to an American hot-rodder at heart, and a civil engineer by trade, it was only a matter of time before he began to experiment with racing suspensions and engine modification. Lotus the second had a Ford Ten engine, and with it Colin won his first race, at the 1950 Eight Clubs' Silverstone. The Mark III was a very successful 750cc machine which, during its active career was never beaten. It was powered with an Austin Seven engine, which Colin drastically re-designed to take a double-choke Stromberg carburetor. Until his clever engine modifications were banned, he literally had a corner on the 750cc class!

Up until this time the Lotus Engineering Company was a spare time occupation for Colin, who was employed as a structural engineer with the British Aluminum Company. His early studies in structural development of light alloys

Continued on next page

Lotus

Continued from page **103**

for them is evident in his later designs.

As is the case with many owners and drivers of the smaller cars, the Lotus organization tired of the 750 cc competition and began to look for more power and speed. The first step in this direction was with a much tuned version of the Ford Consul engine. By using as many standard Ford components as possible, Colin managed to come up with a do-it-yourself kit which enabled buyers to save money, and (a la Jaguar) produced much private experimentation with Lotus components. For the Mark VI he evolved Lotus' first tubular space frame, which enjoyed tremendous success, not only with the hot-rodded Consul engine, but also with MG engines mounted by private owners. So successful was the Mark VI that the plant still turns them out at the rate of one a week for eager buyers. The Mark VIII appeared with the now familiar twin-tailed aerodynamic bodywork, and a de Dion rear suspension. Today the Mark IX version disputes 1,100cc, 1,500cc, and 2,000cc sports car classes with a variety of power units. It is generally conceded however that the 1,100cc Coventry Climax engine as used by the factory at Le Mans and the Nine Hours of Goodwood, is the most startling. Without exceeding 7,000 rpm the four-cylinder single overhead camshaft engine produced (Le Mans) 49 mph in first, 77 mph in second, 104 mph in third, and 130 mph in fourth gear! With (less clutch) a weight of 208 pounds and 78 bhp at 6,200 rpm, it produces 2.66 lb/bhp — this from a production engine!

Based on competition proven construction, the space type frame of the Mark IX is constructed from round and square-sectioned mild steel tubes, which vary in size and weight to the load stress produced. Hanging from the skylight of the Lotus experimental section is a new space frame, which will someday be the basis of a Mark XI Lotus (the Mark X being the 2 liter version of the Mark IX).

However, until his present model begins to "feel" the competition, Colin is staying with his consumer market instead of bringing out drastic model changes. This is not to say that he is resting on his laurels however, his experimental designs are worked out on a drafting board at his home, and what is there will probably confound the competition for some years to come. The success of the Lotus is a testimony to Chapman's engineering prowess, vivid imagination, capacity for hard work, and his fearless ability in the cockpit.

It is difficult to believe that this apple-cheeked young man could conceive and create such a going concern in just a little over three years, but that is a matter of record. With a total of 35 employees, counting the workmen in the body shop of Williams & Pritchard (across the street from the factory), the Lotus plant has produced two hundred cars in three years. The present production schedule calls for the manufacture of one Mark VI, and two Mark IX sports cars a week.

Probably the greatest asset to any corporation is co-operation between department heads. Thus, Colin Chapman as co-ordinating director, designer, test and racing driver is the greatest advantage of Lotus, the fast-growing "Tom Thumb" of England's automotive plants. #

SPLENDID ANCHORS.—*No praise is too great for the Girling 9-in. disc brakes fitted to the works Lotus. Note also the coil-spring front suspension unit.*

PURPOSEFUL.—*A three-quarter rear-view of the tail-finned Lotus, in this instance the car used by Colin Chapman in the T.T. and at Le Mans.*

Continued from page 96

of rubber cord. Lift forward the wafer-thin seat squab and the mysteries of de Dion back-end and inboard disc brakes are immediately apparent!

This starkness notwithstanding, the remarkable TWA Coventry-Climax engine commenced readily and did not run-on after terminating hard spells of motoring, we never had to look at a plug, and carburation is commendably clean over the 1,000/7,000 r.p.m. speed range, the car running without snatch at the former speed in top gear, i.e., at less than 16 m.p.h., and pulling away without hesitation. Moreover, it refused to boil, even in London traffic. The useful range from the aspect of power is from about 3,000 to 6,700 r.p.m.

The splendid performance of this 1,100-c.c. sports/racing car and the excellent understeer handling which enable it to do so well in races also render it a very fast road car. In the hands of a colleague it averaged more than 63 m.p.h., two up, over 195 miles of main-road motoring with Saturday traffic to contend with, 6,700 r.p.m. being the genuine top-gear maximum along the Salisbury straights, equal to nearly 106 m.p.h. This run included averaging 68 m.p.h. between Winchester and Petersfield and 78 m.p.h. from Andover to Lobscombe Corner, which gives some idea of the potentialities of the Lotus as a road car. Moreover, at these high speeds the consumption of Esso Extra worked out at about 24 m.p.g., so that, driven more like a mere sports car, this Lotus-Climax would obviously return economy figures comparable to those expected of a small saloon. Understandably, the engine consumed a lot of oil. The weight is 9 cwt. 1 qtr. 21 lb.*, without passengers, but ready for the road with approximately two gallons of fuel.

The basic soundness of Chapman's design and the excellence of the Coventry-Climax engine add up to a fascinating small competition car, able to challenge many machines far larger than itself.—W. B.

---

* As this weight does not tally with those quoted in other reports, we would emphasise that MOTOR SPORT always uses the same weigh-bridge—the County Council of Middlesex Public Weighbridge at Brentford.

LOTUS MAINTENANCE
The Mark Nine by Mike Costin

THE Mark Nine Lotus, produced in 1955, was developed from the Mark Eight—of which only 10 were made, all but one with Mark Six chassis frames. The Mark Nine chassis was a logical development of the Mark Six unit, without the complicated stressed skin body construction of SAR 5 but with a stressed undertray and propeller shaft tunnel.

Since there was considerable variation in both basic and detail specification on cars fitted with Mark Nine bodywork—and the same general chassis layout was used for the Bristol-engined Mark Ten—a brief resumé of the major differences of specification may help to clear up queries about any particular example.

Altogether some 40 Mark Nines were made, fitted with Ford Ten, MG 1½-litre and Coventry Climax FWA engines. The gearbox used in conjunction with MG and Coventry Climax engines was the MG TC fitted with a Lotus adaptor casting in place of the normal rear casting, and also, in the case of the Climax engine, with a bell-housing adaptor casting. In addition, two Climax-engined cars were fitted with MG J2 gear-

Front end of the Mark Nine showing swing axle suspension and method of mounting coil spring/damper units. This is a Coventry Climax-engined, drum-braked car.

boxes, and very good they were too. The Ford-engined cars retained Ford gearboxes, which were mounted in the same way as in the Mark Six.

Rear axles were either Ford Ten or Lotus de Dion, the latter being fitted only in conjunction with MG or Coventry Climax engines. Brakes varied from standard Ford Ten to Lotus 11 in. x 2¼ in. drums front and rear; both works Mark Nines were eventually fitted with 9½ in. Girling disc brakes.

The chassis of the Mark Nine is a space frame structure requiring little maintenance. Basic dimensions should be:—wheelbase 7 ft. 3½ in; front track 4 ft. 0¼ in; rear track 3 ft. 11¼ in. The suspension units originally fitted were mainly of Girling manufacture, dimensionally similar to those of the Mark Six, but with spring rates of 145 lb per inch at the front and 65 lb per inch at the rear. Ride level should be 5 in. front and rear at the undertray.

SWING AXLE LAYOUT

The front suspension consists of a swing axle and radius arm of Ford Y pattern, with the bottom pick-up for the coil spring/damper unit on a bracket in front of the axle and some 3 inches below the actual axle line. On most Mark Nines the steering gear is similar to that of the Mark Six, but one or two Mark Nines (and all Mark Tens) had rack and pinion steering. In such cases a light alloy casing is used, located by a single Silentbloc bush on the lower offside chassis member, and this connects with a central steering arm which swings vertically as opposed to the horizontal motion of the Mark Six type.

On the cars using a Ford rear axle location is by torque tube and Panhard rod. The de Dion-axled cars use the same type of Panhard rod and twin parallel radius arms. In this latter case the cast hubs are bolted on to the end of the de Dion tube and located by four taper spigots at each side. The rear wheels should have 3 degrees negative camber. The large diameter ball races in the rear hubs should be changed when axial play becomes noticeable, there being no means of adjustment; during stripping and reassembly care should be taken to avoid damage to the Gaco seals; these should be changed if the sharp edge of the seal becomes at all worn.

The differential units fitted in the Mark Nine are from the Austin A40-A90 range, or the Series Two Morris Eight, and all assembly work should be done as indicated in the makers' handbooks. The BMC aluminium differential housing is mounted in the Lotus final drive casing, which is cast in either aluminium or elektron. When a Series Two Morris Eight differential is used the final drive casting should be watched for cracks in the area of the differential mounting flange. The inboard output shafts are mounted in bearings pressed into the sides of the differential casting, and on each shaft runs a further Gaco seal. It is most important that these seals are maintained in perfect condition, in order to keep oil off the brakes.

The standard Mark Nine brakes comprise 11 in. x 2¼ in. Lockheed shoes (with twin leading shoes at the front and a single leading shoe at the rear) in turbo-finned cast elektron drums with cast-in cast iron liners. Mintex M11 brake linings should be used; the fitting of harder linings is not recommended as these brakes run very cool and work well under all conditions. Care should be taken in adjusting the shoes by the screws providing lateral movement, as these control the lateral location of the shoe in relation to the drum. These screws should be set so that the surface of the shoes is parallel to the drum, as mal-adjustment can quickly lead to uneven wear.

Owners of Mark Nines fitted with the FWA Coventry Climax power unit can profitably bring their engine up to latest Stage Two specification; this involves fitting a new camshaft, slight modifications to the interior of the cylinder head and the oil pump idler shaft, and the use of a new rear crankshaft oil seal. Extra power can also be obtained by raising the compression ratio; up to .040 in. can be removed from the cylinder head, but this must be accompanied by 40 thou. shims under the camshaft carrier and 40 thou. thicker tappet biscuits, in order to keep the camshaft drive chain tension constant.

Some trouble has been experienced with the fibre timing gears of the FWA engine, and these have been replaced firstly by cast iron and then by steel gears. In conjunction with the Stage Two camshaft, carburetter needles should be changed from BE to BF.

View of the rear end showing chassis-mounted differential unit and heavily-finned inboard drum brakes.

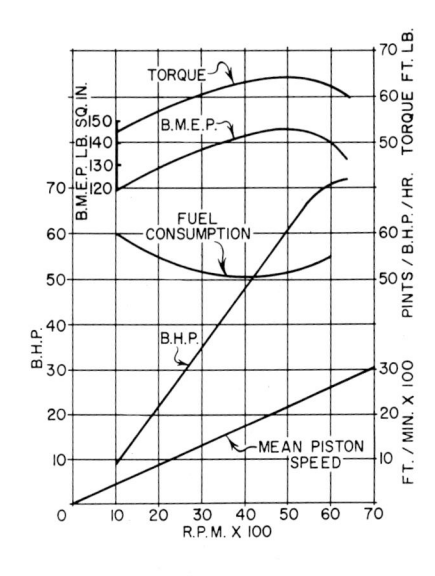

SCI Technical Report:

THE MOST FOR THE

By RUSS KELLY

TO U.S. ENTHUSIASTS who take their racing seriously, a headache of no small proportions is the rapidity with which a ten-thousand-dollar automobile can become obsolete. The history of the under 1500 cc class here, for example, is littered with expensive bones. The MG and Simca Specials gave way to the Porsches. The early Porsches in turn submitted to the dohc OSCAs and the OSCAs to the four-overhead-camshaft Porsche 550. Now it looks as though the new 1500 Maserati could take over in class domination. This quick obsolescence is a major deterrent to those who would like to continue participation and many who would like to begin but can't afford such an all-out financial risk.

One bright spot in this situation has been the famous Miles MG Special. The success of this car points to the chance of some stability in at least one of the smaller classes of racing. MG, from the earliest U.S. tuning efforts to the Ken Miles car, had a long and successful period of competition. There were two good reasons for this. First, it was relatively cheap. Second and more important, it responded favorably to attempts to tune and extract more power from it. In any city where sports cars enjoyed popularity, you could find a mechanic who could return your MG to you running better and faster than when you gave it to him. This meant step-by-step development, which culminated in the Miles Special. Without the introduction of hyper-expensive, esoteric equipment, the 1500 cc class would be fairly stable today. Obviously, however, it is not, and enthusiasts with limited resources, bumped out of the demanding 1.5-litre

View of Lotus from eye level shows beautifully proportioned aluminum covering. Bump on hood accommodates carbs; square holes are for recessed headlight brackets.

LEAST

A Mark IX Lotus at speed. This 1100 cc Coventry-Climax-engined newcomer has aroused a great deal of interest among owners in the small class.

RIGHT: Front suspension is similar to Allard, with a light Ford axle cut in two with plates welded to each half for attachment to frame. Fore and aft location is obtained with radius rods. BELOW: The Lockheed hydraulic brakes are open back type and have Elektron drums with steel liners of 11½ inch diameter and 2¼ inch width.

class, are beginning to watch the smaller classes closely. To ask for a machine in any class that would not become obsolete would be to deny the basic idea of competition. But it is reasonable to wish that another machine would come along with the same possibilities given in another day by the MG.

This is the reason for the tremendous interest aroused by the 1100 cc Coventry-Climax-engined Mark IX Lotus, which is just beginning its career in the U.S. When you keep in mind the basic requirements a car needs to establish a class governed by evolution through skill rather than revolution by the dollar, the Mark IX Lotus looks not only like an exciting newcomer, but like an extremely significant one as well.

Recently I made a trip to the road races at Palm Springs

PRICE:
$4390. FOB factory

ENGINE:
- Cylinders ....4, in line
- Bore and stroke ....2.8 in x 2.6 in (72.39 mm x 66.6 mm)
- Capacity ....1098 cc
- Firing order 1, 3, 4, 2
- Compression ratio ......9.75 to 1
- Output:
  - Max. horsepower ....75 @ 6200 rpm

Valves:	Inlet	Exhaust
Head dia.	$1\tfrac{3}{8}''$	$1\tfrac{3}{16}''$
Stem dia.	$\tfrac{3}{8}''$	$\tfrac{3}{8}''$
Seat angle	30°	45°

- Carburetors: ....$2\tfrac{1}{2}''$ SU semi downdraft

IGNITION:
- Coil and distributor
- Breaker gap ....012 — .014
- Oil capacity ....4 quarts

SUSPENSION:
Independent front, De Dion rear

CHASSIS:
- Wheelbase ....$7'3\tfrac{1}{2}''$
- Front track ....$4'1\tfrac{1}{2}''$
- Rear track ....$3'11\tfrac{1}{2}''$

SPECIFICATIONS   LOTUS MARK IX

CLUTCH: 7¼ Borg and Beck

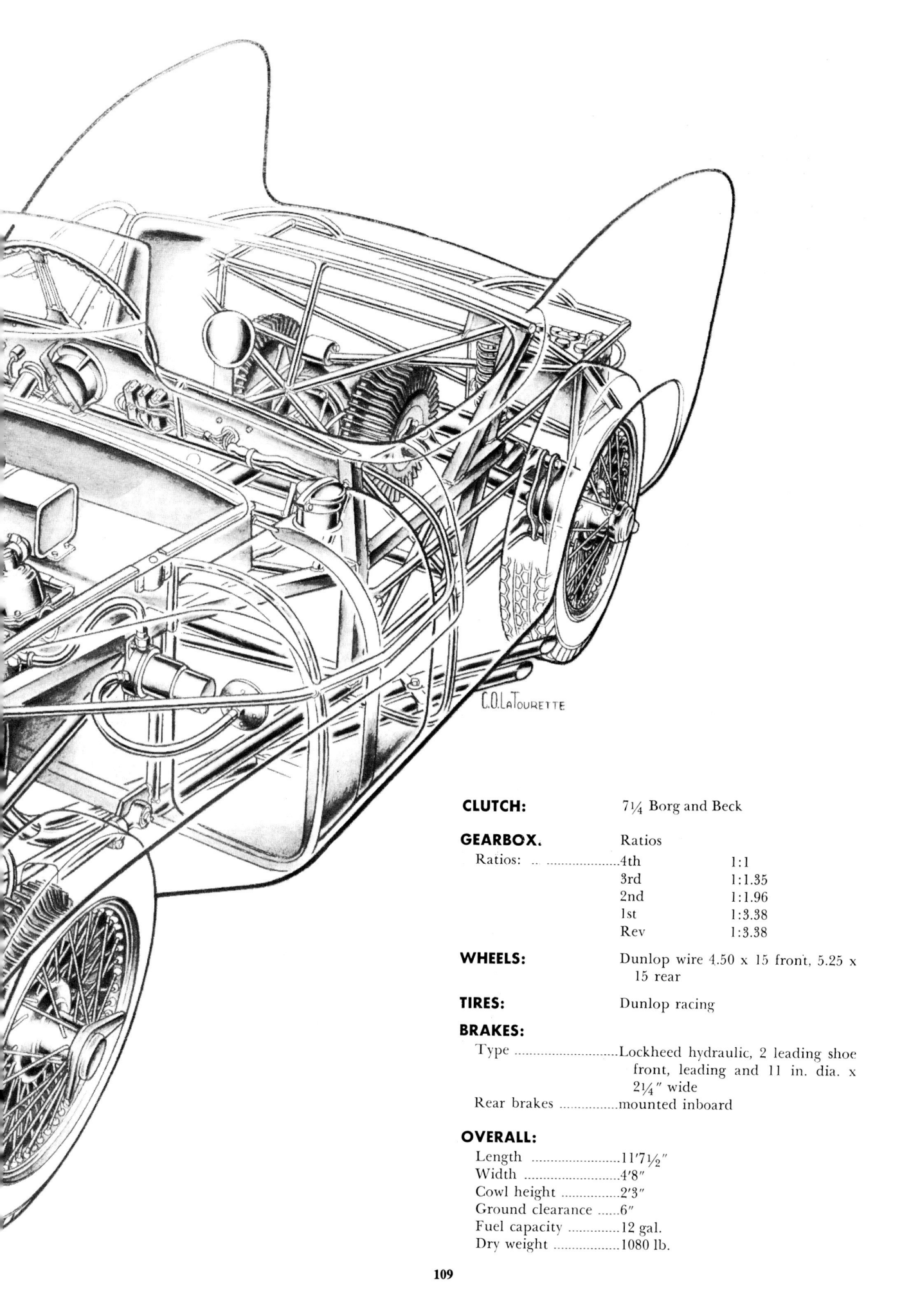

GEARBOX.
Ratios: Ratios
    4th   1:1
    3rd   1:1.35
    2nd   1:1.96
    1st   1:3.38
    Rev   1:3.38

WHEELS: Dunlop wire 4.50 x 15 front, 5.25 x 15 rear

TIRES: Dunlop racing

BRAKES:
  Type .... Lockheed hydraulic, 2 leading shoe front, leading and 11 in. dia. x 2¼" wide
  Rear brakes .... mounted inboard

OVERALL:
  Length .... 11'7½"
  Width .... 4'8"
  Cowl height .... 2'3"
  Ground clearance ...... 6"
  Fuel capacity .... 12 gal.
  Dry weight .... 1080 lb.

Top view of head. Valves have helical springs, and are operated through guided cam followers. Buttons, shown below cam followers, are used to adjust clearances. Standard lift is .300 of an inch.

Combustion chambers are wedge shaped, and the in-line valves are slightly inclined to sit horizontally upon the chamber surface. Note contoured corners around intake valves to accommodate their extra size.

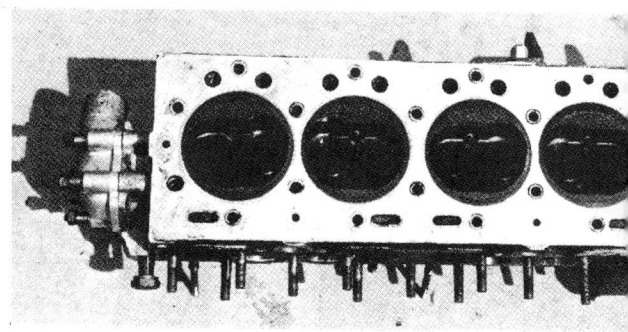

with the specific idea in mind of watching the Mark IX in action. It was a revelation. In the capable hands of Jay Chamberlain of Burbank, a Mark IX finished fifth behind four 550 1.5-liter Porsches and ahead of another Porsche and a pair of OSCAs. In view of what we have learned to expect from 1100 cc cars in the past, the Lotus' ability to hold its own in fast company raised a lot of questions in my mind. As the car headed for its pit, sounding as healthy as at the start of the race, I headed there too. I congratulated the owner on his car, and he urged me to follow him to his shop and check it out as thoroughly as I wished.

At the Burbank shop the Lotus stood in the company of a D-type Jag and a Monza Ferrari, and in looks it suffered not at all by comparison. It had no shiny, mistake-concealing printed finish and it needed none. Its bare aluminum skin was flawless. It had a look of pared-down leanness that contrasted effectively with the rounded, organic lines of the other cars.

Chamberlain offered to let me check out on the road any one of three different Lotus Mark IXs, each with different final drive and gear box ratios. I chose the Palm Springs car because it was soon to be torn down for inspection, and I'd be able to see if any modification had been made in the engine that I'd seen perform so well. Furthermore, driving the car would give me an idea of how far it had been extended to place as it did.

Colin Chapman, designer of the Lotus, is of the opinion that even a sports car designed for racing should be a competent road machine as well. With this in mind, I drove the Lotus to the test area instead of hauling it there on a trailer. This wasn't a mistake. From the time the engine was started and allowed to turn over at a fast, warm-up idle until the time we reached the test area, the car was as tractable as a stock MG. The lowness of the seating position was a little disturbing in the Los Angeles traffic at first, and the desire to raise the busy exhaust note just a bit by foot pressure had to be firmly resisted.

Top speed of the Lotus with a 3.9 rear axle ratio is about 130 mph. Chamberlain's car, with a 4.2 ratio, was clocked at 114 mph on the Straightaway at Palm Springs. The Lotus' acceleration is equally surprising for a car of only 1100 cc. Its 0 - 60 mph time is about eight seconds, and the standing quarter should be covered in under 16 seconds. The aerodynamic form gives this little car a real shot in the arm on acceleration at speeds over 70 mph.

Three-quarter front view shows the all-aluminum body has two main sections, which can be removed in less than one minute.

The Lotus' clutch is light with a pleasingly short travel and a healthy bite. A driving position with arms extended nearly straight to the wheel gives the feeling of lots of room. The TC gearbox will seem like an old friend to many. With the slightest throttle pressure the engine loses all trace of roughness, and the close ratios in the box make full use of the turbine-like power that comes from the little mill. I made a couple of trials runs without exceeding 5000 rpm in any of the top three gears. I noticed no engine vibration, and the absence of body panel drumming and vibration at high engine speeds was welcome and surprising for such a light car.

The ride is flat and solid. Surface roughness noticeable

The Coventry-Climax engine with a total weight, including starter and generator, of only 208 lbs., is fed by two 1½ inch SU carbs through a log-type manifold.

For optimum cooling, the magnesium-alloy steel lined front brakes are finned almost to the hub. This type of rib-fin also strengthens drum.

Because of Dzus fasteners, car can be stripped to this point in less than one minute. Note strong positive chamber due to the divided front axle suspension.

Final drive unit is de Dion type with 11-inch inboard brakes. Ring gear and pinion, however, are Austin-Healey and fitted into massive Elektron casting.

at low speeds becomes less so as speed goes up. To avoid over-controlling at high speeds, this car calls for a light grip on the wheel — a condition to which I'm always happy to accustom myself.

The brakes are phenomenal. They had been used in the race and they probably had been used hard. All my stops from high speeds were in the nature of crash stops. Still, there was enough pedal there to run another race. I can only compare these brakes with those on a 500 cc Cooper, which is saying a lot. As with the Cooper, the Lotus brakes feel as though they could suffer the worst sort of abuse and remain effective.

The Mark IX Lotus has a de Dion rear end and driving it on a winding road, especially a familiar one, is a pleasure indeed. Rough corners that demand caution with live or swing-axle rear suspension can, in this car, be taken on the line chosen almost without regard for surface conditions. The absence of bounce, roll, or squeal makes driving through the slower corners seem effortless. I made many tries in these corners to provoke the unexpected and the potentially dangerous but failed.

In fast corners the car's English airport course breeding thoroughly asserts itself. The long, flat, incredibly fast corners peculiar to English racing have turned out some drivers noted for their command of a fast drift. And what this environment has done for some English cars. The Lotus' steering is almost neutral, with a slight tendency

Lotus

towards understeer

The day after I drove the car it was dismantled and I had the opportunity to take a good look at what was inside. This tiny engine that had been so impressive was as stock as a stove. The ports were rough and the valves, both intake and exhaust, could easily have been enlarged. The compression ratio was just 8.8 to 1 and could have been almost a full point higher. In short, this was the kind of raw material that a good MG man could have a field day with.

The Coventry-Climax engine was primarily designed as an industrial unit, but the possibility of its being used for racing was never overlooked. The result of this approach has been an unusually happy blend of light weight, reliability, high performance, simplicity, and parts availability. Light alloys have been used in the engine extensively and the complete weight of the unit is only 208 lbs., including the starter and generator. With an oversquare bore and stroke of 72.4 x 66.6 mm it develops 72 bhp at 6200 rpm. Piston speeds at this rpm are well below 3000 ft. per min.

The cylinder liners are renewable and the heat-treated cylinder head has shrunk-in austenitic-iron valve seat inserts. A husky, fully counterweighted crankshaft is used. Main and connecting rod bearings are of the steel-backed lead-bronze insert type. The three mains are one inch by $2\frac{1}{8}$ inches and the rods are $\frac{7}{8}$ by $1\frac{3}{4}$ inches.

The con rods' big ends are split diagonally to allow them to be pulled up through the bore. The camshaft is carried in three white metal bearings and is driven by duplex roller chain. The in-line valves are slightly inclined, have double helical springs, and are operated through guided cam followers in the same manner as the Jaguar. Clearances are effected by the use of buttons of various thicknesses inside the follower body. Standard lift is 0.30 of an inch, intake valve diameter is 1.35 and the exhaust is 1.20. The combustion chamber is wedge-shaped. A floating-type oil pickup is used, the engine of course being wet sump. Two $1\frac{1}{2}$ inch SU carburetors of semi-downdraft type are used on a log-type manifold.

The space-type chassis frame of the Lotus uses a square and round section tubes of various dimensions, load being the size-determining factor. It may seem surprising in this day of high-specification alloys that the tubing is mild steel. There's good reason for this however; the chassis is acetylene welded and gas welded nickel alloys joints can be trouble makers.

The frame has two main longitudinal members on each side, the lower ones are of $1\frac{7}{8}$ inches round section and the upper tubes are one inch square. The bracing between these two members and all bracing throughout the frame is designed to eliminate any cantilever loading. To put it a little more simply, the frame is braced at carefully-engineered points so that multiplication of cornering, braking, and acceleration stresses by leverage within the frame is held to an absolute minimum. All of the attachment points for the engine, final drive and suspension are welded to the frame and no bolt-up brackets or clamps are used. Total weight of this frame is given as just 63 lbs.

The front suspension is similar to the Allard's, inasmuch as it consists of a light Ford axle cut in two with plates welded on each side for attachment to the frame. Ford hubs are also used. The pivot point is kept low, resulting in a roll center six inches above ground level. One of the traditional disadvantages of this otherwise excellent and simple form of suspension is gyroscopic "kick" that can be felt through the steering wheel at moderate speeds over rough surfaces. In the case of the Lotus, light weight reduces this tendency of the wheels to steer themselves at high rotating speeds. The fore and aft location of these half axles is obtained by the use of radius arms, again of Ford manufacture, attached to the lower main frame tube by a ball joint.

Suspension is by coil-spring telescopic damper units and each end of each unit is mounted in rubber bushings. The lower mount is a bracket bolted to the half axle that sets the anchor point a considerable distance below the axle center. The top point of anchorage is an orthodox bracket facing outward and forward, welded to the top main frame tube and top front cross tube where they join. The engine is mounted well back from the front wheel center line.

The Lotus steering is by worm and nut. The forged steel steering arms are obviously of special manufacture and are bolted to the stub axles. The linkage between these arms and the steering box consists of divided track rods attached to a bell crank mounted on the bottom front cross tube. The bell crank is actuated by a drag link that angles back to the arm on the steering box.

The Mark IX rear suspension and final drive unit is a moving thing to contemplate. The de Dion layout with its tremendous 11-inch inboard brake drums is responsible for a good share of the Lotus' excellent handling characteristics. Standard layout practice is followed and the execution is ingenious. The axle tube passes behind the final drive unit housing and is of the non-articulated type. This axle is made of three-inch diameter tubing. Housings are fabricated on the ends to receive the aluminum castings that carry the short shafts and bearings for the wheel hubs. The axle tube and hub unit castings are bolted together with four $\frac{5}{16}$-inch bolts, making a very clean, light-looking job.

Acceleration torque is absorbed by two long parallel arms of $\frac{3}{4}$-inch square tubing. They are anchored with rubber bushings to a vertical frame tube at the front, and at the rear to the top and bottom of the wheel hub unit. This method of relieving the de Dion tube of torsional stresses was first used by Ferrari on his grand prix cars. The lateral location is controlled by a husky Panhard rod.

The brakes are Lockheed hydraulics of an open backing-plate type. The Elektron drums have steel liners of $11\frac{1}{2}$-inch diameter and $2\frac{1}{4}$-inch width. There are two leading shoes at the front and one leading and one trailing shoe at the rear. Dual master cylinders are located on the cowl where they can be directly actuated by the foot pedal. A very simple adjustable balance bar mechanism is used to link those cylinders, and provision is made for altering the braking ratio between the front and rear wheels.

The radiator header tank is located on the cowl and a long tube and hose arrangement passes forward to the radiator core. Part of this tube is in close contact laterally with the log-type induction manifold and serves as a heater.

The more time I spent with this car the more I wondered if Colin Chapman, its designer, might not have several heads, all of them busily solving automobile racing problems. The rapid development of this car, its obvious soundness on all engineering points, and its general execution would lead one to believe that it was conceived in a large research laboratory staffed by many British boffins. Research on Chapman established that he is a mechanical engineer and has one head, an excellent little factory, and a lot of enthusiasm.

The Mark IX's U. S. delivered price of $4800 or $1000 less without engine makes it mighty attractive to the small-displacement competitor who wants the most. The large undeveloped potential of the 1100 cc Climax engine would be a rewarding challenge to all those who have served their time on the MG. I believe that the chassis is of advanced enough design to hold its own with any competition it will encounter here for some time. And it's available.

#

Ninth in line

Lovely to look at, delightful to know, the immortal Lotus Mk9 was designed by the combined genius of Colin Chapman and Frank Costin. Mike McCarthy drives a 'Nine' and is exhilarated

Manta-ray nose was designed to force air through the radiator, not around the sides

A Lotus Mk9 on the open road is the distilled essence of exhilaration, a producer of inane grins, of sheer unadulterated joy.

Of course it wasn't built for such nebulous emotions. It was built to win races, to be driven seriously and hard when racing, not to be savoured as a pleasure machine.

But a great car is a great car is a great car. The Lotus Mk9 is a great car. It is the epitome of the phrase 'sports-racer', a car intended for both road and track.

For a start it fits like the proverbial glove, with not an ounce of superfluous space, yet more than enough. You sit low, on a flat cushion with a flat and hard backrest, surrounded by the plastic screen up above and by tubes down below, and if you look right down you can see the two long arms for the rear suspension working away! It feels incredibly stiff, and nothing rattles, not even the doors which is odd considering the amazingly complex door latches – simple bolts... There's a big tacho, a combined oil pressure and water temperature gauge and an ammeter to tell you what's happening engine-wise, and that's it. You ignore the cheap leatherette on the dash.

To be honest, it (at first) showed little sign of greatness and every sign of temperament: more race than road. Second needed an arm-aching tug back from first: when it was all over, there was a sore, red patch in my left palm. So much effort was required that at one point the top of the gear lever knob came orft in me hand. And the engine! Below 2000rpm, zilch, zero, *rien*, nothing. Oh, it ran all right, but any combination of throttle and load, even a feather of a whisper of a touch on the pedal, never mind a hard prod, and it died. Which made following a camera car, at 30 or 40mph, very difficult. With a sharp clutch, and a lock that made a Jumbo jet look positively nimble, U-turns were a pain in the arse. And the elbows, knees and ankles.

I was damned if I was going to let it get the better of me. How could it? How could something so sleek, so svelte, so fluid of line behave so sharply, with such bad temper? I confess I was getting upset. I would not let it take the upper hand.

Perhaps that's what did it, losing my temper slightly, that and the open road without having to follow the camera car: space, in other words. Using the car to its full, using the power, the suspension, the gears, letting it fly – that's when a Lotus Mk9 comes alive. That's what it's all about. Not namby-pamby poodling: the harder you use it, the better, the infinitely better, it becomes.

Start on a straight, a couple of hundred yards, then an S-bend. Boot throttle, wheels spin then grip, needle on tacho swoops round to six grand, snatch next gear, red line it again, click-click into third, corner coming up, steadying dab on brake, back on throttle, into left-hander, a touch more throttle, car darts left: bring steering wheel over centre onto right lock, feed in power quickly, tail squats, rocket out of corner, up to red line again, grab top, click, onto throttle, speed building up incredibly quickly.

For an 1100 there's amazing urge between 2500rpm and 6000rpm, so much so it feels like a 2 litre, and a modern 2 litre at that, very smooth, with a gorgeous exhaust scream. When warm second eases up too, and 3-4 is near perfect in the very close-ratio box. The gear lever is curiously bent but the knob finishes up exactly where you want it.

Now a fast, curved open right hander: power full on, a gentle caress of the steering wheel and it flows through, flat and clean, you feel the back grip and the front just goes where you point it. This is not a sideways-chucking car, neither understeering nor oversteering. The faster you go, the better it is. And, with speed, it's surprisingly supple, absorbing the bumps easily. You can feel the suspension doing the work, not chassis flex.

Another straight with a T-junction: stand on brakes, instant stop. Pause, catch breath. The Lotus Mk9 is – but I said it all at the start. And it's one of the most beautiful cars ever made, in my opinion.

If the Mk6 was the model that put Lotus on the British motoring map, it was the 1954 Mk8, and its successor the 1955 Mk9, that made the company world famous.

By late 1953, Lotus the company consisted of a handful of enthusiasts working in cramped premises in Hornsey, North London. Pay wasn't brilliant, the hours intolerable, but what the hell – they were young, and it was all good clean fun. What's more, they were part of a team that won races, often as not against ostensibly richer, more powerful, faster competition. If the company broke even, fine. The Boss, Chapman, even had a full-time job elsewhere, moonlighting in Hornsey for his own company. Heady days...

The enthusiasm and excitement was generated in great part by Chapman's brilliant and fertile mind. The 6's space-frame chassis was a classic example of minimalistic strength. The split-beam Ford front axle suspension may have looked like something you'd find on Allards, where it didn't work especially well, but Chapman made it highly effective. His cars were a combination of superb, inventive sophistication and readily available bits. If everyone used Ford or MG components, Chapman had to come up with the

Dick Steed, first owner of HUD 139, spins out at Becketts, Silverstone in 1956

Cockpit with space-frame chassis highly visible. Twin parallel arms other side of passenger's seat are part of rear suspension!

unfair advantage. He found it in his genius.

Beneath the light alloy skin, and it's hard to believe visually, the Mk6 isn't all that different to the 8, 9 and 10. (For the record, the Mk7, a developed version of the 6, didn't appear until after the 8, 9 and 10.) There's a spaceframe chassis and swing-axle front suspension. The 8 and 9 have de Dion rear axles, which one or two 6s had as well. Power units are off-the-shelf, Ford, MG, Climax, even oddballs like Bristol, Connaught, and BMW.

By the end of 1953, with the 6's success behind him, Chapman looked to the future. The 6's shape, all square and upright, with cycle wings up front, was fine for 10-lap club events in the UK, but severely hampered top speed, and abroad cycle wings were banned.

Now it so happened that one of the happy band at Hornsey was a chap called Mike Costin, an employee of the aircraft company de Havilland at Hatfield. He'd come aboard in 1953. Much later he'd become the 'Cos' in Cosworth, but that's another story.

It also so happened that Mike's brother Frank was an aerodynamicist at de Havilland.

Frank: "At the time I'd never done anything except bits of aircraft. Mike got in touch, and sent up a model they'd made as bait. It was all-enveloping, and looked like a crunched-up version of the record-breaking Golden Arrow. I wasn't impressed.

"I did a lot of thinking for a couple of months, and decided to make it on the basis of a 'reverse camber line', with a low nose and high tail – there's an RAF aerofoil section, RAF34, which was used on tail-less aircraft between the wars, which gives a very stable centre of pressure. With a small cockpit we could make it near-enough all metal except for a hole for the pilot. We could then use a small wrap-around windscreen instead of the usual flat-plate aeroscreen.

"I made a $1/5$ scale model and used de Havilland's wind tunnel in the middle of the night to make it neutrally stable, which was how the fins came about. I accepted that fins created drag, but it would be acceptable if we used a decent front end. Part of the unknown factor in those days was the radiator, and I was determined that air should go through it, not around, hence the manta-ray like front end with pointed wings. I also ducted the air into and out of the radiator, feeding it out below. From this came full-scale drawings with transverse sections every 10in, and Mike made up a full-scale torsion tube (a long box) to which were fitted cross-section templates.

"We had a thing called a lusting-box, which we'd sit on and have a good lust just looking at the shape – at three in the morning! When Chapman saw what we were up to he said we'd never sell it, it was too advanced. Then *Autosport* had the Mercedes W196 on the cover, and he admitted we were right up with them...

"The Mk9 was a sort of crunched up Mk8. Colin realised that, if it was shorter, he could get two on his transporter instead of one! So on the plans he sent me he scribbled '141 inches, and not a penny more'! So the fins had to go up. They were more rounded too, to reduce sideways drag. And that's how I arrived at the Mk9 shape."

Chapman himself, helped by a couple of draughtsmen, Peter Ross and Mac Mackintosh, drew up the Mk8 chassis. One stage on from the 6's, it was an absolute masterpiece of triangulation, providing 'the utmost rigidity but without an ounce of superfluous weight' as Ian Smith wrote in *Lotus, The First Ten Years*. It was so brilliant in fact that the designer had rather forgotten the fact that engines had to come out: on the prototype, it took 12 hours to remove, 24 to put it back.

Suspension up front was by the tried and tested Ford split axle, with coil springs and telescopic dampers. If you look at it, you can see where Chapman got the glimmerings of an idea for the Chapman strut, since the geometry is that of a wide-based lower wishbone plus a slightly inclined coil-over-shock. Simple, highly effective. At the back there was a de Dion set-up, to keep the wheels and tyres upright and therefore at their most efficient, and yet keep unsprung weight to a minimum. The 25 year-old Chapman had produced a design that any experienced engineer twice his age, and with twice the experience, would have given his eye teeth for, the epitome of lightness, strength and effectiveness.

For the first Mk8, registered SAR 5, the engine was an MG unit, tuned to give 85bhp. That may not sound a lot, but in a car weighing a touch under 10cwt, and shaped like a

Chapman's brilliant Mk9 design revealed

Autocar

De Dion rear axle with massive, finned drum brakes

Lusty Climax engine behaves like a modern 2-litre

High fins were designed for aerodynamic stability – and worked. Perspex screen protects very effectively

The American invasion — Beverley, Massachusets 4 July 1955. Messrs Bastrup (107) and Miller lead off the pack. Bastrup won

Teflon-coated bullet, it could reach 125mph, and reach it quickly at that.

The works Mk8 proved to be one of the fastest 1.5-litre sports car in the country, but was a touch unreliable. Nevertheless, it held up long enough in the curtain-raiser for the 1954 British GP to allow Chapman to beat Hans Herrmann in the Porsche Spyder, at the time the dominant class leader. Six Mk8s were built, John Coombs' being fitted with a Connaught engine, and Dick Steed's with an unusual one, built by a fire-pump manufacturer, Coventry Climax.

For 1955 Chapman planned two new models – and decided to take up running Lotus full-time. The Mk10 was a Mk8 beefed up to take the Bristol engine, and was not the most successful ever Lotus. Cliff Davis raced one, but said: "It was a disaster!"

The Mk9 was basically a cleaned-up 8. The wheelbase remained the same, but no less than 2ft were chopped off the overall length. The tubular inner works were reduced in size and lightened, though without affecting stiffness. Body panels were modified to increase accessibility too. Chapman followed the old rule of 'simplificate and add lightness'.

And it was intended to take the engine that had appeared in Dick Steed's Mk8. Designed and built by Coventry Climax to a Ministry of Defence fire pump specification, the FW (Feather Weight) was a neat, light (so as to be portable) all alloy in-line 1100cc 'four' with a single overhead camshaft. In automotive form (FWA) it initially gave 75bhp at 6250rpm, but the directors of Coventry Climax included ex-Brooklands tuner Walter Hassan, and one thing led to another. The little FWA was, arguably, one of the most important post-war UK engines, almost single-handedly creating a relatively cheap 1100cc sports-racing class, a learner class one up from F3 – and Lotus was in there with the Mk9. Over the next 10 years, the name 'Lotus-Climax' would reach the peak of motor racing – the Formula One World Championship.

The Mk9 was available in two forms, 'Club' and 'Le Mans'. The former used a live Ford back axle on coil springs, Ford drum brakes, and a choice of Ford 10 or Climax engines. The 'Le Mans', announced after the company's first participation at the Sarthe circuit, used a Coventry Climax engine and MG gearbox, a de Dion back axle, and enormous finned drums which filled the wheels. Braking was not a problem on the Mk9 with its all-up weight of 9cwt, especially when, later, disc brakes were fitted.

The first works car, registered 8 EHX, was powered by a tried and trusted MG unit, though, and one or two successes came its way in the 1500cc class. The other works car, and most Mk9s, used the little Climax unit.

The highlight of the year for Chapman was an entry acceptance for the 1100cc car at Le Mans, one of his ambitions fulfilled. He was partnered by Ron Flockhart (who would go on to win this race in 1956 in a D-type Jaguar). The little Lotus easily led the 1100cc class initially, but a slipping clutch put it back a bit, then Chapman slid off the road at Arnage into a sand-bank. He promptly reversed out, but this was a big *non-non* – remember that the terrible accident in front of the pits had happened only a couple of hours earlier – and the car was disqualified.

The only trouble with the Mk9 was that others, notably Coopers down in Surbiton, had Climax-powered cars as well, so there was stiff competition. On the whole, honours were about even, with privateers such as John Coombs, Peter Lumsden, Tom Barnard and Peter Ashdown all adding to the overall success list of the model. Abroad, too, the Mk9 was beginning to get the name of Lotus to the top of the win lists. But it was its successor, the Eleven, that really scored and made Lotus world-famous.

One buyer was Dick Steed, who had first put a Climax engine in his Mk8, and it is his Mk9 that forms the subject of this story. From Steed it went to Tommy Dixon. It was superficially messed about with over the years, being equipped with a Triumph Spitfire engine at one point, but – for example – every body panel is still original. Brian Classic had it briefly for a while 25 years ago, before selling it to an American – for £75. It was bought again by Brian in 1989, for rather more than £75. It was restored to its original form by Mike Brotherwood and fettled by Lou Lorenzini.

The Mk9 is one of the most significant and important of all the Loti, a great in a long gallery of greats. Quite apart from that, the shape is totally redolent of a period of great excitement in motor racing which, had we known it, was coming to an end thanks to that fateful 1955 Le Mans. Its progenitor, Colin Chapman, was on the threshold of revolutionising motor racing for all time.

Mk9's predecessor, the Mk8 – 2ft longer, all in the fins

Lotus MkIX

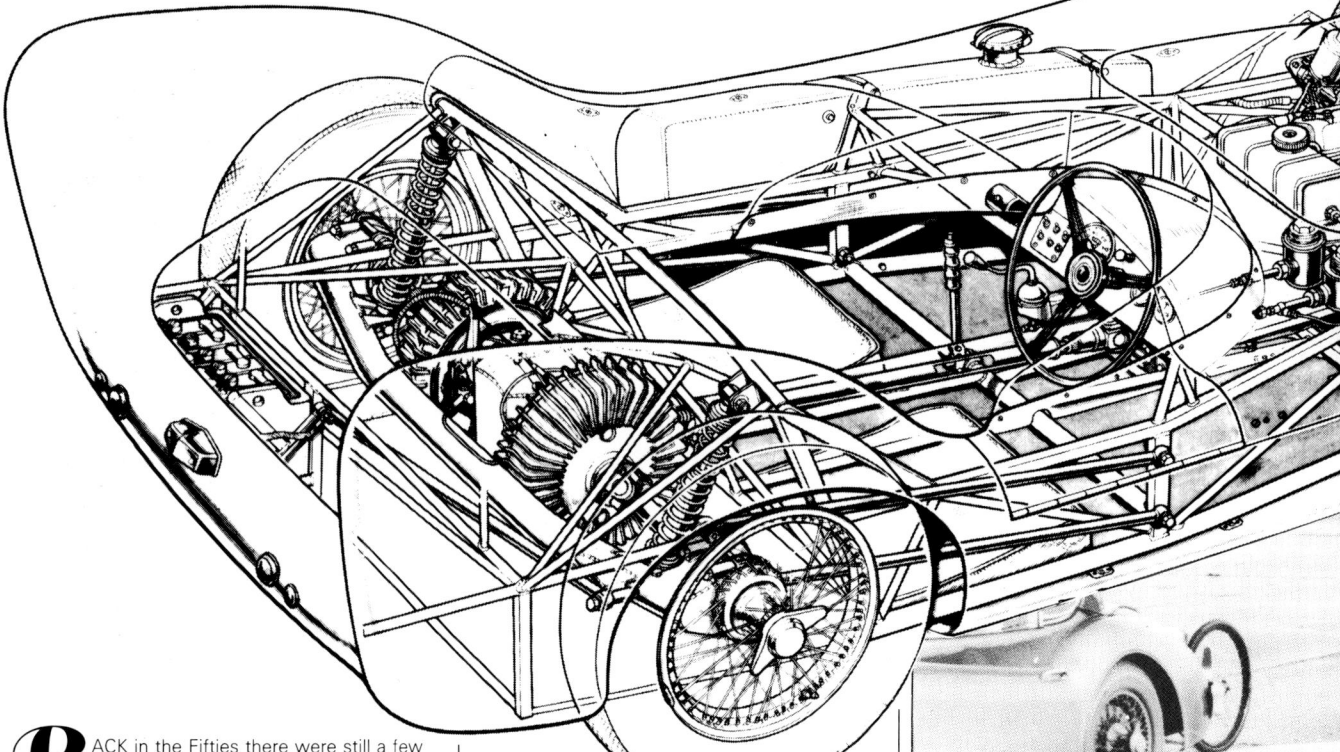

BACK in the Fifties there were still a few cars rugged enough not to lull one to sleep — mostly in the racing sports car field, before the sports-racers had become so highly specialised that they could no longer be used (however tenuously) as occasional road transport. Such a car was Colin Chapman's 1100cc Coventry-Climax-engined MkIX Lotus, current member in 1955 of a line of cars that had started with an Austin Seven-based trials special (the MkI) when the 1172cc Ford-engined cars were taking over from the mighty Ford V8-engined Allards and suchlike. In 1949 had come the MkII, with Ford engine; and in 1951 the Austin Seven-engined MkIII, with inlet ports unsiamesed — a very fast car with its ultra-lightweight body, and Chapman's first racer. The MkIV trials car had appeared in 1951, used by Mike Lawson — Stirling Moss' uncle; and the MkIIIB, seldom, if ever, beaten in 750 Formula events. A MkV 750 Formula car had been produced but did not appear in public, followed by the MkIV, Chapman's first 'production' car, sold as a kit of parts with stressed-aluminium panels, a multi-tube space-frame and a variety of engines, including Ford Ten, MG and Ford Consul 'stroked' to bring it below 1500cc.

The MkVII had been abandoned, becoming the Clairmonte Special; and, in 1953, Frank Costin, Chapman's colleague in his De Havilland days, had joined the company, producing the striking aerodynamic body for the 1954 MkVIII, with its multi-tube space frame, de Dion axle and inboard disc rear brakes and 1100cc FWA Coventry-Climax or 1500 MG engine. In 1955 came the MkIX, an improved MkVIII — and Chapman decided the moment had come to devote the whole of his time to producing Lotus racing-sports cars.

It needs no more than the following list of successes during 1955 to indicate how outstanding this car proved to be:

June
11-12: Le Mans 24-Hour race: Fastest 1100cc car. Delayed initially by slipping clutch, but regained lead in class by 11th hour. Finally disqualified for a regulation infringement.

July
10: Brands Hatch: Second in up to 1200cc sports car class.
30: Crystal Palace: Fourth in 1100cc class in sports car race.

September
19: Tourist Trophy: Second in 1100cc class. Leading class and Index of Performance until fifth hour when delayed by oil pipe fracture. Pit stop of 11 minutes to repair. Recovered position towards end of race; beaten by five seconds for class win.
24: Goodwood: First in up to 1250cc race, and in 1500cc race.
25: Snetterton: First in up to 1500cc race.

October
1: Castle Combe. Second in both up to 2000cc sports car races.
9: Brands Hatch: First in up to 1200cc sports car race.
30: Tarrant Rushton Speed Trials. First in up to 1200cc and in 1101-2000cc sports car classes.

Lap record for 1100cc sports cars taken at: Goodwood, Snetterton, Le Mans, Dundrod Oulton Park and Brands Hatch.

It was with some humility, therefore — and little doubt as to his answer — that, in the middle of the 1955 season when the car was racing almost every weekend, we approached Colin Chapman with the request that *Autocar* might be allowed to drive this masterpiece. We had planned to do a full road test but Colin, while agreeing to our request, suggested: "Why not use it as a road car? Take it on a long run." Not surprisingly, the loan was to be a brief one. That is why, with remarkable nonchalance in retrospect, I decided to drive it down to Cornwall and back over the weekend. Down on the Saturday and back on the Sunday seemed too much like hard work. So, having attended the BARC's annual dinner-dance at London's Grosvenor House on a November Friday night, we (my long-suffering wife, that is, and I) returned to the office, changed out of our 'glad-rags' into 'rompers', packed a cardboard box (no room for suitcases) and set off for Cornwall overnight, the 'luggage' nestling on the floor beneath her knees.

A few concessions had been made to comfort — a sort of wind-deflector on the passenger-side; a sort of seat for the passenger and a single sort of headlamp mounted to the left of the nose. Everything was 'sort of' except the business side of the car. Two glow-worms in front served as side-lights; but at the back . . . a Christmas tree had nothing on it! There were the stop- and tail-lamps, number-plate lamp, reflectors and the two racing-number

118

Peter Garnier recalls his experiences with Colin Chapman's revolutionary sports car in 1955

Left, Autocar Lotus MkIX cutaway: intricate framework covered by streamlined bodywork that was very advanced for its day. Left below, Bob Berry sitting in the Lotus during an Autocar test session with a Jaguar XK 140. Left bottom, two shots en route to Cornwall. Note makeshift screen, headlight and evidence of uncovered pillow for the passenger!

lights, one on the outside of each fin. On taking delivery of the car I stood admiring this array, and asked Mike Costin, Chapman's head mechanic at the time, which combination approximated most closely to the law: "Just turn the lot on — I would,' he said. At least we were visible from behind; from the front we were simply a motor-cycle. So far as noise was concerned, we were an extremely low-flying, unsilenced aircraft. It was possible, though, because of the surprising flexibility of the engine, even with its 9.7:1 compression ratio, to trickle along in top at about 1500rpm — the 4.5:1 rear axle gave 17.2mph per 1000rpm in top gear.

Extremely proud to be sitting behind the wheel, joining the band of famous drivers who had driven the car, but not a little embarrassed, I conducted this projectile through London's sleeping streets until, at last, the Great West Road — the familiar A30 — came up and we could relax. It had felt bumpy and hard in London, but at 45-50 the ride levelled off and became very comfortable. And, being accustomed to cars with much lower-geared steering, one held the wheel far too tight and the car seemed to dart about — but one soon learned to use the lightest grip possible and almost to lean it into corners.

At least we were 'motoring' in the truest sense of the word; but in no way could our progress be compared with the cars of the Thirties that I had driven, or been driven in, along this selfsame road. Our noise, except for those pre-war cars with hand-operated exhaust cut-outs, was excessive and a continuing problem; the driving position with one's behind only inches from the road gave an unaccustomed eyeball to eyeball view of other cars' hub plates, while their occupants looked down upon us from on high; the single headlamp certainly did not light our way as the mighty Lucas P100s had done, and the nose, sloping away in front, was completely out of character, as was the full arms-length driving position. But it was without doubt absolutely enormous fun as we hurried on through the night warmed by the engine and happy.

This initial period of learning the car was terminated by dense fog at Bagshot, which continued down to Honiton. Though it was easier and safer than in a normal road car to keep up a reasonable speed, being able to peer over the screen, it was an anxious period — Borrani wire wheels being expensive at £165 each and kerbs unforgiving; and we carried no spare. Because the undershield-cum-floor had been drilled and cut about in the car's career, water from the wet roads flowed inboard and sloshed about inside — reducing the cardboard box to a brown pulp. It was all too easy to spin the rear wheels, especially the one without much tread, but though the slides were easily started, they were equally easily stopped and, with the ample power available, it was interesting to break the rear end away and corner on the throttle — albeit in a somewhat jerky manner! And, without any question, there was no possibility of dozing-off — one was kept wide awake by the sheer enjoyment.

Our arrival at Newlyn did not, as we had hoped, mean locking the car safely away in the garage until the return journey. No sooner had I called a friend to say we'd arrived in a MkIX Lotus than it triggered-off a succession of telephone calls, each with the inevitable: "Can I come and see it?" — which involved a few "Can we have a go?" requests. It was a miracle the Cornwall Constabulary failed to notice us as we hurtled — not once but several times — along the remaining bit of A30 to Land's End. Such are the penalties of being let loose with an interesting and well-known car. I covered more than 50 miles generously sharing the fun with friends.

Though the return journey was in daylight, our progress was not helped by wet roads all the way and a strong cross-wind. Without having to depend upon our myopic cyclops eye we went very much quicker, and settled down to a lolloping, relaxed 85-90mph where the roads were clear — with a calculated best of 112 (around 6500rpm; there was no speedometer. I need hardly say that there were no out-of-town speed limits either in those days). Sometimes the cross-wind made the car difficult to hold, perhaps because of its extremely light weight at 8cwt. There was no obvious roll on corners, and with the slight negative camber of the rear wheels the cornering power seemed infinite (by my standards, anyway). What I had regarded as pretty inspired cornering at the start of the journey seemed in retrospect only a crawl as I grew more and more accustomed to it. Interesting, and strange, was the way, when

Colin Chapman with the Lotus MkIX in 1955

one closed the throttle, the car seemed to hold its speed unreduced because of its windcheating shape, when an upright saloon would have slowed down of its own accord. One had to do far more check-braking than normally — which must apply nowadays to a great many roadgoing grand tourers, but for me so long ago it was the first experience of driving a truly aerodynamic car.

Only one incident stands out from our return trip, on what was Remembrance Sunday, when

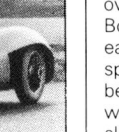

Continued on page 125

Lotus MkIX – State of the Art From '55

Above, Charles Levy in his MkIX with, left, restorer Mike Brotherwood and the Editor
Right, XPE 6 at Castle Combe in 1992: the caring restoration involved few new parts

Any Lotus MkIX is great but the outstanding works Le Mans car has been rescued by American reader Charles Levy; Tony Dron reports

To call this 1955 Lotus Mark IX Colin Chapman's 'make or break' car might seem a cliché, yet it is a fair claim. On January 1 that year he had burnt his bridges by leaving his secure job at the British Aluminium Company; he and Mike Costin set to work full time on Lotus in Hornsey.

Events were moving at a fantastic pace; the Mark VI was in full production and selling well, the cramped factory was expanded with a new building, they divided the company up into the separate functions of production, development and racing and they were moving ahead from the aerodynamic Mark VIII with a new series of advanced small capacity sports-racing cars: the Mark IX was first shown to the Press in March 1955, and the now familiar cutaway drawing by Vic Berris appeared in *The Autocar*. The cars shown were the two Sebring cars just before their despatch to the USA.

What made the Mark IX such a 'make-or-break' proposition for Lotus? After all, one mistake in any part of the rapidly expanding Lotus operation could have brought the entire young business to an instant halt; almost every move had been a make-or-break hazard.

Chapman at that time seemed able to go without sleep but he showed remarkably few signs of the enormous strain that he was putting himself under. He was driven by his mission to show the way forward in car design. Just an inkling of that strain is revealed by Charles Levy who now owns Chapman's Coventry Climax-powered MkIX, registered XPE 6; during his research into the car Charles learnt that while the IX was still in the design stage, Chapman said something like: "If I can create a successful race car with this one I shall go on producing cars. If not, I shall pack it all up."

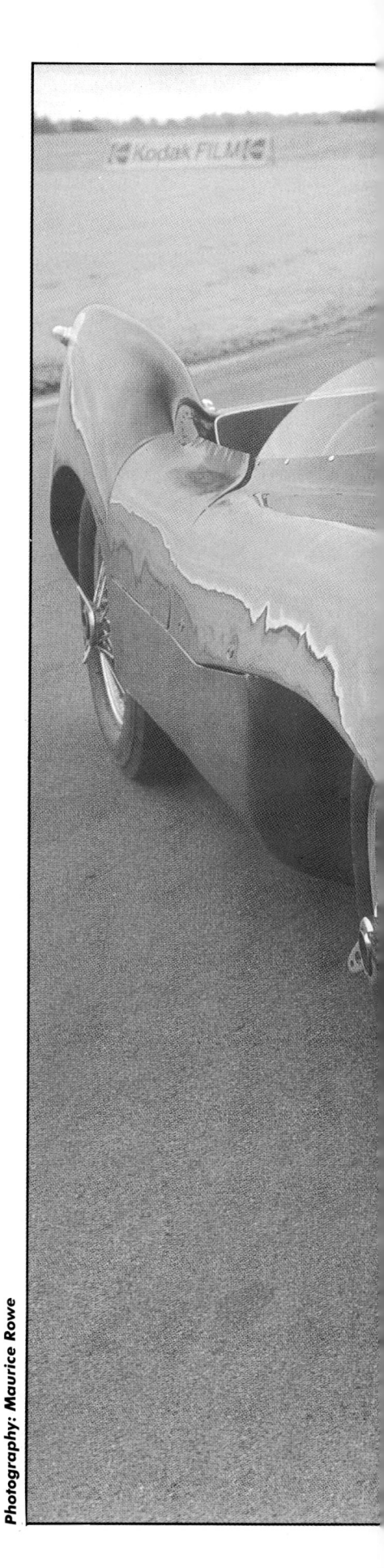

Photography: Maurice Rowe

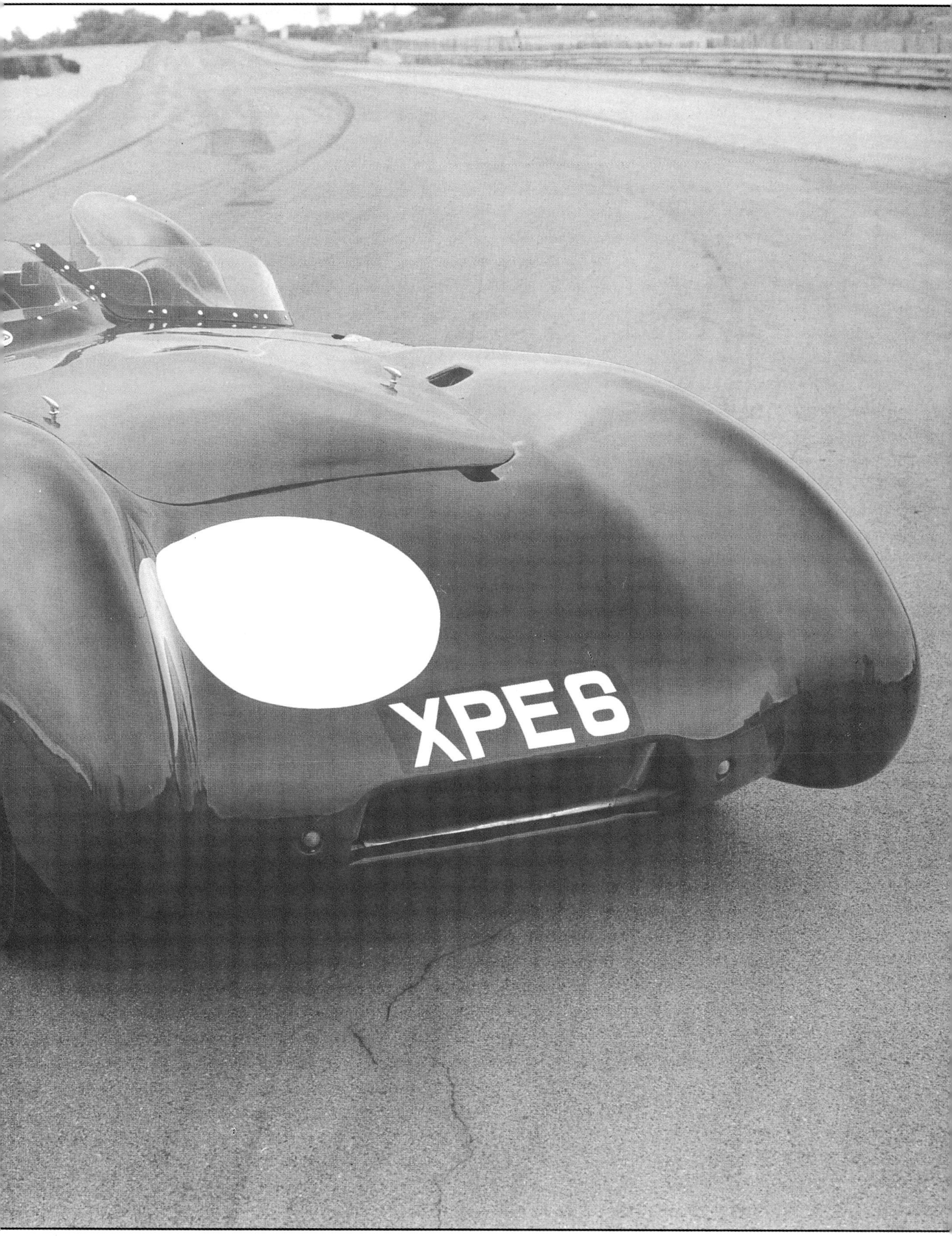
XPE6

Lotus
MkIX - State of the Art From '55

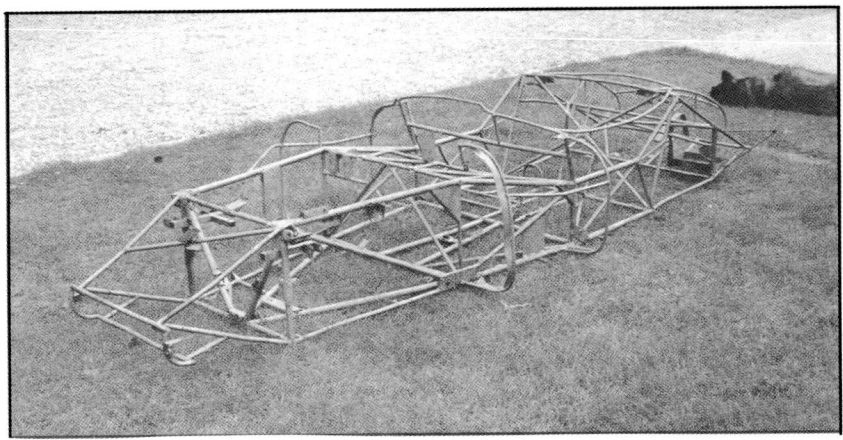

Above, the original spaceframe chassis of XPE 6 after restoration. Compare it with the contemporary cutaway drawing (right) of another Mark IX. The works car was special!

Fortunately the IX was a brilliant car, and XPE 6, the car which Chapman himself drove in the first Team Lotus entry at Le Mans in 1955, has been discovered and restored. It is an amazing story that took American Charles Levy to Australia, where he found that the car's parts had been brought back together incredibly by one Graham Howard, and on to Britain: at the end of it all Levy succeeded in managing an astonishing restoration carried out by British expert, Mike Brotherwood. The full story – history, discovery, restoration and driving impressions – will be told over this month and next. It would be a tragic waste of all the great material found to restrict it to just one article (apologies – you have got to buy next month's issue as well!).

In concept, the Mark IX was a development of the Mark VIII with many new ideas but sticking to the basic philosophy of extracting the greatest possible performance from every drop of fuel used by means of the lowest possible weight and the most advanced aerodynamics.

Aircraft boffin Frank Costin had designed the Mark VIII's shape, agonising over the responsibility he felt towards the drivers of these superlight earthbound projectiles: would they be controllable if caught by a sidewind at speed?

Above, restored de Dion rear suspension: XPE 6 was the first disc-braked Lotus

Above, it could be 1955: the mark of a good job is accurate attention to detail

Right, the ingenious steering arrangement probably unique to XPE 6 (see text). It works very well Below, a good view under the skin. The strange cylinder towards the front is a Serck oil/water heat exchanger

Confidence gained with the Mark VIII led to the Mark IX's body shape, which was considerably shorter and had higher rear fins, though the basic wheelbase and track remained unchanged.

Under the skin, in essence the Mark IX was a tubular-framed, front-engined car with rear-wheel drive, de Dion rear suspension and a divided front axle. Like the Mark VIII, the basic chassis frame was a development of the Mark VI unit, with outriggers to support the fully-enveloping bodies. There were changes but the link is obvious: it can be seen in the Vic Berris cutaway, which also shows the drum brakes and steering box.

Steering box? Look up a Mark IX's specification in a book and you may find it will claim rack-and-pinion steering; which proves that the books are not

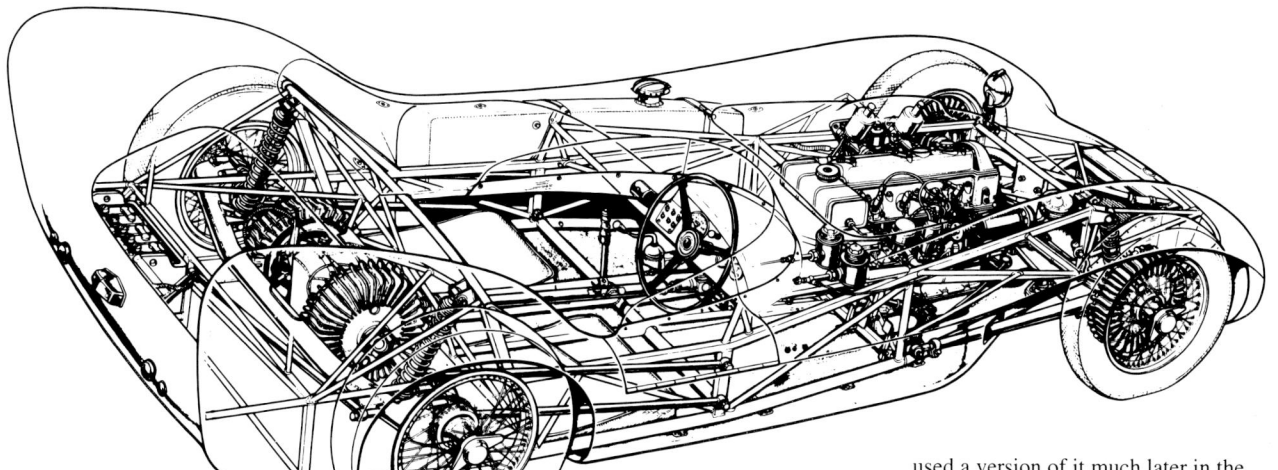

Vic Berris' cutaway from The Autocar, *April 1, 1955. The works Climax-powered car, XPE 6, had many different parts, including chassis, steering and brakes*

always right. I had believed that all the Mark IXs had Mark VI-type Ford steering boxes, but XPE 6 has proved to be an exception. Then look closely at the drawing of the chassis of the Mark IX of March 1955, and compare it with the photographs of XPE 6's chassis, which was built mainly with the Le Mans 24hrs of June that year in mind: they are quite different though none of the books or contemporary magazine articles mentions the fact. The idea of a standard specification for any Lotus cars of those days is hard to sustain.

Chapman's brain was racing ahead; two works Mark IXs were to be built, one for the under-1,500cc class with an MG engine while the other was for the under-1,100cc class, powered by the Coventry Climax 1,094cc engine. He decided that his works Climax-engined car would be the ultimate endurance racer in the 1,100cc class; hence the different chassis, which means that XPE 6 should more properly be seen as a genuine forerunner of the 1956 Lotus Eleven.

It was also the first Lotus to have disc brakes and its rack-and-pinion steering arrangement was most unusual, probably unique, with one end of the rack casing blanked off and swivelling on the chassis, yet it was highly ingenious and effective. Mike Costin, writing in *Motor Racing* magazine in 1959, recalled that "one or two" Mark IXs had this steering set-up but it was used on all Mark Xs (the Mark X was basically a Mark VIII modified to run with a much larger engine, and was a contemporary of the more advanced Mark IX). Experts today suggest that not all Mark Xs had this kind of rack and pinion, so you can take your pick and sympathise with my nightmare in picking my way through the facts: so far I am sure I have not fallen off the tightrope of accuracy!

The rack used was modified from a Morris Minor component. Mike Marsden of the Historic Lotus Register suggests that Chapman kept this unconventional arrangement in the back of his mind and used a version of it much later in the Lotus 63 4WD F1 car. What a marvellous thought.

Chapman had entered XPE 6 for the 1955 *Mille Miglia*, according to Press reports at the time, but for unknown reasons that did not come off. When the Team Lotus entry for Le Mans, 1955, was accepted there were celebrations in Hornsey and the efforts to prepare this very special Mark IX were redoubled. While many components were unique to this car, Chapman was acutely aware of the need to prepare for an endurance race. The body, so the books say, was built from 22-gauge aluminium instead of 20-gauge elektron (magnesium alloy) in this interest. Just a minute: 22-gauge aluminium? I hear tell that Chapman was able to persuade Williams & Pritchard to make bodies out of metal this thin in those days but if you return to this wonderful establishment today for a replacement body you will be told not to be so daft! You'll be lucky to push them below 18-gauge (correspondence for the *Letters* pages?).

The story of this first Team Lotus outing to Le Mans is well known. Although headlights had been built into the front wings and placed behind Perspex, the scrutineers took a dislike to the supplementary lights concealed under

Le Mans, 1955: before the start the winning Jaguar D-type of Hawthorn/Bueb is pushed to its starting place, while Colin Chapman is seated in the works Lotus XPE 6 (no 48) at its pit. Laurence Pomeroy of The Motor *got this shot from the Press box*

Cliff Allison was lucky to escape with minor cuts and bruises from this crash in XPE 6 at Oulton Park's Old Hall Bend on August 27, 1955. The car was repaired in time for the TT at Dundrod on September 17, when it proved sensationally quick

Lotus MkIX – State of the Art From '55

the bonnet (see photographs) which were a standard feature of streamlined Lotus cars in those days. They were relocated before the race.

The Lotus was quick at Le Mans: at the end of the first hour, Chapman and Ron Flockhart were lying 35th overall, one place ahead of the eventual class winners, Duntov and Veuillet in a Porsche 356. Then problems crept in: fire extinguishant was squirted into the Lotus clutch housing to remedy slip caused by the then typical Climax oil seal leak trouble; when the car went off at Tertre Rouge, and ran through the sand, clutch grip was found to have improved so at one point Flockhart was despatched to stop there discreetly and get more sand to chuck at the clutch; apparently this was effective.

All the while a Cooper, which would also retire, and the eventual class-winning Porsche were getting away but the problems of Team Lotus were far from over; the nearside front wing was bent at Arnage by Chapman but later he was black-flagged for unauthorised backing onto the track after (another?) off. This is said to have occurred shortly after 10pm but the Lotus was not disqualified until the 12th hour of the race (ie after 3am) when it was lying 27th. At that moment, the class-winning Porsche was lying 16th. Would the Lotus have been able to catch

October 9, 1955: pressed by Ivor Bueb's Cooper-Climax at Brands Hatch, Chapman set a new outright sports car lap record of 61.2sec in XPE 6. Best time in the big sports car race? C-type – 63.4sec

up? Probably, if the clutch had stopped slipping, as the Porsche averaged 85.5mph for 24hrs and Lotus advertised their fastest class lap at over 97mph after the race.

It was a disappointing race but the works Lotus-Climax Mark IX had shown its mettle and, in the long run, this was no setback. It was noted in *The Motor* that XPE 6 was the fastest car at Le Mans in relation to the power available, a match on the straights for the fastest 2-litre cars.

Despite this pit stop to mend a broken oil pipe, XPE 6 finished 2nd in class and 11th overall in the Dundrod TT. For sheer speed, it was way ahead in class

After the 24hrs, XPE 6 was rebuilt with equal care for the forthcoming shorter races. *Motor Racing* reported that "109lb have been taken off mainly by fitting the original transmission and suspension parts. For Le Mans many 2-litre components of greater weight and strength were fitted." The front bodywork, with its Perspex-covered headlamps, was apparently not seen again.

Chapman then ran XPE 6 in about a dozen meetings in the UK through the remainder of '55. It was always quick and it frequently won, often in Chapman's own hands. A minor disaster struck on August 20 at the Goodwood 9hrs when Tony Gaze spun his DB3S and took out XPE 6 soon after the start. Ron Flockhart, sharing with Cliff Allison for the meeting, was at the wheel. The front suspension was rebuilt rapidly in front of the pits but the car retired later with clutch slip after oil seal failure.

Worse was to come a week later at Oulton Park: Cliff Allison crashed at Old Hall in the 80-lap sports car race and was lucky to get away with minor cuts and bruises after wrecking the body; some events were missed after that and today the car retains the restored body as it was after the Oulton crash repairs.

Soon after that, things looked up: the car was simply a sensation in the TT at the difficult, beautiful but lethal Dundrod road circuit when the Chapman/Allison pairing was literally miles ahead of the class opposition and embarrassing 3-litre Ferrari drivers; only an oil-pipe fracture robbed them of an amazing result but still they were second in class and 11th overall. Timed on the straight the car was 9mph quicker than a privately entered Mark IX, driven by the highly talented pairing of Dick Steed and Peter Scott-Russell. The works car was in a different league without doubt.

Chapman then scored wins at Goodwood and Snetterton before shaping

Last outing as a works car: Chapman (with garland) took a dominant victory at Boxing Day Brands in the rain. The car had already been sold to Doc Wyllie

up for an October duel with Ivor Bueb's Cooper: Bueb won at Castle Combe but Chapman got his revenge a week later at Brands.

During the latter part of the year, the car was loaned to journalists. It was written up in *The Autocar* by Peter Garnier who took it to Cornwall and back with his wife straight after a black tie dinner in Park Lane, remarking on its extraordinary speed, especially the way the streamlined shape allowed it to sail on after lifting off the throttle; Joe Lowrey and Harold Hastings of *The Motor* took it to Belgium for high speed tests (and as regular *Classic Cars* readers will know, ran the headline "49 MPG at a Mile a Minute!"; John Bolster of *Autosport* remarked that all the power could be used nearly all the time but when you had to slow the Girling discs were magnificent; Bill Boddy commented in *Motor Sport* on the distinctive appearance, outstanding performance and controllability of XPE 6.

The car also put in a full day at the Guild of Motoring Writers Test Day at Goodwood during the Motor Show, when it was driven by a large number of other journalists; and it was used for a Team Lotus test day at Brands in November, driven by 12 racing drivers including Ivor Bueb, Graham Hill and Ken Tyrrell; Reg Bicknell was the quickest by nearly half a second from Alan Brown. That Chapman was prepared to expose his product in this way reflected the growing confidence of the entire Lotus enterprise.

Hazel Chapman drove XPE 6 at Tarrant Ruston (a sprint) and she won; the car was then sold to 'Doc' Wyllie in the USA who reluctantly was forced to permit the persuasive Chapman to race at the second annual BRSCC Boxing Day Brands Hatch meeting. Heavy rain fell for much of the race and Chapman just pulled away from the start to win by the large margin of six seconds (a very long way, whatever anyone says!).

So off to the States went the car, where it gave great pleasure and splendid results to Doc Wyllie. For its subsequent history and rebuild, see next month's issue of *Classic Cars*.

Lotus *MkIX*

Continued from page 119

we crawled through Yeovil behind a parade of the Royal British Legion, boy scouts and the rest, headed by a military band. Even though we moved at a tickover in first gear, searching desperately for a bolt-hole into which to vanish, it is questionable whether we or the band made the greater noise. When eventually the chance came to overtake, it had to be done on the lightest possible throttle — a hideous moment that is best forgotten, though there seemed to be more interest than disapproval on the part of the crowds that lined the streets. The only real antagonism we experienced was later on, when a crusty old Indian Army colonel type took violent exception to us — and took a swipe at the Lotus with his stick. It wasn't our noise that hurt his feelings as we were, at the time, going downhill in almost complete silence on the over-run — just the sight of something so outlandish in his town, I suppose.

Outstanding general impression of the car during the 650-odd miles we covered was the manner in which one could afford to drive it restrainedly, knowing that as soon as even the shortest safe opportunity came to overtake, one could change down into third and accelerate from 60 to 90mph by the ninth or tenth telegraph pole, 'exposed' on the wrong side of the road for the briefest possible time. Also, because one is so very much in the public eye driving such a car, one was well aware that any signs of aggression, impatience or other

Top, those early Lotuses were notoriously fragile! Left, metal tonneau enclosed cockpit. Right, Coventry-Climax engine gave top speed of 130mph

misdeeds would be observed and commented upon unfavourably — if not actually reported. Everything was respected, especially speed limits.

Light weight and low drag made the car very economical on fuel, our consumption for the 650-odd miles being between 25 and 30mpg — for an 1100cc car with a maximum of 130mph. A similar engine, used in a Cooper-Climax for long-distance records at Montlhéry and running continuously at 7000rpm, had recorded an overall 35mpg. On the score of noise alone it was not a road car, though this could have been seen to. Even so, the extremely light-gauge aluminium panels, being sensitive, and dented by leaning on them too heavily, were impracticable. For its day, though, when nobody objected to speed on the open road and in safe places, it was a true fun car combining much of the adventure, and required driving skill, of the cars of the Thirties with the latest and greatest developments of the mid-Fifties.

We found it very difficult to reconcile Colin Chapman's noisy, though exciting, masterpiece with the ancient Greek representation of the Lotus plant as producing a state of luxurious dreaminess and distaste for active life!

The Lotus-Bristol Mark X

Although the Mark VIII had been aimed at the sports racing class for cars up to 1500cc, on many occasions, particularly in the unlimited sports racing car events, the 1500cc Mark VIIIs were found to be mixing it with the larger cars, and in particular the 2-litre Bristol engined cars. Archie Scott-Brown proved a constant adversary to Colin Chapman in VIII, SAR 5, and they even had an entanglement at the end of the 1954 season whilst Chapman was leading the Bristol engined Lister in pursuit of a handicap win at Snetterton.

At the Whit Monday Goodwood meeting on 7th June 1954, Chapman in SAR 5 had won the 1500cc class in the 21 lap Johnson Trophy, and finished 6th overall amongst the unlimited capacity cars.

Autosport reported: '....winning the 1½-litre category in really sweeping fashion with eight larger cars between himself and the nearest 1½-litre rival.'

It was, therefore, inevitable that sights would soon be set on the larger capacity sports racing class. However, this did not come from Colin Chapman who was far too busy establishing the first Lotus standard production parts sports car, the Lotus Mark IX during the winter of 1954/5. Credit for the idea to build a 2-litre sports racing car is due to Harlequins rugby football player Mike Anthony, who had been part of Team Lotus in 1954 in his Mark VI, NUF 100. Peter Scott-Russell, who in 1954 had been racing a Frazer Nash, also decided that he would like a 2-litre Lotus. Cliff Davis, the flamboyant Goldhawk Road, West London dealer in American cars who had been racing a Tojeiro, also joined the requests for a car capable of using the Bristol 2-litre six-cylinder engine, which was the state of the art engine to have in the 2-litre class at the time. Chapman succumbed to the combined pressure, or more likely the financial incentives, and set about modifying the production Mark VI/VIII chassis to take the large, and tall 6-cylinder Bristol engine with its increased weight and power.

The chassis modifications were quite extensive. To create an enlarged engine bay two of the chassis tubes had to be removed, and modified to bolt into place after the engine was installed to retain torsional rigidity. As the engine was tall, it was mounted low in the chassis, so that the entire drive line was lowered. At the rear the chassis was strengthened for the increased torque, and modified to mount a Salisbury hypoid differential. The normal Mark IX de Dion axle tube was retained, and the new Dunlop disc brakes were fitted at the front, and mounted inboard on the differential at the rear. To balance the increased weight of the engine, all accessories such as fuel tank, fuel pumps, battery and spare wheel were located behind the rear axle. Williams and Pritchard built the body along similar lines to the Mark VIII in 18 gauge aluminium alloy. The bonnet cover was more humped to allow for the increased height of the engine, but only by 2½ins, and no rear wheel spats were fitted as the car had knock off wire wheels, which most Mark VIIIs later fitted in preference to their original five-stud, bolt on wire wheels. The lessons learned by Frank Costin, strapped to the bonnet of VIII, SAR 5, for high speed wind turbulence tests the year before, had been put to good effect. The Lotus-Bristol body shape featured cutaway pontoons behind the front wheels to aid airflow extraction from the front wheel arches.

The Lotus-Bristol sold for £925, and customers were expected to supply their own engine. The finished car weighed just 11cwt. Apparently, the modifications to the chassis to accommodate the larger engine and take the stronger running gear to cope with the increased power of 140bhp, caused Colin Chapman so many problems and disruptions to his normal Lotus production, that he vowed never to modify another Lotus to customer wishes again. They could buy his cars as he produced them, and do their own modifications in future.

The Lotus-Bristol, as it was originally known, was never intended as a new model of Lotus - it was in fact a modified and more powerful Mark VIII. However, Chapman had already designated Mark IX for his new 1955 sports racing car which was under production. He could have called it a Mark VIIIB, or a Mark VIII Series 2. It was John Bolster, the technical editor of *Autosport* who wrote a ½ page introductory description of the Bristol engined car in the 15th April 1955 edition, who referred to the new car as a Mark X - and it stuck. There was no official track test, no public announcement as had been Lotus policy with the other models, the Mark X just emerged.

The three Lotus-Bristol Mark Xs were built concurrently. Mike Anthony's was registered PCD 13 on 3rd January 1955, but the first appearance was not until the traditional season opening race, the British Empire Trophy at Oulton Park on 2nd April 1955. Both Mike Anthony (PCD 13) and Peter Scott-Russell (JBW 648) were entered, as was Colin Chapman in the new Lotus Mark IX in the smaller capacity class. Scott-Russell's car was not ready, and Mike Anthony got off to a fine start for the 1955 season with the new car by overturning it at the Cascades in practice, suffering cuts and bruises to himself, and also to his new car. Mike Anthony repaired himself and the car for the following weekend at Goodwood on Easter Monday 11th April 1955, where he finished 3rd in the Sports Cars up to 2000cc race behind Archie Scott-Brown in the Lister Bristol, and Tony Brooks in a Frazer Nash. Peter Scott-Russell first appeared with his Lotus-Bristol Mark X at Goodwood on Whit Monday 30th May 1955. Mike Anthony in PCD 13 carrying his favourite race number 13 won the race, with Peter Scott-Russell 3rd. Cliff Davis registered his Mark X, NOY 1, and first appeared with the car painted in silver on 10th July 1955 at Brands Hatch where he finished 4th.

Mike Anthony persuaded paint manufacturers Valspar to supply him with some of their green paint for PCD 13, and in return Valspar used a photo of the Mark X in their advertisements throughout 1955. He must have been given a lot of paint, as he painted his transporter the same colour!

A fourth Lotus Mark X was bought by Dr Vaughan Havard, and raced by Bill Short. This was registered RCR 500. In mid-1955 John Young bought a Lotus Mark X which he registered NBE 806, and installed a John Coombs Formula 2 Connaught engine. Mike Young and co-driver Geoff Richardson drove NBE 806 all the way to Sicily in late 1955 to take part in the 39th Targa Florio race, and Young continued with the car for 1956/7.

In mid-1955, Colin Chapman received an order from his US agent in California, Jay Chamberlain, for a streamlined Lotus for actor James Dean. Cult actor Dean raced a Porsche 550 when not starring in films such as East of Eden, etc. He wanted his car less engine and transmission as he planned to install at 91cu in Offenhuaser. Lotus used up some left over parts, and built a hybrid Mark VIII/IX/X. It had the Mark VIII production (VI) chassis, with Mark IX running gear, and the Mark X body shape. It was shipped to California but arrived a few weeks after Dean was killed in a road accident in his Porsche on 30th September 1955.

Mike Anthony sold PCD 13 to Dimitri Kasterini of the Six Mile Stable Team for 1956. Peter Scott-Russell had crashed JBW 648 at the end of 1955, and the car was heavily damaged in the ensuing fire which involved extensive repair which took until 1958. Cliff Davis continued to race NOY 1 until 1957 when it was painted red and featured in the film 'Checkpoint'. It was sold to Peter Cotterell who continued to race it under the Red Dragon Racing banner. Bill Short did not race RCR 520 much at all, and in November 1956 it was advertised with 'under 2000 miles'. It later went to the USA, and became a road car. The James Dean Mark VIII/IX/X was later acquired by John Timmanus, an official with the Sports Car Club of America (SCCA). He installed an MG XPAG engine and raced it on the West Coast USA. He later installed a supercharged Coventry Climax 1500cc engine, and converted the bodywork to a single seater configuration. Later it was raced with a Buick V8.

Although not wholly successful cars in their time the six Lotus Mark X cars built all survive today.

Graham Capel

The 2-Litre Lotus
Latest Bristol-engined Competition Sports Car Weighs Under 11 Cwt.

THE 2-litre Lotus has a broadly similar specification to the Mark IX which I recently described. It has, however, a new frame specifically designed for the Bristol engine. This is not a particularly easy unit to accommodate, owing to its considerable height. In the Mark X Lotus, the installation problem has been overcome by making two members of the space frame detachable.

In order to get the power unit well down in the car, the whole transmission line has been lowered. This has been brought about by using a Salisbury hypoid final drive, for which ratios of 3.73, 4.125, and 4.56 to 1 are available from stock. This low engine mounting permits the use of a bonnet which is only 2¼ ins. higher than that of the smaller cars. A flute above the front wheel opening prevents the air from eddying upwards, and the body is cut away behind the wheel for air escape from the brakes.

On this model, Dunlop disc brakes are to be standardized. They are normally located in front, but inboard mounted behind, as is Lotus practice. The front suspension is by swing axles and at the rear there is a de Dion axle, with helical springs and telescopic dampers all round.

As this is a larger and heavier engine than previous cars of this make have carried, it has been found necessary to locate plenty of weight in the tail to secure a correct balance. Accordingly, the fuel tank is behind the rear axle, as also are the fuel pumps, spare wheel and battery. The radiator in the nose has a fully ducted air flow.

Fitted with knock-on racing wire wheels, the 2-litre Lotus weighs under 11 cwt. It is thus apparent that the performance will be tremendous, and the acceleration should be quite breathtaking. The first three cars are going to Peter Scott-Russell, Michael Anthony, and Cliff Davis—lucky blokes! If you have a Bristol engine and gearbox, you can get the rest of the motor car for £925.

JOHN V. BOLSTER.

VALSPAR
2-4 HOUR LACQUER

CONGRATULATIONS to Michael Anthony on his excellent performance at Goodwood

MICHAEL ANTHONY uses VALSPAR 2-4 Hour Lacquer on his Lotus Bristol and Transporter.

CARS & DRIVERS
THE JAMES DEAN LOTUS
Colin Chapman Builds a Mystery Hybrid
Story by Graham Capel - Historic Lotus Register

A degree of mystery has surrounded the James Dean Lotus, much as mystery has surrounded the death of James Dean. Dean died on September 30th, 1955 at the wheel of his racing Porsche Spyder (chassis no. 550-0055) when it smashed into a 1950 Ford driven by Don Turnupseed at the intersection of Routes 41 and 446 near the town of Paso Robles, California. Dean was on the way to Salinas for his first race in the car.

The Porsche, signwritten 'Little Bastard', was used following Dean's accident as a mobile accident prevention display by the Los Angeles Safety Council, after the engine and transmission were used on another car. The slogan used in the promotion was "The accident could have been avoided". However, even the remains of the chassis mysteriously disappeared whilst it was returning from one display

But back to the mystery Lotus. The first reference to a Lotus being ordered by the budding and controversial young actor appears in Ian Smith's book "The Story of Lotus - Birth of a Legend". Here the car is referred to as a Mark X, which was shipped less engine so that an Offenhauser powerplant could be fitted.

Jay Chamberlain, who was the official Lotus distributor in the USA, had his workshops on Olive Street, Burbank at the time. As this was close to Warner Brothers' studios, James Dean was a frequent visitor as he started into motor racing in March of 1955. Presumably Jay Chamberlain told him of the exploits of Lotus SAR 5 and the Mark VIIIs on the British circuits during 1954 and this prompted Dean to order one of the streamlined Lotus cars for himself. But he wanted an American engine, and the 91cu. in. Offenhauser 4-cylinder was the motor to have on the circuits at the time, so that was what Dean wanted. The order was sent over to Lotus at Hornsey and would have arrived in April/May 1955 or thereabouts when Mark IX production was just starting and the Lotus-Bristol Mark Xs were taking to the circuits.

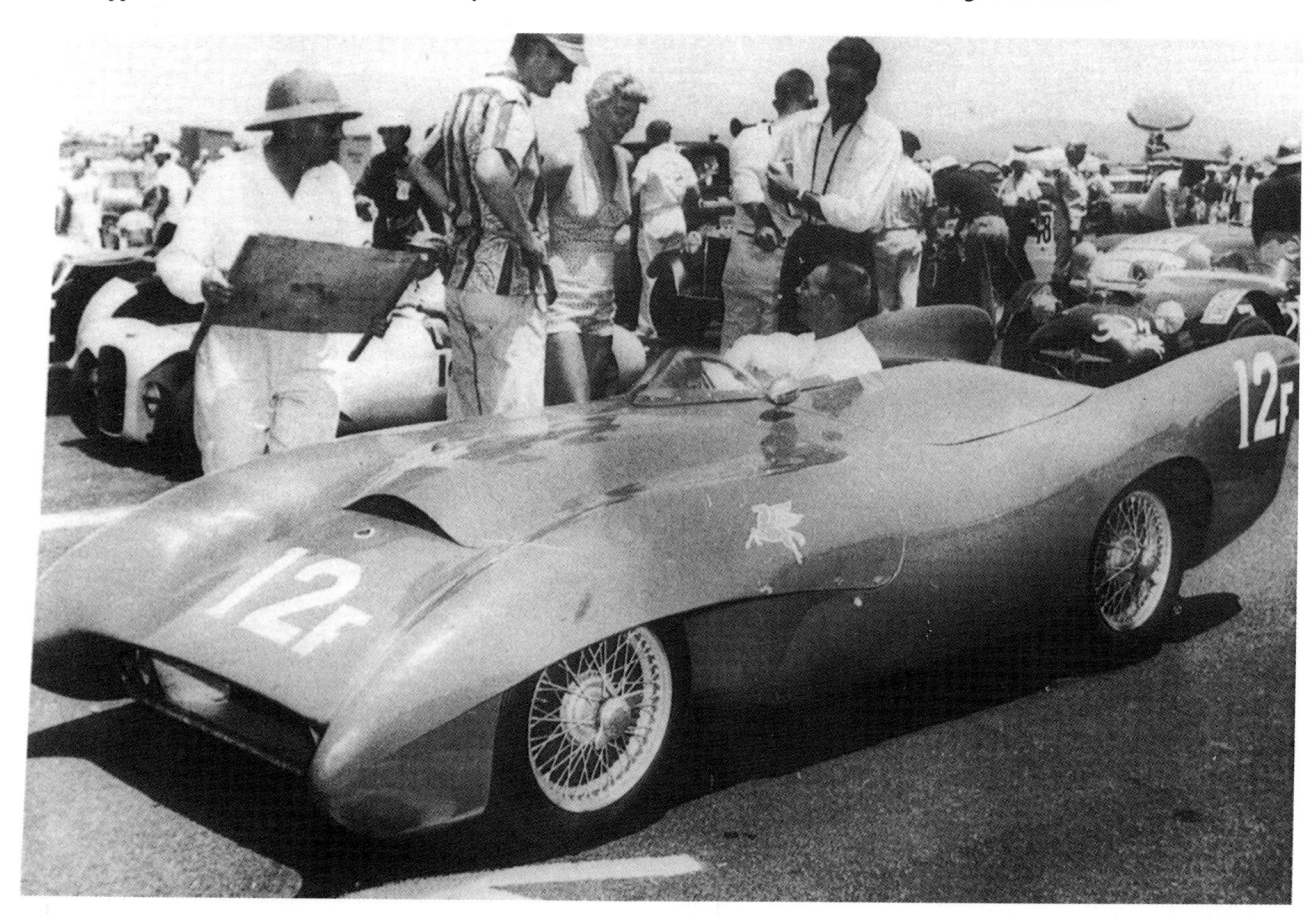

So, Colin Chapman took one of the Mark VI chassis frames that were awaiting sale and fitted the body mounting outrigger tubes that held the streamlined body in place, as had been done for all the Mark VIII and Mark X cars to date. However, as he had a production line of Mark IX parts in stock for the new model, these were fitted to the car destined for the USA.

It was then wheeled along to Williams and Pritchard and a Mark X body fitted - probably because the other Mark Xs had just been completed and, in any event, to fit a tall 4-cylinder engine like the 91cu. in. Offy, you needed a tall engine bay and this is what the Mark X had to accommodate the Bristol engine.

The car was shipped to Jay Chamberlain in July/August and arrived in the US shortly after James Dean was killed. Chamberlain took delivery and it stayed around his works for many months. Eventually, in the late summer of 1956, a year after Dean's fatal accident, John Timanus bought the engine-less car. He fitted an XPAG MG engine and raced it quite successfully in 1957/8. In order to keep the car competitive, Timanus then fitted a Coventry Climax 1500cc. FWB engine with a Marshal Nordec Roots supercharger, which kept him up with the Maseratis and the Porsche 1600cc. 550s. However, when the new Porsche RSK and RS-60s appeared it really was not in the same race so Timanus removed the body and fabricated an open wheel, offset single seater type of thing so that he could go Formula Libre racing using a Coventry Climax 1100cc. FWA engine.

By the time that the Lotus Elevens and Cooper sports cars had reached California in force, the Lotus acquired yet another body - this time a crude sports racing body with which Timanus carried on racing with in the G Modified SCCA class.

John Timanus then graduated to greater things, namely one of the Lotus Eleven Sebring Series 2 cars, and sold the well used, and infinitely variable, ex-James Dean Lotus to Stan Peterson of Oakland. The poor car then suffered the installation of an aluminium block V8 Buick and was further pounded round the circuits in 1960.

After several years it was passed on to Riley Hophins in Tacoma, Washington where Chris Smith, of Westfield Cars fame, found the sad remains in 1979 and had them shipped back home to Britain. Obviously, nothing remained of the original Mark X shaped body, but the Mark IX running gear had survived intact. The poor chassis had been severely cut about on various occasions, not to mention a few involuntary mods caused by curbs, banks and other cars during its long, varied and eventful life.

A new Mark IX chassis was built for Chris Smith by Frank Coltman, ex-Progress Chassis, who used to build the original chassis frames for Lotus. The car was registered with the Historic Sports Car Club in Britain as a Lotus Mark IX. Smith sold the bits still unassembled and eventually Bill Cowling became the owner. He had Crosthwaite and Gardiner build up a Mark IX car using the new Mark IX chassis, the original running gear which was Mark IX, and the car was finished with a Mark IX body and Climax FWA engine. It was later auctioned at Motorfair by Christies in October of 1987.

The original Chassis was discarded after the new Mark IX chassis was built in 1980/1 and was eventually acquired by me. It was then possible to examine it in detail and conclusions to the mystery of what the 'James Dean' Lotus really was are as follows:

It was a modified Mark VI chassis to bring it up to Mark VIII specifications. It was fitted with Mark IX running gear and finally clothed in a Mark X body shape.

A true Colin Chapman hybrid from Lotus! .....and James Dean never even sat in it.

Postcript: It is currently being rebuilt using the original chassis with Mark IX running gear and a Mark X body - has anyone got a 91 cubic inch Offy around?

Victory Lane November 1988

DEPART: Berry (Jaguar, 56), Anthony (Lotus, 13), Sopwith (Cooper, 15), Hamilton (Jaguar, 55) and Brooks (Frazer-Nash, 30) after the Le Mans start of the 21-lap final.

The Lotus Eleven

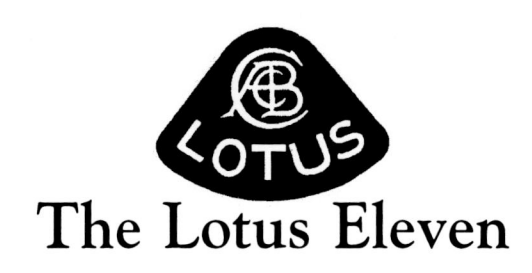

The first big difference with the Lotus Eleven of 1956 was its name. Gone were the Roman numerals of the previous models and in their place just the name Eleven. This also began Chapman's romance with the names of his cars beginning with the letter E.

1955 had established Lotus Engineering Co Ltd on the road to success as a specialised sports car manufacturer. They had sold some 40-50 cars and they had a developing reputation on the racing circuits more or less all over the world, with agents established in the USA and Australia. Stan Chapman, Colin's father, and their new young accountant, Fred Bushell, had produced the funds to build a large assembly building behind the Railway Hotel in Tottenham Lane, Hornsey which could cope with greater volume production. They now employed some ten staff including a young mechanic named Graham Hill, and Colin's school friend, Colin Bennett, had joined them as sales manager which took some of the pressure off the Managing Director, Colin Chapman BSc(Eng).

The new car for 1956 was another multi-tube space frame chassis designed by Colin Chapman, and built by Progress Chassis Co. Gone was any vestige of the Mark VI chassis. The new chassis was all small diameter tubes similar to the two works Lotus Mark IXs that Colin Chapman and Peter Jopp had used as development in 1955. The Costin influence was still apparent in the body shape, but it's final appearance was developed in the workshops of panel beaters Williams and Pritchard. The problems of inaccessibility to internal components on the previous cars, where much of the body was riveted to the chassis, was gone with the Eleven. The whole of the front and the whole of the back opened up like an egg to give easy access to virtually everything in seconds. Even the centre scuttle section could be removed with six screws. It was brilliant.

Mechanically, the major innovation with the Eleven was the rack and pinion steering. Gone was the Ford Popular 1950's steering box. However, the Lotus developed divided front axle remained on the Series 1 cars of 1956/7. Even this was changed in 1957 with the Series 2 which had wishbone front suspension that featured on the subsequent Lotus Seven, Elite, 12 and 16 single seaters, and Fifteen and Seventeen.

The Lotus Eleven was offered in three models. The Sports model featured drum brakes and a live rear axle, and was usually fitted with the tried and tested Ford sidevalve 1172cc engine. The Club model still had the drum brakes and live rear axle, but the engine was a Stage 2 Coventry Climax 1098cc. The top of the range for serious racing was the Le Mans model taking its name from the fact that Lotus had entered this prestigious event in 1955, and planned a serious assault in 1956. The Eleven Le Mans featured a de Dion tube rear axle with Lotus designed magnesium hub carriers, and inboard disc brakes mounted on a Lotus cast magnesium alloy differential carrier. Disc brakes were installed at the front, and the engine was a Stage 3 tuned Coventry Climax FWA 1098cc, but soon the FWB 1468cc was also available. The Series 1 cars used knock off wire wheels, but the later Series 2 cars could also use the later Lotus developed magnesium alloy 'wobbly web' wheels.

Not only were there three models to choose from, there were options on body style as well. A glass windscreen mounted on cast alloy pillars was available and with the open two seater cockpit this was more or less a road car. For a more sporty appearance the windscreen could be wrap-around perspex, with perspex side windows which made for a very sleek appearance. Both options could use a hood, but in either case getting in with the hood up was always something of a problem. There was also an option for a high level tail fairing which fitted onto the rear bodywork behind the driver which gave the car a more purposeful appearance, but a hood was no longer practical. The next option was the closed-in cockpit, almost like a single seater racing car for serious racing, and this looked absolutely stunning. The passenger cockpit was entirely covered over with an alloy tonneau which blended to the body shape entirely. The cockpit windscreen was formed with wrap-around perspex and just the driver's head protruded.

In 1956 the Lotus Eleven sold at £750 for the Sports, £969 for the Club, and £1230 for the Le Mans models, all in self assembly form, as the Purchase Tax on built up cars was still prohibitive. By the beginning of 1957 the prices had increased to £1021, £1309, and £1625 for the three models.

The dry weight of a Lotus Eleven was 854lbs with an overall length of 11ft 2ins, and a height at the scuttle of 2ft 3ins, and even with a tail fin it was only 3ft 1in.

Did they sell? Yes fantastically well. Over a three year production from 1956 to 1959 Lotus Engineering Co Ltd sold a total of 270 units divided into 150 Series 1, 16 Series 1^1/$_2$ and 104 Series 2. It was the major success that Colin Chapman had been working towards for the previous four years since setting up Lotus Engineering Co in a shed in Hornsey in 1952.

The Lotus Eleven was so sensational that it attracted a number of established drivers: Ivor Bueb, Ron Flockhart, Mike Hawthorn, etc. Also a number of up-and-coming drivers made their names with the Lotus Eleven: Cliff Allison, Peter Arundel, Graham Hill, Innes Ireland, Les Leston, Mike Parkes, Alan Stacey, to mention a few.

Just as the Mark IX had made its debut at the Sebring 12 hours in Florida in March, the Lotus Eleven was to have done the same. However, American driver Len Bastrup wrote off the car he was to share with Colin Chapman in practice, so the debut of the Lotus Eleven at Sebring was with American private entrant Ralph Miller and his co-driver Hal Fenner, but the car did not last the distance. The British debut for the Eleven was at Goodwood at the Easter Bank Holiday meeting on 2nd April 1956, but the best that the new car could achieve was 4th place. The first race victory came at Brands Hatch on the same day where Brighton car dealer Bill Frost won in convincing style. Things were a lot better two weeks later at the traditional British Empire Trophy race at Oulton Park. Colin Chapman driving the Team Lotus Eleven won heat 1 and equalled the outright sports car lap record. In the final, Chapman was on pole position ahead of all the larger capacity cars. He led for part of the race from Stirling Moss, but spun and was only able to manage 2nd place, plus sharing a new Sports Car record. However, the potential of the Lotus Eleven was made more than apparent, and orders for the new car came flooding in to Hornsey.

The Lotus Eleven continued its winning ways for 1956 completely dominating the Coopers, and other sports racing cars. At Le Mans on 28/29th July 1956, a team of three Elevens were entered. The Jaguar D-Type of Ron Flockhart and Ninian Sanderson won, but amazingly in 7th place overall came the Lotus Eleven driven by Peter Jopp and Reg Bicknell, who won the 750-1100cc class. In September 1956 Stirling Moss drove a specially prepared Lotus Eleven at Monza to capture the International 50 kilometre and 50 mile World Speed Records for Class G sports cars before the chassis broke due to the rough track surface.

A month later they were back at Monza with Cliff Allison as driver, and captured six World Speed Records up to one hour duration including a top speed of 138mph. At the Earls Court Motor Show in London on 17th-27th November 1956, Lotus exhibited on the ground floor amongst the recognised motor manufacturers. On display they had not only two Lotus Elevens, but the new single seater Lotus 12 for 1957 which caused a sensation.

The success of Lotus Engineering Co Ltd and the Lotus Eleven continued into 1957. In February Colin Chapman was awarded the prestigious Ferodo Gold Trophy. Colin Chapman eventually managed to race at Sebring in March 1957 and with co-drivers Dick Dungan and Jo Sheppard they finished 17th overall and won the 750-1100cc class, plus finishing 3rd in the Index of Performance. On 11/12th May 1957 the editor of *Autosport* took a works Lotus Eleven around Italy on the famous Mille Miglia, and in June three works Lotus Elevens were entered for the 24 hour race at Le Mans, plus two privately entered Elevens. Again, the race was won by Jaguar, with the Ecurie Ecosse D-Type of Ron Flockhart and Ivor Bueb. In 9th place overall came the Lotus Eleven of Mac Fraser and American Lotus agent Jay Chamberlain to win Class G for 1100cc cars. In 13th place came the privately entered Eleven of Walshaw/Dalton to finish second in the class and next, in 14th place, was the amazing 750cc engined Lotus Eleven driven by Cliff Allison and Keith Hall to win the up to 750cc class H, plus the coveted Index of Performance. 1957 had been an all conquering year for the Lotus Eleven with victories in club and international events in Britain, throughout Europe, in the USA and elsewhere in the world.

By mid-1957 Lotus Engineering Co Ltd were producing the Lotus Eleven now in Series 2 format with wishbone front suspension. Plus the new Lotus Seven, the new single seater Lotus 12, and at the year end Motor Show at Earls Court, the Lotus Stand was displaying their innovative GT car, the fibreglass monocoque Type 14 Lotus Elite. A sports Lotus Eleven driven by Ian Walker had won the Autosport Championship, and privateer Lotus Eleven driver Innes Ireland won the Brooklands Memorial Trophy. Lotus went back to Monza to capture more records up to 200 kilometres, and record a fastest lap on the banked circuit of 145.5mph.

At the beginning of 1958, Lotus opened a new showroom at Tottenham Lane, Hornsey. It was a bit small and could only accommodate one car, but it was a significant step forward. Ted Lewis and Dennis Pratt took a Lotus Eleven on the round Britain RAC Rally in dreadful conditions in March 1958 to prove the point that it was basically a road car for the Le Mans organisers who were not too happy at having their Index of Performance taken from French domination the year before! American drivers at Sebring did well, with Sam Weiss and Dave Tallakson finishing 4th overall to win Class G. At Le Mans in June, the Lotus Eleven entry was confirmed, but the only finisher was the 750cc Lotus Eleven of Alan Stacey and Tom Dickson. By July Eric Broadley had brought out his Lola sports racing car, and the writing was on the wall for the Lotus Eleven after three superb seasons of racing.

Production of the Lotus continued into 1959, but by then Lotus were heavily involved in a diverse range of other racing activities including Formula 1, plus road car production with the Seven and Type 14 Elite. The Lotus Eleven underwent a small revival in the mid 1960s with Lotus Eleven GTs winning in the GT class of racing in private hands. Of all of the early Lotus models, the Lotus Eleven was probably the most significant.

Graham Capel

LOTUS ELEVEN

Details of the de Dion rear suspension and disc brakes of the Le Mans model can be seen on the left, while the solid axle and drum brakes used on the Club and Sports model are shown on the right. The axle locating arrangements are the same in each case, so that the two types of axle are inter-changeable.

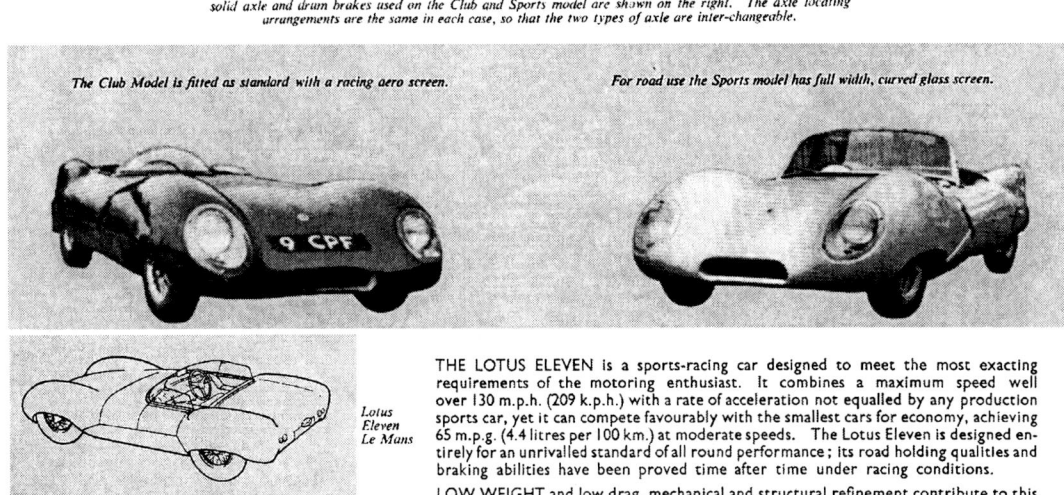

The Club Model is fitted as standard with a racing aero screen.   *For road use the Sports model has full width, curved glass screen.*

Lotus Eleven Le Mans

Lotus Eleven Club

Lotus Eleven Sports

Top kit available on all models

THE LOTUS ELEVEN is a sports-racing car designed to meet the most exacting requirements of the motoring enthusiast. It combines a maximum speed well over 130 m.p.h. (209 k.p.h.) with a rate of acceleration not equalled by any production sports car, yet it can compete favourably with the smallest cars for economy, achieving 65 m.p.g. (4.4 litres per 100 km.) at moderate speeds. The Lotus Eleven is designed entirely for an unrivalled standard of all round performance; its road holding qualities and braking abilities have been proved time after time under racing conditions.

LOW WEIGHT and low drag, mechanical and structural refinement contribute to this paradox of performance. A programme of race development has been pursued over the years following the principles of simplicity and efficiency. The result is a roomy sports two-seater with a performance unequalled anywhere else in the world.

1957 has been a particularly successful year for Lotus, who gained Class wins at Sebring 12-hour race (and 3rd on Index), British Empire Trophy at Oulton Park, Easter Monday at Goodwood, Rouen-Coupe Delamare, Aintree, Roskilde, Spa (3 hours), Silverstone, Karlskoga, etc.

Most outstanding success was the Le Mans victory on Index of performance. This was a double victory in fact, because both first and second places on Index were taken by a 750 cc. and a 1100 cc. Lotus respectively. Had the 750 car not beaten its team-mate the 1100 cc. car would have been the first car of this capacity, ever to win the Index—in the history of the 24-hour race. All four Lotus Elevens which started in the race and which were prototypes of the current model, finished, winning, in addition to first places in the 750 and 1100 cc. classes, 3rd and 4th places in the latter class were also taken by the other two cars. The Biennial Cup was awarded to the 750.

THE LOTUS ELEVEN is available in three versions: the Le Mans model attains the highest standards of performance and is recommended for international competition; it is powered by the Coventry Climax engine and has disc brakes and a de Dion final drive. The Club model is basically similar, having the same engine driving a live axle; it has drum brakes. The Sports model has a similar specification to the Club model but is powered by a Ford 100E 1172 cc. engine. It is eligible as a series production car for the Autosport Championship. Lotus Eleven, Le Mans and Club models have been homologated by the F.I.A. as grand touring cars and as such are eligible for events under Appendix 'J' rules

In accordance with the company's progressive policy, the right to alter specifications without notice is reserved.

LOTUS ENGINEERING CO. LTD.
TOTTENHAM LANE, LONDON, N.8
Telephone: FITzroy 1777

LOGICALLY developed from earlier Lotus designs the frame of the Lotus Eleven, seen on the right, is responsible for the exceptional qualities of road holding for which Lotus cars have an established reputation. Comprising 1 in. (25 mm.) and ¾ in. (19 mm.) square and round steel tubing, it is a welded structure. A sheet metal propeller shaft tunnel acts as a structural member to carry the floor and the rear engine mounting. The frame is devised to accommodate the engine tilted sideways at about 10 degrees from the vertical so as to reduce frontal area, to maintain an efficient induction tract and to facilitate the installation of a variety of carburetter arrangements.

Maintenance and overhaul are facilitated by the extreme accessibility conferred by the design of body. The small drawing (right) shows the four body fasteners and their locations; release of these fasteners enables the front and rear halves of the body to be raised for inspection. As they pivot about pre-loaded rubber bushes, with cam locking devices, the front and rear panelling can then readily be detached simply by lifting off.

This arrangement eliminates the need for opening panels in the front or rear, so making for smooth contours and light weight. These features assist in conferring on the car exceptionally low drag and first class stability. In the opinion of Lawrence Pomeroy, the Lotus "is the fastest car for a given horse-power on any European circuit today". Moreover it is a car which is so well balanced in all its qualities, that all the available power can be used all the time under the right conditions.

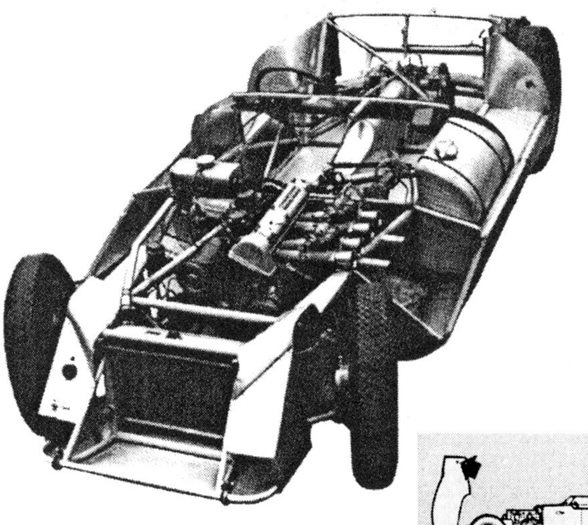

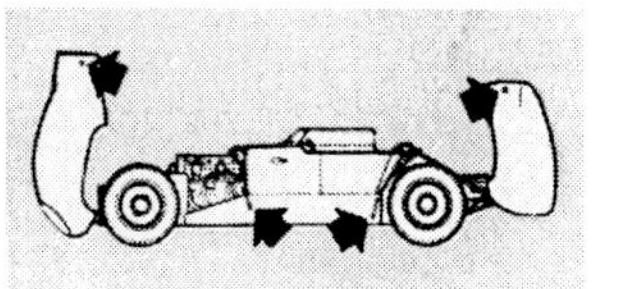

In a few moments the Lotus Eleven can be prepared for inspection, maintenance or overhaul.

THE COVENTRY CLIMAX ENGINE

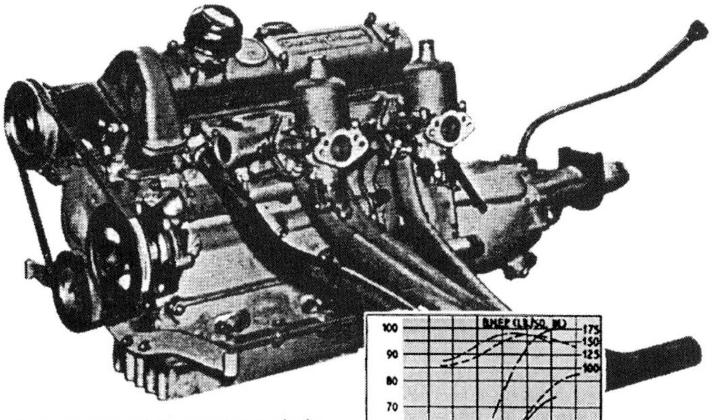

Shown complete with its mountings ready for fitting in the Lotus Eleven, the Coventry Climax 1100 cc. engine is available in two forms; details of power output are given in the graph (right). Two types of 1500 cc. engine are available.

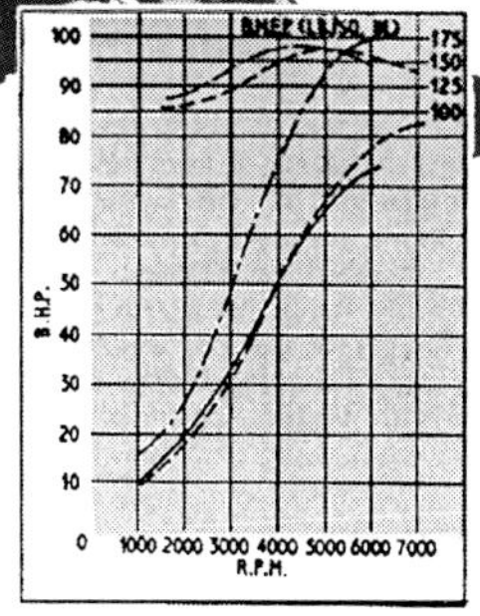

"1100" Stage One ——— "1100" Stage Two — — — "1500" Single o.h.c. — · — · —

LOTUS ELEVEN Le Mans and Club models are fitted normally with the Coventry Climax 1100 cc. engine in standard tune. At extra cost the engine can be obtained in stage two form with a considerable increase in power. Two 1500 cc. units are available in small quantities. Details of the three main types are as follows:

Type	"1100" Stage One	"1100" Stage Two	"1500" Twin o.h.c.
Number of Cylinders	Four	Four	Four
Bore	2.85 in. (72.4 mm.)	2.85 in. (72.4 mm.)	3.2 in. (81.2 mm.)
Stroke	2.625 in. (66.6 mm.)	2.625 in. (66.6 mm.)	2.8 in. (71.1 mm.)
Capacity	66.9 cu. in. (1098 cc.)	66.9 cu. in. (1098 cc.)	90 cu. in. (1475 cc.)
Compression Ratio	9.8:1	9.8:1	10:1
Maximum Output	75 b.h.p. at 6250 r.p.m.	84 b.h.p. at 6800 r.p.m.	145 b.h.p. at 7000 r.p.m.

Features common to all three types are the light alloy cylinder block and crankcase and the easily renewed slip fit cylinder liners. Different liners, pistons and crankshaft in the same block provide the larger capacity of the FWB unit.

The cylinder head has a single overhead camshaft in these models. The camshaft is driven from a gear reduction off the crankshaft to a jackshaft and thence by a duplex chain to the camshaft sprocket. This is located by a dowel and setscrew so that the timing is not disturbed when the cylinder head is removed. Other features are direct valve operation through chilled cast iron tappets working in guides surmounting the valve springs. Tappet adjustment is by the use of hardened discs.

The fully counterweighted crankshaft has three identical lead-bronze steel backed main bearings of 2⅛ in. (54 mm.) diameter and 1 in. (25.4 mm.) width. The big end bearings are also lead bronze, 1¾ in. (45 mm.) in diameter, and ⅞ in. (22.2 mm.) wide. The connecting rods are split diagonally for easy withdrawal.

The aluminium pistons have pressure backed "Dykes" pattern compression rings, and a chromium plated top ring. The combustion chambers are wedge shaped and the XB steel valves seat on shrunk-in austenitic cast iron seatings.

LE MANS SERIES II LOTUS ELEVEN SPECIFICATIONS

	Le Mans	Club	Sports
Frame	Multi-tubular space frame comprising 1 in. (25 mm.) and ¾ in. (19 mm.) square and round tubing of 18 and 20 gauge steel. The propeller shaft tunnel and floor are stressed members forming an integral part of the frame. The tunnel carries the rear engine mounting as well as torque reaction from the final drive unit. The engine is carried on two rubber mountings at the front and a single rubber mounting at the rear around the gearbox; it is tilted sideways through approximately 10 degrees; this has the dual advantage of reducing frontal area and permitting a carburetter arrangement with horizontal induction tracts. The rear framing incorporates a readily detachable spare wheel mounting, to provide ready access to the differential assembly for quick changes of axle ratio.		
Front Suspension	Independent by transverse wish bone incorporating a roll bar. Springing by combined coil spring-damper units reacting through a single attachment point at each end.	Independent by swing axles incorporating combined coil spring-damper units reacting through a single attachment point each end.	
Rear Suspension	De Dion rear suspension with wheels located by parallel trailing arms and a diagonal member on the offside providing lateral location. Bearing housings are picked up circumferentially by the de Dion tube and the out board universal joint is inside the tube thus reducing the loads affecting the assembly. Special seals eliminate unnecessary friction.	Proprietary live rear axle located by similar parallel trailing arms and a diagonal member to provide lateral location. The design of the rear axle has been devised to permit ready replacement by the de Dion system employed on the Le Mans model if required and incorporates identical coil spring damper units.	
Brakes	Ultra light hydraulically operated 9½ in. (241 mm.) disc brakes, outboard at the front, inboard at the rear. Horizontally mounted hand brake operating the rear calipers through inner and outer cables.	Hydraulically operated two leading shoe drum brakes. Cast iron drums, 9 in. (229 mm.) diameter at the front, 8 in. (203 mm.) at the rear. Separate front and rear master cylinders fed from single hydraulic fluid reservoir containing individual front and rear compartments; horizontally mounted hand brake operating rear brakes through mechanical linkage. Operating mechanism in each case similar to Le Mans.	
Steering	Lightweight rack and pinion steering gear with special forged steering arms.	Rack and pinion steering gear.	
Power Unit	Coventry Climax 1100 engine. Details in separate engine data panel. Provision has been made for fitting the 1500 cc. single o.h.c. engine, or the FPF twin o.h.c. 1500 cc. engine producing 150 b.h.p. when available, at extra cost.		Ford 100E 1172 cc. side valve four cylinder engine producing approximately 40 b.h.p. at 4500 r.p.m. in standard form. Compression ratio, 8.5:1.
Transmission	Single dry plate clutch, 7¼ in. (184 mm.) diameter, mechanically operated. Special four speed close ratio gearbox, with following ratios: first, 2.5:1, second, 1.67:1, third, 1.23:1, top, 1:1, Reverse, 2.5:1.	Single dry plate clutch, 7¼ in. (184 mm.) diameter, mechanically operated. Proprietary four speed gearbox with following ratios: first, 4.08:1, second, 2.58:1, third, 1.66:1, top, 1:1, Reverse, 5.17:1. "Le Mans" gearbox available at extra cost.	Single dry plate clutch, mechanically operated. Ford three-speed gearbox as standard, with following ratios: first, 3.664:1, second, 2.007:1, top, 1:1, reverse, 4.79:1. Close ratio gears with following ratios, 2.34:1, 1.33:1, 1:1, available at extra cost.
Final Drive	Hypoid final drive unit. Standard ratio 4.55:1, following axle ratios available at option: 5.375 5.125 4.875, 4.55, 4.22, 3.89, 3.73:1. Typical speeds per 1000 r.p.m. (with standard 5.00 by 15 rear tyres): 3.89:1 = 19.52 m.p.h. (31.41 k.p.h.) per 1000 r.p.m. 4.22:1 = 18 m.p.h. (28.97 k.p.h.) per 1000 r.p.m 4.55:1 = 16.7 m.p.h. (26.87 k.p.h.) per 1000 r.p.m. 4.89 = 15.55 m.p.h. (25 k.p.h.) per 1000 r.p.m.		
Cooling System	Fully ducted cross flow radiator with remote header tank.		
Fuel System	Single light alloy side tank, 8¼ gallons (38 litres) capacity. SU pump mounted alongside tank for Le Mans and Club models. Additional 11 gallon (50 litres) tank complete with pump and pipe lines available at extra cost.		
Bodywork	Full width two-seater bodywork with all wheels enclosed. Front and rear panelling hinge or easily removed for access to engine and final drive, and centre panelling readily removed. Two drop-down doors incorporating map pockets. Dash panel covered to match upholstery. On the Le Mans model a full-width Perspex screen is standard, but a metal tonneau cover and head fairing are available as optional extras. On Club models an aero screen, and on Sports models a full width glass screen are fitted as standard. Slightly modified form of wheel arches has been adopted to give extra clearance for the larger tyres necessary when FPF engine is used.		
Electrical System	Special lightweight 12 volt 31 amp-hr. battery, weight 24 lb. (10.8 kg.) located in tail beside spare wheel. Coil and distributor, centrifugal advance and retard, belt driven dynamo, automatic voltage control. Fuse box mounted on dash panel. Recessed Lucas Le Mans 7 in. (178 mm.) headlamps and separate side lamps, twin stop-tail lights, rear number plate-stop lamp, high frequency horn. Instrument lighting. Screen wiper on Club and Sports models, if required.		
Instruments	3 in. (76 mm.) tachometer 0-8000 r.p.m., oil pressure gauge, water temperature gauge and ammeter. Speedometer available at extra cost.		3 in. (76 mm.) speedometer 0-150 m.p.h., oil pressure gauge, water temperature gauge, and ammeter. Tachometer available at extra cost.
Wheels and Tyres	Knock on 15in. wire wheels with identical rims front and rear are fitted with 4.50 x 15 tyres at the front and 5.00 x 15 tyres at the rear. 4.50 x 15 spare wheel mounted under rear panelling.		
Dimensions	Wheelbase, 7 ft. 4 in. (2160 mm.); front track, 3 ft. 11 in. (1181 mm.), rear track, 3 ft. 11 in. (1194 mm.), overall length, 11 ft. 2 in. (3403 mm.) overall width, 5ft. (1524 mm.) height to top of fin, 3 ft. 1 in. (939.8 mm.), height to top of scuttle, 2 ft. 3 in. (686.8 mm.), minimum ground clearance (adjustable in Club and Sports models) 5 in. (127 mm.)		
Weight	Standard Le Mans model, less fuel, 860 lb. (390 kg.). Weight of other models varies according to specifications.		

SMILING—and well Colin Chapman might, if his latest Lotus performs as well as it looks here, in its racing form with head fairing and wrap-around screen.

THE NEW LOTUS-CLIMAX "ELEVEN"

Exciting New Coventry-Climax-engined car in "Le Mans" and "Club" forms—Dry Weight of $7\frac{5}{8}$ cwts

IN view of the phenomenally successful season that the Lotus enjoyed in 1955, particularly in the hands of its designer, Colin Chapman, one might be excused for anticipating that the current model would continue in production unchanged. Yet the indefatigable Colin has produced a new type which is an improvement in almost every important respect. The new model is called the "Eleven", meaning that it is both Mark XI and 1,100 c.c. in capacity. It comes in two versions.

One of these, the "Le Mans", has disc brakes and a de Dion rear axle. The other, the "Club", is considerably cheaper, and has a normal rear axle and drum brakes. But the chassis, body, suspension units and propelling machinery are identical for both models. Thus, the owner of a "Club" can convert it to a "Le Mans" as soon as he has saved up enough money. The exact prices, incidentally, had not been worked out at the time of writing.

The new chassis frame follows the general principles of the old one, having main steel tubes of 1 in. diameter and subsidiary ones of $\frac{3}{4}$ in. size, in 18 or 20 gauge section according to their work. The transmission tunnel is now a stressed member, and is made from 20 gauge strong aircraft alloy sheet. It takes the final drive torque reaction, part of the floor load, and supports the rear engine mounting.

The front suspension follows tradition, being by modified swing axles. It has a lower pivot than previously to give less front roll stiffness and consequently a shade less understeer. There is a new rack and pinion steering unit, with a short rack to bring the ball joints into the correct position for the suspension geometry. The Girling helical spring units, embracing hydraulic telescopic dampers, are shorter than before and have less travel, due to being mounted nearer the centre pivots. The disc brakes are also of Girling manufacture.

At the rear, a new de Dion axle saves 10 valuable unsprung pounds. The tube is pierced to allow the articulated half-shafts to pass through, giving them considerably greater length and less deflection for the universal joints. The short tubular shafts are still extensions from the Rudge-type hubs, but are now carried on a pair of taper roller races in a light alloy housing. Two pairs of radius arms locate the axle either side, and one of these is triangulated into an A-frame to absorb lateral forces, rubber bushes avoiding binding in roll. Both the propeller shaft and the half-shafts are of Hardy Spicer manufacture.

The disc brakes are inboard on the "Le Mans" car, but the drum brakes are mounted normally on the "Club" model. The axle of this car is a proprietary component built up from various B.M.C. parts, and takes the same nose piece, crown wheel and pinion as the de Dion final drive. The alternative ratios available are 5.1, 4.9, 4.5, 4.2, and 3.9 to 1. Thus, all circuits from the slowest to the fastest are suitably accommodated. Similar helical spring and damper assemblies are employed for both types of axle.

The Coventry-Climax engine is built up in unit with a new gearbox having an Austin A30 case, with Lotus close ratio gears included in the "Le Mans" specification. The reductions are 1.23, 1.67, and 2.5 to 1. Two rubber mountings support the engine low down in front, and a third holds the gearbox in the transmission tunnel. The cylinder head of the Climax engine already has an inclination to the nearside, but the engine is also inclined in this direction to the extent of 10 degrees. This permits a lower bonnet line and a straight induction pipe from the horizontal twin S.U. carburetters. The carburetters are flexibly mounted on rubber induction stubs, and the float chamber is secured on rubber to the frame, with flexible tubes to the carburetters. This is to avoid frothing of the fuel, due to vibration. The well-known single overhead camshaft, over-square, light alloy Climax engine is too well known to require detailed description. For the Lotus, it has a modified sump and oil intake to allow for the inclined mounting.

The body is even better streamlined than last year's model. The scuttle is of the same height, but the bonnet and tail slope down more steeply. They both open on pivots at the extreme front and rear of the frame, but the pivots are ingeniously contrived so that, by a cam action, they unlock on being opened to their limit and allow the two body sections to be taken right off. The consequent accessibility could scarcely be bettered.

Much development work has resulted in a lighter and completely ducted radiator, fed from a smaller air entry, being entirely adequate for the engine. Cooling drag has been reduced, and the piping to the scuttle-mounted header tank has been simplified. Full-sized lamps are now sunk into the front wheel fairings, and covered by profiled transparent plastic shields. For racing, the passenger's seat is covered and a wrap-around screen and head fairing are used. The typical stabilizing fins have been all but deleted, the head fairing

BODY REMOVAL is a simple and speedy business, revealing "the works". The 4 cyl., o.h.c. "over-square" Coventry-Climax engine is inclined at 10 deg. to keep the bonnet line low.

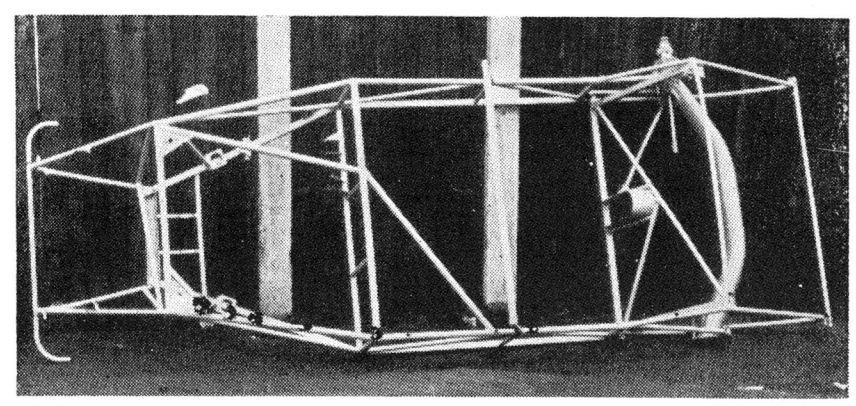

DRY WEIGHT of only 7⅝ cwts. owes much to the chassis structure (above), built up of 1 in. and ¾ in. steel tubes.

HUB DETAIL: (Right) Drive shaft roller bearings are housed in this light alloy casting, to which are attached the de Dion tube and the double radius arms.

having sufficient depth to ensure the necessary stability. For short races, a 9½ gallon fuel tank in the nearside of the body is used, but an extra 11 gallon tank can be installed in the offside outer body panel. There is no rear tank in the tail, only the battery and spare wheel occupying that space.

The body has two doors containing map pockets, which are horizontally hinged and open downwards. Both seats are identical, the light alloy pans resting on the floor with ½ in. Dunlopillo padding beneath the upholstery. The seat squabs have rubberized hair padding. The steering wheel is of duralumin with three spokes, and a leather covered rim. It is attached to a column which turns in rubber-mounted nylon bearings, and has two Hooke's joints running at fairly considerable angles. The throttle linkage is extremely sturdy, and the brake pedal has a compensating bar pivoting directly upon it through a small ball race, and operating two master cylinders with a divided supply tank for safety. The hand brake lever is horizontally mounted under the nearside of the scuttle. A new type of rev. counter is driven at one-third engine speed from the dynamo, which is larger and slower running than before.

Some dimensions of this most exciting new 1,100 c.c. sports car are: Wheelbase, 7 ft. 2 ins.; track, 3 ft. 10½ ins. (front), 3 ft. 11 ins. (rear); overall length, 11 ft. 2 ins. (reduced 6 ins.); width, 5 ft.; height to top of scuttle, 2 ft. 3 ins.; height of front roll centre, 5¾ ins., rear 9½ ins.; tyres, 4.50 ins. (front), 5.00 ins. (rear) on 15 ins. knock-on racing wire wheels. The car has been weighed dry, and without a spare wheel, at 7⅝ cwt.

In addition, the Lotus XI will be supplied as a road sports car. This model will be fitted with the Ford 100D 1,172 c.c. engine and gearbox. It will have a full-width curved glass screen with windscreen wipers, and will also be available with a hard top.

Most certainly, the new Lotus will be most formidable as a competition car, and the lap records held by the 1955 model should certainly be beaten. It is in all ways a more attractive car than its predecessor, and Colin Chapman is to be congratulated on a most remarkable design.

JOHN V. BOLSTER.

BRISTOL ENGINES FOR A.C.

AN agreement has been reached between A.C. Cars, Ltd., and Bristol Cars, Ltd., whereby the well-known and race-proved Bristol 2-litre engine will be made available as an alternative power unit in the A.C. Ace and Aceca models. Performance of these cars should thus be augmented considerably, making them suitable for competition work; speeds approaching 130 m.p.h. will be possible, and the new A.C.-Bristol should prove one of the fastest of 2-litre series production sports cars in the world. The normal Ace and Aceca models, with the well-known six-cylinder single o.h.c. A.C. engine, will still be available.

TAIL END (above) of the Lotus body is blunt in profile but, unlike the "snow plough" Cooper-Climax, has rounded edges.
DE DION back-end (right) is lighter by some 10 valuable lbs.; this type of axle features on the "Le Mans" car, which also has inboard disc brakes.
WITH AND WITHOUT: (Below) The Lotus "Eleven" in competition form with head fairing and wrap-around screen in place and (right) without these accoutrements to speed.

PRODUCT OF GENIUS

New Lotus Shows Further Evidence of Infinite Capacity for Taking Pains

THE value of reducing those arch-enemies of performance—weight and drag—has been demonstrated by Colin Chapman in his evolution of the Lotus sports car. For the coming season this process has been carried a few stages further and the performance of the new Lotus-Climax Eleven Le Mans will be tested first at Sebring, U.S.A., in the twelve-hour sports car race on March 24. Three of the new cars will be fitted with the renowned Coventry-Climax F.W.A. engine with Mark II tuning, and the fourth, belonging to Briggs Cunningham and to be driven by Chapman and L. Bastrup, will be powered by the 1,460 c.c. F.W.B. version of the same basic engine.

The chassis frame is of the space type, constructed mainly from 1in and $\frac{3}{4}$in round and square section tubes for the main members; their thickness is either 18 or 20 s.w.g., dependent upon the load. Gas welding is used throughout the structure. The frame is approximately 2in lower than last year, to give unobstructed access to the carburettor side of the engine. Kerb weight with oil and water, but without fuel and spare wheel, is the remarkably low one of 855 lb ($7\frac{5}{8}$ cwt). On the starting line this should give an all-up weight of 1,150 lb. Performance-wise, this gives about 160 b.h.p. per ton for the 1,100 c.c. version and a shade over 190 b.h.p. per ton for the $1\frac{1}{2}$-litre.

Aerodynamic efficiency has been increased by full enclosure of the front and rear wheels, achieved by hinging the nose and tail sections at their extremities. Thus the whole chassis can be exposed. Furthermore, the hinged-up sections can be removed while the car is on racing-type jacks.

The characteristic stabilizing fins over the rear wheels of the Mark IX have been considerably reduced and a detachable head fairing is now fitted. A metal cover is provided over the passenger's seat. A heat-formed Perspex windscreen wraps round the driver and merges into the head fairing. For normal competition a $9\frac{1}{2}$-gallon fuel tank is outrigged from the chassis frame on the passenger's side, but this can be augmented by a second 11-gallon tank on the right side.

A considerable saving of weight has been achieved on the final drive unit and de Dion rear axle. The nosepiece carrying the spiral bevel and differential assembly is a standard production unit with which alternative ratios 5.125, 4.89,

The nose section of the car hinges forward for access to the engine and suspension. The rear panelling is arranged to hinge upwards in a similar manner for access to the final drive unit, brakes and suspension

4.55 and 4.22 to 1 are available. Special crown wheel and bevel pinions are also being manufactured to obtain ratios of 3.89 and 3.66 for fast circuits. A new magnesium final drive casing has been designed specifically for the Girling inboard disc brakes. The caliper assembly is mounted forward to reduce offset of the de Dion tube, and unsprung weight is reduced by about 15 lb. This redesign of the rear end has saved eight oil seals, for which Chapman claims that he gains approximately one horsepower, which is typical of his approach.

The hub of the de Dion axle carries two opposed taper roller bearings at each side for the wheels and their effective base is wider than with the two ball races previously used. Their use, in conjunction with the closer spacing of the disc brake assembly, has permitted longer axle drive shafts as the outboard universal joint is much closer to the wheel. Thus the angularity of the shafts and consequent movement of the sliding splines is reduced. This hub assembly, with a controlled length of spacer between the two taper roller bearings to achieve a required degree of preload, is locked up by the wheel nut, which results in a very light assembly.

Modifications to the mounting of the integral coil spring and damper unit have resulted in the de Dion tube being relieved of torsional loadings. Location of the axle tube is achieved by tubular rods, the ends of which are rubber bushed. Fore and aft location is by two parallel arms at each side, which obviates torsional loading of the axle tube. Transverse location is by means of a further radius tube on the right-hand side, which forms a modified A bracket with the lower fore and aft arms. This triangular member is so arranged that the effect is of a Panhard rod some six feet long, which results in a near enough vertical movement of the de Dion tube.

Front suspension is by divided front axle, controlled by a radius arm each side. Sooner or later the inherent disadvantages of this type of suspension for racing will have to be recognized. Colin Chapman freely admits that he has managed to keep abreast of increasing speeds by lowering the roll centre from time to time. A further reduction of $\frac{3}{4}$in has been achieved and it is now $5\frac{3}{4}$in above ground level at the front and $9\frac{1}{4}$in at the rear. This type of suspension is very attractive for use in conjunction with space type frames, as the loads are widely spaced.

Rack and pinion steering is used, but now the track rods are mounted directly on the end of the rack.

A weight saving of 31 lb has been achieved on the gear box. The casing and selection mechanism is standard Austin A.30, and a special set of running gears has been designed. In designing these gears it has been possible to obtain

Aerodynamic efficiency of the Lotus-Climax Eleven Le Mans model has been improved by enclosing the front wheels and adopting a head fairing in conjunction with a fully wrapped round screen. Weight has also been saved

A redesigned de Dion tube and hub assembly has reduced unsprung weight and given longer drive shafts. Fore and aft location is by two parallel arms at each side. Transverse location is by a tubular arm which forms an "A" bracket with the lower of the parallel arms on the right-hand side

The Club model uses a live axle with outboard drum and shoe brakes. The locating members are identical with the de Dion version and a conversion to this type is possible without structural alterations

Inboard Girling disc brakes are used at the rear. The caliper assembly is mounted forward to reduce offset to the de Dion tube. The stressed propeller shaft tunnel absorbs the torque reaction loads of the final drive unit

very close ratios to make more effective use of the engine power. A standard 7¼in single dry plate clutch manufactured by Borg and Beck is used for the 1,100 c.c. engine, but to cater for the increased torque and to enable the same size of clutch housing to be used, the firm is developing a twin plate version of the same size for the 1½-litre engine.

To avoid a bonnet bulge to clear the carburettors, the engine is swung over 10 deg from the vertical towards the carburettor side.

The power output of the 1,100 c.c. Coventry-Climax has been increased for the coming season by the use of a new camshaft with increased lift and valve opening period. With this and a new induction system, but still retaining the twin S.U. 1½in diameter semi-downdraught carburettors, the power output has been increased to 83 b.h.p. at 6,800 r.p.m., with a peak b.m.e.p. of 164 lb per sq in at 5,000 r.p.m.

Coventry Climax are also releasing a limited quantity of their F.W.B. engines of 1,460 c.c. capacity, pending full production next year. These are a direct development of the single camshaft 1,100 c.c. unit. Within the same basic structure the bore has been increased from 2.850in to 3in, and the stroke similarly from 2.625in to 3.150in. The same cylinder head and valve assembly is retained and thus by the use of a new crankshaft, pistons and cylinder liners, the larger capacity is achieved. Carburettors are the same size, with different needles to suit the modified power curve. The compression ratio is lower at 8.6 to 1.

The F.W.B. engine gives an extremely creditable output of 100 b.h.p. at 6,200 r.p.m., which is rather surprising when it is remembered that the valve sizes are common to the 1,100 c.c. unit. If the enviable reputation for reliability which the F.W.A. engine has established can be retained, this latest Godiva development should ensure a similar supremacy in 1½-litre classes.

Using the same basic chassis and body, the new car is also available as a cheaper Eleven Club model. In this form a B.M.C. live axle is used but its location is identical with that of the de Dion version, and the car is thus easily converted if desired. This model is equipped with Girling drum and shoe brakes, the sizes being 9in diameter by 1¾in wide at the front and 8in diameter by 1¼in wide at the rear. An Eleven sports model using the Ford 100E 1,172 c.c. engine is also available.

The latest design from this very competent young man Chapman should further demonstrate the value of obtaining performance by reducing drag and weight. By approaching these matters scientifically he has jumped to the front in a very short time, and has also built up a very fine and enthusiastic establishment which is now turning out these specialized cars at the rate of four per week —H. M.

BRIEF SPECIFICATION

Engine: Coventry-Climax 4-cyl, single O.H.C.

	F.W.A. (Mark II)	F.W.B.
Bore	2.850in	3.00in
Stroke	2.625in	3.150in
Capacity	1,098 c.c. (66.9 cu in)	1,460 c.c. (89.2 cu in)
Compression Ratio	9.8	8.6
Max. Power	83 b.h.p.	100 b.h.p.
Revs. at Peak Power	6,800 r.p.m.	6,200 r.p.m.
Max. b.m.e.p.	164 lb per sq in	168 lb per sq in
lb/ft Torque per cu in	1.076	1.120

Transmission:

Clutch	7¼in Borg & Beck single dry plate	7¼in Borg & Beck twin dry plate
Gear Box	4 speed, synchromesh on 2nd, 3rd and 4th	
Ratios	Top gear 1.0	
	Third gear 1.23	
	Second gear 1.67	
	First 2.50	
Axle	Spiral bevel	
	Ratios available, 5.125; 4.89; 4.55; 4.22; 3.89; 3.66	

Brakes: Eleven Le Mans, 9½in dia. Girling discs. Eleven Club, Girling drum and shoe, 9in dia. by 1¾in front, 8in. dia. by 1¼in rear.
Wheels and Tyres: Dunlop 15in dia. rims, identical front and rear. Tyres, front 4.50—15in; rear 5.00-15in.
Main Dimensions: Wheelbase, 7ft 2in. Track, front, 3ft 10½in; rear, 3ft 11in. Overall length, 11ft 2in. Overall width, 5ft. Height (top of fin), 3ft 1in; (top of scuttle), 2ft 3in. Kerb weight less fuel, 855 lb (7⅝ cwt.).

REDUCED in hei[ght]
and overall length, [the]
latest London-built r[ac]-
ing 2-seater is seen w[ith]
passenger seat cove[r]
and a fairing beh[ind]
the driver's head. Pl[as]-
tic covers over fi[xed]
lamps will replace [the]
retractable headlig[hts]
used last year.

A RATIONALIZED RANGE OF HIGH-PERFORMANCE CARS

Lighter, Lowe[r

LOWER tail fins are now used on the full-width body of this ultra-light car. Divided by the propeller shaft tunnel which is now a structural member, the cockpit is comfortably wide, the lightweight steering wheel and Austin gear lever being prominent in the left-hand view.

HINGES now support the nose and tail sections of the body, elimination of a separate bonnet panel contributing to improved streamlining. Air from the cross-flow radiator is ducted out beneath the body.

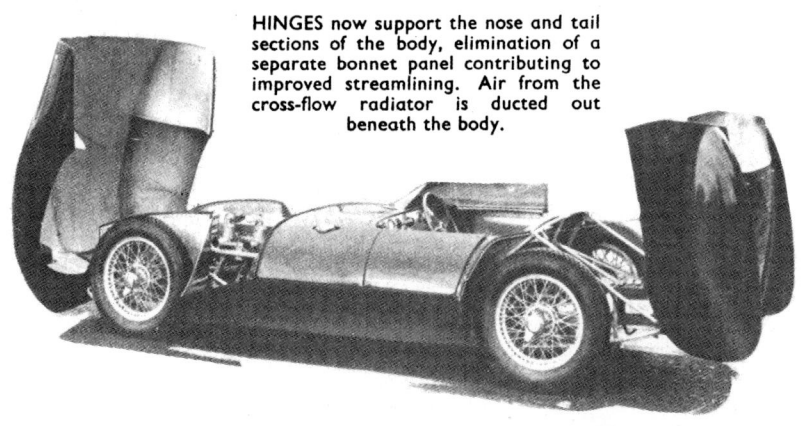

ONE basic type of Lotus only is to be made for 1956, the Lotus XI, but the same body and chassis will be available in three forms. For racing, the Le Mans model illustrated on these pages has been designed by Colin Chapman and his helpers. At a lower price, the Club model uses the same Coventry Climax engine but has a full windscreen, drum brakes and a live rear axle. Finally, components are offered from which a Sports model with 1,172 c.c. Ford engine may be built.

More compact overall dimensions account for the most conspicuous changes since last year, tail fins having shrunk to vestigial form, but a quickly removable head fairing is available. The multi-tubular Lotus frame has been completely redesigned, with savings in weight and overall height as well as improvements in accessibility. The main frame tubes are set at a vertical spacing of approx. 12 in., the lower tubes being of square section so that a light-alloy undertray and boxed propeller shaft tunnel secured with blind rivets can be used as stiffeners.

Swing axle front suspension appears in slightly improved form, with lowered pivot points for the axle halves and a neater inboard mounting for coil springs encircling Girling telescopic shock absorbers. Steering is by pinion and ultra-short rack, with two universal joints in the steering column. The de Dion rear axle has been redesigned to reduce unsprung weight by 15 lb., new hubs large enough to enclose the universal joints allowing the axle shafts to be longer, and a diagonal radius

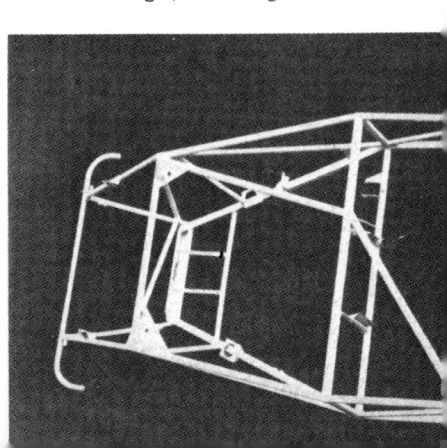

STRIPPED of its nose, tail and centre section panels, the Lotus XI Le Mans is readily accessible for maintenance work. Side mounting of the fuel tank, and the wire wheels which may be of either steel or light alloy, are also evident.

LOTUS

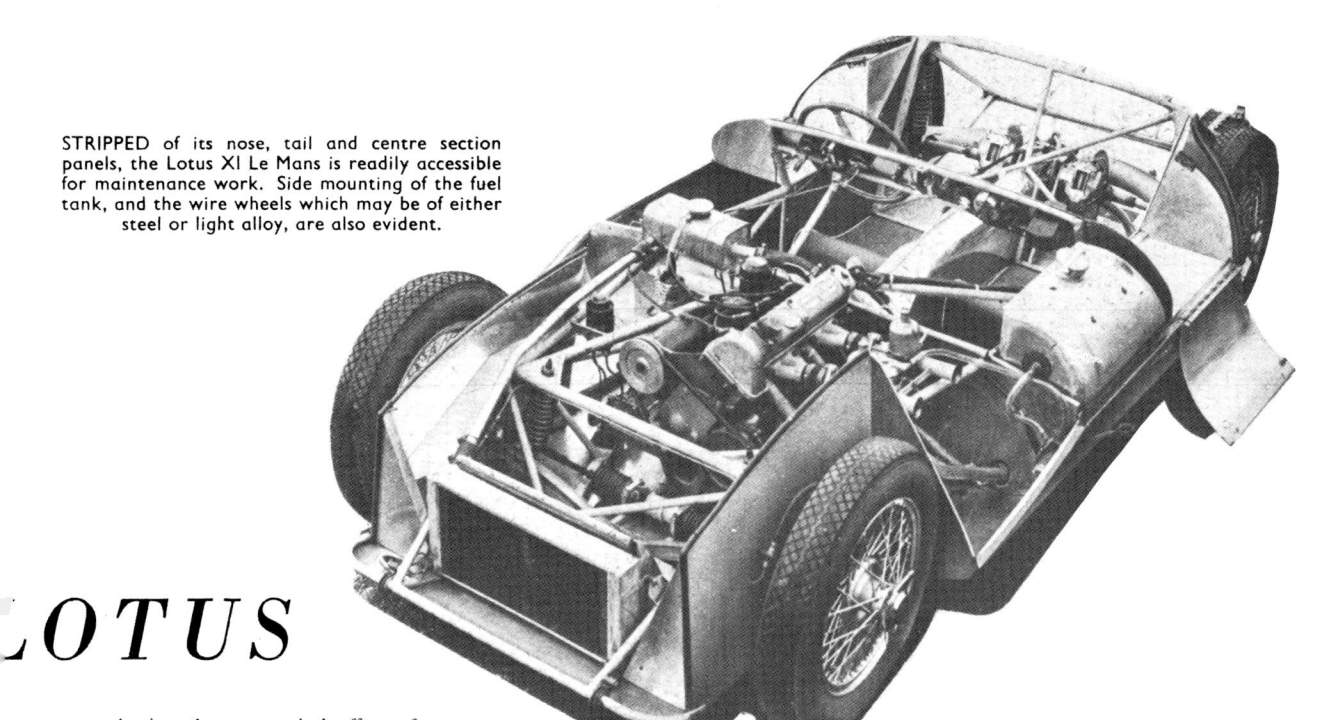

arm having the geometrical effect of a Panhard rod approximately 5 ft. long. Readily interchangeable with the de Dion axle is an Austin A30 live axle, converted to knock-on wire wheels and with a choice of ratios, the same final drive gears being enclosed in a special light alloy casting for the more costly de Dion layout.

For 1956, a more highly tuned version of the 1,097 c.c. Coventry Climax type FWA engine can be obtained, giving 83 b.h.p. at 6,850 r.p.m. instead of 75 b.h.p. at 6,250 r.p.m., the engine being inclined to the left at 10° and the carburetters flexibly mounted. A few 1½-litre type FWB examples of this engine, enlarged to 76.2 mm. bore by 80 mm. stroke, will also be raced this season, these developing approximately 100 b.h.p. at 6,200 r.p.m., and with slight modification this chassis can accommodate a 2-litre Bristol engine tilted over on its side. An entirely new type of gearbox is now used, basically the Austin A30 unit but incorporating close-ratio gears with much wider teeth, synchromesh action being retained. A single plate clutch is used on 1,100 c.c. cars, two plates on the 1,500 c.c. examples.

Girling hydraulic disc brakes continue to be used on the Le Mans model, the rear units mounted inboard but with a lighter and stronger mounting of the calipers. Simpler versions of the Lotus use Girling drum brakes, 9-in. size at the front and 8-in. at the rear. The new body can mount a hard-top for sports use. Fuel is carried in a 9½-gallon side tank, and a second 11-gallon tank can be fitted on the right if required.

LOTUS XI LE MANS

Engine dimensions	
Cylinders	4
Bore	72.4 mm.
Stroke	66.6 mm.
Cubic capacity	1,097 c.c.
Piston area	25.5 sq. in.
Valves	Single o.h. camshaft
Compression ratio	9.8/1

Engine performance	
Max. power	75 b.h.p.
at	6,250 r.p.m.
Max. b.m.e.p.	144 lb./sq. in.
at	5,000 r.p.m.
B.H.P. per sq. in. piston area	2.94
Piston speed at max. power	2,740 ft./min.

Engine details	
Carburetter	Two inclined 1¼-in. S.U.
Ignition timing control	Centrifugal
Fuel pump	S.U. electrical
Fuel capacity	9½ gallons (optional 20½)
Oil filter	Full-flow filter and floating pump intake
Cooling system	Pump
Electrical system	12-volt

Transmission	
Clutch	Single dry plate
Gearbox ratios:	
Top (s/m)	1.00
3rd (s/m)	1.23
2nd (s/m)	1.67
1st	2.50
Final drive	Hypoid bevel, optional ratios 3.66, 3.89, 4.22, 4.55, 4.89 or 5.125

Chassis details	
Brakes	Girling disc
Suspension:	
Front	Coil springs and divided axle I.F.S.
Rear	Coil springs and de Dion axle tube
Shock absorbers	Girling telescopic
Wheel type	Centre-lock wire
Tyre size	4.50—15 front (optional 4.25—15) 5.00—15 rear (optional 4.50)
Steering gear	Rack and pinion

Dimensions	
Wheelbase	7 ft. 2 in.
Track: Front	3 ft. 10½ in.
Rear	3 ft. 11 in.
Overall length	11 ft. 2 in.
Overall width	5 ft. 0 in.
Overall height	Scuttle, 2 ft. 3 in.; fin, 3 ft. 1 in.
Kerb weight, without fuel	7¾ cwt.

Performance factors (At kerb weight)	
Piston area, sq. in. per ton	67
Top gear m.p.h. per 1,000 r.p.m.	17.1 with 4.22 axle
Top gear m.p.h. per 1,000 ft./min. piston speed	39.1 with 4.22 axle
Litres per ton-mile	5,050 with 4.22 axle

TUBES are welded up to form the lightweight girder frame, the lower ones of rectangular section to permit attachment of the undertray by blind rivets. Pairs of parallel radius arms on each side of the car, and a single diagonal arm, can be used to locate either a de Dion (*left*) or conventional (*right*) type of rear axle.

The Lotus Eleven in Le Mans form, though bearing a family likeness to the earlier cars, is lower and more compact. The lamps are now permanently fixed behind perspex covers, instead of on the primitive swinging arms of previous years. The body now has two downward folding doors

The Marl

Photographs by John Ross

The Coventry-Climax engine is now tilted 10 degrees from vertical, thus lowering the bonnet line

The rear of the car showing inboard Girling disc brakes and new de Dion layout. The stressed central tunnel can also be seen

The new lightened space-frame seen from the forward end

The air entry for cooling the rear brakes and final drive

The location of the outer universal joints is within the de Dion tube

The head fairing and tonneau can be quickly removed

The smoothly contoured windscreen and head fairing

Eleven Lotus

ONE of the fastest small cars in sports car racing last year proved to be the 1100 cc. Lotus-Climax. For 1956, a much lighter and improved version has been introduced, and it is by far the best-looking car yet designed by the Lotus factory. The new Mk. XI will be available as a Le Mans car, club version and sports model with touring equipment. The first two will be supplied with Coventry-Climax engines; one suitable for racing in the important international sports car events, and a less expensive version for club racing.

The design of both models is basically the same, but the more expensive Le Mans car has disc brakes, a de Dion rear axle and a wrap-round screen and head fairing, whilst the club model has Girling two-leading shoe brakes with outboard drums, and live rear axle. The third model, designated the Lotus Sports, will have an 1172 cc. Ford engine and gearbox, with a full-width curved screen. A detachable hard top is to be available later on for this and the club models.

The new frame, common to all three cars, follows the logical development of earlier Lotus designs, and is constructed from 1-inch and ¾-inch steel tubing in 18- and 20-gauge steel.

The propeller shaft tunnel is now a structural member and is used to take torque reaction from the final drive unit, as well as carrying part of the floor and the rear engine mounting. Better location of the engine in the frame now permits a variety of carburettor arrangements. Tilting the engine in the frame by some ten degrees has reduced the frontal area and provided a more efficient induction tract.

An 1100 cc. Coventry-Climax engine in stage I tune, providing 72 b.h.p. at 6,000 r.p.m., is fitted as standard in both the Le Mans and club cars. But an engine with stage II tuning is available which produces 83 b.h.p. at 6,800 r.p.m. Naturally, this costs a little more. A ducted cross-flow type of radiator of reduced weight and improved cooling is normal fitting on the new Mk. XI.

Front suspension follows previous Lotus practice, although a slightly lower roll centre is now provided which should still further improve the handling. The de Dion rear suspension of the Le Mans car has been completely redesigned and the tube diameter increased to 3¼ inches. The outboard universal joint is now inside the tube instead of being located in the conventional manner. The new arrangement has meant a valuable saving here of 15 lbs. unsprung weight. The rear wheels are located longitudinally by parallel trailing arms, whilst a diagonal bracket has been introduced on the offside which provides the equivalent of a Panhard rod 64 inches in length.

A wide range of rear axle ratios are available which should meet the requirements of drivers competing on most circuits, fast or slow. The alternative ratios are: 5·12, 4·89, 4·55, 4·22, 3·89 and 3·66.

The new body is smaller and lighter than previous models and much improved in appearance. It should also be stronger as the number of joint lines has been reduced. The entire front now hinges forward to reveal the engine and suspension. The rear panel hinges in similar fashion. The first production Le Mans car, which now weighs only 7 cwt. 70 lbs. was demonstrated by Colin Chapman in determined fashion through several corners, and it was soon obvious that the latest car from the small Hornsey works handles even better than its predecessors.

THE LO

The Latest of t
which has alre

COLIN CHAPMAN, designer and presiding genius of Lotus Engineering, stands beside the Mk. XI "Le Mans". The wheelbase of this car is 7 ft. 2 ins.; widest track, 3 ft. 11 ins.; overall length, 11 ft. 2 ins.; width, 5 ft.; height, 2 ft. 3 ins., and weight, 7⅝ cwt.

WHEN Colin Chapman built his first special out of an old Austin Seven, at a time when he was still in the R.A.F., he could hardly have guessed that, within 10 years, cars designed by himself, and built by his own firm, would have become famous throughout the entire motor racing world. And would be driven from success to success, with power supplied by an engine originally designed to satisfy a Government specification requiring a light fire pump to be carried by two men, and capable of delivering 350 gallons of water per minute! However, so quick and so successful has been the development of the Lotus sports car, that each year has seen the introduction of at least one new model, until now, in 1956, we have the Mark Eleven, the subject of this new Theo Page drawing.

The family tree of the Mk. XI car can be traced back to 1952 and the Mk. VI, the first Lotus to be Chapman-framed, instead of Austin Seven-based, and still winning races four years later. 1954 saw the Mk. VIII, with an aerodynamic body, designed by Frank Costin, and 1955 the first use of the Coventry Climax engine, in the Mk. IX. Put all three together—frame, body, power unit—add the experience of four years' racing all over Britain and on the Continent, and the result is the Mark XI.

The basis of this latest Lotus is a space-frame, constructed from 1 in. and ¾ in. steel tubing in 18 or 20 gauge section. The transmission tunnel, of 20 gauge alloy sheet, is also a stressed member, taking the torque reaction of the final drive, part of the floor load and supporting the rear engine mounting. The aerodynamic, low-drag bodywork is of stressed alloy sheet, the entire front hinging forward to reveal the engine and front suspension, and having a detachable head faring, in place of the prominent fins of the Mks. VIII and IX. The rear body section also hinges, revealing the back axle, while both halves unlock and become detachable automatically, by means of cam action, when they are opened to their limit. The entire car weighs only 7⅝ cwt.

The front suspension is independent, by swing axles and Girling helical spring units, incorporating hydraulic telescopic dampers. The steering is rack and pinion, and the braking system by Girling discs, mounted inboard at the rear. The de Dion tube of the rear suspension has a diameter of 3¼ ins., the ends of the articulated half-shafts piercing the tube, and being attached within it to the outboard universal joints. The rear axle is located on either side by a pair of parallel radius arms.

Although the Lotus Mk. XI "Le Mans" is now being built, and raced by Team Lotus, with the 1½-litre Coventry Climax engine, the 1,100 c.c. unit was originally installed, and inclined towards the nearside at an angle of 10 degrees to permit a lower bonnet line; this required modification to both the sump and oil intake. Having a single overhead camshaft and twin horizontal SU carburetters, the 1,100 c.c. engine gives 72 b.h.p. at 6,000 r.p.m. in Stage 1 tune, and 83 b.h.p. at 6,800 r.p.m. tuned to Stage 2. The power is transmitted to the final drive, for which a wide range of ratios are available, by means of a

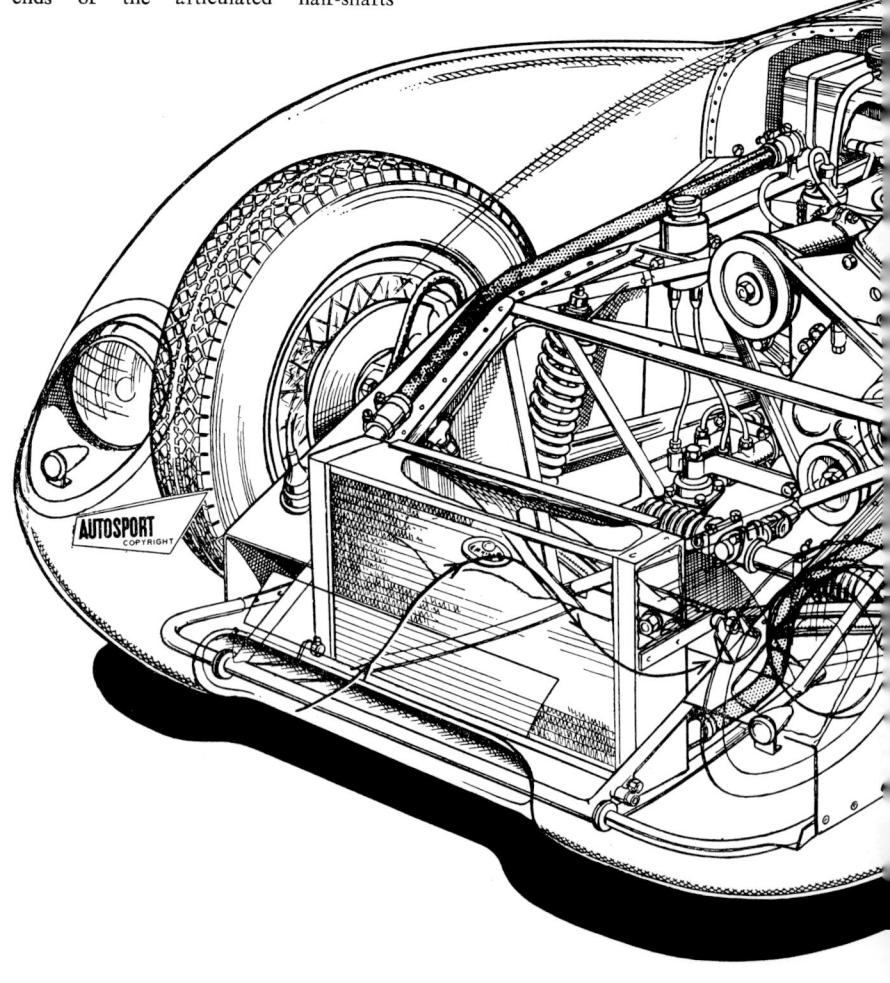

142

US MK. XI "LE MANS"

us Line of Fast Sports-Racing Cars, powered by Coventry-Climax, roved itself extremely successful in 1,100 c.c. and 1,500 c.c. events

Another Exclusive **AUTOSPORT** *Cut-away Drawing by Staff Artist* **THEO PAGE**

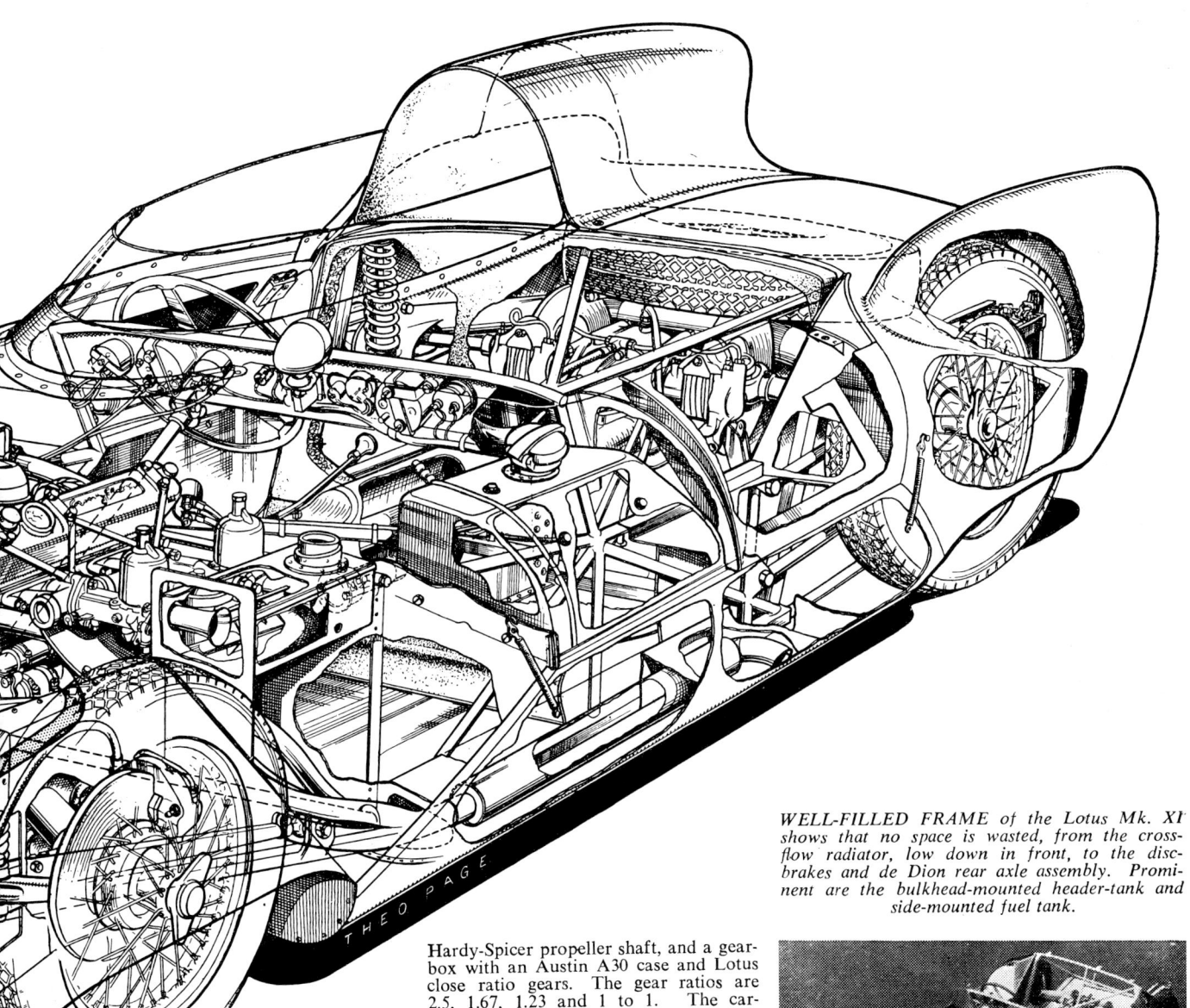

WELL-FILLED FRAME of the Lotus Mk. XI shows that no space is wasted, from the cross-flow radiator, low down in front, to the disc-brakes and de Dion rear axle assembly. Prominent are the bulkhead-mounted header-tank and side-mounted fuel tank.

Hardy-Spicer propeller shaft, and a gearbox with an Austin A30 case and Lotus close ratio gears. The gear ratios are 2.5, 1.67, 1.23 and 1 to 1. The carburetters and float chamber are flexibly mounted and are connected by flexible tubes to avoid frothing of the fuel, while water cooling is effected by means of a ducted cross-flow radiator, the header tank being attached to the bulkhead.

The Mk. XI brings the Lotus story up to date; but future models are planned, using the new twin o.h.c. 1,500 c.c. Coventry Climax engine, and, of course, Formula 2 is on the way. The Lotus tale is far from told.

MAXWELL BOYD.

World Copyright Reserved

JOHN BOLSTER TESTS THE Club Sports Lotus

Fully equipped for touring, this latest Lotus gives 102.2 m.p.h. and 35 m.p.g. from a Ford 10 engine

WHEN one mentions the latest Lotus "Eleven", most people at once think of the 1,100 c.c. and 1½-litre Coventry-Climax-engined cars, that have been covering themselves with glory in all the more important sports car races. There is, however, a simpler and cheaper version with a Ford engine. It retains many of the features of its more exalted brethren, and may in fact be converted to a full Le Mans model by addition of the necessary components. However, it was as a Ford 10-engined car, with conventional rear axle, that I took over my umpteenth Lotus in London recently.

The chassis frame—a genuine "space" type—is constructed of round and square steel tubes. In front is the well-known Lotus swing axle system, but behind is a proprietary rear axle, instead of the de Dion layout of the more expensive models. Normal drum brakes are used in place of the racing discs. The beautifully streamlined body is identical to that of the "racers".

My car had a full-width screen, with wiper, and a detachable hood. I removed the screen and replaced it with a single perspex deflector when timing the maximum speed, but all the other tests were done with the big screen in place. In the tail was a spare wheel, and there was some useful extra space which could be reinforced for carrying impedimenta. There are two shallow doors, but it is best to unfasten the hood when entering, though it can be done without.

The engine of "my" car was a very ordinary "old-type" Ford 10. It had a Ford 8 cylinder head to raise the compression, and enlarged inlet ports and valves. There were twin S.U. carburetters and the export-type water pump. Apart from that, the unit appeared to be aggressively standard, which makes the speed recorded all the more astonishing. Of course, the Ford three-speed gearbox had Buckler close-ratio gears.

On taking my seat, I found that I had plenty of room, and I liked the driving position. First speed was very high, but the Ford engine simply played with the 7¾ cwt. car. (Yes, I weighed it!) Second was a fine gear for fast overtaking, and on top one cruised easily at 80 m.p.h.

At first I was not happy with the steering. It is very light and phenomenally

NO DE DION at the back end, but nevertheless the roadholding is very good indeed. Spare wheel stowage is of the simplest kind, and the 12-volt battery is also housed at the rear.

"quick", so that it is all too easy to wobble, especially after hitting a bump. Eventually, I became fully accustomed to it, and was able to see that it has certain charms. Nevertheless, as a purely personal preference, I would like a little more movement on the wheel. The lock is somewhat restricted, as is usually the case with streamlined bodies, but it is perfectly adequate for normal everyday use on the road.

As the last few Lotuses I have driven were equipped with de Dion axles and inboard brakes, I was interested to try a similar car with an orthodox axle and hub-mounted drums. Of course, the unsprung weight is considerably greater, though the type of springing adopted saves many valuable pounds compared with semi-elliptics. Let me say at once that the roadholding is good for so light a car. Compared with the Le Mans Lotus, one notices the rear axle mostly when accelerating hard from a standing start or away from a bumpy corner. Then, there is more wheelspin, as one would expect. The drum brakes seem just as good as the discs, at least for this 102 m.p.h. version of the Lotus.

That 102.2 m.p.h. maximum speed really does need some comment. For a side-valve 1,172 c.c. Ford—and not by any means a "hot" one—it is beyond all praise. The body shape certainly looks right, and this speed proves that the drag must be phenomenally low. I regret that the road never got really dry during my "ownership" of this car, and so the acceleration figures, good as they are, could easily be improved on a summer's day. It is interesting that, in the first-ever Lotus road test in 1953, I recorded a maximum speed of 88 m.p.h. with an identical engine. Thus, the body alone is worth 14 m.p.h.!

The particular car that I have been driving has often been seen in competition, in the capable hands of Graham

Hill. I, too, drove the little machine at racing speed on Brands Hatch, and found that it was very controllable on a wet track as well as being lots of fun on a relatively dry one. At first, one feels that slight and occasional wandering sensation on the straight, which is typical of front swing axles. One almost forgets this after a few laps, though, and lets the Lotus look after itself.

As a sports touring car, I sampled the vehicle under all conditions in town and country. Colin Chapman advised me to use 18 lb. tyre pressure all round for touring, and 28 lb. (front) and 26 lb. (rear) for racing. Being lazy, I forgot to let the tyres down after a dicing session, and found the ride still quite comfortable at low speeds. The seats are of the competition type, with a minimum of padding, but they are much less tiring on a fast journey than the rock and roll variety.

The headlamps, behind their perspex fairings, are surprisingly powerful, and one can keep up a good speed at night. A very great improvement in the matter of body panel vibration and internal noise in general has been made, compared with the earlier Lotus. The driver and passenger keep warm and dry, even without the hood, and I seldom wore my overcoat during the rigours of a British November. A minor point, easily rectified, concerned the tendency of water off the road to penetrate upwards through the intentional drain holes in the floor. Personally, I would use a couple of corks, but the scientific Mr. Chapman will no doubt design a one-way valve for future models!

It would be no exaggeration to say that the ultra-low streamlined appearance created a real furore. Crowds collected wherever I parked the car, and the interest it aroused was enormous. It has a genuine, functional beauty, absolutely without decoration, and I heard numerous complimentary references from passers-by. I only heard two criticisms. One was from an enormously

Continued on page **164**

WEATHER protection includes a full width windscreen with wiper and a neat detachable hood with a large rear window. These pictures and the one opposite were taken at Brands Hatch.

Specification and Performance Data

Car Tested: Lotus Eleven Sports two-seater.

Engine: Four cylinders, 63.5 mm. x 92.5 mm. (1,172 c.c.). Side valves. 40 b.h.p. at 6,000 r.p.m. Twin S.U. carburetters. Coil and distributor ignition.

Transmission: Single dry plate clutch. Three-speed gearbox with remote control, ratios 4.2, 5.6 and 9.9 to 1. Open propeller shaft to hypoid rear axle.

Chassis: Multi-tubular space frame with stressed light alloy shaft tunnel. Independent front suspension by swing axles with rack and pinion steering. Rear axle on parallel trailing arms, of which one is A-shaped for lateral location. Helical springs and telescopic dampers all round. Knock-on wire wheels fitted 4.50 x 15 ins. tyres (front), 5.00 x 15 ins. tyres (rear). Hydraulic 2LS brakes with twin master cylinders, 9 ins. cast iron drums (front), 8 ins. drums (rear).

Equipment: 12-volt lighting and starting. Rev. counter, ammeter, water temperature and oil pressure gauges.

Dimensions: Wheelbase, 7 ft. 1 in. Track (front), 3 ft. 10 ins.; (rear), 3 ft. 11 ins. Overall length, 11 ft. 2 ins.; width, 5 ft.; height to top of scuttle, 2 ft. 3 ins. Ground clearance, 5 ins. Weight, 7¾ cwt.

Performance: (Damp road) Maximum speed, 102.2 m.p.h. Speeds in gears, 2nd 80 m.p.h., 1st 45 m.p.h. Standing quarter mile, 18.4 secs. Acceleration: 0-30 m.p.h., 4 secs.; 0-50 m.p.h., 9 secs.; 0-60 m.p.h., 12.6 secs.; 0-80 m.p.h., 23.2 secs.

Fuel Consumption: 35 m.p.g. (approx.).

ACCELERATION GRAPH

FULLY ACCESSIBLE, thanks to the completely detachable bodywork, the engine is revealed as that faithful work-horse, the Ford 10, with basic twin-carburetter modifications.

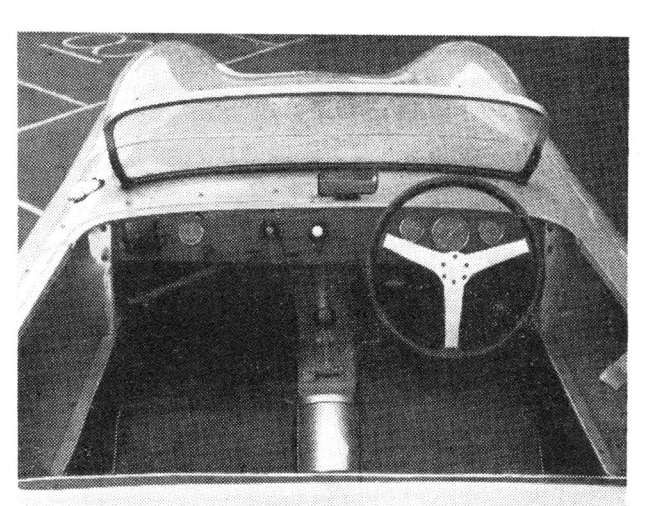

FUNCTIONAL cockpit layout contains all the necessary instruments and a small duralumin steering wheel with sponge-rubber rim, leather covered. The gear-change for the Ford box is of the Dellow type.

LOTUS FOR 1957

Stand 121 at the 1956 International Motor Show, Earls Court, will indeed be a source of attraction for sports car enthusiasts. Lotus Engineering Company Ltd., of 7 Tottenham Lane, Hornsey, London, N.8, will exhibit some of the fastest sporting machines manufactured in this country.

THIS year is the Lotus Company's first at Earls Court, as a full-scale motor manufacturer. That is indeed an important milestone in the life of a company which started only a few years ago making chassis and component parts for specials. Until then the name conjured up thoughts of an exotic flower or perhaps a pair of shoes.

Lotus production for 1957 is based on one model—the " Eleven "—which is offered for several sports car purposes. This design is intended to give an all-round performance of a high standard—road holding qualities and braking abilities have been proved time after time under racing conditions. Light weight and low drag, mechanical and structural refinement contribute to this performance.

Following the principles of simplicity and efficiency a programme of race development has been pursued, with the resultant production of a roomy sports two-seater with a quite astonishing performance. That well-known technical writer Laurence Pomeroy once expressed the opinion that the Lotus, " is the fastest car for a given horsepower on any European circuit today."

Le Mans Model

This version has been developed to meet the most exacting requirements of those who would compete in international class sports/racing car races, and it combines a maximum speed of well over 130 m.p.h. with a rate of acceleration probably not equalled by any other production sports car. The multi-tubular space frame is made up from 1 in. and ¾ in. square and round tubing of 18 and 20 gauge steel and incorporates a stressed shaft tunnel and floor which gives an exceptionally rigid unit.

The engine is carried on two rubber mountings at the front and a single rubber mounting at the rear around the gearbox. It is tilted sideways through approximately 10 degrees to reduce frontal area and also permit a carburetter arrangement with horizontal induction tracts. At the rear is a readily detachable spare wheel mounting, permitting easy access to the differential assembly for quick changes of axle ratios designed to reduce loads affecting the assembly.

The front suspension is independent by swing axles incorporating combined coil-spring damper units reacting through a single point at each end. At the rear a De Dion layout is used with wheels located by parallel trailing arms, and a diagonal member on the offside provides lateral location. The De Dion tube encloses at each end not only the bearing houses but also each outboard universal joint, an unusual feature designed to reduce loads affecting the assembly.

Ultra light, hydraulically operated, 9½ in. disc brakes are outboard at the front and inboard at the rear. The calipers of the rear brakes are carried ahead of the axle to reduce overhung loads, whereas at the front the calipers are behind the discs in order to reduce wheel bearing loads. A horizontally-mounted hand brake operates the rear calipers through inner and outer cables.

Steering is through a lightweight rack and pinion and special forged steering arms. The lightweight steering wheel does not hide the narrow dash panel carrying essential instruments: an 8,000 r.p.m. tachometer, oil pressure gauge, water temperature gauge and ammeter.

Transmission is through a single dry plate clutch of 7½ in. diameter, mechanically operated, and a special four-speed close-ratio gearbox. Final drive is through a hypoid unit and five different axle ratios are available, ranging from 5.125 to 3.89 to cover a speed difference of over four m.p.h. per 1,000 r.p.m. when using standard 5.00 × 15 rear tyres.

Great attention has been paid to the electrical system in view of the annoying petty troubles that can arise. A special lightweight 12 volt, 31 amp-hour battery weighing only 24 lb. is in the tail beside the spare wheel. Engine fittings include coil and distributor, centrifugal advance and retard, belt driven dynamo and automatic voltage control. The fuse box is mounted on the dash panel for easier access and all instruments on the panel are lighted. The Lucas Le Mans 7 in. headlamps and separate side lamps are recessed behind acetate covers and the full complement of twin stop-lights, and so on, are provided.

Knock-on 15 in. wire wheels with identical rims at the front and rear are fitted with 4.50 × 15 tyres on the front and 5.00 × 15 tyres at the rear. The spare wheel with 4.50 × 15 tyre is mounted under the rear panelling.

There are two power units from which to choose—the Coventry Climax 1100 giving 75 h.p. or the " Stage 2 " engine giving 85 h.p. From these h.p. figures are derived the two type numbers for this model, Le Mans 75 and Le Mans 85. The engines are of light alloy construction, having four cylinders of bore 2.85 in. and stroke 2.625 in. giving a cubic capacity of exactly 1,098 c.c. The compression ratio is 9.8 to 1 and maximum output is obtained at 6,250 r.p.m. on the " 75 " and 6,800 r.p.m. on the " 85 " on the " Stage 2 " engine.

Bodywork is well executed, has a noticeably smooth exterior and provides a full width two-seater with all wheels enclosed. The front and rear panels hinge open, or are easily removed for access to engine and final drive, the centre panel can also be taken off very easily. Two drop-down side doors are provided which incorporate map pockets. The dash panel is covered to match the colour of the upholstery which is very tidily and neatly executed. According to customers' requirements, the car can either be supplied with a full width wrap-round screen, or with a metal tonneau cover for the passenger side and a wrap-round screen and head fairing for the driver's side of the car.

Dimensions are—wheelbase 7 ft. 1 in., front track 3 ft. 10½ in., rear track 3 ft. 11 in., overall length 11 ft. 2 in., overall width 5 ft., height to top of tail fin 3 ft. 1 in., height to top of scuttle 2 ft. 3 in. and minimum ground clearance 5 in. Weight is approximately 7 cwt.

The basic prices of this model, less tax, are, Le Mans 85—£1,437, and the Le Mans 75—£1,387, ex works.

A Lotus " Sports " side by side with a " Le Mans " model, the latter with full car-width screen.

The " Le Mans " model, here equipped with wrap-round screen, metal tonneau and head fairing.

THE SPORTS CAR FOR 1957

THE LOTUS ELEVEN

The Lotus Eleven Sports Model

The Lotus Eleven Le Mans

see it on STAND 121 at EARLS COURT

LOTUS ENGINEERING CO., LTD.

7 TOTTENHAM LANE, HORNSEY,
LONDON, N.8

Tel: MOUntview 8353

Sports Model

The last " variation of the original theme " will appeal to those motorists who cannot afford the more costly models but who require a really high performance, yet economical, sports car.

The only difference between this and the " Club " is the power unit, and the Coventry Climax engine is replaced by the Ford 100E, 1,172 c.c. side valve four-cylinder engine. This trusty unit produces 36 h.p. at 4,500 r.p.m. in standard form—a figure that can be easily increased by being " breathed upon " a little. A single Zenith carburetter is fitted with a mechanical fuel lift pump. With all the benefits of low weight, low drag and a basically economic engine, the " Sports " gives an outstandingly favourable petrol consumption (65 m.p.g.) at moderate speeds.

Basic price of this model is £872, excluding purchase tax.

Formula Two Model

The third exhibit on Stand 121 will be the new Formula II Lotus. This will undoubtedly create considerable interest, particularly amongst the racing enthusiasts. A full description and specification of

Ford 100 E 1172 c.c. engine fits snugly into the " Sports " chassis. This particular example has been heavily " breathed upon "—twin SU carburetters augment breathing qualities.

Club Model

To the driver who wishes to use his (or her) car in competition events but either cannot afford the expensive specification or intends only to enter minor meetings, then the second Lotus model must appeal.

The same basic specification applies to this model, the main difference being in the rear suspension and brake departments. A proprietary make live rear axle is located by parallel trailing arms and a diagonal member to provide lateral location. The design of the rear axle assembly has been devised to permit ready modification to the De Dion system employed on the Le Mans model, if required, and incorporates identical coil spring damper units. Drum brakes are fitted outboard at both front and rear and are hydraulically operated two leading-shoe units. Cast iron drums of 9 in. diameter are on the front and 8 in. on the rear. Separate front and rear master cylinders feed from a single hydraulic fluid reservoir containing separate front and rear compartments.

A proprietary four-speed gearbox is fitted to the " Club " with the following ratios : first 4.08 to 1, second 2.58 to 1, third 1.66 to 1, top 1 to 1 and reverse 5.17 to 1.

If required, a full width screen is available (fitted with a screen wiper if necessary) in conjunction with which a hood or detachable hard top are optional. The basic price of the " Club," before tax, is £1,083.

Rear suspension and final drive of the " Le Mans " chassis, showing De Dion tube, suspension units, differential casing and inboard disc brakes.

this car will appear in the December issue of SPORTS CAR & LOTUS OWNER, but we can say that the chassis is very narrow and light in weight. Construction is by stressed tube, front suspension is by coil spring and wishbones incorporating an anti-roll bar. (A departure from the usual Lotus swing axle.) A solid propshaft of ⅞in. diameter, which runs between the driver's seat and the undertray, transmits power to a special 5-speed gearbox in unit with the De Dion rear axle suspended by coil springs.

Disc brakes are fitted all round, inboard at rear and outboard at front. Another departure from usual Lotus practice are the special cast lightweight bolt-on wheels.

The body is of the open wheeled variety and the dry weight of the complete car is only 5¼ cwt. The engine installed in the Show car will be the new twin ohc 1500 c.c. Coventry Climax.

Simplified rear assembly of the "Club" and "Sports" models uses a proprietary make of live rear axle located by parallel trailing arms.

147

Autocar ROAD TESTS

No. 1616

LOTUS 11
Le Mans Model

The Le Mans model has a wrap-round Perspex windscreen, the side sections of which hinge out and downward with the doors (when these are used). The diminutive duct to the radiator is more than adequate, some blanking off being required for best results in normal road work

FOR an 1,100 c.c. two-seater to attain over 112 m.p.h. on a Continental motorway, to cover the standing quarter-mile in 17.9 sec and average well over 50 m.p.g. fuel consumption for normal running is unique in road testing experience of *The Autocar*, yet that was the achievement of the Lotus Eleven Le Mans. On checking records we find only six other cars which have matched or bettered the performance figures—though without approaching the consumption—and all were of over 2-litre capacity.

Some readers may not consider such a comparison to be entirely fair, because the Lotus is built primarily for competition. It is true that there is no luggage accommodation as such, that weather protection is limited and by family car standards there are no more than the bare essentials of trimming and comfort, but to obtain the ultimate in one or two directions invariably necessitates some sacrifices in others. The exhilarating speed and acceleration of this car more than offset its austere furnishings, for the kind of enthusiastic driver who is likely to be found in its cockpit.

There is no reason why the car should not on occasions be used for local shopping or, in fine weather, for taking the younger member of the family to school—and no reason, either, to suppose that the Lotus would be harmed by such employment, for it has all the normal components and an engine which is far from being temperamental. On the other hand a milkman does not usually buy a racehorse to draw his float, nor does an Esquimo choose a whippet.

In the form in which it was tested, the Le Mans Lotus is ready for the track or road course for which it is primarily intended, and according to the merits of the driver, could be expected to finish among the winners. Racing apart, it provides enjoyment and satisfaction in the role of diminutive highway express, and it is under these circumstances also that its exceptional fuel economy is appreciated.

One of the very few specialized manufacturers in Great Britain, the Lotus Engineering company, has built up an enviable reputation since its first trials cars were produced in 1947 and were followed in due course by the Mark III 750 c.c. sports-racers. The present production models have a space-type chassis frame, built up of 1in and ¾in round and square section steel tubing. The thickness of the tubes —18 and 20 s.w.g.—is varied according to the load on the particular section of the chassis. The floor and propeller shaft tunnel are stressed light alloy members which form an integral part of the chassis frame.

The heart of this Lotus is the 1,098 c.c. Coventry Climax engine. Various stages of tuning may be specified by a purchaser. That of the standard model produces 75 b.h.p. at 6,250 r.p.m.; Stage 2 tuning, as applied to the car tested, provides 83 b.h.p. at 6,800 r.p.m. The engine is carried on two rubber mountings at the front and a single one at the gear box, and in order to keep down the frontal area, it is tilted to the left at approximately 10 deg. from the vertical. The compression ratio is 9.8 to 1 and thus high octane fuel should be used, although the admixture of a small quantity

Clips on each side secure the hinged front and rear body sections. The front of the chassis or the rear suspension can be revealed in a moment and the centre section is also quick to remove

of normal premium on one occasion during the testing made no detectable difference to performance.

Whether the engine, which has no "choke," would start readily in very cold weather we were unable to determine, but at temperatures within a few degrees of freezing point there was no difficulty at all. A twist of the ignition key until the S.U. electric fuel pump had finished ticking, one or two exploratory dabs on the throttle pedal as the key was twisted further to energize the starter motor, and the engine came to life readily and was soon firing evenly on all four cylinders. At high r.p.m. the exhaust note is very noisy—more so to the occupants of the car than to those on the road around—but the engine can be warmed up at a steady speed without causing any annoyance to the neighbours. No fan is fitted, and only a few minutes running is required to reach a comfortable operating temperature.

The Climax is at its best at about 80 deg C and, for ordinary road use a radiator blind would be well worth fitting, so that this temperature could be maintained. In traffic it rises rapidly, but was never seen to boil. A short burst in top gear brings the needle down immediately, and with an outside air temperature of about 50 deg F the open road running temperature stayed at little more than 60

Accommodation for luggage is confined to the space within the doors and the sills at their bases. The handbrake lever may be seen tucked away under the facia. Tall passengers have some difficulty in getting in because of the intruding chassis space frame member. There is no speedometer; the central dial records engine r.p.m. only

The Climax engine is inclined to permit an extremely low bonnet level, but the raised wings are easily seen and placed by the driver. The wipers would appear to be unnecessary refinement as neither driver nor passenger normally looks through the screen. The very light aluminium body has no protection against bumps which may occur in parking manœuvres

deg C, in spite of blanking off nearly a quarter of the area of the small transverse radiator.

To complete the specification preliminaries, before turning to the handling, there is the matter of rear axle ratio. Several ratios are offered to suit the various requirements. The car under discussion had a 4.22 to 1 axle which is to be recommended for road work. Others to choice are 3.66, 3.89, 4.55, 4.89 and 5.125 to 1—a good range for high top speed through to maximum acceleration, and calculated to cater for most competition requirements.

Without sacrificing much of the performance a higher than 4.22 back axle gearing could be selected to give exceptional economy on long journeys. On the other hand in England, where maximum speed would seldom be required or attainable, many drivers would prefer to use a little more fuel in order to experience the really exhilarating acceleration, and to increase slightly the tractability in heavy traffic.

Using the 4.22 to 1 axle and driving hard with full use of the gears and r.p.m., a representative figure of 44 m.p.g. was recorded. Jogging along at 60 to 70 m.p.h. and changing to a higher gear at no more than 4,000 r.p.m., nearly 60 m.p.g. was obtained. Such a figure surely provides a lesson in what can be achieved by reducing drag to a minimum. Very light weight, high gearing, outstanding engine efficiency, combine with the exceptionally low frontal area and fine aerodynamic shape to permit such economy.

The recommended pressures for the tyres vary considerably according to the driving contemplated. For high-speed touring 20 and 25 lb sq in front and rear respectively gives plenty of adhesion and a comfortable ride. For high-speed runs on good road surfaces, the pressures should be raised

The Coventry Climax engine unit is inclined at 10 degrees. There is a hole in the bonnet top for the air intake, this air passing through a box to the twin S.U. carburettors. The radiator is mounted very low at the front, and the separate header tank against the bulkhead. There are twin S.U. petrol pumps, of which one only is normally used

The light on the right hand rear wing is for illumination of racing numbers in competition. There is no weather protection other than the screen

LOTUS 11 LE MANS . . .

to 30 and 35 lb and the ride is appreciably harder. It is not surprising that on a car so light and with such high performance, unbalanced or wrongly selected pressures can have a marked effect on ride, stability and steering characteristics.

Until comparatively recently, the carriage of a passenger as well as driver has been the exception rather than the rule on the Lotus, and the readiness with which the suspension bottoms on rough roads indicates that a little more development and experience would be advantageous. The thin foam rubber used for the seats is adequate for this type of vehicle, but it would not be unreasonable to advocate a considerable improvement in draught and waterproofing of the floor and sides.

There is no point in commenting on space and cockpit equipment, for quite obviously the car has been tailored to provide sufficient room for a large, though not outsize man to be accommodated in each seat—and no more. By accommodated, however, we imply with sufficient freedom of movement for all limbs for control of the car on road or track with comfort and safety. As delivered, the car carries no more than the essential instruments and switches and a legal and performance requirement in lamps and horn. If this model of Lotus is purchased mainly for use on the roads, it is up to the owner to specify the additional equipment he desires. There is plenty of room on the panel for a cigar lighter. Also according to specification, a hood can be provided and the makers advertise the availability of a hard top on all models.

Delivered to us almost hot from an economy run of the previous weekend, the shapely and diminutive sports car created quite a stir as it crouched between enormous lorries and vans outside our London headquarters. And such was the timing of our Silver City flight to the Continent for performance measurements that driver and car had to move off at once and get acquainted on the way. By the time the traffic intricacies of the Elephant and Castle had been negotiated, we were already geting along very nicely, though top gear as yet was in reserve.

The clutch is the only control likely to disconcert the inexperienced driver. As with those on most other competition cars, it has powerful springs and a very short, effective travel, being in effect either in or out. After a little practice with more or fewer engine r.p.m. and acclimatizing the foot to feathering the clutch into engagement, a normal, if eager getaway can be accomplished. It is perhaps prudent in traffic to leave rather more than the usual space between Lotus nose and car ahead, because the natural getaway is deceptively rapid and there is more length of Lotus ahead of the driver than he may think.

Even during the warming-up period, the engine pulls without hesitation, and in traffic it is not necessary to use high r.p.m. to obtain responsive running—2,000 to 2,500 r.p.m. in the appropriate gear is adequate for keeping in the stream. Low gear must be used for getaway, but second and third are then selected much as they would be with any other sports car. The satisfying but raucous exhaust note does not become really obtrusive until the higher r.p.m. are used.

The gear lever is short, high-mounted and close to the driver's hand on the wheel. Movements are very small indeed between the gears, and changes are very slick at all speeds. The only occasion when a slight pause was desirable was between third and top at high r.p.m.

On the open road the Lotus takes on a new character, and comes to life at the derestriction sign as if it had been dozing before. The acceleration is such that 80 m.p.h. comes up in a quarter of a mile, and 100 in little over half a minute.

For the believer the exhaust sounds crisp and delightful. Until one is used to it, upchange time as judged by sound comes at perhaps 5,500 r.p.m. but the pull continues and increases, and between 6,500 and 7,000 r.p.m.—the normal maximum—the note becomes true blue. At 7,000 the speed in third gear is 92 and in second 57 m.p.h. By fitting alternative intermediate gear ratios which can be specified, it is possible to have maximum speeds of 100 m.p.h. in third and 75 m.p.h. in second.

Against the howl of exhaust and wind it is impossible to single out mechanical noise, but there is probably none deserving of comment. At low speeds the whine of the back axle can be detected—but then the driver can also see the back axle and inboard disc brakes behind his seat if he lifts the flexible cover.

The speed and acceleration figures quoted in this account were all obtained with two people on board and the road test gear attached. Even on wet surfaces very little wheel spin was experienced on these tests. An easy top gear cruising speed was found to be about 80 m.p.h., with the engine turning at 4,500 r.p.m. During the performance measurements in Belgium the limit of 7,000 r.p.m. was observed in indirect gears, and the maximum speed of 112.5 was reached at 6,200 r.p.m. after a fairly long run. On dry roads and with one occupant, this maximum could certainly be improved. The full width curved screen gives only partial protection to the crew of two.

Driver control of the Le Mans Lotus is ideal. The seat is not adjustable, but the position is such that most drivers feel happy at the wheel. It will be noticed from the data sheet that there are only 1¾ turns of the steering wheel from lock to lock. This is, by all standards, high-geared, even though the lock itself is very restricted by the tight enclosure of the wheels, but the driver is not aware of undue sensitiveness or constant correction of the helm. The car is, in fact, very stable directionally, and a light floating grip on the wheel is best. With load and tyre pressures as mentioned, there is a tendency to understeer, but at all speeds a touch of throttle brings the car neatly round the sharpest of corners and if need be oversteer can be induced with power.

Although it is so light, the Lotus clings to the road in a remarkable manner. Readers who have seen the marque in action at racing circuits will not need to be told that it is one of the safest and most controllable cars built. A driver can cause or experience skids and then correct them as easily as can a man on skates. The response to movement of the steering wheel is instantaneous. On corners there is no roll at all, nor is there any tyre scream. For manœuvring, the steering wheel can be moved from lock to lock with one finger, yet it is not undesirably light at maximum speed.

The Girling disc brakes are more than adequate for the car's performance, and give the driver the greatest confidence in their dependability and stopping power. Pedal pressure required for stopping from high speed is substantial but not unreasonably so; unless the discs are cold there is no squeal. The car pulls up in a straight line and even under maximum braking conditions there is little tendency for the

The wrap-round screen deflects wind but not rain. Weather protection can be provided by hard top or hood

wheels to lock. The brake and accelerator pedals are arranged to permit heel/toe changes. Incidentally the parking brake lever is transversely mounted above the passenger's knees. It is, therefore, reasonably accessible to the driver's left hand.

Two penalties to be paid for the efficient shape of the vehicle which affect ordinary driving are low ground clearance and nearness of the driver to the road surface. Obstacles which the average vehicle would clear easily—bricks or branches in the road—need to be avoided in the Lotus because of its minimal clearance and light construction. At night, dipped head lights and auxiliary lights which would not ordinarily affect the driver of an oncoming vehicle are likely to dazzle the man at the wheel of the Lotus, whose eyes are 18in to 2ft below normal levels.

Provision is made for carrying a spare wheel beneath the tail fairing, and there is no reason why a light luggage grid should not be mounted above it. Few cars can be more accessible than the Lotus, for by unclipping four springs the whole of the front and rear portions of the bodywork can be raised from the centre on hinges at the extremities to disclose engine, brakes, de Dion rear axle, front suspension, tanks and battery.

To summarize, drivers interested in high performance cars willingly sacrifice some of the comforts and other qualities of the conventional sports car to experience the pleasures of driving a car with urge and response like those of the Lotus. It is no great hardship to have to wear suitable clothing to keep out cold and wet if the weather is bad.

The manufacturers are to be congratulated on achieving an admirable compromise between track performance and road docility. The qualities of road holding, steering and braking required for racing place this car above most others so far as safety on the road is concerned.

LOTUS ELEVEN LE MANS MODEL

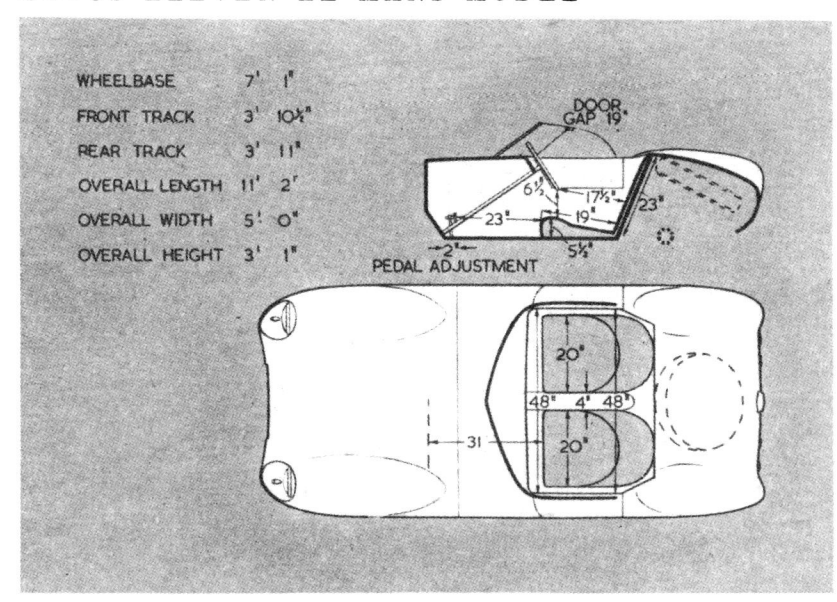

Measurements in these ¼in to 1ft scale body diagrams are taken with the driving seat in the central position of fore and aft adjustment and with the seat cushions uncompressed

PERFORMANCE

ACCELERATION: From constant speeds.
Speed Range Gear Ratios and Time in sec.
M.P.H. 4.22 to 1 5.79 to 1 9.32 to 1 15.30 to 1

M.P.H.	4.22 to 1	5.79 to 1	9.32 to 1	15.30 to 1
10—30	—	—	5.1	2.8
20—40	—	—	4.0	—
30—50	—	—	3.8	—
40—60	—	6.8	—	—
50—70	12.6	6.8	—	—
60—80	11.9	7.1	—	—
70—90	14.0	8.3	—	—

From rest through gears to:
M.P.H.	sec.
30	4.0
50	7.9
60	10.9
70	15.7
80	19.2
90	25.6
100	38.9

Standing quarter mile, 17.9 sec.

SPEEDS ON GEARS:
Gear	M.P.H. (normal and max.)	K.P.H. (normal and max.)
Top (mean)	111.75	179.8
(best)	112.50	181.0
3rd	80—92	129—148
2nd	50—57	80—91
1st	28—34	45—55

SPEEDOMETER CORRECTION—(No speedometer fitted.)

TRACTIVE RESISTANCE: 21 lb per ton at 10 M.P.H.

TRACTIVE EFFORT:
	Pull (lb per ton)	Equivalent Gradient
Top	230	1 in 9.7
Third	340	1 in 6.5
Second	537	1 in 4.0

BRAKES:
Efficiency	Pedal Pressure (lb)
90 per cent	75
61 per cent	50
45 per cent	25

FUEL CONSUMPTION:
47.8 m.p.g. overall for 1,200 miles (5.9 litres per 100 km).
Approximate normal range 44-58 m.p.g. (6.4-4.9 litres per 100 km).
Fuel, premium grade.

WEATHER: Dull, cross breeze, damp concrete and tarmac.
Air temperature 42 deg F.
Acceleration figures are the means of several runs in opposite directions.
Tractive effort and resistance obtained by Tapley meter.
Model described in *The Autocar* of February 10, 1956.

DATA

PRICE (basic), with two-seater body, £1,437.
British purchase tax, £718.
Total (in Great Britain), £2,155.

ENGINE: Capacity: 1,098 c.c. (66.9 cu in).
Number of cylinders: 4.
Bore and stroke: 72.4 × 66.6 mm (2.85 × 2.625 in).
Valve gear: single overhead camshaft.
Compression ratio: 9.8 to 1.
B.H.P.: 83 at 6,800 r.p.m. (B.H.P. per ton laden 137.2).
Torque: 74.5 lb ft at 4,400 r.p.m.
M.P.H. per 1,000 r.p.m. on top gear, 18.00.

WEIGHT (with 5 gals fuel), 9.1 cwt (1,019 lb).
Weight distribution (per cent): F, 53.9 R, 46.1.
Laden as tested: 12.1 cwt (1,355 lb).
Lb per c.c. (laden): 1.23.

BRAKES: Type: F & R, Girling disc.
Method of operation: F, hydraulic; R, hydraulic.
Disc dimensions: F, 9⅜in diameter; R, 9⅛in. diameter.

TYRES: 4.50—15in front; 5.00—15 rear.
Pressure (lb per sq in): F, 20; R, 25 (normal). F, 30; R, 35 (for fast driving).

TANK CAPACITY: 18 Imperial gallons (not standard).
Oil sump, 8 pints.
Cooling system, 12 pints.

TURNING CIRCLE: 42ft (L and R).
Steering wheel turns (lock to lock): 1¾.

DIMENSIONS: Wheelbase: 7ft 1in.
Track: F, 3ft 10½in; R, 3ft 11in.
Length (overall): 11ft 2in.
Height: 3ft 1in.
Width: 5ft.
Ground clearance: 5in.

ELECTRICAL SYSTEM: 12-volt; 31 ampere-hour battery.
Head lights: Double dip; 48-48 watt bulbs.

SUSPENSION: Front, independent, coil springs, swing axle. Rear, de Dion, coil springs.

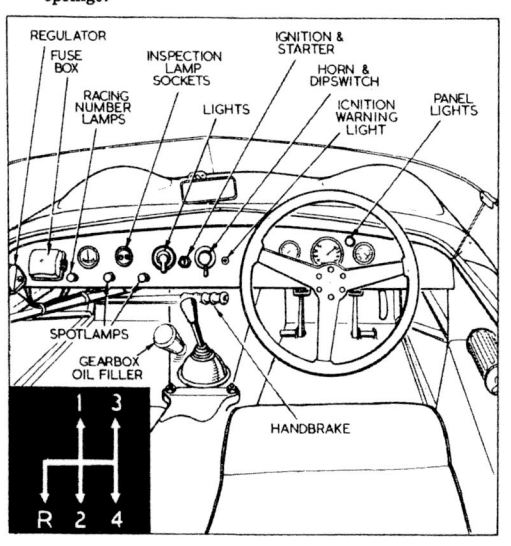

Colin Chapman's latest Lotus brainchild

The Mark XI "Le Mans"

Side and front views, above, show the unusual aerodynamic design of the new body—extreme, perhaps, but more pleasing than the Mark IX. Interior accessibility is simplified by hinging, front and rear, the two halves of the body shell.

photography: Klemantaski

Photos below reveal construction details: At left can be seen the inclined engine, narrow dash, deDion rear end with inboard disc brakes, and coil springs. Placement of gas tank, shown at right, helps to counterbalance driver's weight.

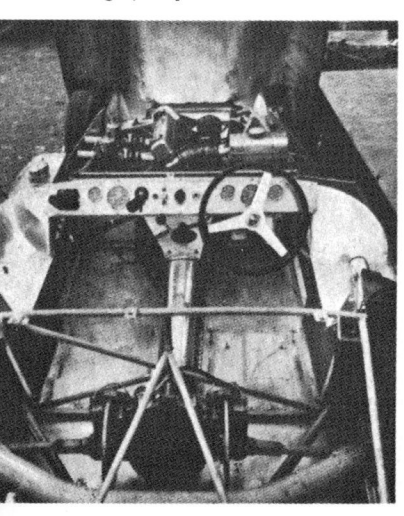

THE NEW Lotus Mark XI "Le Mans" model was shown recently by Colin Chapman, its designer and builder, at his enlarged plant in Surrey. Weight is down, believe it or not, to 826 lbs., and the car has been race-bred into a very smooth product indeed. Last year's high tail fins have been reduced to more balanced proportions, and a general clean-up job has been accomplished both in body shape and engineering.

Consistent success of the Lotus, a relative newcomer to the field, has proved a considerable threat to some of the older firms. While it is true that the car is a hand-made racer first and transportation second and that the Mark XI buyer will not pocket much change from $5000, the outlay is still far less than for an equivalent Italian machine.

As for specifications, there is a multitubular space frame, a Climax 1100cc engine now developing 85 bhp, a special close-ratio, four-speed gear box, rack and pinion steering, a very light deDion rear end, Girling disc brakes and quite a bit more comfort than last year. Always willing to learn from experience, Mr. Chapman has shortened the wheelbase by 1½ inches and mounted the engine at a 10° angle to reduce frontal area and simultaneously allow for various carburetor installations. With no point too small to consider for improving the car's efficiency, even the number of body joints in the metal skin has been reduced to lower drag without impairing accessibility to both front and rear ends; this has been accomplished by using one-piece units hinged outward at each end. New oil seals have been fitted in the rear designed to save ½ bhp over those previously used.

Whereas last season the 1100 cc Cooper had a definite edge in top speed, the new Lotus should equal its rivals in that department without sacrificing its outstanding handling characteristics, which may actually be improved due to a 15-pound cut in the unsprung weight at the rear end. ●

BARE MAXIMUM

AN OPEN VERDICT ON THE BASIC ISSUES

READERS of this journal who have been paying attention in the past few weeks will be aware that there are several ways of Stretching Your Petrol. Right-minded enthusiasts agree that one of the more amusing ways of stretching anything is to pull it out like a piece of catapult elastic and then let go, which is roughly what happens if you let the clutch in at 4,000 r.p.m. on a Mk. XI Lotus. Two basic differences in the performance of the Lotus are that it is very difficult to overstretch the elastic, and that the energy is by no means used up all at once.

The original object of the exercise became rather diverted. We had intended to demonstrate to the Basic public that if they saw gentlemen dashing about in very small racing cars, the chances were that the gentlemen were in fact being even more economical than the public. In the event, it became obvious that anyone who could drive such a car so economically must be possessed of superhuman patience, but if time is really money the Lotus strikes a pretty good bargain.

Like all of its breed, the Mk. XI Club model comes in a variety of trimmings to suit the customer's taste. Being enthusiasts for comfort about this time of year, we spent some days with a privately owned car, with a full-width windscreen and very fully furnished interior, lacking only a hood. In this form, extra weight and the added drag combine to have the worst possible

ESSAY in streamlining. The Lotus is as functional as an aeroplane, and its shape as smooth and uncluttered.

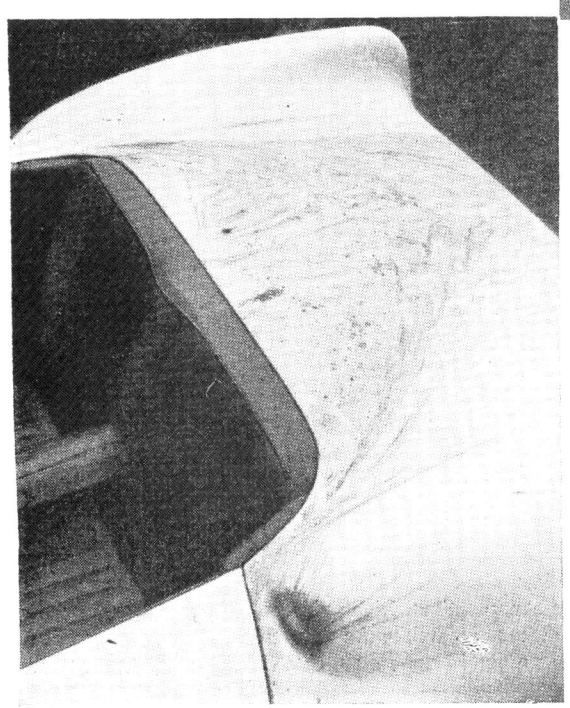

BACKDRAUGHT.—After a long, wet drive, mud forms an interesting pattern on the rear deck of the Lotus. Some more of it forms an interesting pool on the floor.

effect on performance and economy, in a machine which derives both very largely from lightness and good aerodynamic shape. As a purely temporary argument, it could, of course, be reasoned that the owner of this model would need only goloshes and a waterproof bowler to qualify for a supplementary allowance, thereby immediately stretching his six-gallon ration to nine.

However that may be, few who enjoy their driving for its own sake would not agree that the Lotus makes the best possible use of whatever petrol may come its way. On the reasonable assumption that coasting is all very well but nobody can really stay awake at less than 60 m.p.h., we made our most favourable run—80 miles northwards, starting in London—with little use of the indirect gears, and the engine speed held below 4,000 r.p.m. (about 72 m.p.h.), and obtained 46.0 m.p.g. A 200-mile night run to the West Country turned up 41.1 m.p.g., and a more spirited attack on a private record for the return journey was highly successful at

BARE MAXIMUM

STRONG-ARM stuff by designer Colin Chapman, holding the 56 lb. chassis frame of the Mk. XI.

FLAPS-UP effect of a full-width windscreen (still not high enough to cover a six-foot driver) can be judged in this view.

37.6 m.p.g. Possibly the most impressive figure, however, resulted from 56 miles consisting almost entirely of full-throttle acceleration tests and similar goings-on, all for a shade under two gallons, or 29.0 m.p.g. On the whole, it seemed clear that a month's ration for a Lotus would take one a long way, but quite a short time.

There are, of course, snags. If you start with a tubular frame weighing 56 lb. and wrap it in aluminium to make a nice smooth shape, you tend to arrive at a sort of birdcage which human beings enter with ingenuity, whereas water gets in with no trouble at all. As we left the Hornsey works Mr. Chapman cheerfully remarked that if it rained we might find it rather choppy about the ankles. It did, and it was. Then again the headlamp cowls mist up rather when the water behind them splashes about too much, and the windscreen wipers would be more useful if there was a duplicate pair inside the screen, where most of the mud settles.

Light Fingers Needed

But, after all, who cares? A Lotus is for the Jeep-jacketed, the quick of eye and the light of touch. The best way to see through any windscreen is to sit on a cushion and look over it, where the draught is carried over your head and visibility is appropriately that of a racing car. Like any racing car, it is potentially the safest vehicle on the roads. In the Club model, 75 horsepower from the Coventry-Climax engine is transmitted to the road through a live axle, which appears to be a surprisingly small handicap for most conditions. Performance on the primitive highways of Britain being limited more often than not by visibility, a car which is raced at 110 m.p.h. is touring well within its limitations at 70, 80 or 90 miles an hour. Fitted with road tyres, in place of racing types which are not at their best for normal driving in the wet, it enables the driver to ignore most of the slippery surfaces he is used to treating with respect. Slightly lower pressures in front make the car understeer just enough for comfort; but understeer is a relative term, and this steering is a very distant relation of the kind one is used to in the modern saloon. Where earlier Lotuses, however, were sensitive to the extent of making little darts to left or right with every change of camber, this model was more reassuringly straight-running for the tourist.

Frankly, we find it hard to imagine anyone being so pedestrian as a tourist for very long with a Lotus. Even if he insists on driving round all corners without finding out how fast *is* too fast, can there be a man with soul so dead that he finds no simple, childish pleasure in pushing the maximum-reading mark on the rev. counter round to 7,500 r.p.m. just once, to see what happens? As a matter of fact, nothing happens—although we must admit to being circumspect in these matters when entrusted with expensive private property.

The maximum output of the 75 b.h.p. version of the Climax engine occurs at 6,200 r.p.m., which speed we prudently, if not timidly, adopted as a limit for our endeavours in standing-start acceleration. Allowing for the comparatively high axle ratio of 4.22 : 1, and the fact that our car, unlike the standard Club model, was fitted with a gearbox more suitable for racing speeds, one can

Continued on page 164

ROAD TEST **LOTUS 11**

Unusual side view "before and after" comparison shows the instant accessibility of the Lotus, both at the front and rear.

Road Test: LOTUS "ELEVEN"

THE LOTUS MARK XI, with 1100 cc Coventry-Climax engine is now officially called the "Eleven" and this test report brings forth some of the most startling performance data ever published.

It also provided our test department with one giant-size headache (on which more later) and a truly fantastic array of performance figures highlighted by an honest timed top speed of 132 mph, plus acceleration from a standstill to 100 mph in 22 seconds.

First, let us state that the car shown here is not the actual car which we tested, though it is identical in every detail except color. The test car (finished in red) was owned and driven by Lotus distributor, Jay Chamberlain, and ran exactly as it returned from Nassau including battle-scars from a "brush" with a course marker.

As for the headache, there were actually several. The first problem was where, or rather how, to seat the observer. Removal of the cockpit cover would also entail dispensing with the driver's windscreen with attendant loss in performance as well as some discomfort at high speed. Finally a compromise was made which placed the editor *under the cover*. After much twisting and squirming the editor/observer's head emerged alongside the driver's left shoulder, in line for easy reading of the instruments. We should say "instrument" for it was impossible to fit a fifth-wheel to this vehicle and the tachometer was used as a performance gauge (no speedometer is supplied). It is no mysterious trick to get accurate test data with only a tachometer and a surveyed ¼ mile strip as "tools," but the process is a little more involved than normal procedure and by the time the tachometer was calibrated and the "zeros-to" tests were completed the editor was very glad to be released.

Bearing in mind the above, the one-way timed run was made with no internal observer and, as explained in the tabulated data section, the Tapley meter readings were taken with the observer upright (in order to install and read the meter) which necessitated removal of all the cowling including the windscreen and headrest. Accordingly, the Tapley readings in each gear are slightly reduced, especially in the higher gears as the extra drag becomes more important. Also, the total drag loss given in the data as only 68 lbs. would actually be even less with the fairing installed. It is, therefore, not possible to correlate drag data with the engine's output and the recorded top speed but rough figures put the drag coefficient (Cw factor) at about .400. Using this factor and a frontal area of 11.0 sq. ft. it can be shown that about 77 bhp was required to attain 132 mph.

With respect to the timed top speed the driver reported that the tach reached 7100 rpm well before he entered the ¼ mile and would go no higher, yet at Nassau he could touch 7400 rpm on the long straight, equivalent to very nearly 138 mph. Needless to say the lower figure is still extremely good and especially in view of the 4.22 axle ratio which is not ideal for best possible top speed. The optional 3.66 ratio would undoubtedly allow a timed top speed in the vicinity of 145 mph, but most competition is done on "slow" circuits for which builder Colin Chapman will supply further alternative ratios of 5.125, 4.89, or 4.55 if so ordered.

The dry weight is given as exactly 1000 lbs. and this figure includes oil and water but no fuel. Except for the high speed run, all tests were made with a gross vehicle weight of 1360 lbs. plus or minus 5 lbs. because of fuel consumption. We made no fuel consumption checks but Chamberlain reports that he used exactly 13 gallons in the 210 mile Nassau Trophy Race—equivalent to 16.15 mpg. A British road test on an identical machine except for wider-spaced transmission ratios and a full width Le Mans type windshield reports 35 mpg (U.S.) on the road and up to 48 mpg when cruising leisurely. Incidentally, our test car beat all the British test figures by a substantial margin.

During the high speed runs the Desmo "Boomerang" mirrors were bent well back by the air-blast.

The stage II "tuning" includes a pair of huge (for only 1100 cc) S. U. carburetors.

	British test	R&T test
Timed top speed	112.5	132.06
0-60 mph	10.9	9.0
ss ¼ mile	17.9	16.0
Axle ratio	4.22	4.22
Test weight	1355	1360
Frontal area (sq. ft., approx.)	14.0	11.0

Fantastic performance with only 1100cc

Both cars had the "Stage II" tuned engine (83 bhp) and the British figures look suspect to us, if for no other reason than the fact that our standing start ¼ mile time is 1.9 seconds quicker—and there's no question of error in this test—a car either does it, or it doesn't. Possibly the engine of the overseas car wasn't tuned quite up to par, for the addition of a big windshield shouldn't make for much loss over the standing quarter. In any case we once got 15.8 seconds and Chamberlain says he has done better than that at the local drag strips.

Acceleration, naturally, is really fierce even at low speeds. Some care must be exercised to avoid getting too much wheel-spin for the car tends to snake when getting off the mark. A rev limit of 7500 rpm in each gear was used but the tiny C-C engine will scream well past 8000 rpm if you want to risk it. The gearbox unit is very small and light; from an Austin A-30 but re-designed to give closer ratios. It takes a real beating in competition and seems to be trouble-free. Incidentally, the differential unit is also B.M.C. (Austin A-30 or Morris Minor).

We did not drive the car, but there is a small amount of understeer and ample power available to force the rear end out and into an oversteering attitude. The steering takes only 1.75 turns lock to lock but the turning circle is not impressive at 42 feet.

In front there is an Allard type swinging half-axle independent suspension—with a difference. Colin Chapman has cleverly lowered the pivot point (and roll center) to about 12" above the ground and in so doing avoids the usual jack-knifing and front end side-skitter of the older Allards. At the rear we find the tried and true de Dion system and the entire suspension is fairly stiff. This and the high roll axis makes for practically no roll at all, in a corner, but the ride is not designed for a comfortable Sunday trip.

The Lotus Eleven is not a dual-purpose sports car—it is designed to win in Class G and the price of $5467 delivered in the U.S.A. strikes us as being quite reasonable. However, there are lower cost models, as given below.

Model	U.S. Price	Remarks
"Sports"	$3253	Ford 1172cc engine, solid rear axle, drum brakes
"Club"	$4301	C-C engine stage I, solid rear axle, drum brakes
"Le Mans"	$5287	C-C engine stage I, de Dion rear axle, Girling disc brakes
"Le Mans"	$5467	Same except stage II

Even the lowest priced model may not put a Lotus in every garage but it would certainly make an interesting racing class if enough cars of this type are brought over. ●

R & T ROAD TEST NO. 125

LOTUS MARK XI

SPECIFICATIONS

List price	$5467
Wheelbase, in.	85.0
Tread, f/r	46.5/47
Tire size, f/r	4.50/5.00-15
Dry weight, lbs.	1000
distribution, %	54/46
Test weight	1360
Engine	4 cyl.-sohc
Bore & Stroke	2.85 x 2.63
Displacement, cu in.	66.9
cu cm	1098
Compression ratio	9.80
Horsepower	83
peaking speed	6800
equivalent mph	123
Torque, ft-lbs.	74.5
peaking speed	4400
equivalent mph	79
Gear ratios, overall	
4th	4.22
3rd	5.20
2nd	7.05
1st	10.5

CALCULATED DATA

Lbs/hp (test wt.)	16.4
Cu ft./ton mile	95.2
Engine revs/mile	3340
Piston travel, ft/mi.	1460
Mph @ 2500 fpm	103

PERFORMANCE, Mph

Top speed, one way	132.06
3rd (7500)	110
2nd (7500)	81
1st (7500)	54
see chart for shift points	
Mileage range	16/50 mpg

ACCELERATION, Secs.

0-30 mph	3.9
0-40 mph	5.1
0-50 mph	6.7
0-60 mph	9.0
0-70 mph	11.3
0-80 mph	13.8
0-90 mph	17.6
0-100 mph	22.0
Standing start ¼ mile	16.0

TAPLEY DATA, Lbs/ton

4th	270 @ 72 mph
3rd	340 @ 66 mph
2nd	500 @ 39 mph
1st	off scale
Total drag at 60 mph	68 lbs.

(NOTE: All Tapley readings taken with windscreen, cockpit cover and headrest removed. See text.)

LOTUS "ELEVEN" Acceleration thru the gears

TEST REPORT ON THE LOTUS ELEVEN SPORTS

Brilliant Handling Characteristics an Outstanding Feature of Colin Chapman's Least-Expensive, Ford Ten-Engined Aerodynamic Two-Seater.

ON the eve of the petrol famine MOTOR SPORT was loaned for test a bright yellow Mk. XI Lotus two-seater. The Lotus ranks today where Amilcar and Bugatti stood in the eyes of enthusiasts in the gay 'twenties and any version is an exciting proposition. A year ago we sampled the joy of driving a Lotus-Climax, but the car which forms the subject of the present test is a tamed version, powered by a tuned Ford Ten engine. This is not to say that there is anything particularly docile about the Lotus Sports, for it provides spartan accommodation for two *sans* luggage, weather protection is present rather than adequate, and equipment and creature-comforts are reduced to a minimum in the praiseworthy interest of weight reduction.

Although this yellow Lotus is equipped for road work and is perfectly tractable and reliable in heavy traffic, its primary purpose in life is obviously club racing, only the more rabid enthusiasts being likely to crave everyday travel in it. The multi-tube spaceframe is common to all Lotus models. It is formed of 1 in. and ¾ in. square and round tubing of 18 and 20-gauge steel. The propellershaft tunnel and floor are stressed members integral with this frame, and the tunnel carries the rear engine mounting and a torque reaction member from the final-drive housing. Front suspension is by swing-axles and coil-spring damper units, and at the back a rigid axle of B.M.C. manufacture is located by parallel trailing-arms and a diagonal member and sprung on coil-spring damper units. Cast-iron brake drums, 9 in. at the front and 8 in. at the back, are used, with separate master cylinders fed from a common fluid reservoir having individual front and back compartments.

Naturally, on a hand-built car like a Lotus details and even the power unit will vary considerably depending on customer requirements. In the car we had for test the engine was an old-type Ford Ten 100E with two 1½-in. S.U. carburetters. These were mounted 5¼ in. away from the block by inlet pipes with hose connections and each carburetter had a 4⅞ in. long fluted air intake. The engine retained its cast-iron head and coil ignition but had four separate exhaust pipes running into a larger-bore exhaust pipe and silencer terminating just in front of the near-side back wheel. Enlarged inlet ports and valves were used. The power output was in the neighbourhood of 40 b.h.p. and its safe speed in the region of 5,250 r.p.m. A Ford Eight head gave a compression-ratio of 8.0 to 1 and the engine normally prefers 100-octane fuel, but with the Suez Canal blocked we compromised with National Benzole; no pinking or running-on resulted. The usual low-set, fully-ducted, cross-flow radiator was used, in conjunction with an export-type water pump, a right-angle off-take pipe on the centre of the cylinder head being connected to a remote header tank on the off side of the car behind the engine. The radiator provided ample cooling, the temperature only exceeding 80 deg. C. when partial blanking was used, and then only in town driving.

A Ford three-speed gearbox was retained, but with Buckler closeratio gears and a remote-control gear-lever with exposed pivot and substantial push-pull rod, set on the propeller-shaft tunnel. The ratios were 9.9, 5.6 and 4.2 to 1.

That is the specification of the Lotus Eleven Sports, least-expensive car in the Chapman repertoire. As most people know, it differs from the Le Mans and Club models in its Ford (instead of Coventry-Climax) engine and normal in place of the de Dion rear-end employed for the Le Mans car—although ready replacement by this more expensive unit is arranged for. The body is of the famous Lotus aerodynamic form but has a normal (non-folding) windscreen instead of the Le Mans wrap-round screen and head fairing. Indeed, a hard-top, to form a Lotus coupé, can be supplied for the fragile. Incidentally, disc brakes are used on the Le Mans Lotus, whereas those previously referred to are naturally drum brakes.

A dry November changed to a damp December before our test commenced and it was deemed advisable to call at Dunlop's London

FAMILIAR SHAPE.—The efficient, tail-finned lines of the Lotus are well known to motor-racing enthusiasts. A full-width windscreen characterises the Mk. XI Sports, which has a tuned Ford Ten power unit.

depot and have the racing covers on the front wheels changed for road tyres. While this was done under the watchful eye of ever-young "Dunlop Mac" we had visual proof of the excellence of Chapman's frame, because when a jack was raised under one side of the car the opposite front wheel rose in sympathy—rigidity *par excellence*.

Driving away through the night, we were delighted to find that the inbuilt, faired-over 7-in. Lucas Le Mans headlamps gave excellent vision and were easily dipped by a flick-switch from the dash. These powerful lamps and the fact that the Lotus Sports is not at all a noisy car made negotiation of London and its environs light work, although next day we felt rather embarrassed by the vivid colour of the car, racing-number discs on the tail fins doing nothing to mitigate the rippling laughter from the trolley-bus queues!

Colour is of little moment, though, in a sports car as delectable as this Lotus. Simple to drive, this is a very fast little car indeed, in terms of average speed or circuit lap times in the hands of a determined driver. Its absolute performance is obviously governed by the engine, but from the handling aspect there are few cars to match a Lotus. Corners can be taken faster than most drivers are prepared to negotiate them, at all events on early acquaintance, and the brakes are entirely adequate for such driving methods.

The dash equipment is simple in the extreme. Before the driver is a small Jaeger 8,000-r.p.m. rev.-counter, flanked by an oil gauge and a water thermometer. Over on the left of the dash is an ammeter and in the centre the lamps switch (with lettered indicator for side- or headlamps incorporated)-cum-ignition key. There is an electrical junction-box on the extreme left before the passenger, the horn push (the horn has a usefully loud note) is set in the centre of the dipperswitch, and the only other switches are a fuel-pump pull-out switch, dash-light ditto. and the starter button. Two excellent rear-view mirrors are provided, both of which swivel to prevent dazzle from cars behind.

The gear-lever is short and stiff, with a good grip. It is placed exactly right for the left hand, which drops straight onto it from the steering wheel. The action is rather stiff, which causes the ham-handed (or those in a hurry) to crash reverse when coming out of bottom gear, as happens with the normal Ford change, and the lateral movement is short, so that care is needed at first to make sure

SPORTS MODEL.—This view of the Lotus Eleven Sports shows clearly the adequate full-width windscreen, faired-in headlamps and spring-loaded fasteners for front and back hinged body-sections.

158

top isn't selected for bottom, coming out of neutral. After a few miles, however, the Lotus gear-change is a joyful possession.

The driver sits on the low floor, the seat cushion hard and wafer-thin. It is adequate, however, although on the test car it was loose and should have been secured to the floor. Here it must again be emphasised that a Lotus is likely to be largely " made to measure," so that in matters of seating, the substitution of a speedometer for the rev.-counter, etc., the customer would have final choice.

The seating position is reclining, with arms at full-stretch to a steering wheel which is adjustable but normally set within inches of the dash. Seated thus the arrangement is comfortable. Drivers with short legs may need to put a cushion behind them to enable them to fully depress the pedals, and then the top of the screen-frame will be liable to impair forward vision and the elbows, bent, will foul the propeller-shaft tunnel and door. Chapman has chosen a seating position which makes the cramped quarters in a Lotus acceptable to the majority of drivers.

Inside the car there is surprisingly good protection from the wind, in spite of the screen not being as wide as the body, so that a coat is needed as protection from rain, not cold, and a cap stays on the head satisfactorily unless a gale-force wind is blowing into the cockpit. However, drain-holes permit the ingress of rain from the road, so that the floor soon swims in water. While we are not so staid as to be unable to regard this shortcoming philosophically in a car of this nature, in view of the provision of a hood and normal screen, and the high price of the Lotus Sports, the fact that mackintosh trousers are almost a necessity when driving it will be regarded in some quarters as a major disadvantage. Another snag is a single screen-wiper (the motor set well under the dash, where it is necessary to fumble for the switch) that goes about its task half-heartedly and soon ceased to function. Incidentally, although the hood has a good back window it is of simple construction, seriously impedes entry and egress, and there is no provision for stowing it, or its two pull-out alloy hoops.

The hand-brake is also set well under the dash and across the car but it is quite convenient to use, having a short travel, except that the ratchet-release button is very close to the gear-lever push-pull rod, scarcely permitting insertion of the thumb. This brake holds the car admirably.

Qualifying the previous remarks anent comfort, although small hinged side panels serve as doors, to attain the driving seat it is necessary to step onto the seat; in dirty weather a suit from Petticoat Lane is more appropriate for Lotus-motoring than one from Savile Row. There is, of course, no luggage stowage apart from metal pockets in the doors, inspection of the recesses of the tail, by lifting forward the thin seat squab, merely revealing the horizontally-mounted spare wheel and the back axle ! In the case of many cars this would be damning criticism indeed, but as present-day sportsmen buy Lotus for the same reasons that their fathers bought Bugatti there is really no cause for alarm and despondency.

Press the starter, accelerate away to the howl of gears behind the astonishingly willing Ford engine, and commence to fling the car at corners, and little miseries like sodden trouser-legs evaporate.

The suspension is soft enough to subdue rattles from the body, gives a very comfortable ride, yet the " know-how " built into the Lotus enables corners to be taken exceedingly fast without pronounced over- or understeer and under full control. As there is insufficient power to spin the wheels the absence of a de Dion axle is not felt, except when cornering on a rough road. The 15-in. spring-spoke, leather-rimmed steering wheel is set very close to the dash and calls for 1½ turns, lock-to-lock. Actually, there is scarcely any lock to speak of. This rack-and-pinion steering is very light and considerable kick-back is transmitted to the wheel. Over bad surfaces the action of the swing-axle i.f.s. is very pronounced, but if the wheel is allowed to play through the fingers the lightness, high-gearing and kick-back are not objectionable. There is very faint castor action. Steering the Lotus is really a matter of wrist-movement, and slides can be easily corrected.

The brakes are very powerful for a firm pedal pressure and need to be applied discreetly on slippery roads. The clutch calls for care, being either in or out, and it is desirable to keep the revs. well up when starting from rest. One's clutch foot is somewhat restricted when at rest by the prop.-shaft tunnel.

The engine started promptly from cold and displayed absolutely no temperament over warming-up, being ready for play literally at a moment's notice. Water temperature was only 60-70 deg. C. until the radiator was blanked off. Oil pressure (the sump contained Esso 20/30 multigrade oil) varied with engine speed, from 20-70 lb./sq. in. Naturally, in view of the high gearing it paid to make liberal use of all three forward gears, but the engine was extremely docile, pulling away from a mere 1,000 r.p.m. in top gear with very little hesitation. On the overrun there was a good deal of

THE LOTUS ELEVEN SPORTS TWO-SEATER

Engine : Four cylinders, 63.5 by 92.5 mm. (1,172 c.c.). Side valves. 8.0-to-1 compression-ratio. Approximately 40 b.h.p. at 5,700 r.p.m. Safe sustained maximum : 5,250 r.p.m.

Gear ratios : First, 9.9 to 1; second, 5.6 to 1; top, 4.2 to 1.

Tyres : 4.00/4.25-15 Dunlop " Gold Seal " at front, 4.60-15 Dunlop G.T. at back, on centre-lock wire wheels.

Weight : 9 cwt. 0 qtr. 0 lb. (without occupants, but ready for the road, with approximately two gallons of petrol).

Fuel capacity : 7¾ gallons.

Wheelbase : 7 ft. 1 in.

Track : Front, 3 ft. 10½ in.; rear, 3 ft. 11 in.

Dimensions : 11 ft. 2 in. by 5 ft. 0 in. by 3 ft. 1 in. (high).

Price : £872 (£1,308, inclusive of p.t.).

Makers : Lotus Engineering Co., Ltd., 7, Tottenham Lane, London, N.8.

Performance Data

Speeds on gears at maximum safe r.p.m. :
 First ... 35.0 m.p.h.
 Second ... 69.0 „
 Top ... 89.8 „

Standing-start ¼-mile (wet road) :
 Average, two-way runs ... 19.7 sec.
 Best run ... ... 19.4 „

transmission clank, probably magnified by the aerodynamic body.

Before attempting to assess performance we took the Lotus to a measured ¼-mile to check road speed against rev.-counter readings and also paced a Porsche on which the speedometer had been accurately checked and calibrated. These researches showed that an indicated 3,000 r.p.m. in top gear represents 54 m.p.h., and as the rev.-counter was 5 per cent. slow with the tyres fitted, the true speed at 1,000 r.p.m. in top is 17.1 m.p.h. A straight of considerable length is needed for the rev.-counter needle to attain the red mark in top gear and normally the limit is reached at about 5,250 r.p.m., equal to a maximum speed of fractionally under 90 m.p.h. Given a really long run under favourable conditions about 95 m.p.h. is attainable, and if the screen is discarded and the red mark on the rev.-counter ignored this remarkable Ford engine, which runs up to some 6,000 r.p.m., will propel the Lotus at comfortably above 100 m.p.h. Peak revs. in first and second represent, respectively, 35 and 69 m.p.h. Cruising at 4,000 r.p.m., or approximately 68½ m.p.h., the engine is extremely contented. On a wet road, one-up, a standing-start ¼-mile was covered in an average for two-way runs of 19.7 sec., with a best run in 19.4 sec. The engine felt " unburstable " when taken up to peak revs. on these runs, and the very quick gear-change assists rapid accelerating. Dunlop 5.60-15 G.T. tyres were in use on the back wheels, with Dunlop " Gold Seal " 4.00/4.25-15 tyres on the front wheels, the wheels being centre-lock wire type.

We took the car to the usual weighbridge and, with approximately 2 gall. of fuel, it weighed exactly 9 cwt., slightly lighter than the Climax-engined Mk. IX tested a year earlier. The petrol situation did not permit a fuel-consumption check, but better than 30 m.p.g. should be possible even when using the performance to the full. Fuel is carried in a pannier tank, with quick-action filler, on the near side of the car. This tank, on the car in question, held 7¾ gall., which does not provide a very large range for a car of such long-distance potentialities; the solution would be to have the alternative 9½-gall., plus the additional 11-gall. tank, installed.

Accessibility is a highlight of the Lotus. Merely by unclipping a spring-loaded catch on each side, the entire front of the car hinges forward, to be retained by a cord. This lays bare the whole of the vital chassis parts in this area, as well as the engine, with its Lodge plugs under waterproof covers, high-set distributor (with h.t. leads to match the yellow body) and Lucas coil placed below the coolant header tank. A similar arrangement, with the addition of one Dzus fastener, enables the tail of the body to hinge rearwards.

That, then, is the Lotus in its most " bread-and-butter " form and, whether it is being used for club racing, is poodling through traffic at 1,500 r.p.m., or is being accelerated to beyond 5,000 r.p.m. in that extremely usable 5.6-to-1 second gear, it lives up fully to its enviable reputation of being one of our outstanding small sports cars, whose capabilities are restricted in this case by the use of a very docile side-valve power unit. The Lotus Eleven Sports costs £872, or £1,308 inclusive of p.t., and those who can pay this have access to a car which will provide exhilarating motoring and is capable of opening the door to success in club racing.—W. B.

Three-quarter rear view of the Lotus Eleven Le Mans.

Lotus Eleven Le Mans

LOTUS FOR 1958

At the 1957 International Motor Show, Earls Court, a range of cars manufactured by Lotus Engineering Company, Ltd., will be exhibited on Stand 119

"RACE-BRED" is a term frequently used by sports car manufacturers to describe their products. No firm can have a better claim to the expression than Lotus Engineering, which consolidated its position as Britain's chief producer of small-capacity sports/racing cars by its triumph in this year's Le Mans Grand Prix d'Endurance. "Twenty-four hour" reliability is allied to qualities of acceleration, braking and cornering power which have, in 1957, brought Lotus-Climax owners an almost monotonous list of successes in shorter British events. Moreover, in production-car races, and on the road, versions of the Eleven with Ford power units have recorded speeds entirely beyond the dreams of the engine's designers. The programme for 1958 is based on a continuation of the policy which has brought success in 1956 and 1957, detail improvements made on "Team Lotus" and F2 cars being incorporated, when fully tested, in production models. Two versions of the Eleven will be shown at Earls Court, the 1958 Le Mans, and the 1958 Club, while manufacture of the "Sports" version, with Ford engine, will be continued.

Outwardly the appearance of the 1958 Lotus Eleven will remain unchanged. This in itself is a tribute to the aerodynamic efficiency of the bodywork, developed from earlier departures into the sphere of "streamlining" and now familiar to racegoers (and others) throughout the world. The body of the Mark Eight somehow never looked quite right, and was extremely expensive to produce in conjunction with the stressed skin frame ; the exciting tail fins of the Mark Nine brought certain disadvantages in train, but the Eleven has become established as an example of efficiency allied with beautiful simplicity.

Panelled in aluminium, with a smooth, full length undertray, the body is made in three parts, with front and rear immediately removable to facilitate work on engine, transmission or suspension. Drop-down doors are provided, incorporating pockets in which maps or other small articles may be carried. On the Le Mans model the car-width, three-piece windscreen is continued into the top of the doors.

Cockpits are carpeted and fully trimmed. Bucket seats with reclining backs are fitted, and, although lateral space is adequate, leg (and foot) room, for persons of anything above average height, is somewhat limited.

Structural basis of the Lotus Eleven is a rigid space frame welded up from one inch and three-quarter inch, square and round steel tubing of 18 and 20 gauge. Additional stiffness is obtained by the incorporation of floor and propeller-shaft tunnel as stressed members.

THE 1958 LOTUS ELEVEN LE MANS

Most notable feature on this model is the "formula two" front suspension by means of double wishbones acting on coil spring telescopic shock absorber units ; the forward member of the upper wishbone also acts as an anti-roll bar.

Rear suspension is by a De Dion assembly. Fore and aft location is by parallel trailing arms, while a diagonal member from the offside controls lateral movement. The De Dion tube encloses, at each end, bearing housings and outboard universal joints. Girling disc brakes are fitted all round on the Le Mans model, mounted outboard at the front, inboard at the rear. Great attention to detail is noticeable in this department, the rear calipers being carried ahead of the discs to reduce overhung loads, while those at the front are behind the discs to reduce wheel bearing loads.

The brakes are hydraulically operated, with additional cable actuation of the rear wheels through the handbrake. The exceptionally sensitive steering of the Lotus is attributable to its lightweight rack and pinion gear with special forged steering arms. The steering wheel has a leather-covered rim.

Power unit of the Le Mans model is the well-known Stage 2, single cam Coventry Climax, with four cylinders and a capacity of 1098 cc. This, the FWA engine, develops 85 hp at 6800 rpm, and is carried in the chassis on two widely spaced rubber mountings at the front, with a single gearbox mounting at the rear. It is tilted ten degrees to the left, in order to lower the body profile and allow a horizontal induction tract for the twin SU carburetters.

The electrical system is 12 volt, current being supplied by a lightweight 31 amp-hour battery mounted in the tail to the left of the spare wheel. The engine-mounted dynamo is belt-driven, and coil ignition is employed. Acetate mouldings cover the recessed Lucas headlamps and separate sidelamps, while twin tail- and brakelights, rear number-plate light and high frequency horn (rarely needed with the "free" exhaust layout) satisfy all legal requirements for road use. Transmission is taken through a 7¼-in. single-plate clutch, mechanically operated, and a four-speed close-ratio gearbox. The hypoid final drive unit is available with a choice of five different axle ratios, varying from 5.125 to 1 to 3.89 to 1.

It is hoped that in the near future it will prove possible to supply the Le Mans car fitted with the "twin cam" Coventry Climax 1500 cc engine and rear-mounted five-speed gearbox/differential unit, as used in the F2 Lotus. It is typical of the Lotus policy of development by racing that the latter components have not been offered in "production" cars until fully tested. Now, with valve trouble largely eliminated by redesign of the offending parts, and breakage of crown wheel and pinion units overcome by alterations to the axle lubrication system, the incorporation of these features should not be long delayed.

THE 1958 LOTUS ELEVEN CLUB

As already mentioned, there is little outward difference between this, the second Lotus model at Earls Court, and the Eleven Le Mans. Chassis, power unit, and cockpit fittings are also common to both versions, but the Club car is produced at a competitive

Rear suspension on the Le Mans car.

160

LOTUS WINS AGAIN

ROSKILDE	August 17th—18th		SILVERSTONE	September 14th	
1500 cc	1ST Cliff Allison		1100 cc SPORTS CARS	1ST Keith Hall	
	3RD Alan Stacey			2ND Ivor Bueb	
KARLSKOGA	August 24th			3RD Alan Stacey	
1500 cc	1ST Peter Ashdown			4TH Peter Ashdown	
	2ND Alan Stacey			6TH J. Campbell-Jones	
	3RD Bill Frost		1500 cc SPORTS CARS	1ST Ron Flockhart	
SPA 3 HOURS	August 25th			2ND Henry Taylor	
1500 cc	1ST Cliff Allison			4TH Sir G. Baillie	
			also Team Prize and Formula II Record		

MOTOR SHOW
OCTOBER 16-26
EARLS COURT

STAND No. 119 — GROUND FLOOR

LOTUS ENGINEERING CO., LTD.
TOTTENHAM LANE, HORNSEY, LONDON, N.8   Tel: MOUntview 8353

---

price on account of its simplified suspension. At the front is a swing axle system which utilises a divided axle beam acting on coil spring telescopic shock absorber units through a single point at each end. At the rear, similar spring units act on a live axle located, as in the Le Mans version, by parallel trailing arms and a diagonal member. Interchangeability with the De Dion assembly is thus made possible.

Brakes on the Club model are of drum type, outboard mounted at both front and rear. Diameter of the cast iron drums is 9 in. front, 8 in. rear, and the two leading shoe units are hydraulically operated through separate front and rear master cylinders, fed from a single reservoir. Mechanical actuation is provided for the handbrake.

In addition to these models, and the Ford engined "Sports" version, production of the long-awaited Mark VII, an improved version of the Mark VI, will begin in the next few weeks. This is a "basic" vehicle, suitable for road or competition use, of which further details appear on page 243 of this issue.

In many eyes, the Formula Two Lotus was the star of the 1956 London Motor Show. This year, on the turntable on Stand 119 there will be an even more exciting departure in the field of automobile engineering. We are not able to disclose particulars of this car at present, since details will not be released until the eve of the show but we can say that it is a small, compact 2-seater coupe of most unusual construction. A full appraisal will appear in the November issue of SPORTS CAR & LOTUS OWNER.

With a basic car at one end of the scale, and this special new venture at the other, it appears likely that the production resources of Lotus Engineering will be tested to the extreme in coping with the world-wide demand which is certain to arise.

Front suspension on the Le Mans car is by double wishbones. Plug socket on right connects headlamp wiring when bodywork is in position.

161

A Lotus blossoms...

ROAD TEST LOTUS SPORTS

IN March of this year we tested a full competition Lotus, powered by the famous Coventry-Climax engine and selling for nearly $6000. In that report we mentioned that a simpler and cheaper version, known as the "Sports" model, was also manufactured by Lotus. The report ended with "Even the lowest-priced model may not put a Lotus in every garage, but it would certainly make an interesting racing class if enough cars of this type are brought over."

This, then, is a report on the lowest-priced model, powered by an ordinary Ford "10" side-valve engine and supplied by the U.S.A. Lotus distributor, Jay Chamberlain, 2909 West Olive, Burbank, Calif.

The Lotus Sports ("Club Sports" is *not* correct) is very similar to the famous "11" model except for the British Ford engine, three-speed transmission, solid rear axle and drum brakes. The multi-tube frame and low-pivot i. f. s. are used, and the body panels appear to be of identical contour. The racing windscreen is a simpler type, not at all unpleasing, and the rather elaborate cockpit cover and head rest of the 11 are dispensed with. A very neat full-width windshield and a not-too-bad top can be ordered (see photo in R&T for February 1957, page 26).

Parallel trailing arms support the solid rear axle, with coil springs here as well as in front. The brake system has twin master cylinders, two leading shoes, and drums nine and eight inches in diameter, front and rear. The transmission uses special close-ratio gears, giving 1.33 for second and 2.34 for first. While most Lotus (or is it Lotii?) come equipped with 4.50 section tires in front and 5.00 at the rear, our test car had 4.50-15 tires all around.

The seating position feels just right. In the cockpit area, there is a good feeling of neat, functional aluminum—comfortable, but hardly luxurious. All the controls work smoothly and easily, and the shift pattern is standard. In starting off, the high first gear (9.87:1 overall) is noticeable for the first few feet, and for an instant one wonders whether this might not be second gear. But from 5 mph upwards, the surge of power is very good indeed; the Tapley meter swings over to 510 lb/ton and 30 mph comes up in under 5 seconds, even after the initial hesitation. Slightly over 40 mph is possible in first gear (40 mph=5500 rpm), and the engine seems happy at this rate, though low gear is somewhat noisy and of course not synchronized. Second gear is relatively quiet, and gives a good boost with a peak Tapley reading equivalent to acceler-

Expanse of sheet metal in front of passenger will make the Lotus very popular in drive-in restaurants.

I'm a stranger here myself: the little Ford engine looks vaguely uncomfortable in this environment.

ating at the rate of 3.1 mph/sec. Actually, 40 to 70 mph in second gear requires 11.9 seconds, whereas 3.1 mph/sec. would give an elapsed time of 9.68 seconds, but the Tapley reading falls off rather rapidly above 40 mph (3100 rpm). This is, of course, due to the fall-off in engine torque and the increase in wind drag, as the speed continues to increase.

Speaking of drag figures, this car showed—after numerous tests in both directions—a total wind and rolling resistance of only 55 lb at 60 mph, as compared to 68 lb for our Lotus 11 test. From this we can calculate that the Sports model, with racing screen and two persons up, can hold 60 mph with only 9 bhp required at the flywheel.

We made only two timed high-speed runs; the second was the faster, at 99.0 mph. Perhaps a third run would have found the engine just enough freer that the magic three-figure mark could have been attained, but the engine temperature would start to climb under this treatment, and we were re-

an impractical, highly desirable combination

luctant to risk a piston seizure. Incidentally, the speedometer was dead accurate at 99 mph and the engine was held wide open for over two miles on each run, reaching a calculated 5700 rpm at the end. (No tachometer is supplied, which seems deplorable in a sports machine of this price.)

Our test driver was Ignacio Lozano, well known for his support of the marque Lotus. Getting the most and the best out of this car presents no special problems—it is very easy to drive, with one exception: Up to 70 mph or so the steering feels wonderful. With 1.5 turns and a 42-foot turning circle, the overall steering ratio isn't terribly quick. Nevertheless, at 90 mph the car suddenly seems to get as nervous as a wild horse, and frankly it was rather frightening. Experienced Lotus drivers say you get used to this, but for most tastes a slower gear and a smaller turning circle would be preferable.

The ride is quite firm, and on this car at least, the lack of a de Dion rear end is not felt at all. As might be expected from the weight distribution, the car understeers, but the raised roll center in front reduces the understeer to a very modest amount. Insofar as roll is concerned, there is (under normal driving conditions) no such thing. Only when the tires begin to squeak, signifying the approach of one g lateral forces, does the car lean at all perceptibly.

In order to show the range of performance which can be expected from a modified Lotus Sports, we have plotted the results of a British test in dotted lines against our usual acceleration graph. However, the overseas car carried a test weight approximately 200 lb below our figure, and the engine had quite a few internal modifications, including higher compression ratio, polished ports and oversize valves. Both test cars had twin S.U. carburetors. Accordingly, we have estimated that our car had about 40 bhp as compared to 45 or so for the more modified machine.

In short, and with only one or two minor complaints, we liked the Lotus Sports very much indeed. But now we must register what may sound very much like a sermon—and it is.

Here is a car for which we can discover no useful purpose whatsoever!

In two years, Lotus has built up a very good reputation in this country and sold nearly 100 machines. The cars are beautifully engineered, tremendous competition cars in their class, and cost near $5000. Now, in the new Ford-powered Sports, we have an equally fine machine. And, as we quoted earlier, it would make an interesting racing class. But as it stands now, this car is far too expensive ever to get a Ford 1172 class going. It would compete *continued on page* **164**

ROAD & TRACK ROAD TEST NO. 144

LOTUS SPORTS

SPECIFICATIONS

List price	$3690
Wheelbase, in.	85.0
Tread, f/r	46.5/47.0
Tire size	4.50-15
Curb weight, lb	970
distribution, %	55/45
Test weight	1290
Engine	4 cyl, sv
Bore & stroke	2.50 x 3.64
Displacement, cu in.	71.5
cu cm.	1172
Compression ratio	7.00
Horsepower (est.)	40
peaking speed	4600
equivalent mph	79
Torque, lb-ft	52
peaking speed	2500
equivalent mph	43
Gear ratios, overall	
3rd (high)	4.22
2nd	5.62
1st	9.87

CALCULATED DATA

Lb/hp (test wt)	32.2
Cu ft/ton mile	112
Engine revs/mile	3500
Piston travel, ft/mile	2120
Mph @ 2500 ft/min.	70.8

PERFORMANCE, Mph

Top speed, avg.	97.8
best run	99.0
2nd (5500)	71
1st (5500)	40
see charts for shift points	
Mileage range	25/40 mpg

ACCELERATION, Sec.

0-30 mph	4.8
0-40 mph	7.1
0-50 mph	10.6
0-60 mph	14.2
0-70 mph	19.0
0-80 mph	26.0
Standing start ¼ mile	19.2

TAPLEY DATA, Lb/ton

3rd	250 @ 50 mph
2nd	310 @ 40 mph
1st	510 @ 27 mph
Total drag at 60 mph, 55 lb	

SPEEDOMETER ERROR

Indicated	Actual
30 mph	28.6
40 mph	38.8
50 mph	48.7
60 mph	58.5
70 mph	68.5
80 mph	78.3
99 mph	99.0

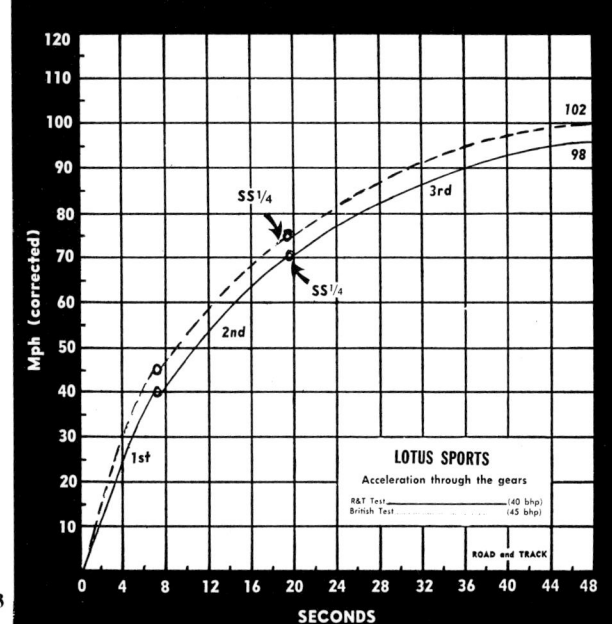

LOTUS SPORTS
Acceleration through the gears
R&T Test .... (40 bhp)
British Test .... (45 bhp)

BARE MAXIMUM

KNEE-HIGH to a visiting journalist, the Lotus has several claims to the attention of passers-by. On the road it is mostly seen from behind.

Continued from page 154

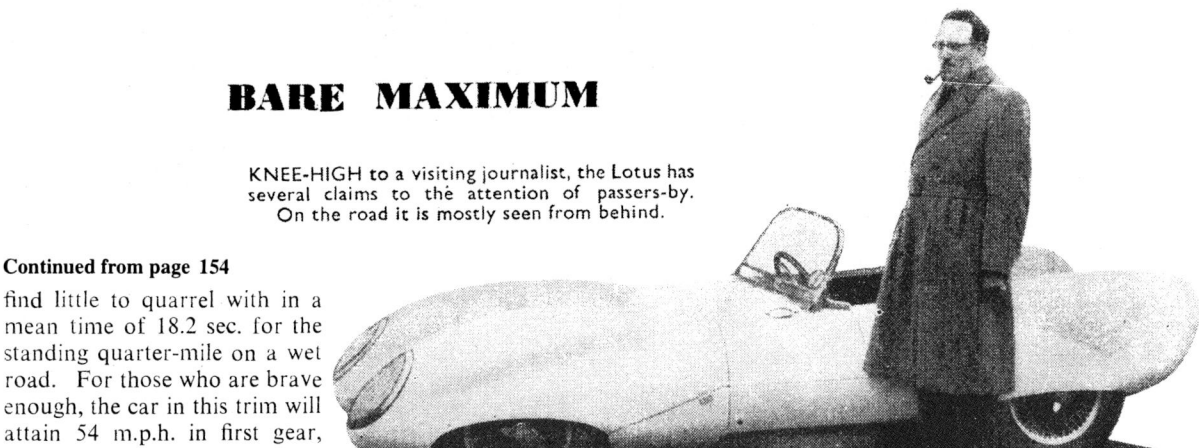

find little to quarrel with in a mean time of 18.2 sec. for the standing quarter-mile on a wet road. For those who are brave enough, the car in this trim will attain 54 m.p.h. in first gear, 81 m.p.h. in second and (theoretically) 109 m.p.h. in third and 135 m.p.h. in top.

Undoubtedly the size of the windscreen makes it a most efficient air-brake on a car of this kind, and it would be an interesting further exercise to see just how big a difference it makes to performance and fuel economy. Part of the service if you buy a Lotus is the ability to choose your own degree of weather protection. It may range from nothing at all, through aero- and wrap-round screens to a hardtop for, we suspect, women and children only; certainly not for our six feet without an extra dome in the roof. We are not, personally, complaining. We should like an aero-screen and a fine day, miles and miles of open road, and a (moderately) generous ration of petrol. — R.B.B.-S.

Lotus Road Test—Continued on page 145

fat lady, who announced that "you wouldn't get me to ride in that thing". The other was from a gentleman who tripped over the Lotus outside licensed premises, and was very critical indeed from a prone position.

Curiously enough, the car was particularly suitable for town work, and one seemed able to judge its exact width to a nicety when hurrying through traffic. I must admit that I was very unhappy about parking it in London streets, though, for most motorists nowadays are accustomed to park by actual bumper contact, and the extremities of the Lotus are alarmingly vulnerable. Some sort of rudimentary detachable bumpers might be developed for use in crowded cities, I feel, though the body looks far better without them.

From a practical point of view, the Ford engine and gearbox can be serviced anywhere, and one can drive at the limit in speed events, secure in the knowledge that a "blow-up" would not be a financial disaster. The Ford 10 is a wonderful engine, and this Lotus at last brings it into the genuine 100 m.p.h. category. Of course, this car is eligible for "1,172 Formula" events.

The Lotus Eleven Sports is spectacular in appearance and performance. It is a perfectly practical means of everyday transport, as well as being entirely suitable for the amateur competition driver. Finally, the fully-opening bonnet and tail must make this about the most accessible car on the market.

LOTUS TEST
Continued from page 163

with its 1460 cc Coventry-Climax-powered cars, a daring but hopeless enterprise.

So, we add the windshield, top and side curtains, securing thereby a very fine and unique dual-purpose car? Almost, but wait. In the first place, the price is $1500 more than the Ford-10-powered Morgan 4/4, although the Lotus weighs 580 lb less. But, more importantly, the Lotus has so little ground clearance that anything larger than a pebble in the street will rake the belly pan from stem to stern. Enclosed front wheels would make parking a matter of finding a space vacated by an Imperial, and what American bumpers would do to that beautiful but unprotected aluminum would be sheer slaughter. Coil springs having at least one inch more loaded height and 5.00 tires would increase the ground clearance to a sensible minimum of 6.5 in. The front fenders could be cut away to give a turning circle of 30 to 32 ft, but that isn't easy.

We would be so bold as to suggest a redesigned 1172 cc car, and possibly a larger all-out competition machine offered for sale at about the same price, without an engine or gearbox. And what would we damn Yanks install for power? An American V-8!

LOTUS "TRAINING"
BY INNES IRELAND LTD.

IN the horse-racing world it is customary for owners to entrust specialist trainers with what might be termed "race-preparation," and a great number never see their animals except when they are actually racing.

Until recently there has been no parallel in motor racing. "Works" cars usually were made and private owners' machines normally being looked after either by the owner-driver himself or by a mechanic he employs—usually in his own garage. But tucked away in the woods in the most rural part of Surrey is an establishment which must be unique of its kind—Innes Ireland Ltd.

On many occasions in the past season racegoers have commented on the number of Lotus Elevens entered by the above concern, particularly when Innes Ireland himself is driving a car entered by an entirely different person. The reason is quite simple; five private owners have put organisation of entries, race-preparation, transportation of cars and spares, and all the other details to be dealt with in getting a car on to the starting line, in the hands of Innes Ireland Ltd. All they need to do is turn up at the circuit in time for practice and drive, a way of life which is normally the prerogative of star works drivers; the only difference is that they, the private-owners, have to pay for this service.

Nevertheless, economics being what they are, this can still be a remarkably cheap way to go motor racing. It inevitably costs more than it would for the man who is also his own mechanic and team manager, and who either drives his car to and from meetings (which can become somewhat impracticable) or tows it on a trailer behind some other vehicle. But by comparison with the cost to a private owner of employing a personal mechanic, and perhaps using a more elaborate transporter in which it is possible to work on the car when, at the circuit, the Innes Ireland method certainly has its advantages. For instance, it is normal to take five cars to a race meeting, three in a very smart ex-Royal Blue transporter and two on a trailer.

And while some drivers can provide a mechanic with a full-time job looking after one car, an owner who takes part in short circuit events may not use his car sufficiently to justify the employment of a full-time mechanic. Conversely, if one particular car should require urgent attention it is usually possible, at Elstead, to get the work finished in time.

From all these angles the system has its advantages. Something of the quality of the work carried out is reflected in Michael Taylor's record of 26 "places" in 27 events (in the odd one he was involved in a multiple shunt). The other owners, Doug Graham, Peter Heath, Chris Martyn and Jack Westcott all have an impressive record of mechanical reliability and Innes Ireland's car has rewarded painstaking work by such successes as a class win in the Reims 12 Hours race and an overall win in the GT event at the Auvergne circuit, when Innes led home a whole host of 250 GT Ferraris. In addition to this, the same car has done remarkably well in British sprint events (Innes set up a new outright circuit record at Full Sutton in September) which rather disproves the contention that it is impossible to use the same car (and engine) for such very different events. But of all the work done on this car during the season, perhaps the most amusing was the arrangement of "Appendix J" luggage space for Gran Turismo events. Interestingly enough, the accommodation thus provided later proved very useful for the carrying of tools and spares.

Until one rounds a bend and sees the front end of an Eleven peeping shyly from a workshop, the grounds of the Golden Acres Country Club are the last place in which one would expect to find a racing car tuning establishment. Pine trees flank the drive as it winds further and further away from what are normally accepted as signs of civilisation and, except when a Coventry Climax engine is being run, the only sound is the song of birds. In this idyllic setting (idyllic except for a lack of plumbing, which dictates the use of a different tree each week) the needs of six cars are catered for by four men; Brit Pearce, Dicky Samuelson, Ted Searle and John Lancaster.

At this point it is necessary to emphasise—if, indeed, it is not already apparent—that the cars at Elstead do not constitute a team in the normal sense of the word. In fact, at most British

a great deal about Lotuses. Innes started his own season disastrously, running out of fuel at Snetterton when in the lead due to increased consumption on Weber carburetters. There followed a spate of gearbox trouble, but once this was overcome the light green car became one of the most reliable—though one of the hardest used—in the country, and several small modifications which had been made were later incorporated—when time permitted—on "customers'" cars.

Six feet six in Eleven

The latter were all fitted with SU carburetters, but all have proved to be very fast, and indeed the Martyn/Graham Eleven was the fastest privately entered 1100 c.c. car in the Tourist Trophy. Michael Taylor's exploits were dealt with at greater length last month; all the other cars have proved almost equally consistent, if not so outstandingly successful. Doug Graham has done well at a number of Club meetings, Peter Heath, on leave from Siam, has had a great personal achievement in managing to get his 6 ft. 6 ins. into an Eleven without major structural alterations (the pedal box was moved forward, special seats were fitted, the steering column and dashboard were raised and one diagonal frame

meetings the drivers are very much racing *against* each other, and particularly against Innes Ireland, whenever they get the chance. Nevertheless, for such events as the Tourist Trophy they have naturally joined forces, and at all times—whether at race meetings or during preparation—they are always willing to lend each other spare parts.

Next season

It may well be satisfaction with the standard of work which promotes this friendly atmosphere among Innes Ireland's "customers," but the confidence of those concerned has not been gained without effort. For instance, soon after the start of the season Innes was given to understand by Michael Taylor's father—in no uncertain terms—that he was not satisfied with certain aspects of the car's turnout. Subsequent improvement was obviously noticed, for the firm has now been given the task of rebuilding a two-litre Fifteen which Michael will drive next year—and this is going to demand considerably more effort than the preparation of an Eleven. However, Brit Pearce, who is in charge of this project, is confident that this car will be really "right" by the start of next season.

All the cars at Elstead have received the same sort of attention during 1958, and particular care has been given to a number of details which have become suspect. Brit Pearce has gained very wide experience of motor racing, and particularly as Mike Hawthorn's personal mechanic, and Dicky Samuelson knows "most of the dodges" as a result of his work at the Connaught and Cooper factories; in addition to this everyone at Elstead has now learned member was repositioned) and Chris Martyn and Jack Westcott have both been placed in a large number of events throughout the year.

One of the reasons for the reliability of all the cars is the attention paid to details. Each car is carefully checked over after every event, and thoroughly inspected after a long distance race or a series of shorter races. Gearboxes are dismantled periodically—not surprisingly after Innes Ireland's own experiences with them—and rear gearbox mountings have been modified during the course of the season.

The same care is given to engine assembly, and in this respect has obviously paid dividends. As far as Innes Ireland Ltd. is concerned, a tremendous amount has been learned about race preparation during 1958, and a number of more ambitious projects are in view for 1959. To assess the service provided at Elstead, one can only look to the car-owners for their opinions; in every case the customers seem to be very satisfied.

Jack Westcott

Doug Graham

Chris Martyn

Peter Heath

Innes Ireland

165

Make: Lotus
Makers: Lotus Engineering Co., Ltd., Tottenham Lane, London, N.8.
Type: XI Le Mans '85'

Test Data

World copyright reserved; no unauthorized reproduction in whole or in part.

CONDITIONS: Weather: Cool and dry with little wind. (Temperature 46°-47° F., Barometer 30.4 in. Hg.) Surface: Dry concrete. Fuel: Mixed British Super-grade and Belgian Premium-grade pump petrols (100 and 92 Research Method Octane Rating).

INSTRUMENTS
Speedometer and distance recorder geared for different axle ratio to that used during test.

WEIGHT
Kerb weight (unladen, but with oil, coolant and fuel for approx. 50 miles) .. 9¾ cwt.
Front/rear distribution of kerb weight 51/49
Weight laden as tested .. .. ..13 cwt.

MAXIMUM SPEEDS
Flying Half Mile
Mean of four opposite runs .. 125.0 m.p.h.
Best one-way time equals .. 126.8 m.p.h.
"Maximile" Speed. (Timed quarter mile after one mile accelerating from rest.)
Mean of four opposite runs .. 120.8 m.p.h.
Best one-way time equals .. 123.3 m.p.h.
Speed in Gears (at 7,500 r.p.m. limit with 1½-litre-size gearbox as used on test car).
Max. speed in 3rd gear .. .. 101 m.p.h.
Max. speed in 2nd gear .. .. 79 m.p.h.
Max. speed in 1st gear .. .. 52 m.p.h.

FUEL CONSUMPTION
— m.p.g. at constant 30 m.p.h. on level.
55.5 m.p.g. at constant 40 m.p.h. on level.
55.5 m.p.g. at constant 50 m.p.h. on level.
52.0 m.p.g. at constant 60 m.p.h. on level.
46.0 m.p.g. at constant 70 m.p.h. on level.
39.5 m.p.g. at constant 80 m.p.h. on level.
35.5 m.p.g. at constant 90 m.p.h. on level.
32.5 m.p.g. at constant 100 m.p.h. on level.
Overall Fuel Consumption for 732 miles, 21.3 gallons, equals 34.4 m.p.g. (8.2 litres/100 km.)
Touring Fuel Consumption (m.p.g. at steady speed midway between 30 m.p.h. and maximum, less 5% allowance for acceleration) 39.0 m.p.g.
Fuel Tank Capacity (maker's figure) 8½ gallons (larger fuel tank optional).

STEERING
Turning circle between kerbs:
Left .. .. 42¾ feet
Right .. .. 41½ feet
Turns of steering wheel from lock to lock 1⅞

BRAKES from 30 m.p.h.
1.00 g retardation (equivalent to 30 ft. stopping distance) with 140 lb. pedal pressure.
0.75 g retardation (equivalent to 40 ft. stopping distance) with 100 lb. pedal pressure.
0.65 g retardation (equivalent to 46 ft. stopping distance) with 75 lb. pedal pressure.
0.42 g retardation (equivalent to 72 ft. stopping distance) with 50 lb. pedal pressure.
0.20 g retardation (equivalent to 150 ft. stopping distance) with 25 lb. pedal pressure.

ACCELERATION TIMES from standstill
0-30 m.p.h. .. .. 4.6 sec.
0-40 m.p.h. .. .. 6.2 sec.
0-50 m.p.h. .. .. 8.0 sec.
0-60 m.p.h. .. .. 10.0 sec.
0-70 m.p.h. .. .. 12.3 sec.
0-80 m.p.h. .. .. 15.1 sec.
0-90 m.p.h. .. .. 18.8 sec.
0-100 m.p.h. .. .. 23.6 sec.
Standing quarter mile .. .. .. 17.3 sec.

ACCELERATION TIMES on upper ratios

	Top gear	3rd gear
10-30 m.p.h.	—	—
20-40 m.p.h.	—	7.9 sec.
30-50 m.p.h.	11.8 sec.	6.0 sec.
40-60 m.p.h.	8.0 sec.	5.3 sec.
50-70 m.p.h.	7.5 sec.	5.2 sec.
60-80 m.p.h.	7.1 sec.	5.5 sec.
70-90 m.p.h.	8.2 sec.	6.4 sec.
80-100 m.p.h.	9.8 sec.	8.6 sec.

HILL CLIMBING at sustained steady speeds
Max. gradient on top gear .. 1 in 6.9 (Tapley 320 lb./ton)
Max. gradient on 3rd gear .. 1 in 5.1 (Tapley 435 lb./ton)
Max. gradient on 2nd gear .. 1 in 3.7 (Tapley 575 lb./ton)

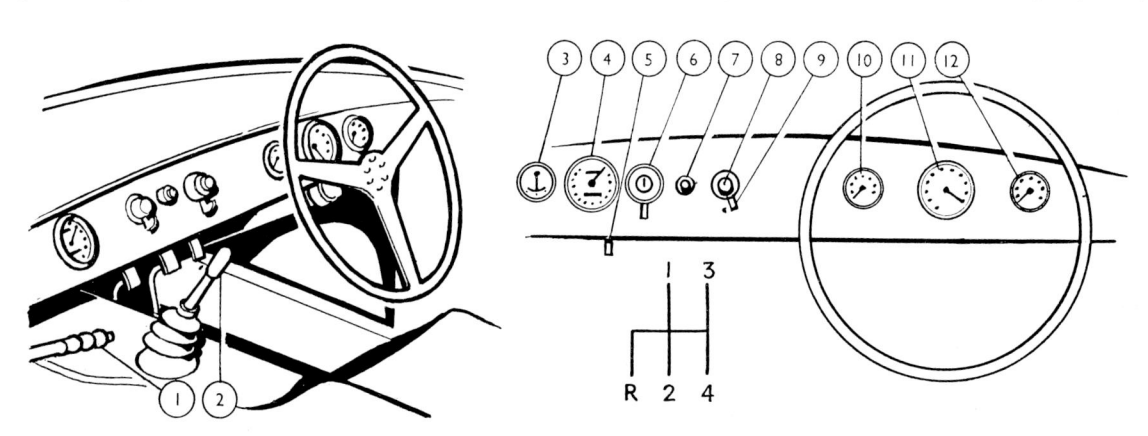

1, Handbrake. 2, Gear lever. 3, Ammeter. 4, Speedometer and distance recorder. 5, Trip re-setting knob. 6, Ignition and lights switch. 7, Starter switch. 8, Horn button. 9, Headlamp dipswitch. 10, Water thermometer. 11, Rev. counter. 12, Oil pressure gauge.

The LOTUS XI Le Mans "85"

A Two-seater with Racing Performance which can be Run on the Road

RECORDING a maximum speed of 125 m.p.h., as an average of timed two-way runs with a passenger as well as a driver being carried, the Lotus XI provides a vivid illustration of the huge gain in small sports car performance which has taken place during the past decade. Able to accelerate the same two-man load from a standstill to 100 m.p.h. in only 23.6 seconds, this car invites incredulity as to its modest 1,098 c.c. engine size, until almost equally miraculous fuel economy figures (which range from 32½ m.p.g. at a sustained 100 m.p.h. to 55½ m.p.g. at a steady 40 m.p.h. on the level) are also observed.

What sort of a car is it that Colin Chapman's brilliant team of young engineers and aerodynamicists has endowed with such astonishing acceleration, speed and economy of fuel? It is, in the form in which we drove it, a somewhat Spartan car in many respects, built to have the minimum weight and frontal area consistent with eligibility for the Le Mans 24-hour race and other sports-car fixtures. Our testing was carried out with a wrap-around windscreen of Perspex, a full-width screen but one so modest in height that a tall man is more comfortable wearing goggles and looking over it than crouching low to peer through its scratchable transparency. No hood is provided, the two doors which open outwards on horizontal hinges do little to facilitate entry or exit from the car, and the frequently-raced test model did not claim to be proof against intrusion of water from the road into the cockpit on wet days. The bucket seats are sufficiently narrow and deep to make full jacket pockets an embarrassment, and the cockpit allows no spare width for a left foot beside the clutch pedal.

Spartan though it is by conventional standards, however, the Lotus XI with its background of success in long-distance races comes to be appreciated after a little while as an oddly comfortable car. Suitably clad and shod, a driver settles down to become very much at home behind the leather-covered steering wheel, with all the controls very conveniently at hand, and comfortably supported by the bucket seat, the curved rear wheel arch which forms a shoulder-rest on the right, and the high transmission tunnel which serves as an armrest on the left. Waste space around the passenger is even more scarce than around the driver, because of the handbrake, an unsymmetrical gearbox cover, some lateral frame tubes, and on the test car some all-too-accessible mountings of the electrical fuse and regulator boxes; yet a passenger also can learn to settle down and really enjoy being motored around with astonishing rapidity. Luggage space is scanty, there being room for a parcel above the enclosed spare wheel and for two more thin parcels just inside the doors, but as tested this was a car to carry its driver and either a passenger or some luggage, fast enough to win awards in racing yet able to run on the public roads without exciting the disapproval of the law. Available variations on the basic body include on the one hand a single-seat windscreen giving extra top speed, and on the other hand a glass windscreen giving two people slightly greater protection from the elements.

For experts on ordinary touring cars to assess the merits of the Lotus XI as a racing machine would be a foolish impertinence, and is unnecessary since results already achieved speak for themselves. Victories all over Europe and in America have confirmed that the speed and handling qualities of this model match one another. During 1957, a wishbone type of I.F.S. replaced the divided-axle layout used on earlier Lotus cars, and the result has been a great gain in ease of control at three-figure speeds on imperfect surfaces by drivers of no more than normal competence, without any offsetting loss of ultimate cornering power being evident.

Several engines can be used in this Lotus, from the 40 b.h.p. Ford 1,172 c.c. side-valve through 1,098 c.c. overhead-camshaft Coventry Climax engines in 75 b.h.p. and 84 b.h.p. forms to single-camshaft and twin-camshaft 1½-litre units of

---

In Brief

Price (including 84 b.h.p. engine as tested) £1,690 plus purchase tax £811 equals £2,501.
Price with 75 b.h.p. engine and normal axle (including purchase tax), £1,937 7s. 0d
Capacity ... ... 1,098 c.c.
Unladen kerb weight ... 9¾ cwt.
Acceleration:
  40-60 m.p.h. in top gear ... 8.0 sec.
  0-50 m.p.h. through gears 8.0 sec.
Maximum top gear gradient 1 in 6.9
Maximum speed ... ...125.0 m.p.h.
"Maximile" speed ... ...120.8 m.p.h.
Touring fuel consumption .. 39.0 m.p.g.
Gearing: 17.1 m.p.h. in top gear at 1,000 r.p.m.; 39.1 m.p.h. at 1,000 ft./min. piston speed.

The LOTUS XI Le Mans

ACCESS to the Coventry Climax engine is easy when the body nose is hinged forward, details in view being the o.h.v. cover, twin S.U. carburetters with intake air box, ignition distributor and coil, hydraulic brake reservoir and rear-mounted coolant header tank.

SWINGING up the tail of the body reveals the battery and spare wheel, removal of the latter giving access to the de Dion rear axle assembly.

limited availability developing up to 145 b.h.p. Our test car had the 1,098 c.c. Coventry Climax engine in stage 2 tune, developing 84 b.h.p. at 6,800 r.p.m. but giving less torque below 4,000 r.p.m. than does the 75 b.h.p. stage 1 engine. Wheel adhesion was improved because a ZF spin-limiting differential supplemented the de Dion rear axle layout on the test model, but this individual car's racing history penalized it to the extent of a 20-gallon petrol tank and extra-heavy gearbox as weight-increasing relics of past service with a 1½-litre engine and in long-distance races.

With only slight silencing of the exhaust and a fair amount of mechanical clatter, the stage 2 engine does not invite hard driving around towns. Numerous journeys in and out of central London at busy times showed a tendency for the coolant to heat up somewhat in traffic jams, and a firm clutch combined with splined rear wheel drive shafts, invited juddery starts from rest, but despite ragged carburation at low r.p.m. there was no plug-oiling or other serious temperament. Even when driven hard, the engine used very little oil. In the absence of choke controls, winter starting from cold required two hands to cover the carburetter intakes while the starter was operated, but the engine soon warmed up enough to pull normally.

In rural surroundings, the stage 2 engine begins to awaken at 3,000 r.p.m., develops its best torque at 5,000 r.p.m., and is still pulling very vigorously indeed at the suggested limit of 7,500 r.p.m. beyond which a risk of harmful contact between valves and pistons soon arises. The cry of a Lotus being driven at high r.p.m. and a wide throttle opening is decidedly audible, but less anti-social than it might be because a Lotus driven in this fashion disappears over the horizon and out of earshot in a brief space of time.

Eight different rear axle ratios are available for the car, covering a range from 3.73/1 to 5.375/1, and our test was made with a 4.22/1 ratio with which almost exactly the maximum permitted r.p.m. were indicated at the timed maximum speed of 125 m.p.h. with full-width windscreen. For our usual standing-start acceleration tests with two people in the car, this axle ratio was too high to give best results, engagement of the clutch at even 5,000 r.p.m. being followed by a drop in r.p.m. to a figure at which there was momentary hesitation, and no wheelspin or clutchslip being evident. But, if a rest-to-30 m.p.h. time of 4.6 seconds and a standing ¼-mile time of 17.3 seconds do not represent the best that a Lotus can achieve in two-up trim (without a 1½-cwt. passenger, this 9¾-cwt. car becomes substantially livelier) such figures as rest-to-60 m.p.h. in 10.0 seconds and rest-to-100 m.p.h. in 23.6 seconds are remarkable for a car of any size and would until recently have seemed wildly impossible for an unsupercharged 1,100 c.c. car carrying two people and using pump petrol. Most people will find that, in the lower gears, they have more power than they know how to use from this 1,100 c.c. Lotus, but once familiarity with the car is acquired the average speeds put up on away-from-towns cross-country running are astonishing, a reminder that the congested state of popular routes on summer week-ends has not eliminated all opportunities to go motoring for fun.

Perhaps partly because the coil springs had settled slightly (Lotus road-holding is based upon flexible springs controlled by exceptionally firm damper settings) the ground clearance of our test model was quite inconveniently small, especially below the disc-type inboard rear brakes but also below the sump and elsewhere, so that moderately rough going or the landing on a normal smooth road after crossing a hump-back bridge at just below take-off speed would produce grating sounds from beneath the car. On rough going, there

TAILORED to fit closely around driver and passenger are the individual seats. Wind protection is by a very low wrap-around Perspex screen, but the speedometer mounting illustrated is a temporary one for test purposes only. Fuel is normally carried alongside the passenger, the test car having a long-range tank in the scuttle.

"85"

LOW BUILD of the Lotus is emphasized in this rear view which shows how, by low mounting of the seats and some sacrifice of ground clearance, the body has been dropped well below the level of the mudguards.

was a considerable amount of rattle from the doors, wrap-around screen sections and elsewhere, the light-alloy body being functionally simple and without a scrap of superfluous weight, but ignoring this sound effect the riding comfort over most surfaces was good. The Lotus does, however, show up to best advantage (in both riding and handling qualities) on reasonably smooth roads.

Built so low to the ground and designed for racing, the car naturally corners without any perceptible roll or sideway. The rack-and-pinion steering has comfortable self-centring action, yet is so precise and light that in ordinary road driving up to and beyond 100 m.p.h., it suffices to hold the wheel rim between the thumb and forefinger of one hand. Whereas earlier designs of Lotus chassis cornered well but needed handling with a very delicate touch in order to run truly straight at speed, this model can be placed precisely without conscious effort by the driver at speeds up to more than two miles a minute. Not pretending to be racing drivers, we confined our explorations of the ultimate limits of cornering speed to occasions when there was spare room for any resultant excitements, and whilst clumsy use of the power in a low gear on a very sharp corner could flick the tail outwards quite quickly, the handling qualities otherwise remained beautifully consistent right up to the cornering speed at which front and rear wheels were sliding outwards together. In fact, experiment confirmed our first impressions that, with consistently good cornering and an outstandingly quick response to any sudden change of plan by the driver, this car could safely be cornered at far more than normal speeds on the road.

Whilst a car weighing under 10 cwt. as it stands at the kerb does not demand great retarding forces from its braking system, a top speed of 125 m.p.h., and wind resistance so low as to let the car run very freely on the over-run, make good brakes extremely important on a car such as this. We did not have a chance to sample this Lotus in the wet, but past experience suggests that the Girling disc brakes would have been as reassuringly adequate in wet weather as they were on dry roads during this test. The pedal pressure needed actually to lock all four wheels is fairly high (there is no servo assistance) but the proportionality of braking response and the sustained firm feel of the pedal in repeated stops from high speeds give a driver great confidence. The handbrake did not earn commendation, but a hard pull to the last obtainable notch would in fact hold the car on gradients.

It is not to be expected that the Lotus XI will be bought as an economy car, but the astonishing m.p.g. figures which it can record are a testimony to its low air resistance and high engine efficiency. At any speed likely to be used outside towns, over the range from 50 m.p.h. to over 100 m.p.h., it would be difficult to find another car able to show equal economy of premium-grade petrol.

Built for the extremely specialized purpose of winning sports-car races, for which present-day requirements of roominess and weather protection are not very onerous, the Lotus XI Le Mans does not represent the average motorist's idea of an everyday car. But, it is a car which can provide extremely fast day or night travel on ordinary out-of-town roads, and can at the same time give immense enjoyment to suitably minded drivers and passengers. As an engineering tour-de-force, this race-proved two-seater of such astonishing speed and roadworthiness certainly suggests that the forthcoming coupé model from the same designers is likely to be worth waiting for.

Specification

Engine
- Cylinders ... 4
- Bore ... 72.4 mm.
- Stroke ... 66.6 mm.
- Cubic capacity ... 1,098 c.c.
- Piston area ... 25.5 sq. in.
- Valves ... Single o.h. camshaft
- Compression ratio ... 9.8/1
- Carburetter ... Two S.U.
- Fuel pump ... S.U. electrical
- Ignition timing control ... Centrifugal
- Oil filter ... Full-flow
- Max. power (net) ... 84 b.h.p.
- at ... 6,800 r.p.m.
- Piston speed at max. b.h.p. 2,980 ft./min.

Transmission (With normal close-ratio gearbox: non-standard gearbox used on test car)
- Clutch ... 7¼-in. single dry plate
- Top gear (s/m) ... 4.22
- 3rd gear (s/m) ... 5.20
- 2nd gear (s/m) ... 7.05
- 1st gear ... 10.54
- Reverse ... 10.54
- Propeller shaft ... Hardy Spicer open
- Final drive ... Hypoid bevel (choice of 8 ratios) on chassis
- Top gear m.p.h. at 1,000 r.p.m. 17.1
- Top gear m.p.h. at 1,000 ft./min. piston speed 39.1

Chassis
- Brakes ... Girling disc (outboard front, inboard rear) with hydraulic operation
- Brake disc diameter ... 9½
- Friction lining area ...
- Suspension:
  - Front ... Independent by coil springs and wishbones, with anti-roll torsion bar
  - Rear ... Coil springs and de Dion axle
- Shock absorbers ... Armstrong telescopic
- Steering gear ... Rack and pinion
- Tyres ... Dunlop racing 4.50—15 front, 5.00—15 rear

Coachwork and Equipment

- Starting handle ... No
- Battery mounting ... Behind seats
- Jack ... None
- Jacking points: Lifting points at front and rear for use with quick-lift racing jacks.
- Standard tool kit ... None
- Exterior lights: 2 headlamp, 2 sidelamps, 2 tail lamps, 1 stop/number plate lamp.
- Number of electrical fuses ... 4
- Direction indicators ... None
- Windscreen wipers. Lucas electrical single-blade
- Windscreen washers ... None
- Sun vizors ... None
- Instruments: Rev. counter, oil pressure gauge, ammeter, coolant thermometer (speedometer and oil thermometer optional).
- Warning lights ... Dynamo charge
- Locks:
  - With ignition key ... Ignition switch
  - With other keys ... None
- Glove lockers ... None
- Map pockets ... Two in doors
- Parcel shelves ... Two inside doors
- Ashtrays ... None
- Cigar lighters ... None
- Interior lights ... Instrument lighting
- Interior heater ... None
- Car radio ... None
- Extras available ... As required
- Upholstery material ... Vynide
- Floor covering ... Carpet
- Exterior colours standardized ... Any colour as ordered
- Alternative body styles: Full-width glass screen and hood, or single-person screen and metal cover for passenger seat, on same basic body.

Maintenance

- Sump ... 7 pints plus 1 pint in filter, S.A.E. 20/30 winter, S.A.E. 30/40 summer
- Gearbox ... 2¼ pints, S.A.E. 90 E.P. gear oil
- Rear axle ... 1¾ pints, S.A.E. 90 hypoid gear oil
- Steering gear lubricant ... Graphite grease
- Cooling system capacity ... 14 pints (1 drain tap)
- Chassis lubrication ... By grease gun every 1,000 miles to 21 points
- Ignition timing ... 2°-6° b.t.d.c. static
- Contact-breaker gap ... 0.015 in.
- Sparking plug type ... Lodge RL47
- Sparking plug gap ... 0.022 in.
- Valve timing: Inlet opens 30° b.t.d.c. and closes 60° a.b.d.c., exhaust opens 60° b.b.d.c. and closes 30° a.t.d.c.
- Tappet clearances (cold):
  - Inlet and exhaust ... 0.006-0.008 in.
- Front wheel toe-in ... $\frac{1}{16}$ in.
- Camber angle ... ½° to 1½°
- Castor angle ... 5° to 7°
- Steering swivel pin inclination ... 9°
- Tyre pressures for road use:
  - Front ... 18 lb.
  - Rear ... 22 lb.
- (For very fast driving: Front 25 lb., Rear 30 lb.)
- Brake fluid ... Wakefield
- Battery type and capacity ... 12 v. 31 amp./hr. Exide lightweight

driving around with WALT WORON

PHOTOS BY CHARLES NERPEL

LOW FRONTAL AREA is typical of all Lotus models. Seating is tight fit; lightweight seats wedge driver into firm, comfortable position so that no safety belt is needed during hard cornering.

LOTUS CLUB performed best on open highway, climbed mountain roads with ease, giving 25-mpg economy on trip.

COVENTRY CLIMAX engine displaces 1100cc, has single overhead cam, develops 75 hp at 6250 rpm in this model.

LOTUS CLUB
slight screamer

DESPITE THE FACT that Lotus "sportscars" have been around on road racing circuits for several years now, few people have seen them close up. Fewer still know anything more about them than that "They're some kind of a special, aren't they?" Even in an area as automotive-conscious as Southern California I was amazed at the questions asked, like:
"What kind of a car is it?"
"Did you build that?"
"What kind of a body is it?"
"What kind of an engine does it have?"
"What country is that built in?"

Of course the people you meet on the street are not the same ones who necessarily attend road races—aficionados who know that the Lotus is a car that has carved a niche for itself in competition. In the hands of the builder, Colin Chapman, it began to appear on road race circuits in 1953. Through its growing pains, using different engines, including a two-liter Bristol, it racked up several wins, including 11th place overall at Sebring, 1957, then fourth, sixth and ninth overall at Sebring, 1958.

New versions of the Lotus are still appearing because of two reasons: Colin Chapman strives to constantly improve the breed, and no one car is run long enough without change. That this is the policy of the Lotus Engineering Co. (London, England) is evident in its brochures, which state, "In accordance with the company's progressive policy, the right to alter specifications without notice is reserved."

My main interest in the Lotus Club was to determine if you can take a sports-racing machine like the Lotus Eleven and, without basic alterations, make it into a street machine. The Le Mans model is the original sports-racing machine, having seating capacity for only one, a built-in headrest-fin, and other minor changes that are more suited for all-out racing, including a windshield screen that wraps completely around the driver.

The basic differences between the Le Mans and Club models are these: The Club model has a live rear axle from a Nash Metropolitan, located by parallel trailing arms, with a diagonal member to provide lateral location; the Le Mans model has a de Dion rear suspension. (The live axle on the Club model can be replaced by a de Dion system at extra cost.) The Club has hydraulically operated, two-leading shoe drum brakes: the Le Mans has disc brakes, outboard at front, inboard at rear. Both models have rack-and-pinion steering, though on the Le Mans model it is lighter. Gearboxes are different only insofar as ratios are concerned, the Le Mans having closer ratios. Both weigh about 850 pounds.

The exceptional road qualities inherent in the Lotus Eleven Le Mans have been carried forward into the Club. These are mainly due to the lightweight tubular frame, a sheet metal driveshaft tunnel that acts as a structural member to carry the floor and the rear engine mounts. The engine is tilted 10 degrees sideways so as to reduce frontal area. Front suspension is by swing axles, incorporating combined coil spring-shock units. The roll center is very low and greatly aids in its handling. The basic difference in handling between the Le Mans model and the Club is due to the latter's live rear axle. On rough roads the Club has a tendency to wander, or walk from side to side, taking real concentration to keep it in a straight line. The de Dion rear axle would more ably swallow up these changes in road contour.

Nevertheless, the handling of the Club model is quite wonderful. It has very quick steering, has marvelous response and, of course, would be easy to overcorrect if you're not familiar with such a car. Taking it around a turn, no matter how many degrees there are, you never have to take your hands off the leather-wrapped wheel for there are only 1½ turns lock-to-lock.

The engine used in both Lotuses is virtually the same—the 1100cc Coventry Climax four. This is an aluminum block engine with steel liners, an overhead cam driven by chain from the crank. The crankshaft is fully counterweighted, uses five bearings, and has split connecting rods to enable their easy removal. The pistons are aluminum, combustion chambers are wedge-shaped, and the compression ratio is 9.8 to 1. Power output is 75 bhp at 6250 rpm or 83 at 6800 rpm, depending on the state of tune.

To get back to the question at hand, is it a street machine—or at least one that you *could* drive back and forth to work? Or is it best for a competition driver who wants to move up in class, and happens to have $4709 in loose change? Let me recount some of my experiences with it after leaving Jay Chamberlain's place in North Hollywood (the U.S. distributor) until I returned it a week later. Then you can decide for yourself.

When you first stand alongside this three-foot-high (at the windshield) machine that fits into your 20-foot garage with more than four feet to spare at either end, you get the impression of fragility. Never forget it! You'll find that the aluminum body is virtually paper-thin. If you lean too heavily on the body when you're washing it, you're liable to leave a dent. You have to make sure you're not parked alongside someone who opens his door suddenly, putting a nice crease in your side. You want to park it where curious onlookers won't paw all over it and give you handprints—handprints that are outlined by the shape of the metal itself.

You can get into the car in one of two ways. I found it was much easier to step directly over the side (which is only 24 inches high) than to open the flap-down door—which makes it a shorter height to step over but increases the spread. If you have dirty shoes and clean clothes, the best

ALL LOTUS COMPONENTS are quickly accessible when four spring hooks are unsnapped, hood and rear section are swung up. Both easily removed from car.

CONTINUED ON PAGE 185

171

Lotus Special - Powered by Nardi

If the significance of our cover photo — two cars with no apparent relationship — escapes you, this should clear up the mystery. The little Lotus Club model and the striking Nardi-Vignale sprint coupe have one very important feature in common — the same engine, a Nardi-modified Fiat-600 which now displaces 750cc (45.5 cubic inches).

An English Lotus with an Italian engine requires a bit of explanation. Jay Chamberlain, U.S. Lotus distributor who owns the car shown, has his North Hollywood shop next door to the firm which imports the engines and the coupes to America, Nardi Automotive Distributors. Jay, intrigued by the possibility of running a Lotus in Class H competition, decided to try one of the Nardi-modified engines.

Although the two engines are basically the same, a drive in the Lotus revealed that Jay has gone just a shade higher in the horsepower department. The engine, as it arrives from the factory in the coupe developing 45.5 bhp at 6500 rpm, is quite tractable and idles nicely below 1000 rpm. It pulls easily at low revs in traffic and really gets going above 3000 rpm.

The engine in the Lotus is another story. It will barely idle below 2000 rpm and doesn't sound very healthy below 4000. Above that point it comes on with a punch that belies its 50-plus horsepower. All this indicates that the Chamberlain crew has increased power by as much as 10 or more horses, a substantial percentage in this league.

The Turin, Italy hop-up firm of Nardi and Co. have done a remarkable job with this tiny engine. Originally intended for Fiat's 600 series of baby cars and Multiplas, the engine cranks out a meager 22 bhp at 5000 rpm. Nardi's major surgery leaves little of the original engine except the block. Bore remains stock (2.38 inches) but a heavier crank lengthens the stroke to 2.56 inches. A new high compression cylinder head (9 to 1) with larger valves and double springs, a cleaner intake manifold with enlarged ports, high compression pistons, a hotter camshaft and all components carefully balanced more than double the original horsepower.

Mounting the engine in the Lotus posed certain problems. The radiator had to be relocated and the most drastic change was running exhaust headers around the front of the engine to get the exhaust onto the left side.

The installation may look a bit peculiar — but it goes. How well is shown by the way in which it beat a factory Ferry Renault — an all-out race car whch cost some $6000. Chamberlain will be happy to deliver a similarly equipped Lotus for about $4000.

The little coupe, while not intended for competition, is a fine Gran Turismo car. It is small and compact, yet spacious. Fuel consumption is in the economy car class — we got 32 mpg — while performance is satisfactorily brisk. A few runs on the dragstrip showed a quarter-mile acceleration figure slightly in excess of 65 mph — not bad for a 1300-pound car. Top speed is over 95 mph and, while it is not recommended, the engine will rev up to 7000 in the indirect gears.

Ready to race, The Chamberlain-built Lotus "Special" has quite a susprise bee under its bonnet. Who'll try for 750cc's?

"Coachwork" by Lotus. Ample room for a spare in the rear area is provided by mounting the tiny Nardi-Fiat engine forward.

The coupe shown here is actually a one-off prototype. Production models will sell for $3193 p.o.e. and there will be minor changes, primarily to make the car more suited to the American market. When the expected 40-per-month delivery starts, the tubular bumpers will cover more area and be steel instead of aluminum. Other modifications will include an extra rear deck airscoop, armrests inside, a fresh air intake for the cockpit, a Weber carburetor instead of Solex, doors with hold-open stops and sealbeam lights.

Driving the coupe is an exciting experience. The gearshift is neatly positioned and slides into the top three synchronized gears with little effort. A short wheelbase is responsible for a softly pitching ride but good shock action makes ride no problem. Swing axles in the rear create an oversteer condition akin to the early Porsches. The car feels skittish at first but actually is quite secure in the turns; just don't become alarmed and try sudden deceleration while cornering.

An interesting contrast is the handling of the Lotus. A comparison is not really fair but the considerably reduced weight of the Lotus and its rock-solid feel give the illusion that absolutely nothing bad can happen in this car. The sense of security is so overwhelming that it could be a danger in itself.

The coupe is finished as a luxury auto should be. Everything fits. Handsome and comfortable individual seats are upholstered in a light tan synthetic similar to Naugahyde. Headliner and door panels match in the same material. There are subtle touches that speak of quality. For example, the knob on the driver's window crank folds flush. On the dash the central instrument is a combined speedo and tach with inner needle for speed and an outer dial which denotes revs. The beautiful laminated wood and aluminum steering wheel is almost enough to sell the car.

If the idea of having one of these lovely Nardi-Fiat engines to cherish, admire and put into a racing special intrigues you — as it did us — Nardi Automotive Distributors will sell you one. The price — reasonable, just under $800. ∎

The Nardi-modified Fiat engine shown below has an unusual manifold treatment. The car, prepared by Jay Chamberlain, has a forward engine mounting, reversing placement by Fiat.

COLIN CHAPMAN EXPLAINS WHY LIGHTWEIGHT CARS ARE SAFER

A GREAT deal of publicity has been given to Juan Fangio's alleged statement that racing cars are becoming too light—and therefore too dangerous—but most of the people closely connected with motor racing, in this country at least, seem to be in agreement that this is not the case.

Two fatal accidents in the Grandes Epreuves, which previously had a wonderful safety record, have been the subject of a great deal of unfortunate—and often ill-informed—publicity; although perhaps purely coincidental, it should be pointed out that these accidents involved the heaviest of the current Grand Prix contenders. Thus, although it would be unwise to say that the "minimum weight limit" addicts—and there are quite a few of them, even in Britain—have got hold of the wrong end of the stick, it would seem to be very easy to show that there is a very strong argument on the other side. It must be obvious that the heavier the car the more difficult it is to control at the limit of adhesion and to slow it from high speed (due to weight increasing its kinetic energy) while in the event of impact with "immovable objects" the extra inertia of the heavier car is likely to result in more damage to everything, and everybody, concerned.

Fangio's statement—if he ever made it—was publicised because Fangio is the acknowledged World Champion driver, and his experience could continue to play an important part in motor racing affairs long after he has finally retired from the cockpit. Moss, whose name is synonymous with fast driving to the general public in Britain, and indeed throughout the western world, deserves equal attention on this subject, and he has said that, given adequate roadholding, the lighter car has the advantage in every wa

Thus, as far as the designer is concerned roadholding is t critical factor. It is, of course, a subject worthy of a comple study on its own.

The roadholding of a Formula 1 racing car is obviously f superior to that of most road cars but this alone demands a f greater awareness of the eventual limits of adhesion on the pa of the driver. A close analogy can be drawn between driving ar flying, for in the latter context there is a critical angle (related speed) at which the wing of an aeroplane will lose all its "lift and consequently will stall; much the same is true of tyre adhesic on a racing car. Whatever the design of the aerofoil section the is a point at which any aeroplane will stall. In the same wa whatever the design of the suspension there is a definite limit a car's roadholding, and this is largely determined by the tread pa tern of the tyre—and, of course, the condition of the road. the pilot can judge the stability of his plane by correlation speed and flying altitude so the driver should be able to balan his car against the forces which are tending to send it off the roa the best drivers have this faculty in the seats of their pants.

The maximum slip angle which the tyres can adopt without lo ing all adhesion is thus the criterion, but the chassis designer ca delay the point at which all "grip" is lost by endeavouring keep as much of each tyre as possible in firm contact with th road, and by equalising weight distribution.

To achieve these ends, it is now generally agreed, the designe needs to use a space frame chassis—the space frame being synon

Allison's car at Oporto, after all the pieces had been collected together.

Inefficiency of the Ferrari F1 space frame results from the use of unequal diameter tubes, the upper tubes taking more load than they should. This frame also has a minimum of diagonal bracing.

mous with light weight and structural efficiency—in conjunction with some form of independent suspension to all four wheels. On this latter subject, of course, there is not yet complete unanimity of agreement, or rather agreement in principle has not yet resulted in universal adoption, in practice, of independent rear suspension. The de Dion system—still widely used—can have many advantages; fixed camber angle under roll; no rear wheel steering due to suspension travel; constant height of roll centre. The disadvantages can be high unsprung weight, the need for sliding splines in the transmission system and—by way of anomaly—constant height of roll centre; this latter can have a very definite influence on cars with variable weight distribution, that is those with fuel tanks at the rear, which for real efficiency demand a self-compensating suspension system, such as on the rear end of the current single-seater Lotus.

The basis of an efficient racing car, however, is the frame, the layout and stressing of which must be planned with reference to the function of each and every tube. Indeed, until the final diagonal member is welded into position a frame of tremendous rigidity may have no torsional strength whatsoever. But once completed such a frame will never fail unless subject to outside influences—that is, if the driver hits something.

IMPACT ABSORBED

And this is where we return to the safety factor. As an example we can take Cliff Allison's practice accident at Oporto. On a left-hand bend Cliff got into a slide (to the right), overcorrected, slid to the left and—at very considerable speed—the rear end of the Lotus struck a lamp post. The rear suspension was torn off—plucked off might cover it more adequately—and in a situation in which a heavier and more "robust" car would almost certainly have slewed round and rolled over the Lotus remained on an even keel, lost its front suspension to the next lamp post, and came to rest looking very much "second hand." The great point was that Cliff got out completely unhurt.

Examined slightly more scientifically, this accident had no ill effect on the driver (other than on his confidence) because firstly the lightweight car dissipated much of its kinetic energy in sliding across the road, in fact between the point at which the car was committed to an accident and the actual point of contact. In the collision with the lamp posts the extremities of the frame took the shock of impact and absorbed it in depth; the driver was not subject to a rate of deceleration at which he would be almost certain to sustain injury against parts of the car. The suspension units, which have been shown to be strong enough for all normal use, did not provide sufficient resistance to throw the car into the air and overturn it, but rather aided the frame in absorbing shock. And although the extremities of the car were very much beyond repair (the engine also was damaged, and the radiator was found some distance away) that part of the frame which surrounds the driving compartment remained intact, so that Allison was able to climb out in the normal way as soon as the car came to rest; an expensive accident as far as the car was concerned, but at least Cliff was able to start in the race—even though it was only in another car.

Weight-saving is a process which is naturally open to criticism if it results in unreliability, or breakages under normal use, but there is no doubt that a well-designed and properly constructed lightweight car can stand up to very hard use, the mechanical parts (engine and transmission) failing far more often than the chassis components. In this connection it must be emphasised that

A Lotus Eleven space-frame. Plan stiffness for the frame is achieved by the close riveting of a strong alloy sheet to the underside; this also forms the floor and undertray of the car.

design is more important than material; despite what might have been said about exhaust pipes dropping off our Formula 2 car it was the design—not the gauge of the tubing—which caused fracture, and it doesn't happen any more. In the same way the original Formula 2 car suffered frame failures when the rear suspension was changed from de Dion to strut; the different load paths required for this layout have since been incorporated.

Instead of reducing weight, however, it is better to design light in the first place, modifying any components which may show signs of stress during development work. This, in the case of the frame, means having links which are all of the same strength, and in this connection it can be said that the Ferrari, although it wins a lot of races (thanks to the most powerful 2½-litre engine in current use) has a frame which is inefficient.

The total weight of a racing car on the starting grid, with driver and fuel aboard, is in the limit determined by the weight of the engine; if this can be decreased by one pound then the rest of the car can be made four pounds lighter. In all this, however, tyres and wheels are the critical factor and their weight has a considerable influence on the car as a whole. The job of the designer is to keep the right relationship between sprung and unsprung weight, and, above all, to keep the greatest possible amount of tyre tread in contact with the road.

So in the end it all comes back to roadholding, and given the suspension (and tyre) qualities which enable the driver to go round corners at very high speed without losing adhesion, the lightweight car will not only have the advantage of safety—in the event of the driver "over-cooking it"—but will also be in a position to defeat cars with more powerful engines and perhaps greater maximum speed. And that is what the Formula 1 Lotus is going to do next year.

LOTUS MAINTENANCE
The Eleven (Series One and Two)   by Mike Costin

THE Lotus Eleven is produced in three forms, Le Mans, Club and Sports, all with basically similar chassis. The Sports version is fitted with a Ford Ten engine and gearbox, the other models with Coventry Climax FWA or FWB power units. The standard gearbox in these latter cases is a Lotus modified BMC "A" series unit fitted with close ratio gears for racing purposes. The final drive unit is also BMC "A" series, thereby allowing changes of gear ratio between 3.7 and 5.3 to 1.

Reverting to the chassis, the Eleven first appeared in 1956 with a tubular steel space frame chassis having independent swing axle front suspension and de Dion rear suspension.

Dealing firstly with general maintenance of the chassis itself, starting from the front, the body hinges are rubber moulded bobbins fitted to the front chassis cross tube. These should be well greased at all times in order to ensure correct functioning. Should they become mutilated or broken they can be replaced by unrivetting the outer portion of the under tray in this area and re-rivetting it after replacing the bobbin.

The body fastening hook has a cam arrangement to ensure that the body is held rigidly in position, and the rollers on which this runs, which are situated immediately behind and above the rubber grommets, should also be kept lubricated.

The front suspension on this car was a development of the Mark Nine suspension except for the addition of Girling disc brakes. The half beam axles are modified Ford Popular components but the radius arms are from an earlier type Ford, the "Y" model, and are rather lighter.

Points to watch on the radius arm and axle beam assembly are:
(a) cracking from the bolt through the rubber bush in the axle beam where it passes through the channel across the front of the chassis,
(b) cracks in the diagonal down tube where it meets the rear pick up of the radius arm,
(c) looseness of the bolt passing through the radius arm and beam. (Note: It is most important that this bolt be absolutely dead tight at all times.)

The suspension units used on the Series One Eleven were of Girling manufacture in the first instance, but Armstrong counterparts are available.

The bottom pick-up for the front suspension unit gave trouble in the early days, when it was made up from a piece of $\frac{1}{2}$ in steel bar; the latter type, which was made from a machined bar of $\frac{5}{8}$ in diameter, proved quite satisfactory. The anchorage for the top of the front suspension unit also gave trouble, particularly on the left hand side, and this was cured by
(a) thickening up the plate through which the peg top of the suspension unit protruded,
(b) raising the gauge of the top chassis member.

Any adjustment of the front suspension which is required for alteration of ride level should be obtainable at the top or bottom suspension pick-up by either adding or subtracting rubbers and although the amount of adjustment available is quite small, possibly in the region of plus and minus $\frac{1}{4}$ in, this actually gives something like plus or minus $\frac{1}{2}$ in on the actual car ride level. The normal ride level of 5 in should give satisfactory road holding characteristics, but for people who wish to experiment for themselves ride levels should be raised to increase understeer or lowered to increase oversteer.

The front stub axles are modified Ford E93A, and the hubs are of a proprietary brand modified to suit the Lotus requirements. The hubs should need no maintenance whatsoever excepting possibly the renewal of the Timken taper roller races and the inboard grease seal. A point to note here is that there should also be an outer seal, which is in the form of a light steel pressed cap, and this should be a press fit into the outer race housing. I point this out because on the majority of Elevens which I have seen recently this outer seal is missing.

The steering gear of the Series One Eleven is of the rack and pinion type, and this again is a modified version of the BMC rack and pinion. This unit should need very little maintenance apart from stripping and re-assembling yearly and

De Dion rear suspension of the Series Two Eleven Le Mans. Identical mounting brackets make this assembly and the live axle of the Club and Sports models interchangeable.

adjustment of the end pads by the addition or removal of shims.

The steering arms used on the Eleven Series One were of Lotus manufacture, and did present some trouble in the first instances in that the two bosses on which the arms are mounted, which are brazed into the steering arm itself, used to come loose and allow play in the steering. This was evident upon inspection and was easily detected by cracks in the braze at the points where the stubs enter the arm. The rack and pinion is actuated by a tubular steering column which has two universal joints. During overhaul these should be washed in petrol and checked for play, and replaced if necessary.

The rear gearbox mounting and the undertray from the engine bulkhead to the seat back are all highly stressed parts of the chassis and should receive some maintenance attention. It is quite likely in older cars that all the rivets holding the undertray on to the chassis itself have become loose, and this can be repaired either by re-rivetting between the existing rivets or better still by drilling out all the old rivets, drilling each hole oversize and re-rivetting using oversized rivets.

The de Dion assembly used on these cars was most satisfactory generally speaking, but there are one or two points which should be watched. Firstly the chassis at the rear of the A bracket pick up on the rear of the prop shaft tunnel should be inspected very closely for cracks. Later chassis have a modification here whereby an angle bracket was inserted joining the right hand vertical member of the rear prop shaft frame on to the seat back tube, which went between the sides of the prop shaft. This would be a worth whole modification on any chassis which is not already so modified.

The de Dion outer drive castings should be stripped and re-assembled and the bearings and grease seals checked for condition.

The Hardy Spicer unions used on the articulated drive shafts were of 1100 series, and these should be carefully checked for any signs of wear and replaced if necessary.

All of the rubber bushes on the radius rod ends should be checked, but these should have an almost indefinite life and should be discarded if they become perished or swollen due to excessive oil or petrol soakage.

The differential housing casting is of Lotus design, and was developed specifically for the Eleven. The drive shaft bearing housings should have provision for a sealing "O" ring, and anyone having a very early casting in which this "O" ring groove is not machined would profit by incorporating this modification, as it certainly helps to keep the brakes free from oil. The differential assembly itself is held into the casting by eight $\frac{1}{16}$ in bolts. Should any of the threads in the magnesium housing be damaged then they can be retained by the use of an Armstrong Heli-coil insert.

The Girling disc brakes used on the Eleven should be maintained as recommended in the February 1958 issue of *SPORTS CAR AND LOTUS OWNER*. Owners of Series One Elevens fitted with discs of chromium plated steel should be careful only to use pad material Ferodo DS1 or Mintex equivalent. Conversely, cars with cast iron discs should use Ferodo DS3 or Mintex equivalent.

The twin master cylinders fitted to these cars are the remote tank centre valve type and should be of $\frac{3}{4}$ in diameter; some early cars were fitted with $\frac{7}{8}$ in diameter master cylinders. The clutch pedal and linkage is assembled in one and fitted in the car through the hole in the side of the driver's foot box. It is essential for correct operation that the assembly should be fitted loosely, and then the bolt through the Metalastik-type bush should be tightened up only when the pedal is pulled backwards to the full extent of its rearwards travel. The reason for this is that the only means of returning the pedal to the normal position is by the spring action of the pivot bush, which is of a special double bonded variety. This special treatment also applies to the brake pedal on Series One cars, although a spring push-off is fitted to the brake pedal of Series Two Elevens.

The throttle linkage also should receive some attention, in particular to the ball joints on the carburetter link, as these have a tendency to come undone when the wear becomes excessive.

In early cars the gearbox oil used to leak from the gearlever attachment plate, and this was cured by soldering a short piece of tube on to the top of the plate and then fitting the normal A.30 rubber moulding over this tube and fastening it into position with a Jubilee clip.

The hand brake on the Series One Eleven is quite effective generally speaking, and maintenance should be confined to greasing the cable, adjusting it—if necessary—at the differential end and replacing the hand brake friction pads.

The Series Two Eleven differed from the Series One in many respects. Firstly the front suspension was replaced by an entirely new wishbone-type layout. The chassis was re-designed to accommodate this new suspension and at the same time the rear suspension was also modified, although it bore a very great relationship to the previous year's de Dion set up.

The front suspension on the Series Two Eleven is completely Lotus in design and utilises only the very minimum of proprietary items. These are the king posts, the stub axle, the hub and the king post bottom bearings. This suspension has proved to be most successful and has remained unaltered even to the latest Formula One car, where it is still precisely the same as on the Eleven but turned back to front. Maintenance on this suspension is confined merely to checking for wear at the stub axle bearings, the top king post ball joint, the bottom king post bearings and the rubber bearings on the bottom wishbone.

The Eleven Series Two de Dion was introduced (a) to widen the base on which the bearings worked and (b) to bring it into line with the 1957 Lotus standard, in order that the cars could be fitted with either spoke wheels or the cast magnesium type. The de Dion is principally the same as for the Series One, but instead of the aluminium grease seals for the outer drive shaft bearings a special seal is now used, which is made of pressed steel approximately 12 thou thick, and this is designed to run on the outside edge of the bearing outer tracks and polish its own line; once it has polished this line it forms a very good grease seal.

On the Series Two Eleven the Hardy Spicer joints were increased in size to 1300 Series, this again to bring the car into line with the firm's 1957 standards.

The spare wheel mountings on early Elevens were made of $\frac{1}{2}$ in tube, but these were later replaced by mountings of $\frac{5}{8}$ in tube.

TRACK TEST

No. 2 Lotus XI Series 1 & 2

by ROLAND DUTT

The Lotus XI Series 1

IN the 1100 cc sports racing class, few cars have retained the popularity and success of the Lotus XI's in their various forms. Although the basic design is now far from new, a Lotus XI is still something to be reckoned with in its class and certainly can be considered a very potent piece of machinery for the club driver. Consequently a magazine with the title Motor Clubman could not be without a description of the handling of such a car. As a result, this month's track test is a little different from usual — instead of dealing with a specific car on a particular circuit, it covers the impressions gained of two cars and a number of circuits, sometimes under racing conditions.

The two Lotus's (or should this be Loti?) concerned were the XI Series 1 and the XI Series 2 and both types are too well known for it to be necessary to give their specifications in any great detail, in any case the various combinations of carburetters, gearboxes, and degree of tune of the engine available make this almost impossible. However, I think the two cars tested can be considered typical of their type. Both cars incidentally although in tip-top condition had covered quite a few racing miles.

The Series 1 was fitted with a 1098 cc Coventry Climax engine, stage two tuned but with a high compression head. In case you don't know, stage three tuning incorporates larger diameter big-end bolts and in the interest of safety, a 5 bearing camshaft. Gearbox was a BMC A30 with special close ratio gears. Continuing in the wording of the typical classified advertisement, DeDion, discs and wire wheels. The familiar all-enveloping body, which really is as aerodynamic as it looks, gives the car a compact and purposeful appearance. The cockpit is roomy and comfortable for the average driver. If you are on the long side and have to sit on the floor with the minimum cushion, there is about 2 inches of adjustment available to enable the steering wheel to clear your knees. This is achieved by undoing one clamp bolt and lengthening the steering column. A detachable headrest is fitted — probably quite effective on the original design which had a wraparound windscreen on the driver's side only but with full width windscreens it looks rather cumbersome, does not appear to serve any real purpose and tends to obscure rear vision.

The propshaft tunnel which is a stressed part of the structure comes fairly high on the left of the driver and acts as a support without restricting arm movement. Due to the perfect position of the pedals one can heel and toe with the greatest of ease, this with the close ratio gearbox makes changing down a joy.

Ones' first impression of the Series 1 is the outstanding acceleration for 1100 cc's particularly at the lower end of the scale. Getting away from the starting line even from a bad position, it is possible to gain several places before the first corner. In spite of the car's good power/weight ratio from a standing start wheel spin can be kept to a minimum.

The roadholding in general is good by most standards, but compared with the heavier IX or the later Series 2, I would not say it was exceptional. On a medium slow bend one tends to broadside with opposite lock, which of course gives a bit of wheelspin coming out of the corner, with a consequent waste of time. However, on faster bends, the car behaves very much better, diving into the corner with the well known Lotus understeer and the minimum of drift. Control through the corner is maintained almost entirely on the throttle, nevertheless it must be said that the general handling characteristics of the car are deceptive. It is particularly sensitive to the slightest error or ham-handedness and at high speed it is very easy to overdo it. In other words the car is by no means as safe as it feels, as I know from experience. This of course is to be expected when one realises the extreme lightness of the vehicle.

The steering characteristics can be altered by quite a considerable amount to suit the individual driver's requirements. Apart from the usual variations of the tyre pressures, the degree of understeer can be varied by adding or removing washers at the top of the front suspension units.

On the straight the car is fairly stable and can be driven "hands off" at quite high speeds, but as the maximum is approached, particularly if there are any slight undulations on the surface, it shows a tendency to snake. This is very slight, but one can't help getting the impression that even the slightest relaxation of effort on the driver's part, and things could very easily get out of hand. I put this snaking tendency down to the front suspension, being of the split axle type. This particular car appeared to have rather hard rear suspension, which had no adverse effect on the roadholding, but did not give the driver a very smooth ride. Braking is extremely good and only the most violent braking produced a slight wheel patter, at the front end. After one particular race when the car had been driven very hard and the brakes had consequently become really hot, it was noticed that grease was melting and throwing from the front-hubs, due to the heat generated by the brakes.

Incidentally on the Series 1 there are no air ducts to the front brakes and the fitting of wire wheels does not materially assist cooling of the discs as the wheels themselves are almost entirely enclosed by the body.

Under racing conditions as distinct from tests when one has not the time (or inclination) to look for faults, the general impression gained is that the car handles well, but does require a certain amount of concentration from the driver.

The revs build up with remarkable rapidity and one goes up to the permitted 6000 rpm through the gears with incredible ease. Changing from third into top at peak revs, when really pressing on, brings about a certain amount of clutch slip before the drive becomes solid. This is accompanied by a strong smell of burning clutch lining. Provided that you are just that little bit inside the limit, the car goes round corners literally on rails, and particularly noticeable is the almost complete lack of roll for a sports car. It does however take sometime before one is sufficiently familiar with the car to know exactly what that all-important limit of the car's cornering ability really is. In the early stages, the driver finds himself taking fast curves well below the car's capabilities. Of course, as can be expected under such conditions and with such a high cornering speed, the limit is met very suddenly with practically no preliminary warning. It is therefore advisable to really get to know the car and build up slowly to this very critical point.

It is an ideal car in every way for the beginner and a good introduction to high speed motoring. At the same time it is a car to be treated with respect and one that does not permit liberties to be taken.

The Lotus XI Series 2

The Series II can be considered the logical development of the I and in the course of this development, the various faults of the I have been eradicated. It is a more robust and slightly heavier car but nevertheless is much superior in performance to the Series I. It is possible that it does not possess quite such good initial acceleration as the Series I. On some circuits of the slower or twisty variety, some drivers prefer the S.U. carb to the more usual Weber to improve the acceleration at lower revs. Although wire wheels can be fitted to the Series II, the majority have light alloy disc type.

This particular car was fitted with an MGA close-ratio gearbox, which is considerably more robust than the A30 BMC, but also a good deal heavier. Gear changing could not be effected nearly so rapidly on this box, neither was the spacing of the ratios all that could be desired. The clutch was incredibly heavy and brake pedal pressure a good deal higher than the Series I. The handling of the car is quite outstanding, the roadholding and cornering capabilities being beyond criticism.

Experimenting with tyre pressures, it was found that the best results were obtained with a pressure difference of 4 lbs between front and rear, the front being the higher. The steering has that firm feel and there is practically no kickback from the road wheels. The bound and padded light alloy stering wheel looks very small indeed, but on driving it fits in well with everything else.

This feeling of firmness, coupled with the high gearing, gives a direct response enabling the car to be placed accurately just where you want it, in a corner. There is absolutely no necessity for any of the dramatic wheel fighting, common to many of the smaller cars. One feels almost relaxed even at quite high coming speeds. Going really fast through a corner at racing speeds, the car remains accurately on the chosen line, with an almost imperceptible amount of drift.

Plenty of throttle is required right through the corner — too much and of course the front-end tends to brake away — but even so, you receive a reasonable amount of warning and a slight easing of the throttle and it is instantly under control. The driver never has that odd moment of doubt coming out of a corner when the outside grass verge comes rapidly nearer and nearer. Under the most extreme conditions it is unlikely that the back-end will break away. In fact I would say that when one is familiar with the car, having set tyre pressures and steering geometry to suit the driver, it is definitely the most 'unspinable' car I have ever driven.

Winding it up on the straight towards the 8000 rpm mark (which incidentally is off the power curve and not to be encouraged), far from showing any tendency to snake, the car seems to sit down on the track even more than usual. At these speeds there is a tendency for the rear of the bonnet to lift due to the pressure of air trapped inside.

Apart from this, the aerodynamics (or to the unitiated and old fashioned — streamlining!) must be very efficient as there is no eddying in the cockpit whatsoever and neither is the driver troubled by wind noise. In spite of the very high pedal pressure, braking is really good even from very high speeds, such as the straight at Aintree. Really hard and vicious braking due to an incident at Melling Crossing, caused nothing more unpleasant than smoke from the tyres, not even a twitch of the steering wheel, but the driver had second thoughts about a safety harness if only to keep him in the cockpit.

On either side of the radiator intake are small air ducts for the front brakes and scoops on the undertray for the back. After several races on widely differing circuits, I have never known the brakes to give trouble or overheat. Incidentally on the disc wheeled car, changing the front wheels interferes with the disc brakes and it is essential that a couple of pumps are given to the pedal after the operation to restore fluid in the calipers and brake-lines. I once forgot with disastrous results at the first corner, due to complete lack of stopping power.

The Series 2 is only slightly bigger than the I, but manages to give an almost big car feel as regards handling. It can be said that it possesses no vices and provided that one remembers that the car is cornering a lot faster than the driver realises, it is a remarkably stable car. To obtain the best results, it is as well to know the proposed circuits and make the necessary alterations to suit that circuit. After all it is only 1100 cc, a fact that the car encourages one to forget. Apart from the obvious choosing of suitable back axle ratio, different carburetters are sometimes more suitable for a particular circuit depending on just what revs you really want the power. This car had the full stage 3 modifications to the bottom-end and a high compression head, but had not been fitted with the 5 bearing camshaft. Although the heavier valve springs that go with this modification had been fitted, no trouble has been experienced with camshaft bearings on the camshaft itself. One cannot fail to be impressed with the roadholding, I once heard one Special enthusiast proudly describing his car by saying it held the road like a Lotus. If he meant an XI he certainly had something. Even under wet conditions it still possesses that little extra.

I shall probably be unpopular for saying so but I think it is a better car than the later type 17.

LIFE WITH THE LOTUS-EATERS

By DOUG BLAIN

SCW's London correspondent tells how a five-year-old sports-racer put fun back in his United Kingdom driving.

LOTUS type-numbers can be confusing, but most enthusiasts know the only car of the marque commonly thought of as roadable at all (aside from the GT Elite) is the dumpy little Seven. Consequently, the question I get asked most often — after "What are you driving these days?" — is "But don't you mean a Lotus *Seven?*"

Patiently, in words of one syllable, I point out that I don't mean a Lotus Seven. I mean a Lotus Eleven. Even then it's surprising how often I have to lead them around the corner into the small sunlit square, lined with its smiling brick-fronted 18th century houses and proudly lift the lightweight plastic cover before their very eyes.

Six years ago, when my car left the little Lotus plant at Hornsey in northern London (it was before it moved out to Cheshunt), you would have been hard-pressed to find a more advanced sports-racer anywhere in the world. Colin Chapman himself was still charging forth on fine weekends and personally giving the opposition some shakeup. Hawthorn was doing likewise, forcing Moss to eat his dust in the weird looking central-seat Cooper 1100. Even the Jaguar and Aston boys were running for cover on the shorter circuits as young Chapman and his Lotus boys set the stopwatches clicking like tommyguns and the marshals crossing out their record laps as fast as they wrote them in. Cars the size of the Lotus Eleven just didn't *go* that quickly in 1956 . . .

"What kind of car?" asked *The Motor*, most conservative of Britain's three motoring weeklies, when it finally got hold of a test Eleven more than a full year later, "what kind of a car is it that Colin Chapman's brilliant team of young engineers and aerodynamicists has endowed with such astonishing acceleration, speed and economy of fuel?" The test report went on: "This car invites incredulity . . . an engineering *tour-de-force!*"

The data panel showed figures that must have made contemporary readers' hair stand on end: 0 to 60 in 10 sec, 0 to 80 in 15, 0 to 100 in 23.6 and a top speed around 127 mph — all from 1098 cc AND with 40 mpg at a steady 80 mph.

But did anyone think seriously of using an Eleven on the road? No sir. *The Motor's* testers thought they were very daring running their evaluation program away from the racing circuit. They were obviously determined to ignore such drawbacks as vulnerability, difficult access, lack of weather protection and, above all, noise just for the sake of recording these figures for posterity. "The cry of a Lotus being driven at high rpm and a wide throttle opening is decidedly audible, but less anti-social than it might be because a Lotus driven in this fashion disappears over the horizon and out of earshot in a very brief space of time . . ."

If you look at the thing logically, there's really no more justification for hacking a Lotus around town at highway speeds now than there was then. But it's an oddity of automotive history that our standards of tractibility as well as of speed tend to broaden as time goes on. Think of the vintage enthusiasts who drive their GP Bugattis to work; in 1928 that would have seemed the height of folly, quite apart from the sacrilege involved. The same with the blown Alfas and Maseratis of the '30s, dope fuel and all. I can even remember how shocked I was when Jack Murray told me he'd just got back from a trip to Adelaide in that immaculate D-Jag of his; and yet here am I behaving worse than anyone, carving up the traffic in a nine cwt, 80 bhp Lotus.

I don't really think there's any particularly profound psychological reason for it. Largely, it's just a matter of getting used to a thing. Today we know there are much faster cars than Bugattis. They have ceased to awe us, we tend to look at them with a historical eye instead of standing back with our jawbones level and our ribs slowly drawing breath.

The same with my Lotus. That tiny single-cam Coventry Climax engine was just about the last word in racing powerplant when it appeared, yet now they have it giving even more power in a street car like the Elite. Even a 9.8 to 1 compression ratio would have brought light to our jaded eyes back in 1956; today the US compacts are charging around on 11 to 1 and more. Expansion of the sports car cult has meant that knowledgeable service is there for the asking in most localities. Personally, I only have to walk 100 yards to find three fully-trained Lotus mechanics just rearing to do business.

But don't let me pretend there's no sense of adventure left. To drive a thoroughbred racing car of the little Eleven's calibre (even if its more recent brethren, not to mention the ubiquitous Lola, will leave it for dead on the tracks) can still be very impressive experience. And to accept, or rather tolerate, the car's almost overwhelming shortcomings as an everyday proposition is not necessarily to lick them altogether.

For example, you can hardly get away from it when your daily hack turns out to have no form of weather protection whatsoever. Not only does the Lotus lack a hood, it also leaks at every seam and has a perspex windscreen so vulnerable I never dare use the single pitifully feeble wiper for more than a few seconds at a time.

And there's still the noise! The exhaust pipe is less than four feet long from manifold to outlet. Of that, about two feet consists of slightly wider pipe than the rest; there is no other form of silencing, and the interior is as hollow as Mother Murphy's head. On top of the shattering racket that billows around you like a cloud whenever you open the throttles, there's the constant rattle from the Climax engine itself with its competition clearance and complete lack of soundproofing. Then there is the clatter from the paper-thin body panels as they slap up and down beneath their flimsy spring fasteners. Oh, and finally the howl of the racing tyres — Dunlop R5s that persist in keeping up a running commentary on whatever outrageous surface it is they're called upon to negotiate. I guess it's what I get for venturing away from Goodwood's baby's bottom smoothness . . .

In fact, my Eleven goes further than words towards proving the truth of what we said recently about racing cars and everyday design. However outstanding it may be as an engineering achievement, however suitable for its one intended task of winning races, the Lotus has very little to offer anyone but the dedicated enthusiast who cares about little else but performance, roadholding and what I can only call driveability. Obviously, if I were not one of these people I could not have considered the car, just as if my wife were not the most tolerant and devoted of females she would never have heard of our indulging ourselves so.

Just to complete my chapter of drawbacks, let's consider the ways in which the Lotus lacks the little things we tend to take for granted in more normal sports cars. First there's vulnerability: my car's panelling is so thin you can dent it

Accessibility — that's the word! Bullet-shaped Lotus opens up like a flower for access to everything from headlamps to final drive. Note flap-type doors.

LIFE WITH THE LOTUS-EATERS

Open the boot, and what do you get? Central assembly includes final drive and Girling brakes. Note alloy de Dion tube passing behind differential.

Hearty beastie: Coventry Climax 1100 gives 85 bhp at racing revs, starts willingly and behaves beautifully on the road. Overheating is a problem in traffic.

Five years of racing have left their scars. It takes little more than thumb-pressure to dent the Lotus's panelling. Extremities are unprotected in traffic.

The gentle art of getting started. Process involves strenuous exercise for almost every bodily muscle, takes hours of practice to avoid dents in thin body.

with the pressure of a thumb, yet it has no bumpers, no form of protection at all. The windscreen, as I've said, is made of Perspex and even a dirty rag will scratch it permanently. The alloy undertray, and particularly the air scoop that reach down for the inboard Girling rear discs, are low enough to be a nuisance on all but the smoothest roads.

Accessibility is another thing — accessibility to the cockpit. Because the Lotus, like all of its ilk, has a properly triangulated space-frame, the doors are no bigger than FIA minimum. They're hardly doors at all. To get in you reach over a fixed Perspex sidescreen and release a crude latch on the inside, whereupon the door drops down like a manhole cover as far as its retaining stay will let it. You then lift a leg inside and hoist yourself laboriously on to an inch-wide frame member that runs beside the thin alloy sill. The final trick is to haul in the other leg without scraping the Perspex and then slide carefully down among the interior plumbing to your seat. On the way you must be careful not to touch the windscreen (it will break off), the tail panelling (it will bend) or the door itself (it will distort and refuse to shut). My wife has given up already; she demands to be lifted bodily in and out.

Inside, what do you get? Very little apart from a flat backrest with a bare quarter-inch of foam padding and no shape, and a piece of bent aluminium with no padding at all for a seat. The floor is a sheet of naked alloy too flimsy to take more than the weight of your boots. Everything you touch is hard, cold and probably greasy.

As for luxuries like luggage space, the less said the better. If you lift the Eleven's befinned tail panel and peer in you'll see wheels, final drive, brakes, battery and sling for the spare. There's no room for anything else, and even if you did squeeze in some luggage the tyres would spray mud all over it. The only built-in accommodation even for odds and ends is on the sills inside the doors, but you have to move everything then before you can get out. Our only hope is a baggage rack on the rear deck . . .

You'll begin to see what I mean. Now for the compensations. What is it that makes it worth putting up with all this?

I guess handling is the secret. Years of testing every kind of sports and sporting car convinced me that the big yardstick in judging any machine is not outright performance but roadholding. That, above all, is what separates the thoroughbred racer from the lowly street machine when the chips go down. I think I would put up with more than I have to already just to get a car I could'nt trust in any turn at any safe (or even mildly unsafe) speed of entry.

Then there's braking. Nine-and-a-half-inch discs on all four wheels give the featherweight Lotus a power and a consistency of braking quite unknown to the average sports car operator. Coupled with the roadholding, they provide a feeling of safety so marked it makes me want to yell for joy whenever I catch myself gasping in a situation that might once have approached the alarming.

And finally I suppose there's performance — the straight-line kind. To have an engine that will rev out happily to 7500 rpm in any of the four forward gears, that will whisk the car and two passengers from rest to 90 mph inside 20 sec and do it day in, day out, without ever seeming to flag and certainly without ever calling for pampering or for more than the most frugal quantities of super grade fuel.

LIFE WITH THE LOTUS EATERS

If you add all these qualities together you have just the usual thing, fun. But it's fun in greater measure than I have found elsewhere within £3000 of the price. It's fun combined with that old, indefinable sense of wind-in-the-hair abandon I used to think came only with vintage driving. Fun in which everything is just that much safer, that much saner than it can ever be in a car designed less with ultimate performance in mind than comfort or appearance or (worst of all) just sales.

But talking will never help. Let's get started!

I'll take it you have a fair idea of the Eleven's specifications. Tubular space-frame, independent front suspension by swinging half-axles and long coil springs, rear ditto by de Dion and coils with inboard brakes, 1098 cc Climax engine driving through a special gearbox using close-ratio straight-cut cogs in a BMC A-type case. You clamber over the side and slither down behind a tiny, leather-rimmed alloy wheel. You look and feel around . . .

Close by your left hand is the business end of a surprisingly long gearstick, without remote control (too heavy!). Movements are short and just a little skew-whiff; you have to reach forward and lift the lever's stump to find reverse. The handbrake is over on the passenger's side, under the dash. Like most others, it is almost completely useless.

Simplicity and function are often synonymous in motordom. Not surprising, therefore, that the Eleven's dash — probably the plainest I have seen — is also the most pleasant to use.

Three dials adorn the flat, plastic-covered surface on the driver's side: 8000 rpm tachometer (with red tell-tale hand), oil pressure gauge and water thermometer. The ammeter lives way over to the left, along with the other electrical equipment including fuse box and cutout. The dip-switch for my matchless Lucas Le Mans headlamps is a simple lever under the horn button in the centre of the panel. A similar combination switch next door controls ignition and lights. The choke knob, which works on only one of the paired SU carbs — they share a single float bowl, incidentally — is the only other manual control in the cockpit apart from the starter. Speedo? The Lotus people, thoughtfully, have provided a hole for one under the plastic on the passenger's side. I suppose one day I'll get around to fitting it, just for the sake of convenience; doing sums with the gearbox ratios for the benefit of the law in built-up areas can get wearisome.

Cockpit furniture is very nearly non-existant. Strengthening plates on the backs of the doors have holes in them that make useful places for maps, screwdrivers and bits of dipstick rag. The shelves over the gaps between doors and frame members will just do for resting bulkier oddments on, but you really need them for elbow room in anything like sporting conditions. Most of the trim is in naked aluminium, apart from a couple of pieces of red plastic at wear points beside the seats.

Pedal placement could hardly be better, with a spoon-type throttle control and steel-capped brake and clutch levers set squarely in front of the wheel at just a shade under full leg stretch. A space for my left foot when it isn't on the clutch would be a help, but so far I have had no cramps through resting it flat on the floor.

The seats themselves are hardly sumptuous; in fact on a longish trip they can get pretty uncomfortable. But at least they locate you properly, along with the very high transmission tunnel and a special shoulder-notch in the side of the body. The passenger's side is very short of legroom for a tall man, but it fits my wife to a T.

The little engine habitually leaps to life at the first touch of the button, although on cold mornings it demands a handkerchief over the one carb intake the choke doesn't serve. Even with the mild Champion N5s I use for running around London, the exhaust crackles and bangs heartily enough to provoke even the staidest passers-by either to wave their walking sticks in fury or else to flourish imaginary starting flags, depending entirely on temperament.

The clutch is sudden death, and it took me hours to get it right. I guess it was designed just to be dropped consistently at around 3000 on the dial, but that kind of thing doesn't seem to go down too well in traffic. Instead I have to call up all my vintage training and feed it *ever* so gently against a slowly increasing ration of throttle. Done properly, the turbine take-up that results is something to experience.

I won't quote any precise gear speeds because I haven't yet had a chance to wind her out in all of them (noise, dear boy, noise); suffice it to say I could hardly wish for a better-balanced boxful, although if the Eleven's eager little Climax engine were not built for everyday revving upwards of 6500 I suppose I would condemn all the indirects as being far too low. As always, it's largely a matter of fitness for purpose.

The shift, incidentally, is so dead easy you can forget synchromesh was ever invented. Double-clutching for upward changing is unnecessary at all but racing revs, and the exhaust racket makes judging by ear a cinch for coming down.

You'll have gathered the Lotus accelerates. It also has high cruising and flat-out speeds. But then so do other cars. Where I can count on my Eleven to see off rivals twice and three times its size is in the cornering and braking departments. Those Girling discs stop my miniscule lightweight like buffers, and with barely a hint on the pedal end at that. Complete absence of body roll means I can hurl the car into any kind of turn in the certain knowledge that I am not committing myself to the judgment of some higher being, that instead I can change my mind right in the middle, even apply the brakes if necessary without throwing the car off balance. This means far more than you might think. It means you no longer get that "Ah, well, here we go!" feeling as you lean into a 60 degree right-hander at around eight or nine tenths, trusting that no one has chosen to dig up the inside verge since last you tried it on. Changes of surface, stray animals, even mobile hazards of the more vicious sort become a lot less terrifying when you get this kind of roadholding. It's the big difference, believe me, between driving even a good production sports car and owning a roadable racer.

And to me that difference is about as important as all the unfavorable ones added together and multiplied by 10. I happen to like driving fast where the elements of risk associated with normal roadwork are at a reasonable level. It's not a passion with me, just a pleasure. I believe the built-in safety I get with this Lotus Eleven gives me more chance of indulging that desire and living to talk about it than most of the available alternatives. That's all!   #

LOTUS CLUB

CONTINUED FROM PAGE 171

method is to lift up the seat cushion every time that you get out; then when you step in you keep the cushion—and your pants—clean. Once you're standing inside, you then place both feet on the floor, and shoehorn your legs under the wheel. This is the *only* way to get in. Otherwise, you'll find that one leg is caught between the tunnel and the wheel, or between the door and the wheel . . . and then you'll have to start the procedure all over again.

Starting was easy enough once the battery situation on this particular car was cured. You turn the key, punch the starter button, choke it if necessary, but don't pump the throttle. You don't let the engine idle too long, since there's no fan; the only cooling you get is when you're moving and air rushes through the radiator.

In town there is a definite tendency to overheat because of the lack of a fan. Several times the temperature went over 100° C, but a few minutes of running at normal road speeds dropped the temperature back to normal. The water won't boil away though, because the expansion tank catches the water that would normally be boiling out.

Since you have to back out of the garage, you reach down to the gear lever on your left, lift up, push over to the right, and drop down into reverse. At first you'll find that you'll be using both hands to do this, but as you get onto it you'll realize it's a safety factor: there is no danger of dropping into reverse (alongside fourth) when you make a snapshift from third to fourth. Incidentally, the top three gears are synchromesh and the shift pattern is the normal H, outside of the reverse position.

The driving position is quite nice, with the wheel in an almost straight-out arm position. The lightweight seats contour to your back and you're wedged down into a comfortable position. (There's no reason for seatbelts.) The pedal positions are good, with ample room between the clutch, transmission housing and steering column, and an equal amount of room for the brake pedal and throttle between the column and the side panel. The driveshaft tunnel traps heat from the engine and the transmission also gets fairly hot; it would be more comfortable if this section were padded.

Watch those water puddles! The water picked up by the tires splatters onto the inside of the fenderwell and comes through the seam where the rear section meets the driver's compartment. For the same reason, take it easy on dirt or on newly tarred sections.

If you take a trip and intend to carry any luggage or clothes other than those that you have on, you'll find there is very little room. We fitted the paraphernalia we carried on our desert and mountain trip with the car into the two small door compartments, on the ledges alongside the driver and passenger, and the rest on the passenger floor. In this way we were able to carry our camera, briefcase, clipboard, jackets, and stopwatches.

For some unaccountable reason the float bowl for the two S.U. carburetors sits between them, and all three units are directly above the exhaust headers. Even though a thin aluminum sheet separates them, the heat from the headers, coupled with the underhood heat, results in the gasoline percolating in the float bowl. This, of course, held down both our performance and gasoline mileage. Even so, we got 25.1 miles per gallon on our mountain-desert-town course of 211 miles.

Is the Lotus Club a street machine? Personally, I look on it as a good base for competition at moderate cost. It has the performance, the handling, and quick access to parts that may need servicing. With the unsnapping of two spring hooks (one on each side at the front) the hood and front fenders lift as one unit, hinging forward. The rear section opens the same way. Both can also be lifted off their cam locks and laid aside.

The Lotus Club with 4.55 rear axle gives 16.7 mph for every 1000 rpm turned in high gear. This means that at the maximum rev limit of 7200, the car is capable of 120.2 mph in top gear and 72.1 mph in third gear. Acceleration is equal to the best sportscars in its category. The Club can turn 86 mph at the end of a quarter-mile through the gears. You can't get much better than that for a sports-racing machine.

It's light, slight, but what a screamer! /MT

THE CAR YOU SEE HERE IS PROBABLY THE BEST OF ITS KIND — ANYWHERE... ADRIEN'S

Top: Back into the SCW files to view not the Schagen Lotus Eleven, but a release picture of the Lotus Eleven Le Mans, "the standard by which all small sportsters may be judged" according to the caption on the back.

Above and left: A Lotus Eleven Le Mans, owned in the early sixties by a former SCW editor, Doug Blain. Note windscreen and small doors. In practice it was wise not to use doors as there was an extreme danger of denting the fragile alloy panel work...

Right: The Schagen Eleven, probably the best in the world and an exemplary restoration job. The car cleaned up in a recent world-wide "photographic concours" of Elevens.

186

MASTERPIECE

Admire the car restorer. He is the man who can take a worn, battered and probably ugly lump of metal, rubber, leather and glass and, having his eyes always fixed on the goal ahead, can transform it into a beautiful classic car. Even among the rare group of men who can do it Adrien Schagen, owner of this Lotus Eleven, is a man apart...

ADRIEN SCHAGEN is a sculptor, working in metal and stone with great feeling for his material, and a prodigious eye for detail.

These same gifts are central to the story of his restoration of a Lotus 11 which, after two years of dedicated work, has become a remarkable piece of sculpture in its own right.

The long chain of events leading to the rebuild is not merely an interesting story in itself, but also an inseparable part of the finished car.

The story starts, on the one side, with Adrien Schagen's long-standing involvement with the sport, including racing an MGTC in Queensland in the 1950s and an almost inevitable meeting with another multi-talented man, Derek Jolly, who was for a time the Australian agent for Lotus. Through Jolly, Adrien bought a Lotus Elite which, when the Schagen family moved to Sydney, was serviced by Tom Sulman and Tom became another good friend until he was killed at Bathurst in 1970 in a Lotus 11.

The Lotus 11-series and its history is the other side of the story. The Elevens collectively (there were two versions, Series 1 and Series 2, externally indistinguishable but significantly different under the skin) were produced between 1956 and 1958, were highly successful in 1100 and 1500 cc sports racing competition, and in terms of numbers produced (about 270) more than doubled the then-existing Lotus population.

Technically, they represented the logical evolution from Chapman's earlier streamlined sports cars. These had begun with the Mk 8 of 1954, which was not all that bad but had an idealistically complex space frame and aerodynamic shell. The Mk 9 which followed in 1955 was a drastic rationalisation, reverting to a variant of the square-rigged Mk 6 chassis clad with a shorter (though still distinctive) high-tailed body. The Series 1 Elevens for 1956 were a further rationalisation, drawing from chassis ideas used in two late-1955 "works" Mk 9s but appearing with an almost minimal full-enclosing shell, an aluminium envelope of simple elegance.

When the Series 1 Elevens had the ultimate development of Lotus' Ford-based swing-axle front suspension, the Series 2 cars for 1957 had wishbone i.f.s. as introduced on the singleseat Formula Two Lotus 12, and could be had, if required, with the distinctive wobbly-web magnesium alloy wheels which also made their debut on the 12. It was one of these Series 2 cars, chassis 305, which British enthusiast John Coombs bought in 1957, to race in Under 1500 cc sports car events with one of the then-new twin-cam Coventry Climax FPF engines, and at the end of the season the car came to Australia for Queenslander Charlie Whatmore (Coombs was getting a Lotus 15, which also eventually came to Australia).

Whatmore got a lot of racing out of this little projectile — though perhaps less success than drivers of the 1100 cc versions — and certainly got a few busy moments. One of these would probably have been his 220 km/h (136 mph) run through the Conrod Straight traps at Bathurst, likely to have been a fairly wild ride in a 450 kg (1000 lb) car with Conrod as rough and bumpy as it was in those days. Just as memorable might have been the time at Lakeside in 1958 when the steering rack detached from the chassis; Lotus and driver went aviating off the rim of the Karussell, and, in due course, a new chassis came sailing out from England.

Tom Sulman bought the car in 1963, viewing it as a more powerful stablemate for his ex-Ron Hodgson 1100 cc car, chassis 343. But in practice the twin-cam Eleven (often incorrectly referred to as a Lotus 15 while in Whatmore and Sulman's hands) was a heartbreak: Sulman had two comprehensive engine blow-ups, and found the relatively peaky twin-cam unsuitable for his major activity, hillclimbing, in which the "little" Eleven excelled. Newcastle enthusiast Malcolm Bailey bought it eventually, and raced it from time to time; Adrien Schagen bought it (less engine and gearbox, destined for another Lotus rebuild) in 1972.

Already owning a spare single-cam Climax engine and BMC-"A" gearbox, Adrien had the makings of a complete Eleven, with the useful advantage that the replacement chassis had done little work.

In other areas, however, the car was only what a second-rank, 14-year-old lightweight racing car could be expected to be. The shell had many cracks and plenty of plastic filler, and the inner alloy panels showed the scars of previous owners more concerned with winning races than with preserving the car.

Mechanically, as well, the car had not aged gracefully and while it may not be obvious against the sheer brilliance of the finished restoration, this car has been apart literally to the last nut, bolt and rivet.

While the mechanical restoration involved headaches mainly arising from Chapman's inspired use of UK components-suppliers parts books (where would *you* go to find a left-hand-thread Lotus 11 tie-rod end?) the panelwork presented an opposite challenge.

Lotuses of this period (apart from the all-fibreglass Elite, of course) were all-metal machines, and their compound-curved bodywork was hand-formed, car by car, by British artisans. The nonchalant accuracy of their flat panelwork is matched only by the sheer impossibility of their skill at shaping and welding more complex shapes.

Here the Schagen Eleven was blessed. Ten minutes drive away from the workshop was Rodney Hoffman, not merely a magical metalworker in a completely different industry, but also married to the delicious London-born daughter of Stan Brown, one-time Lotus body-builder now nicely established in Brookvale crafting aluminium yachts.

Perhaps opposites attract. Whatever the reason, Rodney Hoffman and Adrien Schagen developed a close working relationship and achieved the nearly-impossible, shaping and welding-in strategic sections of new external panels, making from scratch new fuel tanks and almost all the flat panelling.

(Here a word about Lotus flat panels. To start with, Chapman used flat panelling for multiple functions. Thus, the dead-smooth undertray, broken only by apertures for wheels, radiator outlet and sump and rear disc cooling, runs from front to rear, and is tightly pop-rivetted the whole way. Cockpit panels support the driver while they keep out the elements. The tailshaft tunnel not only covers the driveline as required by regulation, but also takes engine and gearbox loads and gives beam strength to the sheet-alloy floor, eight years before the all-monocoque Lotus 25 . . .

As well, Chapman at this time was very concerned with aerodynamic losses caused by air trapped in wheel-wells; thus Elevens have very tight-fitting wheel arches and intricately-shaped inboard panels to enclose the suspension as much as possible and just leave each wheel to itself, inside a sealed little compartment.

As a result, Elevens have many small internal panels and the performance of the car, as much as its appearance, depends on the condition of this sheet metalwork.)

What gives the Schagen Eleven its special character is not the sheer thoroughness of its rebuild, impressive though this is.

But the car is unique in the way its metal surfaces have been finished to distinguish one component from another while at the same time never disguising that the car is a collection of carefully chosen, cleverly shaped pieces of otherwise quite ordinary metal.

The relatively small areas of steel are either painted (grey or black) or plated in cadmium or chrome. The body's external panels — superbly repaired — are painted bright red, with the sill-panel on each side contrasting in unpainted, highly-buffed aluminium.

Under this shell, the all-alloy Climax engine is scrubbed silver-white, with a few machined surfaces polished. The brake calipers are polished castings; the gearbox and differential casing have been glass-bead blasted and glow softly. Internal surfaces of the cockpit have been buffed to a high finish before being rivetted in place, and contrast perfectly with the deliberate satin finish of the fuel tanks, obtained by careful treatment with coarse emery paper and steel wool.

Although intended from the start to be simply a road car, the completed car has won each time it has contested a concours. It won the Racing class at the heavily-supported MG Car Club/Rothmans event in Sydney in 1974, and in 1975 it walked away with a world-wide "photographic concours" conducted by the fanatical US Eleven Register.

Perhaps the greatest compliment paid to the car was by NSW Department of Motor Transport when the Eleven was presented for re-registration. At first, the Department believed re-registration was impossible, since the car was clearly brand new.

But the Eleven finally got a set of plates, and is now in frequent road use (a startling sight) and occasional Club Lotus competition. In the time taken for its rebuild, the Lotus factory sixteen years before had produced the entire output of Elevens. But never an Eleven like this. ☐

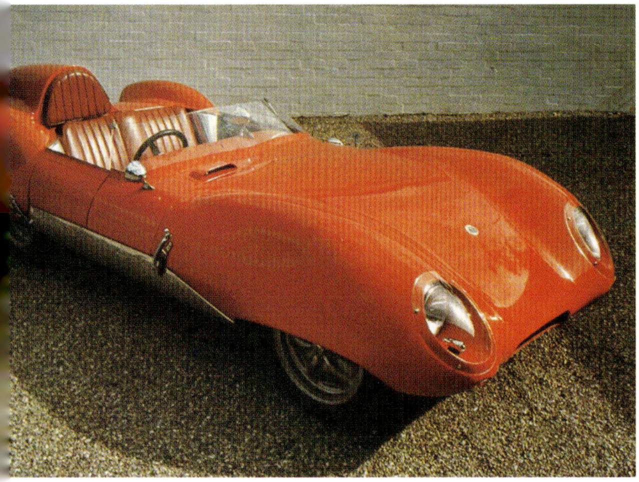
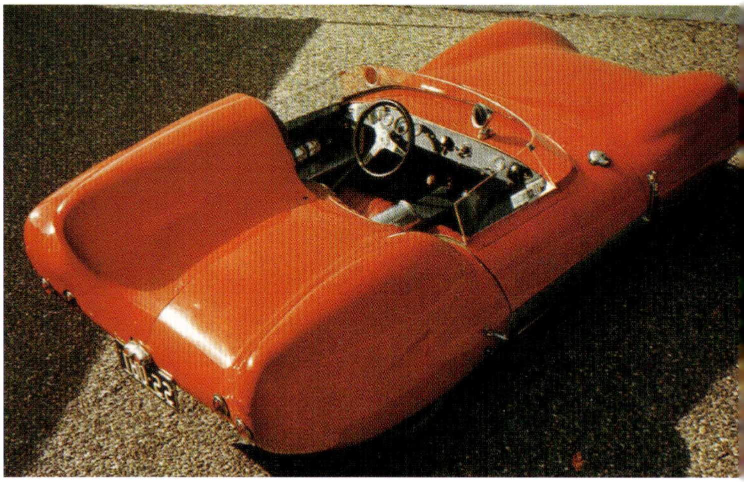
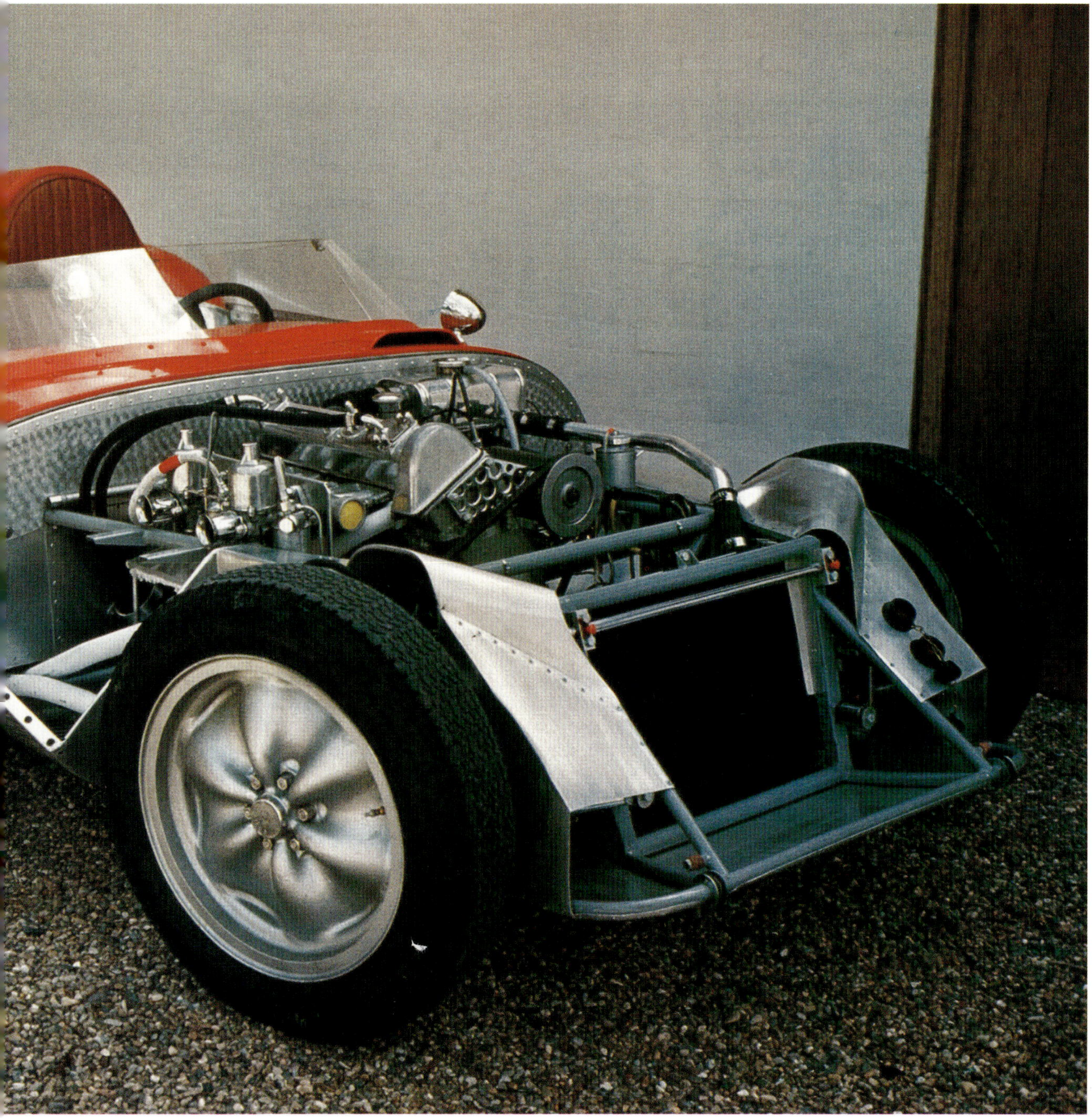

TRACK TEST

SLIPPERY CUSTOMER

Willie Green tries a pristine example of Colin Chapman's Lotus Eleven, with Coventry Climax power and Frank Costin body, on the track

'Simplificate and add lightness' is a phrase that has always stuck in my mind. For the life of me I cannot remember who coined it, nor what they were talking about, but it could well have been about Anthony Colin Bruce Chapman. It summed up all his early thinking, catapulting the name of Lotus from a one-off Austin Seven-based special to a respected car maker in a few short years. And, of those early models, the Eleven was the machine that pushed the company into the big time. Almost every Lotus can be described as 'significant' or 'important', but the Eleven must be counted as one of the *most* significant and important. This year sees Lotus type or model numbers reach the century, with the current 100T in Formula One: without the Eleven it may not have happened…

What was Chapman's genius? That he was a superlative engineer is beyond question, but there have been others of equal ability who never made it. He was also capable of attracting the talented to work for or with him, whether they were drivers or other engineers, though if they didn't agree with him, or couldn't persuade him that they were right and he was wrong – out they went. The astonishing thing about those first few years was that not only did the talented flock to work for him (his innovative approach and track successes ensured that they would at the very least be intrigued) but that they seemed to work all the hours God gave and more (the 25-hour day was the norm) and for fairly ludicrous salaries, if any … It is not going too far to say that Chapman sowed the seeds back then of what is now the British domination of design in the motor racing industry.

But he will probably best be remembered, and rightly so, as the best chassis engineer the world has ever seen. His understanding of the space-frame, and later the monocoque, was unparalleled, while almost every racing car made today has suspension that owes something to him. I have a suspicion that he thought in 3-D: his suspension geometry is uncannily correct, simple yet superb. And if you throw swing-axle front suspension at me, remember that it *worked*…

Loti I through IV were Seven-based specials, built between 1948 and 1952. The VI was the first 'production' car, in that 110 were built, but it was really a kit car, sold in component form, into which an assortment of engines was shoe-horned: it was available between 1953 and 1955. In 1954 came the VIII, of which ten were built, followed in 1955 by the IX and X: between them they account for some 30 cars. The VII, of course, was out of sequence, appearing in 1957 as a successor to the VI.

The VI was the car that really established Chapman's name. Ultra-light, very basic but far from crude in design, it made an ideal weekend racer for

Above: Willie Green at speed in the Lotus Eleven – top speed is aided by careful aerodynamics. Below: Traditional red-rimmed steering wheel. Right: Admiring looks for the Eleven – owner John Grey is in the leather jacket. Opposite page: Delicate lines of the car framed in the Old Hall arch at Oulton Park circuit

the impecunious enthusiast of traditional fame. But, with production engines – usually Ford sidevalve, or, for the less impecunious, MG – it was really only a club racer, not the sort of thing you would enter for Le Mans or the Nürburgring. Still, it set the Lotus style: 'simplificate and add lightness'.

The Mk VIII of 1954 set Lotus on an international course. There was again a Chapman space-frame, but of such purity that it was necessary to strip the engine of ancillaries before it could be taken out or in. *That* didn't last long. There was that apparently crude swing-axle at the front – and a sophisticated De Dion set-up at the back. Two things set it off: firstly its looks, and secondly its performance…

The looks came from Frank Costin, one of two Costin brothers Chapman inveigled into working for him. Frank was an aerodynamicist, who applied his logic to the passing of air over a racing car. The result was a pair of proboscis-like noses either side of the grille, an ultra-clean body, and a pair of prominent tail-fins for straight-line stability. And it was as 'streamlined' as it looked: with Chapman's superlight chassis and the Costin slippery skin, the Mk VIII was as quick as all get-out, as Chapman proved. In spite of a lack of power from an MG XPAG engine, he beat Hans Hermann's works Porsche 550 at the British GP meeting that year. Two future giants of motor racing came together that day, Porsche and Lotus. And their respective approaches paved the way for what we have today, Porsche with their basic strength in engines, and Lotus in chassis.

Something of great importance for Lotus – and other special builders – happened in late 1954: Coventry Climax made their little FWA 1098cc single ohc engine available to buyers. It was initially designed for use in portable fire pumps: since it had to be 'portable', it also had to be light. Since it also had to power a pump that delivered 350 gallons-per-minute, it also had to be powerful. Even so, the FWA might not have been anything special had it not been designed by enthusiasts with a racing background, Wally Hassan and Harry Mundy. They may have designed a fire-pump workhorse, but the end result was a racing workhorse as well. From it was developed a whole family of racing engines which, when applied to the innovative Chapman and Cooper chassis, led to the rise of Britain to the very top in the world of motor racing.

For the FWA, Chapman came up with the Mk IX, a lighter, lower, more compact Mk VIII. It was not wildly successful, mainly because those blacksmiths down in Surbiton came up with the famous 'bob-tail' centre-seat Cooper-Climax. On balance, 1955 turn-

Top: More action on an Oulton corner – low centre of gravity, excellent chassis help to keep the car foursquare. Above: Coventry Climax FWB engine has fire pump motor ancestry. Right: Alloy tonneau and Perspex fairing add to low drag co-efficient. Below: Pure lines from Frank Costin

Left: The Eleven as bought by John – note replica E-type nose and registration. Below left: The Eleven's finest hour – Cliff Allison and Keith Hall celebrate with Colin Chapman (right) after Le Mans 1957. Above right: Stirling Moss in the record-breaker at Le Mans. Right: The Theo Page cutaway from Autosport *of an early Eleven. Note the swing axle front suspension*

ed out to be a Cooper year. The Bristol-powered Mk X (basically a Mk IX with a bigger engine bay) was not a success either, mainly due to a gent called Archie Scott-Brown and his Lister.

And then came 1956, and the Eleven. The Eleven, note, not the XI or the 11. If Roman numerals continued Chapman reckoned that they would eventually be so complicated no-one would understand them (and there's a canny eye on the future for you!), while '11' looked too much like the Roman '11'. Eleven it was...

And, for 1956, there was a clearing of the decks. For the first part of the year, Chapman concentrated on the Eleven and only the Eleven. The chassis was evolutionary rather than revolutionary, a space-frame whose main tubes were 1in in diameter, and those with lesser stress ¾in diameter. Stiffness was increased, though, by the adoption of a stressed transmission tunnel as well. At the front there were swing axles again, but with a lower pivot point to reduce understeer, and rack and pinion steering. For the 'Le Mans' version there was a De Dion back axle again with coil springs. The 'Sports' and 'Club' versions made do with live back axles.

The Le Mans version was the serious racer, and was offered with a choice of engines, the FWA in either stage 1, 72bhp, form, or stage 2 when it pushed out 83bhp. For the works cars, and special customers, there was the new Coventry Climax FWB 1500cc power unit. The Club again featured the FWA engine, while the Sport was stuck with the good old Ford 1172cc sidevalver, complete with three-speed box. The latter two, incidentally, also featured drum brakes all round.

Once again Frank Costin was called in to design the Eleven's party frock. It was far less swoopy than the VIII, IX or X, but by the same token it looked far more purposeful. Frank's almost clinical approach shone everywhere: the radiator intake was a tiny little slot in the nose, quite unlike the maws that others had to resort to, but then he knew all about ducting, and what air did when it went where it did. Elevens never suffered overheating problems through an insufficiency of air. Wheels, too are anathema to good airflow, so Frank allowed as little as possible of them to show, fore as well as aft.

You felt that, if the driver were to wear a specially-shaped helmet, you would have a closed car

The result may have looked bulbous, but by heaven it was clean. For the serious racers too the passenger seat was covered by a metal tonneau, while the driver's head poked out of a perspex surround which flowed into a biggish headrest. You felt that, if the driver were to wear a specially shaped helmet, you would have a fully closed car ... Later, of course, Lotus did fit a bubble canopy for record breaking, and that car must be one of the cleanest ever built. Rounding it all off was a pair of neat tail fins, less prominent than those of the earlier models. The overall result was, and still is, strikingly original, and I personally think very pretty. The lesser models, and some racers, could be fitted with a low, full-width plastic screen, while the Club was even available with a normal windscreen and – believe it or not – a hood, as John Bolster's test of one demonstrated. However, that was about as far as creature comforts went – luggage space was non-existent, as were such luxuries as a heater or sidescreens. The Eleven was a sports-racer, with the emphasis on racer, which is why, to my eyes, the enclosed cockpit 'single-seat' version, for want of a better term, is far and away the best looking.

An Eleven was entered via Briggs Cunningham for the Sebring 12 hours race, but it crashed in practice. Reg Bicknell, a competent but not brilliant driver who'd worked his way up through 500cc racing, took a works car, an FWB-powered version, to a fourth in a race for 1500cc sports cars at the Easter Goodwood, but behind three Coopers.

The first major confrontation between the Eleven and the Coopers came at the Empire Trophy meeting at Oulton Park. The standard of entry was, by today's standards, staggering. Coopers fielded Salvadori, Moss and Jim Russell in bob-tails: Lotus responded with Chapman (in those days a world-class driver as well as a constructor, who could mix it with the best of them), Bicknell and Mike Hawthorn in Ivor Bueb's car. The Trophy was run in three heats, and in that for cars up to 1500cc the result was Chapman, Salvadori, Hawthorn, Moss, Bicknell. Moss, however, won the final. From then on, it was all Lotus...

To document the Eleven's career would take – and has, via Denis Ortenburger – a book. Let's just say that it was everything to everybody, a machine that was equally at home at Le Mans as it was in a five-lap clubbie. Everybody from the famous to complete unknowns took to the tracks, with equally varying degrees of success. You couldn't watch a race meeting between 1956 and about 1959 or 60 without an Eleven appearing somewhere in the programme.

Highlights of 1956 included one of the all-time great battles between Chapman and Hawthorn at Goodwood on Whit Monday, and the Team Lotus foray to Le Mans that year. They ran three cars, one 1500 and two 1100s; the 1500 retired with a blown engine, one of the 1100s was eliminated when it hit a large dog on the Mulsanne straight (yes, really), but the Bicknell/Jopp 1100 won the 1100cc class, finishing seventh overall, and fourth on Index of Performance. Late in the year Lotus went record-breaking at Monza with the bubble-topped car and Stirling Moss behind the wheel. Moss took the 50-mile Class

Right: Autosport's *Editor Gregor Grant took an Eleven to the Mille Miglia in 1957. A ruptured fuel tank meant a slow crawl home to the finish – and a damn good story! Below: In 1956, a youthful Graham Hill was a Lotus employee, and drove a Ford-powered Eleven in the* Autosport *Championship, as here at Oulton Park*

G record at 132.7mph before the Eleven's tail called enough over the Monza bumps, and a sub-frame fractured. A subsequent trip, with the talented American Herbert Mackay Frazer driving, saw the Class G record for the hour standing at 137.5mph. And that from 1100cc...

Chapman started getting involved with Formula 2 in 1956, displaying the single-seater 12 at Earls Court. One beneficiary of this sorry machine was the Eleven Series Two of 1957/58. 'Series Two' because otherwise it would have been the Lotus 13, and that's regarded as unlucky by the superstitious. The Eleven benefited in being equipped with a twin wishbone and coil spring front suspension (in typical Chapman fashion the leading arm of the upper wishbone was formed by part of the anti-roll bar: never duplicate...) from the ill-fated 12. International regulations called for full-width screens and a proper two-seat cockpit, so many Series Two Elevens were so equipped for races abroad, but the 'single seat' configuration was still popular here. The range was broadened slightly to include the Le Mans 150 (powered by the FPF 1500cc twin cam engine), the Le Mans 85 (Stage 2 FWA), the Le Mans 75 (Stage 1 FWA) the Club 75 (Stage 1 FWA but with swing axle front suspension and a live back axle) and Sports 45 (Ford side-valve power).

In 1957 there was no nonsense from the Coopers, and in the UK the Eleven had it almost all its own way. A typical day's racing was summed up in an advert Lotus used which referred to the Goodwood Easter Monday meeting: Eleven's were first and third in the 2-litre class (the winner was Brian Naylor in the Maserati-powered version), first and second in the 1500cc class, first through to *sixth* in the 1100cc class, and first, second and third in the 1100cc Series Production class.

Lotus didn't enter many major events abroad, but there were two exceptions: Sebring, because America took a lot of Elevens, and of course Le Mans. And it was on the Sarthe circuit that an Eleven scored what was perhaps its most famous victory when it took the Index of Performance from under the noses of the French BD-based specials which regarded this award as home territory. It was powered by a very special engine, mind you, a 744cc Climax device, pumping out 59bhp at 8000rpm. What's more, it finished 14th overall, and first in the 750cc class, while an 1100 took its class as well, came ninth overall, and – as if to rub salt into the wound – second on Index...

The 750cc Eleven stole the Index of Performance from under the French noses

The Eleven soldiered on until the end of 1958, winning almost everything in sight as was its wont, but in 1959 Eric Broadley introduced his Lola Mk 1, and the Eleven was instantly relegated to the also-rans whenever it was up against the Lola. Chapman and Lotus, though, had long since moved on: apart from the 12, there was the Seven (a reincarnated VI) and the Elite. The Eleven was succeeded by the 15 – but that's another story...

Before we close the Eleven story, and go on to driving impressions, let's just add a few figures. Some 250 were built all told, of which 150 were 'Series One', the rest 'Series Two'. The quoted weight was 7½cwt, but when *The Autocar* tested DEC494 in November 1956, they found it weighed 9.1cwt, 1019lb. They also recorded a maximum speed of 111.75mph, 0-60mph time of 10.9sec, and a 0-100mph time of 38.9sec. Those figures, they pointed out, were taken two-up, and that added 3cwt to the car, a not insignificant extra load (DEC494, incidentally, being the 1100cc car which finished ninth overall, second on Index and first in the 1100cc class at Le Mans that year). The most astonishing figure, though, was the fuel consumption – no less than 47.8mpg over 1200 miles of testing!

The Motor, on the other hand, seemed to have testers with a heavier left foot – they recorded a maximum of 125mph, took 10.0sec to 60mph, and 23.6sec to 100mph! Mind you, fuel consumption plummeted to 34.4mpg ... Their car was XAR 1, the 750cc Index winner re-engined back to standard.

So on to the test car. It is owned by John Grey and is fettled and looked after by Tony Whitehead whose name has appeared in these pages before – he owned the Halseylec we wrote about in April 1984. John bought it in 1984 from Robin Longdon as effectively, a box of bits.

And what in fact he bought was a mystery. That it was a Lotus Eleven was not in doubt. The wishbone front suspension proved it was a Series Two, the De Dion back axle a Le Mans, and the unusual 'wobbly' wheels' – cast alloys – instead of wires meant that it was one of only 17 Elevens so equipped, and those 17 were either works cars or for especially favoured customers. The mystery? No chassis number.

At some time in its life it had been rebodied as a coupé, with a glass-fibre replica E-type Jaguar bonnet. Now the Eleven's chassis number was stamped on an inner wing panel, and this had been thrown away when it was rebodied...

A log book that came with it showed that it had been road-registered in 1969 as a coupé, and given the number AWR 659G. It is almost certain that it was raced in the seventies by a certain Don Marriott, but once you've said that you've said it all. Is Don Marriott still around? Does anyone remember a coupé Eleven with the number AWR 659G? Does whoever rebodied it have any more information? Are they still around? In fact, is there *anyone* who can add any more information? If so John and Tony would be exceedingly grateful. You can contact them through *C&S* if you can help at all.

The car took about a year to restore. The lot was stripped, the chassis shot-blasted and stove enamelled, and then sent to Williams and Pritchard to be rebodied as per original. In fact, Len Pritchard was one of those who confirmed that it was a genuine Series Two. Wherever possible John and Tony have gone to original Lotus suppliers for parts: Williams and Pritchard for the body, and Ron Welch, who is Edmonton Tool and Engineering, for the hubs, which he supplied back in the fifties as well. As John says, "It's nice to have it going home, as it were."

It was finished by Tony back in 1985, and on its first foray on to the tracks, at Silverstone, the gear lever snapped in Tony's hand on the start line! There were also some rather odd oil pressure problems, like none at critical moments, due to a peculiarity in the pressure release valve area. In all, it's done seven or eight events now, and has proved to be remarkably competitive, about the only car being able to beat it being Peter Walker's Lola Mk 1 with 1500cc. The engine, incidentally, is an FWE, which is the Lotus Elite variant with 1200cc, but it has all the pukka go-faster bits, such as a five-bearing camshaft. Race Engine Services looked after that department...

To outsiders, it looks as if the driver's head is sticking up out of some sort of conning tower, since the gap between the sides of the perspex screen is so narrow. In fact it's not the screen that restricts any movement – there's actually enough room for your shoulders – but rather the high transmission tunnel and side sill, which force you into an elbows akimbo stance. The cockpit is fairly confined, but there's enough room in vital areas for this not to be a bother. And you're far enough away from the wheel for a reasonable straight-arm driving position. Not that you need a lot of arm movement: you don't need a lot of lock, and there isn't much anyway – it has an enormous turning circle! Those all-enveloping wings don't give much wheel movement ... Mind you, as Don Hands (who was having a go in it as well) said, "You seem to just step inside and pull it on..."

It's amazingly easy to drive, and you can get used to it very quickly – you feel very confident very early. You can see why Lotus was happy for ham-fisted journalists to be let loose in it. Apart, perhaps, from a clutch that might make creeping in traffic a bit of a problem, you could use it for shopping.

I don't know what power the engine was giving,

Top left: Track scene, 1957 – Elevens as far as the eye can see... Above left: The classic confrontation, Cooper versus Lotus, 1956. Above: Paddock group, with Loti VI, VIII, IX and Eleven. Left: By 1959 the Eleven (here driven by Tom Threlfall) was already a classic

but I'll say this. Because the car's so light, it feels as if it's a lot more pokey than it probably is! The acceleration is really something else for a 1200, and it don't 'arf go. It will rev to 7500rpm quite safely, though I only used 7000rpm for the purposes of this test, and it pulls very sweetly indeed from about 4500rpm.

The gearbox is the smaller A-series unit, with reverse towards you and back, and the other gears in the normal H-pattern. There's no synchro on first, which is no problem, while the other gears are a bit notchy but all there, and if you feed the lever in gently there are no problems. Gearing was perfect for Oulton.

Loti, and the Eleven in particular, were noted for their handling, and you can see why after a very short space of time behind the wheel. Apart from one problem, which I'll come back to, I can only call the roadholding and handling sensational. The steering literally is finger-light, and from turn-in to the exit of a corner it simply feels glued to the road. Neat, clean, and very, very quick, I reckon an Eleven will out-corner almost anything else in historics, as John has demonstrated when it's been going well. The only car faster in class is the Lola and that has a 1500 engine ... It is dead easy to balance, and very forgiving if anything does happen.

The problem? It goes a little funny under braking into a corner – as you set it up when you're trying, it can lurch badly at the back. I don't think this is serious, though – slightly stiffer rear springs, and a check on toe-out, should be enough. This is emphasised a little by the fact that there's a mite too much braking on the rear. Given that, though, with its light weight, the brakes work superbly, however. As I've said, once you're past the point of instability, the handling is truly fabulous. And Costin got his aerodynamics right, too – it sits dead steady on the straights.

The Eleven really is a sensational little car, and you can see why it was so successful. Superb handling which meant you could simply drive around even more powerful cars, light weight and a clean body shape that allowed a pretty staggering performance for its engine size, and a lovely shape to boot – you've all the ingredients for a classic racer. Colin Chapman and his happy band really were a bunch of geniuses.

To finish, I can but quote from a memorandum defining the philosophy of Lotus Engineering which Tony Rudd wrote, but which was fully endorsed by Chapman: 'The most elegantly effective and traditionally Lotus solution is one with the least number of parts, effectively deployed.'

Or, to put it another way, 'Simplificate and add lightness'.

The Lotus Fifteen

The Lotus Eleven had been a hugely successful sports racing car, and various attempts were made to squeeze bigger engines into the Eleven chassis, notably, the new Coventry Climax FPF twin-overhead camshaft engine that was developed by Wally Hassan and his team at Coventry Climax in 1957 specifically for the new 1½-litre Formula 2. Three Lotus Eleven 150 LMs were built with the FPF engine, but the chassis did not do justice to the increased power. So, in the middle of his first year as a production car manufacturer, with the Seven and the Elite, and forays into the world of Formula cars with the Lotus Twelve, Colin Chapman entered the world of larger capacity sports racing cars as well. Len Terry had been taken on as a design engineer, and some of the credit for the Fifteen multi-tube space frame chassis came from his drawing board.

In the early Lotus Fifteens, in 1958, the FPF twin-cam engine was installed lying at 60 degrees on its side to maintain a low bonnet profile, and the gearbox was at the back incorporated with the limited slip final drive. This had been used on the single-seater Lotus Twelve, with a notable lack of reliability which resulted in it being dubbed the 'queerbox'. It's sequential gear selection created constant problems, and one Team Lotus driver referred to it as a gearbox 'full of neutrals'. Later, a stronger and larger version was used for the Fifteen, but it still contained an awful lot of neutrals on many occasions. The rear suspension was by Chapman strut which had been developed on the Type 14 Lotus Elite, and the Fifteen's version was somewhat stronger. The front suspension was the conventional wishbone arrangement which had appeared with the Lotus Eleven Series 2. Disc brakes were installed, inboard at the rear, and operated by Girling light alloy calipers. The steering was Lotus modified rack and pinion the same as the Eleven. The wheels were the Lotus designed 'wobbly web' magnesium alloy from the Formula 2 Lotus Twelve, but of increased width, and knock off wire wheels were an option. The body was very similar to the Lotus Eleven which had proved so aesthetically pleasing and practical.

When finished, the Lotus Fifteen measured 11ft 5ins overall length, with a scuttle height of just 2ft. The power output of the 1½-litre FPF engine was 150bhp at 7200rpm, which in an overall dry weight of 980lbs made an impressive power to weight ratio. It was even more impressive when the later 2-litre and finally 2½-litre engines were installed.

The first Lotus Fifteen was completed in March 1958, and nine Series 1 Fifteens were built by July 1958, all with the rear mounted 'queerbox'. These were followed by eight Series 2 cars up until the end of 1958, by which time the engine had been raised to 17 degrees off vertical, and a bonnet hump added, plus the troublesome 'queerbox' had been abandoned in favour of the conventional MGA or ZF gearbox mounted directly to the engine. In 1959, the Series 3 appeared. The FPF had now developed to 2-litres, and a stronger and considerably modified 'queerbox' made for the single seater Formula 1 Sixteen was installed and was a lot better. A total of eleven Series 3 cars were built before production finished at the end of 1959. In the two year production, 28 Lotus Fifteens had been built. The selling price in 1960 was a considerable £2800 with the 2-litre engine.

The race debut of the Lotus Fifteen was at Goodwood on Easter Monday 7th April 1958. Graham Hill drove the 2-litre Team Lotus car, but after setting a new lap record at 90.38mph, it failed to finish with the first of a long line of gearbox neutrals. Roy Salvadori was driving Pierre Bercham's 1½-litre car which was chassis No. 601, the first produced. The first victory for the new Fifteen came at Silverstone on 4th May 1958 in the Daily Express Trophy Meeting. There were three Fifteens on the grid for the Sports Car event, and Graham Hill won in fine style.

For the Le Mans 24 Hour event on 21/22nd June 1958, Team Lotus had entered two 2-litre Fifteens for Cliff Allison/Graham Hill and Americans Jay Chamberlain/Pete Lovely. Both cars had knock off wire wheels in anticipation of tyre changes. The Allison/Hill car suffered a blown head gasket, and the Chamberlain/Lovely car was involved in an accident, so neither cars finished.

By August 1958 'Hoot' Gibson was racing a Lotus Fifteen in Australia, and Peter Huth was racing another in Kenya. Pete Lovely had taken the ex-Le Mans car back to the USA, and other Fifteens were racing there. At the beginning of 1959 Tommy Entwistle had his Fifteen in Canada, and Sy Kaback had another in the USA. Two of the last Series 3 Fifteens built at the end of 1959 went to Derek Jolly in Australia, and Jim Palmer in New Zealand, so the Lotus Fifteen certainly attracted an international market.

At the Sebring 12 hours in March 1959 Entwistle, Chamberlain and Fleming were in Lotus Fifteens but none featured in the results. David Piper and Keith Green drove Piper's Fifteen at the Nurburgring 1000kms race on 7th June 1959, but they did not score. At Aintree for the 51 lap British Grand Prix supporting Sports Car race on 18th April 1959, seven Lotus Fifteens were entered. Graham Hill won in the works 2½-litre car, with Alan Stacey 2nd, and David Piper was 4th just behind Jack Brabham.

Although the Lotus Fifteen was not a wholly reliable car, it was most impressive in both its speed and stability, as well as its elegant bodyshape. It was popular in its day, and even more popular in more recent historic racing.

Graham Capel

LOTUS FIFTEEN

I.R.S. on the latest sports car from Hornsey

LOWER STILL—the Lotus Fifteen is the sleekest yet: even the windscreen is smoothly moulded to reduce wind-drag.

Last week the latest of a long line of Lotuses was unveiled—the Lotus Fifteen. This is the 1958 version of the highly successful sports cars and a worthy successor to those which performed so well at Sebring. The new car looks even smaller than its ancestors and, in fact, the frontal area has been substantially reduced, by laying the twin-cam 1,500 c.c. Coventry Climax motor almost completely on its side—in fact only 28 deg. from the horizontal. Overall height has thus been reduced—and yet ground clearance has been increased as well! The other major advancement is that the rear suspension is now strut-type all-independent, in a similar manner to the F2 car and the Elite, and a ZF limited-slip differential is in unit with a five-speed gearbox, out of which Lotus are now confident that the "bugs" have been ironed. In place of the fore-and-aft gate gearchange used in the F2 car, a positive-stop change, similar in principle to a motor-cycle foot-change, is used, while a separate knob, projecting between the seat-backs, is used to select reverse.

Front suspension is of the fabricated wishbone type, now standardised on all Lotuses, and magnesium alloy wheels are fitted. Disc brakes are outboard at the front and inboard at the rear. Rear tyres of larger section are now employed.

The radiator is now fully ducted, so that cooling air does not pass through the engine compartment. Other changes include the "building-in" of the previously detachable head-fairing and re-arrangement of stowage in the tail. The spare wheel is now mounted vertically on the right, and the battery and the three tanks—for gearbox and engine oil, and for fuel—occupy the remaining space. Weight, less fuel, is claimed to be 980 lbs.

COCKPIT layout is functional, yet comfortable. The gearchange is a simple, positive-stop device—move it in one direction for changes up and in the other for changes down.

TAIL is occupied by three tanks for oil and fuel, plus the battery and spare wheel. For suspension details, see the Theo Page drawing on facing page. This is the first sports Lotus to have full i.r.s.

ENGINE is tucked well down on its side, as these pictures show. Dry-sump lubrication is employed and the carburetters are twin-choke Webers.

LOTUS FIFTEEN

THE LOTUS FIFTEEN (Series II) is a sports racing car designed for international competition. Its many unique mechanical features plus the now traditional LOTUS concepts of low weight and low drag with impressive acceleration and fabulous braking make it a formidable contender on race tracks all over the world. Since its introduction in 1958, the racing record of FIFTEENS in four continents, showing many outright wins against unlimited competition has proved that not only is it a "sure fire" contestant in its class, but also very much a proposition for overall success.

THE aerodynamic properties of the FIFTEEN'S bodywork will be appreciated from this picture especially when one considers that with a ground clearance of 5½" the scuttle height is only 24"!! Moulded perspex screen and high back with headfairing are standard. The complete car dry weighs only 980 lbs.

REMOVABLE panels allow instant access to all mechanical components. This vital feature is typical LOTUS practice as are the tubular space frame and wishbone front end. (The latter now standard on all production models including the Formula cars). The crossflow radiator is fully ducted.

ALTHOUGH wire wheels are standard, Formula type magnesium wheels can be fitted and when long distance racing is not contemplated the weight saving is well worth while. Comprehensive instrumentation and complete light weight sports car electrics are provided. Steering is by rack and pinion.

LOTUS FIFTEEN SPECIFICATION

FRAME — Multi-tubular space frame comprising 1 in. and ¾ in. square and round tubing of 18 and 20 gauge steel. The propeller shaft tunnel and floor are stressed members forming an integral part of the frame. The engine is carried on two rubber mountings at the front and a single rubber mounting at the rear attached to the bellhousing; it is tilted sideways through approximately 17° this gives a straight, induction tract. The rear frame incorporates a spare wheel mounting and an easily detachable petrol tank to provide ready access to the final drive unit and rear brakes.

FRONT SUSPENSION — Independent by transverse wishbone incorporating a roll bar. Springing by combined coil spring-damper units reacting through a single attachment point at each end.

REAR SUSPENSION — Chapman strut type rear suspension with single radius arm and articulated drive shafts.

BRAKES — Ultra light Girling hydraulically operated 9½ in. disc brakes, outboard at the front, inboard at the rear. Horizontally mounted hand brake operating the rear calipers through inner and outer cables.

STEERING — Lightweight rack and pinion steering gear with special steering linkage to give higher cornering power at low speeds.

POWER UNIT — Coventry Climax FPF twin overhead camshaft four cylinder engine. Bore 81.2 mm. (3.20 in.), stroke, 71.1 mm. (2.80 in.) capacity 1,475 c.c. (90 cu. in.), compression ratio, 10:1. Maximum power output, 150 bhp (nett) at 7,200 r.p.m. Maximum torque 110 lb. ft. at 6,500 r.p.m. Maximum b.m.e.p. 190 lb. sq. in. at 6,500 r.p.m. Notable features of the engine include aluminium alloy cylinder block and crankcase, wet cylinder liners, fully counterweighted crankshaft running in five 2⅛ in. diameter indium plated lead bronze steel back precision bearings. Connecting rods run in bearings of identical type, the crankpin diameter being 2⅛ in. Light alloy pistons with Dykes pattern compression rings are used. There is one inlet and one exhaust valve per cylinder these being inclined at an included angle of 66 degrees. Camshafts operate valves through piston type tappets. Camshafts are gear driven, one gear of the train driving the delivery and scavenge pumps for the dry sump lubrication system.

TRANSMISSION — Twin dry plate clutch, 7½ in. diameter, hydraulically operated. Special four speed close ratio gearbox in unit with engine. Ratios: Top gear 1:1, 3rd gear 1.23:1, 2nd gear 1.67:1, 1st gear 2.5:1, reverse 2.5:1.

FINAL DRIVE — Hypoid final drive unit incorporating ZF limited slip differential of 4.22:1 ratio, alternative final drive ratios 3.73, 3.9, 4.55 and 4.875:1.

COOLING SYSTEM — Fully ducted cross flow radiator with remote header tank.

FUEL SYSTEM — Single light alloy tank, 19 gallons capacity. SU pump mounted in engine bay.

BODYWORK — A full width moulded Perspex screen conforming with the general body lines and complying with the Appendix "C" regulations is standard.

ELECTRICAL SYSTEM — Special lightweight 12 volt 31 amp-hr. battery, weight 24 lb located in tail. Coil and distributor, centrifugal advance and retard, belt driven dynamo, automatic voltage control. Fuse box mounted on dash panel. Recessed Lucas Le Mans 7 in. headlamps and separate side lamps, twin stop-tail lights, rear number plate-stop lamp, high frequency horn. Instrument lighting. Screen wiper.

INSTRUMENTS — 3 in. tachometer 0-8000 r.p.m., oil pressure gauge, water temperature gauge and ammeter.

WHEELS AND TYRES — Knock-on 15 in. wire wheels with identical rims front and rear are fitted with 4.50 × 15 tyres at the front and 5.50 × 15 tyres at the rear. 4.50 × 15 spare wheel mounted under rear panelling. Magnesium bolt-on wheels can be offered at extra cost giving 35 lb. saving in weight; they are, however, unsuitable for long distance races where tyre changes may be necessary.

DIMENSIONS — Wheelbase, 7 ft. 4 in.; front track, 3 ft. 11 in.; rear track, 4 ft.; overall length, 11 ft. 5 in.; overall width, 5 ft.; height to top of scuttle, 2 ft.; minimum ground clearance 5½ in.

WEIGHT — Standard Fifteen model, less fuel, 980 lb.

EXTRAS — Full list of optional extras may be obtained on request. Hood and sticks and wiper kit for full Appendix "C", necessary for some races, is available at extra cost.

In accordance with the company's progressive policy, the right to alter specifications without notice is reserved

LOTUS ENGINEERING CO. LTD.
TOTTENHAM LANE, LONDON, N.8

Telephone FITzroy 1777 - Cables: LOTUSENG London

THE Coventry Climax F.P.F. 1.5 litre engine has proved outstanding in world racing, it currently produces 150 b.h.p. at 7,200 r.p.m. A modified production B.M.C. four speed gearbox with special ratios gives complete reliability and simplifies servicing overseas. Clutch is a twin dry plate unit.

THE Chapman strut type rear suspension is both efficient and simple. Final drive is a B.M.C. unit in a LOTUS casing and with Z.F. differential. The light alloy petrol tank can be quickly removed to give access to the rear end including the inboard brakes, which as at the front, are Girling disc type with light alloy calipers.

1958 COMPETITION CARS

THE LOTUS

Inclined Engine, Rear Gearbox and All-independent Suspension

THE latest in the line of sports cars from Colin Chapman and his team is announced, and bids fair to be the fastest machine yet from the Lotus stable. Easter Monday at Goodwood should see the début (probably in 2-litre form) of the twin-cam, five-speed, all-independent, lower and longer Mark Fifteen which will be the mainstay of the Lotus attack in sports-car races this season, and is already entered for Le Mans.

Outwardly similar in aerodynamic shape to its predecessor, the Fifteen is new right through. Lessons learned in all fields of racing activity have produced a new, light tubular space frame in which the twin o.h.c. Coventry-Climax FPF engine is laid almost on its side, driving through the rear-mounted five-speed gearbox hitherto employed only for the F2 single-seater. The rear suspension has abandoned the de Dion axle layout in favour of the strut-type independent suspension also developed for the F2 car, while the front wheels are attached by the coil-spring and wishbone system now standardized on all Lotus models. Naturally enough, the car is designed specifically to comply with Appendix C of the Sporting Code, and the swept-over windscreen is now extended so that a minimum gap is left between it and the high tail, with only the driver's headrest prominent above it.

Aerodynamics, always highly developed by Lotus, are considerably improved by a floor which is completely flat throughout the length of the car apart from the gearbox and one small projecting lug on the clutch bell-housing. Both floor and propeller shaft tunnel are stressed members integral with the multi-tubular frame in 18 and 20 gauge steel. Wider and considerably deeper in front than the earlier model, the frame supports the Climax engine at 28° to the horizontal by three points only: fore and aft on the crankcase, and at the forward end of the cylinder head. The offset of the crankshaft is such that the engine also makes an angle of 7½° with the centre line of the car in the horizontal plane.

Surprisingly few of the expected troubles have been encountered with the new engine layout, which may be because the ancestry of this unit goes back to one half of a 90° V-8. Power output was initially down on account of the inevitable added contortion of the inlet tracts, but after experimental work with Webers the manufacturers have now returned to the original S.U. carburetters and development proceeds. Overhead valves, inclined at an included angle of 66°, are operated through piston-type tappets by twin overhead camshafts which are gear-driven. Five 2½-in.-diameter lead-indium main bearings support the crankshaft in an aluminium-alloy crankcase, the cylinder block also being of alloy with wet liners. The dry-sump lubrication system employs two scavenge and one pressure pump in the crankcase, with an oil reservoir in the tail and a cursory but effective cooler in the shape of an exposed length of finned aluminium connecting pipe, flush with the underside of the body. Ignition is by Lucas coil and distributor, with one plug per cylinder.

The rear-mounted gearbox marks a new departure for Lotus sports cars, although it had a first season of proving last year on the single-seater. A tubular propeller shaft transmits power from the twin dry plate, 7¼ in. clutch (now hydraulically operated) to the combined gearbox and differential assembly. Lotus designed and manufactured, this extremely compact unit contains five constant-mesh forward gears engaged by a single sliding dog. The gears revolve

A positive-stop change has been fitted to the five-speed gearbox. On the left is the rod to a separate knob in the cockpit for selecting reverse. Disc brakes are by Girling.

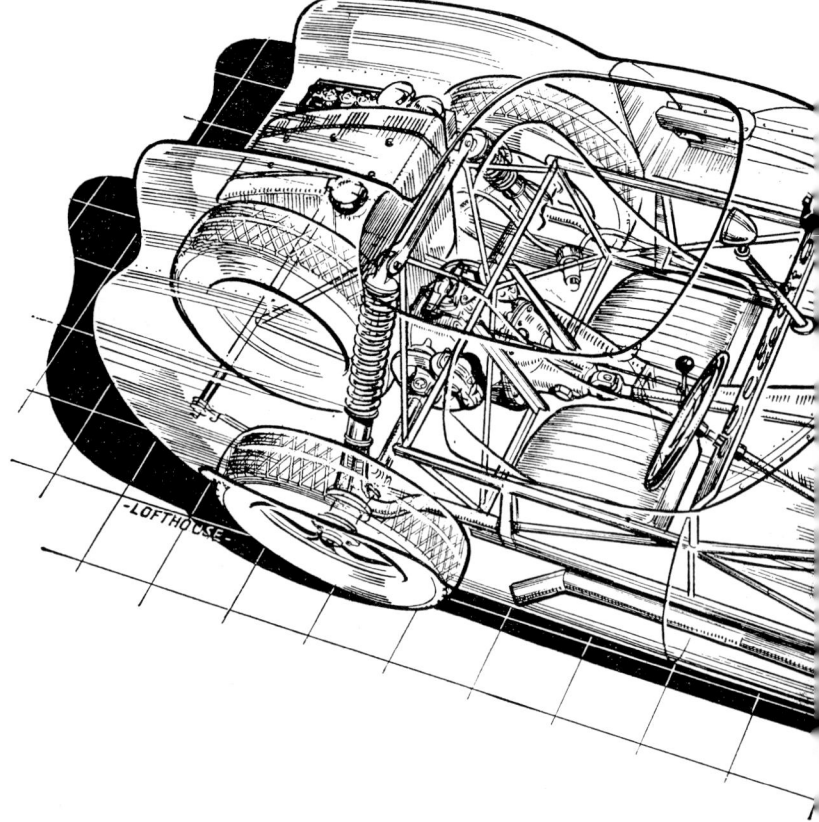

The tilted and offset engine, rear-mounted transmission incorporating a five-speed gearbox and ZF limited-slip differential, strut-type rear suspension and disc brakes can all be seen in this drawing. Wider and deeper than hitherto, the tubular frame is reinforced by a stressed floor and propeller shaft tunnel.

FIFTEEN

This Year's Sports Car

freely on a sliding sleeve on the input shaft which incorporates the engagement dog, while the mating gears immediately above them are locked on to a shaft integral with the spiral bevel pinion of a ZF differential.

The gear lever presents an unusual sight in a racing car, for its movement is simply straight forward or backward with a positive stop, motorcycle-fashion, so that there can be no mistake about gear selection. Reverse is engaged by a separate lever projecting from the rear bulkhead. Complete with the inboard rear brakes and the short, tubular drive shafts, the transmission assembly weighs only 85 lb. It is separately lubricated by pressure and scavenge pumps driven from the input shaft, a six-pint reservoir being fitted alongside the engine oil reservoir. All five pairs of gear wheels can be interchanged, so that 10 final drive ratios are available with an almost unlimited selection of intermediates.

The strut-type rear suspension patented by Colin Chapman is somewhat different in detail from that of the F2 car, the Armstrong combined coil-spring and damper unit being inclined more steeply towards the centre of the car, where a ball race takes the place of a rubber bush at the top pivot. The bottom of the strut is integral with the alloy hub casting, to which is hinged a slightly cranked, 1-in. mild-steel radius arm, rubber bushed at its forward end. The front suspension also uses Armstrong spring and damper units, in a wishbone arrangement employing a torsion anti-roll bar as one arm of the upper wishbone. The steering swivels consist of a threaded lower trunnion and an upper ball joint. Tortuous steering columns are nothing new to Lotus; on the Fifteen there are two universal joints to take the column beneath the engine and upwards to the rack and pinion gear.

Girling disc brakes of the latest, light-weight pattern with cast iron discs and quickly detachable pads are fitted front and rear. Cooling air for the latter is directed onto the discs by scoops where the line of the floor panelling is broken by the projecting gearbox. Centre-lock wire wheels or six-stud cast magnesium alloy disc wheels can be supplied.

Except for long-distance races, for which extra side tanks will be fitted, fuel is supplied by a 19-gallon tank held in place over the gearbox by elastic shock cord. The problem of space for the spare wheel is neatly solved by placing it upright inside the head fairing of the tail. The estimated dry weight is 8¾ cwt., which should give the car a respectable power-weight ratio even in 1½-litre form. The chassis will nevertheless accommodate either 2-litre or 2.2-litre Coventry-Climax engines.

S.U. carburetters as normally fitted on the twin-cam Coventry-Climax engine will replace the Webers shown here during development. The 1,960 c.c. unit has the same external dimensions as the 1½-litre engine illustrated, while a capacity of 2.2 litres increases the overall length by only ¼ in.

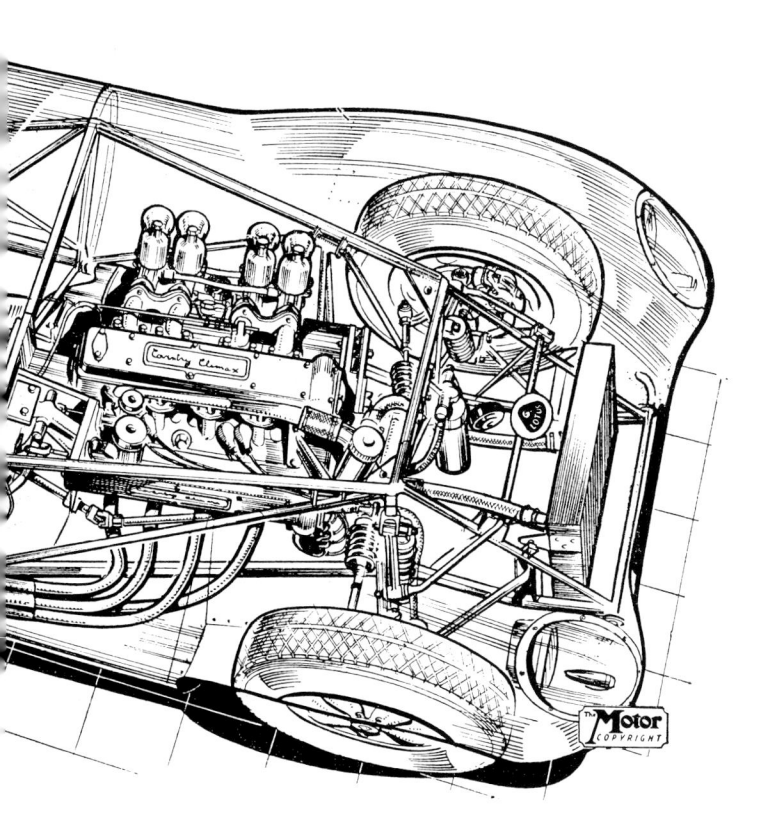

Engine: (Coventry-Climax FPF)
Cylinders : 4
Bore and stroke :
  81.2mm. × 71.1 mm.
Cubic capacity : 1475 c.c.
Piston area : 32.2 sq. in.
Valves : Twin o.h.c. inclined
Compression ratio : 10:1
Max. power : 150 b.h.p.
  at 7,200 r.p.m.
Max. b.m.e.p. : 190 lb./sq. in. at
  6,500 r.p.m.
B.H.P./sq. in. piston area ; 4.56
Piston speed at max. power :
  3,360 ft./min.
Carburetters : Two twin-choke
  Horizontal S.U.
Fuel pump : S.U.
Fuel capacity : 19 gallons
Oil capacity : 20 pints
Battery : 12-volt, 31 amp./hr.

Transmission:
Clutch : Twin dry plate
Gear ratios :
  Top 4.1
  4th 4.55
  3rd 5.61
  2nd 7.38
  1st 10.5
Final drive : Hypoid bevel with
  ZF limited-slip diff. Alternative ratios : 3.25, 3.42, 3.61,
  3.80, 4.0, 4.22, 4.43, 4.68, 4.93,
  5.20.

Chassis
Brakes : Girling 9½ in. diameter disc, outboard front, inboard rear.
Suspension :
  Front : Independent, wishbones with combined coil-spring and damper units.
  Rear : Independent, strut and radius arm with combined coil-spring and damper.
Wheel type : Wire centre-lock (bolt - on magnesium disc available).
Tyre size : Front 4.50-15
  Rear 5.50-15
Steering gear : Rack and pinion.

Dimensions
Wheelbase : 7ft. 4 in.
Track : Front 3 ft. 11 in.
  Rear : 4 ft. 0 in.
Overall length : 11 ft. 5 in.
Overall width 5 ft. 0 in.
Height (to scuttle) : 2 ft. 0 in.
Ground clearance : 5½ in.
Turning circle : 38 ft.
Dry weight : 8¾ cwt.

Performance factors
(at dry weight) :
Piston area, sq. in./ton : 73.5
Top gear m.p.h.
  per 1,000 r.p.m. : 18.2
Top gear m.p.h. per 1,000
  ft./min. piston speed : 39
Litres per ton/mile : 5,560

LOTUS FIFTEEN

In the last few years it has become customary for most new Lotus creations to be hailed as "sensational," and the Fifteen is no exception to this rule. Basically a most advanced 1½-litre sports/racing car, this is also the means by which Lotus, using a 2.2-litre engine, will make a first attempt at a "Distance" win at Le Mans.

Recent Lotus models have come to be regarded by a wide section of the motoring public as the (current) ultimate in chassis design, aerodynamic efficiency, and general layout. As a means of obtaining high speed from comparatively modest power outputs, the Eleven created entirely new standards—as witness the performance of the "750" at Le Mans in 1957. Now, with only 2.2-litres and a total weight (less fuel and driver) in the region of 9 cwt, the theoretical maximum speed of the Fifteen is 205 mph.

The Fifteen also marks an advance, in Lotus sports car design, in the incorporation of all-independent suspension of Formula Two pattern, together with a composite, rear-mounted gearbox/final drive unit and, of course, disc brakes.

By comparison with earlier models the new model also exhibits several detail features of great technical interest. Despite the use of a larger engine, frontal area is reduced, chiefly as a result of the tilting of the "twin-cam" engine through approximately 60 degrees towards its right-hand side. To accommodate this unusual layout the twin, horizontal Weber carburetters are mounted on specially designed manifolding.

Height at the top of the scuttle is exactly 2 feet; the higher tail lines blend with the top of the windscreen (which is of "Le Mans" type) and provide for the fitting of three tanks (fuel, engine oil and gearbox oil) as well as a spare wheel. Careful thought has been given to the oil-cooling system and all piping is recessed into the nearside of the body. With regard to the rear suspension, whose novelty has aroused a certain amount of scepticism, it should be pointed out that each wheel is positively located by three separate elements, the radius arm, the drive shaft, and the suspension unit. It must also be emphasised that the system is *not* based on the swing axle principle, although it has a swing axle effect. On bump the increase of negative camber promotes stability and compensates for extra weight—as when the fuel tank is full, for instance. There is also slight toe-in on bump, which promotes understeer.

The gearbox/final drive unit is that first used on the Formula Two car last year. Lubrication problems, which resulted from the carrying of the oil in suspension—well away from crown wheel and pinion—have now been overcome, and the Fifteen should be capable of using this lightweight, composite unit to full advantage. Full use of all five ratios will also be facilitated by the fitting of a positive-stop gearbox change system.

The gearchange lever is centrally mounted and operates in one plane only, with neutral situated between first and second. Reverse gear is obtained with the lever in neutral, by means of a separate linkage; the selector knob is situated on the driver's left at the rear of the passenger seat.

So much for the more novel features of the design. The basis of the Fifteen is a multi-tubular space frame of the well-known Lotus type. It is welded-up from 1 in and ¾ in square and round tubes of 18 and 20 gauge steel. As is customary, the propeller shaft tunnel and floor are stressed and form an integral part of the frame. Complete with mounting brackets this chassis weighs 65 lb.

As at the rear, the front suspension is that of the Formula Two car, also tried and tested on the series two Eleven.

The layout consists of twin transverse wishbones, the upper link incorporating an anti-roll bar. Coil spring/telescopic shock absorber units are used all round, and consist of a "firm" damper—part of the reason for the car's smooth ride and high cornering power—in conjunction with a "soft" spring in conjunction with the car's smooth ride and high cornering power.

The standard Fifteen engine is the Coventry Climax FPF unit of 1475 cc, fitted with twin SU double choke carburetters. At Le Mans one works car will be fitted with a 2.2-litre engine; there will also be 1960 cc versions at other major events, of which the first are Goodwood and the British Empire Trophy. Thus Lotus make an entry into the "big sports car" category, albeit with a smaller vehicle than the 1100 cc Eleven.

The "Frank Costin" bodywork of the Fifteen follows lines very similar to those of the Eleven, and particularly of the 1957 Le Mans cars. The aerodynamic "high tail" is aligned with the top of the curved, moulded Perspex windscreen, and the seating position is arranged so that the driver looks over the top of, rather than through, the screen. A canvas tonneau cover for the passenger seat, attached at the top of the windscreen, adds to aerodynamic efficiency. Full lighting equipment, including instrument lighting, is fitted and there is also a regulation windscreen wiper. Body panels are hinged front and rear, and are quickly removable (sockets being provided for lighting wiring) in the usual Lotus manner.

Centre-lock wire wheels are fitted as standard equipment on the Fifteen, but magnesium bolt-on wheels, representing a saving of 35 lb, will be fitted on works cars for races where tyre changes should not be required. They are also available for sale, but at extra cost. Wider section tyres (5.50 x 15) of Dunlop manufacture, are fitted at the rear and tend to augment the "high-powered" appearance of the rear end when the tail-section is removed.

A feature of the driving compartment is the attention which has been paid to the arrangement of control pedals. Greater lateral space is made available by transference of the gearbox to the rear, and this is reflected by the use of offset clutch pedal to the left of the steering column. All this represents a considerable improvement by comparison with the Eleven, and attention to detail is shown in the throttle pedal, which is provided with a wide

Complex rear end features gearbox-final drive unit (with forward gear selector on the right and reverse selector on the left) inboard disc brakes and Chapman-strut type rear suspension.

Wide-section rear tyres give the unclad rear end a powerful appearance. Tanks for fuel, engine-oil and gearbox oil bring to mind advertisements for a famous chocolate beverage. Note ingenious spare wheel mounting.

This view of the engine "on its side" shows the twin cam boxes and well-designed exhaust manifolding.

Alternative final drive ratios (with intermediate ratios to suit) are as follows:—3.25, 3.42, 3.61, 3.80, 4.22, 4.43, 4.68, 4.93, 5.20.

Cooling System
Fully ducted cross flow radiator with remote header tank.

Fuel System
Single light alloy tank, 19 gallons (86.3 litres) capacity. SU pump mounted in engine bay.

Bodywork
A full width moulded perspex screen conforming with the general body lines and complying with the Appendix "C" regulations is standard.

Electrical System
Special lightweight 12 volt 31 amp-hr. battery, located in tail. Lucas magneto, centrifugal advance and retard, belt driven dynamo, automatic voltage control. Fuse box mounted on dash panel. Recessed Lucas Le Mans 7 in (178 mm) headlamps and separate side lamps, twin stop-tail lights, rear number plate-stop lamp, high frequency horn. Instrument lighting. Screen wiper.

Instruments
Three in (76 mm) tachometer 0.8000 rpm, oil pressure gauge, water temperature gauge and ammeter.

Wheels and Tyres
Knock on 15 in wire wheels with identical rims front and rear are fitted with 4.50 x 15 tyres at the front and 5.50 x 15 tyres at the rear. 4.50 x 15 spare wheel mounted under rear panelling. Magnesium bolt-on wheels can be offered at extra cost giving 35 lb saving in weight: they are, however, unsuitable for long distance races where tyre changes may be necessary.

Dimensions
Wheelbase, 7 ft 4 in (216 cm); front track, 3 ft 11 in (118 cm); rear track, 4 ft (119 cm); overall length, 11 ft 5 in (340 cm); overall width, 5 ft (152 cm); height to top of scuttle 2 ft (686 cm).

Weight
Standard Fifteen model, less fuel, 980 lb (444.5 kg).

Careful attention has been paid to pedal layout, with clutch pedal offset to left of steering column and accelerator provided with basal extension for "heel-and-toe" gear changing.

being inclined at an included angle of 66 degrees. Camshafts operate valves through piston type tappets. Camshafts are gear driven, one gear of the train driving the delivery and scavenge pumps for the dry sump lubrication system.

Transmission
Twin dry plate clutch, 7¼ in (184 mm) diameter, hydraulically operated. Special five-speed close ratio gearbox in unit with final drive. Interchangeable all indirect gears give ten optional final drive ratios and virtually unlimited selection of intermediate ratios.

Final Drive
Hypoid final drive unit incorporating ZF limited slip differential which, with standard gears, has 4:1 ratio. Intermediates are as follows:—first, 2.56:1; second, 1.80:1; third, 1.37:1; fourth, 1.11:1; fifth, 1:1, and reverse.

Aerodynamic from every angle, the Fifteen appears particularly sleek and low built in this view.

Functional driving compartment features two non-adjustable bucket seats and central, positive-stop gearchange lever. Instruments include tachometer, oil pressure gauge and water temperature gauge ahead of the driver, gearbox oil pressure and engine and gearbox oil temperatures in a central grouping and on extreme left where the light switch and fuse box are also situated.

base to facilitate heel and toe gear-changes. The bucket-type seats are fully upholstered but, as on earlier models, seem to be designed only for drivers of less than average height.

Instrumentation, in addition to tachometer, oil pressure gauge, water temperature gauge and ammeter, includes special dials for gearbox oil pressure and engine and gearbox oil temperatures on the prototype car. The lamps are controlled by a simple, positive switch and, although the exhaust note is such that it is rarely likely to be required when the car is driven on the road, a regulation high-frequency horn is fitted.

While the 1½-litre engine is standard equipment, the 2- and 2.2-litre versions of the Fifteen will probably attract the greatest attention; not only is their overall performance potential greater, but the better torque characteristics of the larger units will add to the car's suitability for racing on tortuous circuits.

With the 2.2-litre engine fitted the Fifteen will be virtually an all-enveloping F1 car. In terms of sports car development it may well lead to the growth of a new conception of circuit performance. If it is true that "good engineering wins races," then this is a car which is going to take a lot of beating.

SPECIFICATION

Frame
Multi-tubular space frame comprising 1 in (25 mm) and ¾ in (19 mm) square and round tubing of 18 and 20 gauge steel. The propeller shaft tunnel and floor are stressed members forming an integral part of the frame. The engine is carried on two rubber mountings at the front and a single rubber mounting at the rear attached to the bellhousing; it is tilted sideways through approximately 60°; this has the advantage of reducing frontal area. The rear frame incorporates a spare wheel mounting and an easily detachable petrol tank to provide ready access to the final drive unit.

Front Suspension
Independent by transverse wishbones incorporating a roll bar. Springing by combined coil spring-damper units reacting through a single attachment point at each end.

Rear Suspension
Chapman-strut type rear suspension with single radius arm and articulated drive shaft.

Brakes
Ultra light hydraulically operated 9½ in (241 mm) disc brakes, outboard at the front, inboard at the rear. Horizontally mounted hand brake operating the rear calipers through inner and outer cables.

Steering
Lightweight rack and pinion steering gear with special steering linkage to give higher cornering power at low speeds.

Power Unit
Coventry Climax FPF twin overhead camshaft, four cylinder engine. Bore 81.2 mm (3.20 in), stroke 71.1 mm (2.80 in), capacity 1,475 cc (90 cu in), compression ratio 10 : 1. Maximum power output, 150 bhp (nett) at 7,200 rpm. Maximum torque 110 lb-ft (1.52 kg-m) at 6,500 rpm. Maximum bmep 190 lb/sq in (1.34 kg/sq cm) at 6,500 rpm. Notable features of the engine include aluminium alloy cylinder block and crankcase, wet cylinder liners, fully counterweighted crankshaft running in five 2½ in (63.5 mm) diameter indium plated lead bronze steel back precision bearings. Connecting rods run in bearings of identical type, the crankpin diameter being 2⅜ in (60 mm). Light alloy pistons with Dyks pattern compression rings are used. There is one inlet and one exhaust valve per cylinder, these

203

NEW LOTUS FIFTEEN

Outwardly similar to the Eleven, but with even less frontal area, the Fifteen is the first Lotus designed to take an engine of over [2] litres capacity.

ALTHOUGH completely new and untried, and very much in undeveloped prototype form, the Lotus Fifteen, driven by Graham Hill, went well enough at Goodwood to suggest that it will have a very bright future in sports car racing. It failed to finish in the Sussex Trophy event for sports cars of unlimited capacity, retiring on the penultimate lap (when in fourth place) when the gear selector refused to select any forward gears. Hill had earlier set up a new Class E lap record (1501-2000 cc) in 1 min 35.6 sec—90.38 mph, and had worked his way through a field of larger cars from a position at the tail end of the line-up for the Le Mans type start.

Time for development of the Fifteen has clearly been lacking, for the first full trials of the new design did not take place until 2 April. The only mechanical difficulties experienced at this time—as on Easter Monday—were connected with gear selection, and it should not be beyond the Lotus staff to achieve a speedy and complete solution of this problem. One other feature noticeable at Goodwood was the fitting of an aluminium air deflector on the driver's side of the windscreen—clear indication that Lotus drivers look over, rather than through this regulation equipment.

Basically a 1½-litre sports/racing car, the Fifteen is far more than just an addition to the Lotus range of small capacity machines. Works entries with 2- or 2.2-litre Coventry Climax engines will compete in both 3-litre (Sports Car Manufacturer's Championship) and unlimited capacity events. In 2.2-litre form the Fifteen will be the means by which Lotus will make a first attempt at a "Distance" win at Le Mans; here its theoretical maximum speed should be no less than 205 mph.

More than this, the new car has the same general layout, albeit in full width form, as the 1958 Formula One and Two single-seaters. Its major technical features include the customary space frame, all-independent suspension (for the first time on a Lotus sports model) a composite gearbox/final drive unit, and disc brakes; probably the most interesting design feature, however, is the fitting of the Coventry Climax "twin-cam" engine

This view of the power unit " on its side " shows the twin cam boxes and well-designed exhaust manifolding. The engine is in fact tilted 60 degrees towards the offside of the car, and is also offset 7½ degrees from the chassis centre line.

Functional driving compartment features two non-adjustable bucket seats and central, positive-stop gearchange lever. Instruments include tachometer, oil pressure gauge and water temperature gauge ahead of the driver, gearbox oil pressure and engine and gearbox oil temperatures in a central grouping, and ammeter on extreme left, where the light switch and fuse box are also situated.

t an angle of some 60 degrees from the vertical. This layout has the advantage of reducing bonnet height, and therefore frontal area.

No lubrication problems are experienced, since the engine is of the "dry-sump" variety, with an oil tank mounted in the tail and the connecting piping recessed into the nearside of the body. The unconventional layout has brought one disadvantage, however, in that power output (in the case of the 1½-litre engine) is down by about 9 per cent (12 hp) as a result of the use of a curved induction tract. This initial setback is unlikely to persist, however, as there would appear to be several means of rectifying the situation once development work is really under way.

The Chapman-strut type rear suspension, which is now subject to an Application for Patent, is very similar to that used on the 1957 Formula 2 car, and on the Elite. Each wheel is located by three separate elements, the radius arm, the drive shaft and the suspension unit. Advantages claimed for the system are that the increase of negative camber on bump promotes stability and compensates for extra weight, as when the fuel tank is full. There is also slight toe-in on bump, which promotes oversteer. Front suspension of the Fifteen is of the type now standard on all Lotus models, by double wishbones, the upper link incorporating an anti-roll bar. Co-axial coil spring/damper units act on all four wheels, the combination of "soft" spring and "firm" damper having a great influence on the car's visibly excellent roadholding qualities.

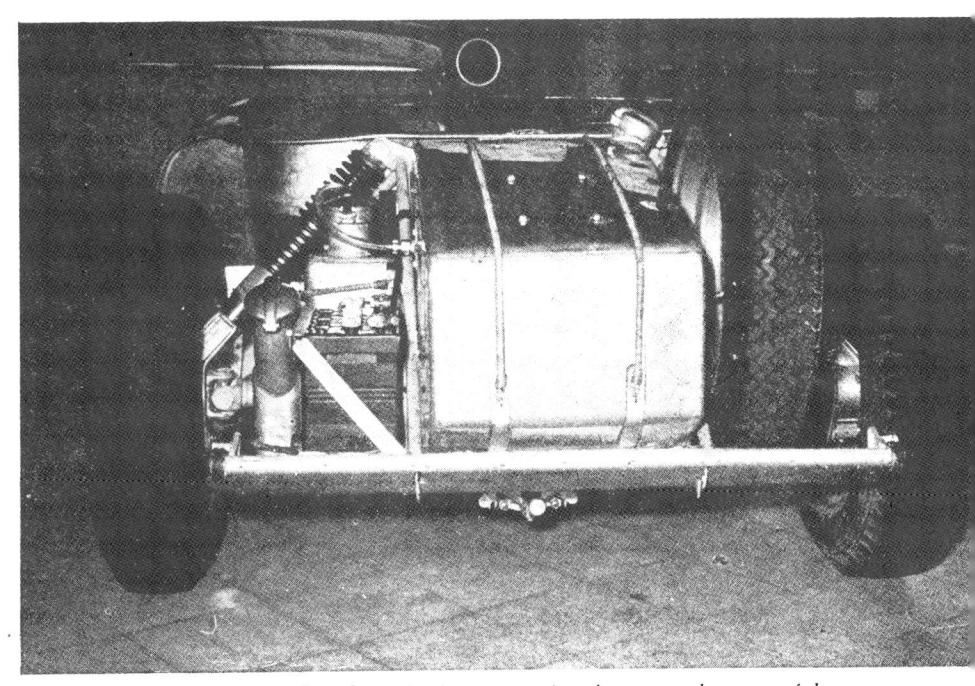

The gearbox/final drive unit, on which lubrication problems —resulting from the carrying of the oil in suspension, well away from crown wheel and pinion—have now been overcome, is fitted with five forward ratios and reverse. Selection of forward gears is carried out by a centrally mounted lever, which operates in one plane only and is of the "positive-stop" type. Neutral is situated between first and second. As mentioned above, difficulties in gear selection at Goodwood, culminating in a complete lack of forward ratios, should be speedily overcome. Reverse gear, obtained by means of an entirely separate linkage (operated by a knob behind the passenger seat) can only be engaged when the main lever is in the neutral position.

With bodywork removed, wide-section rear tyres give the rear end a powerful appearance. Tanks accommodate, from right to left, fuel, engine-oil and gearbox oil. Note ingenious spare wheel mounting, which utilises the space within the driver's head-fairing.

A multitubular space frame is no novelty on a Lotus, but it is interesting that the chassis of this "larger" car, complete with stressed floor and propeller shaft tunnel, and all mounting brackets, weighs only 65 lb. The frame itself is welded-up from 1 in. and ¼ in. tubes of 18 and 20 gauge steel.

The bodywork shows a close resemblance to that of the Eleven, and incorporates the aerodynamic high tail first used on last year's Le Mans cars and now the subject of a Patent Application on the part of Frank Costin. Frontal area is reduced, by comparison with the Eleven, and height at the top of the scuttle is exactly 2 feet. The curved, full width windscreen, made in three pieces with welded joints, is aligned with the tail and can be fitted on the passenger side with a canvas tonneau, a further aid to aerodynamic efficiency. There is also a very smooth undertray, the line of which is broken only at the rear where the gearbox/final drive unit protrudes and cooling scoops are provided for the inboard rear brakes. Body panels are hinged front and rear and are quickly removable, in the usual Lotus manner.

While it is intended purely for use as a racing car, the Fifteen has a full two-seater cockpit and complete lighting equipment, including instrument lighting. An important improvement in the driving compartment concerns the arrangement of the control pedals. Greater lateral space is made available by the use of a rear-mounted gearbox and this is reflected in the use of an offset clutch pedal, together with foot space to the left of the pedal. In addition the throttle pedal is provided with a wide base in the interests of heel-and-toe gear changing.

While the 1½-litre Coventry Climax engine is standard equipment on the Fifteen, the 2- and 2.2-litre versions will probably attract the greatest attention; not only is their overall performance potential greater (in terms of maximum speed) but the better torque characteristics of the larger units will add to the car's suitability for racing on tortuous circuits.

Students of motor racing will not be slow to notice that this new Lotus represents a most important advance in sports car design. The Eleven set unprecedented standards in obtaining high speeds from comparatively modest power outputs. Even with only a little over two litres the Fifteen will probably cause acute embarrassment to the manufacturers of larger and more powerful cars.

Complex rear end features gearbox-final drive unit (with forward gear selector on the right and reverse selector on the left) inboard disc brakes and Chapman-strut type rear suspension.

...And Now The FIFTEEN

New Lotus Sports Car; Tilted Engine, Formula 2-Type Five-speed Gear Box

FEW firms, even those engaged in the rather specialized business of sports-racing car production, have produced so many new designs as have Lotus in the six years of their existence. Apart from the formula 2-Mark XII and the Elite-Mark XIV (a Mark XIII was not designated for reasons of superstition) ten distinct models have been produced since the first true Lotus commenced with the Mark VI. Latest of the line for the coming season is the Fifteen, and two examples of the car will be seen for the first time at the Goodwood Easter Monday meeting.

The new model follows the general lines of the Eleven series, but further reduction in frontal area has been made and the gear box is the five-speed, Lotus-designed type first used on the formula 2 car and placed at the rear in unit with the hypoid bevel final drive. Compared with last year's cars the scuttle height has been reduced by 2in (it is only 24in from the ground) and the tail incorporates a built-in headrest on the driver's side.

The multi-tubular frame follows established Lotus practice, comprising 1in and ¾in square and round tubing, with the material thickness varying between 18 (0.048in) and 20 (0.036in) s.w.g. Frame stiffness is enhanced by the propeller-shaft tunnel and floor, which are stressed members forming an integral part of the frame. Compared with the Mark XI the frame is much deeper, being approximately 5in greater at the scuttle section, yet weights are almost identical.

To achieve the reduction in frontal area, the engine has been swung through 60 deg from the vertical axis towards the exhaust side. At the same time it is skewed in the frame with the axis of the crankshaft, as viewed from above, running from left to right at an angle of 7½ deg—at the front the crankshaft is offset towards the left-hand side, and at the clutch slightly towards the right-hand side.

The twin plate, 7¼in dia clutch is mounted behind the engine, and from it the propeller-shaft connects to the centrally mounted transmission unit at the rear, at a slight angle from right to left. Thus a compromise has been struck between the amount by which the engine can be placed at a compound angle to achieve a low frontal area, and that which can be accommodated by the maximum desirable angle of a static propeller-shaft. By this layout the two-seater body complies with the minimum dimensions laid down in Appendix C of the International Sporting Code.

Another factor which determined the amount by which the Coventry Climax 1½-litre FPF engine is swung over in the frame is the avoidance of steam pockets within the cylinder head. Fortunately the roof line of the internal coolant passages is such that a natural water rise is obtained and the standard water take-off flanges may be used without the need for additional bleed-off pipes to eliminate trapped steam.

Modifications have had to be made on the induction side to accommodate the carburettors. The normal induction flange has been machined back consider-

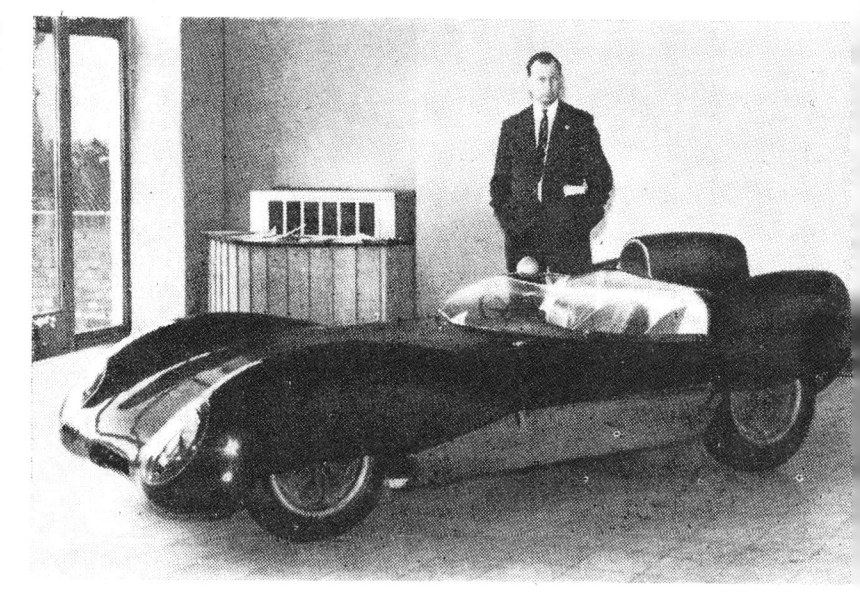

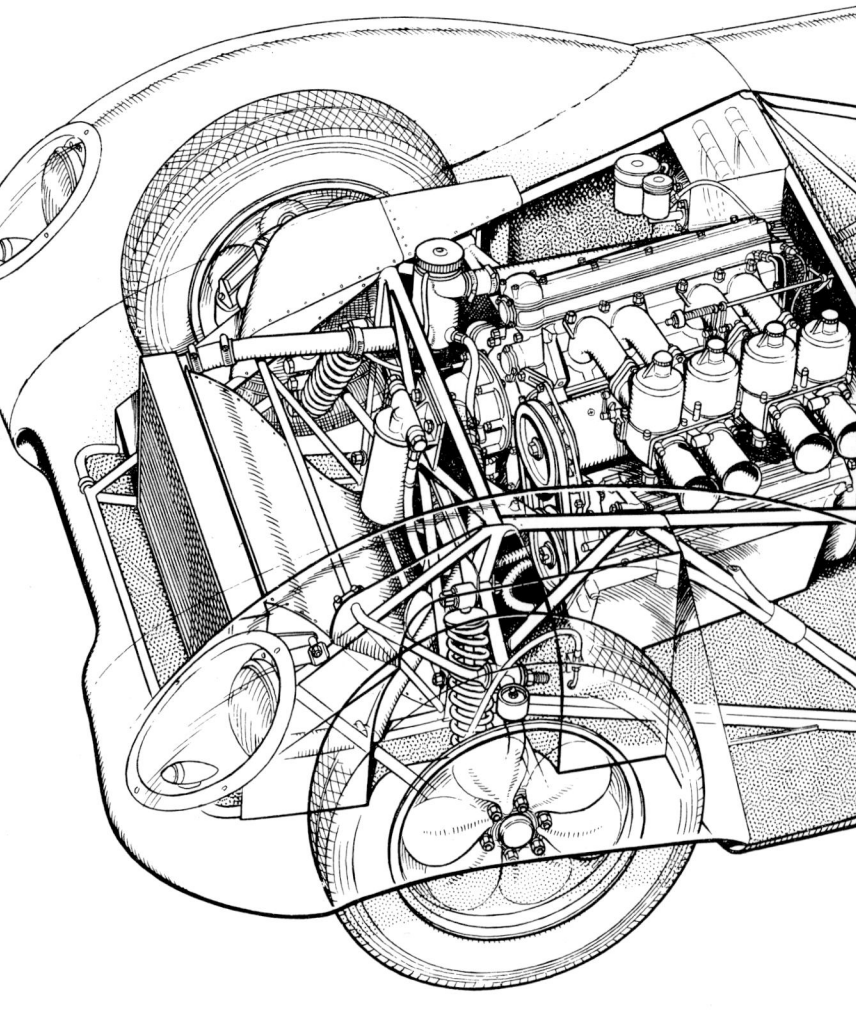

206

RIGHT: A moulded Perspex screen meets competition regulations but is cleverly devised to minimize drag. Tail fins are reminiscent of the earlier Mark IX

LEFT: The new Mark XV follows established Lotus practice in the use of minimum drag body form and is 2in lower than last year's car. Mike Costin, chief development engineer, provides scale effect

ably, and the ports counterbored to take individual tubular induction pipes connecting the head to the horizontal carburettors. These pipes each seat against the face of the counterbore with a rubber sealing ring, and they are clamped with plates welded to the stubs.

As shown in the photographs, two twin choke 40mm dia Webers are fitted to the prototype car, but in standard form carburation will be by two twin choke S.U. HDU6 (1¾in dia) units.

Without the modifications peculiar to the induction side of the Lotus, the engine develops 142 b.h.p. at 7,250 r.p.m. with a 10 to 1 compression ratio, running on 100-octane fuel in accordance with sports car regulations. All engines are turned out from Coventry Climax with a minimum sustained reading of 140 b.h.p., but generally the power is 2 to 3 h.p. in excess of this; it is interesting to note that when some engines have been returned after taking part in several races, the power has risen to 145 b.h.p.

The figures recorded for the vertical engine with standard induction system are not being achieved in the Lotus set-up, and some difficulty is being experienced in recovering the lost power. In carrying out the modifications, the straight portion of the ports which assists in obtaining ram effect has been sacrificed. This, combined with the fact that the mass of gas has to be turned through an angle of 70 deg in a comparatively short distance, has resulted in some filling losses. Development work is proceeding, but so far the power is down by approximately 9 per cent, i.e., about 12 b.h.p.

As the engine is of the dry sump type, there have been no major problems on the lubrication side. The true bottom face of the sump has been machined off, and a plate of aluminium welded to it to produce, as installed, a vertical side face. Normally one pressure pump and

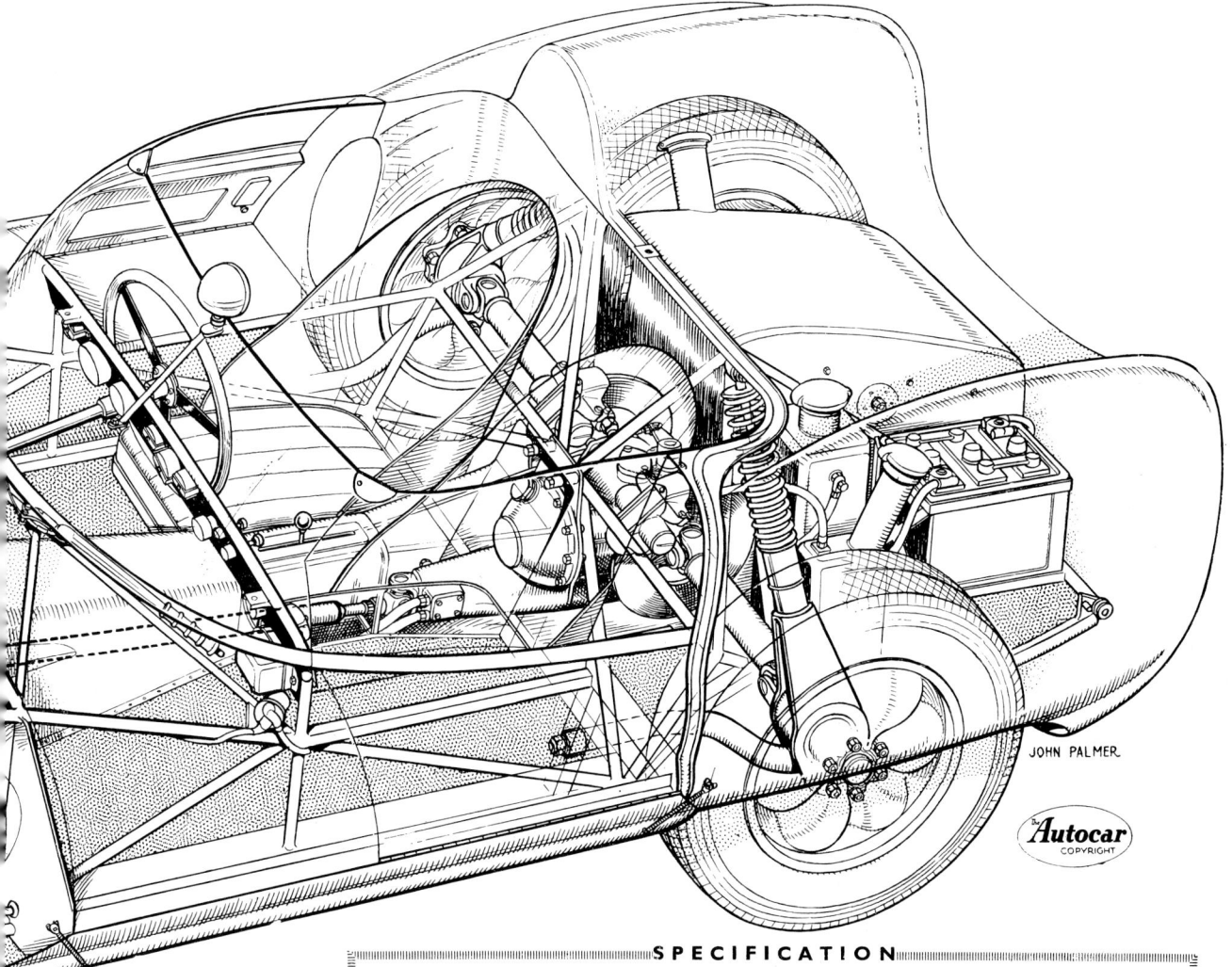

A low frontal area has been achieved by tilting the engine to one side. To restore weight distribution and minimize propshaft angles, the engine is also placed at an angle in plan. The five-speed gear box is in unit with a hypoid final drive which incorporates a ZF limited-slip differential

SPECIFICATION

ENGINE: No. of cylinders, 4, in line; Bore and stroke, 81.2 x 71.1mm (3.20 x 2.80in); Displacement, 1,475 c.c. (90 cu in); Valve position, Twin overhead cam haft; Compression ratio, 10 to 1; Max b.h.p., 142 at 7,250 r.p.m.; Max b.m.e.p., 188 lb per sq in at 5,600 r.p.m.; Max torque, 112 lb ft at 5,600 r.p.m.; Carburettors, Two twin-choke S.U.; Fuel pump, S.U.; Tank capacity, 19 Imp. gals (86.3 litres); Battery, 12 volt, 31 ampere-hour.
TRANSMISSION: Clutch, Twin dry plate, 7¼in dia; Gear box, Five speeds; Overall gear ratios, 1st 10.24, 2nd 7.2, 3rd 5.36, 4th 4.44 and 5th 4.0 to 1; Final drive, Hypoid bevel, with ZF differential; standard 4.0 to 1; 10 optional axle ratios available.
CHASSIS: Brakes, Girling disc front and rear; Disc dia, 9½in; Suspension: front, Independent, wishbone and anti-roll bar with coil spring damper units; rear, Strut type with single radius arm; Wheels, Knock-on wire; Tyre size, F, 4.50—15in; R, 5.50—15in; Steering, Rack and pinion.
DIMENSIONS: Wheelbase, 7ft 4in (223cm); Track: front, 3ft 11in (119cm); rear, 4ft 0in (122cm); Overall length, 11ft 5in (348cm); Overall width, 5ft 0in (152cm); Overall height, 2ft (61cm) to top of scuttle; Ground clearance, 5½in (14cm); Dry weight 980 lb (8¾ cwt) (444. 5kg).

Transmission and rear suspension. The right-hand lever and rod above the transmission controls selection of the forward ratios; the one on the left engages reverse only. The central fuel tank has been temporarily removed

The Fifteen . . .

two scavenge pumps are attached below the main bearing housings, and driven from gears at the front. The rear scavenge pump has been discarded and the centrally mounted pressure pump provided with a modified pick-up pipe to suit the new lowest point to which the oil settles. The dynamo, mounted on the side of the crankcase just beneath the carburettors, is driven by a single belt from the crankshaft.

To eliminate possible failures from vibration everything on the engine, including the water take-off pipes and carburettors, is rubber mounted, as is the engine itself.

There are three engine mounting points; those at the front are high up, with fabricated tubular arms picking up to the normal engine mounting foot on the induction side, and to a bracket bridging two cylinder head nuts on the exhaust side. At the rear, a single mounting point on the left-hand side picks up on one of the bolts by which the clutch casing is fixed to the crankcase. From the riser pipe coolant water is taken to a minute header tank with a pressurized filler cap, and thence forward to the fully ducted cross-flow radiator.

The five-speed gear box and combined differential is identical with that of the formula 2 car, but a positive stop type of change has been incorporated, to eliminate the rather cumbersome gate type which the drivers found difficult last year. The five ratios are obtained within a total length of 3⅜in over the running gears. First gear has sliding tooth engagement, as it is required only for starting, but the upper four are of the constant mesh type. There are two shafts, with all the gears free running on the first one. Drive is transmitted to each gear in turn by a single six-sided spline (with staggered faces for ease of engagement in each direction) formed on a sliding sleeve on the input shaft. It is an extremely light unit in which the weight has been kept down to 49 lb; ready for installation with drive shafts, and inboard disc brakes, the dry weight is only 88 lb.

By a cam and pawl arrangement a push forward on the centrally mounted gear lever (spring-loaded to the neutral position) selects the next upper ratio, and a pull backwards effects a change down. Reverse is selected by a separate lever situated in the panelwork behind the driver's seat, which he presses with his left elbow for engagement when the forward gear is in its neutral position.

Last year's lubrication problems have been overcome, and the differential is now arranged to dip in a controlled amount of oil carried in the rear part of the casing, in addition to a jet which feeds oil into the nip of the gears on the driving side. A further supply line feeds oil through the hollow first-motion shaft to the gear box gears, and this is scavenged and returned to a separate oil tank mounted in the tail. At the moment the engine and transmission oil tanks are entirely separate but placed side by side; these two units will be replaced by a single one having separate compartments for the two oil systems.

The tail also accommodates the battery, a 19-gallon light alloy fuel tank, and the vertically mounted spare wheel on the right-hand side.

Front suspension is identical in layout to that used on last year's car, comprising transverse wishbones, the triangulated upper one incorporating a roll bar, with combined coil spring and damper units acting through a single attachment point at each end. Chapman has pinned his faith for this year in his strut-type rear suspension, in which lateral location of each wheel is controlled by its driving shaft; the de Dion layout is no longer available. One detail change is that the forward-facing arm is now made from 1½in dia tube, and it is anchored in plain bearings to the underside of the aluminium casting inside which are the wheel bearings. This casting also forms the attachment point for the telescopic damper, the lower end of which is pressed in after the casting has been heated to obtain an interference fit. The combined coil spring and dampers have a steeper inward inclination at their top attachments.

Girling disc brakes of 9½in dia are standard, those at the rear being inboard; rather surprisingly, a common master cylinder is used for the front and rear hydraulic systems. For the first time on a Lotus, hydraulic clutch operation is used; this has reduced the operating loads considerably. Access to the engine and transmission is achieved by arranging for the complete nose and tail sections to hinge upwards at their extremities, and a full-width, moulded Perspex screen (front and side) to minimize drag, follows the pattern of last year's Le Mans cars.

Knock-on wire wheels with 4.50—15in tyres at the front and 5.50—15in at the rear are standard equipment, but magnesium bolt-on wheels are offered which effect a 35 lb saving in unsprung weight; they are suitable only for short races where tyre changes are not necessary.

Export price of the Fifteen is £2,885. This is also basic price in this country, to which purchase tax must be added. For anyone wishing to buy a set of components and build a replica in his own workshop, the kit price amounts to approximately £2,395.

Engine bay, showing how the induction side of the engine has been modified to accommodate the new carburettor arrangement necessary because of the angled engine position. The Weber carburettors are a temporary set-up on the prototype

A SERIES TWO LOTUS FIFTEEN

Lotus casing for BMC final drive unit is chassis-mounted, with inboard rear disc brakes alongside. Rear suspension is "Chapman-strut" type, as on standard Fifteen, single-seater racing cars, and Elite. Note lip on windscreen ahead of driver

OUTWARDLY identical with the curent "up-right-engine" car, the Series Two Lotus Fifteen differs from the standard model in that it has a rather more conventional transmission layout. The standard car, with its composite five-speed gearbox/final drive unit, will continue to be made, and despite the designation "Series Two" the new car is not expected to out-perform it; the more conventional transmission is designed largely for export to countries where Lotus spares may not be immediately obtainable, and indeed the first car to be completed has been shipped to American Pete Lovely.

Basically the transmission of the Series Two Fifteen consists of a BMC "B"-series four-speed (and reverse) gearbox—front-mounted—together with a BMC final drive unit or, to be accurate BMC gears in a special chassis-mounted Lotus casing. The gear lever operates in a normal "H" gate, by contrast with the quadrant change of the five-speed box on the standard model, and during recent tests at Brands Hatch, the new car made a very favourable impression. Gear Ratios are 1:1, 1.25:1, 1.67:1 and 2.5:1, and a variety of final drive ratios is available.

In all other respects the specification of the Series Two Fifteen is the same as that of the standard model. The chassis is a lightweight space frame, and suspension is independent to all four wheels, by means of double wishbones—incorporating an anti-roll bar—at the front, and by Chapman-strut at the rear.

The engine is the well-known 1½-litre Coventry Climax FPF unit with twin double-choke SU carburetters. It is installed in the frame at an angle of 17 degrees from the vertical, i.e., tilted towards the left as seen from the driving compartment, which arrangement permits the use of a straight induction tract. Maximum power output is 141 hp at 7000 rpm and this, with a weight of under 8½ cwt, gives a bhp per ton figure of over 330.

Gearbox is front-mounted with the gear-lever slightly offset towards the driver. It is reported that on test the gear change was excellent

LOTUS IS THE WORD FOR GO!
Colin Chapman's New Sportscar Blossoms Into The Mark 15
BY GORDON WILKINS

PHOTOS BY GEOFFERY GODDARD

Lotus 15 resembles earlier Mark XI but has greatly reduced frontal area via inclined engine, lower windscreen and seats.

New seats slope back, have thinner cushions, placing passengers lower. Windscreen fairs cleanly into rear of the body.

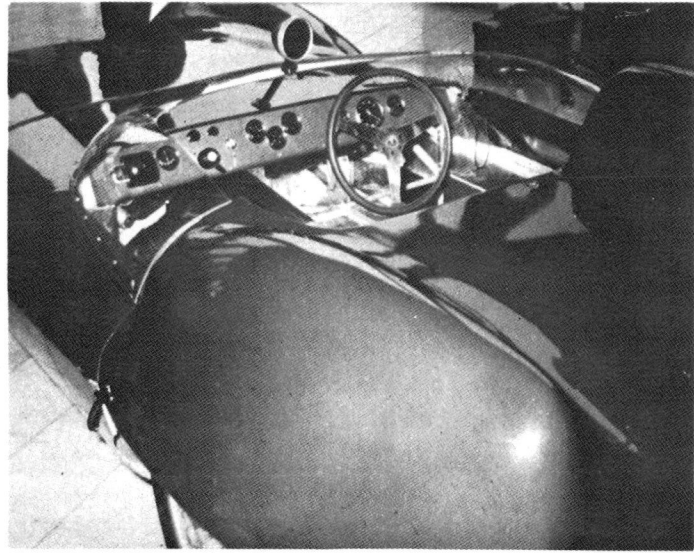

Passenger's side will have a detachable cover for racing. The unique rear-view mirror is mounted above windshield.

The worldwide success of the Lotus XI, with engines of 750 to 1500cc, has induced no complacency in the Lotus organization. Colin Chapman is currently producing the Lotus 15 designed to take Climax twin camshaft engines of 1500 to 2200cc. This car is the mainstay of the Lotus attack in this year's sportscar races.

Although outwardly resembling the Mark XI, the car has a lower frontal area — eight square feet instead of 12 — partially obtained by tilting the engine 28 degrees to the horizontal. The body complies with Appendix C of the International Sporting Code. A boldly curved windscreen blends into a high tail leaving only a small open space through which the heads of driver and passenger protrude. The underside is completely enclosed with no interruptions except for the engine sump and a radiator outlet. The belly-pan and the tunnel over propeller shaft and gearbox are of light alloy riveted to the tubular steel chassis frame and form part of the stressed structure. The frame, which is wider and deeper than that of the Mark XI, is of square and round section steel tubes of one-inch and ¾-inch diameter — 18 and 20 gauge.

Normal power unit is the Coventry Climax FPF four-cylinder, 1475cc, engine, giving 150 bhp at 7200 rpm. It has overhead valves at an included angle of 66 degrees operated by two gear-driven camshafts. Cylinder block and crankcase are of light alloy. The two twin choke SU carburetors have been specially designed for the car.

Lubrication is by dry sump with an oil tank in the tail of the car. The pipe delivering oil to the tank is finned to act as an oil cooler. The engine is cooled by a cross-flow radiator with a tiny cylindrical tank functioning as filler, header tank and swirl tank.

The five-speed gearbox and ZF limited-slip differential unit has been improved as a result of last year's racing experience with Formula II single seaters. It has its own dry sump lubrication system with pressure and scavenge pumps and a separate oil tank in the tail. All five pairs of gears are in constant mesh, unique in an automobile but normal practice on motorcycles.

Gear shifting is the progressive type. First gear is engaged by pulling the lever back; neutral and the other four ratios are obtained by repeatedly pushing the lever forward. Downward changes are made by pulling the lever backwards and reverse by pulling a separate knob on the bulkhead between the seats.

The entire transmission unit with Girling disc brakes and driveshaft weighs only 85 pounds. Ratios on the upper four gears can be changed by simply drawing the gears off the shafts. First gear is used only for starting and it is unnecessary to vary its ratio.

Rear suspension is the Chapman strut type as on the Formula II, but it is not fastened at such an acute angle. At the top it is attached to the chassis frame and at the bottom it rests in the light alloy hub casting. Front suspension, now standardized on all Lotus cars, consists of coil springs and wishbones.

For long distance racing where tire changes are involved, center lock wire wheels are used, but for shorter events the special Lotus magnesium bolt-on disc wheels save some 30 pounds per set of four.

Even though the engine has been lowered, the fenders are the same height and the drivers have not been changed in size. Just how has the reduction in frontal area been obtained? The driving seat has been inclined to the rear at a greater angle and the cushion is now a thin plastic which is only ¼-inch thick when compressed. It has thus been possible to set the windscreen lower, reducing the height by about 1¼-inches.

The old 1100cc Lotus XI with the 84 bhp engine reached 151 mph. The Mark 15 with either the 1.5 or 2.2-liter engine will exceed this easily, making the car a match for larger machines. ■

Right: Vertical spare fits inside the driver's headrest. Fuel tank is quick release for access to gearbox and differential.

Below: Twin camshaft Coventry Climax engine is angled 28 degrees from horizontal; 1500cc version develops 150 hp.

Right: Fuel tank removed reveals ZF differential, five-speed gearbox, Girling disc brakes and independent rear suspension.

1959 COMPETITION CARS

LOTUS

A New 1,100 c.c. Model and an Improved "Fifteen"

LOTUS SEVENTEEN

Engine.—Coventry Climax single overhead camshaft, 4-cyl., 72.4 mm. × 66.6 mm., 1,097 c.c., compression ratio 9.8 : 1, 84 b.h.p. at 6,800 r.p.m.

Transmission.—7¼-in. single-plate clutch, 4-speed gearbox with ratios 1.0, 1.23, 1.67 and 2.5 (reverse 2.5). Hypoid bevel final drive mounted on frame with optional ratios 3.73, 3.9, 4.22, 4.55 or 4.875. ZF differential optional.

Chassis.—Multiple tube frame reinforced by floor. I.F.S. by telescopic damper struts, coil springs and low-set wishbones. I.R.S. by telescopic damper struts carrying coil springs, non-telescopic drive shafts and trailing arms. Girling 9½-in. lightweight disc brakes, inboard mounted at rear. 4.50–15 and 5.00–15 front and rear tyres on bolt-on magnesium disc wheels. Rack-and-pinion steering.

Dimensions.—Wheelbase 6 ft. 10 in., front track 3 ft. 6 in., rear track 3 ft. 9 in., overall length 10 ft. 11 in., overall width 4 ft. 7½ in., scuttle height 1 ft. 11 in., overall height 2 ft. 5 in., ground clearance 5 in., weight without fuel 6.7 cwt.

LIGHTWEIGHT car with the single o.h.c. 1,097 c.c. Coventry Climax engine, the new Lotus 17 has strut-type independent springing of all its four cast magnesium alloy wheels. Also seen in the photograph and in our artist's drawing below are the cross-flow radiator and simplified frame of straight ¾-in. and ⅝-in. tubes.

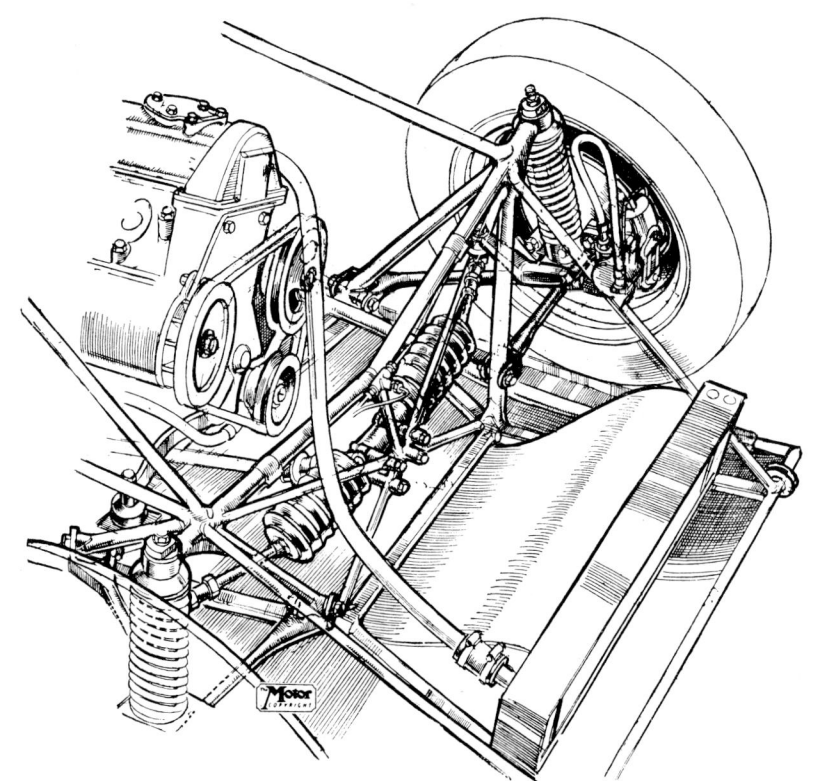

FOR the 1959 season, the Lotus Engineering Co., Ltd., of Hornsey, N.8, will themselves race a team of single-seaters in Formula 1 and Formula 2 races, and will sponsor some entries of the Elite coupé for Grand Touring events, but will not race sports cars. Private owners are, however, being offered new Coventry Climax-powered sports cars in 1,100 c.c., 1½-litre and 2-litre sizes, and the Lotus 7 which is sold mainly as a build-it-yourself kit to accommodate the Ford 10 engine also continues in production.

Smallest of the new season's models, the Lotus 17, keeps to the company's practice of using a frame welded up from multiple 20-gauge steel tubes, these tubes being of ¾-in. and ⅝-in. size as appropriate, and mainly of circular section, but of square section where light-alloy floor panels and transmission covers are attached by rivets to reinforce the frame. Featured on this model is a type of I.F.S. which is new to the company, although bearing a resemblance to the Lotus layout of independent rear wheel springing. Each front stub-axle is mounted on a telescopic strut, permitting 5 in. total movement and incorporating a hydraulic shock absorber, the top of the strut attaching to one corner of the chassis, and the base of the strut being linked to the

LOTUS

FASTEST sports Lotus, the Fifteen, with 2-litre (or 1½-litre) twin-o.h.c. engine, has its spare wheel beneath the driver's head-fairing. I.F.S. is of unequal-length wishbone layout, the upper link being a torsionally non-rigid X-section arm braced by the ends of an anti-roll torsion bar located behind it.

LOTUS FIFTEEN (SERIES III)

Engine.—Coventry Climax FPF twin overhead camshaft, 4-cyl. 86.4 mm.× 83.8 mm., 1,960 c.c. (or 81.2 mm.×71.1 mm., 1,475 c.c.), compression ratio 10 : 1, 176 b.h.p. at 6,500 r.p.m. (or 150 b.h.p. at 7,200 r.p.m.).

Transmission.—Twin-plate dry clutch. Four-speed gearbox with ratios 1.0, 1.23, 1.67 and 2.5, and frame-mounted hypoid bevel final drive (with ZF differential) with ratios of 3.73, 3.9, 4.22, 4.55 or 4.875. Alternative rear-mounted 5-speed gearbox, with wide choice of ratios for all gears and " positive-stop " change.

Chassis.—Multiple tube frame reinforced by floor and transmission tunnel.

I.F.S. by transverse wishbones, coil springs on telescopic dampers, and anti-roll torsion bar. I.R.S. by telescopic damper struts carrying coil springs, non-telescopic driveshafts and trailing arms. Girling 9½-in. disc brakes, inboard mounted at rear. 5.00—15 and 5.50—15 Dunlop R5 front and rear tyres on bolt-on magnesium disc (or knock-on wire) wheels. Rack and pinion steering.

Dimensions.—Wheelbase 7 ft. 4 in., front track 3 ft. 10 in., rear track 4 ft. 0 in., overall length 11 ft. 5 in., overall width 5 ft. 0 in., scuttle height 2 ft. 0 in., ground clearance 5¼ in., weight without fuel 8¾ cwt.

frame by a swept-forward wishbone member. In respect of the suspension itself and the frame mountings needed for it, this new I.F.S. is a valuable contribution to keeping the 1,097 c.c. car as light as possible. Steering is by a rack-and-pinion gear mounted on a vertical X-bracing of the chassis, behind hub level, and the steering column incorporates two sharply angled universal joints.

At the rear, the Lotus 17 has the strut-type I.R.S. already seen on the Lotus 15, Elite and Formula models, the driveshafts (each with two universal joints but no telescopic coupling) acting as transverse radius arms, and a trailing arm maintaining rear wheel alignment. A Girling disc brake of 9½-in. size is mounted on each front hub and at the inboard end of each rear axleshaft, operation of the front and rear brakes being from twin hydraulic master cylinders.

Inclined Engine

Powering the Seventeen, the single-overhead-camshaft Coventry Climax engine is tilted towards the left at an angle of 10°, and in unit with it are a hydraulically actuated 7¼-in. s.d.p. clutch and an A-series British Motor Corporation gearbox with close-ratio gears. The frame-mounted final drive can accommodate a choice of gear ratios, and a spin-limiting ZF differential is available to order. When the 750 c.c. Coventry Climax engine becomes available, this car will be able to accommodate it, the weight in 1,097 c.c. form with bolt-on magnesium wheels being quoted as only 6.7 cwt.

To accommodate the twin-overhead-camshaft Coventry Climax engines of 1,475 c.c. and 1,960 c.c., the Lotus 15 has been redesigned to incorporate useful improvements. I.F.S. of the wishbone type is retained for this more powerful model, but the anti-roll torsion bar which forms a part of each upper wishbone has been moved from ahead of the suspension to behind it, a change which diminishes the stresses on the front part of the chassis and leaves more room for radiator air ducts in the nose of the car. Strut-type rear suspension is used, with the refinement of three different mounting points for the top of each rear strut, wheel camber changes resulting from the choice of mounting point varying the car's handling characteristics to suit the tastes of any individual driver.

This type of I.R.S. has been carefully laid out so that, when the car rises on its springs due to a reduction in fuel load, the rear wheel camber changes slightly, diminution of their inward inclination offsetting any tendency for altering weight distribution to cause an unwanted increase in the car's chosen degree of understeer. The shock absorbers built into the rear suspension struts incorporate the latest Armstrong adjustable bleed valves, these further increasing the scope for adapting the suspension to either " 5 lap " or " long distance " fuel loads in the rear-mounted 22-gallon petrol tank.

Four Speeds or Five

On the Fifteen and on the single-seat Formula car, with which it shares a great many mechanical features, the engine is tilted over towards the left at an angle of 17° in order to lower the car without introducing the lubrication difficulties associated with horizontal cylinders. With the 1½-litre engine this car uses the Lotus 5-speed gearbox mounted in unit with the final drive gears. When the 2-litre engine with its greater torque is chosen, a 4-speed gearbox is thought adequate, and a B-series British Motor Corporation gearbox with close-ratio

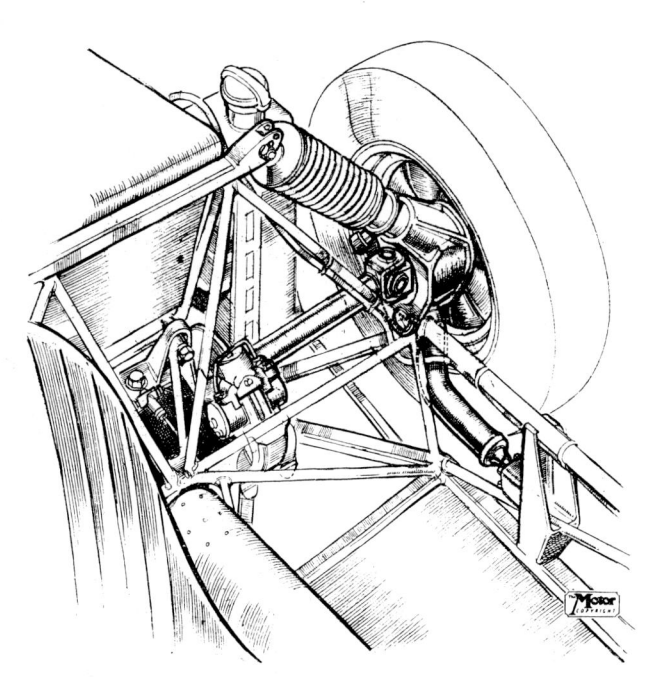

LOTUS

INDEPENDENT rear springing on Lotus cars is by the layout drawn here on the Fifteen sports car. Rear brakes are inboard mounted, and each wheel is located by the driveshaft, a trailing link and the spring-cum-damper strut.

gears is installed in unit with the engine and twin-plate clutch —overseas buyers can ease their servicing problems by choosing to combine the 4-speed gearbox with the smaller engine.

Our photographs show these sports models in chassis form, but the ultra-low bodies with tail sections fairing off the curved windscreens closely resemble those which have already been seen. Unusual is the vertical spare-wheel mounting on the Lotus 15 which makes use of the space in a fairing behind the driver's head. An interesting detail of this model is the provision of two swirl chambers in the coolant pipes to a very low radiator, to get rid of any steam or air which might be trapped in the fast-circulating water. The weight of this car, with 150-b.h.p. or 176-b.h.p. engine, is quoted as 8¾ cwt. without fuel in the 19-gallon tank.

To be raced by Team Lotus, the 6¼-cwt. single-seat model has not been significantly changed since it was exhibited at the Motor Show in October. Rather more comfortably wide in the cockpit than originally, it will for this season have an improved Coventry Climax 4-cylinder engine of full 2½-litre size. Already a few engines have been raced successfully with their cylinder dimensions "stretched" from 86.4 mm. × 83.8 mm. to 89 mm. × 89 mm., this raising the swept volume from 1,960 c.c. to 2,205 c.c., but as the 2-litre engine was itself already a "stretched" version of what had originally been designed as a 1½-litre power unit it has not hitherto been possible to gain fully proportional power advantage from swept volume increases beyond 2 litres. Now, about a dozen engines are to be built by Coventry Climax for Lotus and one other car manufacturer, with the light-alloy cylinder block and crank-case casting re-designed to permit a further increase in cylinder bore to 94 mm., this with a 90 mm. stroke giving a 2,495 c.c. displacement which fully exploits the 2½-litre Formula 1 limit on engine size.

Balanced Crank

In addition to having extra swept volume, this latest engine will have room for full counterweighting of its five-bearing crankshaft, something which was not practicable in the 2.2-litre unit. There is the hope that engine speeds up to as much as 8,000 r.p.m. may be safe with this new Formula 1 engine, which should permit an exceptionally light and well stream-lined single-seater to perform very competitively indeed under the existing formula—although when and if the projected 1½-litre Formula comes into force in 1961, Colin Chapman expects race-winning performance to depend upon availability of multi-cylinder engines able to operate up to speeds in the 12,000-16,000 r.p.m. range.

On the single-seat Formula car, in order to leave room for a low central driving seat, the propeller shaft is arranged to run diagonally across the car from a twin-plate clutch to the rear-mounted 5-speed gearbox, suspension layout being on the same lines as the Lotus 15 at both front and rear. From the lessons learned in races during 1958, the Lotus team believe that they have now developed this car to a pitch at which it can be expected to perform successfully during the remaining two seasons of the 2½-litre G.P. Formula; a victory (with its alternative 1½-litre engine) in the Formule Libre race at Brands Hatch on Boxing Day having given morale a boost.

LOTUS FORMULA CAR

Engine.—Coventry Climax twin overhead camshaft, 4-cyl. 81.2 mm.×71.1 mm., 1,475 c.c., or 94 mm.×90 mm., 2,495 c.c.

Transmission.—Twin-plate dry clutch. Rear-mounted five-speed gearbox with facilities for altering any ratio independently of remainder. Positive-stop gearchange.

Chassis.—Multiple-tube frame. I.F.S. by transverse wishbones, coil springs, on telescopic dampers, and anti-roll torsion bar. I.R.S. by telescopic damper struts carrying coil springs, non-telescopic driveshafts and trailing arms. Girling 9½-in. disc brakes, inboard mounted at rear. 4.50—15 and 5.50—15 Dunlop R5 tyres on cast magnesium disc wheels. Rack-and-pinion steering.

Dimensions.—Wheelbase 7 ft. 4 in., front and rear track 3 ft. 11 in., overall length 11 ft. 8 in., height at head fairing 2 ft. 11 in., ground clearance 4 in., weight 6¼ cwt.

MOUNT for Team Lotus drivers during 1959 will be the single-seat Formula car with alternative engine sizes. Cockpit details are the diagonal transmission line, rear gearbox, and padded knee-rest.

Further Thoughts On
THE 2-LITRE FIFTEEN

By Graham Hill

The author in the 2-litre Fifteen at Aintree (above) and at Oulton Park (below).

THE Series Three Fifteen shows quite a number of changes from the car we raced last year, the most obvious being the use of a stiffer chassis frame, "reversed" front suspension and a conventionally-mounted four-speed gearbox.

My first outing with the new car, at Goodwood, was extremely disappointing, for in practice the handling was not right and on race day the distributor drive sheared on the warming-up lap, which explains why the engine would not fire following the Le Mans-type start.

As the engine was taken out for repairs the following week there was no time to test the car before the British Empire Trophy meeting at Oulton Park. It went very well in practice, however, and I managed to do the fastest lap with a time of 1 min 52.2 sec—quicker than all of the Formula Two cars but 1.4 sec slower than my record lap last year, which was set up in a similar car with a five-speed rear-mounted gearbox and with the engine inclined at 60 degrees. Despite this I regard the current car as potentially quicker than last year's—everyone was going a little slower on 10 April, possibly because the circuit was slightly damp in places.

It was more than slightly damp on race day, and all thoughts of fast times were forgotten. Despite my pole position I made a poor start—too much wheelspin —and got rather boxed-in on the inside of the corner, so that I was well behind the leaders at the end of the first lap. I managed to work my way up to third place, passing Flockhart's Ecurie Ecosse Lister-Jaguar and Brabham's Cooper Monaco in the process, but I could make no impression on Jim Russell and Roy Salvadori, whose Coopers finished first and second respectively. In the wet the car understeered a great deal, rear end adhesion being so good that the back end would not come round in the normal way, and attempts to un-stick it on the throttle only resulted in pushing the front end out even further.

At Aintree, where I managed to do fourth fastest lap in the practice session for sports cars over 1100 cc, the Fifteen still understeered, and the handling seemed rather indefinite. After practice the amount of toe-in on the rear wheels was adjusted, and the car felt much better in the race, and from fourth place at the end of the first lap I managed to move up to second on lap three, in which position I stayed until the finish. I was unable to make a challenge to Salvadori, whose 2¼-litre Cooper-Maserati finished nearly half a minute ahead of me, but I was not seriously threatened by Masten Gregory's Ecurie Ecosse Lister-Jaguar, which was 7.4 seconds behind at the end of the 17 laps. There are few passing places at Aintree, particularly on the infield loop, where you have to gain at least three car's lengths between corners to get lined-up for the next bend, but I managed to pass both Bueb's and Gregory's Listers—which are faster than the Lotus on the straight—at Village Corner and to get just far enough ahead round Bechers to avoid being caught on Railway Straight. But it was a near thing, especially in the case of Gregory, who was right alongside me again just before Melling Crossing.

By comparison with twenty gear-changes per lap in last year's Formula Two car, which had the 1½-litre Coventry Climax engine and five-speed gearbox, I make only twelve changes to the lap in the Series Three Fifteen—due partly to the greater torque of the 2-litre engine and partly to the wider ratios of the four-speed box. Coming out of Tatts in second I change up into third and then top going past the pits, and stay in top (dropping to about 5000 rpm) through Waterways. I go down to second for the right-hander at Anchor Crossing, up to third and down again for the left-handed Cottage Corner, using second for Country Corner (a left-hander) and third for Village Corner (a right-hander). On Valentines Way I get into top just before Bechers, go through Bechers in third and take top again by the gate just before the straight. Maximum revs in top are 6500 (final drive ratio is 3.7 to 1) and I drop to third again for Melling Crossing and second for Tatts.

FASTEST LAP

My fastest lap was 2 mins 6.6 sec, by comparison with Salvadori's 2. 05.4 (which is a new 2000-3000 cc class record) and Cliff Allison's 1500-2000 cc class record, set up in last year's 2-litre Fifteen with five-speed gearbox—2. 6.2.

From the driver's point of view the latest 2-litre Fifteen is a wonderful car— lots of steam low down, tremendous roadholding, high maximum speed considering the engine size and an excellent gear-change. I have never had any trouble with the five-speed box, but I know other people have; they couldn't have any difficulty with the BMC box, the change being absolutely conventional and particularly good "across the gate" between second and third. The driving position is comfortable, the brakes work well and maintenance should be quite straightforward.

COMMON

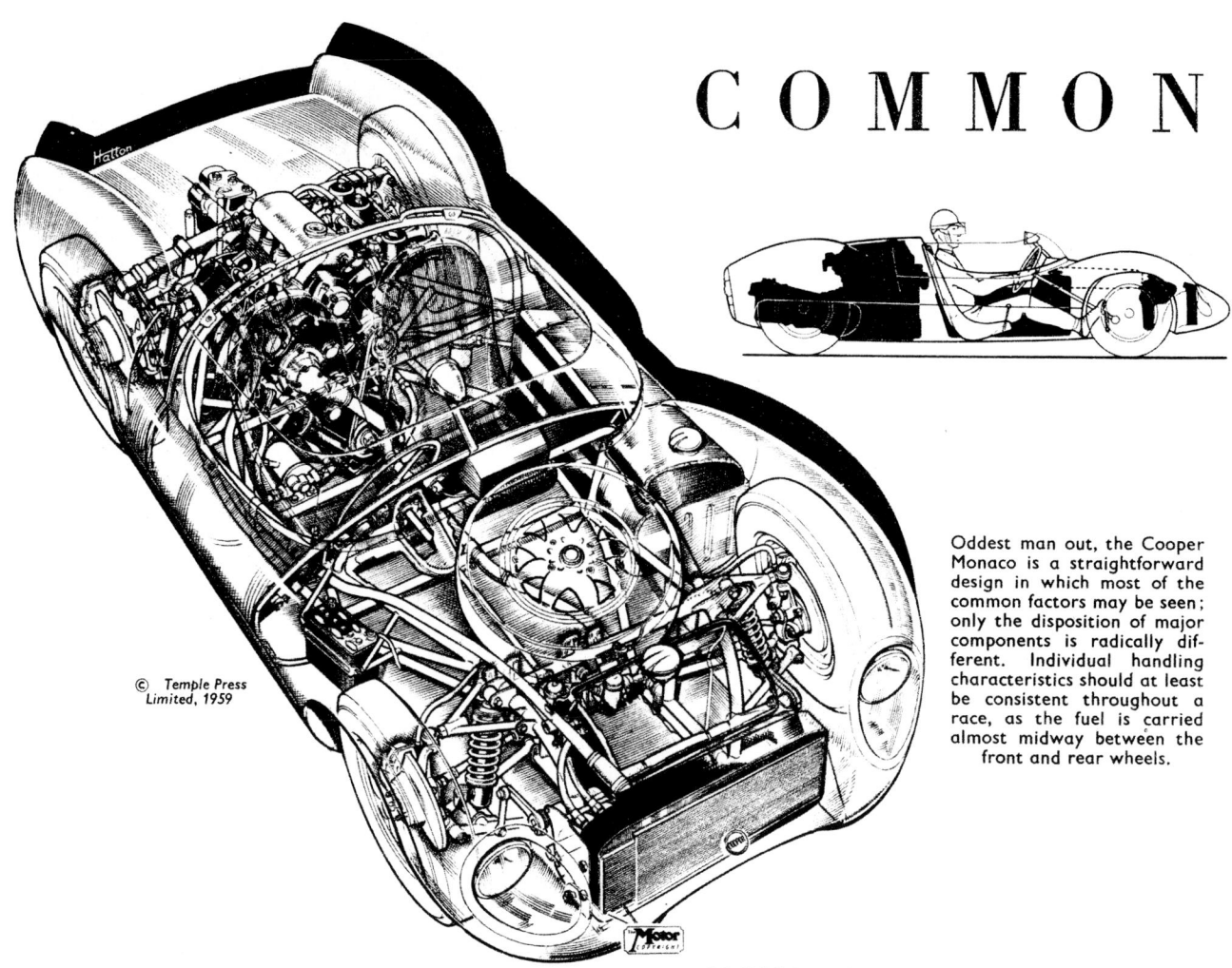

Oddest man out, the Cooper Monaco is a straightforward design in which most of the common factors may be seen; only the disposition of major components is radically different. Individual handling characteristics should at least be consistent throughout a race, as the fuel is carried almost midway between the front and rear wheels.

© Temple Press Limited, 1959

COOPER and LOTUS DATA

Engine: Coventry-Climax FPF 1½-litre (2-litre figures in brackets). Cylinders, 4. Bore, 81.2 mm. (86.4). Stroke, 71.1 mm. (83.8). Cubic capacity, 1,475 c.c. (1,960). Piston area, 32.3 sq. in. (36.3). Valve gear, twin o.h.c. Compression ratio, 10.0:1 (12.4). Max. power, 145 b.h.p. at 7,250 r.p.m. (176 b.h.p. at 6,500 r.p.m.). Max. b.m.e.p., 187.5 lb./sq. in. at 5,600 r.p.m. (204 at 5,050). Carburetters, 2 twin-choke S.U. or Weber horizontal. Lubrication, dry sump.

	Cooper	Lotus
Transmission		
Clutch	Borg and Beck 2-plate	2-plate
Gearbox	Four-speed Ersa	Five-speed Lotus or four-speed B.M.C. "B" series
Rear axle	Combined with gearbox	ZF differential in Lotus casing
Chassis		
Frame	Multi-tube	Multi-tube with floor stiffening
Front suspension	Coil springs, wishbones and anti-roll bar	Coil springs, wishbones and anti-roll bar
Rear suspension	Transverse leaf spring and wishbones	Independent, coil springs on telescopic damper struts, non-telescopic drive shafts and trailing arms
Shock absorbers	Telescopic, front combined with coil springs	Telescopic, combined with coil springs
Steering	Rack and pinion	Rack and pinion
Brakes	Girling disc	Girling disc (inboard rear)
Dimensions		
Wheelbase	7 ft. 7 in.	7 ft. 4 in.
Track	3 ft. 11 in.	Front 3 ft. 10 in., rear 4 ft.
Overall length	11 ft. 8 in.	11 ft. 5 in.
Overall width	4 ft. 10 in.	5 ft.
Overall height	2 ft. 9½ in.	2 ft. (to scuttle)
Dry weight	10 cwt.	8¾ cwt.

THE comparison of racing cars is an instructive but sometimes misleading occupation. Instructive if pursued at length by engineers qualified to appreciate the merits of this or that suspension, weight versus aerodynamic, or the effect of changing weight distribution, it can on the contrary produce doubtful answers when enthusiastic laymen match rival specifications one against the other. Fortunately there is plenty of opportunity to put private theories to the test by observation. After the Sebring Grand Prix and the Easter race meetings in Britain, all four of the cars illustrated here have made a representative public showing, some with success and some without. Certainly there must be some head-scratching amongst designers at this moment, and checks to see which calculations were wrong.

The fact is that details of design have only a minor effect in themselves, whereas the thing which really rings the bell and ducks under the chequered flat is a coherent whole, assembled after usually well-known principles, with care and accurate mathematics. For proof it is evident that the most important instruments of higher speed in recent years have become almost universal just as soon as the designers were able to acquire them.

A shining example is the Dunlop R5 racing tyre; another (with exceptions at this date) the disc brake; a third, the Coventry-Climax engine without which an endeavour to build a successful British sports-racing car for the 1,100 c.c. or 1½-litre class is little more than a forlorn hope.

With these things in mind, it is still useful to make a few detailed comparisons, for details are interesting whether their effect is profound or not.

If one is looking for contrasts, there could be no more obvious

216

FACTORS

Four Sports-racing Cars Which are Not as Different as they Look

one than that between Cooper and Lotus in their respective, most advanced sports-car forms. Flattery by imitation has never been a habit in either Surbiton or Hornsey, and the 1½/2-litre cars from both factories (each using alternative versions of the twin o.h.c. Coventry-Climax engine) stick to their designers' original guns. The stub-tailed Cooper of four seasons ago, which was the first serious competition car to use the Climax, was not greatly different from today's Monaco model. The frame is now a little more complex, the front suspension a little more orthodox, and the driver sits to one side instead of in the middle. Cooper chassis tend to be based on experience rather than theory, and experience has in the past brought home plenty of victories with—or in spite of—frames which were not fully triangulated to obtain the maximum stiffness with minimum weight, even going so far as to use curved tubes where sudden changes in width made it convenient. For reasons as yet unknown, but possibly connected with the latest, wider frame, the Monaco seems to be a difficult car to handle in the wet. The frame consists basically of four car-length tubes, forming a girder on each side, and as lightweights go the car is probably rather heavy at an estimated dry weight of 10 cwt. Such weight as is saved by dispensing with the propeller shaft may well be made up by long pipes carrying water between the rear engine and front radiator.

Being out of the driver's line of sight, the engine can stand higher in relation to him than usual without obstruction. In practice the engine is tilted 18° on its right, or exhaust side, to lower the centre of gravity, while a header tank for the cooling system is mounted directly over it without exceeding windscreen height. The inclination of the engine works to the disadvantage of the inlet ducts from a pair of twin-choke horizontal S.U. carburetters which have to be sharply curved. Following normal rear-engined practice, the final drive unit is sandwiched between engine and gearbox, the latter being an all-indirect four-speed Ersa, originally based upon the Citroen design but without synchromesh.

Although the front suspension now employs the almost universal coil spring and wishbone layout, with an anti-roll bar passing through a frame tube, the Cooper still exhibits its Fiat ancestry with a transverse leaf rear spring clamped to the chassis at two points to increase roll stiffness without losing flexibility. Alternative designs use a pair of wishbones to each rear wheel, or a single lower wishbone in conjunction with the leaf spring. Very short drive shafts are universally jointed and splined. Girling 9-in. disc brakes, with two separate master cylinders, are

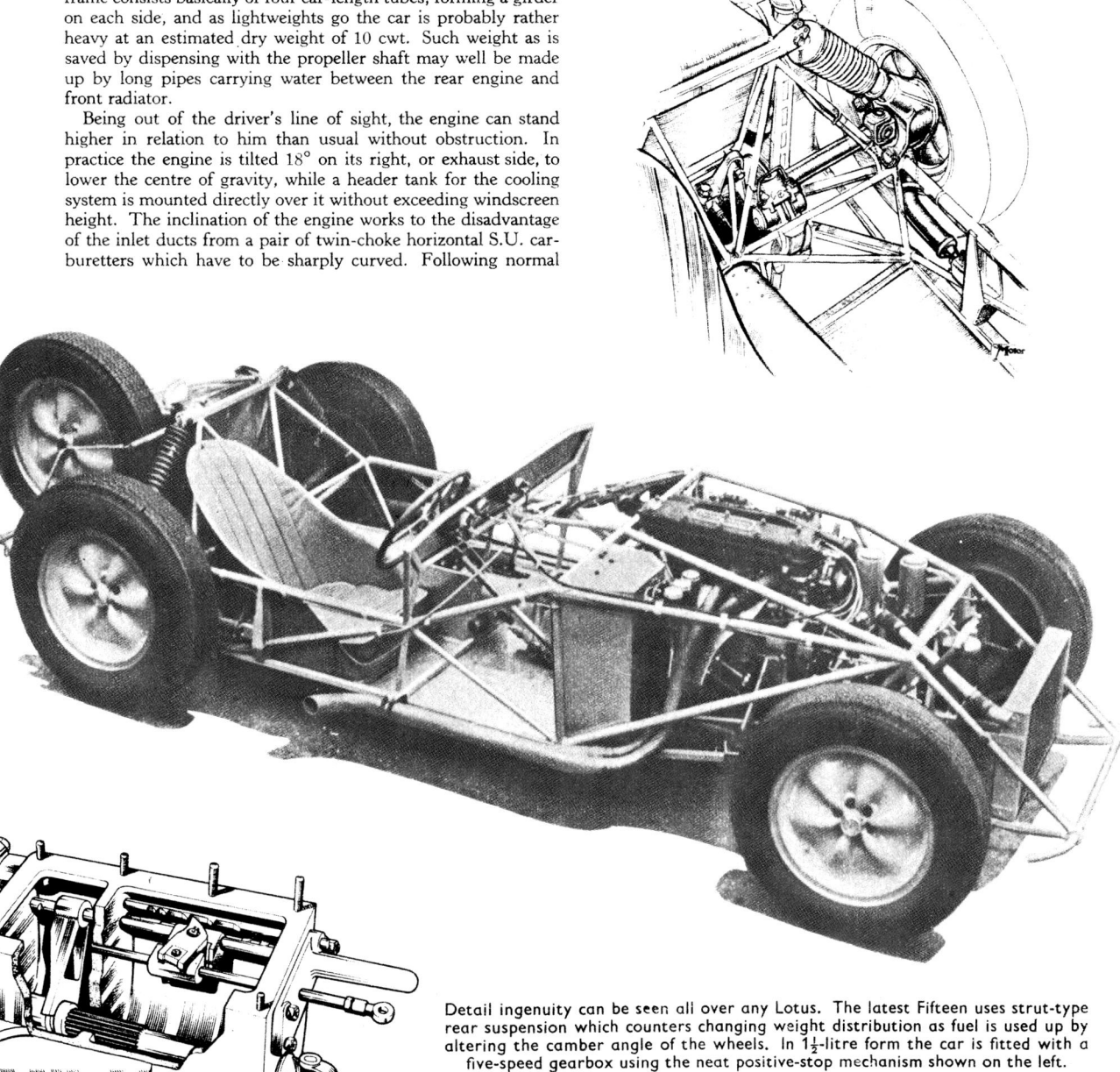

Detail ingenuity can be seen all over any Lotus. The latest Fifteen uses strut-type rear suspension which counters changing weight distribution as fuel is used up by altering the camber angle of the wheels. In 1½-litre form the car is fitted with a five-speed gearbox using the neat positive-stop mechanism shown on the left.

COMMON FACTORS

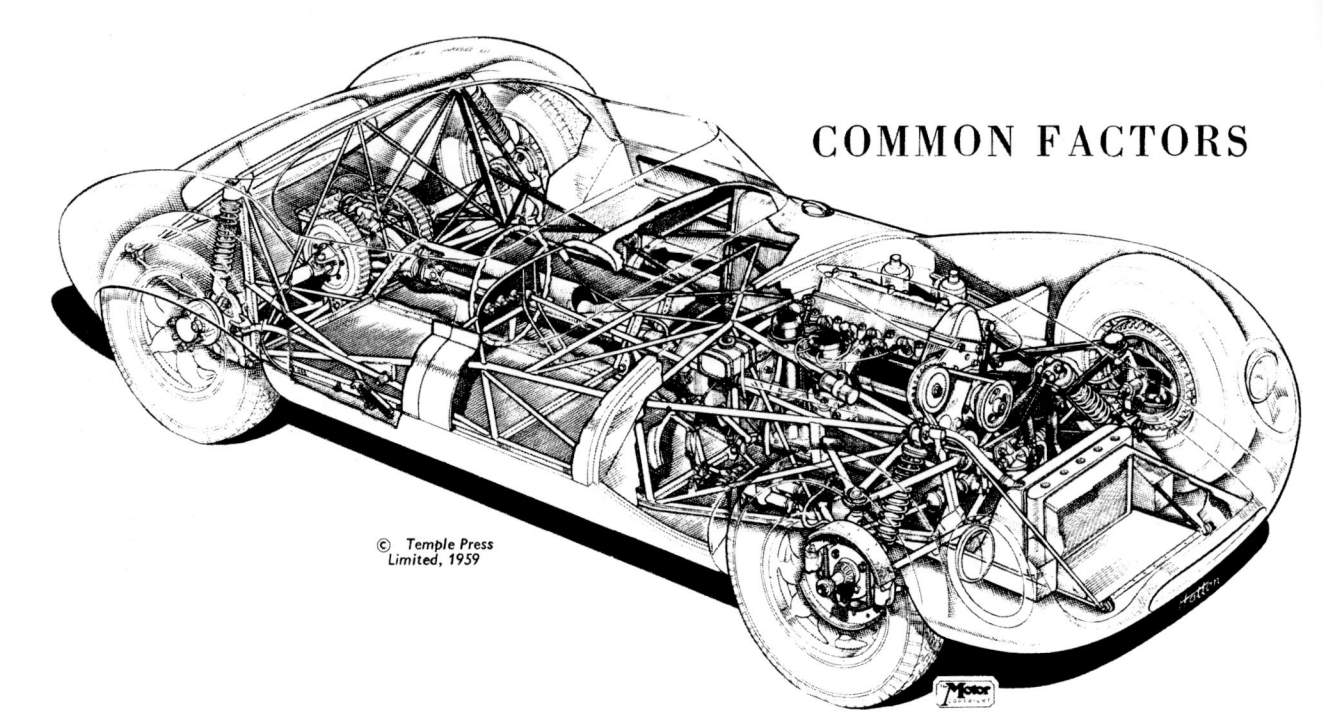

© Temple Press Limited, 1959

Lola—last season's prodigy. Very low and very light, it shares with Elva the use of drum brakes which have so far proved adequate for short-distance racing, putting up an 1,100 c.c. class record at Goodwood. The independent rear suspension also has common principles with the Elva.

ELVA and LOLA DATA

Engine: Coventry-Climax FWA Mk 3. Cylinders, 4. Bore, 72.4 mm. Stroke, 66.6 mm. Cubic capacity, 1,098 c.c. Piston area, 25.5 sq. in. Valve gear, single o.h. camshaft. Compression ratio, 10.5:1. Max. power, 90 b.h.p. at 7,200 r.p.m. Max. torque, 72 lb. ft. at 5,250 r.p.m. Carburetters, 2 twin-choke S.U. or Weber horizontal. Lubrication, wet sump.

	Elva	Lola
Transmission		
Clutch	Borg and Beck s.d.p.	Borg and Beck s.d.p.
Gearbox	MGA with Elva gears	B.M.C. "A" series with special gears, or MGA
Gearbox ratios	1.0, 1.26, 1.60, 2.64	1.0, 1.239, 1.659, 2.64
Rear axle	B.M.C. nose-piece and hypoid bevel in Elva casing	B.M.C. nose-piece and hypoid bevel in special casing
Axle ratios	3.73, 4.22, 4.55, 4.88	3.73, 4.22, 4.55, 4.88, 5.375
Chassis		
Frame	Multi-tube	Multi-tube with floor stiffening
Front suspension	Coil springs, wishbones and anti-roll bar	Coil springs, wishbones and anti-roll bar
Rear suspension	Independent, coil springs and wishbones using drive shafts as upper wishbone, with trailing torque arms	Independent, coil springs and trailing/transverse wishbones using drive-shaft as upper wishbone
Shock absorbers	Telescopic, combined with coil springs. Adjustable at rear	Telescopic, combined with coil springs
Steering	Elva rack and pinion	Lightweight rack and B.M.C. pinion
Brakes	Lockheed hydraulic in linered, ribbed light-alloy drums. Front, 10 in. x 2¼ in. Rear (inboard), 10 in. x 1¾ in. Lining area 163 sq. in.	Lockheed hydraulic in ribbed Al-fin drums. Front, 10 in. x 2¼ in. Rear, (inboard), 10 in. x 1¾ in. Lining area 163 sq. in.
Dimensions		
Wheelbase	7 ft.	7 ft. 1 in.
Track	3 ft. 10½ in.	4 ft. front, 3 ft. 11½ in. rear
Overall length	11 ft. 6 in.	11 ft.
Scuttle height	2 ft. 3½ in.	1 ft. 11½ in.
Ground clearance	5 in.	5 in.
Dry weight	7½ cwt.	7¼–7½ cwt.

mounted outboard on each of the eight-spoked, cast light-alloy wheels.

Reading from front to rear, the heavy elements of the Cooper are radiator and oil-cooler; oil tank; spare wheel (horizontal); fuel tank beside the driver; engine and gearbox. For its rival, the 1½-litre Lotus Fifteen, the equivalent sequence is radiator and oil cooler; engine; driver; gearbox; fuel and oil tanks; and spare wheel (for the 2-litre class Lotus uses a four-speed gearbox behind the engine). Like all Chapman designs, the Fifteen is based on a frame of light, straight tubes, fully triangulated and additionally stiffened by a stressed floor and transmission tunnel. Here again the twin-cam Climax engine is inclined, by an almost equal angle to that of the Cooper, but this time towards the inlet side after some unsatisfactory experiments last year with an engine laid over the other way to a near-horizontal position. Although lubrication problems were solved with that arrangement, curvature of the inlet pipes caused too big a drop in power, and the present system allows a reasonable profile with good breathing.

If novelties are to be found in racing car design, a Lotus is often the place to look for them. One such is the five-speed gearbox which was developed first for the Formula 1 car of last year and now appears in the 1½-litre sports car. Mounted integrally with the final-drive unit, the gearbox has two shafts only, lying longitudinally with the output immediately above the input. All five pairs are in constant mesh, the output gears being solid upon their shaft while their mates revolve freely upon a hollow input shaft until they are locked to it in turn by a selector sliding inside the shaft. The box is light and compact, with a positive-stop motorcycle-type change in which the driver simply pushes the lever forward for a lower gear or backward for a higher one.

Lotus front suspension, which began five years ago with divided Ford axles and in the latest 1,100 c.c. Seventeen has evolved into a strut-type similar to the current Fords, is still at the orthodox wishbone stage for the Fifteen. The lower wishbone is widely spaced to absorb braking reaction, the upper consisting of a single arm combined with the end of the anti-roll bar. The rear suspension is an entirely original Chapman lay-out, also pioneered on the single-seaters, which gives the rear wheels a somewhat similar geometry to that of the strut-type front suspension mentioned above, by employing a non-telescopic drive shaft as one arm of the "wishbone."

As a detailed drawing on page 359 shows, each wheel is

218

located by the drive shaft, a trailing link and the strut containing the coil spring and damper, which can be mounted at one of three points on the frame to suit drivers' tastes in handling characteristics. The geometry compensates changing weight distribution as fuel is used up, by reducing negative camber and hence understeer, as the tail becomes lighter. Cast magnesium bolt-on wheels reduce unsprung weight, as do inboard rear brakes. Girling discs are used at front and rear.

Although Cooper sports-car activity is now confined to the upper classes (of engine, that is), the Lotus Seventeen will be in hot competition with two formidable 1,100 c.c. adversaries, the Mk. 4 Elva and last season's prodigy, Lola. The latest Elva which made only one or two tentative appearances in 1958 is largely the work of Peter Nott, who is no longer with the company, in collaboration with the founder of the business, Frank Nichols. One of its most striking characteristics is a determined effort to put most of the weight on the back wheels, by placing the engine so far back in the frame that the propeller shaft between gearbox and final drive is no more than a pair of universal joints back-to-back. The single overhead camshaft (wet sump) Coventry-Climax engine is inclined 10° to the left, as is standard practice with this unit, and mated to an M.G. gearbox containing Elva close-ratio gears. Conversely, the final drive unit consists of an Elva casing with B.M.C. nose piece and differential.

The straight-tubed space frame carries wishbone front suspension which reverses Lotus practice by using the anti-roll bar as part of each lower link. The rear suspension is another essay into combining low unsprung weight with controlled geometry. A short non-telescopic drive shaft and a long lower transverse link to each wheel act effectively as wishbones, the lower link taking most of the cornering loads and being adjustable to vary the handling characteristics, which approximate to those of a low-pivot swing axle. Thrust is transmitted to the chassis by a trailing link which is ball-jointed to the frame but bolted rigidly to the hub carrier, and carries the attachment for the usual coil spring and damper unit.

There is no brake torque to cope with, as inboard brakes are used at the rear. Like its rival Lola, the lightweight Elva at present relies on Lockheed drum brakes, using radially finned magnesium alloy drums containing ferrous liners and drilled back plates. The wheels are of special Elva pattern, cast in magnesium with four indentations like broad, shallow spokes and eight holes for brake cooling air.

The first season for Eric Broadley's "production" Lolas, after the success of last year's prototype, started in mixed fashion at Snetterton a fortnight ago, when two cars ran away from the field and the third was wrapped firmly round a piece of scenery. At Goodwood three cars left a field of Lotuses and Elvas far behind, demonstrating considerable verve which springs largely from lightness, obtained by a straight-tubed chassis with no surplus weight anywhere, braced by the floor and transmission tunnel. The engine and transmission arrangements are strictly orthodox, using, like Elva, special ratios in a B.M.C. gearbox (A-type or MGA) and B.M.C. final drive gears in a special light alloy final drive casing.

The front suspension is likewise conventional; upper and lower wishbones are angled forwards to resist brake reaction. The independent rear which joins a united opposition to Count de Dion in this class of racing, is a good example of our thesis that details differ more than principles. Again the geometry is approximately that of a low-pivot swing axle, drive shaft and trailing arm forming an upper wishbone while the lower link is a composite wishbone consisting of a single tube ahead of the hub and a triangle behind it.

Lola brakes are of the finned Al-fin drum type currently available for the Triumph TR3, and are mounted outboard at the front, inboard at the rear and in both cases the circulation of cooling air is assisted by open back plates. The cast light-alloy wheels are of the same type as those used by Cooper.

Writing at the very beginning of the season, one would be bold to wager on the probable fortunes of one car or another. At least a study of the drawings on these pages should demonstrate the sometimes unappreciated similarity of design which prevails amongst superficially dissimilar cars. Time and the timekeepers will demonstrate the accuracy of rival slide-rules.

The World Copyright of this article and illustrations is strictly reserved © Temple Press Limited, 1959

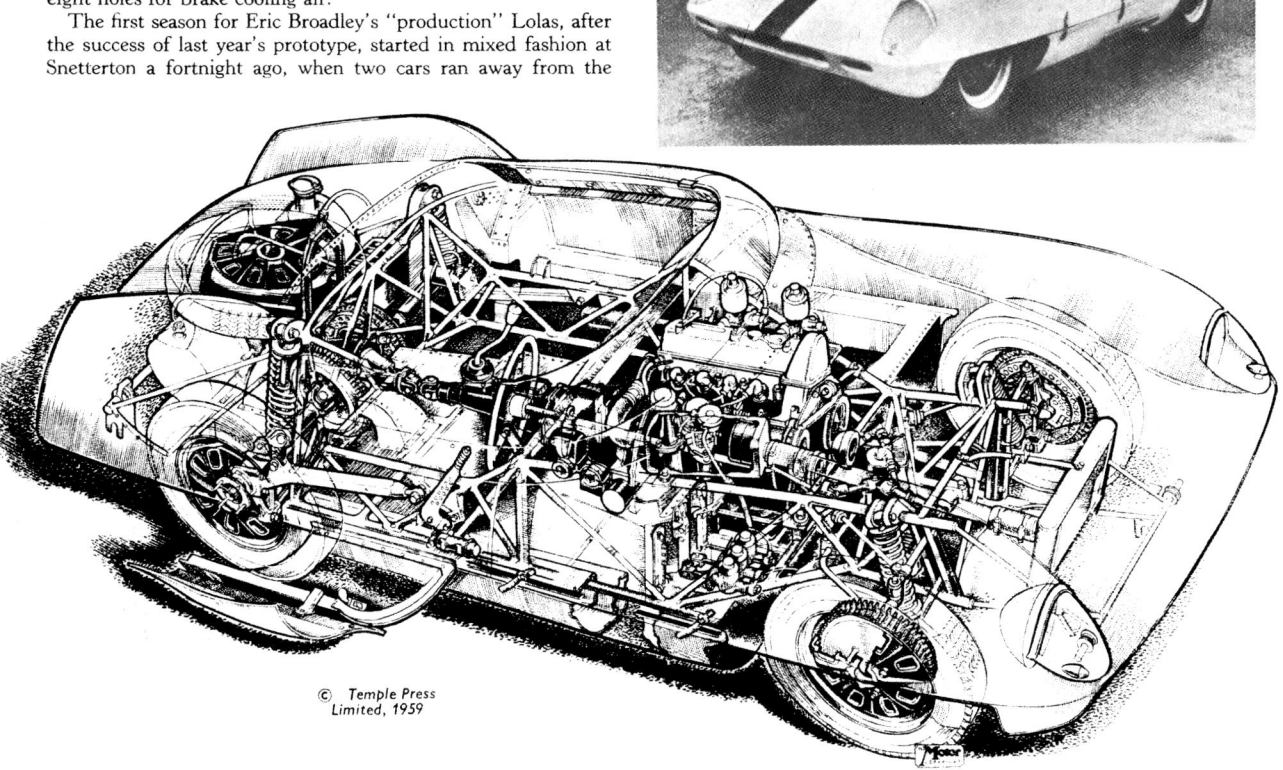

© Temple Press Limited, 1959

At the cost of a little, calculated, rear-wheel steering, the Elva contrives to have independent suspension with very low unsprung weight and the effect of a low-pivot swing-axle. A salient feature is the engine mounting, far back in the frame

FERTUS? LORARI? Who Knows; It Goes!

by Russ Kelly

▶ Nothing is more like a game of musical chairs than the California sports car engine swap. Engines of various price and muscle pass from one hot hand to the next and when the music stops, even the new owners are sometimes startled by the hybrid they start the season with.

However, when Jean Pierre Kunstle, of Sebring Porsche fame, found a two-liter Ferrari four (that had lost its place to a three-liter engine of the same make) and gave it a push fit into a Lotus 15 chassis, he wouldn't have been as startled if it had turned and bit him as were the RSK proponents when it rolled onto the grid at Laguna Seca.

That JP should have decided to roll his own instead of depending as before on normal factory delivery isn't surprising. Ever since Count Zorobrowski and his Chitty-Bangbangs, drivers have felt that they knew better than all others the combination that could carry all before it. Miles with his Porsche-engined Cooper represents a recent example of this conviction.

With the RSK's threatening to dominate the under two-liter class there is little doubt that beating them was uppermost in JP's mind and few people know the weaknesses of racing Porsches better.

With the two-liter Ferrari four he selected a power plant that is probably at the peak of Modena development. It is the direct descendant of Ferrari's first four cylinder effort that made its appearance in 1951 powering his Formula II car of that year and met with considerable success (something like winning all its races). In 1953 this design again powered the Formula II machine and proved itself so reliable and suited for competition that it was used in two sports models the following year.

In original delivery form this twin overhead cam four claimed 190 bhp from its 1984.8 cubic centimeters at 7000 rpm. With Kunstle's engine, a rebore and new pistons raised the total displacement to 1993 cc's. The new pistons raised the compression ratio from 8.7 to 9.5 to one. With the up in compression and the up in displacement there's another up in the claimed horsepower, standing now at 200 bhp at 7000 rpm.

JP's decision to use a Lotus 15 chassis was probably not only influenced by what he had seen on various race courses but also by the charming lightness of this Colin Chapman creation. In 1956 the little 2-liter Ferrari four was forced to wrestle around a 1510 pound (dry) sports car body and chassis. Now it only has to contend with 1350 pounds. This figure is wet and includes 19 gallons of gas, 17 quarts of oil and water. Weight distribution without the driver is 730 pounds at the front wheels and 620 at the rear. Even Junior without using all of his fingers can figure this out . . . that's 6.75 pounds per horsepower which is very healthy, indeed.

Squeezing the Ferrari engine, clutch and transmission into the Lotus chassis was a little touchy but other than the fabrication of new engine mounts, little alteration in the space frame chassis was necessary. New firewall and transmission cover were hammered out to accommodate the larger Ferrari unit. The only way the new power plant would fit into the Lotus chassis was in an upright position and this left about four inches of Ferrari head and cam cover sticking out above the Lotus hood line. A Lister-type bulge was fabricated to cover these bits of machinery and a small air duct was provided at the forward edge of the bulge to

PHOTOGRAPHY: KELLY — VESTA

First appearing at Laguna Seca, California, Jean Pierre Kunstle's startling 2.0 Ferrari-engined Lotus 15 really shook up the opposition. Teething problems sidelined it but the future of this Yankee-built Anglo-Italian looks good.

Fertus? Lorari?

provide additional cooling for the upper portion of the engine and the magneto.

The Ferrari twin plate clutch drives a four-speed box that has the following ratios: first gear is 2.01 to one; second is 1.53 to one; third, 1.23 to one; and fourth, 1 to one. The Lotus drive shaft couples to the Ferrari transmission and carries the power back to a stock Lotus rear end with a final drive ratio of 4.2 to one. All the Lotus running gear remains stock with swinging half axle independent suspension in the front and a de Dion layout in the rear. Brakes are, of course, Girling disc in the front and inboard Girling discs at the rear.

Work on the car was started only two weeks before the Laguna Seca race date and was barely completed in time for technical inspection. Saturday with its race practice and preliminary races was the first opportunity JP had to test the car. The concensus of opinion in the pits was that it was too fragile and would not last. But as Kunstle turned in a few conservative practice laps, then began steadily lowering his time, the pits divided into two factions: those who hoped he would last, and those who hoped he wouldn't. For his first race with his new mount Kunstle shared the first row of the grid with Sammy Weiss driving a 1600 cc Porsche RSK.

With the drop of the flag, it was Katy bar the door between these two up to the first turn, where Kunstle had to drop back in behind Weiss from an almost even position in order to get his proper line for the turn. However, within a couple of laps the Lotus Ferrari was safely in the lead and had started to leave Weiss further and further behind. Then as Kunstle would lift his foot going into the corners, large puffs of white smoke began billowing from the engine room. Kunstle checked the instruments and although everything looked OK, he decided to take no chances and slowed down and the white clouds diminished in size. Weiss caught up and went into the lead with Kunstle following at a steady, slower pace neatly calculated to keep him in front of third place Charles (Sea Biscuit) Howard in another RSK Porsche.

In the pits it was discovered that the white smoke was caused by a leak in the fuel system that spewed gasoline over the manifold whenever the throttle was shut off. Although cheated of first place, the two-liter hybrid was guaranteed a place on the front row of the grid for Sunday's two-liter main event.

The next day in practice Kunstle offered the car for a trial ride to Ken Miles. Miles completed less than a lap before he pulled off to the side of the course with the rear end gone. By the time a tow car had pulled his car back to the pits, Kunstle found that friends and rivals alike were anxious to see his car make the two-liter race. Arrangements were made to borrow the center section from Stan Petersen's Lotus 1100. Bill Breeze offered his help and up to a few minutes before the start of the race, Kunstle's pit looked like a Who's Who of West Coast racing.

Unfortunately, final drive ratios suitable for an 1100 left the two-liter engine sadly under geared for the course. With an anxious foot and under geared, Kunstle almost disappeared from the other drivers' sight when the flag fell. During the first lap J.P. found that he would only be able to stay in the race by dangerously over revving the engine. So after holding an easy lead for several laps, he decided to save his engine for another day and reluctantly pulled into the pits.

Determined not to be let down by what he considers a weak link, the Lotus rear end, Kunstle has decided to do some testing with a Halibrand quick change rear end or some other equally rugged equipment.

Kunstle has a lot of enthusiasm for his Lotus-Ferrari and we are inclined to go along. A little bench racing trigonometry should show that this car will be a serious contender on the West Coast. However, Colin Chapman has just shipped to the West Coast the first Lotus with a twin overhead cam 2-liter Coventry Climax engine . . . Say . . . do I hear music again?
—rk

Jay Chamberlain's 2-litre Fifteen leads a Talbot Special and Ken Miles's Porsche at Santa Barbara.

QUICKER THAN SOMEWHAT —

A side view of the Lotus-Alfa with bonnet and tail strapped down gives a good idea of its clean low-drag lines. The steeply-raked and curved plastic screen sweeps around to meet the high sides of the tail to cut the drag of the open cockpit to a minimum.

Lotus-Alfa XV

For the benefit of readers who take a more-than-academic interest in the performance and behaviour of sports-racing machinery, CAR has arranged for a special series of articles — entitled "Quicker Than Somewhat" — to be written by L. Symons, the prominent trials driver and motoring journalist. The articles will reflect his impressions—those of a person who has some claim to being a competent driver but who is not used to the more potent carriages — of the speed, handling and road-holding of such cars as the Lotus-Alfa XV which is the subject of this first article. Other cars it is hoped to feature in the series include the Alfa S.S., the Dart-Alfa, the Maserati 200SI and the D-type Jaguar.

Because it is both impractical and inappropriate to conduct full road tests of such cars, the Specification and Performance tables are given in abridged form.

Pictures: ALTON BERNSTEIN

TWO famous names in motoring — one old and one comparatively new — are combined in the pugnacious-looking little red Lotus-Alfa.

There is an old saying about good things coming in small packages, and neither this nor the car's looks have been belied by its performances in this country. In two months of racing it has considerably shaken both onlookers and other drivers in races from Cape Town to Bulawayo, and it is worth setting down its achievements for the record.

The car is basically a Lotus XV, designed and built by Colin Chapman and his fellow-wizards to comply with the international definition of a "sports" car — but with racing as the object. It was imported, second-hand and sans engine, by Gene Bosman of Pretoria, shortly before the third Nine-Hour Endurance Race at Grand Central, last October 29. The plan was to instal an Alfa engine, much modified, and gearbox and to run it in this race and anything else available.

It ran in its new form a bare week before the race. In the race itself Gene and Ernest Pieterse shared the wheel and were second on distance — missing what seemed a certain win because the rough track caused

What the driver sees — the stark but reasonably comfortable cockpit. Only essential instruments appear on the dashboard, and the bulges over the front wheels and engine provide useful "aiming marks"—while the windshield is for looking over, not through.

A close-up of the inlet side of the engine shows the wide mouths of the air-intake extensions and the massive bodies of the twin Webers. The accessibility of oil and water fillers, hydraulic fluid reservoirs and coil will be noted, as well as the small size of the radiator, airflow to which is ducted when the bonnet is closed.

the car to "bottom" and wore a hole in the diff. housing. At Bulawayo, in November, the same drivers used it to score 3rd overall and second in class in a scratch race and 2nd in a handicap race. At Killarney in December Gene won the race for sports cars and "specials" which rung up the curtain for the Cape G.P., and in the G.P. itself was 6th overall and second South African home.

In the South African G.P. at East London, Ernest was lying 8th after about 50 laps when the rear suspension came adrift and he was forced to retire. A week later, at the Fairfield meeting at Pietermaritzburg, Gene won the "Petit Prix", was 3rd in the race for sports and modified production machinery, and 7th in the Fairfield "100". On January 14 he scored a 1st and a 2nd in short scratch races during a Club meeting at Grand Central.

Impressive performance

This is pretty impressive for a car which is, after all, a two-seater "sports" job with enveloping bodywork, competing, in many of these races, against "real racing" single-seaters. But no less a person than Jack Brabham was heard to remark thoughtfully at East London that he could not remember a 1500cc sports car which travelled faster.

When the car arrived the Lotus gearbox was still in position, in unit with the spin-limiting diff. There was no time to remove it before the 9-Hour, so the drive was taken through it from the five-speed Alfa SS gearbox which is mounted on the engine. The engine itself has been both bored and stroked to raise its capacity from the normal 1290cc to almost exactly 1500cc.

The Lotus box has since been removed, and the engine has also been run with several different cylinder heads. Odd jobs like replacing pads for the disc brakes have also been done but, apart from this, neither the engine, gearbox nor back axle have been "down" since the car started racing here.

These facts, and the car's race history, are worth bearing in mind when digesting the performance recorded. In conjunction with the lack of odd knick-knacks like dynamometers and, perhaps, a slight natural reluctance to disclose too many "trade secrets", they also explain why some figures in the specification are approximate.

The brief performance figures, however, were recorded as accurately as was possible. I think they are impressive enough, but make no bones about my conviction that they could be considerably improved by taking them after the car has been given the going-over which it is now starting to need, and by letting a more experienced rocket pilot do the driving.

It is, after all, one thing to believe fondly that one is something of a Moss when it comes to driving fairly ordinary touring or sports cars, however potent they may be in their class. It is quite another to put belief to the proof in a vehicle which looks little bigger than a healthy roller-skate and disposes of about 300 b.h.p. per ton.

So there was a good deal of trepidation mixed with the pleased anticipation when it came to the actual driving — which was to be done alone as the passenger compartment is definitely for emergency use only. I could not help wondering what would happen if I was clot enough to lose or break it. I consoled myself with the thought that, assuming I survived, I might be able

With the Lotus-Alfa doing circa 120 m.p.h. the driver is not concentrating fiercely on his instruments — merely trying to get his head down far enough to prevent the breeze under the peak of his crash-hat from taking it — and his head — off.

223

The smooth, gradual curves of the "bunch-of-bananas" exhaust system, giving minimum interference with the gasflow, catch the eye when looking at the near-side of the engine.

to outrun Gene — who anyway is a fairly friendly and easy-going type.

In the event I found that I need not have worried. Trying afterwards to find something with which to compare the experience, the nearest personal parallel I have been able to draw is with the first flight in a Spitfire. There was the same frightening noise, the same shattering performance — and the same viceless good manners. It is no car to suffer the fool or the ham-handed gladly, but responded wholeheartedly to the best I could do in the way of combining firmness with sensitivity.

Standstill to 120 m.p.h.

"Docile" would be a wildly inappropriate word for a car which goes from a standstill to 120 m.p.h. in well under 30 secs. without breathing hard. Yet it is certainly quite tractable.

Real power starts arriving between 4,000 and 5,000 r.p.m. and goes on growing up to near the limit of 8,000 — though I tried to keep down to about 7,500 for safety's sake. Using the power to get the car going can provide some of the trickiest moments of the drive — as Gene has also discovered.

The car snakes fiercely as the rear wheels spin — the spin-limiting diff. finds itself quite unable to stop it completely and has to be content with keeping it even on both wheels — and any unevenness or loose patches tend to start a slide before things finally settle down and the car is really on its way, using all the power and leaving two long black streaks of rubber on the road. And it is not only in first from a standstill that the wheels can be spun, either.

If acceleration from a standing start is impressive, that available for overtaking at normal road speeds is even more so. The driver doing 70 - 80 in the normal car is travelling fairly fast, but at that speed the Lotus is merely at comfortable revs. in third and can rocket up to 20 m.p.h. faster in about five seconds. To the driver it feels like nothing, flat, accompanied by a strong kick in the back, but for the man being passed it is probably even more surprising.

To the accompaniment of a noise like ripping canvas, what was a little red car in the rear-view mirror becomes a small red dot, disappearing rapidly over the next rise ahead.

Having established that the car can go, the next question is whether it can stop. Ettore Bugatti's remark about making his cars to go and not to stop notwithstanding, the ability to come to anchor rapidly can be very comforting.

A time of exactly 21.0 secs. to go from a standstill to 100 m.p.h. and back to a standstill, the same time being recorded on each of four consecutive runs in rapid succession and in opposite directions, answers that question.

The suspension could hardly be soft with a clearance of just over three inches, but there is surprisingly little harshness about its firmness. There is very little lost motion in the rack-and-pinion steering box and the linkages which connect the small, leather-covered steering wheel to the road wheels, but the lock at low speeds appeared surprisingly poor. The turning circle at such speeds was not measured, because of lack of room — it appeared that it would need something like the Grand Parade to do it on.

It was thus all the more disconcerting to find that at speed the steering seemed desperately "quick" — until it dawned that this car is steered at least as much with the throttle as with the steering wheel. Until then I frightened myself several times by finding myself far too close to the inside of a bend far too soon, coming out wide and most untidily.

Once the penny had dropped completely and I realised just how much more effective this type of "power steering" is on a car which really has the power for it,

Open wide, please. Accessibility of the essential "works" at both front and rear would surely win the approval of dentists, though mechanics have known tubes of the space-frame chassis to get in the way at the wrong moment.

SPECIFICATION

MAKE AND MODEL: Lotus-Alfa XV (sports-racing).

ENGINE: 4-cyl., in-line, water-cooled, twin o.h.c., 2 horizontal Weber 40DCO3 twin-choke carbs., compression ratio about 10 : 1.

BORE AND STROKE: 79·0 x 76·5 mm.

CUBIC CAPACITY: 1,499·5 c.c.

MAXIMUM HORSEPOWER: About 140 b.h.p. at 7,500 r.p.m.

TOP GEAR M.P.H. AT 1,000 R.P.M.: (Fifth) 20·3. 4th (Direct) 17·3.

BRAKES: Girling hydraulic disc; 10 in. diam. outboard at front, 9 in. diam. inboard at rear.

SUSPENSION: (Front) Independent, by coil springs enclosing dampers and twin wishbones, the upper incorporating an anti-roll bar. (Rear) Independent, swing axle, by Chapman strut and radius rod on each side.

TRANSMISSION: Single dry-plate clutch, mechanically operated. Five-speed, manual, all-synchromesh gearbox, central lever.

OVERALL GEAR RATIOS:
- 1st: 13·684
- 2nd: 8·337
- 3rd: 5·699
- 4th: 4·2
- 5th: 3·587
- Rev.: 13·658

FINAL DRIVE RATIO: 4·2. **TYRE SIZE:** 165 x 15 rear, 155 x 15 front.

LENGTH OVERALL: 11 ft. 7¾ ins. **WIDTH:** 5 ft. 2¼ ins.

HEIGHT: 37¼ ins. (Headrest).

CLEARANCE (Laden): 3½ ins.

STEERING: Rack-and-pinion, 1¾ turns lock-to-lock.

TANK CAPACITY: 22 gallons. **SUMP CAPACITY:** 2 gallons.

BOOT CAPACITY: Zero. **WEIGHT EMPTY:** About 1,050 lbs.

WEIGHT AS TESTED: About 1,250 lbs.

PRICE: ?

INTERIOR DIMENSIONS:
- Width of driver's seat: 14¼ ins.
- Width of passenger's seat: academic.
- Headroom: Unlimited.
- Driver's seat to clutch pedal: 22¼ ins.

PERFORMANCE

ACCELERATION THROUGH GEARS:

M.P.H.	Secs.	M.P.H.	Secs.
0—60	6·75	0—100	16·1
0—80	10·35	0—120	27·7

ACCELERATION IN 3RD IN SECS:

M.P.H.	Secs.
80–100	5·5

ACCELERATION IN 4TH IN SECS.

M.P.H.	Secs.
100–120	11·3

STANDING QUARTER MILE: 15·1 secs.

REASONABLE MAXIMUM SPEEDS IN GEARS:
- 1st: 40
- 2nd: 65
- 3rd: 100
- 4th: 135

MAXIMUM SPEED IN TOP: (Actual) 140-plus; (Recorded on test): 130·4 m.p.h.

ACCELERATION AND BRAKING: 0–100 m.p.h.–0 — 21·0 secs.

FUEL CONSUMPTION: 10–13 m.p.g.

TEST CONDITIONS: Fine, warm, dry tarmac, no wind. Altitude 4,500 ft.

---

the car became a positive delight. On the straight, even where fairly bumpy, it ran very true, but anyone who feels the need to hang on tight to something at speeds of 100-plus is recommended not to use the steering wheel of the Lotus for the purpose. He will need a wider road than South Africa can provide.

Furniture and fittings, as is to be expected, are reduced to the minimum, but it is still a very comfortable car for the driver. He sits in a well-fitting bucket seat, right down on the floor, with legs straight out in front of him and supported, respectively, by the cover over the prop-shaft and a vertical aluminium panel inside the body. There are sponge rubber pads at strategic points, and the pedals are well arranged, with brake and accelerator just right for heel and toe operation.

The steering wheel is where it should be, at arms' length, and the only instruments he has to watch are a chronometric tachometer, oil pressure and water temperature gauges, and an ammeter. So he can really watch the road, "aiming" between the bulges over the front wheels and able to see it to within a few feet of the front of the car, in spite of the fact that his personal rear end is only about six inches above its surface. He looks over the windshield, and a crash-hat without a peak is to be preferred unless he wants to give his neck muscles plenty of exercise keeping his head on against the force of the breeze getting under the peak.

It is a sobering thought that this car, with a few mods. which would still leave it with a fabulous performance, could easily be made into a road car which even traffic cops could not fault. In the hands of a reasonably competent driver it would be about twice as fast — and twice as safe — from A to B as the great majority of other cars on the road — but I still feel it would not be quite the thing to take Aunt Agatha shopping in. ●

A close-up of the off-side rear suspension, showing details of the Chapman strut, with its coil spring enclosing the damper, the substantial single radius-rod running forward from its lower end and the swinging half-shaft with dual universals. Mounting the rear disc brakes inboard still further cuts unsprung weight.

TRACK TEST

by

John Blunsden

DIZZY ADDICOTT is a test pilot for the Vickers aircraft company, and like most test pilots he enjoys living dangerously. Some of the things he does as a matter of course—such as locking up a Swift's wheels on a runway at around 200 mph 'to check the coefficient of friction of the runway'—would turn the average man's blood to water. So it comes as no surprise to hear that when he goes motor racing he prefers a real hairy motor car, 'something that will get the old adrenalin juices moving'.

His old Lotus 11, a car with which he did remarkably well against some considerably younger cars, he found on the tame side, so when he drove past the Dorchester Service Station on the way back from Oulton Park one day last year, and saw the ex-David Piper Lotus 15 lying there waiting for a buyer, he stopped. After the inevitable haggling, he signed a cheque and became the new owner of the car, less engine.

John Dabbs, Dizzy's young racing mechanic, now comes on the scene. Last year, when he was working for Jack Brabham, he spent quite a lot of time with John Timanus and Paul Camano, two of Lance Reventlow's mechanics, who leased a couple of adjacent lock-ups when they came over with Lance's Ford Galaxie, prior to the Silverstone International Trophy meeting.

The Americans were full of the strides which had been made in 'competitionising' some of the Transatlantic power units, and in particular they spoke highly of the Buick all-aluminium 3½ litre V8—the unit which Scarab had earmarked for his single-seater Scarab. Dabbs was 'sold', and in due course convinced Addicott that this was just the unit for the Lotus 15.

Bill McCowen and Andrew Hedges had a batch of them in London, and soon the first of these was nestling in its crate alongside the Lotus. The installation, which involved quite an elaborate chassis conversion, was carried out entirely by Dabbs, and the car was made ready just in time for the Boxing Day meeting at Brands Hatch. There was no time to really sort out the car, and it was handling badly that day, and consequently did not perform very well. But since then, the suspension has been sorted out, and the engine 'tweeked', and the result is a very potent sports-racing car!

The Buick V8 has not been extensively modified, because Addicott wants reliability as well as power. The single Rochester carburettor has been replaced by a pair of Holleys, there is an Edelbrock inlet manifold, an Iskenderian camshaft, pushrods and tappets, and special high-compression pistons and bearings. The combustion chambers have been modified, the cylinder heads gas-flowed and the valves have been polished.

Dizzy has been told that the compression ratio is approximately 12 to 1, but this seems to be somewhat on the high side, while the output is quoted as 240 horsepower between 6,000 and 6,500 rpm. About 180 horsepower is developed at 5,000 rpm, and there is even a reading of 70 horsepower as low as 2,000 rpm.

Dabbs has carried out a very clever chassis conversion. Several of the Lotus frame tubes forward of the cockpit bulkhead have been cut away, and the engine has been bolted rigidly between two transverse plates of 3/16 inch Duralumin. The main plate, behind the engine, comes between the power unit and the clutch bell-housing, the three being bolted together as a solid unit. This has the dual advantage of simplicity and excellent heat dissipation, for the Duralumin becomes quite hot during a race, while the unit itself is able to run reasonably cool. Although not originally intended for such a purpose, the bulkhead has solved an overheating problem which has been causing quite a lot of trouble across the Atlantic!

At first, Addicott ran the car with the normal Lotus 15 five-speed combined gearbox and back axle, but the positive-stop gear change was unreliable, and after finding neutral more often than a gear, he decided that he had better invest in an alternative transmission!

20 FORWARD GEARS!

So now the car is running with a Jaguar XK140 four-speed box mated to the Buick single-plate clutch, while as a temporary measure the Lotus-ZF transmission still fits snugly at the back. This gives a remarkably adaptable transmission, with a choice of no less than 20 forward speeds! And there are no problems about changing ratios—this is simply a matter of selecting the appropriate cog in the rear box. But the double gearbox involves quite a big transmission drag, and the intention is to fit a 1952-type Austin A90 back axle.

The remainder of the car is fairly standard, with 10-inch disc brakes for the front wheels, and 9-inch inboard discs at the rear. The front suspension is by coil springs with lower wishbones and single top links, and the Chapman

Blunsden (**above left**) *treads lightly on the right pedal on a slippery Paddock Bend, while Addicott* (**below**) *finds that the situation calls for a quick fag! Well, wouldn't you?* (4986/23A and 4986/17A).

Dizzy Addicott's
LOTUS-BUICK

Above: *The neat installation of the Buick V8 engine to the Lotus 15 chassis was carried out by Addicott's young mechanic John Dabbs. The light-alloy bulkhead behind the engine acts as a mounting plate and a heat dissipator.* (4986/15A).

Below: *Fuel tank for a thirsty car! When tested, the Lotus-Buick still had the Lotus-ZF five-speed rear-mounted gearbox-axle unit, as well as four-speed Jaguar box in the conventional position. Gearing for the circuit was no problem!* (4986/12A).

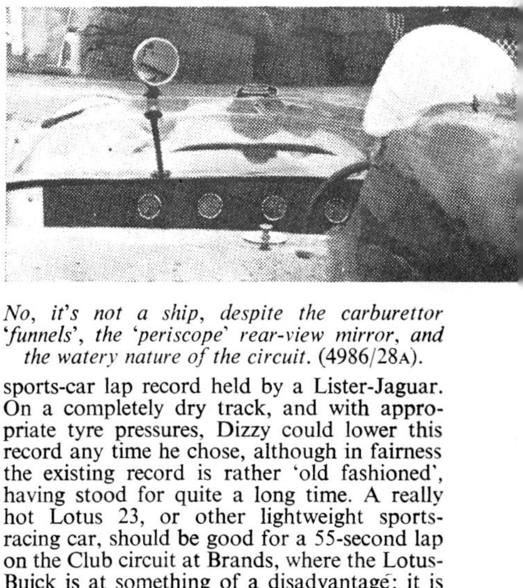

No, it's not a ship, despite the carburettor 'funnels', the 'periscope' rear-view mirror, and the watery nature of the circuit. (4986/28A).

strut system is used at the rear, with the drive shaft acting as one link.

Of course, it had to be pouring with rain when I met up with Dizzy and the Lotus at Brands Hatch for the track test! Not exactly the ideal conditions under which to sample a car like this, and after Dizzy went out for two laps to see that everything was screwed together, and gave a wonderful demonstration of ice driving—the car snaking under power all round the circuit—the adrenalin was flowing freely—mine, not his!

He pulled in, and with a wry smile said 'OK, it's all yours . . . Oh, in case you hadn't noticed, it's like a b . . . ice rink!' And how right he was. Believe me, I took it very gently during my first spell in the cockpit, and I was thankful to find that the engine, although very powerful, had a comfortingly smooth torque curve. With a little care it was not too difficult to stop the rear wheels spinning, or to prevent the tail and the nose changing ends. Fortunately, later in the morning, the weather improved quickly, and I was able to go out again on an almost dry circuit, and really appreciate the engine power.

Being longer in the leg than Dizzy, I found the cockpit somewhat cramped, and the tops of my legs were touching the steering wheel for most of the time. This could have been adjusted had there been sufficient time, but with the wheel where I really needed it, it would have been too close to the screen, which had been specially modified for Dizzy.

The Buick V8, despite its 'wuffling' exhaust, is a very smooth unit indeed, with tremendous torque right through the range. So much so, that I was able to lap Brands at racing speeds using third gear throughout, with the rear box fixed in fifth. From the transmission point of view, this must be one of the most restful of all circuit cars!

All Lotus 15s seem to understeer slightly, and with the Buick unit installed the tendency is more pronounced. In fact, on the slower corners I found that a lot of power half-way round will tend to push the nose straight on. The technique, therefore, is to give a short dab of throttle, then lift off to let the front dig in again, and the back end to come round slightly.

On the faster curves the best result seems to be gained by approaching the bend almost too fast, then putting on some lock to break the tail away. Then, immediately the understeer has been killed the car can be driven round smoothly under power.

I found the Lotus-Buick an exhilarating car to drive. The engine power is such that it has to be fed in carefully coming out of corners if the back end is to remain stable, but it is a refreshing change to find a competitive car with more power than roadholding, instead of the other way round.

The dry spell lasted for only a few minutes, and there was not really time to adjust the tyre pressures from their 'wet' settings of 25 pounds front, 24 pounds rear. (Something like 32 front, 30 rear would have been preferable in the dry).

The result of the softer tyres was to still further increase the car's inherent understeer, and to give a slight build-up in body roll. The steering also became heavier, due to the higher cornering speed, and I found that I was having to use every inch of the track coming out of the bends.

In view of all this, it was pleasing to find the car lapping consistently in 59 seconds dead, which is some 1.6 seconds outside the existing sports-car lap record held by a Lister-Jaguar. On a completely dry track, and with appropriate tyre pressures, Dizzy could lower this record any time he chose, although in fairness the existing record is rather 'old fashioned', having stood for quite a long time. A really hot Lotus 23, or other lightweight sports-racing car, should be good for a 55-second lap on the Club circuit at Brands, where the Lotus-Buick is at something of a disadvantage; it is on the faster circuits that its abundant horse-power stands to be used most effectively and enjoyed to its maximum.

By current standards, Dizzy's car calls for quite a lot of work in the cockpit, the brake pedal in particular demanding a heavy push, although the stopping power is there. But it is a most enjoyable car for all that, not least because it has to be treated with considerable respect.

To mate a 'foreign' engine, born thousands of miles away, with a not-so-new British sports-racing chassis, is a bold effort, but I am glad to say that it is already being rewarded by the sight of the chequered flag. But success is not everything; the main thing is that this hybrid Lotus is giving its owner a lot of pleasure on the circuits and the hills. As Dizzy put it to me, 'I like to go through life with a little bit of fear, and the Lotus-Buick gives me just about the right amount'. After sampling it in the wet, I know exactly what he means!

Full Bore Lotus 15

Michael Bowler tries a lightweight sports-racer, product of Chapman and a pair of Costins; centre spread shows owner Mike Weatherill at Silverstone

UNLESS you were really well versed in Lotus lore at the time, you may find it rather difficult to sort out Colin Chapman's early forays into lightweight streamlined sports cars in the 1954–9 period; that would take you from Mks8 to 17, before the mid-engined cars came along. Fifteen years on, the latest F1 car is the 77; it is an output which averages three creations a year from the dawn of Lotus. We'll return to the lead-in later, but this is concerned with a 1959 Lotus 15 series 3 which is one of a pair of XVs entered for Le Mans in 1959, in the days when Chapman was still speaking to the organisers and regarded the 24-hours as one of the great challenges.

Mike Weatherill, who used to race 7, 11 and Elite in those days, owns this one and was taking part in a test day at Goodwood where I joined him. Goodwood, with its air of sad neglect, is still a nice circuit to drive round and with its dips and adverse cambers is much more of a challenge than, say, Silverstone. I tend to use Silverstone because I know it so well and don't have to waste valuable track-test time learning the circuit; also, there is so much space and the corners come up one at a time, that it is not too hard to assess someone else's valuable motorcar in minimum time with minimum risk. Sadly I never raced at Goodwood although I have watched many races there, including those historic 9-hour events, and was once driven round by Bruce McLaren in an M6B; which leads up to the fact that no demon lap times were recorded for obvious reasons.

The 15 came with a choice of Climax engines from $1\frac{1}{2}$–$2\frac{1}{2}$-litres. Awaiting the installation of a 2-litre, this one was fitted with the $1\frac{1}{2}$-litre twin-cam FPF with a preservative rev limit of 6000rpm, against the originally quoted 142bhp at 7200rpm. In common with the production series 2 and 3, a normal four-speed gearbox is fitted, rather than the Chapman integral gearbox/final drive of the early 15s and of course the F1/2 12 and 16.

There is actually a door, which opens enough for one to put a gentle foot on to a convenient chassis tube on the inside of the sill and then lower away into the narrow confines of the seating area.

Mike Weatheril is somewhat bigger and drives without a seat; I had to sit on and be pressed forward by suitable sorbo padding. Like a lot of "fours" in racing vehicles, the engine isn't particularly smooth at rest, but as you move off with a bit of revs and a bit of load, it smooths out and pulls strongly from the middle range and would be quite happy beyond 6000rpm.

Despite sorbo the driving position was ideal; not much room for feet or even for twirling elbows, but then a Lotus never has required much twirling and the lock is fairly limited by the bodywork. You sit back and steer at arm's length with the gear lever within a handspan of the left hand. With a slight kick-up on the driver's side of the perspex screen, 5ft 8in can look over the top without getting windswept; it was only in the left-handed St. Mary's dip that I found I had to look through it. The mirror sits on top of the screen with stays down to the scuttle top and gives a view that can be described as adequate, without being at all comprehensive.

With well under 10cwt and around 120bhp to play with – up to 6000rpm – the acceleration is brisk without being startling; it just moves up rapidly to 100mph (5300rpm) and beyond without any obvious effort so good are the aerodynamics. The bonnet starts to flap a bit beyond 90mph. The necessary silencer for Goodwood made it very quiet, too, at the expense of a rather warm right thigh – the system runs inside the sill to its outlet just in front of the rear wheel. The gearbox is the ZF unit that was available on Elites at the time and is very slick in its short travel movement, with ratios that suit the car well.

It is difficult to put across the level of roadholding on any car without a g-meter, but in their heyday those Lotus sports cars were always beating cars of considerably greater capacity, so the roadholding was obviously better than most. Even now, it still feels very good even on appropriately narrow tyres – $5.00L \times 15$ front and $5.50L \times 15$ rear, Dunlop's, of course. There is a complete absence of apparent roll and the car just responds to the steering wheel; on the overrun and under braking the rear suspension design countersteers which would lead to oversteer under power but the overall system is set up to understeer under power for slower corners, which the aerodynamics adjust to slight oversteer on faster corners. Apart from spring rates and damper settings there isn't a lot of adjustment available as roll- bars require replacement. In fact on slow corners there is enough power surplus to get through the understeer – round Woodcote for instance and out of the chicane.

Light cars don't take a lot of effort to stop with $9\frac{1}{2}$in dia discs all round, and the 15 seems to go almost impossibly deep into corners before the slightly soft pedal anchors the car firmly down. It is a very reassuring car to drive in all ways and as long as you have enough engine spares – FPFs are getting rare – it is easy to maintain and keep going; Herald uprights, ZF box (or an MGA equivalent) and BMC A-series differential are easier to find than many equivalents on other makes. I enjoyed it very much and it seemed an eminently suitable car in which to go historic racing, although doubtless one would soon start wanting the extra power of the 2 or $2\frac{1}{2}$-litre.

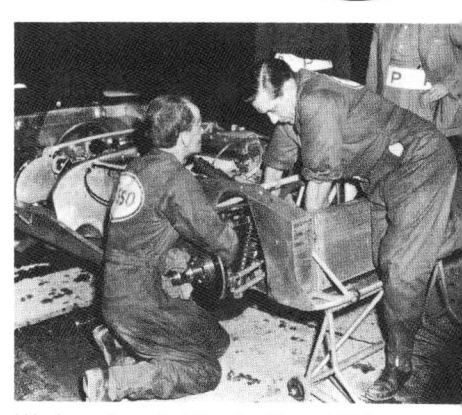

Work on the sole 15 at Le Mans 1959 to replace broken suspension; note centre-lock adapter hub and oil cooler alongside radiator.

Le Mans 1959 and final drive change after practice; engine canted to left on series 3. Positive stop five-speed box mounted vertically was used on this car.

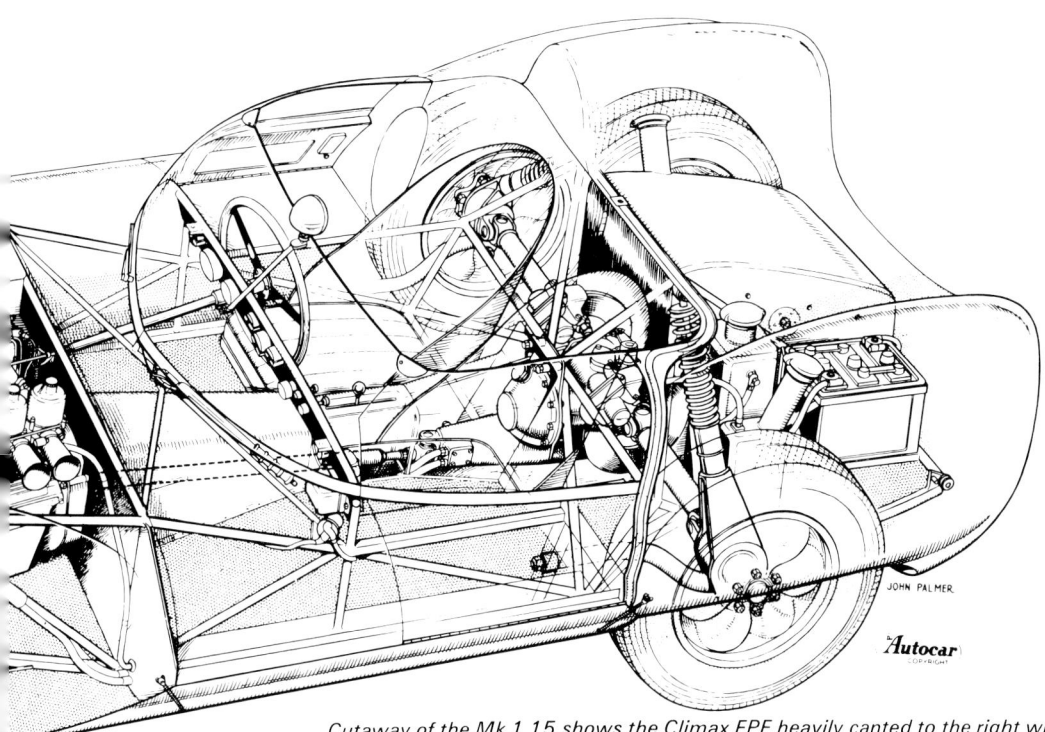

Cutaway of the Mk.1 15 shows the Climax FPF heavily canted to the right with twin-choke SUs on long curved manifolds. Front suspension has forward upper link as part of anti-roll bar. Final drive gearbox uses oil from the engine; lever gate is fore-and-aft zig-zag.

Graham Hill leaps out of the car during the night at Le Mans while mechanics prepare to inspect the front suspension, above. Graham Hill in a 15 (the same perhaps) at the 1959 TT.

Lotus 15

History

It is logical to start the story of the 15 with the 8 which was the first of the aerodynamically shaped Lotus sports-racers. Peter Gammon's MG-engined Mk6 was doing well in 1953 and Chapman wanted to take on the 1500cc "establishment", which at that time meant Cooper, Tojeiro, Connaught and, of course, Porsche. Lotus, at that time, meant Colin Chapman and Mike Costin, so Frank Costin was brought in to design the bodywork of the new car while Chapman evolved a chassis better than that of the 6. It was still a lightweight space frame and retained the divided or swing-axle front suspension but used a de Dion at the rear with inboard drums and it was sprung by a single transverse helical spring above. Brakes were drums all round with air ducting. The body was certainly a departure from that of the usual sports car and was effectively Frank Costin's first essay into automobile aerodynamics. Thus, it had a long, penetrating nose, coming almost to a point at hub-height with the extension of the full-length undertray, while the tail extended back and up, into pronounced fins to give the course stability required in the aircraft world; the rear wheels were faired in with spats – removed or cut back on some cars – while the front wheel arches followed the shape of the wheel in front but were cut vertically behind close to the wheel. The exhaust system was contained in the sills and exited in front of the rear wheel. The popular choice of engine was the uprated TC of 1467cc, but the Climax 1100 was also fitted and John Coombs used a 1¼-litre Connaught engine, which was eventually the fastest 8. The final drive incidentally was cooled by a prop-shaft-driven pump and oil from the engine.

For 1955 some were wanting to install ever larger engines in their 8s, notably Mike Anthony who wanted to put a Bristol engine in. Enlarging the engine compartment and putting a bulge in the bonnet-top to clear even a lowered Bristol was all that was outwardly necessary, but underneath, disc brakes were added, while the de Dion was located on the usual radius arm and transverse rod with conventional coil/damper units. This was the Lotus 10.

Meanwhile, Chapman had been working on a version of the 8 for smaller engines, notably the 1100 FWA Climax and perhaps the 1500 FWB version. The idea was to use as many common parts as possible in the 9 in its competition form and the 10, hence the revised de Dion location with special cast elektron hub-carriers. Lighter than the 8, the 9 used the same wheelbase, but was two feet shorter overall, losing a little in the nose, but rather more behind, although taller fins kept the course stability the same; this had been as a result of wool-tuft tests with Frank Costin strapped to the bonnet for some runs! The rear of the front wheel arch was less suddenly chopped into the body with a more gradual escape path for the air around the wheels.

The 9 came in Club form with normal drum brakes and a Ford 10 rear axle, using the de Dion locating linkage; in its Le Mans competition form, the drums were steel-lined Elektron castings of, initially, 9in diameter, rising to 11in. At the front the divided axle was retained but the roll centre lowered by dropping the pivot point. Chapman's fears of gyroscopic reaction at high speeds had not been realised and it was reasonable to continue with the swing axle.

The Le Mans came after Chapman and Ron Flockhart had taken a 9 to Le Mans; Chapman had been racing with the 1½-litre MG engine, but took an 1100 Climax car to Le Mans. This had heavier gauge panelling and discs to help negotiate Mulsanne. After one hour the Lotus was leading the 1100 class just ahead of the Duntov/Veuillet Porsche which eventually finished 13th, but that and another 356 were soon ahead and the Lotus was fighting it out with the Wadsworth/Brown Cooper-Climax. Unfortunately the car was disqualified after 11 hours, when Chapman reversed out of a sandbank at Arnage without being ushered by a marshal; at this point they were 27th overall and ahead of the Cooper which went on to take 21st place and 3rd in the 1100 class.

With the 9 and 10 in various forms running concurrently in 1955, Chapman decided to produce just one model for 1956 and that was the 11. This was to be available in three forms under the same skin; the 11 retained the same scuttle height as that of the 9 but the bonnet dropped away more quickly, which accentuated the wheel humps. At both ends the wheels were hidden to just above hub height. The rear finning had all but gone, although high speed competition cars could have a headrest fairing to retain the sidewind stability. It was six inches shorter than the 9 and the new frame gave a wheelbase 2½in shorter; like the 9, it was designed to take the Climax engine in FWA and FWB forms, giving 83 or 100bhp. All models retained the divided axle, but the Le Mans still had de Dion rear suspension, still with upper and lower radius arms, but with an inclined arm on the off-side to make up an A-bracket with the lower radius arm and provide lateral location. 9½in dia discs were fitted all round and the car scaled just under 8 cwt. The height to the scuttle top was just 2ft 3in, while even to the top of the fin it was only 3ft 1in.

The Club model came with a BMC axle, using the same location as the de Dion version, drum brakes all round and the 1100 Climax. Finally the Sports model was tailored for the Ford 1172 engine. This year's return to Le Mans saw three cars built specially, with slightly wider cockpit areas and full-width screens for the regulations – there were two 1100s and one 1500. Cliff Allison's 1100 was put out by a dog on the Mulsanne straight at dawn, then Chapman's 1500 broke a big-end bolt with 4 hours to go when it was lying 18th, although it had been as high as 11th. However the remaining Bicknell/Jopp 1100 kept going till the end and finished an astounding 7th, winning the 1100 class from the Hugus/Bentley Cooper, 8th.

Meanwhile, Chapman had been working on the first single-seater Lotus, the 12 for the 1500 F2, with the new dohc FPF "four" giving some 142bhp at 7200rpm. This used a space frame chassis, but dispensed with the divided axle front suspension in favour of wishbones in which the forward link of the upper wishbone formed an arm of the anti-roll bar. At the rear, the original design had included a de Dion tube with single radius arms, a central link and a semi-trailing Panhard rod, but this was dispensed with, in favour of a design which allowed camber change with lessening fuel loads and the Chapman strut was born; this used a MacPherson strut arrangement with an aluminium hub carrier, a shrunk-in coil/spring damper strut, with the lateral location on the drive shaft and an inclined radius arm.

The gearbox arrangement used a Lotus design integral with the final drive. Using a low transmission line with a two-piece prop shaft the gearbox was a simple two-shaft unit with five pairs of gears in constant mesh, engaged by dogs and controlled by a lever, which zig-zagged forwards for higher gears and back for downchanges – an ingenious device which required a little early sorting in its lubrication but otherwise worked fairly well for that torque application. The 12 marked the first appearance of the wobbly-web bolt-on magnesium alloy wheels, too.

For 1957, the 11 continued, but in series 2 form for the two Le Mans models – the Le Mans 85 and Le Mans 150 the latter using the FPF unit. The Series 2 changes were to use the wishbone front suspension from the 12 and enlarge the de Dion tube to take bigger bearings, while the bodywork was flared out to take the wider wheels; some were using wobbly-webs instead of the old knock-on spoked variety.

Le Mans 1957 saw five 11s entered with one on the reserve list – a 1500 FPF, three 1100s and a 750 with only the latter, which would probably not need a tyre change, on the bolt-on wheels. Unfortunately, the FPF dropped a valve in practice and that was that, so four cars started and four cars finished, with the MacKay-Fraser/Chamberlain car finishing 9th overall and winning the 1100 class, and the Allison/Hall 750 winning its class and the Index of Performance in 14th place overall, averaging 90mph – 10mph faster than the previous DB Panhard's speed.

With the 1500 breaking the class record in practice, Chapman's thoughts for 1958 were turning towards outright victo.y when he conceived the 15 to

John Clark of PAO Preparations, above, who rebuilt the Lotus. Below, Climax FPF in 1½-litre form; oil cooler behind right front wheel.

take the FPF in 2 and 2·2-litre forms. This was really the successor to the 10 for bigger engines, but embodied all that had been learnt in the series 2 11s with the addition of the 12's strut rear suspension. The radius arm was mounted farther out than with the single seater and was a dog-legged trailing radius arm. For the gearbox, the Lotus 12 unit was used with the gear selection changed to the 16's positive-stop motor-cycle system, back for downchanges and forward for upwards. As a successor to the 10 the 15 used the 88-in wheelbase – three inches up on the 11 and three inches longer, too. The engine was canted over 60° to the right with special long curved manifolds for the Webers or twin-choke SUs, which the 12s had been using, this allowed the car to be even lower than the 11 at 2ft to the top of the scuttle. The fins were similar to those of the 11, while the head-fairing became standard, since it housed the vertical spare wheel; it was a very slippery shape which had a theoretical maximum of 205mph on the 2·2-litre FPF. To cater for the Appendix C rules, the cockpit was larger than an 11's and the screen was a full-width item carefully profiled. They were very fast first time out at the British Empire Trophy in 1958, with Hill taking the lap record at Oulton Park, which Moss had to equal in the DBR2 Aston to stay in front of Allison in the final.

Le Mans 1958 saw six specially prepared Lotus, four works cars and two privateers. The canted engine with the long curving inlets had proved to lose power so the 2-litre car had the FPF canted 17° to the left, like the 12. Hill and Allison were to

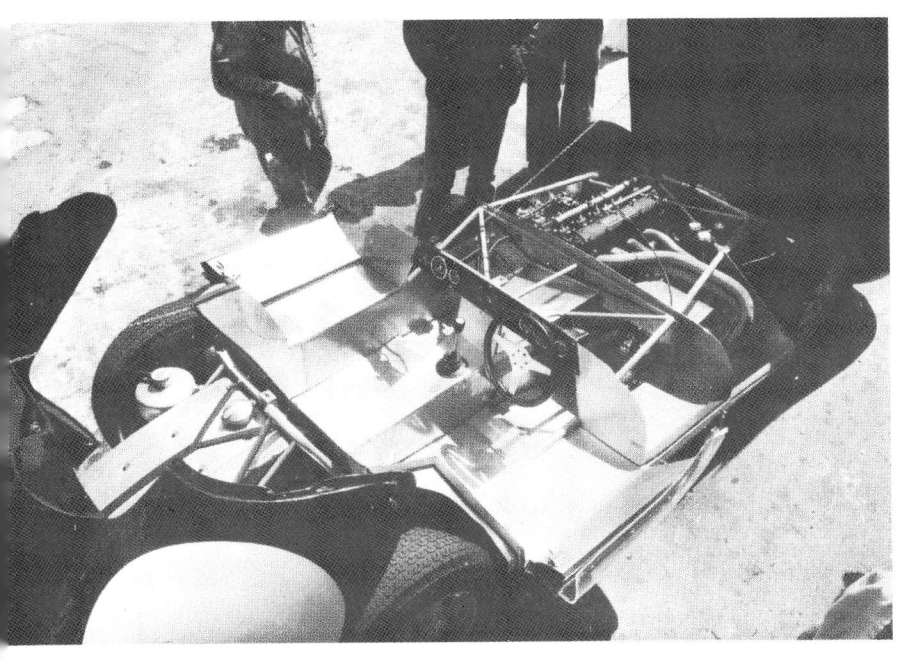

General layout and design is shown above with round and square tubes for the chassis. Below left, battery is forward on this car compared with Le Mans '59 car and Series 1 15s. Overhead light reflects the 15's slippery curves, below.

Above, front suspension shows anti-roll bar behind transverse top link. Below, Chapman strut rear suspension uses fixed length drive shaft and dog-leg trailing arm.

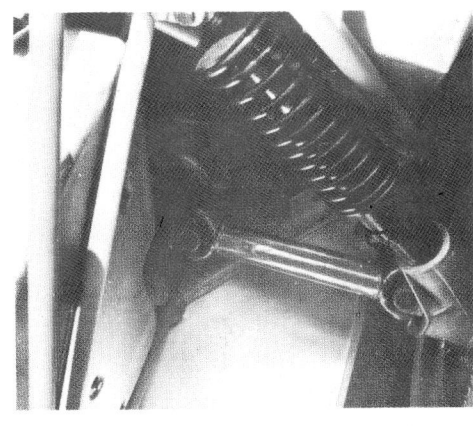

drive the 2-litre 15 with an eye to possible outright victory. Chamberlain/Loveley had the 1·5-litre, Ireland and Michael Taylor the 1100cc 11, and Stacey/Dickson a 750cc 11, with the FWM single-cam engine up to 750, rather than the modified FWA of the previous year. Another FWM 11 and an 1100cc 11 were private entries.

The 750cc cars saved transmission losses with live axles and were using drum brakes and magnesium wheels, while the 15s had knock-ons. Unfortunately it was a disastrous year for Lotus; the 2-litre had gone impressively fast in practice, but blew a gasket after three laps, the 1·5-litre had ignition trouble and was finally shunted. One 1100 wasn't allowed to restart after spinning on the Mulsanne straight, but the other kept going and had been up to 12th place, before the distributor failed after 19 hours, when it was the sole 1100 running; one 750 was involved in a White House shunt while the Stacey/Dickson 750 was the sole surviving Lotus in 20th position and well behind the other 750s.

In mid-'58 a series 2 version of the 15 was announced as an export version for easier servicing; consequently it used a conventional BMC B-series box with a BMC A-series final drive in a Lotus casing. By now, the F1 16 was in regular use as an improved 12 using the positive stop gearbox under a new Costin designed skin. One of the 15's more memorable performances in 1958 was at the British GP where Salvadori in Coombs' 2-litre came second to Moss' Lister-Jaguar to win the 2-litre class, while Allison was third winning the 1500

class and Stacey fifth to win the 1100 class in his 11.

The year 1959 saw the arrival of the 11's replacement for small capacity engines and that was the 17, shorter, narrower and even lower than the 11; it followed on from the 16 in using some glass-fibre panels. The rear suspension used the Chapman strut system and the front suspension, too, used a strut although this was changed to wishbones later. It was available with the FWM or FWE engines. The 15 continued as the series 3 with a stiffer chassis, the upper wishbone was reversed to allow a bigger radiator – the anti-roll bar was now behind hub-centre line – and the engine was now angled like the Le Mans 2-litre at 17° to the left; the transmission followed the series 2 in having a separate gearbox and final drive.

For Le Mans outright victory was again the goal and a 2½-litre FPF was entered for Hill and Derek Jolly while Ireland/Stacey were to have a 2-litre. A pair of 17s had FWM engines with an eye on the Index of Performance. In fact only one 15 arrived with a 2-litre engine, using a version of the 16 gearbox, which now lay on its side in the single-seater but was vertical in the 15. The 2-litre unit was replaced by a 2½-litre before the race and the car, driven by Hill/Jolly was 7th at the end of the first hour but lost time with a prop-shaft bearing failure, then broke a wishbone and finally dropped a rod. The two 17s suffered distributor trouble which caused overheating, and it was left to the Elites to maintain the Lotus name, with Lumsden/Riley finishing 8th and Clark/Whitmore 10th.

At the Brands F2 meeting Hill won in the 2½-litre 15 from David Piper's 2-litre. The TT saw 15s out with 2-litre engines; Hill's car had ignition trouble and Piper's crashed when a tyre failed.

It is probably fair to say that at that time, the 15 suffered from lack of development while the accent was on Grand Prix racing. At the end of 1959 the mid-engined era had arrived and the 18 was Lotus' ubiquitous single-seater, which led to the Monte Carlo 19 and the 15 was instantly obsolete.

Whether this was the final sole Le Mans 15 is not certain, but it was sold by the works to Malcolm Templeton at the end of 1959 and he raced it in Ireland. The next owner was Roy Pierpoint who had some stirring dices with Dizzy Addicott on the Buick-engined 15 during the mid-sixties. I'm not too sure what happened in the interim, but come 1972 it was in the hands of Lotus enthusiast Alan Brownlee, and Chris Renwick drove it in the Le Mans Cinquantenaire in 1973. Mike Weatherill acquired it at the end of that year and since he was involved with PAO Preparations (see September issue) they rebuilt the car from stem to stern in their immaculate fashion. Where appropriate everything is cadmium or nickel plated or stove-enamelled; the chassis is rust-proofed with stove-enamel on top of zinc spray, while the wheel arches are coated in a sort of undersealant, called Body Schuts which stops stone chipping. The undertray is polished aluminium. As is often the case, it is probably in far better condition than when it was racing Internationally, and as I said before a very pleasant car to drive as well as look at.●

From the days when the racing was richly flavored and sports cars had their engines at the front. The last of the greats was a Lotus, the...

FINE FIFTEEN

The Lotus Fifteen was a remarkably successful sports-racer, a beautiful little machine that wrote a fitting finale for the front-engine brigade as the rear-engine models began opening a whole new chapter. Three Fifteens came to Australia. Their distinguished careers are here unravelled for the record by Graham Howard, who also gratefully acknowledges assistance given by Adrien and Marc Schagen, tireless Lotus historians and the justly respected Archivists of Club Lotus Australia.

"THE CANNONBALL FIFTEEN," Gordon Wilkins called it in his description of the prototype Lotus 15, nearly 20 years ago in SPORTS CAR WORLD.

It was Lotus's big-banger sports car of the late 1950s, with the still-stretching Coventry Climax twin-cam four of either 1.5 or 2.0 litres as propellant, and a compact Chapman/Costin chassis (just 60 cm high at the scuttle) controlling the trajectory.

While probably not more than 30 Fifteens were built in all (Series One and Two in 1958, and about a half-dozen of the Series Three in 1959), they were very successful machines in short-distance UK racing, in the hands of private owners as well as works drivers.

And so they should have been. With a dry weight of 445 kg (980 lb, or 8.6 cwt in those days) the Fifteen offered 140 pre-Metric horsepower and 112 lb-ft of torque in 1.5-litre form, or about 170 horsepower and 160 lb-ft as a two-litre, in a chassis which got its power to the ground very well indeed.

Thus during 1958, especially in the more flexible two-litre form, well-driven Fifteens left D-type Jaguars astern, and would only be challenged for outright victories by works Listers and Aston Martins of nearly twice the capacity.

Yet major successes — long-distance races like Le Mans or the Tourist Trophy, where the earlier Elevens had scored some notable wins — eluded the Fifteen in Europe, and its career as a front-line contender was fading by the 1960 season.

But what was wilting in Europe was beginning to blossom in Australia. Three Fifteens — a surprising number, considering the small total production — found their way here, and led amazingly long and successful racing lives. The three were: chassis 608, imported by Derek Jolly in 1958; 609, imported by Ann Thomson in 1961; and 623, imported by Leaton Motors in 1959.

Each car carved a place for itself in Australian racing history of the 1960s — 608 taking the-then Australian Lotus agent Derek Jolly to some classic sports-car wins, then rebounding into prominence driven by young Bevan Gibson; 609 racing for eight years straight in Queensland and — like 608 in Gibson's hands — defying the rear-engine brigade, in this case with Glynn Scott at the wheel; and 632, the ultimate Cannonball, rocketing Frank Matich to stardom.

Each of these cars is significantly different, and also interestingly special mechanically, so that before looking more closely at these ones, some briefing on the Fifteen in general is a good idea.

The very first Fifteens differed from all later ones in having the engine laid over some 60 degrees to starboard, permitting a perfectly flat (and aesthetically stunning) bonnet line between the wheel arches, albeit at the cost of available space for any diagonal bracing for the top of the engine bay. In all other ways, the early Series One cars did not noticeably differ from the finalised Series One. Derek Jolly's car, as landed in 1958, arrived in the later Series One form, whereas Ann Thomson's — originally owned by John Coombs and raced by Roy Salvadori — was built with an inclined engine.

Chassis of the Fifteen was a 30 kg spaceframe in 18 and 20 gauge mild steel; it was of elegant simplicity, and reminiscent of the concurrent Lotus 16 GP car. While this was the era of "Team Shambles" in Lotus racing, the actual design of the cars was shrewd indeed, with the 15 and 16 having many components in common. In the case of the front suspension (with wishbones incorporating the anti-roll bar as the front half of the top A-arm) components were common with the Series Two Elevens, the Sevens, the Elite and the Formula Two 12. Rationalisation indeed. The 15 and 16 also shared the variations in engine inclination, and of course shared the Chapman-strut rear suspension principle, although the wider chassis of the 15 required that the radius arm be shorter, and cranked into an S-shape — a necessary violation of the designer's creed of straight tubes.

Like the smaller-capacity Eleven, the Fifteen was available with either wire or cast-magnesium 15-inch wheels, which (again like the Eleven) had the same rim width front and rear. On the 1958 cars, this width was a mere four inches, carrying 4.50 front and 5.50 rear tyres. Possibly the 1959 cars ran four-and-a-halves, but (at least in the case of chassis 623) widths were still the same front and rear. Remember, the wide-tyre revolution was still some years away, and Chapman's primary concern until at least 1960 was minimisation of unsprung weight by keeping both wheel and tyre as small as possible.

Despite its small overall size, the Fifteen had the *standard* Lotus track and wheelbase of the day — that is, in units of that period, 88-inch wheelbase and just under 48-inch track. These dimensions had been established with the Eleven, and were used with the Seven, the Twelve, and the Sixteen.

Australian debut: Derek Jolly's 1.5-litre Fifteen on the Bathurst grid in October 1958, prior to start of Australian Tourist Trophy. Note "Team Lotus" insignia on door, early-style short bonnet with separate scuttle panel. In background, on left of trio behind car 8 (the Prad Holden) is bodybuilder Stan Brown, who worked with Lotus bodybuilders Williams & Pritchard before emigrating to Australia.

Carried over from the 12 was the somewhat controversial Lotus five-speed gearbox, a thing of Swiss-watch subtlety and elegance, but still of doubtful reliability nearly a year after its introduction. Rear-mounted, in unit with the differential, it carried its five ratios in less than nine cm (3½ inches) of length, with the output gears fixed on the long differential pinion shaft, and the input gears spinning free until progressively selected by a migrating spline which was itself splined to the tailshaft. This gearbox was very much the Achilles Heel of the Fifteen, and in fact substitution of the less-subtle, but infinitely more reliable, BMC B-series gearbox bolted to the engine, and of the proven Lotus Elite diff-case, distinguished the Series Two cars introduced later in 1958.

However, to start with it was the engines that gave the biggest headaches. Present-day Climax FPF enthusiasts would shudder to hear the heresies Lotus committed on those early engines, and the very conservative gentlemen at Coventry Climax undoubtedly felt the same way. To accommodate the inclined engine, one of the dry-sump scavenge pumps was discarded and the other modified, and the sump itself was drastically reshaped; the inlet ports were counterbored to take spigots for the manifolding, which had to incorporate a 30-degree droop. No matter how hard Climax tried (and to give them their due, they tried hard) the inclined engine was about nine horsepower short of upright-engine figures, and suffered cooling and oiling problems.

None of these things was happening to the FPF engine in rival Coopers, so for Le Mans Lotus bit on the bullet and produced two cars (a 1.5 and a two-litre) with engines inclined a mere 17 degrees the other way . . . just one degree different to the Cooper! This gave the upright-engined Fifteens a distinctively long and slim bonnet-blister which was reputedly damaging aerodynamically, but the reliability must have been some compensation. Apart from a continuing series of enlargements to the water and oil cooling radiators, the 1958 Fifteen had been finalised.

For 1959, the Series Three car was announced, offering a simpler chassis mainly resulting from re-positioning the front anti-roll bar to become the rear link — instead of the front — in the top wishbone. Engine position, and the important diagonal across the top of the engine bay, carried on from the upright-engine 1958 car. A small change was visible in the cockpit, where the Series Three now had two small down-tubes from the dash, meeting a transverse tube which ran across the floor, whereas the earlier Fifteens had relied solely on the stressed tailshaft cover to strengthen the floor and to provide gearbox mounting for the B-series box.

Press pictures of the 1959 car show it with the BMC gearbox but at least two cars were built with the very compact, front-mounted ZF S4-12 all-synchro four-

Sprint winner: Graham Hill in one of the early works 15s, racing at Silverstone in May 1958, where he won a short Under-1500 sports car event. This angle shows the ultra-low bonnet line obtained with the steeply-inclined installation of the twin-cam Climax engine; compare with the visibly taller bonnet line of the following car (Westcott's Lotus 11) which has its single-cam Climax at only 10 degrees from vertical.

"He loved that car": Glyn Scott in Ann Thomson's 1500 cm³ pushrod Ford-engined Series I Fifteen, hammering through the BP sweeper at Lowood.

speed box, and another had a probably-unique development of the Lotus five-speeder which carried the gears astern of the differential.

The existence of at least two ZF-gearbox cars can be supported because there are two such cars in Australasia — one the Leaton Motors 2.5-litre car, the other a 2.0-litre which went to New Zealand for 19-year old Jim Palmer. And we are fortunate in having the unique five-speeder too, because this box was fitted to Derek Jolly's car. That raises the question of how a 1959 gearbox found its way into a 1958 car. The answer involves what is probably the most contentious item of Fifteen history, here settled in print for the first time.

Jolly's car, chassis 608, was one of the two Fifteens that Team Lotus ran at Le Mans 1958. One was a 1.5-litre, the other a 2.0 which caused quite a stir with its fast practice laps, but which retired embarrassingly early (blown head gasket) in the race itself. The 1.5, shared by the American Lotuseers Jay Chamberlain and Pete Lovely, went well in patches between pit stops, and became one of the victims of violent rainstorms during the night when it crashed avoiding a slower car and was in turn centre-punched by a spinning Ferrari.

The sparse published information of the period merely notes that Jolly bought "an ex-Le Mans car", but considering the damage the 1.5-litre car suffered, and the very original appearance of his car when it turned up at Bathurst in October 1958, it may be reasonable to conclude Jolly had bought the two-litre chassis and had a 1.5 engine fitted. Jolly's approach to his racing — do it right, do it reliably — also hints that he may have preferred the smaller-capacity engine anyway, both as a stepping-stone from the 1100 single-cam Climax used in his Decca Special, and also as a gentler companion for the Lotus-12-type gearbox which is what his car used at that stage.

I remember watching the car's Bathurst debut, and feeling that it didn't seem to have such brilliant acceleration — not surprising really with that peaky 1.5-litre engine, compared with three-litre Astons and Maseratis, or 3.4-litre D-types and Jaguar-engined devices such as the Phillips Cooper, or the Cantwell Tojiero.

Nonetheless, Jolly drove a controlled race and duly finished second, in a race won after a great drive by MacKay in his ex-works DB3-S. Next day, Jolly scored his first win, walking away with the sportscar support race to the memorable Davison/Jones/Gray duel in the Australian Grand Prix. It was a very impressive start.

Then it all came crashing down at Albert Park, when Jolly put the car heavily into a tree, doing himself a lot of hurt, and smashing the car badly. He had been suffering from exhaust fumes from a broken tailpipe, and there is also indication that a rear radius arm tore out from the chassis. But whatever the story, the car — having shone brightly in a very brief period — had come to a rather comprehensive stop.

So back the wreck went to the factory, and chassis 608 did not run in Australia again until late 1959. There is no doubt items of the crashed car were incorporated in the rebuild, but no doubt either that the opportunity was taken to use Series Three features wherever possible. Externally, the most easily recognised is the later style of bonnet, which extends right to the dashboard and carries the centre section of the carefully-curved perspex screen — whereas Series Ones and Twos had a shorter bonnet and a separate scuttle panel, very much in the style of Lotus Elevens.

The Jolly car in rebuilt form also had a very different style of engine bulge — wider based, more gently curved, and open at both ends. There may have been areodynamic reasons for this, but as well the engine under the bulge was now a late-series two-litre, with the taller and far stronger 2.5-litre block and bottom end. Additionally, the original five-speed gearbox — in which the gears were carried just ahead of the differential — had been replaced by a new design, with the gears astern of the crown-wheel and pinion, but on the same fore-and-aft centreline. This meant gears could be swapped far more easily, and it was announced this box would be an option for sports cars. In fact, it seems likely that only the one box was ever built, although the same principles were used — in a slightly different casing — for Grand Prix Lotus 18s, and the closely-related Lotus 19 sports car.

Team Lotus had, earlier in 1959, announced its intention to contest Le Mans with a pair of customer-owned 2.5-litre Fifteens. But as noted earlier this was a time when Lotus resources were spread very thin, an illustration being that only one Fifteen arrived at Le Mans, and that with two-litre engine; the first appearance of the rebuilt Jolly car, still carrying its original chassis number.

So the Jolly car emerges (after nearly 20 years of conjecture) as the *real* 1959 Le Mans 2.5-litre, an identity which has on occasion been claimed for the Leaton Motors car, and, more recently, also claimed for a copiously-restored two-litre Fifteen running in UK historic events. Jolly's car is probably also the only Lotus other than an Elite or two (for example, the very historic Elite best known by its UK registration, WUU-2, now owned by Adelaide collector John Blanden) to have ever contested more than one Le Mans race. And for 1959 Jolly shared the car with Graham Hill.

The two-litre engine was replaced with a Lotus-owned 2.5 after the first practice session, and the untested gearbox showed itself keen to unscrew the nut on the end of the pinion shaft because this shaft now rotated in the opposite direction to previous gearboxes. Nonetheless, despite these indications of haste, the car survived practice and in fact ran for more than 10 hours of the race. Graham Hill at one stage had the car as high as seventh outright — before its habit of jumping out of gear caught co-driver Jolly at 120 mph, changing up to fifth on the very fast run to Arnage. In traditional Climax fashion, number four rod hacked the block almost in half, demolished the starter-motor for good measure.

Having again failed at Le Mans, the car was returned to the factory (now moved from the cramped Hornsey site to a large factory in Cheshunt) to be readied to continue an Australian career so its reputation could be recovered. Jolly's two-litre engine was fitted, and the car was shipped to Australia on the same boat which carried the Palmer two-litre. Sister car (at least originally) to Jolly's 608 was the two-litre bought by UK enthusiast John Coombs for Roy Salvadori to drive. This car — 609 — is shown in all its UK photographs to have the flat bonnet line which distinguished the early Fifteens with 60-degree inclined engines, and the fact that its chassis number is one later than the Jolly car raises the possibility 608 may originally have had a 60-degree engine too, but had been modified prior to Le Mans.

That in turn would indicate 608 had some UK racing history, which 609 — the Coombs car — certainly did. It was not as unsuccessful as the two-litre Fifteen that Team Lotus was then running, but Salvadori put 609 amongst the top privately-entered Fifteens in 1958, and the car, distinctive in its all-white paint with blue stripes fore-and-aft over each wheelarch, was even used to illustrate Lotus advertisements of the time.

There's little doubt that originally this car used the 12-type five-speed gearbox. This is indicated by the car's specification when it arrived in Australia in 1961, the chassis in the area of the differential modified to accept the Series Two-style Elite diff case, but with basic tubing still in place to show where the fragile five-speed gearbox differential had been. When this very tidy modification was done isn't known, nor is the car's history between 1958 and 1961, when it arrived, still in Coombs colors but with a very ordinary 105E Ford engine and gearbox, to start yet another Lotus Fifteen second life in Queensland.

Chassis 623 was built in 1959 as a *works* Fifteen Series Three, and had one of the-then very scarce 2.5-litre Coventry Climax FPF engines and the ZF four-speed gearbox which was at that time becoming an option (nowadays a highly prized one) in the Elite coupe. Just as a passing note on Lotus interchangeability at that time, the standard Elite box was the BMC B-series unit, the same unit in-

The 15 now owned/driven by Mike Ryves had to have the body's wheel cutaways enlarged when previous owner fitted wide wheels.

The Ryves car has non-original green-painted chassis but the Norman Gunston red cockpit trim is 100-percent historic Lotus.

troduced along with an Elite differential case in the Series-Two Fifteens.

This 2.5-litre car was briefly among the kings of short-distance UK sports car racing. It had one memorable race against Jack Brabham in a 2.0-litre Cooper Monaco at Aintree, and won, and must have left the traditional Jaguar-powered opposition feeling very breathless. Second was Alan Stacey in another works Fifteen with ZF and a two-litre engine, which probably became the Palmer car.

Leaton Motors bought 623 late in 1959 for Frank Matich to drive, and announcement of George Leaton's acquisition rather upset some of the Australian Gold Star brigade, who were finding 2.5-litre engines very difficult to get for their Coopers. They might have felt a little better to learn that the car arrived with a highly *interim* 2½ which notably lacked the main-bearing cross-bolting which was almost crucial for engine reliability. But it was this car, in its sponsor's unexciting cream and black paintwork, which quickly became the most impressive Fifteen of all. With Matich driving, and the 2.5 Climax delivering about 240 horsepower and more than 210 ft-lb of torque, it was a cannonball indeed.

Number 623 made its debut at Easter Bathurst, 1960, and I watched it come through the fast sweepers between Reid Park and McPhillamy in one long smooth surge of acceleration, the almost concealed wheels rippling over the bumps as it vanished away at quite unbelievable speed. The only sound left behind was the gasping disbelief of the crowd, and the distant noise of the rest of the field — still to come into view on the first lap.

It reminds me now of Bruce McLaren's comment that a 2½ Climax delivered around 170 horsepower at quarter throttle...

All three Australian Fifteens went on to have remarkably long and successful careers, yet of the three the Leaton Motors car — on paper clearly the fastest of the three — was less successful than its present legendary reputation might suggest. For one thing, it was inclined to be unreliable and missed out at two Bathurst meetings (including its 1960 debut, where it left Whiteford's Maserati 300S and Phillips' Cooper Jaguar well behind) and one Warwick Farm, with various rear suspension and differential failures, and the story that the tiny BMC A-series differentials were replaced between a practice and a race might well have been true.

Matich didn't in fact race the car for very long. Leaton's number two driver, the very smooth Johnny Martin, took over late in 1961 when Matich's even-faster Lotus 19 was looming. The 2.5-litre Fifteen had been meant as a front-line car, but with the arrival of rear-engine sports cars its brief dominance was eclipsed.

Nonetheless, Matich drove 623 to win (amongst other events) the Victorian and NSW sports car championships in 1960, and Warick Farm's *Little Le Mans* 23-lapper in 1961, where he beat Stillwell's 2.5-litre Cooper Monaco. Interestingly, Stillwell's best lap at Bathurst in October 1961 (when the Fifteen suffered a seized differential) was 4.8 secs slower than Matich's 2m 40.1s lap record from that Easter. Moreover, when Martin beat Stillwell at the Farm in 1962, Matich's record there (1:46.3) was a second and a half faster than Stillwell's best in pursuit of Martin.

The writing was on the wall with Matich's new Farm record early in 1962 — 1:44.6 with the Nineteen. Matich didn't finish and Stillwell beat Martin. The Fifteen's last victory as a front-line car was Sandown in March 1962, where Martin not merely beat Stillwell, but set a new lap record in 1:16.1. What a way to go... This Fifteen had won about two dozen races in two years, and set lap records on every circuit it visited.

With that history established, it was understandable that the car's next owner, Sydney's Mick Crampton, was a bitterly disappointed man by the time he sold the car after fruitless searching for reliability. Next owner was Town & Country engineering's John Schroder, another skilled tuner-driver, who installed an alloy Oldsmobile V-8 with suitably startling results and actually finished some races, although not without another rear suspension breakage. By the end of 1966 it was clear the car's handling was quite severely limited against wider-wheeled rear-engine opposition. Rather than cut the car about, the decision was made that Alice (as the Fifteen had become known at TACE) would be gracefully retired.

Care having been taken not to butcher the chassis when the Oldsmobile was fitted, it wasn't difficult to give Alice a TACE-rebuilt 1.5-litre Climax, and in that form the car was bought by Sydney's Mike Ryves. A nice twist to end the history of this car, which still appears occasionally in Historic races, is that in his search for a *proper* 2½ for the car Mike has become an accomplished rebuilder of these engines — as the off-the-clock cold oil-pressure of his leak-free renovated 2½ testifies.

Chassis 609, the John Coombs car, started its Australian racing modestly, as befitted its cooking 105E Ford engine, and owner Ann Thomson often had mere males driving the car. Nonetheless, she won a minor race in 1962, and co-driver Alan Reed another in 1961. An indication of what the 105E could really do was that Frank Matich, attending Lakeside to lecture a driver's school, took Mrs T. around in the passenger seat of her Fifteen more than six seconds faster than she had until then managed.

Top Queensland driver Glynn Scott then got involved with the car, and significantly changed its history. First, the very strong pushrod Cosworth Ford from his Lotus 27 was dropped in during 1964, almost doubling the power. Second, Scott himself was offered some of the driving, and against the then-new shoals of rear-engined Lotus 23s he went exceptionally well, often finishing ahead of the not-so-quick-23s, and sometimes winning outright.

Ann Thomson went faster and faster, winning (amongst other events) the last-ever race at historic Lowood in October 1966, and being probably the only woman ever to lap this very fast circuit in less than two minutes. Her pinnacle with the car was 1968, when numerous placings, including two wins at Lakeside in September, brought her Queensland Motor Sporting Club's "Driver of the Year" award. It was after the September meeting that Glynn Scott persuaded her to fit a roll-bar and harness, and only a fortnight later the Fifteen tangled with a slower car at Lakeside, overturned, and was very badly damaged. Mrs Thomson was unhurt, but the Fifteen has not raced since.

This was a sad, but suitably heroic end for the car's career. It had been racing continuously since 1957, and had admittedly become, as Mrs Thomson put it: "so tired in so many places". Still, it had remained a highly competitive car through to the end of the 1966 season. "He (Glynn Scott) loved that car," Mrs Thomson said, and it's not hard to understand why.

Kingaroy farmer Allan Swenson bought the wreck and straightened the chassis most successfully, but was eventually

Number One: the car that confirmed Frank Matich as a star, the ex-works 2.5-litre Series III Fifteen, here in action at a wet Warwick Farm. Picture shows the high bulge over the tall-block 2.5-litre Climax engine, the spring-racing magnesium-alloy Lotus wheels, and the very wide air-intake for radiator and dual oil coolers, the latter a most unusual 15 feature.

persuaded to sell the project. Present owner Barry Bates, supervising the daunting panel repairs in Newcastle, is emphatic the car will duly return to racing.

Even more than the John Coombs-Ann Thomson Fifteen, the Derek Jolly car became a never-say-die racer; first for Jolly, then for the young Bevan Gibson, and into the 1970s for the other Gibson brothers.

Having finished second in the 1958 Tourist Trophy, Jolly then ran the rebuilt car in the 1960 race at Longford and won, sharing fastest lap with Whiteford's 300S Maserati. This was one of Jolly's last races with the car, and one of his greatest successes. Another was his 1962 win in the Caversham Six-Hour race where a report noted that the car's restrained motoring reflected "some differential trouble, but not serious enough to retire." Jolly put the car up for sale, and had the accomplished Frank Coad run it at occasional Victorian meetings to keep it visible. An indication of how thoroughly the sports-racing scene had changed is that a buyer did not come along until late in 1964.

The buyer was Hoot Gibson, a long-time Victorian motor sport identity, who bought the car for his son Bevan as the next stage in a motor racing career which had started with karts and then a Triumph Spitfire. Bevan had just two races with the car before end-for-ending it five times at Warwick Farm in a highly spectacular crash which left him unhurt on the grass as his car somersaulted onwards. Two months later the car reappeared at The Farm, and Gibson won race from the back of the grid.

That was the start of a period in which the Gibson team campaigned the car at virtually every available Victorian and NSW meeting until the end of 1968. Engine capacity stretched to 2.3 litres, which put small-capacity lap records out of consideration, while the Over 2.0-litre class was by then the territory of the big V-8 cars, so that outright and class wins were relatively few, although the car held the Phillip Island sports lap record for many years. The vigorous racing left its mark: the bodywork was progressively hacked about to repair minor damage and to accommodate wider rims and tyres, and the gearbox — of course — needed a lot of repairing. But by the time the car was retired in early 1969 it had served its purpose of getting Bevan a faster drive, with the Bob Jane team. It was tragic that very shortly afterwards he was killed in Jane's Elfin 400, during a drive at Bathurst which had showed his really impressive talent and heart.

The Lotus is still with the Gibson family, and Bevan's brothers are active sports-racing drivers. Of all the Australian Fifteens, this one has raced furthest, hardest and longest — and certainly looks it. From a once-sleek, British Racing Green works car, it has become a battle-scarred work-horse which, somehow, looks what its sisters never did: a *real* racing machine, able to do great things in the right hands. □

Rationalisation: Series Three had gearbox mountings from a tube across the floor, supported by a pair of downtubes to the dash; earlier versions relied on a full-length alloy gearbox/tailshaft cover to give beam strength to a gearbox mounting direct into the sheet-alloy floor. This shot also shows the close-ratio BMC B-series gearbox, offered as an alternative to Lotus' own fragile five-speed.

Series Three: Immediate identification of the 1959 "production" model can be made by this shot, which shows the front suspension with a rear-mounted anti-roll bar; earlier cars mounted the bar ahead of the top transverse link. This shot also shows the upright engine installation, which gave better engine performance at the price of frontal area and drag. High-mounted water pump indicates this is a 1.5 or 2.0-litre Climax engine.

A long way from Le Mans: Jolly's 1.5-litre 15 in the pits at Bathurst, October 1958. Note the Costin-devised inflatable tonneau cover over the passenger's seat, the mounting position for the spare wheel, a dry-sump tank which is divided to serve both gearbox and engine, and a massive battery of truly 24-hour dimensions. The fuel-tank has been removed, from between the oil tanks and spare wheel, probably to get at the gearbox.

The Lotus Seventeen

The Lotus Seventeen was supposed to be a lower, lighter and faster successor to the Lotus Eleven which would vanquish the all conquering Lola, designed by Eric Broadley. The Lola had stolen the glory from Lotus Eleven domination in the period 1956-1958 in the small capacity sports racing class. Unfortunately, it did not live up to its expectations. It was lower, and it was lighter, but it was not faster, and worse, it did not beat the Lolas which were now being driven by the cream of ex-Lotus drivers who had defected to the new make.

The Lotus Seventeen was designed by a combination of Colin Chapman and his new recruit, design engineer Len Terry. However, Chapman was very heavily committed in his Formula 1 programme with the Lotus Sixteen, re-design of the Lotus Fifteen sports racing car into the Series 3 version, production of the Lotus Elite - Type 14, and Lotus Seven, plus some remaining orders for the Lotus Eleven as well as moving Lotus Engineering Co Ltd to new premises in Cheshunt.

The Chapman strut rear suspension was well tried and tested on the Lotus Elite, and the Fifteen, and was used on the Seventeen, but the strut front suspension was a radical difference, which quite frankly did not work as well as expected. It was such a problem that within a few months from the beginning of the 1959 racing season, customers were bringing back their new Seventeens to be modified into conventional wishbone front suspension. It was not quite a factory recall, but it was not far off!

The specification of the Lotus Seventeen included the now traditional Lotus multi-tube space frame chassis, but in smaller tubing than before comprising $5/8$in and $3/4$in tubes in lightweight 20 gauge steel. Girling disc brakes were fitted all round, and inboard at the rear. The steering was by lightweight rack and pinion, and the engine was the Coventry Climax FWA 1098cc in Stage 3 tune with Weber carburettors. The power output was quoted at 84bhp at 6800rpm. Lotus developed magnesium alloy 'wobbly web' wheels from the 1957 Formula 2 Lotus Twelve were used, and the external bodywork was full width moulded fibreglass. The overall length was only 10ft 1in with a dry weight of a mere 750lbs.

The first Lotus Seventeen was bought by Ian Walker Racing and was registered on 2nd April 1959. Team Lotus for the 1959 Le Mans 24 Hours race consisted of two Lotus Fifteens, two Lotus Seventeens for Alan Stacey/Keith Green and Michael Taylor/Jonathan Seiff, plus three privately entered Lotus Elites. Both of the Seventeens were fitted with the Coventry Climax 750cc engine in the hope of regaining the Index of Performance. The Taylor/Seiff car only lasted five hours when it retired with ignition trouble, and the Stacey/Green car retired after 14 hours with head gasket problems. It was a bad year for Team Lotus with none of their sports racing entries finishing, although a privately entered Elite won its class to retain some honour for Lotus. Production of the Lotus Seventeen continued until 1961 with a total of some 20 cars being produced.

Graham Capel

A BIT OF OVER-ENTHUSIASM causes Rudi de Waldkirch (Lotus Seventeen) to spin, at Oulton's Old Hall Corner, to the alarm of Keith Francis (Lotus), A. G. Wood (Cooper-Ford) and Bill Pinckney (Lotus). De Waldkirch had to let the field go by but managed to finish third.

Lotus Developments

NEW MODEL : OTHERS REFINED

The single-seater as it will be raced by the works team consisting of five cars

SUCCESS in sports car competition is the foundation upon which the fortunes of Lotus have been built, and although the company is now entering the series production field with the Elite, the major part of its activities is still concentrated on the building of competition cars. As discussed in *The Sport* on page 96, there is to be some curtailment of racing activities for 1959 so far as works-entered cars are concerned, but a new range of models for private sale has been announced. These are in the established Lotus tradition of low weight and drag, and should ensure continued success for the marque.

Works cars will be entered for **formula 1 and 2** events only, and the design will be very similar to that evolved for the single-seater racing car which made its first appearance at Rheims in July last year, but was never properly developed for that or subsequent races. Since the end of last season development work has been completed and, fitted with a 1½-litre formula 2 engine, one of these cars driven by Graham Hill lapped Brands Hatch consistently in 56.3sec, which is 1.1sec faster than the present lap record.

In their full formula 1 guise these cars will not be for sale to the public; this arises from the engine supply position. Coventry Climax are developing a 2,495 c.c. version of their type FPF four-cylinder twin overhead camshaft unit. It will be recalled that this engine started life as a 1½-litre with a bore and stroke of 3.2 × 2.8in, and was progressively increased to 1,960 c.c. (3.4 × 3.3in); last year a few engines were enlarged further to 2,205 c.c. (3.5 × 3.5in). Not unnaturally, these later versions lost something in reliability, largely because it was impossible to increase the degree of crankshaft balance in the same proportion as the capacity, and overloading of the main bearings occurred.

This year the crankcase and crankshaft are being redesigned, not only to eliminate last year's failures, but also to enable the capacity to be increased to 2,495 c.c. (3.7 × 3.5in). These 2½-litre engines can be built in limited numbers only, and will be available to Lotus and to Cooper Cars, Ltd., exclusively, during their period of development. The 1½- and 2-litre versions can, however, be supplied to private customers. Apart from the difference in engine size they are technically identical.

This latest single-seater car is developed

Above right: The Seventeen has a new design of front end, with a single lower wishbone in conjunction with a strut type of suspension. Below, left: Chassis of the Seventeen, which supersedes the Eleven. It is powered by the 1,098 c.c. single camshaft Climax engine, and has strut type independent rear suspension. Right: This season's Fifteen, refined and developed from last year's car, has a redesigned front suspension and can be powered by either a 1½- or 2-litre twin camshaft engine

Lotuses for 1959...

directly from the original 1957 formula 2 car, but bears little resemblance to it. Bodywork is more aerodynamic, and the gear box is offset to permit a lower seating position. The gear box is like the original five-speed sliding mainshaft type, but it is now equipped with a positive stop type of gear change, and the earlier lubrication problems have been overcome.

A completely new car for sports racing events is the **Seventeen**, which supersedes the Eleven, compared with which it is smaller in overall dimensions and has an even lower frontal area. Following basic Lotus practice, the frame is a light, tubular structure fabricated from ⅝in diameter and ¾in square 20 s.w.g. gauge tubing; the propeller shaft tunnel and floor are stressed members forming an integral part of the frame.

This car has independent suspension on all wheels, based on the pattern of the formula cars and the Elite. At the rear the Chapman strut type is used, and a development of this is also fitted at the front. At each side at the front there is a single fabricated tubular lower wishbone which has a ball joint at the outer end. Pivoting on this is a tubular stub axle, caliper mounting plate and steering arm, retained at the base of the strut by four bolts. This strut comprises a telescopic damper surrounded by a helical coil spring, and it is attached at the top to an extension of the frame front cross member. Opposed conical rubber bushes permit the required degree of oscillation at this point.

Girling 9½in dia disc brakes (inboard at the rear) are used and, as on all Lotus cars for this season, the front and rear systems have independent master cylinders linked to the pedal by an adjustable balance bar, by means of which the degree of front to rear braking can be adjusted. Cast magnesium wheels which effect a nett weight saving of 35lb over the spoked centre-lock type are standard equipment on these cars.

The power unit is the Coventry Climax FWA single camshaft engine with stage 3 tuning—which means that the camshaft has five bearings (the standard unit has three). In this form the engine develops 84 b.h.p. at 6,800 r.p.m. with a compression ratio of 9.8 to 1. As originally designed, this car was intended to be powered by the Climax 750 c.c. FWM engine, and the chassis has mounting points to accommodate this unit as and when it becomes available.

Compared with the Eleven, it is claimed that the new car is 110lb lighter, and will have a similar body to that used by the works team at Le Mans last year, with the high back and multi-curved transparent plastic windscreen.

For competition in larger class events, last year's **Fifteen** is continued, but modified considerably in detail. It can be fitted with either the 1½- or 2-litre version of the Climax FPF twin camshaft engine. Most important design changes are a modified frame, basically the same as last year but increased in stiffness, and a revised front suspension. The elements of this are the same, but the anti-roll bar at the top, which also doubles for the upper wishbone arms, is moved as far behind the hub centre line, as previously it was in front. This has given more space for the radiator, which has been increased in size, and for the oil cooling system.

Last year considerable trouble was encountered with overheating of the coolant system when the twin cam engines were fitted, and to overcome this a clever system has been devised. On these engines the water pump is located high up on the timing gear train, and it is difficult to fit a normal header tank without giving away height and hence increasing frontal area.

On the outlet side of the cylinder head there is a tubular canister in the pipeline to the front-mounted radiator. This canister is pressurized, and is also arranged to centrifuge out any trapped air bubbles. Previously the overflow vented to atmosphere, and when the system cooled down after a run, air entered the system. It is now arranged for a second canister to take the overflow from the blow-off valve, and this part of the system is vented to atmosphere but is arranged to have a weir effect. In other words, when the engine cools down, instead of sucking in air as previously, it now takes back the blown-off water trapped in the overflow canister.

Two types of gear box are available with this model. A close-ratio, four-speed MGA type, mounted directly to the engine, can be supplied, and this is offered mainly for overseas markets to assist servicing and spares facilities. The alternative is the Lotus-designed five-speed gear box as fitted to the formula cars, and mounted on the front end of the hypoid final drive unit, which has a Z.F. limited slip differential, on the chassis centre-line.

This is a very comprehensive range of competition cars, particularly from such a small establishment which, by its virile technical approach to problems, has had a profound influence on racing car design.

Chassis of the single-seater formula 1 and 2 car. The engine is swung over through 17 deg and angled at 10 deg in the frame to permit a low seating position

Revised front suspension of the Fifteen. The top anti-roll bar, which also forms the legs of the upper wishbone, is now placed to the rear, an arrangement which gives more space for the radiator. The engine is swung over at an angle of 17 deg to the inlet side, but the transmission line is on the centre of the chassis

New Lotus Seventeen

ANOTHER new 1100 cc Lotus—the Seventeen (briefly described last month)—will invade the racing circuits this season, and can reasonably be expected to be even more successful than its predecessor, the Eleven. It is, of course, a logical development of the Eleven, but incorporates features hitherto restricted to larger Lotus models—becoming the first 1100 cc Lotus with all-independent suspension—at the same time being 110 lb lighter and considerably less complex than previous versions. In addition, it is generally smaller (particularly in respect of frontal area) than the Eleven, and can be expected to have even better roadholding; early tests (sans bodywork) have shown that it has improved acceleration and that wheelspin is much reduced.

Like the Eleven, the Seventeen has a multitubular space frame chassis, which is built up from $\frac{5}{8}$ in. and $\frac{3}{4}$ in. square and round tubing of 20 gauge steel. As usual, the propeller shaft and floor are stressed members forming an integral part of the frame, but on the new car a shortened propeller shaft tunnel is all that is necessary to take braking and accelerating loads from the chassis mounted differential unit. The engine is carried on two rubber mountings at the front and on a single rubber mounting, attached to the gearbox, at the rear; as on the Eleven it is tilted sideways at an angle of 10 degrees to the nearside to give a straight induction tract, but the gearbox is now mounted upright.

One of the most interesting features of the new car is the front suspension, which is of strut type, with each wheel located by a wide-based lower wishbone. The tubular stub axle, brake caliper mounting plate and steering arm are all retained at the base of the strut by means of four bolts, which give a very strong yet light assembly incorporating the absolute minimum of components.

This new, simplified suspension system has been designed to reduce weight—and to reduce load problems at mounting points—and to permit further refinement of the chassis frame, which now weighs only 41 lb complete with brackets, yet is extremely strong. It is also designed to allow wheel loads to react through the wishbone rather than through the strut, and thus the wishbone mountings are as near as possible to hub height, the forward arm being mounted part way up a vertical frame member. The suspension struts—Armstrong co-axial coil spring/adjustable damper units — are mounted almost upright at the front (in fact at $8\frac{1}{2}$ degrees from the vertical) to restrict camber change; at the rear, on the other hand, camber change is required, to cope with variations in load (the difference between full and nearly empty fuel tanks); the rear struts are therefore at 45 degrees.

The front suspension will naturally be compared with the swing axle system of earlier Lotus models, and while the two have some features in common the strut-type gains considerably in that it has a roll-centre height of only two inches, compared with six inches on the swing axle Eleven. On this basis alone it can be predicted that the Seventeen will have a higher cornering power than the Eleven. The relatively narrow (3 ft. 6 in) front track is designed to accommodate the wheels within the bodywork and yet permit a reasonable turning circle (39 feet).

At the rear, fully independent strut-type suspension, similar to that used on the Formula cars, the Fifteen and the Elite, is fitted for the first time on a small-capacity sports car. As on the other models, the locating elements in this suspension system are the tubular drive shaft, the suspension strut and a longitudinal radius arm, all reacting through a magnesium hub casting.

The brakes are of Girling manufacture, hydraulically operated, with $9\frac{1}{2}$ in. discs mounted outboard at the front, inboard at the rear. The front and rear braking systems have independent master cylinders linked to the pedal by an adjustable balance bar. The use of these smaller and lighter brakes has been made possible by the extremely low weight of the complete vehicle. Lotus cast magnesium "wobbly-web" wheels are fitted as standard and effect a saving of 35 lb over a wire-wheel set-up. Steering is by a new type lightweight rack and pinion gear.

The bodywork is neat and extremely attractive, and although, naturally enough utilising aerodynamic experience gained on previous models, and incorporating the high tail and two-dimensionally curved windscreen first used at Le Mans in 1957, the Seventeen nevertheless has sufficiently distinctive lines to ensure that it cannot be confused with earlier models. By comparison with the Eleven, the Seventeen is 3 in. shorter, $4\frac{1}{2}$ in. narrower, $3\frac{1}{2}$ in. lower at the scuttle and $7\frac{1}{2}$ in. lower overall. Frontal area is 9 sq. ft. Ground clearance is unchanged but the turning circle is reduced by 6 feet.

Power units which will be fitted to the Seventeen are the Coventry Climax 1100 cc FWA engine in Stage Three tune and the same manufacturers' 750 cc FWM engine when it becomes available. The 1100 cc unit has a single overhead camshaft and produces 84 hp at 6800 rpm with a 9.8 to 1 compression ratio.

Power is transmitted by a single Borg and Beck dry-plate clutch of $7\frac{1}{4}$ in. diameter, hydraulically operated. There is a special lightweight four-speed, close ratio gearbox in unit with the engine. Ratios are: first 2.5 to 1, second 1.67 to 1, third 1.23 to 1, top 1 to 1, reverse 2.5 to 1. The final drive is a hypoid unit of 4.22 to 1 ratio and alternative ratios of 3.73, 3.9, 4.55 and 4.875 are available. A ZF limited slip differential is available at extra cost.

A single light alloy fuel tank of eight gallons capacity and an SU petrol pump are mounted at the rear, as is the special lightweight, 12 volt, 31 amp. hour battery, which weighs 24 lb. The fuse box is mounted in the cockpit. Electrical equipment includes recessed Lucas six inch headlamps incorporating side lights, twin stop/tail lights, number plate/stop light, instrument lights, screen wipers and horn. The instruments comprise a 3 in. 8000 rpm tachometer, oil pressure gauge, water temperature gauge and ammeter.

The magnesium wheels, with identical rims front and rear, are fitted with 4.50 by 15 tyres at the front and 5.00 by 15 at the rear. A 4.50 by 15 spare wheel is mounted in the tail.

The car is fitted with a full-width moulded perspex screen; hood and sticks to full Appendix "C" specification, may be had at extra cost.

The dimensions of the Seventeen are: wheelbase 6 ft 10 ins, front track 3 ft 6 ins, rear track 3 ft 9 ins, overall length 10 ft 11 ins, overall width 4 ft $7\frac{1}{2}$ ins, height to top of scuttle 1 ft 11 ins, overall height 2 ft 5 ins, ground clearance 5 ins. The weight of the car, less fuel, is 750 lb. For production reasons the car will initially be offered for sale on the home market only.

Front end of the Seventeen, showing the new, simplified chassis frame and front suspension. At the time of going to press the bodywork had not been fitted.

The rear suspension of the Seventeen, showing tubular drive shaft, longitudinal radius arm and Armstrong strut unit.

LOTUS for 1959

New sports and single-seater cars from Hornsey, plus an improved version of the Lotus Fifteen

Photography by Theo Page

For the coming racing season Lotus Engineering have three competition models lined up. First on the list is a small car to replace the highly successful Lotus Eleven. This is the Lotus Seventeen.

On this new car the overall dimensions are reduced and the frontal area is considerably less.

The chassis follows basic Lotus practice and is a light tubular steel structure, suspension is now independent on all wheels, using the reliable and remarkably efficient Chapman strut type at the rear. This, although standard on the Fifteens, Formula cars and the Elite, is fitted for the first time to a small Lotus. Front suspension is entirely new, also using a light strut type arrangement with one low mounted wishbone for location

SMOOTH LINES of the F1/2 single-seater Lotus (above) are well shown in this illustration. Outwardly the car is little changed from last year's model, but extensive changes have taken place underneath.

REAR SUSPENSION (below) is the Chapman strut type with Armstrong adjustable dampers.

of the lower end of the strut. A tubular stub axle, calliper mounting plate and steering arm are all retained at the base of the strut by four bolts which give an immensely strong, yet extremely light, assembly incorporating the absolute minimum of components. The use of these new suspension systems has allowed the design of a more refined chassis frame which, whilst giving no concessions in respect of strength, has produced an appreciable weight saving. Again a stressed floor/undertray gives plan stiffness to the chassis but now a reduced prop shaft tunnel is all that is necessary to accept part of the braking and acceleration loads from a chassis-mounted differential.

An aluminium alloy petrol tank of approximately eight gallons is rear-mounted, as is the pusher-type petrol pump. The lower weight of the complete vehicle allows for the use of smaller Girling disc brakes. Front and rear brake systems have independent master cylinders linked to the pedal by an adjustable balance bar. To reduce further the unsprung weight, cast magnesium wheels will be standard in the specification of the Seventeen, and effect a net saving of 35 lb. over the standard wire wheel set-up. The Coventry-Climax 1,100 c.c. engine will be mounted inclined at 10 deg. to the nearside as in the Eleven, but the hydraulically operated clutch is new. The chassis and mounting points are also designed to accommodate the Climax 750 c.c. FWM engine as and when it is available. In fact the car was originally intended as a 750 c.c. contender, so light weight and careful design will be a big advantage now that a 1,100 c.c. engine is fitted. Bodywork will be distinctive, although using aerodynamic experience gained with previous models. First introduced by Lotus at Le Mans, the high back and two dimensionally curved perspex windscreen are incorporated.

Altogether the Seventeen will be lighter (110 lb.), smaller, more aero-

ALL NEW This is the chassis of the "little" Lotus—the Seventeen. As can be seen from the photograph, the engine is inclined to the nearside. Note the new front suspension.

STEERING on both the Seventeen (left) and the Fifteen (right) is of the rack and pinion type. The different types of suspension used on these cars can be clearly seen.

dynamic and have better road-holding than the Eleven.

For production reasons the car will only be offered for sale on the home market for the time being.

The 2-litre Lotus Fifteen for 1959 is not a completely new model, but a refined and developed car based on last year's experience with its predecessor. These cars offer two main developments: firstly, the front suspension has been reversed, giving the dual advantages of more space available for radiator and oil cooler arrangements required for the 2-litre engine, and also a refinement of chassis frame construction which increases strength, stiffness and simplicity. Secondly, with the greater torque available from the 2-litre engine, it is possible to offer an alternative transmission which incorporates a four-speed gearbox in unit with the engine and a conventional final drive unit. This four-speed transmission system will also be offered on 1½-litre cars for export, where servicing and spares facilities for a proprietary box may prove easier than for the specialized five-speed unit. A further developed and improved version of this latter gearbox will still be offered on either model to special order. An interesting detail of the improved cooling system used are the new double swirl and overflow pots, which ensure that the system works effectively at all times.

Due to the water pump location on this power unit and the low bonnet line necessary for minimum frontal area, a conventional header tank system cannot have sufficient water head over the pump effectively to separate out air bubbles and prevent their entry into the eye of the impeller, causing cavitation. Lotus have, therefore, evolved this system which removes these bubbles by a centrifuge and allows the water expelled by thermal expansion to be returned again on cooling.

The Single-seater

Although the Lotus sports cars have frequently taken an indecently short time to make the journey from the drawing board to the circuit, the single-seaters have proved slightly more difficult.

NEW POSITION for the gearbox on the Lotus Fifteen is the orthodox one, i.e., in unit with the engine. Last year's box was combined with the final drive.

SPECIFICATION OF LOTUS SEVENTEEN

Frame: Multitubular space frame comprising ⅝ in. and ¾ in. square and round tubing of 20 gauge steel. The propeller shaft and floor are stressed members forming an integral part of the frame. The engine is carried on two rubber mountings at the front and a single rubber mounting at the rear attached to the gearbox: it is tilted sideways through 10 degrees to the nearside—this gives a straight induction tract. The rear frame incorporates a spare wheel mounting and an easily detachable petrol tank to provide ready access to the final drive unit and rear brakes.

Front Suspension: Independent by strut type including telescopic hydraulic shock absorbers and coil springs with wishbones picking up at the bottom of the shock absorbers.

Rear Suspension: Independent by Lotus strut type with coil springs and telescopic shock absorbers.

Brakes: Ultra light Girling hydraulically operated 9½ ins. disc brakes, outboard at the front, inboard at the rear. Horizontally mounted handbrake, operating the rear callipers through inner and outer cables.

Steering: Lightweight rack and pinion steering gear.

Power Unit: Coventry-Climax 1100 engine Stage III. Single o.h.c. four-cylinder engine, bore and stroke 2.85 ins. x 2.625 ins. = 66.9 cu. ins. (72.4 mm. x 66.6 mm. = 1,098 c.c.). Max. 84 b.h.p. at 6,800 r.p.m. Comp. ratio 9.8:1. Provision has been made for fitting the 750 c.c. FWM engine as and when available.

Transmission: Single dry plate clutch 7¼ ins., hydraulically operated. Special lightweight four-speed, close-ratio gearbox in unit with engine, ratios: first, 2.5:1; second, 1.67:1; third, 1.23:1; top, 1:1; reverse, 2.5:1.

Final Drive: Hypoid final drive unit of 4.22:1 ratio, alternative ratios available, 3.73, 3.9, 4.55 and 4.875, a ZF limited slip differential is available at extra cost.

Cooling System: Fully ducted crossflow radiator, remote header tank.

Fuel System: Single light alloy tank, 8 gallons capacity. SU pump rear mounted.

Bodywork: Full-width moulded Perspex screen conforming with the general body lines and complying with Appendix "C" regulations.

Electrical System: Special lightweight, 12 volt, 31 amp. hr. battery, weight 24 lb., located in tail. Coil and distributor, centrifugal advance and retard, belt-driven dynamo, automatic voltage control. Fuse box. Recessed Lucas 6 ins. headlamps incorporating side lamps, twin stop tail-lights, rear number plate stop lamp, high frequency horn. Instrument lighting. Screen wiper.

Instruments: Three ins. tachometer, 0-8,000 r.p.m.; oil pressure gauge; water temperature gauge and ammeter.

Wheels and Tyres: Magnesium bolt-on wheels with identical rims front and rear, fitted with 4.50 x 15 tyres at the front and 5.00 x 15 tyres at the rear. 4.50 x 15 spare wheel mounted under rear panelling. Wire wheels may be had as an alternative.

Dimensions: Wheelbase, 6 ft. 10 ins.; front track 3 ft. 6 ins., rear track 3 ft. 9 ins.; overall length, 10 ft. 11 ins.; overall width, 4 ft. 7½ ins.; height on top of scuttle, 1 ft. 11 ins.; overall height, 2 ft. 5 ins.; ground clearance, 5 ins.

Weight: Standard Seventeen, less fuel: 750 lb.

Extras: Hood and sticks for full Appendix "C" necessary for some races is available at extra cost.

with a Formula 2 engine fitted, Graham Hill circulated on test at Brands Hatch in 56.3 secs., and for 15 consecutive laps at higher speeds than Stirling Moss's record of 57.4 secs. Subsequent testing throughout the winter in the hands of numerous drivers has produced even more performance and controllability. Mechanically, this model is very different from the 1957 "cigar-shaped" models, only the engine, front suspension, wheels and some gearbox internals being the same. A new chassis with an additional removable chassis member over the engine and a detachable rear sub-frame, new aerodynamic bodywork with part-faired front and rear suspension, and headrest in the tail; a modified gearbox casing and a new positive stop gear-change mechanism, new petrol and oil tanks and mountings, strengthened rear suspension, altered water and oil cooling systems, new engine mounting arrangements, bigger cockpit, etc., are now used.

The engines in the 1959 Lotus Formula 1 and 2 cars are inclined 17 deg. off vertical and are angled at 10 deg. in the chassis. Extra heat insulation around the exhaust is provided

Completely new Lotus sports-racing c[ar] is the Mk. XVII powered by the 1100 c.[c.] single-camshaft Coventry Climax power un[it]

New Lotus models

The Seventeen is an entirely new 750/1100 c.c. sports racing car. A Formula Two car with a new chassis and bodywork [is] ready; a new Fifteen with improved chassis, revised cooling and other modifications is announced. Coventry Climax engine[s] are used in all these types

IT WOULD not be unfair to either constructor to draw something of a parallel between Ferrari and Lotus. Both are highly individual in their approach to motorcar design and construction, and both have a talent for getting things done with commendable dispatch. Not for them a fairly leisurely progression from drawing board to road test. They think, and act, in terms of weeks; and both Enzo Ferrari and Colin Chapman are of like temperament in regarding each achievement as a challenge to their resource and experience—the next development is foreseen almost before the latest creation has won its spurs. And so the untiring striving after that something closer to the ultimate goes on . . .

At the present time, by way of illustration, Colin Chapman and his keen young team are engaged in finalizing production arrangements for his Elite coupé. They are also planning shortly to move, in stages, design and commercial office and manufacturing facilities to a new factory at Cheshunt, Herts., near the northern approaches to London. Meantime, the desirability of producing certain new models has not been overlooked, and it says much for the enthusiasm and drive of Team Lotus that this has actually been achieved.

We were invited to see the new cars last month, and when we went to the Hornsey factory for the purpose of taking pictures and notes Mr. Chapman indicated that the current programme of work and racing was of a more circumscribed character than last year's undertakings. This is a wise move in our view for last year Lotus attempted too much in too many directions. The 1959 season will not see any works' entries for sports car racing events but private owners will naturally be able to count upon works assistance so far as other commitments will allow. Lotus themselves will concentrate on *grand épreuve*. Two Formula One cars will be run in as many major events as possible, with a third car always available for practice. Formula Two will, as in the past, continue to interest the Hornsey firm and a number of events will be officially supported. One of the new cars we saw (and which is briefly described below and illustrated) is a Formula Two machine and this is to be available to private purchasers.

This last-mentioned new model gives a very good illustration of our earlier comments about Lotus being quick workers. Two prototypes of the F2 car were first raced at Rheims last July and continued to be used during the rest of the season. The experience gained on the circuits was incorporated in a developed vehicle and this was shown at Earl's Court—four months after the prototypes were first pushed on to a starting grid. Later in October, it may be recalled, with a Climax 1½-litre engine installed, Graha[m] Hill beat Stirling Moss's Brands Hatch record during tests of th[e] car. His best time was 56·3 secs., against Moss's 57·4 secs. recor[d] lap.

The Seventeen is a completely new car designed to have a[n] even better performance than its successful predecessor, th[e] Eleven. Overall dimensions of the Seventeen are reduced and most important, the frontal area is considerably less.

The chassis follows basic Lotus practice, being a light tubula[r] steel structure. Suspension is now independent on all wheels using the now proven Chapman strut type at the rear. This although standard on the Fifteens, Formula cars and the Elite is fitted for the first time to a small Lotus. Front suspension i[s] entirely new, also using a light strut type arrangement with on[e] low mounted wishbone for location of the lower end of the stru[t]. A tubular stub axle, brake caliper mounting plate and steering ar[m] are all retained at the base of the strut by four bolts which give [a] strong, yet light, assembly incorporating the minimum of com[po]nents. The use of these new suspension systems has allowe[d] the design of a strong chassis frame which shows an appreciabl[e] weight saving. Again a stressed floor/undertray gives plan stiffnes[s] to the chassis but now a reduced prop shaft tunnel is all that i[s] necessary to take care of part of the braking and acceleratio[n] loads from the chassis-mounted differential. An aluminium allo[y] petrol tank of approximately eight gallons capacity is rear mounted, as is the "pusher" type S.U. petrol pump.

The lower weight of the complete vehicle allows for the use o[f] smaller Girling disc brakes. Front and rear brake systems hav[e] independent master cylinders linked to the pedal by an adjustabl[e] balance bar. To further reduce unsprung weight Lotus cas[t] magnesium wheels are standard; they effect a net saving of 35 lb[.] over the equivalent wire wheels.

The generally unchanged Coventry Climax 1100 c.c. engin[e] will be inclined at 10 deg. to the near side as in the Eleven, bu[t] the hydraulically-operated Borg & Beck clutch is new. The chassi[s] and mounting points are also designed to accommodate the Clima[x] 750 c.c. F.W.M. engine when it is available, but at the time o[f] writing the Coventry firm had only got into production with th[e] ingenious outboard marine version. Actually, the car was originall[y] intended as a 750 c.c. contender, so light weight and careful desig[n] will be a big advantage now that a 1100 c.c. engine is fitted Bodywork will be distinctive although using aerodynamic experi[i]ence gained with previous models. First introduced by Lotus a[t]

244

Le Mans the Costin-conceived high back and two-dimensionally-curved Perspex windscreen are incorporated.

Altogether the Seventeen will be 110 lb. lighter, smaller, more aerodynamic and have better roadholding than the Eleven. For production reasons the new car will only be offered for sale on the home market for the time being.

Two-litre Fifteen

The 2-litre Fifteen for 1959 is designed, Lotus explained, to give the private owner of means the best possible chance of success in this year's big sports car racing. It is not a completely new model, but a refined and developed racing car based on last year's experience. The two main developments are important ones. The front suspension has been revised, giving the dual advantages of more space available for the larger radiator now required for the more powerful 2-litre engine, and also a refinement of chassis frame construction which has been introduced to increase strength, stiffness and simplicity. Secondly, with the greater torque available from the 2-litre engine, it is possible to offer an alternative transmission which incorporates a four-speed M.G. gearbox in unit with the engine and a conventional final drive unit. This four-speed transmission system will also be offered on 1½-litre cars for export because servicing and spares facilities for such a widely used box will naturally prove easier to obtain than for the specialised Lotus five-speed unit introduced in a limited manner some time ago. A further developed and improved version of this gearbox will, however, still be offered on either model to special order.

An interesting new detail of the improved cooling system, aimed at conserving water, is the use of two swirl and overflow pots fitted with sealable cups. These are in front of the engine and ensure that the system works effectively at all times; one takes the place of the header tank. Due to the high water pump location on the twin-cam Climax power unit, and the low bonnet line necessary for minimum frontal area, a conventional header tank system cannot have sufficient head of water over the pump to effectively separate out air bubbles and prevent their entry into the eye of the pump impellor to cause cavitation. Lotus have therefore evolved the cooling system modification mentioned, which removes air bubbles by centrifugal action and allows the water expelled by thermal expansion to be returned to the second pot after cooling. Only in the event of engine temperature and cooling system pressure rising excessively for one reason or another will the "safety valve" of the system operate and allow water to be discharged to waste and excess pressure lowered.

Formula Two

Mechanically, the Formula Two car for the 1959 season is very different from the 1957 cigar-shaped model, only engine, front suspension, wheels and some gearbox internals remaining unchanged. A new chassis is used and has an additional removable chassis member over the engine and a detachable rear sub-frame. New aerodynamic bodywork with part fairing over the front and rear suspension, and headrest in the tail will be used. A modified gearbox casing and new positive-stop gearchange mechanism figure among the improvements, and there are new petrol and oil tanks and mountings, strengthened rear suspension, altered water and oil cooling systems, new engine mounting arrangements and a bigger cockpit.

These modifications have revolutionised the car those who have tried it consider and the new season is therefore approached with great confidence.

New 2½-litre Climax engine

Of matching interest to the new Lotus cars is the new Coventry Climax FPF 2½-litre engine which is to be used to power the Formula One machines. Inasmuch as this larger engine has four cylinders and twin overhead camshafts it is similar to the earlier Climax twin-cam unit we described and illustrated in our issue for May, 1957. All its major components are, however, of new design, it is in no sense an enlarged edition of the earlier type.

With a bore and stroke of 3·7 in. and 3·54 in. respectively, the cubic capacity is 2492 c.c. At the time of writing the engine was very new and no programme of dynamometer testing had been carried out so no power figures could be quoted. Peak revolutions are of the order of 7,000 r.p.m. and we imagine that an output in the region of 100 b.h.p. a litre will be reached when development is completed. Different cylinder heads are being tried and various compression ratios are also being investigated; at present the ratio is 11 to 1. It is hoped to standardise twin-choke S.U. carburettors but Webers will also be tried; both, it will be recalled, have been used with satisfaction on the smaller Climax racing engines.

The new well-stiffened light alloy crankcase is of improved design as is the massive three-bearing counterweighted crankshaft. Great attention has been given to achieving stiffness of these components in the interests of trouble-free running at high speeds. Pistons and connecting rods are new and no doubt the satisfactory experience with Dykes-type compression rings and Vandervell indium-flashed lead bronze thinwall bearings will result in these being standardised in the new engine.

A Lucas racing-type magneto is employed and the head is of single-plug type. As before, a single inlet and single exhaust valves are used, but the development work in hand when we were in touch with Coventry Climax Engines Ltd. last month also included investigation of valves of different sizes as well as heads of various designs. A flywheel of larger size than previously figures on the new engine and a larger starting motor is also fitted.

Power will be transmitted through a Borg & Beck racing clutch of new design, this being a twin-plate dry-type clutch arranged for hydraulic operation. A clutch of this type will also be used on the Fifteen and Formula Two Lotuses for this season.

The Mk. XV will be continued in similar form to last year using either 1.5 or 2 litre Climax engines. The chassis has been stiffened with little alteration to weight

The mounting of the engine in the XV is tilted off the vertical. The interesting oil cooling arrangements will be noted

LOTUS

NEW MODEL SEVENTEEN

IMPROVED MODEL FIFTEEN AND FORMULA CAR

Formula 1 Lotus in background will be fitted with a full 2½-litre Coventry Climax engine this year. Minor chassis modifications have been carried out since last year. The entirely new Lotus Seventeen was originally designed to take the 750 c.c. Climax engine but is shown here in 1,100 c.c. form. A development of the Chapman strut suspension is used at the front and the car is 110 lb. lighter than the Eleven which it replaces

EVERY year sees the introduction of new models or modification of the existing range of Lotus cars. The *marque* has had impressive successes in competition since 1952 when the first Lotus Mark IV appeared at a race meeting. Since then they have come a long way and today are internationally famous in sports car racing, Grand Prix and record breaking.

This year, with the production of the Elite getting under way at their new Cheshunt premises, Lotus Engineering have announced that they will no longer directly participate in any form of sports car racing. They will, however, sponsor private stables in the 2-2½-litre, 1½-litre and 1,100 c.c. class and some of these cars will be run under the auspices of Team Lotus. Lotus Engineering will be confining their activities to Formula 1 racing backed up with a limited number of Formula 2 and Grand Touring events.

They intend to enter all the major *Grandes Epreuves* abroad, and all major International events in this country. Three cars will be prepared and two raced; Graham Hill is a nominated driver.

The Formula 1 car which is very much different from the original Formula cars introduced in 1957, is basically the same as that shown at the Motor Show last year. Detail improvements are incorporated and include a "double pot" header tank similar to that fitted on the improved Fifteen model, a modified selector shaft for the positive stop mechanism in the gearbox with bigger detents preventing a neutral being obtained between each gear, and strengthened rear suspension components. The unreliability of the bottom end of the enlarged 2,205 c.c. FPF Coventry Climax engine which was originally developed from the 1,500 c.c. engine has prompted the design of a new full 2½-litre unit. Only a few of these new engines will be made and the entire quota will be absorbed by Lotus and by Cooper Cars Ltd., so the unit will not be available to the public. The crankcase and crankshaft of the new engine has been completely redesigned to eliminate bearing trouble and a new cylinder block is featured giving a capacity of 2,495 c.c. Later in the year it is hoped to produce a new cylinder head with improved breathing which should give a power output in the region of 100 b.h.p. per litre.

The completely new Lotus Seventeen announced recently replaces the Eleven and is 110 lb. lighter and as well as being more aerodynamic it is smaller with reduced frontal area. It is claimed that the road holding is better, too. Construction follows basic Lotus practice with light tubular steel frame and a stressed floor/undertray and prop-shaft tunnel gives additional strength. For the first time on a small Lotus all-independent suspension is employed with the Chapman strut system as used on the Elite, at the rear.

Close-up of the front end of the Seventeen shows the new type of suspension. A single lower wishbone locates the strut/damper/coil spring which is attached at the top to an extension of the chassis

FOR 1959

Modified Fifteen for 1959 has had its front suspension reversed which allows more room for the radiator. The latter has been enlarged and the cooling system has been redesigned to eliminate the formation of air bubbles within the coolant. The deeper radiator core is visible as is the new alternative four-speed gearbox in unit with the engine

Front suspension is a development of the strut with a low mounted wishbone to locate its bottom end while the top of the strut is attached to an extension of the frame. A tubular stub axle, caliper mounting plate, and steering arm are all retained at the base of the strut by four bolts giving a very strong front assembly with the minimum of components. The new suspension has resulted in a considerable saving in weight, this in turn allowing the mounting of smaller 9½-in. Girling disc brakes which are inboard at the rear. These have independent master cylinders for front and rear systems linked to the pedal by an adjustable balance bar, enabling the degree of front to rear braking to be adjusted at will. Magnesium wheels are standard, again for lightness—they are 35 lb. lighter than the total weight of a wire wheel set-up.

An 8-gallon aluminium-alloy fuel tank supplies petrol via a rear-mounted S.U. "pusher"-type pump to the 1,100 c.c. Climax engine which is inclined at 10 deg. to the chassis. The chassis and mounting points are designed to accommodate the 750 c.c. FWM Climax engine when it is available. The bodywork of the new car will incorporate the high back and the two dimensional curved acetate windscreen first introduced by Lotus at Le Mans. It is intended for production reasons, to limit the sale of the Seventeen to the home market for the time being.

The 2-litre Fifteen for 1959 has one or two refined and important modifications based on experience in racing over the last two years. The frame has come in for some minor stiffening and the front suspension has been reversed with the high-mounted anti-roll bar which serves as part of the top wishbone, behind the hub centre line. This has allowed more space for the oil cooling system and for the radiator which this year has been considerably increased in size. Last season, trouble with overheating was encountered when the twin-cam engines were fitted. This stemmed from the location of the water pump high up on the timing train and which necessitated the fitting of a very high header tank. As this was out of the question in the interests of a low bonnet line, a conventional header tank system could not be used. Lotus fitted a tubular canister in the pipeline to the radiator. The canister is pressurized and is arranged to remove bubbles from the cooling water by centrifuging them out and allowing the water expelled by thermal expansion to be returned again on cooling. On the previous model air was sucked in through the overflow vent of the canister as the water cooled at the end of the race, but now a second canister vented to the atmosphere takes water from its overflow and prevents this from happening.

Two types of gearboxes are now available; the Lotus five-speed rear-mounted unit as fitted before and an alternative B.M.C. four-speed box in unit with the engine. The offering of the latter is likely to be of interest to overseas competitors who have not the servicing and spares facilities that Lotus owners have in this country.

Preparation of the Formula cars on which British hopes will be partly resting now that Vanwall have withdrawn from racing for the 1959 season will be undertaken by Stan Elsworth who has spent the last 18 months with Vanwalls.—D.S. ★

Modifications on the Fifteen model include a deeper radiator and "double pot" cooling system. To accommodate the former the front suspension has been reversed, bringing the anti-roll bar as far behind the front hub centre line as previously it was in front

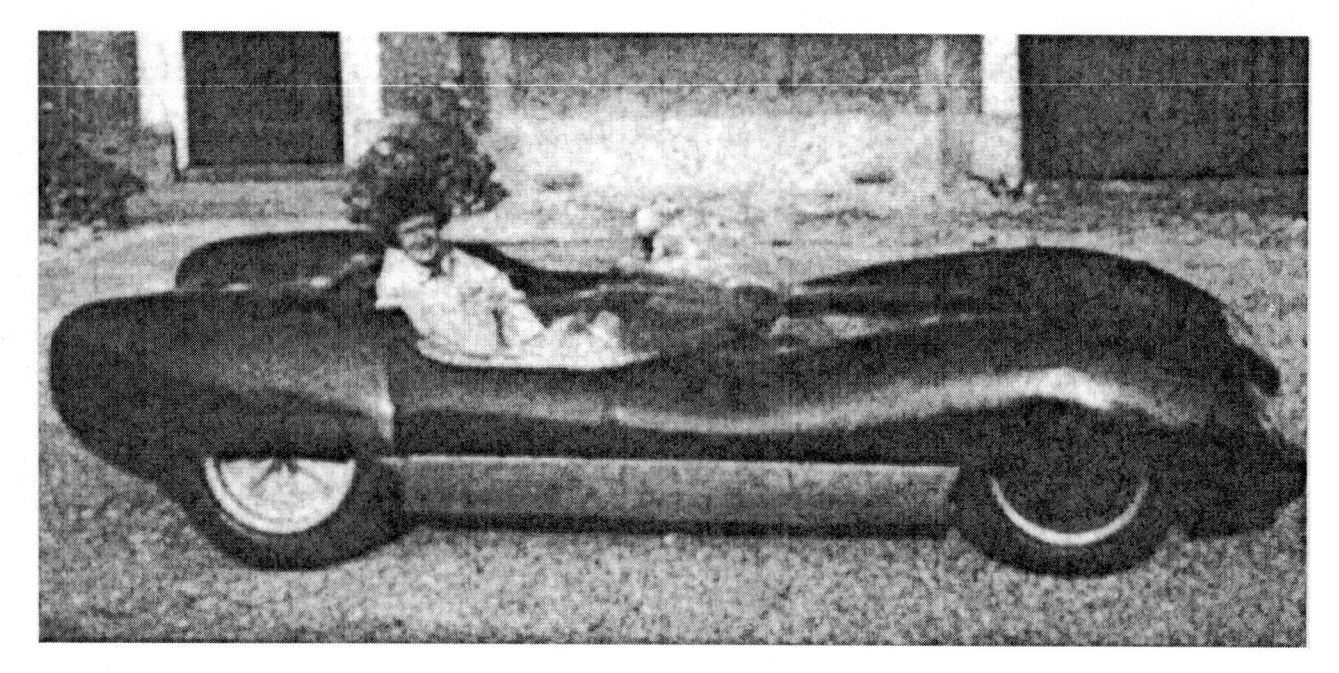

ROAD IMPRESSIONS

LOTUS SEVENTEEN

by David Phipps

"**Visibility is not impaired by the windscreen**"—goggles are essential for fast motoring in the Seventeen.

DRIVING a car which is basically designed for circuit racing on the open road is hardly the best way to assess its possibilities for "on the limit" use, but as a result of an afternoon's run in Hertfordshire and Cambridgeshire I can definitely assert that the Lotus Seventeen is an excellent means of transport on a fine summer's day.

SUSPENSION

Since the Seventeen was first announced, new and untried, to the Press, a number of modifications have been made, mostly to the suspension. Basically the car consists of a lightweight tubular space frame, with independent suspension front and rear, propelled by the well-known 1100 cc Coventry Climax FWA engine in Stage Three tune and clothed by extremely light glass-fibre bodywork. The floor and the rear part of the propeller shaft tunnel are stressed members, forming an integral part of the frame. Strut-type suspension is used all round, with each front wheel located by a wide-based lower wishbone, and the rear wheels by the drive shaft and a longitudinal radius arm; the struts are of Armstrong manufacture. Steering is by shortened rack-and-pinion gear of the type used on the Triumph Herald.

The engine on the car I tried was "just as it came from the works" except for the fitting of twin choke 38 mm Weber carburetters. The basically Austin A30 gearbox was fitted with the latest type of Lotus close-ratio gears.

On the Road

This latest "works" Seventeen is normally equipped with a lightweight bucket seat which provides very good lateral support—too good, in fact, for my hips, so I arranged for the seat to be removed and replaced with a full-width seat back. Rather surprisingly, there is more leg room in this car than the Eleven, and ample room around the pedals for large feet. The leather-rimmed steering wheel is set at just the right height and the long gear-lever projects to a point where the left hand drops naturally upon it. Hidden away under the dashboard on the passenger side is the handbrake which, in customary Lotus fashion, works on a horizontal plane. Immediately to the driver's right, at the leading edge of the door sill, are the ignition/starter switch (operated by a key) the lights switch and the horn button. The latter is fitted mainly to comply with regulations, as it seems pretty obvious that anyone who has not heard the exhaust note is unlikely to hear the horn.

INSTRUMENTS

Directly ahead of the driver is the tachometer, flanked by a combination oil pressure/water temperature gauge on the left and an ammeter on the right. All instruments are of Smiths manufacture.

First impressions are that this is an extremely easy car to drive. The engine starts first time, the gear lever slips easily (with a surprisingly short travel) into bottom gear, and the hydraulic clutch takes up the drive smoothly but very firmly. Up to second and third, and down to second again (the most suitable ratio for Cheshunt traffic)—this is just like driving a saloon car, but a little noisier than most. Visibility is not impaired (as it will be, thanks to the CSI's new regulations, on next year's racing sports cars) by the windscreen, and the bonnet line falls smoothly away, with the relatively high front "wings" assisting accurate placing of the car for corners, or overtaking.

ACCELERATION

Cheshunt becomes Wormley, and then Broxbourne and then Hoddesdon, so we bumble along with the traffic stream, either in second or in third, with the engine spluttering somewhat as the revs drop to around 2000 but picking up smoothly and crisply at about 3500, from which point the tachometer needle rushes round to 7000 in second and third in the short distance needed to overtake a string of three lorries. This tremendous acceleration is a wonderful asset on the road, and once out of restricted areas the Seventeen is rarely held up by other traffic, almost always being able to slip by before the next corner or blind brow.

The semi-open road after Hoddesdon becomes very much built up in Ware, but

248

after this, on the undulations of A10, we get into top for the first time, and soar through Wadesmill and up the hill on the other side with the Seventeen imparting a tremendous feeling of security. Approaching Puckeridge at around 90 mph a firm application of the brake pedal (Girling discs with Ferodo pads) slows the car to 20 in a few seconds and we thread our way through parked and parking vehicles to B1368.

STEERING

After the frustrations of London and suburban traffic, the "road-through-the-villages" is like the entry to another world. It is by no means straight, or particularly fast, but provides a succession of fairly open sections on which one can obtain a very good impression of a car's real potential. Through the open bends before Barkway the Seventeen can be steered almost entirely with the throttle, and indeed, except for the sharp turning in Barley, the steering wheel rim is not moved more than three inches in fourteen miles. Together with the acceleration and "iron-hand-in-velvet-glove" braking, this light and direct steering is yet another factor which makes a major contribution to safe high speed driving.

Between Barley and Flint Cross some idea is gained of the Seventeen's potential in the way of straight-line speed. Then, turning right on to A505, the open road really unfolds and, accelerating hard, the little car sweeps through the gentle left, right, left bends which precede a two mile straight, coming out of the third "kink" at about 6000 rpm in top, running rapidly up to 7800 rpm (about 120 mph with the 4.9 to 1 "Brands Hatch" final drive ratio fitted) and holding this for about a mile before slowing for what turns out to be the mirage of a lorry shimmering over a slight rise. (I was also loath to move the tachometer tell-tale, which had been pushed round to this figure a few days earlier when the Seventeen lapped Brands Hatch during tests in 58.2 seconds, although no mention of rev limits was made when I collected the car.)

IMPECCABLE

For this type of use the road-holding of the Seventeen can only be described as impeccable. Initial break-away of the rear wheels can be induced quite easily, but there is obviously a very wide margin between this condition and complete loss of adhesion. For normal cornering the steering characteristic is virtually neutral,

The strut-type rear suspension of the Seventeen.

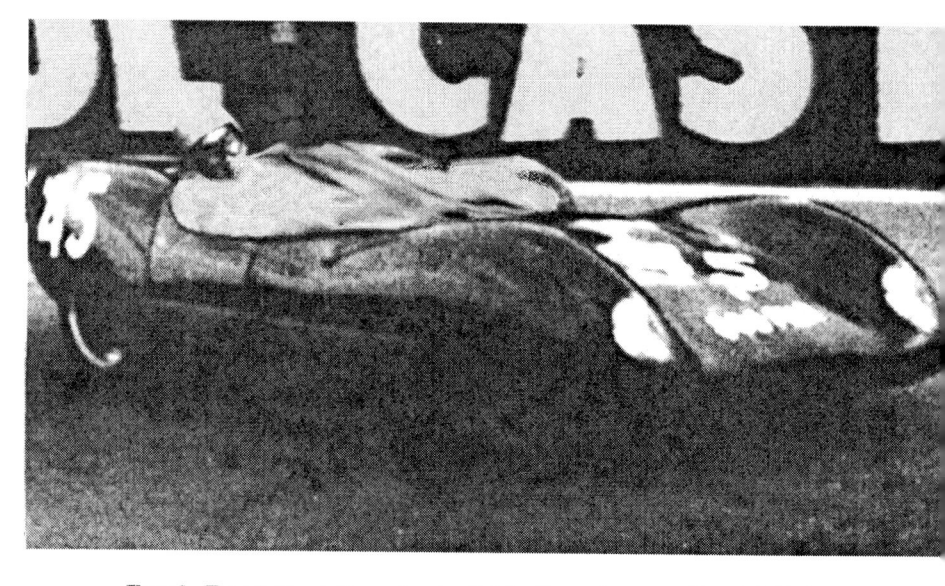

Derek Randall at the wheel of his Seventeen at Crystal Palace.

with a slight tendency towards understeer, but "lifting-off" in a corner produces oversteer, the retarding influence of the engine having much the same effect as putting the brakes on.

Despite the lack of upholstery (other than my own) I found the ride surprisingly comfortable, the relatively soft springs of the Seventeen smoothing out road surfaces which transmit all manner of jolts and jars into the more austere types of saloon cars. The propeller shaft tunnel became rather warm (something which might not have been evident with the bucket seat in use) but very little heat came through from the engine compartment, and on the whole I was much more comfortable than in certain current "luxury" sports cars.

FLEXIBILITY

Thus, although it is first and foremost a racing car, there seems to be no reason why the Seventeen should not be used regularly on the road. The steering lock is adequate, full lighting equipment is provided, and with a Stage One rather than a Stage Three engine fitted the car would lose little in acceleration, and gain a great deal in terms of flexibility. With road use in mind it might be reasonable also to consider the observations of a passenger, one who has to put up with long journeys in vehicles of all types (including transporters)—my wife.

For the Passenger
by Priscilla Phipps

I find the motoring gentlemen of my acquaintance singularly unimpressed by the opinions of a mere female passenger. They listen with avidity to my husband holding forth on handling characteristics, solemnly concerned with oversteer and understeer, gear ratios, and "what it'll do in third," and utterly ignore my practical comments on the toute ensemble. After all, the passenger has the opportunity to assess the general feel of a car, without being blinded by prejudice about its gearbox or its carburation. I maintain she (or even he!) is the only one who can truly calculate the amount of roll, for instance, having no steering wheel to hang on to in corners, the only one who knows anything about the adequacy of the suspension and interior comfort, and whether or not a car feels "safe."

Now, generally speaking, I feel happier in the passenger seat of a sports car—preferably a sports/racing car—than a saloon. There are exceptions to this but they are few. I like to travel close to the ground, and close to it I most certainly was the other day when I lowered myself into a Lotus Seventeen. We couldn't roar away from the new factory in best racing style for fear of tall men in dark blue, and had in fact to put up with many miles of irritating slowness and heavy traffic before we could take advantage of the phenomenal acceleration. When David really put his foot down, at last, the result was better than flying! It was a perfect summer day and the warm air rushed through my hair, encouraging it to stand on end even more than usual, and I abandoned myself to the tremendous exhilaration I feel at speed in an open car, as the grey road unrolled, miraculously smoothed of bends and corners—in a Lotus, at least.

COMFORT

I can't say it's as comfortable as a ride in a family saloon; after a few miles I forbore to touch the propshaft tunnel which looked normal enough but felt like a tin oven. Being close to the ground means being close to the potholes and boulders too; and as it was too hot to stretch my feet out ahead in the approved style, I bent my knees up under my chin.

But all this is not important. The Seventeen impressed me by making what once seemed dangerous corners look like gentle curves; by taking roundabouts steadily without that horrible wallowing one often experiences; by flicking in and out of a long line of traffic by virtue of its almost unbelievable acceleration; by braking, when necessary, as though we had run gently into a giant, invisible marshmallow; by taking me safely along a straight road at 120 mph without vibration or directional instability, and by just looking beautiful anyway.

APPEARANCE?

Of course, when we stopped, I looked a perfect fright. In racing overalls several sizes too big, with hair like a coconut doormat, and a face as black as Harry Schell's at the end of a race, I undoubtedly merited the outraged stares of more normal folk waiting at a 'bus stop, as I stepped reluctantly, on to firm ground again.

NEW LOTUS LOWER STILL

The Seventeen is much smaller, with a wheelbase of 82 in., and a lower frontal area. It weighs 110 lb. less than the Lotus Eleven. Springing is all independent with a new strut type front suspension which beats even Lotus records for lightness. A coil spring and damper strut acts as the steering swivel and has a light tubular stub axle with mounting plate for the disc brake caliper and the steering arm attached at the base by four bolts. Top end of the strut is attached to the frame; the lower end rests on a single wishbone. Rear suspension is the Lotus strut type swing axle as on the single seaters, the Fifteen and the Elite. Widely separated mounting points of the suspension have permitted the creation of a strong but extremely light space frame. The sheet metal floor is a stressed unit and a small sheet metal drive shaft tunnel takes part of the braking and acceleration loads from the chassis-mounted differential. A light alloy fuel tank of 8 gallons is mounted at the rear.

Engine normally supplied is the Coventry Climax 1,100 with single overhead camshaft in stage three tune with five bearing crankshaft giving 84 b.h.p. at 6,800 r.p.m. on a 9.8 to 1 compression. Mounting points are also designed to take the Climax 750 c.c. FWM engine when it becomes available.

Transmission is through a 7¼ in. single plate clutch, hydraulically operated and a lightweight four-speed close ratio gearbox in unit with the engine. A choice of four ratios is available for the hypoid final drive and a ZF limited slip differential is an optional extra.

Brakes are Girling discs — 9½ in. diameter — operated through two master cylinders with an adjustable balance bar. The body will be very well streamlined on familiar Lotus lines. Dry weight is only 750 lb. for the complete car.

The Lotus Fifteen already raced so successfully by private owners has been refined and developed. Front suspension has been reversed so that the anti-roll bar forming part of the top wishbones passes rearwards, allowing more space for radiator and oil cooler and simplifying the chassis frame.

Torque produced by the 2-litre twin camshaft Climax engine is now such that a four-speed gearbox is considered adequate and a BMC box is now fitted in unit with the engine. The same box will also be available to export buyers of the 1,500 car as they may find it easier to service than the Lotus five-speed box which forms a unit with the differential, although this is still available to order.

The Lotus Elite, now in regular production will be raced at Sebring, Le Mans and Rheims. For the Formula I and Formula II cars Stan Elsworth, former Vanwall mechanic, will take charge of preparation.

**LOTUS SEVENTEEN—
TECHNICAL DETAILS**

ENGINE: Coventry Climax 1100 engine, Stage III. Single O.H.C. 4-cylinder; bore and stroke, 72.4 mm. x 66.6 mm.; 1098 c.c.; 84 b.h.p. at 6,800 r.p.m; comp. ratio, 9.8 to 1; light alloy cylinder block and crankcase, slip fit cylinder liners. Overhead camshaft driven from a gear reduction off the crankshaft to a jackshaft and thence by a duplex chain to the camshaft sprocket. Direct valve operation through chilled cast iron tappets working in guides surmounting the valve springs. Tappet adjustment by hardened discs. Fully counterweighted crankshaft in five copper lead steel backed main bearings of 2⅛ in. diameter and 1 in. width (Stage I and Stage II engines have three bearings) big end bear-

So much torque pours out of that two-litre Coventry-Climax motor that Chapman decided to use a four speed B.M.C. gearbox instead of the normal five-speeder. Instrument panel is perfectly simple.

ings are copper lead 1¾ in. in diameter, and ⅝ in. wide. Connecting rods split diagonally for easy withdrawal. Aluminium pistons with pressure-backed "Dykes" compression rings and a chromium plated top ring. Combustion chambers are wedge shaped and the XB steel valves seat on shrunk-in austenitic cast iron seatings.

TRANSMISSION: Single dry plate clutch, 7¼ in., hydraulically operated. Four speed close ratio gearbox in unit with engine. Ratios 2.5:1, 1.67:1, 1.23:1, 1:1; reverse, 2.5:1. Hypoid final drive of 4.22:1. Alternative ratios, 3.73, 3.9, 4.55 and 4.875. ZF limited slip differential optional at extra cost.

SUSPENSION: Independent front by strut and single wishbone with telescopic hydraulic dampers and coil springs. Independent rear by Lotus strut with coil springs and telescopic dampers.

BRAKES: Light Girling hydraulically operated 9½ in. discs outboard at front, inboard at rear. Horizontally mounted handbrake, operating the rear calipers through cables.

FRAME: Multi-tubular space frame of ⅝ in. and ¾ in. square and round tubing of 20 gauge steel. The propeller shaft and floor are stressed members. Engine carried on two rubber mountings at front and single rubber mounting at rear attached to the gearbox; it is tilted through 10 deg. to the vertical to give a straight induction tract. Easily detachable fuel tank for access to final drive and rear brakes.

ELECTRICAL SYSTEM: Lightweight 12 volt, 31 amp. hr battery (weight 24 lb.) in tail. Coil and distributor, centrifugal advance and retard, belt driven dynamo, automatic voltage control. Fuse box. Recessed Lucas 6 in. headlamps incorporating side lamps, twin stop tail-lights, rear number plate lamp, high frequency horn. Instrument lighting. Screen wiper.

INSTRUMENTS: 3 in. tachometer, 8,000 r.p.m., oil pressure gauge, water temperature gauge, ammeter.

WHEELS AND TYRES: Magnesium bolt-on wheels with identical rims front and rear. Tyres 4.50-15, front; 5.00-15, rear. 4.50-15 spare wheel under rear panel. Wire wheels as alternative.

DIMENSIONS: Wheelbase, 82 in.; front track 42 in., rear track 45 in.; overall length, 131 in.; overall width, 55½ in.; height to scuttle, 23 in.; overall height, 29 in.; ground clearance, 5 in.

WEIGHT: Standard Seventeen, less fuel, 750 lb. #

Lotus 17 sports car is newest of Chapman's designs, features strut-type independent rear suspension, inboard disc brakes and alloy wheels.

Further evidence of Chapman's brilliance: see how the Lotus XV's anti-roll bar forms part of upper wishbone, allowing lower radiator mounting.

THE MANY FACES OF LOTUS

Colin Chapman's full line of sports and Grand Prix cars makes an imposing list. Here is a partial lineup including the Formula I, Formula II, Mark 15, Two-Liter and Mark 17.

Far left: Lotus Formula I, driven by Graham Hill at Monaco, has long, low distinctive silhouette. Car is best on short tight course.

Left: Engine on Formula I/II car is set 17 degrees to vertical and 10 degrees to horizontal to permit driveshaft to pass on left side of cockpit.

Below left: Lotus front suspension on Formula car is marked by lightness, simplicity. Disc brake is set into magnesium alloy wheel.

by Gordon Wilkins

Profiting from last year's lessons, when they attempted to do far too much and suffered setbacks in racing, Lotus have pulled their factory team out of sportscar racing but are giving limited support to approved stables and private owners. The bounding vitality of this vigorous young outfit is now concentrated on production of an extended range of cars including a new small sports model and full-scale participation in Formula I and Formula II Grand Prix races.

The single-seater which takes either size of engine has been redesigned from 1958 with a new chassis frame and cleaner body which has no blisters over the engine. For Formula I events the latest Coventry Climax engine displacing 2495cc is employed. After experimenting with two different mountings, the power unit is canted 17 degrees to the vertical and 10 degrees to the car's horizontal center line to take the driveshaft past the left side of the cockpit. The Lotus five-speed gearbox in unit with the differential has been redesigned with a positive stop shift in which the lever returns to the same position every time instead of the five-notch quadrant which drivers found difficult to use. There is now more room in the cockpit and the exhaust system is mounted externally. Cooling systems for water and oil are redesigned and rear suspension is stronger. The car weighs about 700 pounds dry.

The new frame has a removable tube over the engine for additional stiffness while suspension at front and rear is partly enclosed by the body.

Using the car in Formula II form with 1500cc Climax engine, Graham Hill was able to lap the Brands Hatch circuit in 56.3 seconds and put in 15 consecutive laps well below Stirling Moss's old racing record of 57.4 seconds.

The entirely new sports-racing car is the Mark 17. Conceived originally as a 750cc machine, it is very small and extremely light. As now offered, with the Climax 1100cc engine, it is very potent indeed. At present it is only being supplied on the British market but whatever the United States market wants it usually gets.

The 17 is much smaller than any previous Lotus models, with a wheelbase of 82 inches and a lower frontal area; it weighs 110 pounds less than the Lotus 11. Suspension is all independent with a new strut-type front suspension which beats even Lotus records for lightness. A coil spring and damper strut acts as the steering swivel and has a light tubular stub axle with mounting plate for the disc brake caliper and the steering arm attached at the base by four bolts. Top end of the strut is attached to the frame; the lower end rests on a single wishbone. Rear suspension is the Lotus strut-type swing axle as on the single seaters, the 15 and the Elite Coupe. Widely separated mounting points of the suspension have permitted the creation of a strong but extremely light space frame. The sheet metal floor is a stressed unit and a small sheet metal driveshaft tunnel takes part of the braking and acceleration loads from the chassis-mounted differential. A light alloy fuel tank of eight gallons is mounted at the rear.

Engine normally supplied is the Coventry Climax 1100 with single-overhead camshaft in stage three with five-bearing crankshaft. This unit gives 84 bhp at 6800 rpm with 9.8 to 1 compression. Mounting points are also designed to take the Climax 750cc FWM engine.

Photos by Gunther Molter, Geoffrey Goddard and Bob D'Olivo

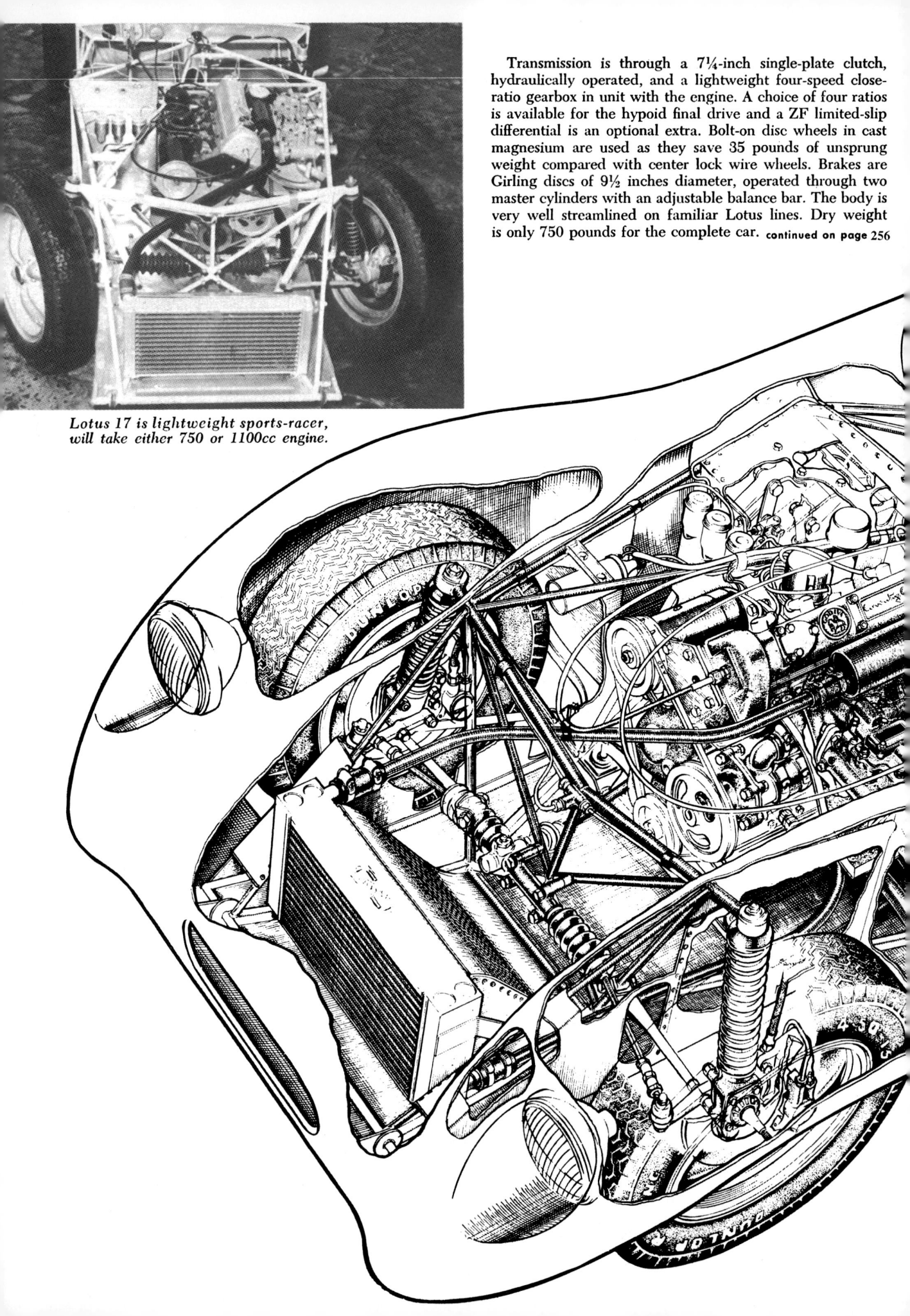

Transmission is through a 7¼-inch single-plate clutch, hydraulically operated, and a lightweight four-speed close-ratio gearbox in unit with the engine. A choice of four ratios is available for the hypoid final drive and a ZF limited-slip differential is an optional extra. Bolt-on disc wheels in cast magnesium are used as they save 35 pounds of unsprung weight compared with center lock wire wheels. Brakes are Girling discs of 9½ inches diameter, operated through two master cylinders with an adjustable balance bar. The body is very well streamlined on familiar Lotus lines. Dry weight is only 750 pounds for the complete car. **continued on page 256**

Lotus 17 is lightweight sports-racer, will take either 750 or 1100cc engine.

THE MANY FACES OF LOTUS

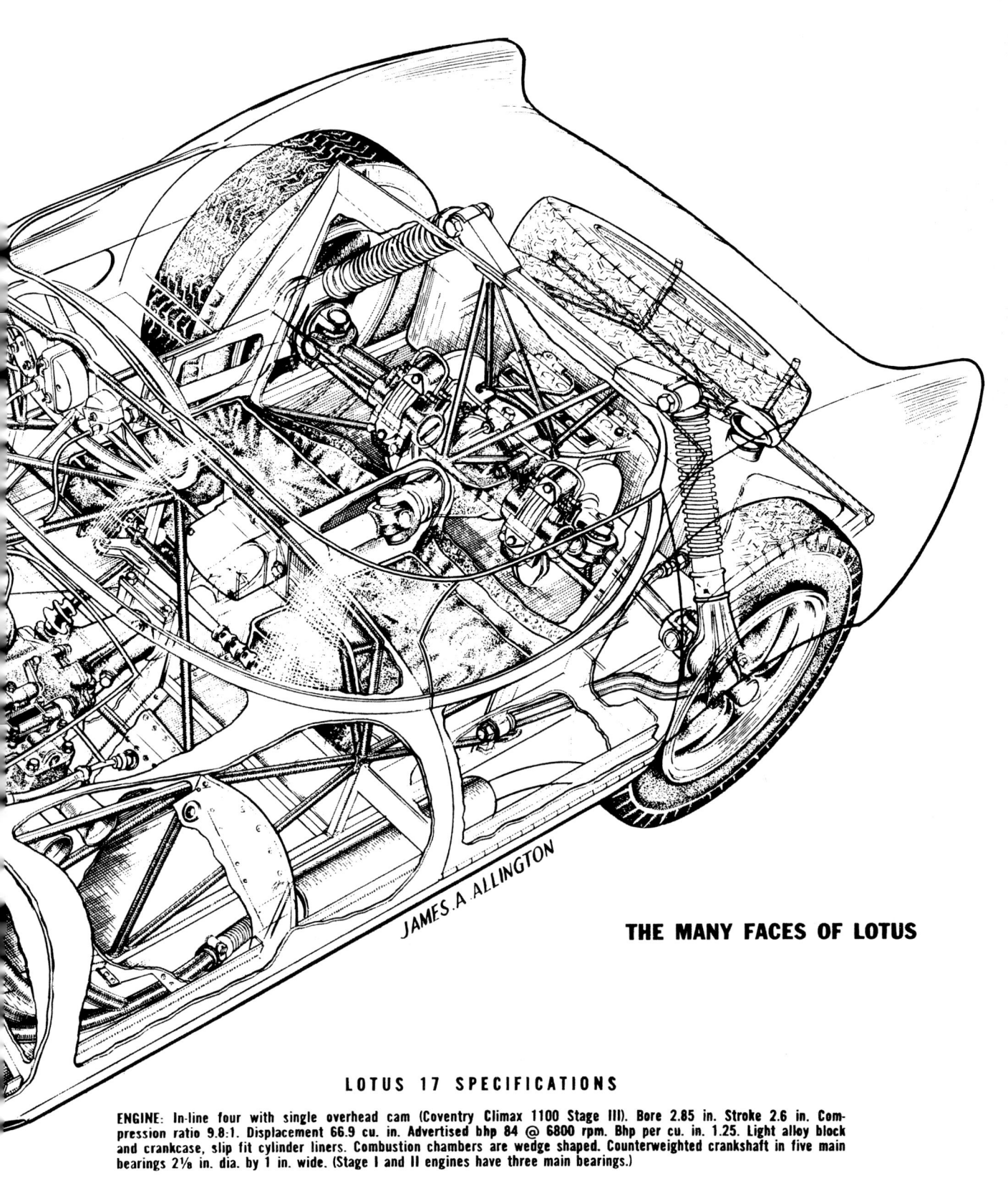

LOTUS 17 SPECIFICATIONS

ENGINE: In-line four with single overhead cam (Coventry Climax 1100 Stage III). Bore 2.85 in. Stroke 2.6 in. Compression ratio 9.8:1. Displacement 66.9 cu. in. Advertised bhp 84 @ 6800 rpm. Bhp per cu. in. 1.25. Light alloy block and crankcase, slip fit cylinder liners. Combustion chambers are wedge shaped. Counterweighted crankshaft in five main bearings 2 1/8 in. dia. by 1 in. wide. (Stage I and II engines have three main bearings.)

TRANSMISSION: Single dry plate clutch 7 1/4 in. hydraulically operated. Ratios 2.5:1, 1.67:1, 1.23:1, 1:1. Hypoid final drive 4.22:1. Alternate ratios 3.73:1, 3.9:1, 4.55:1, 4.875:1. ZF limited-slip differential optional.

CHASSIS: Welded tube space frame of 20-gauge steel square and round tubes. Propeller shaft and floor stressed. Engine mounted 10 degrees to vertical for straight induction tract. Front suspension — Strut and single wishbone with telescopic shocks and coil springs. Rear — Independent by Lotus strut with coil springs and telescopic shocks. Brakes — 9½-in. Girling discs, outboard at front, inboard at rear. Wheels — Magnesium bolt-on; center lock wire wheels optional. Tires — 4.50 x 15 front, 5.00 x 15 rear.

DIMENSIONS: Wheelbase 82 in., overall length 131, overall height 29, overall width 55.5, ground clearance 5, front tread 42, rear tread 45, dry weight 750 lbs., 8.9 lbs./bhp.

The Lotus 15, already raced so successfully by private owners, has been refined and developed. Front suspension has been reversed so that the anti-roll bar forming part of the top wishbones passes rearwards, allowing more space for radiator and oil cooler and simplifying the chassis frame.

Torque produced by the two-liter twin-camshaft Climax engine is now such that a four-speed gearbox is considered adequate and a BMC box is now fitted in unit with the engine. The same box will also be available to export buyers of the 1500cc car as they may find it easier to service than the Lotus five-speed box which forms a unit with the differential although this is still available to order.

The low body line does not allow a conventional radiator header tank to have a sufficient head of water above the pump to separate air bubbles and prevent cavitation at the impeller in all conditions. Two swirl pots are therefore being used to separate the air by centrifugal action and allow the water displaced by thermal expansion to be returned again on cooling.

Lotus-builder Colin Chapman never ends the development of his various models which makes it very difficult to make firm statements about his cars and be certain of their accuracy. The important fact is that his development has always been for the good of the automobile so we can't feel too embarrassed when occasionally caught in misstatements about the Lotus.

As in Formula cars, engine in Mark 15 is tilted 17 degrees to vertical but driveshaft is parallel to car's center.

THE MANY FACES OF LOTUS

Two-liter Lotus, based on Mark 15, is intended for U. S. market, promises to give strong competition to Porsches. Car handles easily, offers comfortable racing.

Two-liter Lotus unfolds for easy access to mechanical components. Magnesium wheels are light but not quick change.

256

No matter how outstanding a car appears on paper, the proof is in the driving. Our test drive in a new two-liter Lotus 15, provided by U. S. distributor Jay Chamberlain, North Hollywood, Calif., proved many things. Not the least of them is that it is becoming increasingly more difficult, under F.I.A. rules governing sportscars, for builders to disguise a pure racing machine as a two-seater touring car. Colin Chapman, a man who enjoys the comforts of life, apparently appreciates the fact that some of this comfort must apply to the driver of his sportscars. He has crowded the little two-liter car full of a really potent engine, good brakes, plenty of fuel capacity, a husky gearbox, and still preserved adequate seating, good wheel position, pedal room and wind protection. Best of all, one of the greatest comforts of competition driving is the peace of mind in knowing that under you is a superb handling chassis.

Chamberlain, no stranger to competition driving, eased his rather ample bulk into one of the first two-liter machines on the West Coast and proceeded to turn some hot laps on the Riverside International Raceway road racing course. Track, gear ratio and climatic conditions dictated a carburetor jet size change after which the car was turned over to us for some hot laps. The contrast between our driving experience and Chamberlain's is wide-spread. Jay, with many years of competition but never a race at Riverside, and my own — no Lotus competition but hundreds of miles every year testing all sorts of automobiles on this course. Strangely, we both arrived at virtually the same conclusions. Here they are:

The two-liter has a flat handling chassis with suspension designed to provide good support in the corners without bone-jarring rebound or wheel bounce in the rough stuff. Built-in understeer provides a little front wheel washout in hard cornering without the necessity of micrometer corrections at the wheel rim to negotiate fast S-bends. The car sticks like crazy to the limit of adhesion at which time it really lets go. (This occurs in a common racing maneuver known as "being over your head.") The 3.7 to 1 rear end ratio was too low for the Riverside mile-long straight where the 6500 rpm red-line set for the tests (136 mph) was reached about one-fifth of the way into the straight. The car is easy to drive, plenty of cockpit room and ventilation, and not much vibration or engine noise. We learned one other important thing — a healthy respect for turn seven, a downhill, undulating camber, 180-degree left-hand corner with a blind over-a-hill approach. It caught us both "over our heads" and screeching sideways into slides that seemed to last forever.

A series of quarter-mile acceleration runs indicated that the car gets off the mark exceptionally well. Elapsed time was 13.2 seconds and speed at the end of the quarter was 115.5 mph.

This two-liter machine is a remarkable bit of race car. On the basis of its known performance it should prove to be a strong class contender. —**Charles Nerpel**

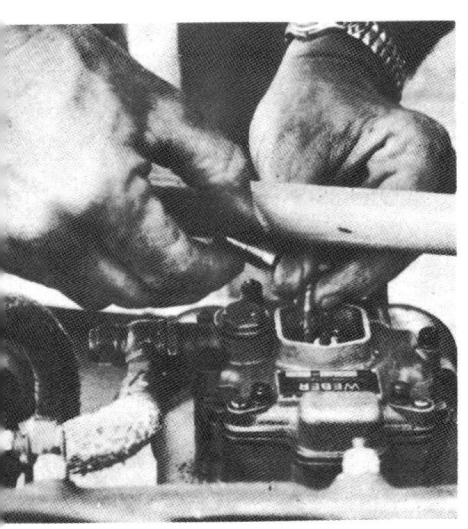

Lotus cornered very flat in our tests, stuck well to limit of adhesion, then car broke loose with little warning.

Frame tube across one of the Weber carburetors makes changing jets difficult.

Rear suspension is Chapman strut type; elastic cords hold gas and oil tanks.

Car accelerates well as shown by ¼-mile elapsed time of 13.2 secs. and 115 mph.

Before modification. The Lotus Seventeen being driven through the new hairpin at Prescott. Note the 'nose-dive' position of the body and the very small clearance at the front.

MODIFIED SUSPENSION FOR A LOTUS SEVENTEEN

by Antony Reardon-Smith

LAST November I bought a Lotus Seventeen chassis and body complete with latest modified front and rear suspension from a well-known Midland firm. This was in place of my Lotus Seven, in which David Peregrine and I completed our first season of hill climbing last year.

The new car was my attempt to find a class winner. We thought that the independent rear suspension, disc brakes all round and the 4.9 crown wheel and pinion, would be ideal for hills.

STAGE TWO CLIMAX

In recent years it has been proved that it is not sheer power one needs, but first-class roadholding. We therefore retained my FWA stage two 1,098 cc Coventry Climax engine for the new machine. We had found this an adequate power unit last year, and as we did not have the time to do any circuit racing, the more costly and temperamental stage three tuning was shelved for the time being.

During the winter the Seventeen was prepared by our local wizard, Norman Moss, who spent very many hours fitting engine and gearbox into the frame—as this chassis had not been built for a Climax unit.

Many people expressed their doubts as to the suitability of the Seventeen for hill climbing. We were told that the front suspension was at fault, and tended to wander while cornering, especially when accelerating out of a hairpin, such as the new loop at Prescott. In fact we only experienced this at our first meeting there on June 6.

We found that the front end broke away under power in the hairpins, and we also experienced bottoming when under severe braking on the approach to Pardon. This also proved that the front coil springs were not strong enough, and our clearance was so small that we began to worry about the sump.

PROMISING DEBUT

Despite these difficulties David Peregrine took the Seventeen up the hill in a time of 56.05 seconds. We thought this time very good, since it compared with a fastest time of 58.7 seconds put up last year by our Lotus Seven Climax. Another point to be taken into account was that neither of us had even driven the car before this meeting.

At the next meeting at Shelsley Walsh the car bottomed during our first practice climb sufficiently to tear the corner off the sump. We returned home to South Wales determined to rectify the faults for good.

Our problem was how to raise and stiffen the front end at minimum cost. Again, after a lot of thought and discussion, the ingenuity of Norman Moss came to our aid with a simple answer.

On the Seventeen, with double wishbone front suspension, the bottom ends of the shock absorbers are mounted on to the bottom wishbone but at a lower level—that is, underneath them. So to raise the clearance the lower wishbones were removed, reversed right to left and vice versa, and turned upside down. Therefore the lower ends of the shock absorbers were now mounted on to the top of the lower wishbone, as will be seen from the picture.

This also increased the angle of the

After modification. Seen again in action, this time at Westbrook Hay. The greater clearance at the front can be seen clearly.

dampers, and when the car stood on its road wheels they were more contracted than they had been previously. So we obtained our stiffening effect as well.

The overall clearance had been increased by about two-and-a-half inches, and to our surprise the stability of the front end was very much better. We then decided to test it further at Silverstone. A day's testing was needed at this stage anyway, since we had never really driven the car before, and the adjustable rear shock absorbers also needed setting.

Close-up view of the modified front offside suspension.

This was all achieved during the day, but the stage two Climax transmitting through a 4.9 to 1 back axle found the track a little too fast, so the result was that we went home with a broken tappet and a bent inlet valve. Even so, before the mishap, we found we were able to lap at about 90 miles an hour.

The day at Silverstone had also shown us that the front suspension was very much better in its modified form, and was now a match for the very excellent rear suspension layout.

The next hill climb meeting was at Westbrook Hay, where we again found that the handling was very much improved (although it could not be taken to the limit because of the wet track conditions on that day).

A time of 26.4 seconds was put up by the car under these damp conditions. Comparing this with the Seven's time of 29.78 seconds on a dry course last year this improvement over a 650-yard course was most pleasing, especially bearing in mind the damp surface.

There are still many hill climbs yet to come this year, and we are certain that our simple and inexpensive modifications will improve our chances on the hills. But whatever we do I don't think we will be able to go faster than that b . . . . . Lola which always appears in our class.

Sorting out The Seventeen

A DESCRIPTION OF TESTING AND DEVELOPMENT WORK

BY ALAN STACEY

Leaving the "pits" for another session to find the effect of the latest "mods."

I WAS very pleased when David Phipps suggested that I should contribute a few words on the new Lotus Seventeen, if only to help reduce the endless questions from enthusiasts and prospective customers—" Is it quick, yet?" . . . " Will it beat the Lolas?" As it hasn't done the latter yet, although I think it is certainly capable of doing so, I must try to give an idea of the development work which has taken place on the car.

QUICKER

To start with let me just say that I believe it will be quicker than all its predecessors. To all the pessimists and members of the Lola fan club who suggest " It's too narrow," I would say "What is the fastest car round a corner?" —a '500 with a 3 ft 6 in track. The point is that, as cars are going increasingly quickly these days and reaching a higher state of development, there is little chance of an entirely new design being " right " straight off the drawing board.

The need for a certain amount of modification became apparent in practice for the Goodwood Easter Monday meeting. I managed to record 1 min 40.2 secs despite atrocious handling qualities, but decided it would be unwise to race the car and treated practice as a testing session, which allowed me to make a few suggestions to the powers-that-be.

The next meeting for which the Seventeen was entered was Aintree on 18 April, and although I was busily engaged preparing the new Fifteen I was assured that all my suggestions concerning the roadholding of the Seventeen had been carried out.

In practice I thought we really had got somewhere. It was wet, but I had little difficulty in recording fastest practice time. However, in a " free for all " practice session in the dry the increased cornering forces brought out the old oversteering tendencies. Nevertheless, I decided to race the car, and although I lost my pole position on the grid due to some last minute carburetter trouble, starting from the back row, I managed to take the lead within two laps, when second gear went. Still, the car had shown its potential.

SUSTAINED EFFORT

Practice for the Silverstone International Trophy meeting revealed the same interent trouble, and now I had got my Fifteen going quickly, I decided a sustained effort would have to be made on the Seventeen. After two days' practice, with Mike Costin working full time on the Seventeen, we discovered the cause of the disconcertingly sudden oversteer. Unfortunately, in the time available this could only be cured by adjustments giving a completely oversteering tendency. The race thus became a test again, but it did prove that the " twitch " had gone.

After Silverstone, due partly to the not undeserved adverse publicity and lack of improvements we decided to do another day's testing at Silverstone. An early start was made and Colin and Mike

Sorting out The Seventeen
Continued

Discussion period; left to right, Graham Hill, Don Badger of Dunlops, Alan Stacey, Colin Chapman and another Dunlop representative.

Almost neutral-steer characteristics at Becketts.

brought the car and two mechanics with them, complete with an assortment of springs and anti-roll bars.

The test began with a few laps warming up and making sure the faults encountered during the last race were still present, and sure enough the oversteer was still pronounced. The first step taken to overcome this was the resetting of the ride level. This was found to be very critical, and was definitely too high. Lowering it improved the handling immensely, but with a full load of fuel it was found that the rear of the car bottomed through Becketts.

To prevent this, stronger rear springs were fitted. This, we knew, would bring back the oversteer, but it is is a principle of such tests to try only one thing at a time. With the new springs fitted the car certainly oversteered, but it was more gentle and easier to control. We had two ways of getting back to an understeering tendency, either by fitting a stronger roll bar or by stiffening up the front springs. As the car was not rolling excessively, stronger front springs were fitted, and as a result, the car handled very well indeed. After 79 laps of the Grand Prix circuit throughout the day I got down to 1.49.5 —this with an engine that was 300 rpm down on Derek Randall's standard-engined Seventeen. From this lap time it seems feasible to suggest that with a few more horses times of around 1.48 would be possible.

In comparison with the Fifteen and Formula cars, the Seventeen now has much more neutral steering, that is, less understeer. I believe it is quicker into a corner, and that with the increase in roadholding gained with the strut type rear end, it was essential to incorporate something similar at the front to maintain stability through the corner at the increased speed. This season all the quick cars using independent rear suspension seem to suffer from understeer. I believe the Seventeen has the answer.

After a quick check all round on the engine in an attempt to regain the lost horsepower, we took the car to Crystal Palace for the Whit Monday meeting. Practice showed that the horses hadn't returned, but a time of 1.4.0, under Keith Hall's 1100 cc lap record, proved that the roadholding was now very good. During practice private timing showed that the Seventeen was easily the fastest up to 1500 cc car, including Salvadori's Cooper Monaco and the Lolas, through the notorious Ramp Bend.

On Sunday we rounded up the horses ready for Monday and for the first time were feeling slightly confident. However, in the first 25 yards of unofficial practice the crankshaft broke. Who said there's no luck in motor racing!

Well, that's the story to date. We've proved that the Seventeen is the lightest 1100 yet built and also that its roadholding is on a par with the best. Doesn't that mean its the fastest?

Very fast until the gearbox packed up; the Seventeen at Aintree on 18 April.

Lotus Nineteen

The Lotus Fifteen had been Colin Chapman's introduction to large capacity sports car racing, and hoped for overall race victory. Although fragile, the Fifteen had proved itself a very quick car, and sometimes a race winner.

With the rear engined Lotus 18 in 1959, the scene was set for a rear engined large capacity sports racing car to carry forward Lotus aspirations in international competition. This was the Lotus 19, or Lotus Monte Carlo in recognition of the first Grand Prix win for Lotus by Stirling Moss in Rob Walker's Lotus 18 at Monaco in May 1960. Gone, also, were the roman numerals depicting Lotus models. Instead it was Nineteen or just 19.

Using the Len Terry inspired perforated hoop bulkheads as the main bracing points in the tubular chassis as per the 18, this was widened to accommodate two drivers and the Lotus Nineteen Sports Racing car was born part way through the 1960 racing season. *Autosport* of 31st March 1961 produced a centre spread introduction with a James Allington cutaway drawing. The market for the Lotus Nineteen was predominantly America and track tests were published in *Road & Track* April 1961, *Sports Car Graphic* May 1961 and *Car and Driver* June 1961.

The power unit for the Lotus Nineteen was the Coventry Climax FPF, twin-overhead-camshaft engine that had been used in the Lotus 15, plus single-seaters 12 and 16. Originally in 1500cc capacity this had now grown to 2.0 and 2.5-litres producing up to 240bhp. Most Nineteens were fitted with the Mark 2 Lotus 'Queerbox' from the single-seater Lotus 16, but some were later replaced by more reliable forms of transaxle.

The introductory race for the Lotus Nineteen was at Karlskoga, Sweden in August 1960 where, continuing Lotus tradition, the new car won first time out driven by Stirling Moss. The following day Swedish driver Jo Bonnier set a new Swedish record with the Nineteen at 161mph over a 1000 yard run. In 1962 Dan Gurney won the Dayton Continental 3 Hours race in the USA. The Lotus Nineteen was a very successful sports racing car with many victories to its credit over its 3-4 year competition history from 1960-64.

A total of twelve Lotus 19s were built of which nine were sold to the USA, the remaining three being raced by the British UST-Laystall Team.

Graham Capel

Here's the sleek new golden yellow Lotus MK-19 that will carry the name of the Bardahl International Oil Corporation in sports car competition throughout North America in 1963. The speedy roadster, with sensational young Jerry Grant at the wheel, will compete in 20 major sports car races. Bardahl has been a consistent competitor in the Indianapolis 500 Mile Memorial Day Classic and in unlimited hydroplane racing. This is the first time the Seattle based additive oil firm has entered sports car racing competition.
"300 bhp Aluminum Buick V-8"

Lotus Nineteen Sports Racing Car

Above: The Lotus Nineteen sports car is based on the very successful 1960 Formula One car, and has proved formidable in trials at Silverstone. It won its first race at Karlskoga in Sweden driven by Stirling Moss. The space frame is wider in the central section to accommodate the driver and passenger. The controls are also offset to suit the new driving position, but the gear level is central.

Left: The rear of the new Lotus is cut off sharply and the large cooling vent behind the transmission, which was introduced on the formula cars this year, is retained. The bodywork is reinforced plastic with a one-piece nose section and a detachable engine cover at the rear. The spare wheel is housed in the front above the driver's knees, and the fuel capacity of 18 gallons is carried in two side pannier tanks. The engine is the latest Climax FPF unit fitted with a starter, and is used in conjunction with a Lotus five speed gearbox, which also has a reverse gear.

Below left: Colin Chapman corners the Lotus Nineteen during tests at Silverstone. The body is wider but has the same track and wheelbase as the Formula car. The battery and radiators for oil and water are mounted in the front, and both oil and water pipes are exposed as they pass along the side of the car. Cooling vents for the front disc brakes and the outboard mounted rear disc brakes are also visible.

Lotus Monte Carlo, M. Costin at the wheel

Lotus Monte Carlo

This promising newcomer to the sports racing car field is described by David Phipps

HAVING gone over to an entirely new rear-engined design for his 1960 Formula One and Formula Junior cars, it is hardly surprising that Colin Chapman has used the same basic layout in the Lotus Monte Carlo sports car. Within the works the new model is known as the Nineteen, its more exotic title resulting from the fact that the firm scored its first Grande Epreuve victory in the Principality this year, albeit with a privately entered car.

In principle the Monte Carlo is an exact copy of the Formula One car, but in practice it has been necessary to make numerous alterations to turn the basic single-seater into a sports car. First and foremost, the space-frame chassis has been widened out to provide the seating space required by Appendix "C" of the International Sporting Code. It remains a three section unit, as on the Formula One car, and in fact the front bulkhead (just behind the radiator) and the rear bulkhead (through which the gearbox protrudes) are Formula One components. Immediately behind the front bulkhead, whose location is determined by the forward front wishbone mountings, the chassis side rails begin to diverge. A second bulkhead coincides with the rearward front suspension mountings. Diagonal bracing on five sides of this front suspension bay makes it exceptionally stiff and fully capable of absorbing all the loads passed into it by the front suspension and steering (the steering rack is mounted on the front bulkhead at the apex of two triangles).

An unusual feature on a Lotus is the location of the front coil spring/damper units on tubes in bending. This divergence from the Formula One practice of locating the suspension unit and forward top wishbone mounting by a common bolt has been made necessary by the widening of the chassis. To compensate for the extra loading involved, the short tube between the two top wishbone mountings is of $1\frac{1}{8}$ inch, 14 gauge mild steel, as against the 1 inch and $\frac{3}{4}$ inch 16 and 18 gauge tubing used for the rest of the chassis.

Chassis

Forward of the front bulkhead the chassis consists of a sub-frame carrying mountings for the radiator, oil tank and bodywork. Within the front suspension bay are mountings for brake and clutch master cylinders, throttle, brake and clutch pedals and battery. The front section of the frame extends to the scuttle hoop, which is a tubular and perforated sheet steel structure designed to eliminate the need for diagonal bracing. The other five sides of this section are all fully triangulated—by the stressed aluminium undertray in the case of the floor. In addition to acting as a major structural member, the scuttle hoop also provides mountings for steering column, gear-lever, seats, instruments and brake and clutch reservoirs. The hand brake is mounted on the top diagonal tube just forward of the hoop. From the scuttle hoop rearwards the chassis side rails run virtually parallel to the engine bulkhead. As on the Formula One car, this centre section is only braced on three sides, and with the greater width of the sports car becomes even less stiff than on the single-seater, but the rigidity of the front and rear sections compensates for this and gives the whole chassis adequate torsional stiffness.

From the engine bulkhead the main frame rails converge towards the rear bulkhead, constructed on the same lines as the scuttle hoop. Although not straight sided, the rear bulkhead is an effective triangle, its shape being determined by the need to accommodate the inboard brake discs. The upper tubes meet this bulkhead just above the pick-ups for the rear suspension units, while the lower ones converge more rapidly to meet at the bottom of the hoop, at the lower wishbone pick-ups. Fore and aft suspension loads are taken out into the chassis through parallel radius arms anchored at the top and bottom of the engine bulkhead. As the latter is considerably wider on the Monte Carlo than on the single-seater this results in a slight alteration of geometry, but the suspension is otherwise identical to that of the Formula One car.

The upper part of the rear bulkhead is removable, together with a Y-shaped top diagonal, on the release of four fitted shear bolts and one tension bolt. In addition to absorbing suspension loads at either end, this member also deals with engine loads, the gearbox being located at its centre via two rubber cone-bushed mountings. Each front engine mounting is located at the apex of two triangles, consisting of the side frame diagonals. Complete with all its brackets, the chassis weighs 70 lbs.

Suspension

Front suspension is by double tubular wishbones, with proprietary (Standard-Triumph) uprights and machined steel hubs, as on the Formula One car. The upper wishbones have threaded, ball-jointed outer ends to allow alteration of camber angle, and an anti-roll bar is fitted, located on the chassis beneath the rearward top wishbone mounting and connected to the top wishbones below the ball joints in spherical bearings. Steering is by rack and pinion gear mounted just ahead of the wheel centre line. A straight steering column is used, bolted to a 14 inch alloy wheel with leather-covered rim.

Rear suspension elements are the lower wishbones and the drive shafts for transverse location, and parallel radius arms for fore and aft location. At their outer ends these components are linked by castings which also carry the wheel hub bearings. The lower wishbones are threaded at their inner ends for alteration of camber angle and at the outer for alteration of toe-in. The rear anti-roll bar, located on the chassis at the suspension unit mountings, is connected to the lower wishbones by upright links incorporating spherical bearings. Wheels are of cast magnesium, 15 inches in diameter and fitted on six studs. Rim section is 5 inches at the front, $6\frac{1}{2}$ inches at the rear, and tyre sizes are respectively 5.00 and 6.50

Detail arrangements

Formula One brakes are used, consisting of outboard mounted $10\frac{1}{2}$ in. front discs and inboard mounted $9\frac{1}{2}$ in. rear discs. Provision is also made in the hub castings for mounting the rear brakes outboard; in hot climates it may well be worth the sacrifice of increased unsprung weight to move the brakes away from the engine and gearbox.

The main 12 gallon fuel tank is mounted on the left of the car—on the far side from the driver—with a 10 gallon auxiliary tank alongside and behind the driver. The space above the driver's legs, used for the main fuel tank on the Formula One car, contains the spare wheel on the sports car. The battery is alongside the pedals. The cross-flow radiator and 6 gallon oil tank are as on the Formula One car, with the oil tank breathing through the chassis to a number of small holes at the rear. Aluminium water pipes link engine and radiator, and oil is circulated between engine, oil radiator and oil tank—and gearbox and gearbox oil radiator—by pipes which run outside the body panels over much of their length.

The standard power unit is the 2495 c.c. four-cylinder

Rear end of the Lotus Monte Carlo sports car from which the very close affinity to the formula one car can be gauged

Front of the new Lotus Monte Carlo sports car showing radiator, oil tank, battery alongside pedals, and main fuel tank mounted outside chassis on nearside of car

Birds-eye view of Lotus Monte Carlo showing general layout and compact dimensions of the car

Coventry Climax FPF engine, which develops 239 b.h.p. at 6750 r.p.m. For sports car use this has Lucas coil ignition, dynamo and starter. Fuel is supplied to the two twin choke Weber 58DC03 carburettors by two S.U. electric fuel pumps.

Transmission

Bolted directly to the engine is the Lotus five speed gearbox/final drive unit, the front casing of which incorporates the clutch bell housing and starter mounting. The two gear trains are mounted behind the rear wheel centre line and the drive, taken through a Borg and Beck twin plate clutch with sintered copper linings, enters the box beneath the differential unit and is transmitted in a vertical plane. Hypoid bevel final drive gears are used and the unit has its own lubrication system, with a reservoir mounted ahead and to the right of it.

In addition to being extremely compact, this gearbox has the great advantage that third, fourth and fifth ratios can be changed in a matter of minutes; it is only necessary to remove the rear cover, attached by nine bolts, and slide the gears out. First and second are fixed, but seven pairs of gears are available for third, fourth and fifth, giving a total of fourteen alternative ratios. Final drive ratio is fixed at 4.1 to 1, and thus on fast circuits it is customary for both fourth and fifth gears to act as "overdrives". Gears are engaged by a selector sleeve which is splined to the input shaft and incorporates external dogs which engage on internal dogs in the gears. Each pair of gears is in constant mesh, but the drive is only transmitted by the pair receiving it through the selector sleeve.

To comply with sports car regulations a reverse gear is fitted just ahead of first; it is operated through first and engaged, with the gear lever in neutral, by a spring which pushes it into mesh with first gear. Positive disengagement is ensured by a Bowden cable. A migratory gear change is used, as on the Formula One car, but due to the need to accommodate two seats it has been found necessary to incorporate a lever in the selector linkage, and thus the direction of gearchange movement is reversed—forward for upchanges, backward for downchanges.

Glass fibre

The bulk of the bodywork is in glass fibre, consisting of two removable panels hinged at front and rear. The horizontally hinged doors, the lower bodysides and the undertray are in aluminium. Lighting equipment consists of two 7 in. Lucas Le Mans headlamps mounted behind plastic fairings, side, tail and brake lamps. To facilitate removal of the body panels the electric wiring passes at both front and rear through waterproof plugs and chassis-mounted sockets.

The 7 ft. 6 in. wheelbase, 49 in. front track and $47\frac{1}{2}$ in. rear track are as on the Formula One car. Overall length is 11 ft. 9 in. width 5 ft. 5 in. and starting line weight, less driver, is approximately 11 cwt. with 8 gallons of fuel. Weight distribution at normal ride level, with driver aboard, is 46 per cent front, 54 per cent rear.

Driven by Stirling Moss the prototype Lotus Monte Carlo won its first race, at Karlskoga in August, with ease. On the following morning Joakim Bonnier used the car to set up a new Swedish speed record, being timed at 161 m.p.h. after a run-in of only 1000 yards and *using only fourth gear*. All of which suggests that, even though restricted to $2\frac{1}{2}$ litres, this new Lotus is really going to make its presence felt in International sports car racing.

JAMES.A.A

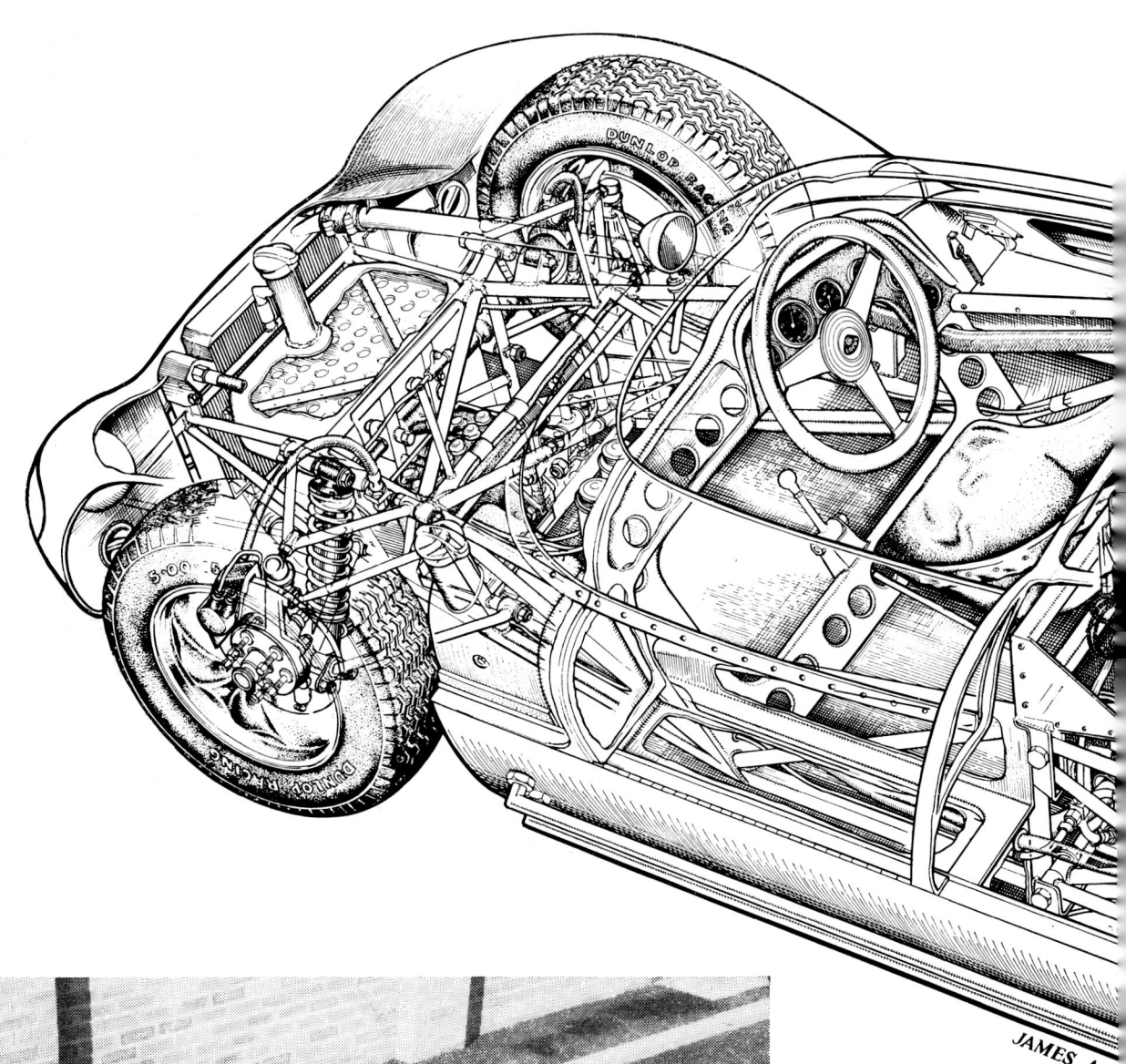

The Lotus N

teen

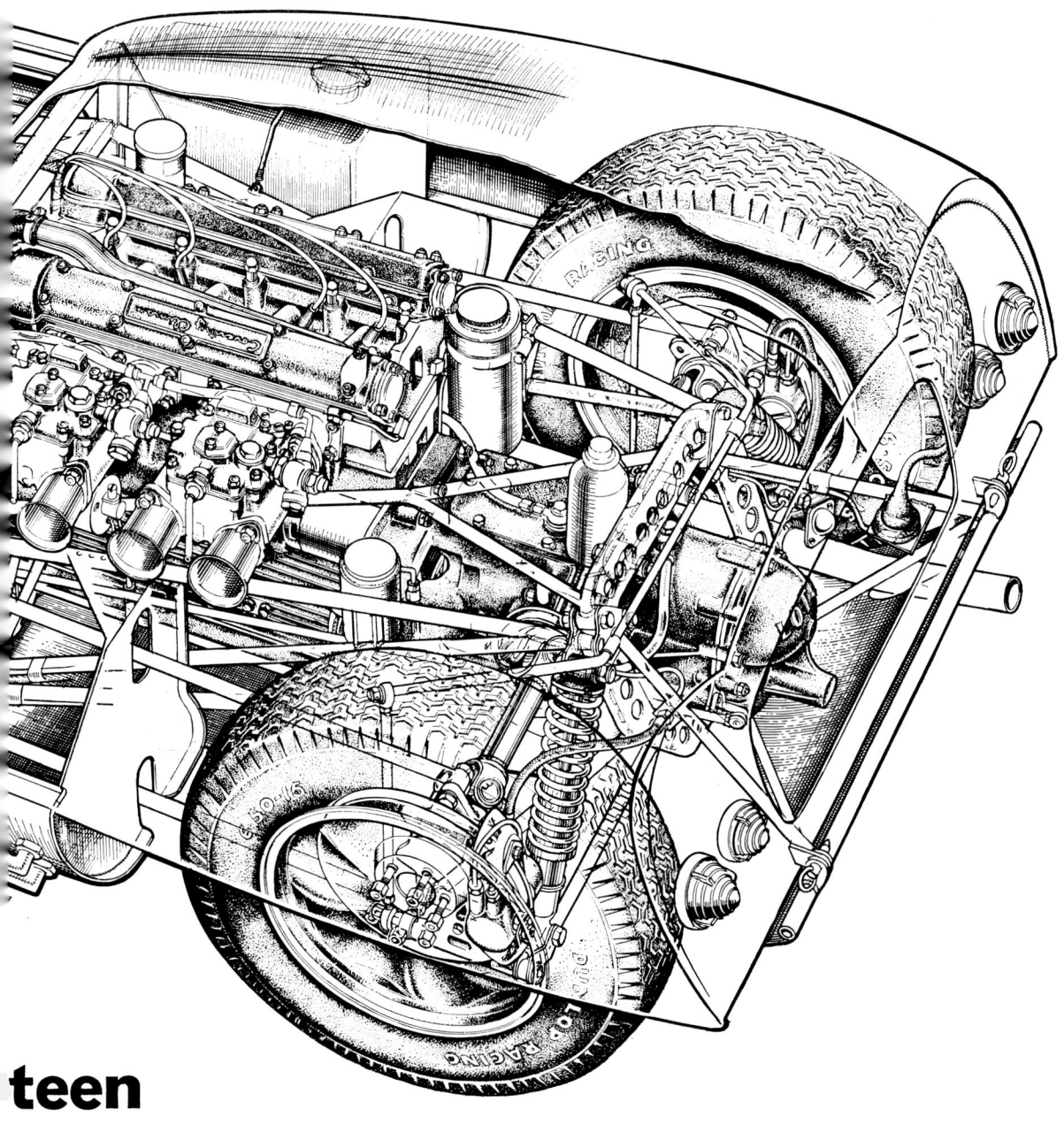

TECH REPORT:
Lotus Mk. XIX

THE WINNER THEY DON'T WANT TO BUILD

THE NEWEST LOTUS sports-racing car is proving to be a thorn in Colin Chapman's side. This is unique, as the Mk XIX has thus far proven a highly successful "thorn." Busily engaged in development of a '61 Formula machine and increasing production of his trim Elite coupes, the British designer decided to stretch a Formula 1 chassis into a two-seater on a let's-see-what-happens basis. The resultant prototype exhibited so much potential that prospective buyers were soon hard after Chapman for similar machines. Among them were Rob Walker, Stirling Moss' sponsor, and West Coast contractor Frank Arciero, the man who gave Dan Gurney his first ride in a really hot modified car, Arciero's 4.9 Ferrari. Dan practically camped at the Lotus factory, trying to get the machine finished in time for the Riverside and Laguna Seca USAC races.

Arriving barely in time for qualifying at Riverside, Gurney's hastily-assembled machine was out of the main event after 17 laps when a cylinder liner chipped at its upper ridge and lost the compression seal. Moss' Lotus lasted but 10 laps before transmission trouble put him out of the race. But before that, the cars were magnificent. Gurney had qualified his Mk XIX over four seconds faster than the existing lap record, set two years earlier by Chuck Daigh in one of the extremely fast Scarabs. Moss qualified his Lotus three seconds slower, but still almost a second ahead of the old record.

A week later, at Laguna Seca, Moss set a new course record in qualifying, then went on to win both 102-mile heats in the Mk XIX. Gurney was still having bad luck and sheered the flywheel bolts during practice. After frantic work in the pits, the car made the starting grid, but an un-

Front and rear sections of the Fiberglas body are quickly removable. Scoop in the aluminum rocker panels was installed to duct air to the differential and inboard disc brakes.

Instruments are placed in forward bulkhead, switches on flat panel at right. Note well-insulated radiator return hose to the right of driver's seat, gearshift in center of cockpit.

completed petition to delay the race kept the USAC officials from letting it run, even though the delay had been granted.

Nassau, however, allowed Arciero's chief mechanic, Bill Fowler, time for adequate preparation. Gurney's relaxed win demonstrated that Arciero's crew has the know-how to do the job. Dan's smooth handling of the car is given a great deal of credit by pit crew for the car's reliability, but, from a performance standpoint alone, the reputation of the Lotus Mk XIX as a Birdcage-eater is obviously well-deserved.

In changing his F1 design to fit FIA sports car specifications, Chapman altered very little of the basic layout. Wheelbase, track, and suspension design remain nearly identical. The Climax 2.5-liter powerplant and the compact transaxle lie in the same position with only the widened frame causing small changes in mounting. The light-tube, semi-bulkhead, modular construction is likewise identical.

Despite a weight addition of over 400 lbs., changing to a full-fendered, aerodynamic body apparently helped — not hindered — top-end performance. The "Monte Carlo" (a moniker suspected as a gentle jibe at John Cooper's "Monaco") reportedly pulls 100 more rpm in 5th gear than the F1 car when gearing is identical. The body construction is both unique and extremely practical. Underpanning and the oversized rocker panels are formed from aluminum. The removable nose and tail sections are molded in color-impregnated Fibreglas, the subject vehicle being a brilliant orange. Aside from collision damage, this assures a dent-free, shiny car no matter how much it's handled or campaigned. Once off, these sections allow major service without further skin removal and it only takes seconds to part them from the chassis.

The much-discussed and oft-condemned transmission seems to have most of its problems eliminated. Jay Chamberlain, well-known Lotus driver filled us in on its development history, relating how it was ahead of the differential in the front-engined '58 GP car, then moved behind it in '59 with the advent of the rear-mounted engine, finally assuming its present compact form in this position for the '60 F1 car. An amazing piece of engineering, the five-speed box is "progressive" both in the way it's shifted and the gears' relationship to each other. Foregoing the usual shifter-fork design, a sliding sleeve engages the gears internally and also serves as a carrier shaft for this primary set of gears. The sleeve, in turn, is internally splined at one end to accept the output shaft from the clutch. Six small pawls on the sleeve, with *no* synchronizing and only a slight amount of taper, are forced into engagement with the gears. Spacers in between each cog act as neutral positions. Aside from being one of the most compact five-speed boxes ever constructed, it has a quick-change advantage whereby *all* transmission ratios may be individually altered in a slightly longer time than it would take to swap one secondary set in a Halibrand rear! All this is accomplished in a 10-inch length.

An elaborate lubrication system for the transaxle has been further augmented on the Arciero car. Basically consisting of two pumps (one pressure, one scavenger) and an external filter, a front-mounted oil cooler now supplements this system. We get to the reason for this modification further on.

Tying in closely with the transaxle design, the rather wild rear suspension has caused even more controversy. While long, trailing arms absorb power and stabilize the rear, the actual suspension consists of low-mounted, *reversed* A-members *and* the half-axles themselves. Cast hub-carriers extend downward to connect with the outer ends of these arms while the axles, with U-joints acting as pivot points, serve as the upper members. Naturally, with this design there can be no slip-spline incorporated in the axles and it would seem that lateral load against the wheel would be

LOTUS MK XIX

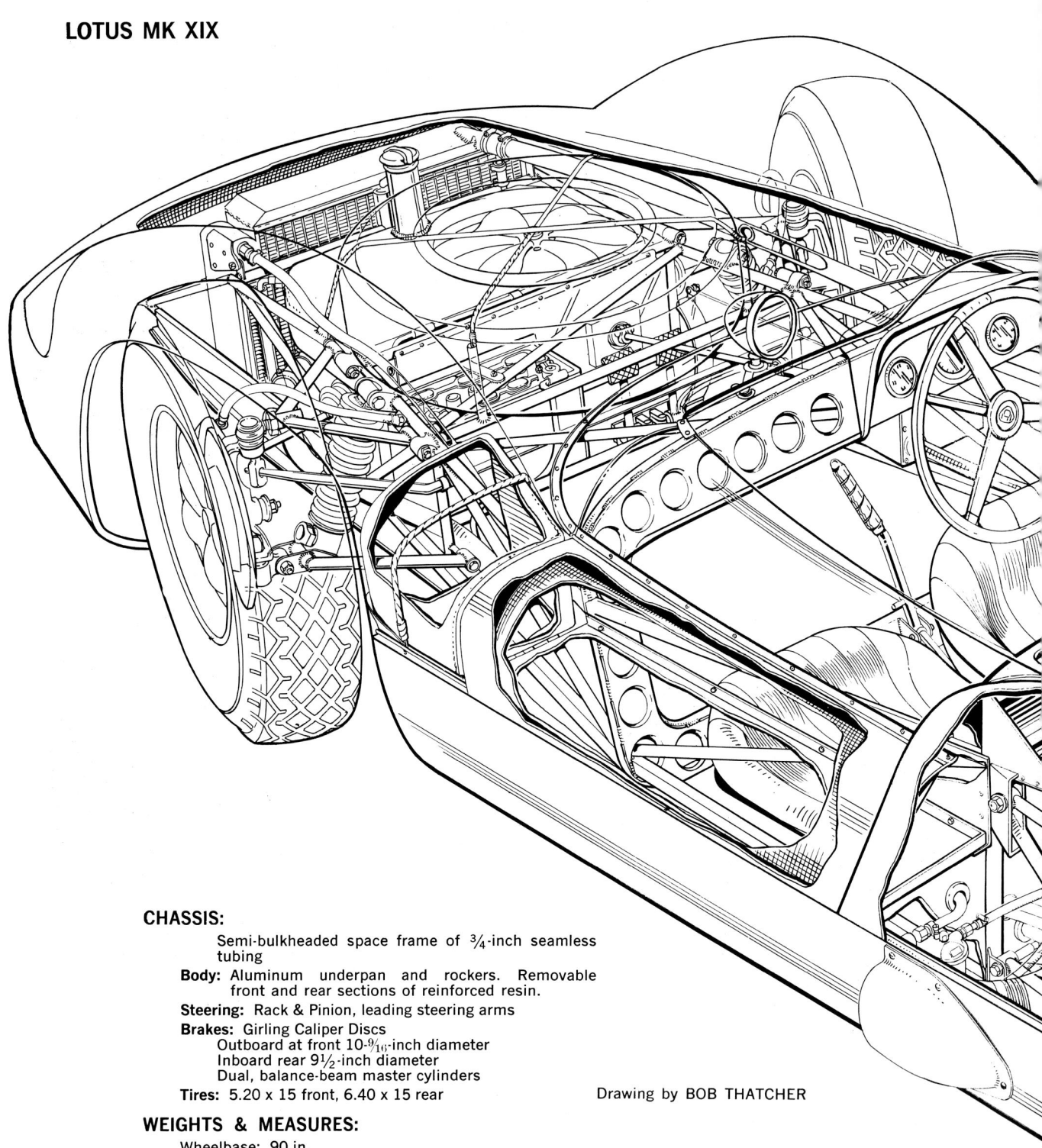

CHASSIS:
    Semi-bulkheaded space frame of ¾-inch seamless tubing
Body: Aluminum underpan and rockers. Removable front and rear sections of reinforced resin.
Steering: Rack & Pinion, leading steering arms
Brakes: Girling Caliper Discs
    Outboard at front 10-9/16-inch diameter
    Inboard rear 9½-inch diameter
    Dual, balance-beam master cylinders
Tires: 5.20 x 15 front, 6.40 x 15 rear

WEIGHTS & MEASURES:
    Wheelbase: 90 in.
    Front track: 51 in.
    Rear track: 50 in.
    Overall height: 31 in.
        width: 60.5 in.
        length: 139.25 in.
    Ground clearance: variable
    Curb weight: 1240 lbs.
    Lubrication system: 2½ gal.
    Cooling system: 16 qts.
    Fuel capacity: 32 gal. (2 tanks)

Drawing by BOB THATCHER

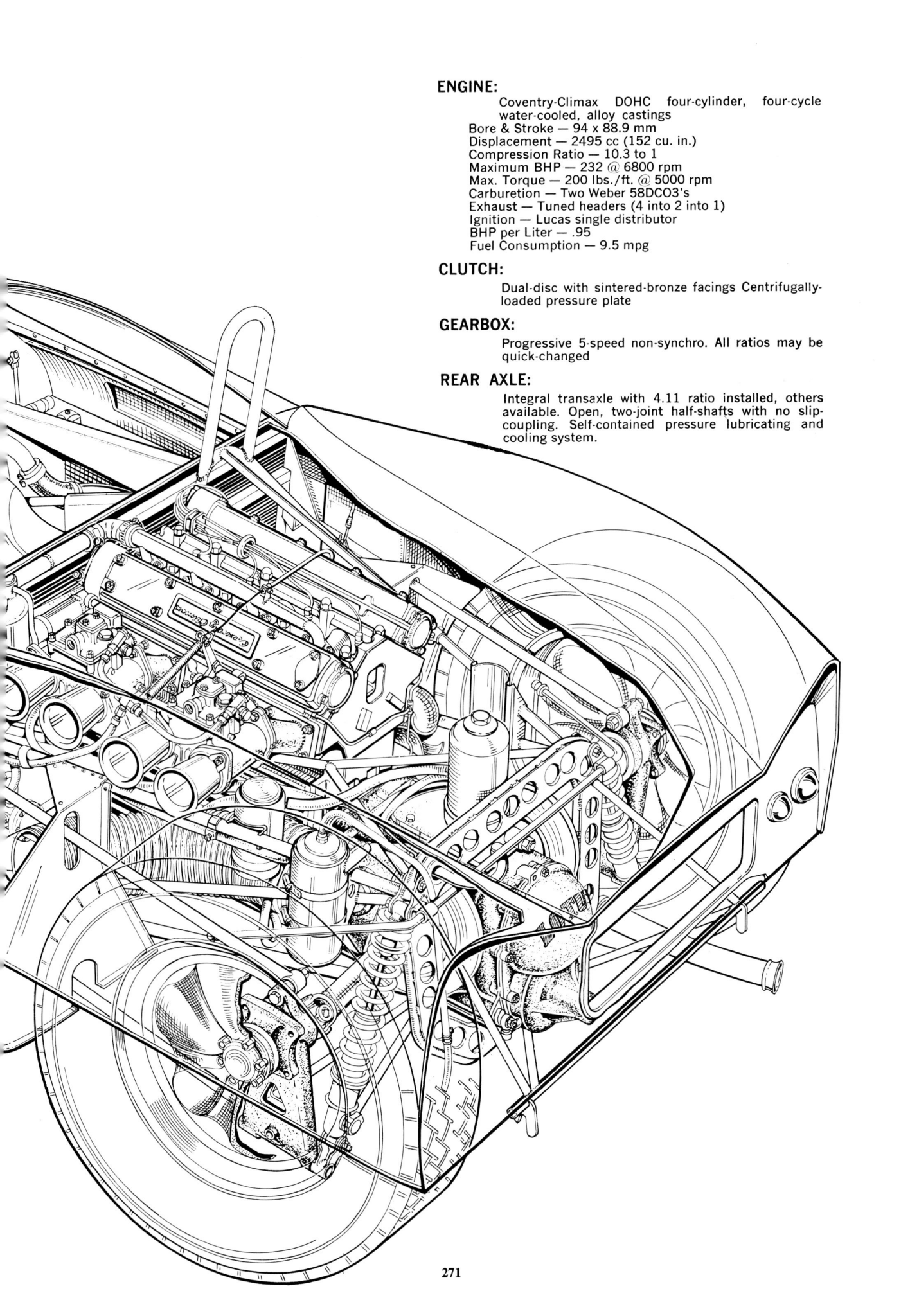

ENGINE:
Coventry-Climax DOHC four-cylinder, four-cycle water-cooled, alloy castings
Bore & Stroke — 94 x 88.9 mm
Displacement — 2495 cc (152 cu. in.)
Compression Ratio — 10.3 to 1
Maximum BHP — 232 @ 6800 rpm
Max. Torque — 200 lbs./ft. @ 5000 rpm
Carburetion — Two Weber 58DCO3's
Exhaust — Tuned headers (4 into 2 into 1)
Ignition — Lucas single distributor
BHP per Liter — .95
Fuel Consumption — 9.5 mpg

CLUTCH:
Dual-disc with sintered-bronze facings Centrifugally-loaded pressure plate

GEARBOX:
Progressive 5-speed non-synchro. All ratios may be quick-changed

REAR AXLE:
Integral transaxle with 4.11 ratio installed, others available. Open, two-joint half-shafts with no slip-coupling. Self-contained pressure lubricating and cooling system.

The Gurney-driven Arciero car will be campaigned in pro races this season with possibilities of Formula Libre participation as well. Bill Fowler is responsible for maintenance.

THE WINNER THEY DON'T WANT TO BUILD

transmitted directly into the differential bearings. The geometry is such, however, that the axles remain in stretch-tension, rather than compression, most of the time. This tends to neutralize any load trying to get in at the differential. Adjustable Armstrong coil — shocks provide the spring — dampening media and a thin stabilizing bar completes the design, the latter located high in a leading-arm position, but with a long connecting link to the lower ends of the hub carriers.

Good points of the design are lightness, a degree of simplicity, a low roll-center, and ideal caster-camber changes. Like the gearbox, however, it has exhibited enough "bugs" to consider them bad points. One example; the hub carriers extend so low that a flat tire lets them contact the road surface. This fact alone caused considerable consternation on the Formula One circuit. There have also been axle failures. When an axle is also a suspension member, breakage can get horrendous in a hurry. Moss confided that, as a safety precautions, these shafts were replaced before every race on the Rob Walker F1 cars. Differential failure is likewise not unknown, though overheating, rather than load on the tiny ring gear, has been diagnosed as the cause. On the prototype Mk XIX, the inboard disc brakes were moved out to the hubs, but Fowler chose to install large cooling ducts *and* the oil radiator we mentioned earlier, leaving the brakes mounted to the differential and utilizing the sprung advantages. Installation of a temperature gauge has thus far indicated his modifications to be a success.

The gearbox, from the driver's standpoint as well as the designer's, has been a nightmare on the earlier cars. Chamberlain remembers several instances of approaching corners at above 150 mph only to discover a downshift had netted a "false" neutral! Outright failures were frequent, too, enough so, to discourage everyone but Chapman who stuck doggedly to his design and made linkage, spacer, pre-load and sleeve changes to bring it to its present state of development. Gurney uses caution, but has thus far experienced no difficulty in fast, positive shifting.

Front suspension is light, compact, and conventional. The Armstrong coil-shocks are used here and the short, unequal upper-and-lower A-members have minimal geometry changes in deflection. A tie-rod end on the upper members serves as a ball joint and provides easy camber adjustment. Roll stabilization is controlled by a thin transverse bar mounted like the one in the rear, except that it links directly to the upper arms, instead of the lower. The steering arms are the "leading" type and connect through short tie-rods to the rack-and-pinion reduction.

While adequate on the light F1 car, the Girling discs are reportedly critical on the Mk XIX; prone to fading and high wear when used excessively. In combination with the over-all design, however, their stopping power is excellent. In the two races in which this writer was able to observe these cars, only the best RSK Porsche was, at times, able to equal the depth in corner-approach that the Mk XIX's were using consistently. No servo mechanism is used, but dual master cylinders, now pretty much S.O.P. on high-potential racecars, actuate the binders under moderate foot pressure.

The "office" is extremely comfortable, with a low-slung bucket holding the driver's entire torso snugly. Centrally located on the floor of the right-hand-drive machine is the gearshift. All switches are at the driver's right hand on the wide, flat panel directly under the door. The instruments are mounted directly in the forward bulkhead, centered behind the wheel and running down to the right. Hidden under the dash is a small, meets-FIA-requirements emergency brake. From this, a cable leads to the brake pedal, rather than to any mechanical actuation that would normally be associated with such a device. Clutch engagement is hydraulic, depressing the centrifugally-loaded pressure plate and, in turn, releasing the dual discs that are lined with sintered bronze.

Pumping out an estimated 232 horsepower (SAE), almost a hundred-per-liter, the Climax engine is conservatively red-lined at 6800 rpm. No attempt is made to air-ram the huge 58DCO3 Weber carburetors which use 51 mm venturis to draw oxygen through their side-drafted dual throats. Cam overlap is 85 degrees, with the intake valve opening at 40° BTDC. Via three pumps buried deep in the crankcase (one pressure, a separate scavenge for front and rear sections) the dry-type sump is fed oil from a 2½-gal. tank in the front. The oil is used, filtered, then sent back up front again to be circulated through coolers on both sides of the radiator and cored integrally with it. Crankcase breathing is cleverly — but Fowler admits, rather messily — exhausted into the frame tubes. Dozens of tiny holes in the lower rails let fumes and any blow-by to atmosphere. Aside from meticulous re-assembly, little else has been done to the powerplant in the Arciero machine. Replacing the single Lucas distributor with a magneto of the same make is being considered but no ignition problems have been encountered. Forged replacements for the cast pistons are being made up to enhance the reliability margin as much as possible. The two 16-gal. fuel tanks now have a crossover system incorporated so that either one of the dual electric pumps and separate filters can be used with either tank in another effort to eliminate problems before they occur.

Investigating the handling how's-and-why's gave us some insight into the car's remarkable flexibility. As it stood, the suspension was set up for the Nassau course; an extremely rough surface with hard acceleration, cornering and braking. "Fudging rings," or spacers under the coils, lifted the car above its normal ground clearance — both front and rear.

CONTINUED ON PAGE 274

The two photos above demonstrate ease with which the Mk XIX can be "skinned" to facilitate repairs. Gas tanks are located behind left front wheel, ahead of right rear. Located behind the radiator and under the spare tire is the three-gallon oil tank.

Due for gusseting before further races is the delicate front end. Disc brakes and ball-joints are clearly visible here.

Huge velocity stacks of the twin Webers will accommodate a hand. Fill-expansion tank for water is object to their left.

The Chapman-designed gearbox is probably the most compact 5-speed ever built though its shift linkage is oft-cursed.

Which twin is the phony? More than just similar are the rear ends of a Lotus Formula I (above) and the Monte Carlo.

It's hard to believe that the entire power train of the potent sports car is contained in this small section behind seats and with room to spare, but it's true.

273

A NEW LOTUS and a MENDED MOSS...

THE SPORTING SIDE

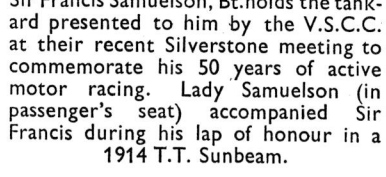

Sir Francis Samuelson, Bt. holds the tankard presented to him by the V.S.C.C. at their recent Silverstone meeting to commemorate his 50 years of active motor racing. Lady Samuelson (in passenger's seat) accompanied Sir Francis during his lap of honour in a 1914 T.T. Sunbeam.

...tried each other out at Silverstone on July 25. The outing was evidently successful, the combination unofficially breaking the sports car lap record with a reputed time of 1 min. 41·5 sec., just under 104 m.p.h. The new 2½-litre Lotus is Colin Chapman's answer to the all-conquering Cooper Monacos that have dominated sports car racing in this country this season, and it is based on the Formula 1 Lotus Chassis. Right: Moss at speed with lady passenger.

THE WINNER THEY DIDN'T WANT TO BUILD

CONTINUED FROM PAGE 272

The front wheels where slightly decambered, the rears sat almost neutral with unladen gas tanks. Heim joints at the outer ends of the rear arms allow adjustment of both camber and toe-in and goodly amounts of the latter were aiming the rear wheels inward. Goodyear sports-racing tires, with their diamond-shaped tread, are used with satisfactory results: 5.20 x 15's in front, 6.40 x 15's in the rear. We weighed the front and rear segments of the car and discovered over 65% of the 1210 lbs. was rearward! Both gas tanks and driver are located centrally, so it's doubtful that percentage of distribution would vary much by filling the former and including the latter. The radiator, oil tank, spare tire and battery constitute the only major weights up front and two of us easily lifted the front end to set it on horses.

At this point, we would have liked very much to quiz Gurney concerning the handling traits, but Fowler was able to pass on his generalized comment... Dan considers it the best he's ever driven, almost dead neutral in terms of over-or-understeer and extremely high in adhesion under all circumstances.

In overall concept there's nothing too radical about the Mk XIX. While somewhat fragile, it is, as we mentioned, an extremely flexible machine, able to cope with any kind of competition on any kind of course or surface. It is every inch a racecar, built to do its job *and* be maintained with a minimum of wasted effort. There is some conjecture that the forthcoming rear-engined Maserati may offer it a challenge, but there seems to be nothing on the existing scene that is real competition.

Proof of its potential is that Arciero, in addition to his plans to campaign the little bear in "money" races this season, is also considering Formula Libre events. It is, after all, every bit as quick as the *average* F1 car and, as reliability is steadily increased, it may well be able to outlast the hottest ones. Not bad for a car conceived on a "let's see" basis.

— *Jerry Titus.*

Contributing Editor Griff Borgeson puts the watch on a deceptively fast befendered Grand Prix car, a prototype of great road machines of the future.

▶ The day before Dan Gurney was due to fly to New Zealand to drive for B.R.M. we convened at Riverside International Raceway. Also present were Dan's enthusiastic father (with a new Honda 'cycle in his station wagon), mechanic Bill Fowler, photographer Lester Nehamkin and a very rare and choice sports car, the Lotus XIX owned by Frank and Phil Arciero, general contractors and flat-out racing men of Montebello, Calif. Purpose of the get-together: get acquainted with the Birdcage Cleaner.

Sports cars usually are derived from road machines. While flaying the British sports car industry for its archaic chassis designs John Bolster recently said in AUTOSPORT, "The prospective sports car owner is a man who knows his stuff, and if you offered him a car with chassis features that were straight from Grand Prix designs, he would never again touch the old cart-sprung horrors."

The Lotus XIX's greatest significance is that it is a prototype of the kind of superior sports car that, with a few economy-dictated changes, can and should go into volume production in the not-distant future. It *is* the Lotus G.P. machine, slightly modified.

The car is 31 inches high and an inch short of 12 feet in length. It weighs about 1250 pounds ready to go and with the 152-cubic-inch, 240-bhp Coventry Climax FPF engine has a weight to power ratio of just over five to one. This favorable state of affairs is, of course, just the starting point for chassis wizard Colin Chapman.

The Arciero brothers purchased their XIX specifically for Gurney to drive and Dan put in time at the Lotus plant (the botanical allusion is irresistible) during which he specified assorted minor design changes as the car was being built. His first real outing with the machine was in the Times Grand Prix for sports cars held at Riverside last October. He took three laps for qualifying: one starting lap, one timed lap, one for slowing down. The timed lap was a fairly good one but, since it was the first time Dan had been able to stand on it, it was a bit sloppy here and there. Result: a new lap record for sports cars of 2:00.9.

Gurney was clocked at 156 mph down the back stretch which, with 4.11 cogs, is the limit for the Climax, which is all done at 6800 rpm. There were faster cars on the straight, with times all the way up to the 170s. Nevertheless the new Lotus got through the corners so rapidly and effortlessly that it had the best overall lap time, hands down. "It was no particular driving feat," says Gurney; "it was just the car."

Next came Laguna Seca. During practice Gurney was within one or two mph of the Scarab that had the fastest *trap* time and, unofficially, Dan turned the fastest lap times. Then all eight of the flywheel cap screws sheared and, while there was miraculously little damage, racing was ended for Gurney for that weekend.

Then came Nassau. There, there were a couple of Chev-powered specials that would out-accelerate the Lotus on the straight. But the moment there was a combination of turn and straight the Lotus flashed out of sight. The Nassau course is incredibly rough and, knowing that anyone who goes gung-ho there is begging for disaster, Gurney saved his car and drove to finish. In spite of the soft pedal Gurney won the 250-mile Nassau Trophy Race along with $10,000 and, in the process, effortlessly raised the race record by a full two mph to 89.54 mph.

So we went motoring at Riverside. The Lotus XIX is a razor's edge exercise in stress anaysis and its ring and pinion gears, for example, tolerate very little rough usage. It is therefore the Arcieros' rule that no one but Gurney drives the car. I am a very poor passenger under normal conditions but quite cheerful about entrusting my safety to great talent and it was a memorable privilege to ride *copiloto* to the tall, shy but warm Californian.

First I'd like to comment on Gurney's style. I've ridden with Moss, Miles, Ginther and many others and never have witnessed smoother cockpit performance. It is consummately, ultimately smooth and beyond that I'm at a loss for words. At terrific speed he laps a road course not in a succession of acts connected by transitions but in one act which is a flowing continuum. A very nice driver indeed.

Now for the car. It doesn't feel terribly fast on the straight; there is not a sensation of brutal acceleration. Its performance is markedly sensitive to the load of fuel it's carrying, a way of saying that its endowments of power and torque are not fantastic. The accompanying acceleration curve (Gurney alone aboard, driving and operating stopwatch) shows what the car does aside from subjective impressions. Fragile ring and pinion or not, Gurney made the XIX perform like a fairly sudsy dragster and it did not

Many laps of Riverside were turned with Borgeson as intrepid passenger. Prime impressions were of smooth performance of Gurney and the lusty Lotus.

Road Test: LOTUS XIX

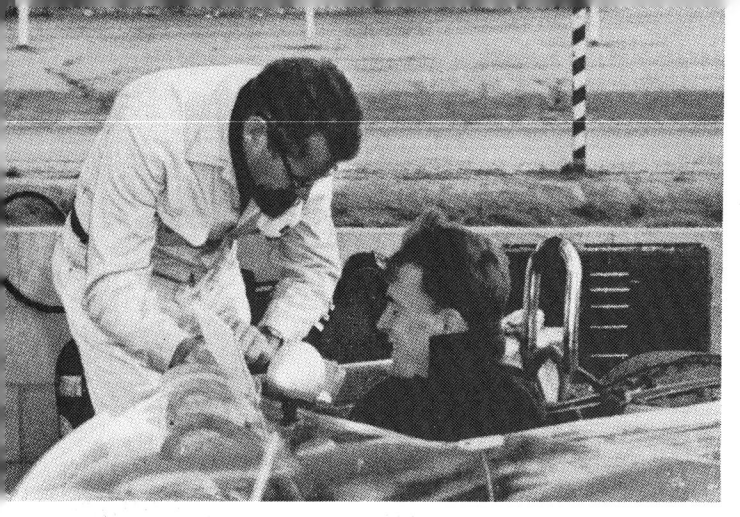

Griff and Gurney check out times posted by the Lotus, which Dan drove "like a fairly sudsy dragster" in spite of fragile ring and pinion.

Stark cockpit shows Grand Prix car frame layout expanded to fit driver and passenger. Big positive-stop shift lever is at left of the wheel.

PHOTOGRAPHY: NEHAMKIN

Dan clocked the times solo during acceleration runs. Built under Gurney's supervision, the Arciero-owned Nineteen varies from "stock" in many details.

protest in the least.

Handling and roadability of course are the car's strongest points. They are not absolutes since all depends on how the chassis is adjusted and practically everything is adjustable: camber, toe-in, damper settings, riding height, gear ratios, tire pressures. You can pretty much make the car do what you want and can tailor it to cope with a broad range of conditions. At Nassau Gurney and Fowler were concerned about front-tire wear on the rough, abrasive course and therefore set the chassis up to oversteer slightly, to plow less at the front. This probably was unnecessary since, after about 350 miles of practice and racing, the remarkable new Goodyear Sports Car Specials had lost only 1/16 inch of tread.

Normally — as at Laguna Seca and Riverside — Gurney likes to have the machine set up for pretty neutral steering tendencies. He has driven almost everything and states that when the chassis is properly set up it is one of the easiest, best-handling sports cars in the world. Some of the Birdcages and Porsches go around corners admittedly well and the Cooper Monaco is very good; none of them are any better than the XIX. In fact, Gurney says that while the XIX still is not a G.P. car in handling it approaches that status closer than anything he has driven in the sports car line. It's just a total pleasure to drive.

The passenger senses this strongly both on the straight and in the turns (he sits in the wind with no seat belt and little to hang on to). Diving down the hill and whistling over the Riverside back straight at 150 mph the ride is like that of — I have to say it — a Cadillac. It utterly puts to shame the typical American straightaway machine, to refer again to "cart-sprung horrors." In the turns, large or small radius, it sticks fantastically and stays dead flat. You can't believe that such side-bite is possible yet there it is, happening.

And now we come to the subject of the rear engine or, as is now more fashionable, the center engine, and its effect upon handling. Since the days of the G.P. Auto Unions it has been axiomatic that a car with its engine behind the driver is inherently squirrelly, that it's a dangerous layout because by the time you sense that the rear end is breaking loose it's already swung around in front of you. Hardly anyone bothered to regard John Cooper's F.3 machines as legitimate automobiles and the Auto Union-based concept or prejudice endured. And out of Cooper's rear-engine F.3s evolved today's fine English G.P. cars and the Lotus XIX.

Mechanic Bill Fowler stands by as Gurney disdains the door while boarding the Lotus. Automobile demands and gets extremely meticulous maintenance.

Positively packed with machinery, the bared back end of the Lotus shows the compact gearbox and coil suspension. Crew uses Goodyear racing tires.

From what has been said here already it is clear that the XIX isn't just as good as any front-engine car. It's one of the very few best-handling sports cars ever built, one of the easiest to drive. Swooping around big, fast Turn Nine at Riverside at immense speed you can feel the threshold of rear-end breakaway approaching. It comes on very slowly and you have all the time in the world to back off, in which case bite immediately returns to optimum — or to keep your foot just where it is, in which case you continue around the turn with the rear end hanging out a bit. The point is that you get *plenty* of message from these cars.

That was the big problem that had to be conquered before the rear- or center-engine race car could become a thoroughly practical proposition, and it has been conquered. There are many beneficial side effects. One, as Phil Hill has pointed out, is that a driver seated amidships is tossed from side to side during cornering far less than is a driver who is seated closer to the extremities of a vehicle and therefore must devote a lot of his energy to merely hanging on. Another virtue is that with the engine behind the driver there is very little noise to fatigue him. And, from the design standpoint, consolidating engine, transmission and final drive into a single unit is a more economical procedure in every sense.

The Lotus five-speed gearbox leaves something to be desired in the slowness with which the spur-cut gears must be engaged. However it has an advantage over other gearboxes in that any ratio can be changed in about five minutes. *A la* Halibrand quick-change the rear cover plate can be snatched off, exposing all the innards of the transmission. This is a well-proved device, having been around since the days of the Lotus front-engine G.P. car. Its placement in the rear-engine G.P. car was as it is in the XIX: aft of the rear axle.

There are variations from car to car in the few XIXs that have been built to date. The 9.6-inch Girling rear discs are mounted outboard on the machine which Moss has been driving; they are inboard on the Arciero car. On standard XIXs there are two one-inch aluminum tubes which run the length of the body from wheelwell to wheelwell. These are for carrying oil and water between radiators and engine and Gurney, distrusting their exposed position, had them moved inboard. The body is fiberglass and has proved to be extremely durable. It can be removed in moments.

One problem with all Climax-engined cars is that the engines are in short supply and parts are not too readily available. At this writing one gentleman has just ordered a XIX without engine. In this vehicle he plans to install one of GM's new 215-cubic-inch "all aluminum" V8s. This is not as shocking a plan as it may appear to be at first sight. The weight of the two engines is closely similar. With a little Chev-type tuning one bhp per cube should be readily available and with a little boring and stroking the cubes can be increased. The engine is relatively cheap and, most important, parts are cheap and more or less universally available. Which gets us that much closer to the volume-produced super sports car.

The nominal cost of the XIX is $17,000, which probably was pretty accurate when the first specimens were being made. Now, with all the prototype-type problems overcome, the price is considerably lower. Chapman originally planned to build only 12 of these cars per year but that was before he had any way of knowing the market that evidently exists for them or how successfully they would perform. Where it all goes is anybody's guess but, to repeat, the XIX is today's blueprint for tomorrow's superior sports car.

—GB

ROAD TEST:

LOTUS XIX

Price: $15,650 POE East Coast

Manufacturer: Lotus Cars, Ltd.
Delamare Road
Cheshunt, Herts.
England

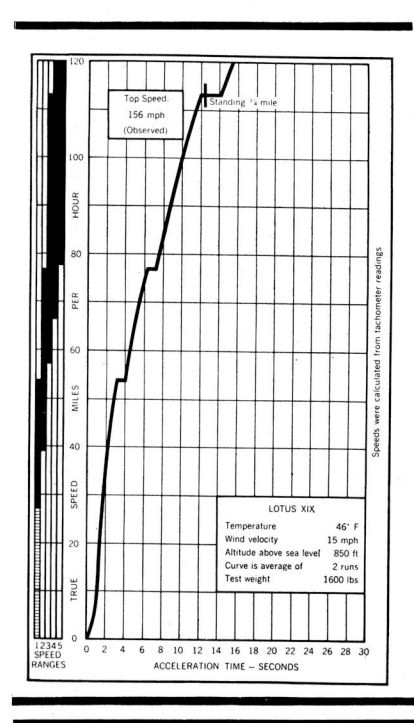

ENGINE: (Coventry Climax FPF)

Displacement	152 cu in, 2495 cc
Dimensions	Four cyl, 3.70 in bore, 3.54 in stroke
Valve gear: Gear-driven double overhead camshafts with 0.41 in lift; valves at 66° included angle.	
Compression ratio	10.0 to one
Power (SAE)	240 bhp @ 6800 rpm
Torque	212 lb-ft @ 5200 rpm
Usable range of engine speeds	3300-7000 rpm
Corrected piston speed @ 6800 rpm	4100 fpm
Fuel recommended	Superpremium
Mileage	about 10 mpg
Range on 32-gallon tank	about 320 miles

CHASSIS:

Wheelbase	90.0 in
Tread	F 51.0, R 50.5 in
Length	143.0 in
Ground clearance	4.0 in
Suspension: F, ind., coil, wishbones, anti-roll bar; R, ind., coil, lower wishbone, unsplined driveshaft, trailing arm.	
Turns, lock to lock	2¼ (was 2½)
Turning circle diameter between curbs	40 ft
Tire and rim size: F 5.00/5.20 x 15, 15 x 5; R 6.40 x 15, 15 x 6½.	
Pressures recommended	28 psi
Brakes; type, swept area: disc, F 10.6 in, R 9.6 in; 387 sq in	
Curb weight (full tank)	estimated 1250 lbs
Percentage on driving wheels	66%

DRIVE TRAIN:

Gear	Synchro?	Ratio	Step	Overall	Mph per 1000 rpm
Rev	No	2.50		10.28	−7.7
1st	No	2.50		10.28	7.7
2nd	No	1.75	43%	7.19	11.0
3rd	No	1.20	46%	4.93	16.1
4th	No	1.03	17%	4.21	18.9
5th	No	0.88	17%	3.60	22.1

Final Drive Ratios: 4.11 to one, 4.55 optional.

Top Speed: 156 mph (Observed)

LOTUS XIX
Temperature 46° F
Wind velocity 15 mph
Altitude above sea level 850 ft
Curve is average of 2 runs
Test weight 1600 lbs

Speeds were calculated from tachometer readings

LOTUS nineteen MONTE CARLO

The hottest sports car going is derived from a successful Formula I car

STORY BY DAVID PHIPPS

Having developed an entirely new rear-engined design for his 1960 Formula I and Formula Junior cars, it is hardly surprising that Colin Chapman used the same basic layout in the Lotus "Monte Carlo" sports car. Within the works the new model is known as the Nineteen, its more exotic title resulting from the fact that the firm scored its first *Grande Epreuve* victory in the Principality last year, albeit with a privately entered car.

In principle, the Monte Carlo is an exact copy of the Formula I car, but in practice it has been necessary to make numerous alterations to turn the basic single-seater into a sports car. First and foremost, the space frame chassis has been widened out to provide the seating space required by Appendix C of the International Sporting Code. It remains a three section unit, as on the Formula I car and, in fact, the front bulkhead (just behind the radiator) and the rear bulkhead (through which the gearbox protrudes) are Formula I components. Immediately behind the front bulkhead, whose location is determined by the forward front wishbone mountings, the chassis side rails begin to diverge. A second bulkhead coincides with the rearward front suspension mountings. Diagonal bracing on five sides of this front suspension bay makes it exceptionally stiff and fully capable of absorbing all the loads passed into it by the front suspension and steering (the steering rack is mounted on the front bulkhead at the apex of two triangles).

An unusual feature on the Lotus is the location of the front coil spring/damper units on tubes in bending. This divergence from the Formula I practice of locating the suspension unit and forward top wishbone mounting by a common bolt has been made necessary by the widening out of the chassis. To compensate for the extra loading involved, the short tube between the two top wishbone mountings is of 1.125-in., 14-gauge mildsteel, as against the one-in. and 0.750-in. 16 and 18 gauge tubing used for the rest of the chassis.

Forward of the front bulkhead the chassis consists of a subframe carrying mountings for the radiator, oil tank and bodywork. Within the front suspension bay are mountings for brake and clutch master cylinders, throttle, brake and clutch pedals and battery. The front section of the frame extends to the scuttle hoop, which is a tubular and perforated sheet steel structure designed to eliminate the need for diagonal bracing. The other five sides of this section are all fully triangulated—by the stressed aluminum undertray in the case of the floor. In addition

Skip Hudson looks on as mechanic makes adjustments to Frank Arciero's Lotus at Riverside.

Cockpit of Moss's Lotus shows personal touches.

Spare tire is carried in front among the tanks.

to acting as a major structural member, the scuttle hoop also provides mountings for steering column, gear lever, seats, instruments and brake and clutch reservoirs. The hand brake is mounted on the top diagonal tube just forward of the hoop. From the scuttle hoop rearward the chassis side rails run virtually parallel to each other to the engine bulkhead. As on the Formula I car, this center section is braced on only three sides and, with the greater width of the sports car, becomes even less stiff than on the single-seater, but the rigidity of the front and rear sections compensates for this and gives the whole chassis adequate torsional stiffness.

From the engine bulkhead the main frame rails converge toward the rear bulkhead, constructed on the same lines as the scuttle hoop. Although not straight sided, the rear bulkhead is an effective triangle, its shape being determined by the need to accommodate the inboard brake discs. The upper tubes meet this bulkhead just above the pick-ups for the rear suspension units, while the lower ones converge more rapidly to meet at the bottom of the hoop, at the lower wishbone pick-ups. Fore and aft suspension loads are taken out into the chassis through parallel radius arms anchored at the top and bottom of the engine bulkhead. As the latter is considerably wider on the Monte Carlo than on the single-seater, this results in a slight alteration of geometry, but the suspension is otherwise identical to that of the Formula I car.

The upper part of the rear bulkhead is removable, together with a Y-shaped top diagonal, on the release of four fitted shear bolts and one tension bolt. In addition to absorbing suspension loads at either end, this member also deals with engine loads, the gearbox being located at its center via two rubber cone-bushed mountings. Each front engine mounting is located at the apex of two triangles, which consist of the side frame diagonals.

Complete with all its brackets, the chassis weighs 70 lb.

Front suspension is by double. tubular wishbones, with proprietary (Standard-Triumph) uprights and machined steel hubs, as on the Formula I car. The upper wishbones have threaded, ball-jointed outer ends to allow alteration of camber angle, and an anti-roll bar is installed, located on the chassis beneath the rearward top wishbone mounting and connected to the top wishbones below the ball joints in spherical bearings. Steering is by rack and pinion gear mounted just ahead of the wheel center line. A straight steering column is used, bolted to a 14-in. alloy wheel with leather-covered rim.

Rear suspension elements are the lower wishbones and the driveshafts for transverse location, and parallel radius arms for fore and aft location. At their outer ends these components are linked by castings, which also carry the wheel hub bearings. The lower wishbones are threaded at their inner ends for alteration of camber angle and at the outer for alteration of toe-in. The rear anti-roll bar, located on the chassis at the suspension unit mountings, is connected to the lower wishbones by upright links incorporating spherical bearings. Wheels are of cast magnesium, 15 in. in diameter and mounted on 6 studs. The rim section is 5 in. at the front, 6.5 in. at the rear, and tire sizes are, respectively, 5.00 and 6.50.

Formula I brakes are used, consisting of outboard-mounted 10.5-in. front discs and inboard-mounted 9.5-in. rear discs. Provision is also made in the hub castings for mounting the rear brakes outboard; in warm climates it may well be worth the sacrifice of increased sprung weight to move the brakes away from the heat of the engine and gearbox.

The main 12-gal. fuel tank is mounted on the left of the car—on the side away from the driver—with a 10-gal. auxiliary tank alongside and behind the driver. The space above the driver's legs, used for the main fuel tank

With changes in bodywork, this would look like the back of the Formula I Lotus which, in effect, it is.

on the Formula I car, contains the spare wheel on the sports car. The battery is alongside the pedals. The cross-flow radiator and 6-gal. oil tank are as on the Formula I car, with the oil tank breathing through the chassis to a number of small holes at the rear. Aluminum water pipes link engine and radiator, and oil is circulated between engine, oil radiator and oil tank—and gearbox and gearbox oil radiator—by pipes which run outside the body panels over much of their length.

The standard power unit is the 2495-cc, 4-cyl, dohc Coventry Climax FPF engine, which develops 239 bhp at 6750 rpm. For sports car use this has Lucas coil ignition, generator and starter. Fuel is supplied to the two twin choke Weber 58DC03 carburetors by two SU electric fuel pumps.

Bolted directly to the engine is the Lotus 5-speed gearbox/final drive unit, the front casing of which incorporates the clutch bell housing and starter mounting. The two gear trains are mounted behind the rear wheel center line, and the drive, taken through a Borg and Beck twin plate clutch with sintered copper linings, enters the box beneath the differential unit and is transmitted in a vertical plane. Hypoid bevel final drive gears are used and the unit has its own lubrication system, with a reservoir mounted ahead and to the right of it.

In addition to being extremely compact, this gearbox has the great advantage that 3rd, 4th and 5th ratios can be changed in a matter of minutes; it is only necessary to remove the gear cover, attached by 9 bolts, and slide the gears out. First and 2nd are fixed, but seven pairs of gears are available for 3rd, 4th and 5th, giving a total of 14 alternative ratios. Final drive ratio is fixed at 4.1:1 and, thus, on fast circuits it is customary for both 4th and 5th gears to act as "overdrives." Gears are engaged by a selector sleeve which is splined to the input shaft and incorporates external dogs which engage on internal dogs in the gears. Each pair of gears is in constant mesh, but power is transmitted only by the pair receiving the drive through the selector sleeve.

To comply with sports car regulations, a reverse gear is fitted just ahead of first; it is operated through first and engaged, with the gear level in neutral, by a spring which pushes it into mesh with first gear. Positive disengagement is insured by a Bowden cable. A migratory gearshift is used, as on the Formula I car, but, due to the need to accommodate two seats, it has been found necessary to incorporate a lever in the selector linkage, and thus the direction of gear change movement is reversed—forward for up-changes, backward for down-changes.

The bulk of the bodywork is of fiberglass, consisting of two removable panels hinged at front and rear. The horizontally hinged doors, the lower body sides and the undertray are aluminum. Lighting equipment consists of two 7-in. Lucas Le Mans headlights, mounted behind plastic fairings, and side, tail and brake lights. To facilitate removal of the body panels, the electric wiring passes at both front and rear through waterproof plugs and chassis-mounted sockets.

The 90-in. wheelbase, 49-in. front track and 47.5-in. rear track are as on the Formula I car. Over-all length is 141 in., width 65 in., and starting line weight, less driver, is approximately 1232 lb with 8 gal. of fuel. Weight distribution at normal ride level, with driver aboard, is 46% front, 54% rear.

Driven by Stirling Moss, the prototype Lotus Monte Carlo won its first race at Karlskoga in August, with ease. On the following morning Joakim Bonnier used the car to set up a new Swedish speed record, being timed at 161 mph after a run-in of only 1000 yards and *using only 4th gear*. All of which suggests that, even with only 2.5 liters, this new Lotus is the car to beat (or buy, if you can get Chapman to build another one).

Minimum clearance, overhang and weight, but not speed. This is the Arciero/Gurney car at Riverside Raceway, a few weeks before the GP.

Gurney's car supported another winner at Laguna Seca.

The Lotus Twenty-Three

The Lotus Twenty-three of 1962 was, for Lotus, the revival of Lotus' fortunes dating back to the Lotus Eleven of 1956 - but with the engine behind the driver as was the popular revolution of the 1960s. As with the Lotus 19 this car also had a plain number designation, the Twenty-three or 23.

The Lotus 23 was the all-purpose sports car, the same as the Eleven had been six years before. Designed for a variety of engines and planned to race in international, national and club competition, it fulfiled its promises and did everything that had been expected from it. The Lotus 23 was the car to have for 1962-3 and its development the Lotus 23b of 1963-4 through to 1966 was to car to beat.

The early Lotus 23s from April 1962 had the Ford 105E Anglia 1100 single-overhead-cam engine from Formula Junior development. At 1100cc, with some 90-100bhp, the power was transmitted via a Renault transaxle. However, it was not long before the Lotus developed twin-cam cylinder head from the 1500cc Ford Cortina 116E, which was the mainstay of Lotus Cortina, Lotus Europa and later Elan production, was being installed as the new Sports Racing Class up to 1600cc ensured race victories instead of just class places. The VW gearbox modified by Hewland was *the* transaxle by the beginning of 1963. This soon gave way to the 1600cc engine with a fully Hewland-built gearbox. With the increased power up to 160bhp it was necessary to strengthen the chassis with additional bracing tubes from the side rails to the Len Terry inspired, perforated chassis bulkhead hoops that had been introduced with the Lotus 18 in 1959. This became the Lotus 23b later in 1963.

The first motoring press announcement of the Lotus 23 was in *Autosport* on 5th January, 1962 by David Phipps, with superb cutaway drawings by James Allington. This was followed by *Sports Car Graphic* in May 1962 who dubbed it 'Monte Carlo in miniature'. Other introductory articles and track tests followed as the car's popularity and potential became apparent.

Undoubtedly race of the year for the Lotus 23 was Jim Clark in the Essex racing 23 in the Nurburgring 1000Km race. At the end of lap 1 the '*Flying Scot*' was 27 seconds in the lead, ahead of an international field including Ferrari and Porsche. The Lotus 23 entries for Le Mans marked the end of Lotus official participation in this 24-hour classic. Chapman and the French scrutineers had never got on well, but this year the 23 was excluded on the grounds that the wheel stud fixings were different front to rear. Despite Mike Costin flying back to England and machining new four-stud rear hubs, when the car was represented the car was again excluded on the grounds that if the rear hub had been designed for six studs then four *might* be dangerous. Chapman vowed never to return, and during his lifetime no Team or Works Lotus cars ever appeared at the French circuit again.

From its introduction in April 1962, until final production in May 1966, a total of 131 Lotus 23 and 23Bs were built. The car sold all over the world, and achieved success on every continent, dominating the 1500cc and 1600cc Sports Racing classes for five seasons until Lotus interests concentrated on Formula 1 and World Championship races with top international drivers, and racing car production for mass market single-seaters. The Lotus 23 was the last of the line of small capacity sports racing cars that had been the backbone of development by Lotus for a decade.

Graham Capel

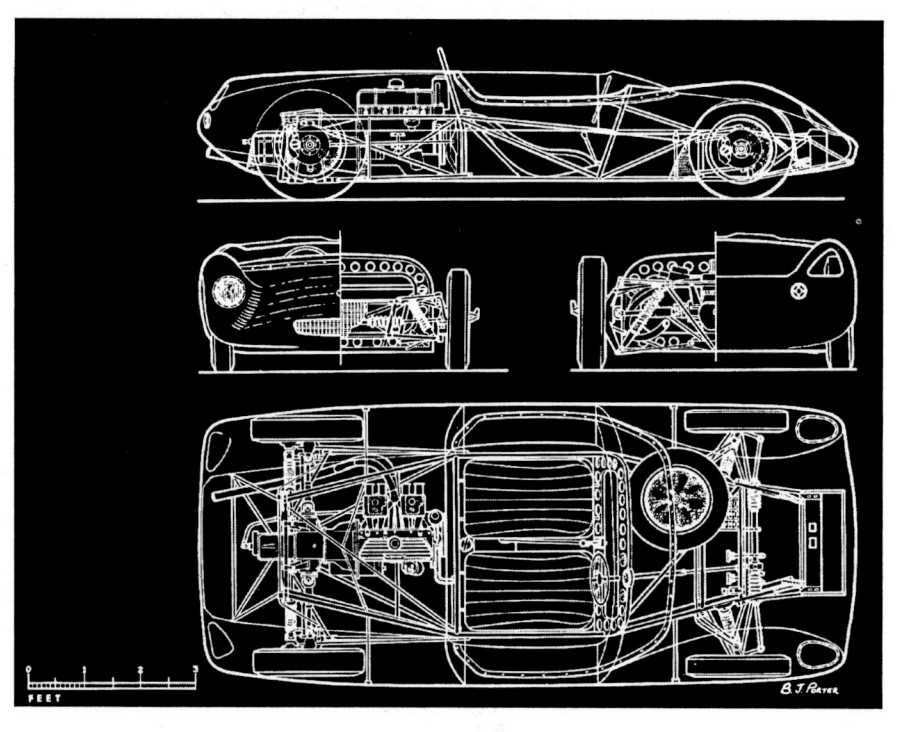

John Bolster Tries The Lotus XXIII Sports Car

J.V.B. takes the sports car through Madgwick. The roadholding of this car is very similar to that of the 22 although it understeers a little more.

THE new Lotus rear-engined sports car is very closely related to the Formula Junior design. The independent suspension is identical, as are the 9½ ins. Girling disc brakes. A Cosworth-Ford engine of 1,100 c.c., with Weber carburetters, is again employed. Naturally, a much wider multi-tubular frame is used.

I was able to put this one through its paces, too. The performance is almost as great as that of the single-seater and the ride just as comfortable. The test car was considerably noisier than the Junior, but this was partly due to incomplete bodywork. However, I wore ear plugs and was quite happy.

The sports car has inherited the extremely high cornering power of the racer. It understeers a little more, but in general it is very well balanced. On the short Lavant Straight, both cars had about the same maximum speed, but one would expect the all-enveloping sports car to go ahead on a long Continental straight. Against this, however, is the greater effect that gusts of wind have on a streamlined shell.

I formed the opinion that this 1,100 c.c. sports car will be just as formidable in its class as the F.J. car. It costs £1,650 in component form, or £1,725 complete and ready for export.

ABOVE: The oil tank for the 1,100 c.c. F.J. engine which is mounted right behind the radiator. Note the outboard-mounted Girling discs.

BELOW: Two ultra-reclining seats and an under-dash mounting of the spare wheel keep the body line low.

SPECIFICATION

Frame: Multi-tubular space frame constructed of round, square and rectangular section tubing, incorporating fabricated load carrying sheet metal driver's bulkhead.
Front Suspension: Fully independent by unequal length double wishbones incorporating coil spring and telescopic Armstrong dampers.
Rear Suspension: Fully independent by double wishbone type, incorporating parallel radius rods and also a top link.
Brakes: 9½ ins. Girling disc hydraulically operated front and rear mounted outboard.
Steering: Lightweight rack and pinion unit with adjustable steering column and lightweight leather covered steering wheel.
Power Unit: 1,100 c.c. Cosworth-Ford o.h.v. four cylinder, fitted with two 40 DCOE Weber carburetters. Mounted in rear of chassis.
Transmission: Single dry plate hydraulically operated clutch 7¼ ins. diameter with either Renault or Volkswagen modified close ratio four-speed gearbox. Final drive spiral bevel crown wheel and pinion mounted between engine and gearbox. Available gear ratios are: Renault: Standard 4.86; Optional 5.24; 4.59. Volkswagen: Standard 5.04; Optional 5.34; 4.73; 4.43.
Cooling System: Cross flow radiator mounted in nose with integral oil cooler. Oil and water flow through chassis tubes.
Fuel System: Light alloy fuel tank basically, approximately nine gallons, but other fuel tanks available as optional extras for long distance racing. Single SU high pressure electric fuel pump.
Bodywork: Resin bonded glassfibre panels, quickly detachable on front and rear hinges. Lightweight bucket seats.
Electrical System: Special lightweight battery. All other parts are Lucas equipment, incorporating dynamo, starter, automatic voltage control, fuses, headlights, side lights, tail lights, stop lights, windscreen wiper and horn.
Instruments: 0-9,000 r.p.m. tachometer, oil pressure gauge, water temperature gauge, ammeter.
Wheels and Tyres: Lightweight cast magnesium wheels 13 ins. diameter front and rear. Fitted with 450 x 13 front and 550 x 13 rear Dunlop R.5 racing tyres.
Dimensions: Wheel base 90 ins., front track 51½ ins., rear 50 ins., overall length 140 ins., overall width 59½ ins., overall height 27 ins., ground clearance 3¾ ins. at normal ride.
Price, in component form: Ex works £1,650.

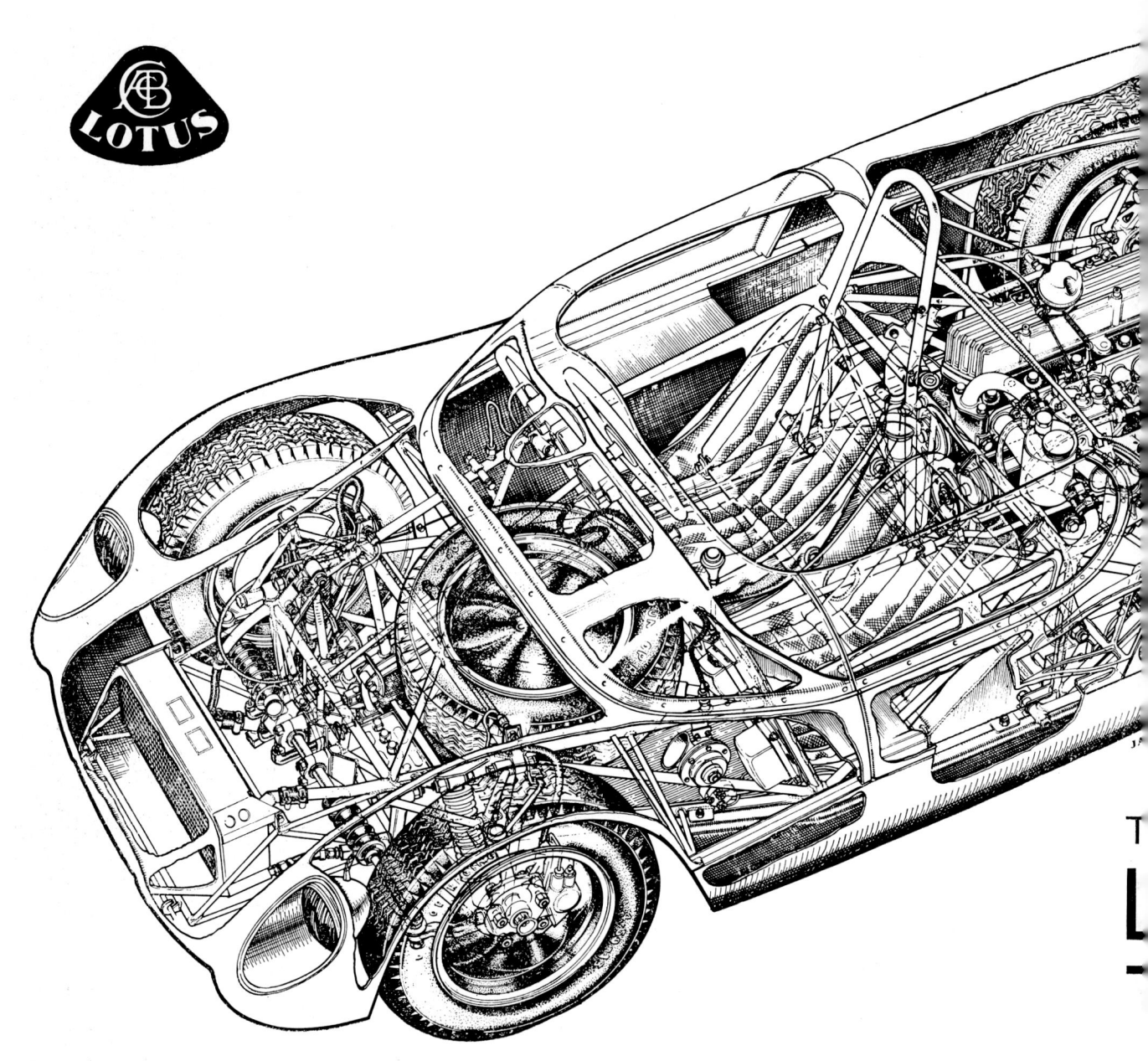

COSWORTH-FORD ENGINE—1,100 c.c., 103 b.h.p.—*is mounted behind the driver in a space-frame, all-independent chassis.*

In 1960 Lotus produced the Nineteen or Monte Carlo, a sports version of their current Formula 1 car. Now comes the 23, a two-seater based on the all-conquering 1961 Formula Junior Lotus and incorporating most of the modifications found on the 1962 model. If early tests are any guide—Peter Arundell has lapped the Silverstone club circuit in 1 min. 7.6 secs., well inside the 1,100 c.c. lap record, in a bodyless prototype—this car is going to take a lot of beating.

The basic specification of the 23 includes an 1,100 c.c., 103 b.h.p. Cosworth-Ford engine mounted behind the driver in a space-frame chassis, with all four 13-in. wheels independently sprung. Disc brakes are fitted as standard, and 1,470 c.c. or 997 c.c. engines are available at extra cost. Transmission is by a modified 7½-in. Ford clutch and either Renault- or Volkswagen-based four-speed, close ratio gearbox/final drive unit.

As with the engine and gearbox, the front suspension is similar to that of the

LOTUS TWENTY-THREE

BY DAVID PHIPPS

1961 F.J. Lotus, consisting of unequal length double wishbones, the lower one acting on co-axial coil spring/damper units; the dampers are the latest Armstrong GT7 "upside down" type, designed to minimize unsprung weight by mounting the piston at the inboard end. The four-stud cast magnesium front wheels are fitted with 4.50 x 13 tyres on 5-in. rims. Steering is by Lotus rack and pinion gear.

The rear suspension is based on that of the 1961 F1 Lotus, with a top lateral link, a wide-based lower lateral link and parallel longitudinal radius arms. Coil springs and GT7 dampers are used, and power is transmitted by splined drive shafts. In this case six-stud wheels are used with 5.50 x 13 tyres on 6-in. rims. Anti-roll bars are fitted at both front and rear, to offset the effects of using fairly low roll centres, and the brakes—9½-in. Girling discs—are mounted outboard all round.

The chassis is basically similar to that of the 1961 Lotus Junior, but widened to accommodate two seats. It consists of three bays, and every frame except the one through which the driver's body projects is fully triangulated. Thanks to increased cross-section area it is considerably stiffer than that of the Junior. The forward bulkhead provides mounting points for the front suspension, the steering rack, the battery, the pedals and the cross-flow radiator (with integral oil-cooler). The scuttle bulkhead—of the "perforated hoop" type, consisting of two tubular rectangles linked by sheet steel—locates steering column, seats, gear lever, instruments (9,000 r.p.m. tachometer, oil pressure and water temperature gauges, ammeter) and switches. The rear radius arms are mounted on the engine bulkhead, which also supports the nine-gallon fuel tank, helps to locate the seats and takes loads from the engine mountings (at the junction of two side-frame diagonals). Engine loads are also accepted, via the gearbox mountings, in the rear bulkhead; the latter also provides mountings for the remaining elements of the rear suspension.

The top left and bottom right longitudinal chassis members are used as water pipes linking engine and radiator, whilst the top right and bottom left members act as oil pipes; the interior of these tubes is specially treated to produce an anti-corrosive phosphate film.

The bodywork, of resin-bonded glass-fibre, complies with Appendix J, Group IV, 1962, in respect of windscreen height, luggage space (alongside the engine), ground clearance and turning circle. There is also ample room for extra fuel tanks for use in long distance races. Full electrical equipment is fitted, including SU fuel pump, Lucas dynamo and starter, voltage regulator, fuses, head-, side-, tail- and brake-lights, windscreen wiper and horn. Overall length is 11 ft. 8 ins., width 4 ft. 11½ ins. and maximum height 2 ft. 3 ins. (to the top of the windscreen). Weight, ready to go, is 880 lb.

Early reports on the 23 are that the handling is every bit as good as that of the 1961 Junior, while the brakes are described as "fantastic". The queue starts at Delamare Road, Cheshunt, Herts.

PHOTOS: GEOFFREY GODDARD

LOTUS TWENTY THREE

BY JOHN BLUNSDEN

REMEMBERING COLIN CHAPMAN'S beautifully streamlined and monotonously successful Lotus 11, and trying to forget the comparative limitations of its successor, the Lotus 17, it has always seemed inevitable that sooner or later 'The Guvnor' would renew his interest in the small-capacity sports-racing car.

The first hint that a new Lotus of this type was on its way came last Fall, at a press conference at the Piccadilly, London, showrooms of Coventry Climax. The occasion was the introduction of new marketing arrangements for the Elite, whereby the Grand Tourer would be sold as a kit and thereby escape the levy of close to $2,000 in purchase tax. But Chapman, flying home after a sales-boosting tour of the United States, chose the opportunity to outline his 1962 plans in a tantalizing lack of detail.

Although only the briefest reference to the new sports-racer was made, it did not call for a crystal ball to speculate that the car would be a sort of mixture of the Lotus 19 Monte Carlo and the 1962 model Junior. Its debut at the Racing Car Show confirmed the thought; briefly, the Lotus Mark 23 is the closest thing to the Mark 22 Junior that it is possible to make that will carry a scaled down and smoothed out Appendix 'C' Monte Carlo body. It is a car which, design-wise, offers a few if any surprises. On the circuits, however, there are likely to be surprises aplenty. Sufficient at this stage to record that its early development trials on British circuits have made existing 1,100 cc sports car lap records seem somewhat comical.

The car has been built up on a fairly conventional space-frame of mild steel tube of round, square and rectangular section, the complete structure being shot-blasted, primed and stove enamelled. The most interesting feature of the frame is its use as a carrier for oil and water to and from the engine — a system first used by Chapman in 1961. For this reason the four main side tubes, all of which have different cross-sectional dimensions, are treated in an acid solution to prevent impurities in the oil and water systems.

Apart from the floor pan, which consists of a sheet of stressed 20-gauge aluminum, the frame structure is fully triangulated, lateral reinforcement being provided by three bulkheads. Immediately in front of the driver there is the now familiar diaphragm arrangement consisting of 18-gauge sheet which forms a double skin over a framework of ¾-inch 20-gauge tubing, the sheet being liberally drilled with flanged holes for lightness and stiffness.

The fireproof bulkhead between the driver and the engine is a sheet of 18-gauge aluminum, and the third bulkhead is a smaller sheet adjacent to the pedals, and is sealed against the front body panel by sponge rubber strips. This forms a draft shield, and helps to keep radiator heat off the

286

Monte Carlo in Miniature

driver's feet, as well as trapping the road dirt thrown up by the front wheels.

Reverting to the engine's coolant and lubrication systems, the water passes out of the cylinder-head to the swirl pot mounted against the bulkhead behind and to the left of the driver, and then into the 1¼-inch diameter round tube which forms the top left main frame member. This takes the water to the radiator, from which it is returned via the bottom right main tube, which is a 1½-inch by ¾-inch rectangular-section member, to the water pump and the block.

The oil, meanwhile, leaves the engine to enter the bottom left main tube, which is of ¾-inch square section in order to clear the bottom wishbone bushes, passes through the radiator, to return via the top right 1-inch round tube to the engine bearings. The take-off points for the water temperature and oil pressure gauges are in the top tubes, just forward of the diaphragm bulkhead, thereby minimizing the chance of lead failure through vibration and/or excessive length.

The front suspension of the Mark 23 is almost interchangeable with that of the Lotus 19, the only difference being its adaption to the Triumph Herald type hub, as used on the Juniors. It is a double wishbone layout, with the latest Armstrong GT7 shock absorbers mounted coaxially with steeply inclined coil springs, and fitted in 'reverse,' with the heavier end of the unit attached to the chassis frame in order to reduce unsprung weight. A ⁹⁄₁₆-inch anti-roll bar is Rose-jointed to the suspension uprights.

The rear suspension is the same as that used on the latest Junior, the Mark 22. It comprises a pair of lower wishbones with single inboard pivots, linked to a new magnesium casting forming the hub carrier and suspension upright. A single transverse arm is attached to the top of each upright, and is bushed just forward of the shock absorbers on an extension of the main frame. Fore and aft location is by paired tubular radius arms, the upper arms being at approximately wheel hub height, and a ½-inch anti-roll bar is connected to the suspension uprights by drop arms and rubber bushes. The shock absorber settings are slightly harder and the springs slightly stiffer on the sports car than on the new Junior, and in fact correspond to the settings used on last year's Lotus 20 Junior.

Girling 9½-inch disc brakes are used all round, the discs being ⅜-inch thick. The AR type caliper, with 2-inch piston, is used at the front and the NR type, with 1½-inch pistons, at the rear, the latter being the same brake as is used on the front of the early Lotus Elite. The pad material is Ferodo DA2, which gives a pretty hard pad. The rear wheels have a six-stud fixing, but the front wheels are fixed with four studs to enable them to be used with proprietary hubs.

The Lotus 23 is catalogued with a Ford 105E engine, modified and tuned by Cosworth Engineering, and producing a minimum of 95 horsepower at 7,400 rpm as a pass-out figure. A cylinder bore of 3.346 inches (85 mm) and a stroke of 1.906 inches (48.4 mm) gives a displacement of 1,097 cc. Fuel is fed through twin Weber type 40 DCOE carburetors and the compression ratio is 10 to 1. The wet sump holds approximately 2.2 (U.S.) gallons of oil, which is circulated at 60 to 65 psi. Normal inlet valve clearance is 0.020-inch, and exhaust clearance 0.022-inch, with 0.390-inch lift on the valves. With the 'production' camshaft fitted, the inlet valve opens 50 degrees before top dead center and closes 75 degrees after bottom dead center, while the exhaust valve opens 86 degrees before bottom dead center and closes 50 degrees after top dead center.

The electrical equipment includes a Lucas HA12 sports coil, and the distributor is virtually standard, apart from the lack of any vacuum advance mechanism. An Exide 12-volt battery is carried on the floor of the car, to the left of the driver's feet, and normally Champion L58R or Lodge R47 plugs will be fitted.

Although the prototype car was fitted with a Renault gearbox with four speeds, a four-speed VW box is being offered as an alternative, although this has involved some redesigning of the rubber couplings which are fitted between the Lotus-designed side plates of the gearbox and the drive shafts. These couplings, which were first used by Lotus on the Mark 21 Formula 1 car, help to cushion some of the road shocks from the transmission. Their use has also been facilitated by the positioning of the rear disc brakes outboard, where any slight lack of balance is unlikely to impose any stresses on the couplings. Another, more practical reason for the outboard mounting, of course, is that there was insufficient room within the Formula Junior frame for inboard discs, and by bringing the Mark 23 into line with the single seater at least one production problem has been overcome.

When the Renault gearbox is used the normal final-drive gears will be 8 x 35, giving a ratio of 4.37 to 1, but 7 x 33 (4.71 to 1) is offered as an alternative, and 7 x 29 (4.14 to 1) will be available to special order. The ratios in the

LOTUS TWENTY THREE

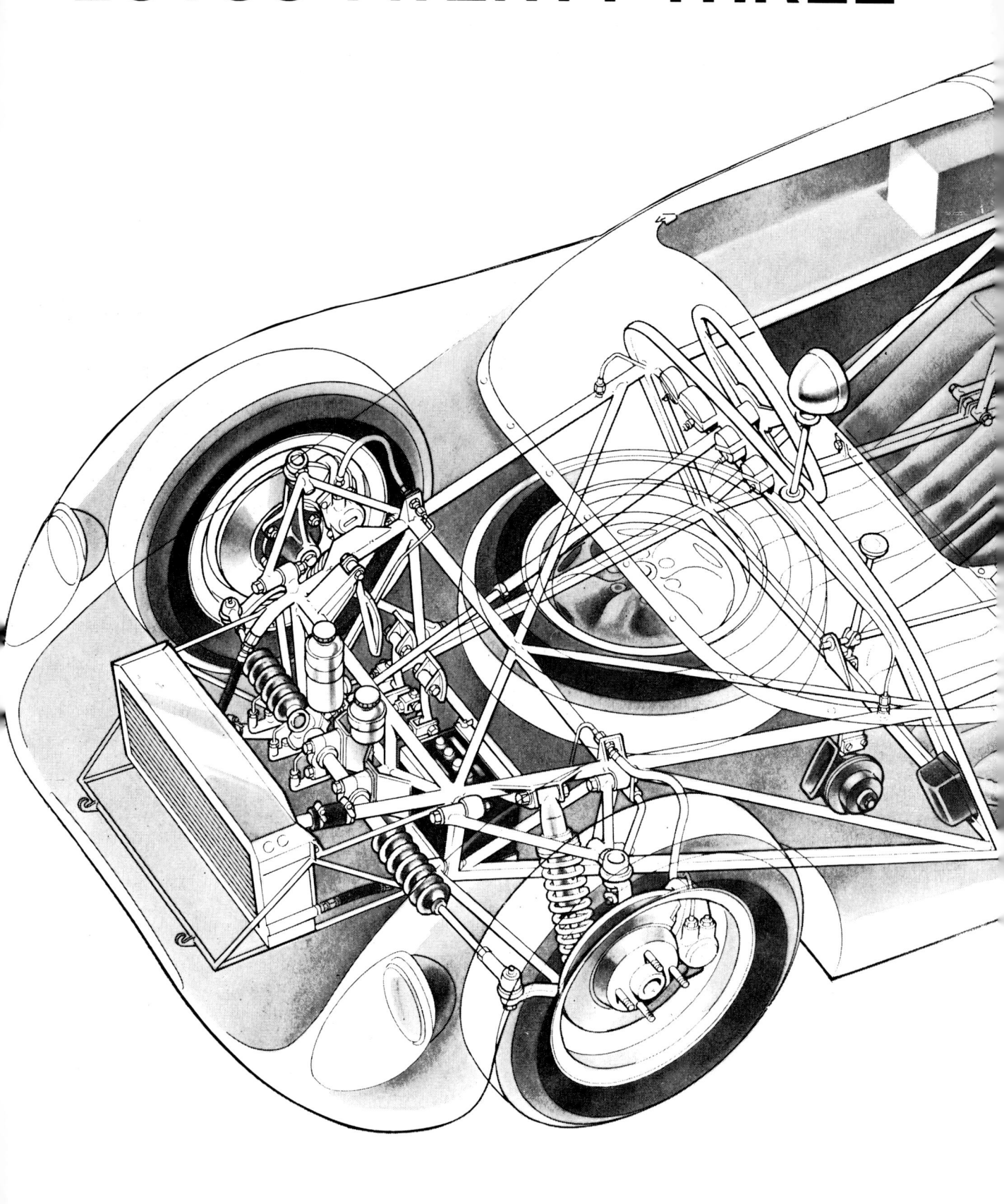

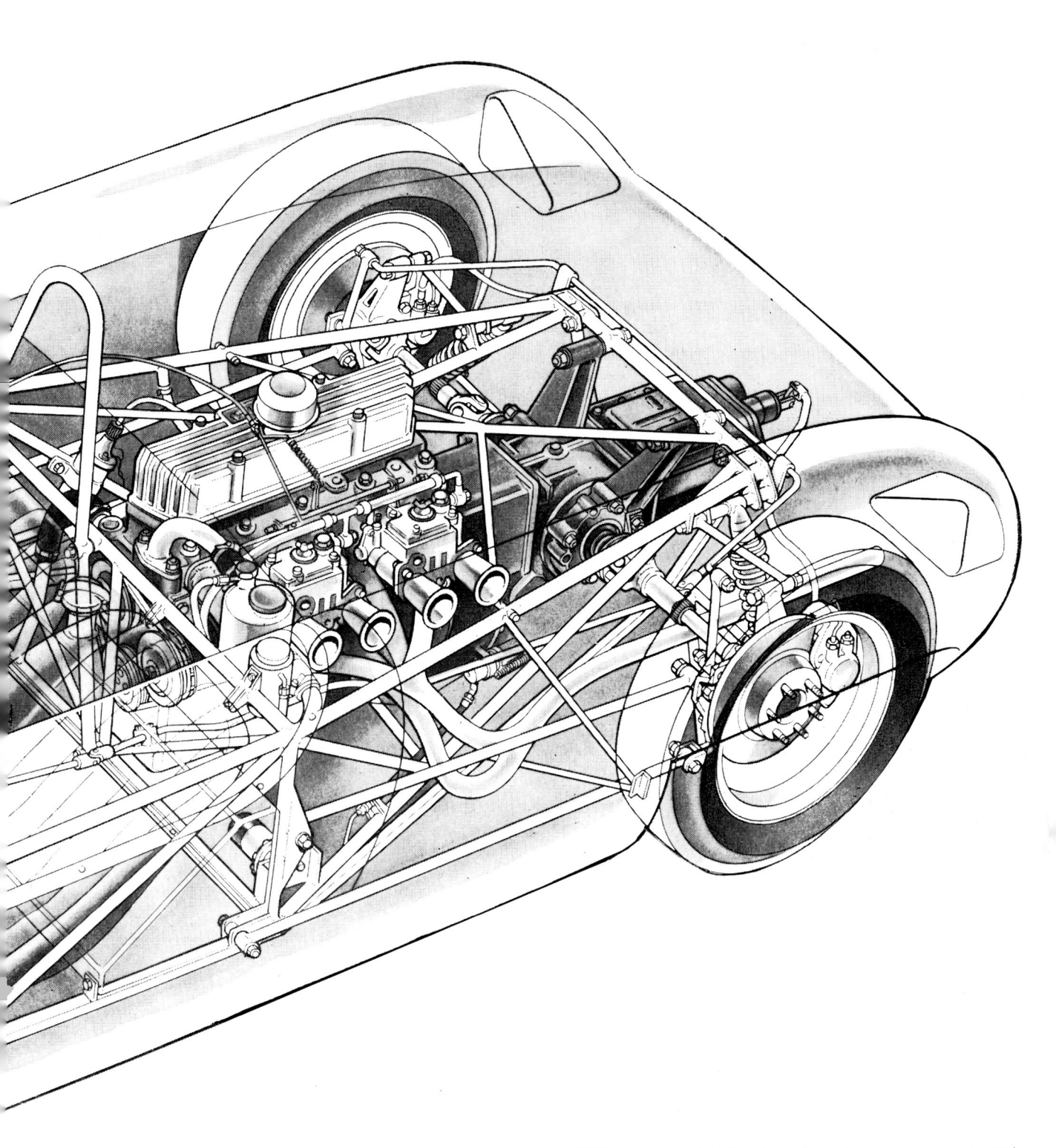

ENGINE: Cosworth-Ford. Standard 1100-cc version of 100 hp. Optional engines in 997 or 1470-cc versions.
TRANSAXLE: Either VW or Renault available in close-ratio, four-speed form.
CHASSIS: Space-frame of ¾-inch steel tube. Removable body panels of Fiberglass.
WHEELS: Cast magnesium, 13-inch diameter. 4.50 x 13 Dunlop R5 tires in front, 5.50 x 13 rears.
REAR SUSPENSION: Reversed "A" lower member, single upper, slip-coupled halfshafts, double-trailing radius arms, coil/shocks, reversed swaybar, cast-alloy hub carriers.
BRAKES: Outboard 9.5-inch Girling discs. Inboard-mounted rears optional.
FRONT SUSPENSION: Reversed upper "A's" with lower arm and swaybar joined to form member. Armstrong coil/shocks, rack & pinion steering to leading spindle arms.

WEIGHTS & MEASURES:

Wheelbase	91 in.	Overall Length	140 in.
Front Tread	50 in.	Width	59.5 in.
Rear Tread	48 in.	Height	27 in.
Curb Weight	880 lbs.	Gas Tank	9 gallons

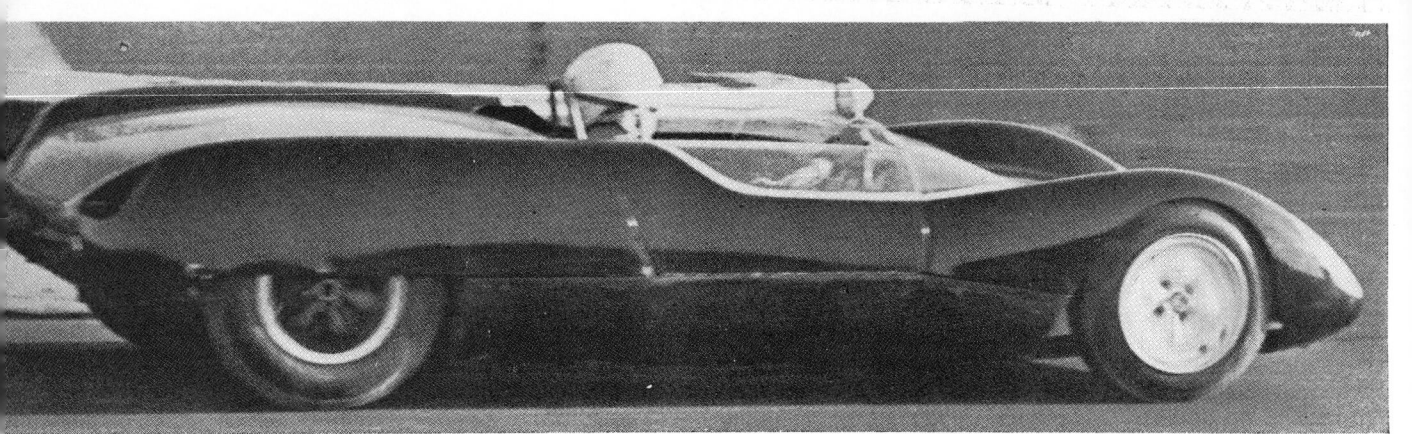

SCG's John Blunsden takes new Lotus 23 through a sweeping turn on the Goodwood circuit, found car extremely stable.

LOTUS TWENTY-THREE

Renault box are 2.92, 1.81, 1.36, and 1.11 to 1.

With the VW gearbox, which has ratios of 3.80, 2.06, 1.55 and 1.22 to 1, the 8 x 33 (4.125 to 1) final drive will be standardized, with 8 x 31 (3.875 to 1) as an alternative, and 8 x 29 (3.625 to 1) available to special order only. Irrespective of the gearbox, a 7¼-inch single-plate clutch is supplied.

The engine-transmission unit is secured to the chassis at four points, two transverse arms from a junction point of three side tubes, terminating in plates which are secured to the sides of the cylinder block, and two more support arms linking the final-drive casing with pins running forwards from the top rear transverse frame member.

Unlike the Junior, the Mark 23 has the engine mounted vertically in the frame, and being on the centerline of the car, this poses a gear linkage problem, the gearshift for the sports car also being on the car's centerline. This has been overcome by cranking the linkage round to the left side of the engine, with the aid of two universal joints and three guides. When the VW box is fitted, the forward positions are in the conventional position, with first and second to the left of the neutral gate, and third and top to the right, but on the Renault box the positions are transposed, first and second being towards the driver of a right-hand drive model, and third and top away from him, to the left.

The lightweight steering rack and pinion are placed forward of the front wheel line, between the combined six-row oil and water radiator, with its separate header compartments, and the bulkhead just forward of the pedals. It is linked to a 13-inch leather covered wheel by an adjustable column. As set up at the factory, the Lotus 23 is given zero degrees camber and a total of ⅛-inch toe-in, while the non-adjustable caster angle is seven degrees. Between 2 and 2½ degrees of negative camber is given at the rear, and each wheel has a toe-in of ¼-inch.

The prototype car was fitted with a wedge-shaped fuel tank lying immediately behind the two seats, but on production models this is being replaced by a longitudinal tank, of quadrant cross section, resting amidships to the left of the cockpit. In this position it conveniently fills the space between the frame side tubes and the outer skin of the glass-fiber body, the body being attached to the frame by two outriggers of ½-inch 18-gauge tube on each side, and by two brackets securing it to each bottom chassis tube. This left-hand tank, holding approximately 10 (U.S.) gallons, can be supplemented by a second tank, a little more than half the size, on the right, in which case a second SU electrical fuel pump will be fitted.

Apart from the center sections, which as just described, are secured rigidly to the chassis frame, the body is built up of just two large sections, each of which hinge on ¾-inch 18-gauge outriggers extending from the main chassis frame. When closed, these body sections are secured in position by two pairs of vertical spring clips in the corners of the cockpit. The front outriggers incorporate quick-lift jacking points, but at the rear the lower wishbones (of ⅞-inch 14-gauge mild steel tube) have strengthening pieces welded to the rear arms, just inboard of the outer pivots, which act as bearing surfaces for a jack, as on the Junior cars.

The body is of resin-bonded, color impregnated glass-fiber throughout, and incorporates an intake duct forward of the radiator. It complies with the International Appendix 'C,' and incorporates a three-piece windshield extending around three sides of the cockpit, and blending in neatly with the two bottom-hinged doors. Full lighting equipment is provided, and the Mark 23 is supplied with detachable roll bar, bolted to a frame cross member.

Instruments include a 9,000 rpm tachometer, flanked by an oil pressure gauge on the right and an ammeter on the left, with a water temperature gauge further to the left, while there is provision low down on the right side of the diaphragm bulkhead for an oil temperature gauge. The combined ignition-starter switch is mounted centrally in the dashboard, and the minor controls, for lights, horn, and so on, are of the toggle switch type, as fitted to most of Britain's latest production cars.

The two seats are based on those used in the Lotus 21 last year, and have higher shoulder pieces than those used on last year's Junior. They have a glass-fiber shell, with plastic foam padding and vynide trim ... and they offer that armchair comfort which seems so much a part of present-day competition cars. How times have changed!

Track Test

The Lotus day of track testing at Goodwood is becoming something of an annual event. Each year, as soon as the new production models have passed their preliminary circuit trials, Colin Chapman invites down a selection of journalists and potential customers to sample his latest wares. In 1960 it was the Lotus 18 Junior, last year it was its successor, the Mk. 20. This time he brought along two models, the Mk. 22 Junior and the Mk. 23 sports-racer. Amazingly, both cars survived the day's ordeal without harm, although each had had close to a score of different bodies in the cockpit in the space of a few hours, and several times they were over-revved unmercifully, if inadvertently.

Although I drove both cars, it would be wrong to try to assess them on a direct comparative basis, for not only did I drive the Junior in the wet, and the Mk. 23 in almost dry conditions, but they are, for all their technical similarity, fundamentally different cars, and should be considered as such. I will just mention in passing, therefore, that the Mk. 22 Junior appears to have noticeably more cornering power than the Mk. 20, has an even more compact cockpit, and is undoubtedly better braked. Driver and power being equal, therefore, I would assess it as at least a second per minute quicker in lap times, and perhaps up to two seconds per minute on the really tortuous circuit. In short, the top Lotus drivers will have to buy one if they plan on still winning Junior races.

The first impression on climbing into a Lotus 23 (you never use the door!) is that this is the first car from Cheshunt to combine restfulness with spaciousness within a compact package size. There is no need for the contortions practiced by Junior drivers in reaching the pedals, and the only hazard en route is a frame diagonal on the right, which can catch the right knee of the taller driver.

With pedals and steering column adjustable for reach there are no driving position problems for those with moderately standard dimensions, and as equipped, the Mk. 23

The Lotus 23 comes with Ford 105E Cosworth-tuned 1100 cc engine that gives a minimum of 95 bhp at 7,400 revolutions.

offered adequate lateral support from the sides of the well-upholstered seat. Obviously, a customer would tailor this to his specific requirements before going motor racing seriously.

The roll bar, being bolted to a frame member, serves to comply with certain race regulations rather than to offer any substantial degree of protection to the occupant. In any case, there is a stronger case for the removal of this item from sports cars, the cockpits of which offer more room for maneuvering than there is in single-seaters.

Once in position, the feet have full freedom of movement for pedal operation. The clutch has the now customary light action, but the accelerator spring was on the heavy side, with the result that one tended to take 'lumps' of throttle at a time instead of a steadily progressive opening. A small matter of adjustment.

The test car was equipped with the Renault transmission, on which the wide gate of the gearshift simplifies the selection of the ratios, and although considerable stick movement is involved, the action is light.

The Cosworth-Ford engine has a reputation for robustness and for a fairly substantial usable rev range. The real 'meat' is found from 5,000 rpm upwards, so that with a peak engine speed of 7,800 rpm, this offers a range which makes the use of only four speeds in the gearbox fully justifiable. The engine of the test car, which had earlier been doing work in another chassis, had a sharp and crisp note throughout the usable range, and picked up cleanly after an over-run, although considerable popping and banging accompanied the closing of the throttle at high speed.

A fault peculiar to the test car was the unreasonably high engine noise level in the cockpit. This was due to the length of the exhaust pipe, which fell just short of the tail of the body, so that the rear panels deflected some of the exhaust pulses and acted as an echo chamber for them, to the considerable discomfort of the driver's ears! About an inch added onto the tail pipe would have overcome this, and I understand that this is being rectified on future models.

As set up, this prototype Mk. 23 had almost neutral handling characteristics, with exceptionally stable cornering power, despite a discernible amount of body roll, when really pressed. Under most conditions, a geometrical line can be steered through a bend, the breakaway point, in the dry at least, being beyond the limit set by the average club driver. A purposely induced rear-end slide need not become an embarrassment, however, for it is catchable, and if there is sufficient power on hand it can be maintained. In this respect, the car handles rather like a Mk. 19 Monte Carlo, the main difference being that under most conditions the power available will not allow the slide to be maintained for any length of time.

Both the steering and the brakes of this newcomer are apparently up to the very high standards established in Formula Junior racing, and they contribute notably to the feeling of 'at home-ness' which prevails after the first few seconds on the circuit.

The riding comfort of the car was difficult to assess, for this was the first time I had driven at Goodwood since it has been completely resurfaced. The transformation of this track is remarkable, for the old, abrasive, bumpy and in places undulating surface, has given way to a smooth but not-too-slippery top dressing which seems likely to please tire technicians, if not their sales staffs. Bumps which used to be there, and which did their best to unleash a car on a bend, are no longer, so that any car would seem a vastly improved machine when taken down there for the first time. Nevertheless, these improvements apart, the Lotus 23 obviously maintains the marque's reputation for high standard of riding comfort.

This really is a compact sports-racing car, with a 90-inch wheelbase, and a track of 51½-inches at the front and 50-inches at the rear; ground clearance is a nominal 3½ inches. If anything, when viewed from outside, it seems even smaller, but from the cockpit it has quite a big car feeling of solidarity.

The wind protection probably contributes to this feeling, and I found that the slight lip in the screen over the instruments helps to deflect some of the air over the top of the crash helmet, while the wrapped side screens take a lot more well behind the shoulder line. Obviously, the body line is aerodynamically very efficient, and this is unlikely to be a tiring car to drive in a long-distance race. The only cause for criticism of the body during the test concerned the 'passenger's' door, which dropped open after a spot of sharp cornering, and trailed on the ground, scoring its edge.

With the car still in the process of development at the time of the test, it is perhaps difficult to assess accurately its ultimate potential, but it would be fair to suggest that this good-looking newcomer should be able to lap any given circuit within five percent of the time set up by the latest Lotus Junior, and that on a fast circuit such as Reims, where its shape will compensate for its unladen weight of 948 pounds, it might even prove to be faster. We shall see!

The extremely low front profile of the Lotus shows here as Blunsden gets ready to test it at Goodwood.

HOW GREEN IS MY EAR-'OLE

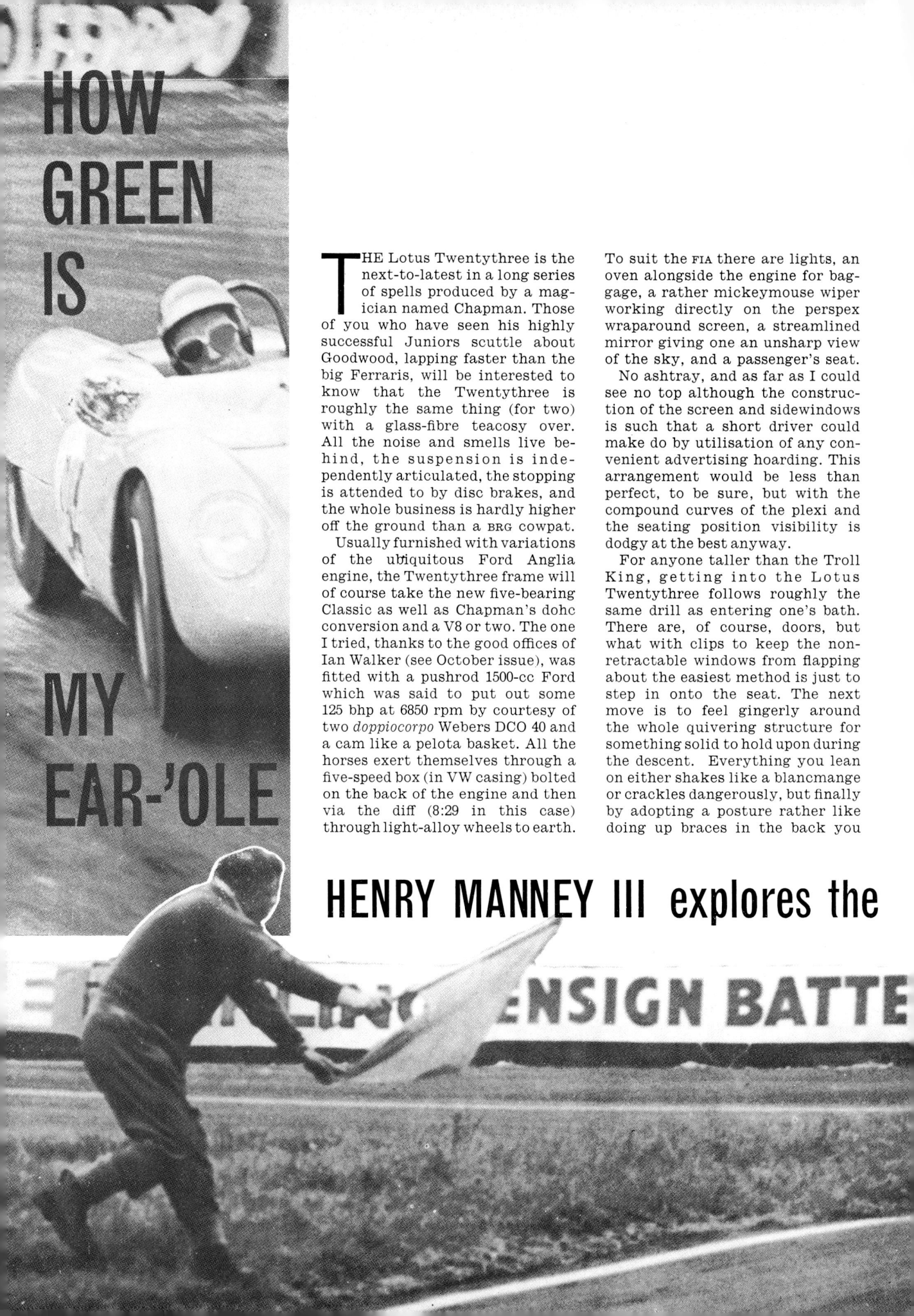

THE Lotus Twentythree is the next-to-latest in a long series of spells produced by a magician named Chapman. Those of you who have seen his highly successful Juniors scuttle about Goodwood, lapping faster than the big Ferraris, will be interested to know that the Twentythree is roughly the same thing (for two) with a glass-fibre teacosy over. All the noise and smells live behind, the suspension is independently articulated, the stopping is attended to by disc brakes, and the whole business is hardly higher off the ground than a BRG cowpat.

Usually furnished with variations of the ubiquitous Ford Anglia engine, the Twentythree frame will of course take the new five-bearing Classic as well as Chapman's dohc conversion and a V8 or two. The one I tried, thanks to the good offices of Ian Walker (see October issue), was fitted with a pushrod 1500-cc Ford which was said to put out some 125 bhp at 6850 rpm by courtesy of two *doppiocorpo* Webers DCO 40 and a cam like a pelota basket. All the horses exert themselves through a five-speed box (in VW casing) bolted on the back of the engine and then via the diff (8:29 in this case) through light-alloy wheels to earth.

To suit the FIA there are lights, an oven alongside the engine for baggage, a rather mickeymouse wiper working directly on the perspex wraparound screen, a streamlined mirror giving one an unsharp view of the sky, and a passenger's seat.

No ashtray, and as far as I could see no top although the construction of the screen and sidewindows is such that a short driver could make do by utilisation of any convenient advertising hoarding. This arrangement would be less than perfect, to be sure, but with the compound curves of the plexi and the seating position visibility is dodgy at the best anyway.

For anyone taller than the Troll King, getting into the Lotus Twentythree follows roughly the same drill as entering one's bath. There are, of course, doors, but what with clips to keep the non-retractable windows from flapping about the easiest method is just to step in onto the seat. The next move is to feel gingerly around the whole quivering structure for something solid to hold upon during the descent. Everything you lean on either shakes like a blancmange or crackles dangerously, but finally by adopting a posture rather like doing up braces in the back you

HENRY MANNEY III explores the

SPORTING DRIVER

Yes, mister, you *are* looking down the multiple throats of the world's fastest small sports car engine: the Cosworth 105E

find support. The preferred method is to straighten out the legs, not putting undue pressure on the floorboards, and emulate a snail retracting into its shell. The feet must be pointed, otherwise a bulkhead three-quarters of the way in halts progress, but once you're there there is a surprising amount of room—not enough for the Twist perhaps, but enough to change gear and that without coming away covered in bruises.

The driving position of the Twentythree is rather like lying on the beach. Not only are you at shoelace level but the currently fashionable reclining position ensures that you are looking straight up Ian Walker's nose instead of out front where the accident is.

This is further exaggerated by a handy cutout in the back deck to put the noodle in; now I know why Twentythree-drivers always look as if they are asleep. Very comfortable. The only trouble is that the dash is so far away a telescope is essential to see the dials. Not that there are many; water temp, oil pressure, tach, and two or three odd switches to cut out the brake lights and so forth. But it would be nice to know what is going on without sitting bolt upright and dropping 600 rpm at once.

The leather-covered wheel, roughly the size of the average pub porkpie, is likewise out of reach. The only really handy item is the gearshift. Played by the left hand, it is most surprisingly a large unsubtle piece of iron—apparently a concession to the fact that hired hand 'Awkins doesn't know his own brute strength.

The gate, a six-bar H, is fitted with the usual Lotus system of sliding baulks to protect the drivers from themselves; reverse, second and fourth are up, working from the left, if you follow me. In spite of the lack of synchromesh, the clutch must be depressed fully to give scrunch-proof entry from rest (regardless of what Mr Issigonis says) unless, of course, you are trying to engage reverse while creeping gently forward.

Actually I was excess baggage on this caper as the celebrated P. Arundell was thrashing the Twentythree arounds Brands with a view to sanitising the roadholding. After he, Ian, and boss mechanic Stone had got through fiddling about with shockers and all, they crammed me into Ian's crashhat and said, with unanimity but not without serious misgivings, 'Go'. Now some of you young people may have got the idea from the more exuberant dailies that all we motoring correspondents are picked for our looks, sexiness, and ability to

OVER ▶

Brands Hatch verges in a Lotus Twentythree —

And here it is all bolted in behind a Lotus Twentythree. Driver's ear is about 4½ in. from camshaft, which is a help

—driving lying down with cuff buttons interlocked

lap the Nurburgring in under 10 minutes. That is not only disputable, generally speaking, but the only feature Fangio and I have in common is two arms, two legs and a head. Therefore it is perfectly understandable (I keep telling myself) that I zigzagged all over the lot and lost myself in the gate instead of rushing out and Showing Arundell Where to Get Off just like in the movies. But why not?

Frankly, the Twentythree is a real giggle. It commences either by pushing (to spare the aircraft-type battery) or by the starter, and moves off without fuss in second unless haste is indicated. As with many competition cars, there is not all that much racket going on from the engine; what you hear are the dentist-drill sorts of noises from the gearbox and rear end.

Therefore it pays to keep an eye on the tach, but unless you are braver than I am you won't have time to (i) look, (ii) go that fast anyway. The short straights at Brands seem miraculously to contract into nothing once you've actually got there.

Now everyone knows what to do as you arrive at a corner . . . brake, shift down, turn the wheel and so forth. The first of these is uncomplicated enough; the brake pedal is large, close and easy to find. The next is confused by the necessity to remember what gear out of five you are in, where it is on the gate and just where you look for the next one. Additionally, the gearshift itself, while moving easily enough, has little feeling of being connected to anything. The gear goes in silently on its last half-inch

of travel, so it is difficult to tell whether you are home safe or way out in limbo instead.

The third thing, steering, is perhaps the most difficult of the three because of the combination of odd-odd driving position and simple mechanical leverage. I personally can't exert much force with my arms straight out in front of me with the cuff buttons practically interlocking, especially when lying on the back of my neck, and the effort required on the Twentythree is surprisingly great. Rounding a sharp hairpin like Druids makes for the old gritted-teeth stuff lest one run out of road on the outside.

As I trundled around a few times, though, I got to feeling a little more reasonable simply by the expedient of sitting up whenever I could.

SPORTING DRIVER

This sort of manoeuvre is especially difficult on corners because the Twentythree sticks like glue (so the only thing leaning is the driver) but a policy of bobbing up like a prairie dog, setting the line and then disappearing again works wonders. As far as comfort is concerned, I found none of the traditional racing-car oozes or drips and the ride was really marvellous: so soft and comfortable. No, really.

For obvious reasons acceleration figures were not taken but as Ian claimed the car was good for 150 mph in top gear, maybe it's just as well I stuck to the first four. As a sop to those who are going to Monte Carlo by Lotus, though, it returns 15 mpg or so under give-and-take conditions (whatever that means). What it will do with a Chrysler V8 in is anybody's guess. In its original state, though, it is a fine sports and racing car for those who like Junior handling but don't necessarily want to be shunted every event.

School cars like this brought up the current crop of British drivers and will no doubt contribute to the next. I don't know what they cost or whether you can get them in a kit, but Ian Walker probably can tell you. And if he can't Lotus can. If I wasn't lumbered with a family I'd enquire myself. ●

Twentythree habitually turns miles into metres. SMALL CAR'S Henry Manney never found fifth gear during entire test

TRACK TEST of MIKE BECKWITH'S LOTUS 23

by PATRICK McNALLY.
Photography by Geoffrey Goddard

This is as much a story about the driver who conducts the car as it is about the car itself, for together, they proved a winning combination. Mike started with Normand, Ltd., in March 1960 as a car salesman. In 1961 he bought his own Lotus 11 and started racing early in the year, scoring nine first, nine second and four third places. This success gave him encouragement to proceed but, unfortunately, he just did not have the money and had to look around for a sponsor. This was where Normand, Ltd., stepped in, and after a certain amount of discussion it was decided to sponsor a Lotus 23 for the 1962 season.

The car was delivered in March and work started immediately to get it ready for the first meeting of the season—Goodwood on the 24th of the month. This meeting was not a success, as the car was bent due to the chassis and rack being out of alignment which caused violent toe-in on full braking. Undaunted by this unfortunate incident, the car was rebuilt and a week later Mike set off for Aintree where he was unsuccessful once more due to failure of the gear lever, which fell to pieces. This was duly replaced by the top of an old M.G. TC gearbox, which has proved 100 per cent reliable ever since! Following this depressing start to the 1962 season the car was finally "sorted-out" and went on to score 20 class and outright wins, five second, one third and two fourth places (including even *Formule Libre* events). Mike also holds five class lap records: Snetterton, Goodwood, Oulton Park, Castle Combe and Silverstone.

Sharing the success was Colin Knight, who is a personal friend of Mike's and has been his mechanic since the beginning. The car has always been brought to the line as immaculate internally as it was externally.

The car is basically a Lotus 23 fitted with a Cosworth wet-sump 1,100 engine which is mated to a four-speed Renault gearbox—not the five-speed Hewland which is now fitted as standard. Suspension is standard but set up to Mike's taste. The brakes have undergone a lot of development and are one of the best features of the car.

We took the opportunity to try the car just as raced and spent an enjoyable afternoon lapping Silverstone. The first thing which makes itself obvious is the perfect trim of the car, which feels absolutely right. The gear lever is on the left and comes easily to hand, the steering wheel is so placed as to enable the driver to adopt a straight-arm driving position, whilst the pedals are so arranged as to make gear-changing easy work. The rev. counter can also be viewed without difficulty. We set off for a few warming-up laps and were immediately impressed by the gear-change, which was slick, without any excessive movement, and the brakes, which imparted the utmost confidence. After five laps one really had the feel of the car and was able to experiment with different lines through the corners. There was definitely a tendency towards understeer; this may be caused by the lack of weight on the front wheels, but it could easily be changed by a "fistful of wheel" to get the car going nicely. These handling characteristics suit most drivers.

On the club circuit the car was not as interesting as it would have been over a longer course, but the gearing was still ideal. Except on take-off, where first and second gear coped admirably, we used third and top for the rest of the time except on one occasion where we tried second at Becketts, with apparently little advantage. Third gear was also used at Woodcote where the technique was to brake at the 200 ft. board, to accelerate hard by the time one passed the Shell stand and to give the car a good twitch as one passed the last of the barrels. If one didn't grab another handful of wheel at this spot there was no doubt at all that one would have been on the grass, as the understeer was fairly severe. Third gear, too, was used at Copse, the twitch being necessary just before one shaved the wall; the piece of concrete on the outside of the circuit was needed on most occasions! Maggots Corner, naturally enough, was taken flat, the change-up having taken place just before entering the slight twist. The 200 ft. board again was our braking point before we swung through Becketts; it was on this corner that the understeer was most pronounced. The rev. limit was 8,000, which we had on the clock as we crested the slight rise before starting to brake for Woodcote. On several occasions we saw 8,300 and 8,500, but rather than ease off, which would probably have caused more damage, we let the revs. climb.

Oil and water temperatures always remained constant and oil pressure remained steady even after a good many laps. The engine never missed a beat and I gather from Mike it has proved extraordinarily reliable and trouble free through the season. The rain came to confirm my opinions on the handling, and shod as it was with D12s, surprisingly it never gave me a nasty moment—obviously I wasn't going quickly enough. The brakes definitely deserve a special mention, for even on a very slippery track they proved extremely satisfactory. How they have been made so reliable, progressive and potent is no doubt the secret of Colin Knight, who told me these were his most difficult problem.

The car has now been sold to Robin McArthur, who drove a Lotus 7 last year. Robin was up with us at Silverstone and showed promise at the wheel in extremely difficult conditions.

Mike Beckwith himself, whose performances throughout last season were favourably noted by many people, is to take a further gradual step forward. Mike is to drive one of two 1½-litre twin-cam Lotus 23s which are to be entered by Normand, Ltd. The other driver is to be Tony Hegbourne. Tony, of course, was one of Mike's greatest rivals during the 1962 racing season—he drove a Lola-Climax with considerable skill and won the Brooklands Memorial Trophy.

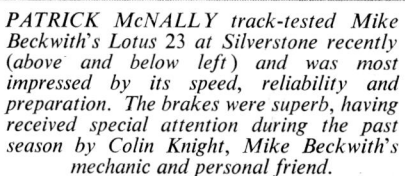

PATRICK McNALLY track-tested Mike Beckwith's Lotus 23 at Silverstone recently (above and below left) and was most impressed by its speed, reliability and preparation. The brakes were superb, having received special attention during the past season by Colin Knight, Mike Beckwith's mechanic and personal friend.

JUST LOOK how clean the car is! The cockpit (above) is absolutely shining white—with not a stain in sight! Note the spare wheel in the front portion of the body. The engine (below) has proved very reliable during the past season.

Peter Arundell was able to get the Lotus around somewhat faster than our Manney (no fool he).

DRIVER'S REPORT: LOTUS 23

from our suitably impressed correspondent (was Manney Appreciably Faster in the Turns?)

STORY AND PHOTOS BY HENRI L'AFITT

ONCE UPON a time, dear reader, if people wished to get from one place to another they walked. Those who wished to get the choicest dinosaur cutlets, or to avoid being eaten instead, ran. The quicker folk needed no advertising to set themselves apart from others, as they were the only ones left alive. As conditions grew more reasonable, fleetness of foot grew to be less important and even the Hunchback of Notre Dame could escape creditors, alimony, and the King's tax collectors by availing himself of a rapid horse. Cowboy movies notwithstanding, this age too passed and once past the age of puberty the only running seen these days is out the back door of someone's pad when the fuzz comes to check on smog violations potwise.

Generally speaking, the internal combustion machine now sees to our locomotion and very nicely too, even if the problem of evading triceratops, alimony, *et al* now requires jets. Human nature being what it is, the automobile has taken various forms ranging from the Morgan-JAP three-wheeler to Pomeroy's stately Rolls-Royce, with solid citizens like the VW or Model T supplying the real meat in the stew. Possibly remaining as an atavistic urge, though, there will always be some nit who wants to get there *first* and it is for him that sports and racing cars are built.

Until fairly recently, the real seeker after speed had to confine his kidneys to the tender caresses of a Bentley, Mercedes, Bimotore Alfa, V-12 Maserati or, postwar, any of the various Ferrari variants. All of these were large and made noise. The little stuff, like Panhards, made noise too but it was of a sort not fit to describe in a family magazine. All this has changed. As demonstrated at the last 1000 km of the Nurburg Ring (Sept. R&T), a 100-bhp 1500-cc-engined Lotus 23 was skunking Porsches on their home ground and the might of Ferrari as well until a split exhaust manifold caused its retirement. Admittedly, it was a bit wet and Jim Clark was the driver but even so . . . there were enough people afraid of it for heavy pressure to be brought to bear on the AC de l'Ouest to keep it from running at Le Mans. We were interested, we thought that you might be interested, and so negotiations were undergone with Colin Chapman to try one. Because it was some time before all three (Chappers, the Lotus, and I) all got in the same place, eventually it came to pass that I was foisted off on poor long-suffering Ian Walker, who has been running a successful team of Juniors and 23s this year. He was testing a 23 with pushrod 1500 Ford at Brands Hatch on Wednesday. Could I make it? I could.

Because the FIA feels that *prototipi*, or for that matter sports cars, should be at least vaguely road-mannered we will approach the test from that direction. The 23 *is* a sports car, a two-seater roadster to be exact, and besides stating that it has a tubular space frame, four-wheel independent suspension, and fiberglass bodywork I will leave you to the mercies of the

Technical Ed. who understands all the reasons thereof. The dry-sump engine lives in the back as does the 5-speed gearbox and clutch, and the requisite baggage space as well for those clothes that won't be harmed by heat. A muffler of sorts is fitted (ensuring that the car makes less noise than the average boulevard hop-up), as are headlamps and a windshield wiper. There is no ashtray.

Even to those accustomed to competition machinery, the Lotus 23 is a trifle low. This has led to heartburning among drivers stuck behind the blind spot of bigger machinery and for extended road use some form of mainmast with a winking light would be recommended. This ironed-out look, however, has, as an unexpected dividend, the advantage that one may forego wearing out the door hinges, always a weak spot on fiberglass bodywork, and step in over the side windows, which incidentally do not wind down. Inserting oneself under the wheel and pointing the toes to clear the forward bulkhead, one eventually comes to rest in an exceedingly comfortable bucket seat. Adjustment relative to the pedals can be accomplished in a few hours by any competent mechanic but in fact a simple skunching up and down seems to suit most people.

The controls fall, to coin a phrase, readily to hand. The only snag lies in the fact that a sizeable scoop is cut out of the rear deck to facilitate the fashionable reclining position and one's arms are at extra-full stretch. In fact, far-sighted drivers can easily dispense with bifocals in reading the water-temperature or oil pressure gauges and of course the tach, which is redlined at 7500. There is a surprising amount of room dimly discernible around the generous pedals, as one would expect in a competition car where a slight mixing up of feet TC-wise might lead to disaster.

The throttle is on the right, as is the steering wheel; a 7- and a 9-gallon tank occupy the sides, while the streamlined driving mirror perches in a high central position on the screen to clear the rear deck. This fitment is largely a formality, as it vibrates too much to be really useful. Ignition key and starter button are on the right, and the functional gear lever (cut down from a Caterpillar tractor, I suspect) is on the left. It works in a rather vague six-slot gate with sliding balks in Lotus fashion to keep one from selecting the wrong gear in moments of stress; in the left-hand row reverse is up and 1st down, 2nd and 3rd rows are like any normal shift with 2nd and 4th up and 3rd and 5th down, always going in but difficult to feel actually engaged.

Lotus Jr champion Peter Arundell was engaged in thrashing this little varmint around, bright in its yellow and green

I hope I don't break it, these things are expensive.

paint, testing it for an appearance at Oulton Park the following week. The matter of rear shock absorbers and springs seemed to be mostly under discussion, suitability thereof being judged by the amplitude of hop over a nasty bump on the downhill paddock bend, but nevertheless the car looked very steady in spite of some 54-sec laps, just outside the record. Eventually Ian and the cheerful mechanics got it to their satisfaction and in a borrowed crash-hat and goggles, I inserted myself and made ready to depart. Availing myself of a push-start to save the rather dinky battery, and with last-minute warnings like the price of new frames and bodies ringing in my ears, I set forth and trundled around for a few slow laps (Ian Walker .. Hah!) to get acquainted before the motorcycles started their next short practice session. After they were through, I had another go at a slightly more enterprising speed.

With the Ford engine bunged out to 1498 cc (85 x 66), breathing through two double-throat DCO 40 Webers, giving approximately 12 mpg and delivering 125 bhp at 6850 rpm, one would expect the rather light Lotus to be propelled at an

Manney tries the Lotus on for size and wishes they had been around when he raced his Crosley Hotshot.

A mighty small frontal area faces the wind.

And a mighty small rear view faces the competitors.

LOTUS 23

alarming rate but be rather a fire-breathing monster. Of course it does go like the clappers (with Arundell driving) but what surprised me is that there was so little noise, fussiness, cam effect, and other ill winds inseparable from getting a quart from a pint pot. In addition, the 23 rode very softly indeed over any bumps without overdoing it, just as well with my seat so close to the road, and it would be entirely practical in its present state of tune to take on quite a long road journey. From that point of view, or that of an endurance race, wind noise and buffeting are reduced to a minimum for an open car, as the plexiglass screen and windows curve gently all around to form what is almost a coupe with sunshine roof. As a detail refinement, a tab was fitted to the screen in front of the driver which ensured that the slipstream wouldn't catch under his visor with the head tilted back.

As far as performance was concerned, the 23 was marvelous and it almost shot out from under me. Corners presented a novel control problem as the leather-covered steering wheel is about the size of a pie plate and way out at the end of my arms; as the steering itself is a little on the heavy side anyway, the unwary and recumbent driver finds himself undercontrolling just from not putting enough pressure to bear. The gears also got me lost from time to time as there wasn't time to think with Brands' already short straights shrinking to the length of a pencil and the last thing I wanted to do was knock teeth off; accordingly I got to use only the first 4 of the 5 and was going too fast for my comfort when I did that. As the 8:29 final drive was fitted, giving a theoretical 155 mph, perhaps it is just as well that I didn't. As expected, the roadholding was superb and although I got fairly brave (Peter Arundell . . . Hah!) around one downhill corner it never even felt like slipping. One's progress, as Jennings remarked about a Junior, seems limited more by sidewise g in the seat than any dubious coefficient between car and road.

The most valuable thing I found out, I think, is that I ain't ever going to be a race driver. For those who are, though, the 23 would be hard to beat as a small, handy package which can take a variety of engines from the small to middling large. If it were mine, a 750 would just about do, but with the new 1500 Ford 5-main production engine, suitably breathed upon by Cosworth or yourself, there is no reason why you can't give much larger cars fits. Walker's address is 15/17 Brunel Rd., East Acton, London W3; Lotus' is Delamare Rd., Cheshunt, Herts., if your home dealer (look at the R&T ads) can't supply you. Wisht they'd had them when I was running my Hotshot.

The inner workings laid bare show the engine/transmission layout complete with muffled exhaust for mid-week testing.

LOTUS 23

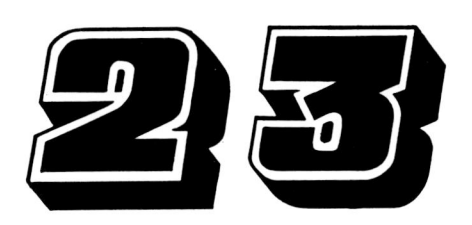

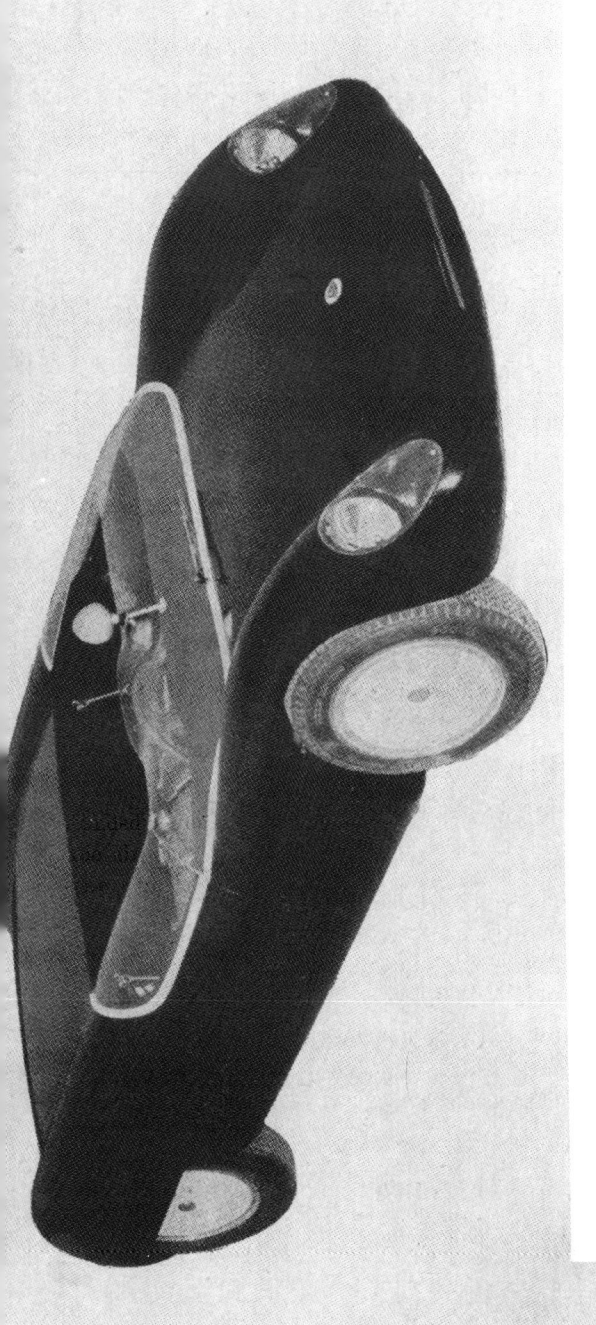

One of the most exciting new Lotus cars for 1962 is the **Lotus Twenty-three Sports Racing Car.**

This new car complies with the F.I.A. Sports Racing regulations for a category which is expected to become just as popular as Formula Junior. Promoters throughout the world are taking great interest in this class of racing and all the major Formula Junior manufacturers are planning production of similar cars.

The Twenty-three is based on the highly successful Formula Junior car but, because it is lighter and has better aerodynamics, it will have an even better performance and a maximum speed of 150 m.p.h.

Like the Formula Junior, it is powered by a Cosworth tuned Ford 105E engine with the usual benefits of easy and low-cost maintenance. During development the car broke lap records for its class at several leading English circuits.

Overall height to the top of the screen is a mere 27 inches.

The engine is mounted at the rear and coupled to a close ratio four speed gearbox. Front and rear suspension are identical with the 1962 Formula Junior layout, together with the disc brakes, steering and cooling system.

By Chris Beck

Riding the 23

UNDOUBTEDLY the most successful small sports/racing car of the last decade is the tiny Formula Junior-based Lotus 23.

Its performance, roadholding and handling are so outstanding that it has been able to lap with much bigger-engined machinery. Last year a 23 raced away from all opposition, including works-prepared Ferraris, during the arduous 1000 kilometre race for sports and GT at the twisty Nurburgring in the Eiffel Mountains. The car was powered by a twin overhead camshaft Lotus-Ford motor of 1600 cc—then in the development stage—and Jim Clark led the race in it until mechanical trouble forced his retirement on lap eight.

Clark said it was the most amazing sports car he had ever driven.

To understand these hairy little race-winning machines, which have consistently trampled on all opposition on circuits in Britain, Europe and the US, one has to ride in and drive one. Only then can the genius of Colin Chapman, its designer/builder, be fully appreciated.

Derived basically from the Lotus 22 FJ, it uses a slightly modified version of the same space frame. A variety of engines can be fitted to the car, ranging from a 750 cc single overhead camshaft Coventry Climax to a 1600 cc twin overhead camshaft Lotus Ford, but the most popular version is the pushrod Cosworth Ford. The five bearing 1475 cc motor develops 126 bhp at 7000 rpm. Situated amidships, the power unit is mated to a VW gearbox containing a Hewland five speed close ratio gear train.

The only thing original in the Wolfsburg transmission, other than the casing, is the crown wheel and pinion.

Suspension is independent all round by unequal length wishbones and telescopic dampers encircled by coil springs.

Nine inch Dunlop disc brakes are fitted on all wheels, which are made of cast alloy with round ripple centres. The discs pull the little car up very quickly from its top speed of more than 140 mph.

Covering the stark nakedness of its typically British frame is a low, beautifully contoured fibreglass skin. Headlights are faired in, similar to most of Chapman's other sports/racers, and the front slopes gently down to the mouthlike radiator intake onto which is fitted a wire mesh screen. Permanently attached to the front panel, the multiple curvature perspex screen is really nothing more than a wind deflector.

To conform with FIA regulations the Lotus has two bottom-hinged hatch-type doors. The side panels of the windscreen are fixed to the leading edge. A spring fastener holds the doors in place. In fact, the whole body is held to the frame in the same fashion.

The hindquarters are obviously the result of intensive wind tunnel testing and have a clean, neat, eye-pleasing line. Two red "pimple" brake lights adorn the blunt back end. Trafficators are not fitted—who needs them on a race track?

After a recent Catalina Park meeting where the Geoghegan 23 had shown a clean pair of heels to all comers I was able to do a special track test of the car.

No difficulty arose in getting the car. Tom Geoghegan, the team's manager, and Total Oil, its sponsor, were very co-operative but co-ordination was the troublesome point. Either the car was not available, or the photographer could not make it, or the weather was against us.

Eventually, after more than a month's wait everything fell into the correct slot and we got the car, the photographer, and the Warwick Farm circuit all available together.

John Sheppard, the equipe's mechanic, unloaded the car from the trailer which had brought it to the Farm, and warmed it up on starting plugs. When it reached the required temperature, he shut it off and changed to cooler racing plugs. After checking the tyre pressures to make sure they were 31 lb/sq in all round, several other small adjustments were made and the car was ready.

While all this was going on I was putting on my visorless helmet and goggles borrowed from Leo. Leo hopped in and beckoned me to do the same. Now, when you're a portly 13½ stone, it isn't easy. I wondered if the frail looking machine would accommodate my bulk. Leo undid the flap door and, after placing a foot on a chassis crossmember and a hand on the roll bar behind his head I levered myself into the small, austerely padded passengers seat with a varied assortment of grunts and groans. Settling down in the hip-hugging bucket seats was no easy job. The spare wheel located under the bonnet on the passenger's side fouled up my legs and when I managed to straighten them out they reached the aluminium bulkhead at the front of the car.

Right in front of me on the dash, which was covered in a red plastic material, was a little

On left hand corners the centrifugal force was so great that the upper rail of the space frame gnawed into the writer's arm.

Track Test of the Lotus 23, the world's most consistent race-winning small sports-racer.

An ideal place to bury yourself. All body panels hinge or can be easily detached. Access is a mechanic's dream.

RIDING THE 23... continued

metal plaque which said: Lotus Components Ltd, Cheshunt, Hertfordshire, England. Below this, the various chassis and type numbers were given. Once settled, I found myself peering over the perspex excuse for a windscreen.

The self starter whirred, the engine coughed once and then roared into life. Leo selected first gear, feathered the clutch slightly and we were away. At 3500 rpm real power began to come in and it lasted well up to 7000. Leo shifted the stubby little gear-lever forward into second gear, keeping the power on all the time. As we came out of Paddock Bend he shifted into third and poured on more power. Approaching the Causeway, which is very difficult on the short circuit, he eased off a little and gave it the gun as we made our exit.

On the small straight run up to Polo Corner, he hit 6000 rpm in third before braking fairly heavily. Accelerating briskly through Polo, we shot up the back straight, changing into fourth gear for Leger Corner and Pit Straight. Cruising down Pit Straight at a mere 5000 revs, he changed down to third for Paddock Bend.

Before Leo left the pits he had told me that he would not be going hard at first because the front wheels were locking and some brake adjustment was necessary before we could really pull out all stops. After four or five laps he brought it in and John adjusted the brakes, screwing a thing in here and there. Another slow lap and Leo was satisfied the system was working properly and then flattened it.

A healthy 126 bhp kicked me in the back and by the time we had reached the braking area in Pit Straight the 23 was pulling 6300 rpm in fourth gear—more than 109 mph. The wind buffeted my helmet and whistled around my ears and I braced myself.

Through Paddock Bend full bore in third, the car stuck to the bitumen like a new brand of stick-it-all adhesive and the chassis tube beside bit into my arm under centrifugal force. Picking up 300 rpm through the corner Leo backed off slightly on the Causeway approach and used all the available power for the exit, accelerating hard to 6000 rpm before braking quickly for the tricky Polo Corner.

Again we picked revs all the way through the corner. Leo changed into fourth just before Leger and played the throttle carefully through it and then flattened it again on the entry to Pit Straight.

Not until the second time around did I fully appreciate the car's magnificent roadholding and shattering performance. Above the staccato rasp of the hard-revving little four cylinder motor I could hear the whine of the straight cut gears.

Leo knocked off another half dozen of these fast laps in quick succession; on left hand corners I was compressed against the chassis tubing and on right-handers flung over the gear lever. I had to keep my feet firmly planted against the forehard bulkhead during this hard cornering. Basically an understeerer, oversteer could be provoked by easing off the throttle in the middle of a corner—rather like a Mini.

Useable torque is between 4000 rpm and 6250 rpm and there is very little reason why this ceiling should be exceeded, although the engine will rev quite willingly to more than 7500 rpm.

After the high speed track impressions, I took the wheel for a few laps. Immediately in front of the driver is a small aluminium-spoked, leather-covered steering wheel, a little less than an arms length away. On the facia there is quite a comprehensive array of instruments, by sports/racing car standards, including a water temperature guage, an oil pressure guage and a tachometer redlined at 7000 rpm. Behind one's head there is a tubular steel roll bar.

Lotus is rather an amazing car because it seems to be able to accommodate a body of any stature. Everything is well within reach, and the driver's hand falls, almost automatically, on to the short,

Cockpit is very functional as far as a sports/racing car goes. Tachometer is redlined at 7000 rpm.

The little car was very stable even when the most difficult corner was taken flat out.

black-knobbed gear lever with its small shift throws. The gate is a rather unconventional H pattern, with first to the far left and straight back and fifth all out on its lonesome to the far right and back.

A pull-up hand brake, similar to those seen on some BMC and Ford products, is mounted horizontally under the dash. This is only to cope with the fairly stringent FIA regulations.

Slipping behind the steering wheel gives one a rather odd sensation. Once you're settled in you feel completely at home and know that the little beast will do almost anything you want. A turn key starter is used and, after a short period of pumping petrol into the cylinders through the twin DCOE40 Weber carburettors, the engine bellows into life.

Letting the clutch out is a tricky problem. A gradual build up of revs is needed as the clutch is feathered in and the unit gets under way. Below 3000 rpm the motor is very lumpy, but about 3500 the cam begins to come in and at 4000 revs there is a real wallop. Changes can be made quickly and easily, but double declutching is needed on down shifts.

Flung into corners the driver does not work hard. Under power and at high cornering speeds the understeer becomes more pronounced, but it never gives the indication of getting out of hand.

Speeds in the gears are: First, 50 mph; second, 76.5 mph; third, 97 mph; fourth, 121 mph; fifth, 140 mph. With a special set of high ratio gears for long, fast circuits the car will pull 155 mph in top. Gearing of this sort would be suited to such European circuits as Sarthe, Spa and Rheims.

My brief association with the little fireball from Cheshunt has left an indelible impression of perfection at speed.

Wherever it goes the little black Lotus leaves a trail of devastating victories behind it. At the recent winter meeting at Warwick Farm it took the coveted RAC Trophy and at Lowood two weeks later it had an effortless win in the Australian TT. Both times the car was driven by Ian Geoghegan, the younger of the two brothers.

At the Easter Bathurst meeting conducted by the ARDC it clocked 142 mph through the flying eighth which is mighty quick for a car with a 1475 cc motor, in fact, even the 1500 cc racing cars were slower.

Not since the days of the famous D-type Jaguar has a racing/sports car caught the public imagination as much. In England nearly all the leading teams who participate in sports car events in the small capacity class have a 23 in their stable. At the Racing Car Show in London earlier this year the Brabham organisation and Elva released sports racers similar to the 23. Until then Lotus had been alone in this field, but to be copied is the greatest compliments Chapman's organisation could be paid.

The space frame in the 23 is a slightly modified version of that used in the 22 single seater. Chapman uses every weight saving device possible. Note how the coolant runs through the chassis tubes.

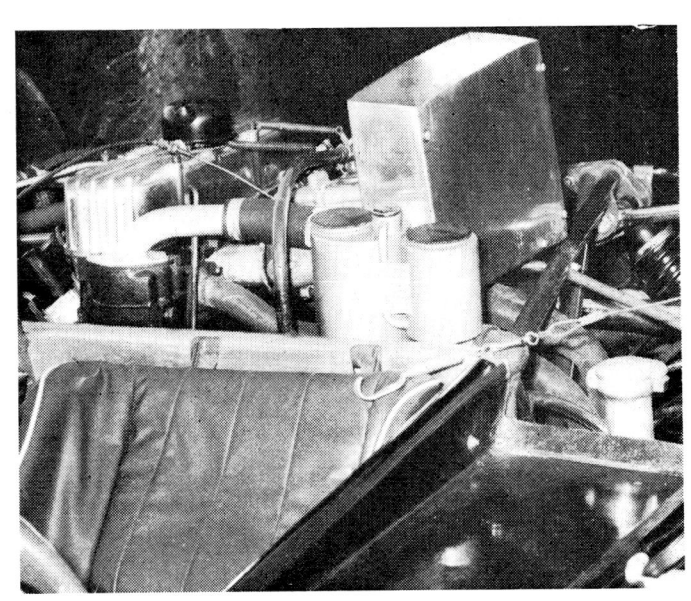

This amazing little 1475 cc Ford motor pushes out 126 bhp. On long straights the car can be wound out to more than 150 mph without any trouble.

Above: *Warming up the 143 horsepower Ford-based 1.6 litre twin-cam engine, which drives the 10 cwt Lotus 23B through a Hewland five-speed gearbox and limited-slip differential.*

TRACK TEST

by John Blunsden

ONE day it may be possible to forecast British weather accurately more than a few hours ahead. When that day arrives, life will become a lot simpler, and probably more pleasant. It will certainly mean that track testing can be planned in the knowledge that it will prove (a) informative, and (b) enjoyable.

Meanwhile, we have to carry on gambling with the calendar, and accept that sometimes the gamble doesn't come off. This time the gamble didn't come off! After several days of dry weather (during which it was not possible to carry out the test) Brands Hatch was saturating under a non-stop downpour when Mike Beckwith and Tony Hegbourne kept their date with a pair of Normand Lotus 23Bs. The test couldn't be postponed, so we did the best we could in the circumstances. Inevitably, some of the comments which follow, including all those relative to performance in the dry, have had to be based on information supplied by the two Normand team drivers, rather than on personal experience.

In view of the weather conditions, only one of the cars was off-loaded from the Normand transporter, this being the model used by Jim Clark on four occasions during 1963 (and featured on the cover of the June issue of MOTOR RACING), but as all three Normand Lotuses are virtually identical, the remarks can be considered as valid for all.

And what impressively successful cars they have proved. During the past season, the team have made 49 starts, and suffered only three mechanical breakdowns (all concerned with transmitting the drive from the differential through to the rear wheels). A lot of the credit for this outstanding run of reliability must go to Normand chief mechanic Colin Knight and his colleague Alan Jarrett, who have maintained a meticulous standard of pre-race preparation, and to Cosworth Engineering, whose twin-cam 1.6 litre Ford engines have given the team no trouble at all throughout the season.

STIFFENED FRAME

The Lotus 23B, as most people know, is a development of the Lotus 23, which was designed for 1,100 cc engines producing in the region of 100 horsepower. As the twin-cams have been turning out something like 143 horsepower at 6,800 rpm, it is not surprising that quite a few chassis modifications have been necessary, amongst them a considerable stiffening up of the frame to prevent it from doing some of the work intended for the suspension!

Normand have gone about this in a very businesslike way, and have fully outrigged the chassis frame on each side to achieve the effect of a triple, instead of a single 'A' frame. At the same time, the front end has been stiffened up considerably by inserting an extra steel floor pan below the pedals, repositioning the suspension pick-ups so that the loads are put through stronger frame members, and revising some of the cross-bracing. By re-routing one of the diagonals, it has also been possible to give the driver considerably more vertical leg room.

On the Lotus 23B the power is transmitted through a Hewland five-speed gearbox and final drive, with a Hewland limited-slip differential—a transmission arrangement which has stood up extremely well to a full season of racing. The 13 inch wheels have 4.50 tyres at the front, and 5.50s at the rear, and after a lot of experimenting with tyre pressures the team have hit on 30 pounds front, 33 pounds rear as about the right set-up. But both Beckwith and Hegbourne agree that the effect of pressure variations from these figures is very marginal, and that even in the wet they prefer to ease off the dampers, rather than to drop the tyre pressures more than a token amount.

However, as the test car had been set up for the dry, Colin Knight wisely removed some air as well as clicking back the adjustable dampers to 10 turns, front and rear, before letting me loose with it. The result of this, I soon found, was to produce an unusually soft ride, through which all the undulations of Brands Hatch could be felt very distinctly. But the considerable vertical

306

The Normand Lotus 23B

Top: *Care was necessary in feeding the power through to the slippery surface, but the wide rev range was a comfort.*

Above left: *Driver's eye view of Paddock Bend. Despite the rain, the cockpit kept remarkably dry.*

Above: *Umbrella for the ignition. This neat clip-on cover for the twin-cam engine was given a chance to prove its effectiveness.*

Left: *Kidney Bend in the wet, when a steady right foot and quick reactions are highly desirable!*

body movement was a most acceptable alternative to the probable lateral movement that would have resulted from a firmer ride on such a slippery surface!

Colin Knight had dropped in a set of very close ratios for the test, and I was able to make use of the top four gears, even though I was keeping well under the peak rev limit. Normally, this is 7,000 rpm, which means changing up as the needle points to 6,800, but I settled for a 6,000 rpm peak, giving 6,100 or 6,200 on the tell-tale.

This was the first Ford twin-cam power unit I had driven, and apparently I was not alone in finding that it is quite a deceptive engine until you have had quite a lot of experience with it. It has an unusually good rev range, starting from 4,500 rpm, and it will even pull cleanly (though without giving particularly brisk acceleration) from as low as 3,500 rpm.

Unlike, for example, a top Formula Junior engine, it has no specific point in the rev range where the exhaust note suddenly becomes a lot more crisp, and where you expect to get a considerable build-up in power. Instead, there is only a subtle change in exhaust note all the way through, but somewhere along the way you realise, by the way the back end breaks away, that this is no 1100!

Through the hairpin, I found that the car had a lot of understeer, but this was probably because I was unable to feed sufficient power through to the rear wheels. At the same time, I found that a lot of care was necessary when negotiating the puddles (which were getting larger all the time), notably on Bottom and Kidney Bends, because of their tendency to break the tail away. Fortunately, the Lotus 23B seems to respond extremely well to steering and throttle corrections, and I was more than relieved to find it possible to bring the car back from about 30 degrees-on after I had stabbed it a bit too hard in fourth over that little hump in front of the pits.

A FINE GEARCHANGE

The gearchange was excellent (a spring-loaded safety catch has to be lowered in order to select first, after which it becomes virtually a four-speed box) and the clutch action very light for the initial depression, and only a little heavier for the rest of the travel. The brake pedal was pleasantly firm, but of course I didn't have to use the pads at all hard. Apparently the team has done a lot of meticulous work on the brakes, to get the maximum possible efficiency, as both Mike Beckwith and Tony Hegbourne consider that the 23B with the twin-cam engine tends to be under-braked.

In further reference to the car's handling, roll bar thicknesses, front and rear, play an important part in deciding characteristics, and it seems that the most critical settings for the dampers are around the 15-turn mark, where one turn either way can noticeably alter the firmness of the ride. A typical setting for a dry track is 12 turns on at the front and 14 turns at the rear.

A most surprising feature was that even in driving rain I did not get unduly wet, despite the low profile of the body, and the fact that I was well clear of the steeply raked screen. Also, at the end of the test, I discovered that very little water had found its way into the body. This, it seems, was not always the case, and is the result of some careful body modifications by Colin Knight, who had to wrestle with the conflicting problems of keeping the drivers dry and the rear tyres cool.

The driving position is a slightly unnatural one, the legs being angled somewhat to the left, but this is not uncommon in a sports-racing car, nor does it prove uncomfortable. The instrument layout is straightforward, the rev counter being the focal point, and the cut-out button conveniently placed to the immediate left of the dials for instant use.

It would be foolish as well as false to suggest that this track test was a particularly enjoyable task. But it was valuable, if only to get a limited impression of a remarkably successful car; to meet, away from the tensions of race day, the people who help to make it tick; and to appreciate more fully the hard work that has gone on behind the scenes in order to earn Normand a respected place on the racing map.

R&T Track Report

LOTUS 23 & ELVA MK 7

Six of one and half a dozen of the other (would make a great race)

LOTUS PHOTOS BY RALPH POOLE   ELVA PHOTOS BY GORDON CHITTENDEN

THE RESURGENCE of Class G (1100-cc displacement limit) modified sports car racing is one of the most interesting and, we think, encouraging developments of the recent past. Formula Junior, which was to be the great club-racing battleground, has evolved into a struggle between factories, destroying much of its original usefulness to the new-to-the-game driver.

Class G is a logical replacement. Regulations governing cockpit dimensions, etc., and the current impasse in suspension design will, or so it appears, insure that a first-rate Class G car acquired now can be updated and refined enough to keep it in contention for at least a couple of seasons. This is, obviously, better than the situation prevailing in Formula Junior, where a car ordered from England may become obsolete before it arrives. Developments in Class G should be, for a time, restricted to engine and transmission refinements (in all likelihood, tires will be responsible for any improvement in road-holding) and these can of course be applied to existing machines.

Many racing car manufacturers are now producing Class G machines, and they are all fairly evenly matched. However, there are two that seem to have the slight edge needed to win. The most prominent of 1100-class cars is the Lotus 23, which has been a consistent winner since its introduction, and it is definitely one of the cars with an "edge." The other, Elva's Mk 7, is quite new on the scene, but it has already shown itself to be a match for the Lotus 23 and we may expect some fine tussles between these cars.

To get a view of this tussle from the inside, looking out, we borrowed a Lotus 23 and an Elva Mk 7, and spent a lot of time in each boring around the fast and difficult Riverside Raceway: a track with a mixed bag of tricks that never fails to tell us a lot about the car we are driving and sometimes, in a most unflattering way, about ourselves.

There are numerous points of similarity between the Lotus and the Elva. Both have space-type frames constructed of small-diameter, thin-wall tubing (mild steel of course; chrome-moly offers no advantage if the structural layout is correct) and both are fully triangulated, with a removable Y-brace over the engine bay. The Elva derives rigidity through the cockpit area from a double tetrahedron structure along the sides of the cockpit, while the Lotus achieves the same end through the stiffening effect of a large cowl hoop, in the same manner as the Lotus 22, their space-frame Junior.

Independent suspensions are, as goes without saying, featured all around on the Lotus and the Elva, and there is little difference in either overall layout or constructional details. The Elva does have special, cast magnesium alloy vertical links that carry the front wheel bearings (the spindle is bolted solidly to the wheel and extends through the vertical link) and this is said to save a few pounds as compared to the forged-steel, off-the-shelf, upright and spindle arrangement used by Lotus. This may very well be true, as the conventional hub has been eliminated in the Elva. And, on the other hand, the Lotus uses a rubber "Metalastic" U-joint on the inboard ends of the drive axle, which not only provides for angularity but end-motion as well, eliminating the splined section that is necessary on the Elva's axle shafts. As these splines tend to bind when the shaft is carrying a heavy torque loading, which restricts, to some extent, the motions of the rear suspension, the Lotus layout would appear to have an advantage. Also, the rubber U-joint and its 3-point spiders must be lighter than the conventional Hooke-type joints and splines used on the Elva.

Both cars' suspensions have coil springs concentrically mounted around adjustable Armstrong dampers. The spring rates are very low, as per modern practice, and while the damping, even at the softest setting, is a bit too heavy to give the cars a true "boulevard" ride, the Lotus and the Elva are a far cry from the jolting spine-crunchers that were

The Lotus 23 is low and chunky, and very, very efficient.

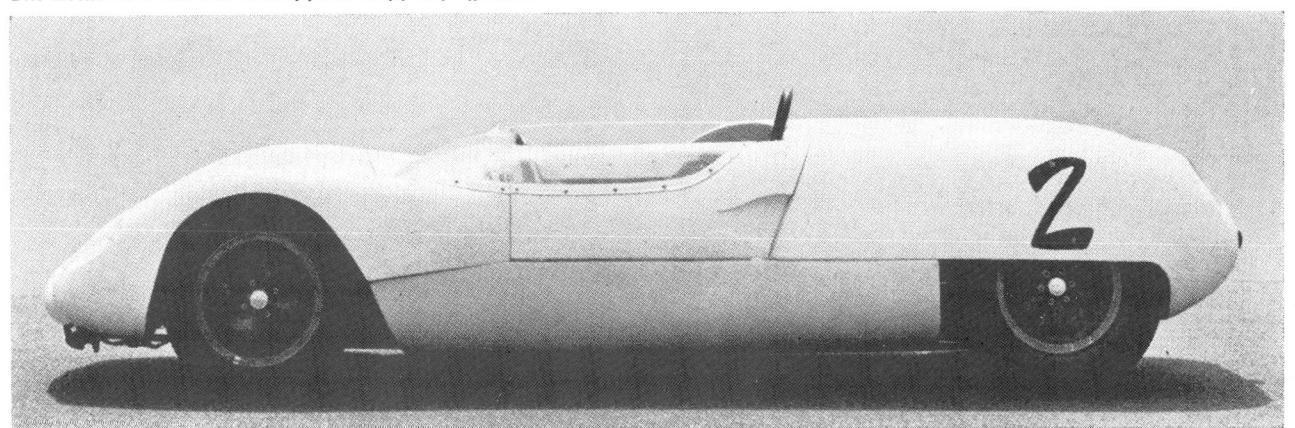

Elva's Mk 7 is also low, somewhat more pleasing of line and also efficient.

LOTUS 23 &

until comparatively recently typical of the racing car breed.

The Lotus' and Elva's respective suspension geometries are quite similar, too, giving raised roll centers that provide a mild "swing-axle" effect to keep the outside wheels upright when the chassis is heeled over in a corner. Chassis roll would be moderate in any case, but torsional anti-roll members are provided. The Elva has its front suspension arranged to give an anti-dive action (braking torque acting on the suspension links provides an upward force roughly equivalent to the effects of weight transfer trying to force the nose down) and this should be an aid to stability under hard braking. Unfortunately, the theoretical promise of braking stability was not realized in the Elva we tested. The brakes themselves were extremely powerful, but the car had a tendency toward snaking back and forth when the brakes were applied hard. This was particularly true when attempting to brake while still turning slightly; the car could be held steady only if aimed straight-on when braking. The Lotus did not have this deficiency, but it did require an uncomfortably high amount of pressure at the pedal—much more than was true of the Elva, which would pull down with much less struggle on the part of the driver (if one overlooks the effort put forth in keeping it pointed properly).

Several combinations of engine and transmission are available for both cars. They are least expensive with the 1098-cc, 96-bhp (@ 7600 rpm) Cosworth-Ford engine, which is equipped with Weber carburetors and various internal modifications—including a special camshaft and mainbearing caps—much like, but not identical to, the Cosworth-Ford engines used in Formula Junior cars. At a slightly higher cost, the Mk XI Cosworth-Ford engine may be had, and it is in very highly tuned form, developing a minimum of 100 bhp @ 7800 rpm. In either instance, wet or dry sump lubrication systems may be specified. Each engine is tested on a dynamometer after assembly and the carburetors are jetted for maximum performance on the individual engine at that time.

As an alternative to the Cosworth-Ford, Elva also offers the Coventry-Climax FWA 1098-cc engine in stage 5 tune,

Our Hero Driver working hard.

A Cosworth-Ford engine powers the Lotus 23.

Hairy Flatters down the straight.

Open oh Sesame; the Lotus blossoms.

ELVA MK 7

with a very reliable 98-bhp, and there will soon be pistons available to boost the displacement to 1150 cc, and these extend the output to just over 100 bhp.

To accommodate those who cannot be content with level of performance in Class G, these cars are also available with the new, 1600-cc twin-cam Ford engine made by Lotus. This unit is a development of the one used in the Lotus Elan, but is modified by Cosworth to produce a minimum of 140 bhp @ 6500 rpm.

The Elva has two transmission options: an all-synchro 4-speed and a "crash" 5-speed; both in a VW gearcase with the gears themselves produced by Hewland. There is an almost endless selection of ratios, intermediate and overall, for the Hewland-VW transmission in either form, and ratios may be juggled about with great freedom to suit individual courses.

The Lotus uses a modified Renault 4-speed transmission as standard, with close-ratio gears, and the Hewland-VW 5-speed is available at extra cost. The purchase of this 5-speed transmission would definitely be money well spent. We were fortunate to have the Lotus 23 equipped with the Renault 4-speed, and the Elva with the Hewland-VW 5-speed, because this gave us an opportunity to compare them. As one might expect, the 5-speed unit provides an advantage, but what is rather surprising is that it is a very great advantage. With that extra ratio, all of the ratios are brought closer together, and there is never a time when the driver has to choose between using too few, or too many, revolutions. With the Renault-based, 4-speed transmission, there was rather a long jump between 2nd and 3rd gears (1st is used only in getting started), even though 3rd and 4th were grouped close enough. It should be understood that the Lotus Cosworth-Ford engine has a fairly wide range of power, and that the ratio staging does not force the engine down "off the cam" after the change from 2nd to 3rd, but an 1100-class car has a rather limited amount of power in any case, and it is better to have available all that can possibly be obtained—and in that regard the 5-speed transmission is most useful.

Prospective purchasers should understand that these cars are—even though being made in some quantity—essentially

The Elva Mk 7, with innards exposed.

Weber carburetors on the Coventry Climax engine.

Incongruity: large driver; small car.

Only the necessities.

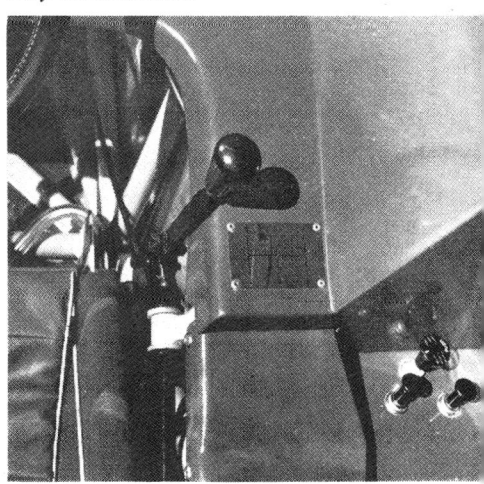

311

LOTUS 23 & ELVA MK 7

custom-built, and that when ordering it is possible to ask for and get almost anything the heart desires. We have not even attempted to list all of the miscellaneous items of equipment, because these change from week to week, and it is wise to obtain the latest listings just before ordering. Those who sell the Lotus and the Elva can help in selecting the proper combination for the type of racing that is contemplated.

Cockpit room is always at a premium in racing cars, and neither the Lotus nor the Elva provided an exception. Both have sharply reclined seats, and this serves to get those of medium to small stature down out of the direct air-stream in the very low bodies. Foot-room is surprisingly good especially in the Elva; the Lotus' front anti-roll bar is placed so that it is necessary to hook one's toes under it to get at the pedals. Frame tubes intrude on the over-sized driver dreadfully. Indeed, the only way a 6-footer can be accommodated in the Lotus 23 is by sawing out one diagonal frame member and replacing it with another running across the other way. This had, fortunately, been done to our test car, and our 6 ft 1 test driver was thus able to settle down into the Lotus 23 in a reasonably comfortable position. The Elva was absolutely standard, and in that form it offers quite poor accommodations for the tallish person. There is room, but for some reason, which we were unable to fathom, the seats are placed with a lot of clearance between them and the firewall and floor. Slight modifications in the seat mountings would, we are sure, provide the necessary room and make the Elva the more comfortable of the 2 cars for tall drivers.

Instrumentation is held to the essentials, and the tachometer/water temperature/oil pressure group on the Lotus is right under the driver's nose—so to speak. The same basic instruments in the Elva are on a small, square panel mounted over toward the left side of the car, far away from the driver. The cockpit is obviously too small for the instruments to be *too* far away, and it is not awfully difficult to catch a quick tachometer reading when required; but we would have been

Very minimal lean.

The Hewland/VW 5-speed transmission is an optional extra on both the Lotus and the Elva. With 18 different intermediate gear sets, and 2 final drive ratios, there is an almost endless number of combinations possible.

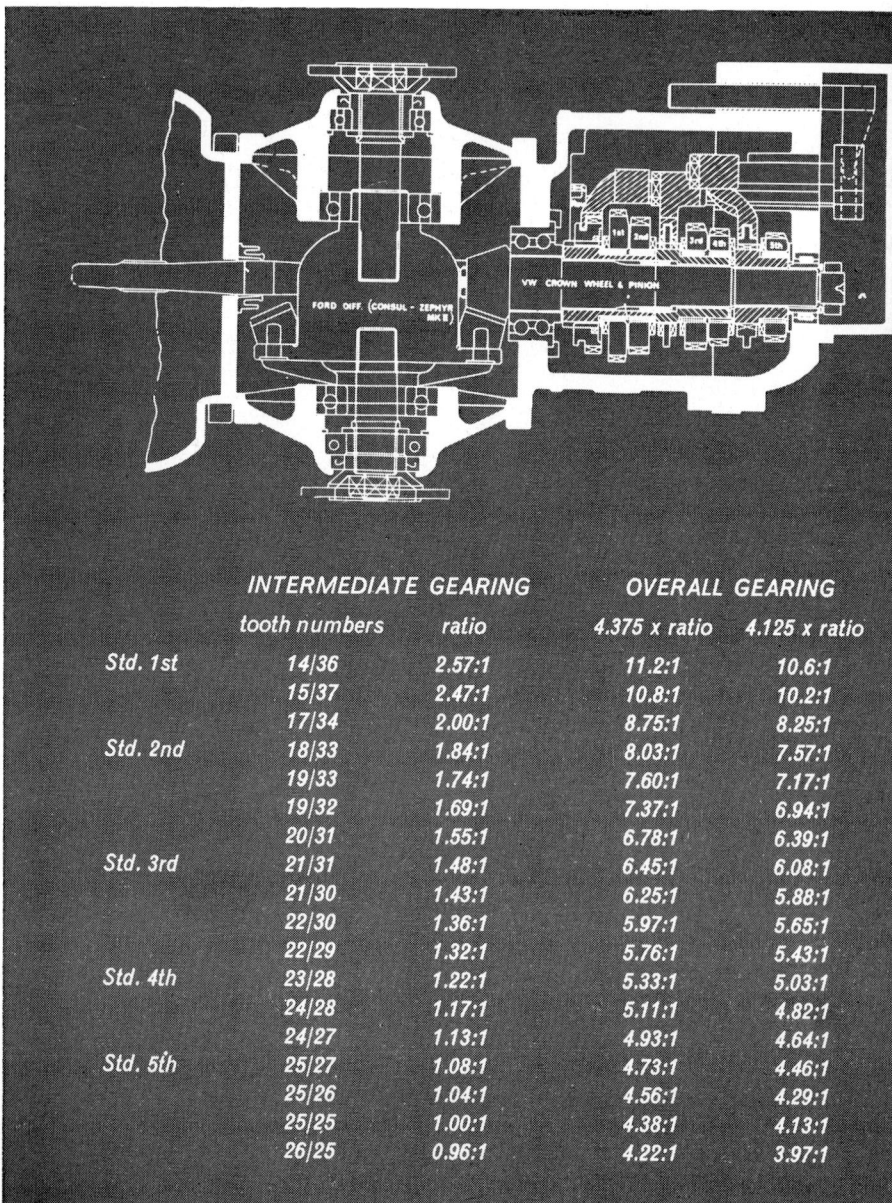

	INTERMEDIATE GEARING		OVERALL GEARING	
	tooth numbers	ratio	4.375 x ratio	4.125 x ratio
Std. 1st	14/36	2.57:1	11.2:1	10.6:1
	15/37	2.47:1	10.8:1	10.2:1
	17/34	2.00:1	8.75:1	8.25:1
Std. 2nd	18/33	1.84:1	8.03:1	7.57:1
	19/33	1.74:1	7.60:1	7.17:1
	19/32	1.69:1	7.37:1	6.94:1
	20/31	1.55:1	6.78:1	6.39:1
Std. 3rd	21/31	1.48:1	6.45:1	6.08:1
	21/30	1.43:1	6.25:1	5.88:1
	22/30	1.36:1	5.97:1	5.65:1
	22/29	1.32:1	5.76:1	5.43:1
Std. 4th	23/28	1.22:1	5.33:1	5.03:1
	24/28	1.17:1	5.11:1	4.82:1
	24/27	1.13:1	4.93:1	4.64:1
Std. 5th	25/27	1.08:1	4.73:1	4.46:1
	25/26	1.04:1	4.56:1	4.29:1
	25/25	1.00:1	4.38:1	4.13:1
	26/25	0.96:1	4.22:1	3.97:1

happier had the instruments been placed directly in front of the driver's seat. Here, the Lotus scores a point or two over the Elva.

Elvas have always handled quite well, and the Mk 7 differs from its predecessors only in that it is better—and must be rated as absolutely top-notch by any standard. The frame is very rigid, the suspension supple, and the car scuttles along in a reassuringly steady fashion at any speed. There is a light understeer that lends a lot of stability and makes high-speed cornering seem very easy. For us, the best method for getting the Elva around a high speed bend was to swing smoothly into the bend, feathering the throttle, and then, after the car had assumed the position, bang on plenty of power. When all was finely judged, the Elva would proceed around in a truly satisfying drift, with the steering wheel held virtually stationary. The slight understeer makes the car extremely steady when cornering at speeds over 80 mph, and we appreciated that. On slower corners, the understeer becomes more noticeable and can become a bother.

Riverside Raceway's turn 7 is a fairly difficult, off-camber left-hander, and a race held the day before our test had left a fog of oil that made it quite slippery. In that turn the Elva showed an unfortunate tendency to slide straight off, no matter how much steering lock was applied. However, we are of the opinion that some well directed jiggery-pokery with the suspension settings and tire pressures would overcome this. On other low-speed turns, less slippery, the Elva behaved much better; perhaps because on the other turns it is not necessary to hold the "line" quite as closely as is true of turn 7, which exits abruptly into the right-hand turn 7A.

The Lotus handled much the same as the Elva, but without the understeer—or oversteer, for that matter; the handling is absolutely neutral. It responds best to a technique (if our test driver may be permitted to dignify whatever it is he is doing out there with such a high-flown word) that consists of simply cranking it over quickly to start the car drifting and then to apply all power—holding the drift attitude with small corrections at the wheel. This works well on either fast or slow turns and although the Lotus would skate to the side on that same slippery turn 7, the slippage occurred evenly at both ends of the chassis. The only fault we could find in the Lotus' handling was that when cornering hard on

Below: a side-view of the Hewland/VW transmission and a chart showing the 18 gearing combinations, in terms of rpm/mph, that can be had with a ring-and-pinion ratio of 4.375:1. All one's crew must do is select the proper 5.

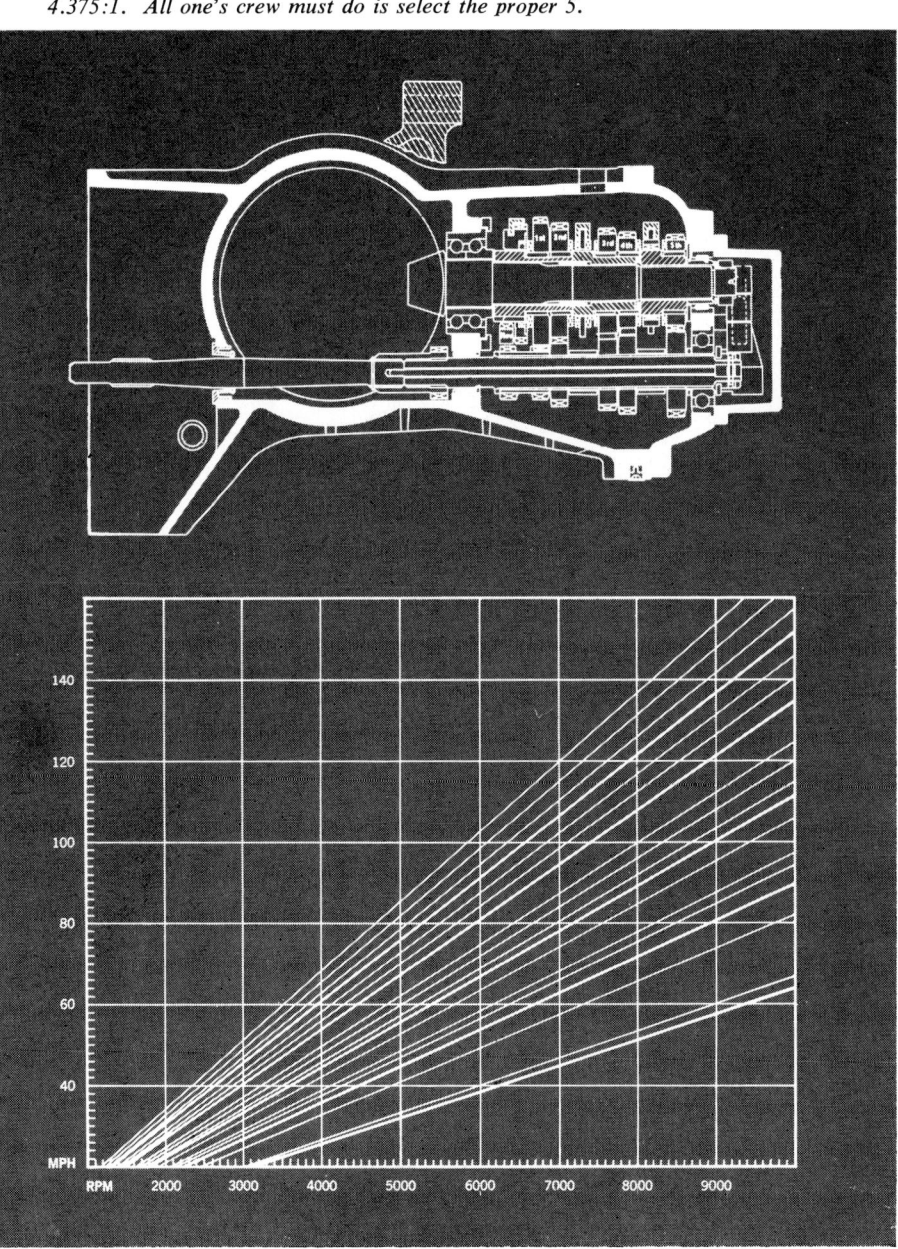

Motor racing anyone?

LOTUS 23 & ELVA MK 7

medium-fast turns (up to 100 mph) the steering felt quite heavy, and considerable effort was required at the wheel to hold the car in its line. In fairness to the Lotus, we must mention that the steering does get a bit lighter when teetering around on the ragged edge. It seems likely that in the heat of battle, when a great deal of teetering on the edge is being done, the driver would not notice any steering heaviness.

Driving this pair of sports/racing cars was enjoyable beyond the telling. Both are absolute marvels of stability and roadholding (not always the same thing) and the man who manages to clout one of these machines into a banking will not have the excuse that the car played him false; it will be, quite simply, due to clumsiness or gross over-exuberance.

It may be (probably is) pointless to discuss such things as appearance and finish when dealing with out-and-out racing cars; we will do it anyway. In both respects, the Elva was better than the Lotus. The Lotus is probably every bit as good as the circumstances require, but its overall finish gave us the feeling that the people who had built it had done the job many times before and were getting a trifle bored. The Elva, on the other hand, had the appearance of a machine put together by a person or persons who wanted very much for it to look good. There were no signs of haste anywhere, and the little things like wiring and plumbing were done neatly. The bits and bobs often seen dangling from tubes and across compartments were entirely absent. The Elva's styling, if we may be permitted to venture into an area of pure opinion, was also impressive; the Lotus is, no doubt, aerodynamic, but it is also a trifle stubby and featureless. Both cars are very "clean" and will run up to the top speed permitted by their respective rev limits very quickly, but the Elva seemed to be especially good. Neither car showed any signs of lifting, and side winds had little effect.

It is worth mentioning that despite track temperatures near 100° F, there were no problems with overheating. We had been apprehensive about the Elva, which has a pair of really tiny radiators flanking the spare wheel, and supplied with air from small vents above and below the sharp-edged nose, but the temperature remained normal at all times—as did that of the Lotus.

Because of the disparity of engines and transmissions, it was impossible to assess the relative performance of the Elva and Lotus. With the cars equipped as they were, the Elva was faster, but there is no reason why the cars should not be equal, given the same engine and transmission. We were unable to weigh the cars (our scales, the 300–1500 lb K-D individual wheel units, do not read that low), but the maker's weights, with water and oil but no fuel, are 960 lb for the Lotus and 850 lb for the Elva. This would indicate that the Elva enjoys a 100-lb advantage, but we are inclined to doubt that the weight difference is that great. Certainly, the cars have shown themselves to be very evenly matched in British races thus far. In any case, they are both potential winners, and anyone interested in Class G (or even Class F) should see both cars before coming to a decision. Prices vary with equipment, and here again the Lotus and Elva are essential equals. Would that we had the wherewithal to purchase either.

	LOTUS 23, series two	ELVA MK. 7
WHEELBASE	90.0	90.2
TREAD, front	51.5	50.0
rear	50.1	50.0
OVERALL length	139	138
width	60.0	59.0
height	26.0	27.0
FRONTAL AREA, sq. ft.	9.38	9.22
WEIGHT (mfg, w/water & oil)	960	850
distribution, %	42/58	40/60
TIRE SIZE, front	4.50-13	4.50-13
rear	5.50-13	5.50-13
BRAKES, maker	Dunlop	Lockheed
disc diameter	9.5-in.	9.0-in.
WHEELS, material	magnesium alloy	magnesium alloy
rim dimensions, front		13 x 5K
rim dimensions, rear		13 x 6L
OIL COOLER	in unit with radiator	behind seats
ENGINE OPTIONS, std. first	Cosworth-Ford, Mk. IV 3.35 x 1.91 & 1098 cc 96 bhp @ 7600 rpm	Coventry-Climax, FWA, stage-5 2.85 x 2.625 & 1097 cc 98 bhp @ 7000 rpm
	Cosworth-Ford, Mk. XI 3.35 x 1.91 & 1098 cc 100 bhp @ 7800 rpm	Coventry-Climax, FWE, stage-5 2.92 (?) x 2.625 & 1150 cc 100 bhp @ 7000 rpm
	Cosworth-Ford, Mk. IX (5-m/bear.) 3.19 x 2.86 & 1499 cc 125 bhp @ 6500 rpm	Cosworth-Ford, Mk. IV & Mk. XI
	Cosworth-Ford, Mk. XIII 3.29 x 2.86 & 1594 cc 140 bhp @ 6500 rpm	Cosworth-Ford, Mk. XIII 3.29 x 2.86 & 1594 cc 140 bhp @ 6500 rpm
TRANSMISSION OPTIONS, std. first	Renault 318-3 gearcase w/close-ratio Colotti gear-set.	VW gearcase w/4-speed, close-ratio gears. All synchromesh.
	VW-Hewland, w/quick-change, close-ratio, 5-speed gear-set.	VW-Hewland, w/quick-change close-ratio, 5-speed gear-set.

New sound on the circuits

A Lotus 23 powered by Ariel Arrow—six of them!

By JOHN BOLSTER

To the mechanically minded, the tendency to use only a few makes of engine in racing must somewhat reduce the interest nowadays. The new Rotorvic will therefore be of considerable interest.

This car, designed by R. V. Marchant and driven by Bill Hill, has a Lotus 23 sports-racing chassis, modified to take the unusual engine. This consists of no fewer than six Ariel Arrows, making in effect a 12-cylinder two-stroke engine of 1,482 c.c. The air-cooled power units are inclined outwards at 45 degrees, giving an angle between the cylinders of 90 degrees. Each engine has a straight-toothed pinion on its mainshaft which engages with a similar pinion on a shaft which runs down the centre of the engine.

These gears are enclosed in housings and the shaft has a flywheel on its end, which carries the single dry plate clutch and drives the two distributors of the electronic ignition system by toothed belts. The transmission is via a Hewland five-speed gearbox.

Lubricated on the petroil system, the engines are at present cooled by air collected in large scoops, though a Porsche-type fan may be the eventual solution. The whole assembly is installed in a most workmanlike manner, a starter ring being arranged on the flywheel as push starting on the grid is now forbidden.

The car is in its early stages of development but already shows promise. The exhausts are arranged to collect three cylinders apiece into four separate megaphones, and the shape of these ducts will be the subject of elaborate experiments. Though eventually 10,000 r.p.m. will be exceeded, at present the machinery does its best work at 7,500 r.p.m.

Seen in action at Snetterton, the Rotorvic travelled at a good speed and made a splendid sound. Apart from the fierce note of the 12 two-stroke cylinders, there is little mechanical noise, in spite of all those pinions. It is difficult to tell if one or two cylinders are "out", but an ingenious system of thermocouples will indicate by lamps on the instrument panel if any of the exhaust branches are not maintaining working temperature. Listen for a new sound on the circuits!

SIX Ariel Arrow motor-cycle two-stroke engines go to make the Rotovic Lotus 23 into a 12-cylinder 1½-litre vehicle (above). THE INSTALLATION of the engine in the car, which was recently on test at Snetterton, can be seen (below).

UP-DATING THE LOTUS 23

Two Excellent Conversions

The Lotus 23 chassis has been one of Colin Chapman's most successful designs. It has been volume-produced (by race car standards, anyhow) with several small-displacement engines fitted, and its good handling made a minor star of many a mediocre driver. While it has proven strong, it is not especially light as compared to other G and F-Modified machines, so it was only a matter of time before bigger engines were installed. We show here two of the best conversions we've seen to date: the Chevy II four-cylinder and Porsche 904 powerplants. The former puts it in Class D, the latter in E. Neither engine increases the total weight very much, and are below the point of exceeding practical stress on the chassis. So the logic and benefits are obvious; increased performance and reliability.

Glenn Baldwin's LOTUS 23/CHEVY II

BY JERRY TITUS

A LOTUS 23 AT THE AMERICAN ROAD RACE of Champions last November that tremendously impressed us was the one Glenn Baldwin of Birmingham, Michigan, brought out. The 53-year-old GM Quality Control Engineer had installed a highly modified Chevy four-banger. It went extremely fast, but Glenn had the misfortune to bend the pan during the early laps of the race, jamming the centrifugal oil-pump pickup, and leaving the engine without oil pressure in the corners. While this detracted from the results, it didn't reduce the impressiveness of the conversion.

Glenn first became interested in the Chevy II when he heard that midget builders were obtaining up to 225 horsepower from its 153 cubic inches. Knowing it was roughly "half a V-8" and light, due to thin-wall castings, he decided to purchase a Lotus 23, less engine, and mated the reworked engine to its Hewland five-speed. Installation in the chassis was relatively simple, the main problem being adequate pan-to-ground clearance. The oil pan had to be reduced in height by 1½ inches. The block was bored to four inches, bringing the total capacity to 2.6-liters. Ansen forged pistons were installed on Chevy con rods that were boxed,

The flyin' grandpa, Glenn Baldwin, drifts his Chevy/Lotus in the ARRC event last November, finishing 2nd in class despite oil-pickup damage.

bronze-bushed at the pin end, heat-treated, shot-peened, and finally Magnifluxed.

Borrowing a page from the midget boys, Baldwin purchased an Ansen aluminum cross-flow cylinder head for the Chevy, and bolted Rassey Mfg. intake and exhaust systems to it. Carburetion is a pair of 48DCOE Webers. This provides a total intake length of 14½ inches. The exhaust headers are variable in length, from 31 to 38 inches. A Dempsey Wilson camshaft, driven by a Chevy truck alloy timing gear, and timed at 38-78-78-38, contacts Pontiac chilled-iron lifters. Pushrods and rockers are stock. Total valve-lift is 0.513 inches.

The stock crankshaft was ground for extra clearance, the mains grooved for maximum oil flow, and then nitrite-hardened. The five main bearings were reinforced with additional steel caps. Oil pressure was increased to 60 psi by installation of a heavy-duty pump. Total oil capacity including the filter, a cooler, and the reworked sump, comes to 8½ quarts.

In mating the Chevy to the Hewland transaxle, a VW flywheel was shaved and a Carerra clutch bolted on. The adaptor plate is half-inch aluminum. A VW starter is used.

Modifications to the electrical system include reworking the stock distributor to a double-point setup, running 50 degree dwell and a total advance of 42 to 45 degrees. The alternator was changed to a positive ground and a larger aluminum drive pulley added to cut down revolutions. An Ansen bronze distributor drive gear was added for reliability in this area. A Smith electric tach is used.

About the only chassis modification necessary in this conversion was the addition of 3½-inch brake-cooling ducts to cope with the increased performance of the engine. The latter is turning out a conservative estimate of 200 horsepower and a very healthy amount of torque. While designed with a maximum-rev potential of 7000 rpm, the engine is held to 6200 as a redline and the final-drive ratio was lowered to insure against the necessity of exceeding it. Total weight of the converted car is 1050 pounds. Some four months of spare time went into the project, but it was certainly well-spent; Baldwin winds up with a superb-handling chassis and a very hot engine built from non-exotic parts. Its reliability enabled him to garner enough Class D Modified points to win his SCCA Division last year, and a second-in-class at the ARRC, despite the aforementioned oil-pickup problem. In all, it's a very logical and admirable machine.

About the only modification necessary to the chassis with installation of the Chevy II was increased ducting (visible on the raised rear deck in this photo) to provide brake cooling.

Chevy four-banger, equipped with Ansen cross-flow head, highly-tuned exhausts, and Webers, is an easy fit in the wide Lotus engine bay. This Under-3-Liter powerplant has top potential.

UP-DATING THE LOTUS 23

George Follmer's LOTUS 23/PORSCHE 904

LOS ANGELES INSURANCE MAN, GEORGE FOLLMER, purchased his Lotus 23 chassis almost two years ago, and first considered installation of a Corvair engine sleeved down to two-liters. He modified the rear bay to accept the wide configuration of the powerplant, but never developed enough horsepower or reliability to make the swap worthwhile. Several months ago, with a practically new chassis on his hands, Follmer decided that a Porsche 904 engine was a more logical source of competitive power.

After incorporating modifications to the engine that pumped its output well above 190 horsepower, George's mechanic, Bruce Burness, flopped over the Hewland five-speed gearbox to match the Porsche's rotation, and proceeded to again modify the rear bay. The side rails have all been replaced, but the majority of the rear bulkhead has been retained. A large aircraft-type oil cooler was installed up front and larger saddle-type gas tanks fabricated to handle the 200-mile USRRC races without a pitstop. A raft of minor improvements were included to make the car more race-worthy and reliable, but the chassis still uses the original 23 spring and shock rates, as well as suspension settings.

The recent Pensacola USRRC race was the fourth outing for the Follmer Porsche-powered machine. Leading Under-2-Liter, he moved up to win Overall as four of the big-bore cars dropped out. It was very impressive, but George has no illusions that a good small car can beat a good big car of Chaparral quality unless there is a lot of luck involved. It definitely proved, however, that Follmer and his very rapid little car are going to be major contenders for both the Under-2-Liter and the overall Driver's Championship in 1965. The team's sponsor, Trans-Ocean Motors —a Pasadena VW/Porsche dealer— has already given them the green light to make the whole USRRC circuit. It's sure an entry to watch!

Lower right, George Follmer and Bruce Burness check out the aft end of the converted Lotus after it is returned home from its Pensacola outing. At right, the wide Porsche engine is a tight squeeze transversely, even with side rails altered. Ignition is dual. Below, only minor modification to the body was required.

PHOTOS: PAT BROLLIER — DARRYL NORENBERG

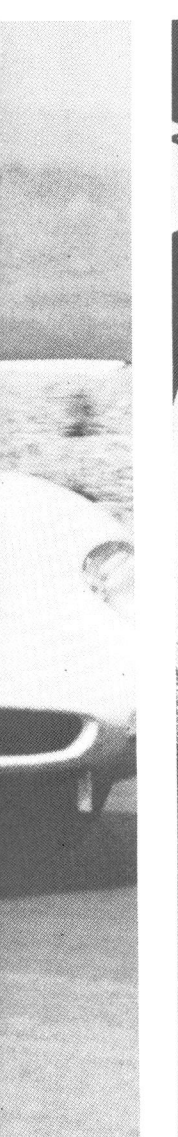

T&T LOTUS 23B TRACK TEST

CT&T moved West to find an example of the over-the-counter class of racing machinery . . . in this case the Lotus 23B driven this season by Bob McLean of Vancouver. The car was brought over from Britain in March by Bob's sponsor, Tim Matson, after a Brabham had failed to materialize. It had some racing miles on it but was still fairly new and, more importantly, it had the Mk 13 Cosworth-Lotus-Ford 1600 twin-cam motor which incorporates all the mods necessary to prevent it blowing apart like some earlier racing variants tended to do.

Initial tests made at Westwood revealed problems in the handling and braking departments. The considerable understeer was reduced by playing with the toe-in and camber until the present settings were arrived at: zero degrees and 1/16 inch toe-in at the front; two degrees negative and 3/16 inch at the rear. The shocks are set on the firm side, 12 clicks front and 14 rear, and the Dunlop R6 tires carry 27 lbs. up front (4.50 -13) and 32 lbs. at the rear (5.50 -13) . . . both tire pressures and shock settings being softened for wet weather. Bob was helped in the initial setting-up by Brian Dunlop, his regular mechanic, and Roy Shadbolt, who has built specials of his own. The final configuration gives first class handling as far as Bob is concerned, although the settings are nothing like the factory recommendations.

The next area of modification was in the brake department. Cooling was found to be the answer, and ducting was added to provide ventilation to all four 'stoppers'. Since then there have been no further problems.

The only other mod to the bodywork was the addition of a spoiler to the rear of the car to stop it becoming airborne over the Deer's Leap at Westwood which has been the undoing of more than one West Coast driver.

Another piece of redesign work was aimed at the gear shift mechanism, which resembled a "stick in a bucket of mud" when received and made the selection of the desired ratio in the Hewland five-speed box a matter of chance. Some re-routing of the linkage improved the situation although there are still five universals between the stick and the box. Another gearbox fault appeared at the Player's 200 this year when the drain plug dropped out during the first heat. The expansion differential between the alloy casing and the steel plug seems to have been the cause, but luckily no damage was done and Bob collected sixth place in the second heat. The offending plug was replaced by an alloy one.

So far Bob and the Lotus have not had a happy season, as after a win in the rain at its first race at Portland, Ore., the various troubles outlined here have kept it out of the winner's circle. But he seems unperturbed, perhaps remembering that it took a season to sort out the Cooper Junior in which he notched up 19 wins in 22 starts last year. As his home circuit is naturally Westwood we got him to describe a typical lap of that tight little course.

"For Westwood," said Bob "the car is geared to give 130 mph in fifth at our rev limit of 7,000 rpm, which is the same gearing as we use for Mosport and Kent, Washington. For a flying lap I would cross the start-finish line at about 118 mph (7,000 rpm in fourth) and shift into fifth taking the sweeping left-hander under the bridge flat. At Marker 3 before the 'Caroussel' right-hander I brake and downshift to third, taking the corner at about 85 mph and then accelerating hard to Turn 2, a left-hander. I brake hard at the hump just before the corner to bring the speed down from 95 to about 60 mph, and then accelerate through, still in third, to take the downhill right-hander No. 3 at around 85 mph with scarcely any braking and a touch of opposite lock with the throttle feathered as I go in. This corner gives the appearance of having adverse camber and the line through 2 is very important in setting up for 3, as going through this fast means extra speed on the back straight. Once through 3 I go up through fourth gear to hit fifth at the bottom of Deer's Leap, going over the top at 125 mph but keeping on the ground thanks to the spoiler — although only just. The car is doing just on 130 mph as I reach Marker 6, where I start braking hard and getting down to second for the hairpin which is taken at about 40 mph, then flat up the hill through third, going into the esses at 100 mph in fourth and staying in that gear as we cross the start-finish line again."

When this was written the lap record was held by Gerry Grant in a 465-hp Traco-Chev powered Lotus at one minute 12.5 seconds, while Bob's fastest lap to date is 1:14.7, which is fair going considering the horses he is giving away.

LOTUS 23B SPECIFICATIONS
Engine:
Cosworth-Ford 1594-cc dohc Mark 13. 145 hp at 7,000 rpm. 2—40 DCOE Weber carburetors.
Transmission:
Hewland five-speed box with quick change ratios on fourth and fifth.
Brakes:
9.5-inch Dunlop disc.
Tires:
Dunlop R6, 4.50x13 front, 5.50x13 rear.

It's now a permanent fixture on the Formula 1 calendar, but the Japanese GP hasn't always had such a high profile. **Mike McCarthy** *unearths the story of the first race in 1963*

Your starter for 10, as Bamber Gascoigne used to say: who won the first Japanese Grand Prix? What was he driving? And what was one of his prizes? The answers may astound you.

The winner was Peter Warr, later to become famous as team manager at Lotus; he was driving a little Lotus 23 sports-racer; and part of his prize was a year's supply of Coca-Cola.

The year was 1963, and the grand prix was actually an invitation race for European drivers which had been organised by French journalist and renowned Lotus enthusiast Jabby Crombac.

The grand prix was the feature race in a Japanese national meeting at Suzuka, the only other significant factor being the first appearance of a four-wheel Honda in a race — an S600 driven by American Ronnie Bucknam. Also on the grid for the grand prix were Mike Knight in another Lotus 23, Jose Rosinski in an Aston Martin, Frank Francis in a Jaguar D-type and Huschke von Hanstein in a Porsche.

But Warr had an unfair advantage. "I phoned Bill Brown at Cosworth, told him what was happening and asked if he could help," remembers Warr. "He said he'd lend me a development 1650cc motor — if he could come along as my mechanic. So I had a built-in advantage.

"At scrutineering there were lots of oohs and aahs — they'd never seen such cars before. There was a *major-domo* type wearing white gloves, and when he clapped his hands, a group would come forward and check this and that. Another clap and another group came hurrying forward. After a while I realised they were actually measuring the suspension and writing down all the details.

"The final indignity came on the final clap. One man came forward with a piece of tracing paper and did a rubbing of the tyre tread. We were on Dunlop R5s that year. When we went back the following year we were on Dunlop R6s, but all over the paddock were Yokohamas — with the R5 tread pattern.

"Having won the race, I was given this fortune in Yen — a cheque with lots and lots of zeros on the end. Then I was told that because of currency controls I couldn't take it out of Japan, so I went on a massive shopping spree, buying the most advanced radios of the time and jewellery for my wife-to-be.

"After being presented with the cup, another Japanese gentleman stepped up, bowed a lot and presented me with another large cup and an envelope. The letter was in Japanese, so I had it translated and it informed me I'd won a year's supply of Coca-Cola.

"I thought no more of it until a month or so later when a large truck pulled up outside my home and unloaded a huge amount of Coca-Cola. I thought 'That'll last a long time', and the next month exactly the same thing happened. And this carried on for 12 months."

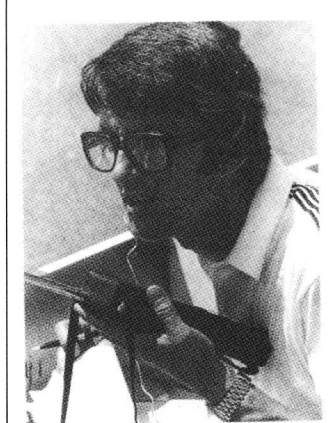

Winner Warr went on to manage Lotus F1 team

Lotus 23 won first Japanese GP. Coca-Cola provided the second surprise

Hindsight

Lotus 23B Built to win

Tony Dron traces the history of the Lotus 23 and drives a newly restored example

As Lotus restoration expert Simon Hadfield points out, there were at least 131 Lotus 23s built in the early Sixties and probably about half of them are still running today. It says a lot for these cars which look incredibly flimsy by modern standards that they should have survived so well, but in truth most of them have been rebuilt and some several times over. Their survival is more a tribute to the fact that they are so well-loved by competitors rather than that they were built to last. They were built to win races and they remain very easy to keep in good winning order.

We have been testing a Lotus 23B, chassis number 85, which was delivered to Span Inc in the USA as a 1600cc Twin-Cam powered version on April 30, 1963. Chassis number 85 does not appear to have had a distinguished history for all that is known about it is that it was discovered by a British dealer as 'a nasty festering mess of bits, but complete' when he was in the States a couple of years ago. He bought it and brought it back to Silverstone with the idea of restoring it for himself but somehow never got around to it. Simon then acquired it for Nick Brittan and a total rebuild was commenced. We snatched a few laps in the car before its despatch to Australia, where Nick will use it in historic events.

The original Lotus 23 made a sensational debut in the hands of Jim Clark, when it led the 1000km race at the Nürburgring in May 1962. It had an equally sensational, but utterly distressing, rebuff at Le Mans the following month which left Colin Chapman to vow that he would never enter Team Lotus cars at Le Mans again. He never did, nor was there ever a truly successful Lotus sports-racing model after the 23B. Lotus was beginning to focus its attention on Formula 1 and the forthcoming all-important battles for Grand Prix honours.

The Lotus 23 was descended directly from the Lotus Grand Prix single-seaters: the first mid-engined Lotus racing car was the 18 of 1960, and the 19 was simply a widened example with enclosed bodywork, made for sports car racing.

The single-seater line continued with the 20 and its direct successor, the 22, all these cars being simple spaceframe lightweight designs which became lower and sleeker with each successive model. Once again, the Lotus 23 was simply a widened 22 with enclosed bodywork and many of the parts are interchangeable. In fact, a high proportion of the original parts from Nick Brittan's car are stamped '22 and 23'.

The 23's debut really was something, though. It had long been Chapman's aim to produce a complete Lotus engine, and a significant step on the road was the Ford Lotus Twin-Cam, a highly modified production engine created in-house by Harry Mundy.

The Nürburgring was chosen as the first outing for this brilliantly-designed engine, and it was entrusted to John Ogier's Essex Racing Team, with Jim Clark at the wheel of the new 23. Although the engine had been tuned for 140bhp on the dynamometer, this first actual race engine, based on the Ford Classic 1500 unit, was tuned conservatively to produce a reliable 104bhp. Even so, Clark achieved a stunning practice time of under ten minutes, which put him seventh on the grid and well up among the Porsches and big Ferraris.

As the 67 cars got away after the Le Mans start, steady drizzle was falling on the murky Eifel mountains. Clark was second as they descended into the woods: 14 miles later, as he completed his first lap, he was leading the race by 28sec, with Dan Gurney's Porsche second. After six laps, Clark had stretched his lead to 1min 41sec, but the the track started to dry and the pressure was on. At the same time the Lotus front brakes became almost useless and the exhaust had broken, and Clark was suffering from the fumes. On the eleventh lap, still leading, the car jumped out of fourth gear under braking, the rear wheels locked and Clark and his 23 slid off the road and out of the race.

For Le Mans, the works 23 was fitted with a 997cc version of the new Twin-Cam engine, while UDT-Laystall's entry had the more traditional Coventry Climax twin-cam, in this case the 747cc FWM unit. The cars were rejected by the scrutineers because the turning circles were too big, fuel tanks were too large, door openings did not comply with the regulations, there was insufficient ground clearance and, most important of all, the wheels were not interchangeable front and rear. Back wheels had six studs, and front wheels just four.

Safety squabbles

Colin Chapman explained that he had written to the organisers in advance and had had no indication that his cars would not be passed at scrutineering. New rear four-stud hubs were flown out from England immediately and the cars were modified in time for the scrutineers to inspect them before Wednesday practice. All the points had been attended to but once again they were rejected, this time on the grounds of safety. The scrutineers argued that if the rear hubs required six studs then they were unsafe with four studs. Chapman flew out with Dean Delamont of the RAC to back him up but it was all to no avail. Patriotic English fans suggested that the performance of the racing 23 at the Nürburgring had shown that the cars would be easy winners of the important Index of Performance, and the French officials had acted chauvinistically to block their chances. It was an ugly business that did little for the sport.

Despite this setback, the Lotus 23 was a sensational success, winning races all around the world from the very start. All that was needed to keep it ahead in 1963 was the

Built to win the Lotus 23B

installation of the latest 1600cc Twin Cam Lotus Ford engine and some beefing up of the chassis to accept the extra power and weight. This strengthening took the form of the addition of narrow tube triangulated bracing for the top outer chassis tubes, plus stiffening of the rear wishbone pickups. Many different engines were fitted to 23s by private teams, notably the Porsche-powered car of George Follmer in the USA and the one-litre BRM example of Robin Widdows in the UK. Both were extremely quick, and far more successful than the few attempts to install much larger engines into these very light and small cars.

Going over Nick Brittan's 23B while Simon Hadfield made the finishing touches in his workshop it was clear that this car has been rebuilt to comply pretty closely with the original specification. Throughout the job, Simon has kept in close contact with the Australian historic racing authorities and they have made it clear all along that the kind of modifications seen in other countries, including the UK, would not be welcome down under.

Original spec

While most of the 23s racing here have nylon bushes and ball-joints built into the suspension, this example has still got the original type of rubber joints. Once the car has been built, there is very little that can be done to adjust the suspension. At the back the lower, inboard wishbone pickup is adjustable and that, apart from the ride height, is it as far as altering the geometry goes. The 23 followed the 1961 Lotus F1 rear suspension design in not using the driveshafts as locating arms. It had two Hooke's joints and sliding splines at first, later going over to rubber 'doughnuts', as in this car, which has a Hewland gearbox.

Rear uprights were specially fabricated and, following crack testing, the originals have been retained in this case. The front uprights, as was the case for so many years in small race design in this country, were of Triumph road car origin. The front suspension is adjustable for camber at the outboard end of the

Below, detail of the engine bay of Nick Brittan's car. The 1600cc twin cam marks this as a 23B rather than simply a 23. Bottom, many, many drivers drove 23s. This is Peter Gethin in an 1150cc car during the Norbury Trophy race at Crystal Palace gasping for breath after an oil leak filled his cockpit with smoke

Built to win the Lotus 23B

top wishbones, but otherwise it is fixed. Even the anti-roll bars are non-adjustable, front and rear.

The original magnesium 'wobbly web' wheels were very light but none too safe after some years of use. Restored cars can look right with new alloy wheels, made in Birmingham to the original shape, but they are much heavier if more durable. Simon points out that modern brake pads and tyres ask much more of a chassis than was the case two decades ago, and there is no point in risking your neck needlessly. Even so, the wheel nuts are of the original type which were banned in 750 racing about 25 years ago but in this case there are more studs per hub and there is no record of failure over the years.

The chassis itself is a gleaming new-looking item today, which is hardly surprising as it was found necessary to replace 60 per cent of the spaceframe with new tubing. The job has been done properly, with the water and oil routed to and from the radiators through the chassis tubes themselves. The option of separate tubing is messy as well as being non-original.

The engine rebuild was put out to Racing Fabrications of Bury St Edmunds. The 1600cc Twin-Cam has been tuned to give what should be a very reliable 160bhp. It would have been possible to go for 185bhp but this car will be expected to run for many races before it is rebuilt, and Nick Brittan does not want the aggravation of having to change the engine several times a season.

By the time we got the car down to Donington for its first private shakedown test, the winter day was showing signs of fading into darkness, which was all right for us as drivers but which did no favours for photographer Tim Wren, but then he is famous for being able to get a good result with a box camera and no flash equipment in a dark cellar!

The circuit was at its worst, damp and treacherously slippery as only Donington can be. Lotus 23s are famous for their tendency to turn round at high cornering speeds in the hands of the unwary, so care was called for. I also know from experience that most freshly rebuilt cars feel dreadful on the track until they have done a good few laps and settled down. This car, however, just like the Ferrari 250GT racer written up last January, felt just right straight away, which is most unusual.

With the seat removed, and some padding fitted instead, I was, well, reasonably comfortable and there was certainly plenty of room for me despite the tiny nature of the car (I am 6ft 5in tall). Nick was unable to be present as he was working on the RAC Rally, and he had asked me and Simon to check the car out before it was despatched to the docks for shipment to Sydney. With this in mind I set off in the gathering gloom with some misgivings, checking the brakes. Not surprisingly there was a tendency for the fronts to lock, especially on the nearside, for the track was not offering much grip.

Under the best of conditions, a Lotus 23 feels light and one is always aware of the fact that there's not much motor car around the driver, who tends to feel almost as exposed as a motor cyclist. Gathering darkness and almost no grip did not add any sense of security as I steered the car into Redgate. Very little effort was needed to turn the wheel and the car began to understeer; at the apex I gave it a little power and immediately the 23 took on a neutral stance and eased out of the corner, gathering speed towards the Craner Curves. Such impeccable balance was very welcome and very confidence-inspiring, for I certainly had not expected this newly-rebuilt car to feel so good straight away. Admittedly it would have been very easy to put the car off the road in those conditions and a slightly unsympathetic gearchange or heavy right foot would have been enough to send it careering towards the sand and concrete. Sticking to the 'book' of race driving technique, however, there was no problem and I enjoyed teasing it through the downhill Craner Curves, putting on as much speed as I dared even though the feeling was something akin to being on a helter-skelter without any retaining sidewalls! It was immediately apparent how Jim Clark was able to humiliate the bigger cars in the 1000km at the 'Ring 23 years ago in the first works prepared Lotus 23, and how much he must have enjoyed those opening laps in the drizzle. His predicament when the brakes and gearchange began to give him trouble was equally understandable, for it must have taken all his brilliance to keep the car on the road, let alone to continue to lead the race until the virtually inevitable accident.

We wish Nick Brittan the best of luck with chassis number 85 in his forthcoming historic races in Australia.

323

The Lotus Thirty

In 1964 Lotus decided to build another sports racing car after six consecutive single-seater models. This was the Lotus 30. No more numerals, just the number 30. This was the beginning of the Can-Am era of large V8-engined sports cars, all of which were impressively noisy and fast.

Ron Hickman had designed the sheet steel fabricated 'backbone' chassis for the Elan for Lotus road car production and Colin Chapman used the same principle to build a 'backbone' chassis for the Lotus 30. The only difference was the power. The Elan chassis had to contend with some 150bhp but the Ford V8 engine in the 30 produced some 300bhp. The first three cars for Ian Walker's Team Lotus showed a severe lack of torsional rigidity amongst other problems, so for further cars the chassis fabrication was increased to eighteen gauge. In 1965 further modifications were incorporated to gain easier access to the transmission and this was the Mark 2 Lotus 30.

The first publicity for the new Lotus 30 came from *Autocar* of 24th January, 1964 with a detailed Dick Ellis cutaway drawing, and technical specification. Other articles followed and a track test of the JCB Lotus 30 by John Blunsden appeared in *Motor Racing* in October 1965.

Jim Clark drove the first Lotus 30 into second place at Aintree which was a promising beginning. Clark scored a third place at Riverside, and was leading the Tourist Trophy race at Goodwood before retiring. With the stronger Mark 2 in 1965 Clark won at Silverstone and Goodwood early in the season. Although not equal to the McLaren and Lola 'big bangers' the Lotus 30 was sleek and impressive, although it was largely the skill of Jim Clark that produced some success. Other drivers found it a handful.

A total of twenty-one Mark 1 Lotus 30s were built in 1964 and twelve Mark 2s, making a total production of thirty-three cars in all over a two year period.

Graham Capel

LOTUS 30 – FORD V8

Chapman Goes Big Bore For '64

Courtesy AUTOCAR, London

Power-packed Lotus

The new sports car from Cheshunt has a Ford Fairlane power unit developing 350 bhp

Long, low and wide line for the new Lotus Thirty, which is to be raced by Ian Walker's team and driven by Jim Clark when available

Prominent wheel arches may restrict the view at some points, but driver comfort is well looked after

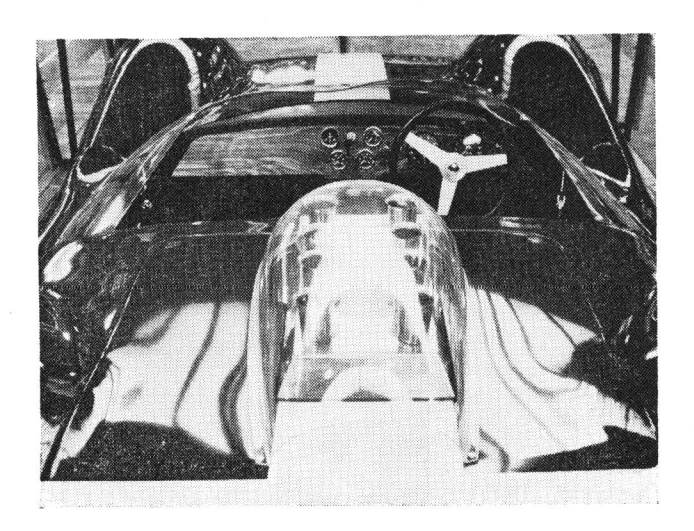

AS mentioned briefly in Sport Report last month, Lotus have announced their new sports-racing car, the Lotus Thirty, which was exhibited at the Racing Car Show. It is designed to accept a 4.7 litre Ford Fairlane V8 engine or a Cosworth Lotus-Ford 1,600 cc engine without any modification to fittings.

Success of the Lotus Elan design has encouraged Colin Chapman to use the same formula again, employing a central backbone box-shaped fuselage frame which also houses flexible bags containing fuel and oil. Glass-fibre box-section outriggers carry more fuel to bring the capacity to the maximum permissible 31½ gallons.

Behind the driving position the chassis divides in a Y-shape, to accommodate the power unit, and a bridge across the top of the Y supports the rear suspension and forms an engine-gearbox mounting. Thus the backbone, constructed of 16-gauge steel, is immensely rigid with high resistance to torsional stresses.

The bodyshell is made of glass-fibre and appears to be an extreme example of modern styling for this type of car —exceptionally low, with wheel arches dominating the profile, but unusually wide and long for a Lotus. Wheelbase and track are dictated by the engine output and potential speed of the vehicle, so that despite its apparent size the bulk of the car shows only a slight weight penalty; kerb weight is said to be about 15 cwt.

Suspension is derived from experience with the Lotus 29 raced at Indianapolis, and with the Twentyfive formula one car, but the springing is harder than usual to counteract excessive weight transfer under acceleration and braking. Metalastik rubber couplings replace universal joints on the inner ends of the driveshafts in order to cushion shock as the great power of the engine is transmitted to the wheels.

The Fairlane engine (constructed with a cast iron block, and not the lightweight alloy Indianapolis block) has a swept capacity of 4,730 cc and should develop some 350 bhp. Four twin-choke Weber carburettors deliver fuel, and drive is transmitted through a twin-plate Laycock diaphragm clutch and a five-speed all-synchromesh ZF gearbox. An alternative power unit is the twin overhead camshaft Lotus-Ford engine developed by Cosworth currently producing 145 bhp at 6,500 rpm. This unit, the Mark 13, has a capacity of 1,594 cc.

Steering is Alford and Alder rack and pinion, and 11-inch Girling disc brakes are used on all four wheels. Maximum height of the car, at the top of the rear wheel arches, is 31 inches. The front wheel arches are 30 inches from the ground, and the windscreen is four inches lower, although the driver's line of vision is above this. In overall size the Lotus Thirty is 13 ft 9 in long and 5 ft 8 in wide.

Due to the width of the bodywork there is a comfortable amount of working space inside the car, and a fairly hardy passenger should not have too many complaints. Backrest angle is reclining at about 45 degrees from vertical, but all ideas of starkness are removed by the use of simulated wood veneer on the fascia panel!

Maximum speed of the car has been calculated at 200 mph, or more, with Le Mans type gearing. For most purposes the gearing will be quite a bit lower and a choice of six final-drive ratios is available.

BIGGEST YET

New LOTUS 30 Sports Car uses Ford Fairlane 4·7-litre V-8 engine

Autocar copyright

DICK ELLIS

© Iliffe Transport Publications Ltd. 1964

THE coming racing season promises to be one of the most exciting in the prototype sports and G.T. categories. Latterly Ferrari has been way ahead in this field, but with the advent of a new generation of cars, many of them powered by tuned-up versions of large capacity American vee-8 engines which develop enormous torque, if modest power, in comparison with European racing engines, competition undoubtedly will become very much keener.

Colin Chapman, who never misses an opportunity to compete in any rewarding form of racing, has produced a new car for this category. Initially, there will be an open sports version, but this will be supplemented later in the year by a G.T. coupé. Ultimately a fully equipped road version of the same car will be produced.

After his co-operation with Ford of America in producing the car which made a sensational début at Indianapolis last year, in which Clark finished second, Colin Chapman perhaps hoped the American company would link up with him instead of Eric Broadley when they decided to expand their competition activities. Maybe this new Lotus 30 is also an attempt to demonstrate to them that their choice, though politically understandable, was not necessarily the wisest.

The power unit, which is mounted in the now orthodox rear position, is based on the Ford Fairlane 4727 c.c. vee-8 engine and is basically similar to the one fitted in the A.C. Cobra. Among the changes made are the substitution of mechanically adjustable valves for those using hydraulic tappets and the addition of an oil scavenge pump for the dry sump lubrication system, which includes a cooler in the circuit. Initially, these engines will be fitted with four twin-choke Weber downdraught carburettors, in which form the maximum power output is 350 b.h.p. at 5750 r.p.m.; the peak torque is expected to be just over 300 lb. ft.

Development work is proceeding on a new British type of fuel injection system, which is expected to improve the power output and extend the engine's speed range slightly. Power is transmitted through a twin-plate Laycock diaphragm-type clutch to a new five-speed, all-synchromesh ZF gearbox; the same makers, incidentally, are also producing a new five-speed gearbox for the latest formula 1 Lotus car.

Regulations for prototype racing are very stringent in respect of seating dimensions and door apertures. It seemed obvious to Chapman, therefore, that a backbone type of frame as evolved for the Lotus Elan was the best solution. Such a construction is not only light, but provides the desired degree of rigidity. The frame of the Lotus 30,

Brief Specification

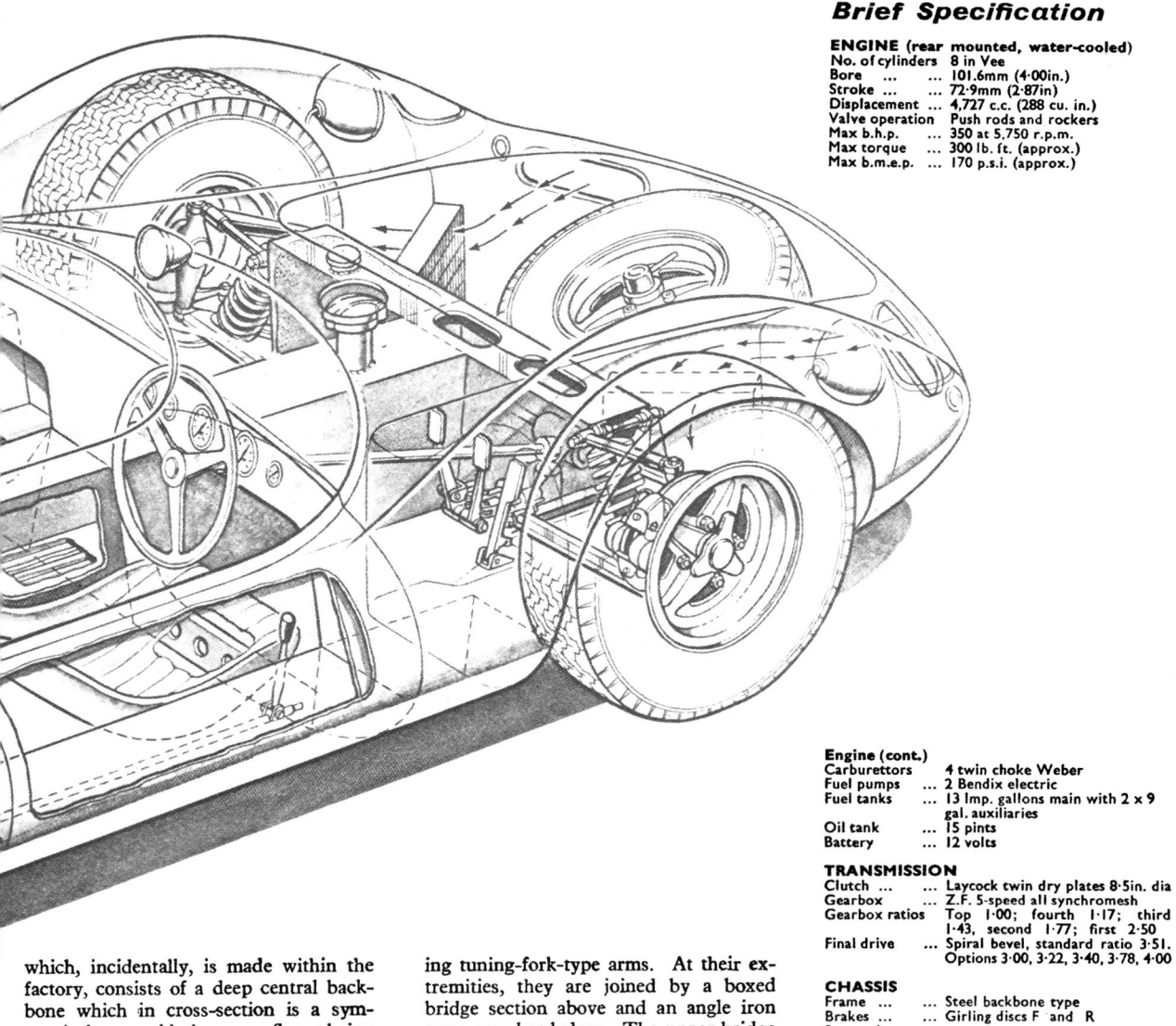

ENGINE (rear mounted, water-cooled)
No. of cylinders	8 in Vee
Bore	101.6mm (4·00in.)
Stroke	72·9mm (2·87in)
Displacement	4,727 c.c. (288 cu. in.)
Valve operation	Push rods and rockers
Max b.h.p.	350 at 5,750 r.p.m.
Max torque	300 lb. ft. (approx.)
Max b.m.e.p.	170 p.s.i. (approx.)

Engine (cont.)
Carburettors	4 twin choke Weber
Fuel pumps	2 Bendix electric
Fuel tanks	13 Imp. gallons main with 2 x 9 gal. auxiliaries
Oil tank	15 pints
Battery	12 volts

TRANSMISSION
Clutch	Laycock twin dry plates 8·5in. dia
Gearbox	Z.F. 5-speed all synchromesh
Gearbox ratios	Top 1·00; fourth 1·17; third 1·43, second 1·77; first 2·50
Final drive	Spiral bevel, standard ratio 3·51. Options 3·00, 3·22, 3·40, 3·78, 4·00

CHASSIS
Frame	Steel backbone type
Brakes	Girling discs F and R
Suspension:	
Front...	Double wishbones, coil springs and Armstrong adjustable dampers
Rear ...	Wishbones with single lower radius arm, coil springs and Armstrong adjustable dampers
Wheels	Lotus cast magnesium, centre lock, peg drive. Rim widths: F 5·5in., R 7·0in.
Tyres	Dunlop R6, F 6·00 x 13in., R 7·00 x 13in.
Steering	Rack and pinion

MANUFACTURERS DIMENSIONS
Wheelbase	7ft 10·5in.
Track F and R	4ft 5in.
Overall length	13ft 9in.
Overall width	5ft 8in.
Height (to top of screen)	2ft 2·5in.
Ground clearance	4·5in.

which, incidentally, is made within the factory, consists of a deep central backbone which in cross-section is a symmetrical trapezoid, the upper flange being 6in. wide, the lower 9·5in. wide and the depth 12in.; material thickness is 18 s.w.g. (0·048in.). This member also forms the main fuel reservoir for inside it is housed a bag type fuel tank provided with the necessary anti-surge baffles and having a capacity of 13 gallons. There is provision for two auxiliary tanks each holding 9 gallons, accommodated in each body sill below the doors. The total fuel capacity is thus within the limit of 140 litres permitted in this class of racing.

At the front end, the frame terminates in a transverse member of deep box section. To this the front suspension assemblies, comprising fabricated double wishbones with adjustable telescopic dampers and co-axial coil springs, are bolted directly. In the left-hand section there are apertures for the pedal linkages and the steering column, which connects to a forward-mounted rack-and-pinion assembly. The right-hand section of the front member is completely enclosed to contain the 15 pints of oil for the engine lubrication system.

Aft of the cockpit rear bulkhead, the backbone frame member opens out into two symmetrical box section and tapering tuning-fork-type arms. At their extremities, they are joined by a boxed bridge section above and an angle iron cross-member below. The upper bridge structure forms a mounting point for the power unit and to it the rear suspension assemblies are attached. Each suspension unit consists of an upper wishbone having a screwed adjustment for camber; at the lower end there is a single transverse arm and a long forward-facing radius arm. The wheelposts, as at the front, are made from aluminium castings.

Girling disc brakes, mounted at each wheel, are used front and rear; the wheels are machined from magnesium castings, provided with driving pegs and fastened with a centre-lock nut. Tyre sections are truly enormous, being 6·00-13in. at the front and 7·00-13in. at the rear, the rim widths being 5·5in. and 7·0in. respectively; Dunlop R.6 tyres will be used. The spare wheel is mounted centrally and in a near horizontal position in the nose of the car. It acts as an air deflector for the twin coolant radiators mounted obliquely forward of the frame front cross-member.

A glass-reinforced plastic body will be used for each version of the car, but the one currently on exhibition at the Racing Car Show is a prototype constructed in aluminium. It is planned to sell these cars at between £2,500 and £3,000, which is extremely cheap.

Team Lotus will race two cars in selected events, the drivers being Clark and Gurney. There will be many more around, however, for several have been ordered already by private entrants in this country and America. Colin Chapman is still sticking to his resolution not to enter a car again at Le Mans after his disagreement with the organizers in 1962, but it is quite probable that one of the new cars will compete in that race as a private entry.

LOTUS THIRTY

The Cheshunt-Dearborn combine takes the next logical step and blends 289-cu in Ford power with the latest sports/racing chassis

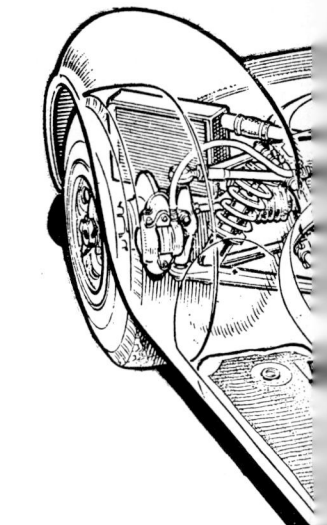

THE LATEST LOTUS sports car is certainly the most exciting one yet. It is evolutionary rather than revolutionary by Cheshunt standards—since his virtual abandonment of multi-tubular frames Colin Chapman shows signs of reaching a period of design stability, although this may be only temporary. Like the Lotus Elan, this model has a glass-fiber body and a central backbone chassis frame but is turned end for end to accommodate a 4.7-liter 350-bhp Ford V-8 engine at the back. In some ways it can be thought of as a derivative of the Indianapolis Lotus which had a basically similar engine; in suspension layout it resembles both this and the F-I car far more than most of the sports range. With an unladen power/weight ratio approaching 500 bhp/ton and a maximum speed which wind-tunnel tests suggest may be well over 200 mph, it should be more rapid than any of the single-seaters on some fast circuits.

The chassis is shaped like a tuning fork, bifurcated at the back to contain the V-8 engine. The central backbone, fabricated from 16-gauge steel sheet, forms an enormously rigid box of trapezoidal section 6-in. wide at the top, 8.5-in. at the bottom and 10.5-in. deep, although its sides continue downward for another 1.5 in., forming the sides of an inverted channel which carries two water pipes, two oil pipes, the brake and clutch hydraulic lines, the throttle cable and the wiring harness. Into the tube is inserted the flexible rubber bag main fuel tank which holds 13.5 gal. and this is supplemented by similar flexible tanks holding 9 gal. each in the fiberglass box-section members which run below the door sills of the body, bringing the total capacity to the maximum allowable figure of 31.5 Imperial gal.

The central tube is joined to a front cross member of similarly massive proportions containing the clutch and brake master cylinders on one side and another flexible bag to hold some three to four gallons of oil on the other, the V-8 engine being converted to dry sump lubrication. This engine is a Shelby-modified version of the 4.73-liter Ford Fairlane power unit and not to be confused with the one used in the Indianapolis Lotus 29; the latter was specially made of light alloy, this one retains the normal cast-iron block and crankcase, although mechanical tappets replace hydraulic lifters and mixture is supplied by four 48-mm. double-choke downdraft Weber carburetors.

This engine, of course, has a two-plane crankshaft and, although it is therefore capable of being balanced to very fine limits, no attempt has been made to bolt it solidly into the chassis. The rear mounting, a rubber bush in the gearbox cover, is held in the channel section bridge piece which joins the chassis side extensions and supports the rear suspension.

A special twin-plate Laycock diaphragm clutch of 8.5-in. diameter transmits the enormous torque to a ZF 5DS 20 gearbox—like the F-I box a much-modified descendent of the ZF commercial vehicle range but fitted with five very close ratios. The spiral bevel final drive is in unit with the gearbox, it has a limited slip differential and there is a choice of six ratios varying between 3 and 4 to 1; even the highest of these gears will only allow about 175 mph at the rev limit so that an even higher one may be needed on occasion if its theoretical speed capabilities are to be realized in practice.

Very large diameter Metalastik couplings take the place of inboard universal joints in the half shafts. These perform the triple function of cushioning drive shocks, allowing angular shaft deflection and, because they permit something like an inch of axial movement, act as frictionless splines. Similar couplings have been used on most recent Lotuses and were only omitted from the Indianapolis car in favor of much more expensive Saginaw universals because it was impossible to find room for rubber couplings of adequate size.

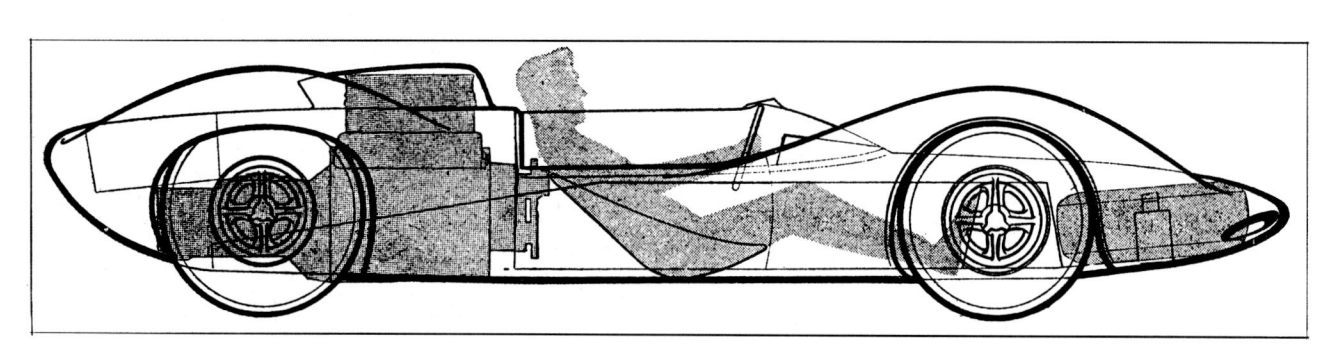

Most Lotuses have very soft suspension and very limited ground clearance, a combination which makes it advisable to bring the bump rubbers (often of Aeon hollow cushion type) into operation early in the upward suspension stroke and thus produce a rapidly rising spring rate. In the Indianapolis car it was found that an extremely powerful engine in a very light car could produce quite a considerable nose-up pitch angle when accelerating hard even at very high speeds and, of course, a reversal of this angle when braking. With variable rate suspension these changes of trim affect the handling by altering the ratio of front/rear roll stiffness, by changing the wheel camber angles and by modifying high-speed aerodynamic lift effects and, although spring rates have not yet been settled, it is likely that the Lotus 30 will be considerably harder sprung than most previous models to minimize these effects. A similar trend may be expected in the very powerful Grand Prix cars of 1966 onwards.

As the drawing shows, the rear suspension design follows current racing Lotus practice, with outboard Girling 11-in. disc brakes, cast magnesium alloy hub carriers and 2° of negative camber on each back wheel. The rear roll center has been kept low (about 2.5 in. to 3 in. above ground level) in order to reduce weight transfer on corners, but otherwise, although a considerable rearward weight bias may be expected, no particular efforts have been made to build in understeer. Roll understeer has been avoided because geometrical roll-steer effects of any kind are inimical to high-speed stability on the straight.

Many cars with all-enveloping low-drag bodies have had extremely limited steering lock but the Lotus finds room under its wheel covers for 35° of movement. Control is by an Alford and Alder rack and pinion of Triumph pattern; steering geometry is arranged with considerable regard to structural convenience and none to Ackermann—because in racing nearly all the cornering is done on the outer wheel, and the direction in which the inner one is pointing is of little concern. The castor angle is 5°, the camber 1° negative and the front suspension is of ordinary double transverse wishbone layout with Armstrong coil spring/damper units.

Even for a Lotus the body is exceptionally low. The top of the windscreen is only 26-in. high, 5 in. lower than the rear wheel covers and 4 in. lower than the front ones so that the view to left and right will be rather obscured. Otherwise it is certainly not a small car, with its overall length of 13 ft 9 in. and width of 5 ft 8 in. Much of this is accounted for by overhang of the light fiberglass body, which is molded in one piece, trapped in place by the front suspension mountings and supported by light cross members at intervals. The whole chassis frame is fed into it through the large engine compartment opening in the tail.

From two very small oval entries in the nose cowling, air flows into a sealed plenum chamber and can only escape through the two small radiators, 8 in. x 15 in., one in front of each wheel arch. The spare wheel lies flat in the nose.

At the time of going to press, many of the design details remained to be finalized, so that even in prototype test form it is likely that there will be departures from this description. Before it makes its first appearance in competition (probably in the spring) further modifications may be necessary. Recent Le Mans history has shown that the fastest cars, such as the Ferraris, become intensely critical to aerodynamic lift and pitching moments at speeds approaching 200 mph, and the Lotus will be lighter than any of these.

REPRINTED COURTESY OF THE MOTOR, LONDON

Having won the 1963 Formula One Manufacturers' Championship, and having started a design revolution at Indianapolis, Lotus now is setting out to dominate large-capacity sports car racing. The means to this end is a long, low projectile which is fitted as standard with a 350-bhp version of the 289-cu-in Ford Fairlane V-8 engine. It should be a worthy successor to the Mark 19. Even with the cast-iron Fairlane engine, it weighs only about 1400 lbs, which gives it a power to weight ratio of around 4.0 lbs/bhp, or 5.1 lbs/bhp with driver and a full load of fuel. It is also extremely low: the height to the top of the windshield is only 26.5 inches, with front and rear fenders respectively four and five inches higher. However, it is possible that the size of the front fenders could bring the center of pressure too far forward, and also that they might have an adverse effect on visibility.

One of the most surprising features of the Mark 30 is the use of 13-inch wheels. They are fitted with a new type of wide-section Dunlop R-6 tire—6.00 on 7-inch rims at the front, 7.00 on 8.5-inch rims at the rear. The speed potential of this car, certainly over 200 mph with longer gearing, could well lead to overheating problems—in regard to braking as well as engine cooling. There is also a possibility of front-end lift at high speed, but a model is being wind-tunnel tested at present, and any necessary modifications will presumably be incorporated before the car goes into production.

The chassis is of the backbone type, and in principle is similar to that of the Elan. It is made of sheet steel, folded and welded into box section, and consists of a central channel, a front crossmember (which provides mountings for front suspension, steering, radiators, and spare wheel) and "wheelbarrow arms" on either side of the engine, the latter being linked by a removable rear diaphragm which incorporates mountings for the rear suspension and the gearbox. The engine is flexibly mounted, and does not contribute to the overall stiffness of the structure. The interior of the main backbone member is occupied by a 13.5-gallon rubber fuel tank (there are additional 9-gallon tanks beneath each door sill), and extensions beneath it provide for oil and water pipes, fuel lines, brake lines, clutch line, accelerator cable, and electrical leads.

Suspension is by double wishbones and coil springs all around, but at both front and rear, the layout differs in detail from recent Lotus

The inscrutable Colin Chapman, sweeping all before him in '63, turns his attention to the coming unlimited sports car season

LOTUS 30

ENGINE
Water-cooled V-8 cast-iron block, 5 main bearings
Bore x stroke....4.00 x 2.87 in, 101.6 x 72.9 mm
Displacement..................289 cu in, 4727 cc
Compression ratio................12.0 to one
Carburetion...Four twin-choke downdraft Weber
Valve gear...Pushrod-operated overhead valves
Power (SAE)............350 bhp @ 6500 rpm
Torque.................278 lb-ft @ 4500 rpm
Tank Capacity..................37.25 gallons

DRIVE TRAIN
Clutch........Laycock 8.5-inch dry twin-plate
Transmission...5-speed all-synchro ZF gearbox

Gear	Ratio	Over-all	mph/1000 rpm	Max mph
1st	2.50	8.91	10.1	75
2nd	1.765	6.26	14.4	108
3rd	1.43	5.11	17.6	132
4th	1.172	4.17	21.5	162
5th	1.00	3.56	25.2	188

Final drive ratio..3.56 to one standard (limited-slip) 3.00, 3.22, 3.40, 3.78, and 4.00 optional

CHASSIS
Backbone frame fabricated from mild sheet steel
Wheelbase........................94.5 in
Track......................F 53, R 53 in
Length..........................165 in
Width...........................68 in
Height.........................26.5 in
Ground clearance................4.5 in
Curb weight....................1400 lbs
Weight distribution front/rear %........40/60
Suspension: F: Ind, unequal length wishbones and coil springs
R: Ind, double opposed wishbones, lower radius arms, coil springs
Brakes..Girling 10 9/16-inch disc front and rear.
Steering....rack and pinion, adjustable column
Tires........6.00 x 13 front, 7.00 x 13 rear
Revs per mile (rear)..................810

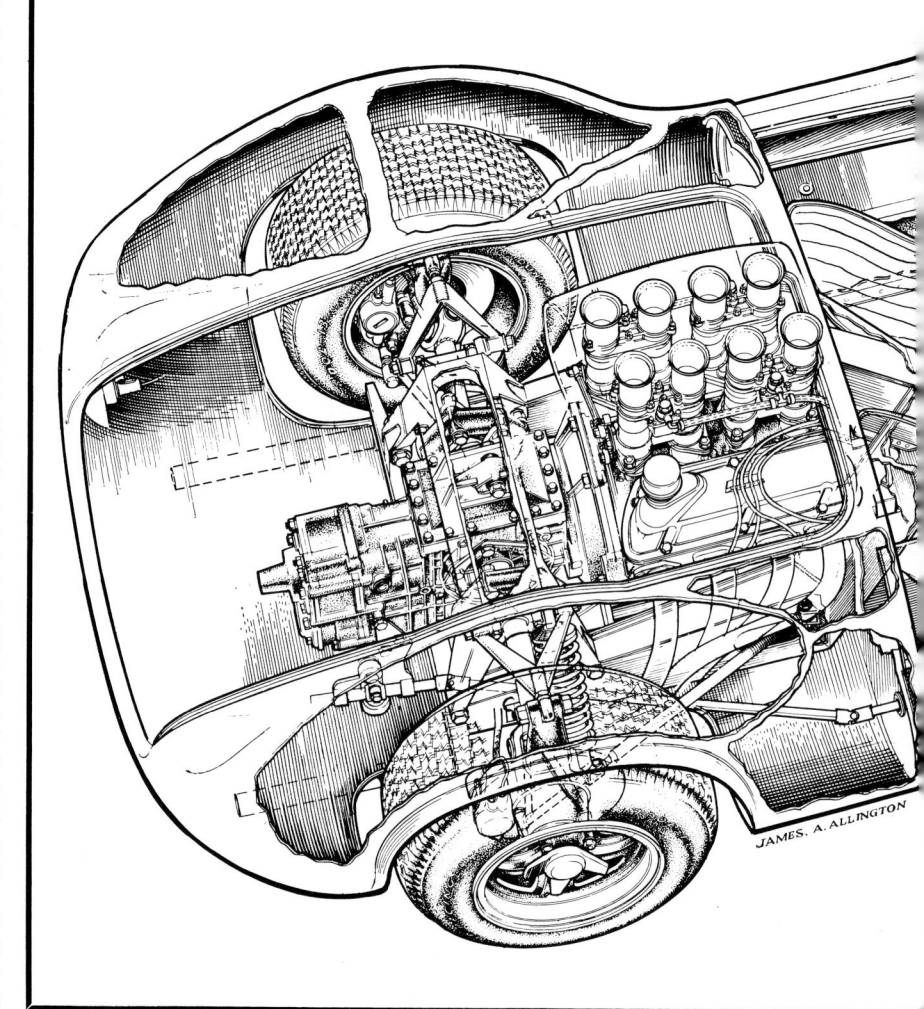

JAMES A. ALLINGTON

Car built for London Racing Car Show was halfway between mock-up and race car.

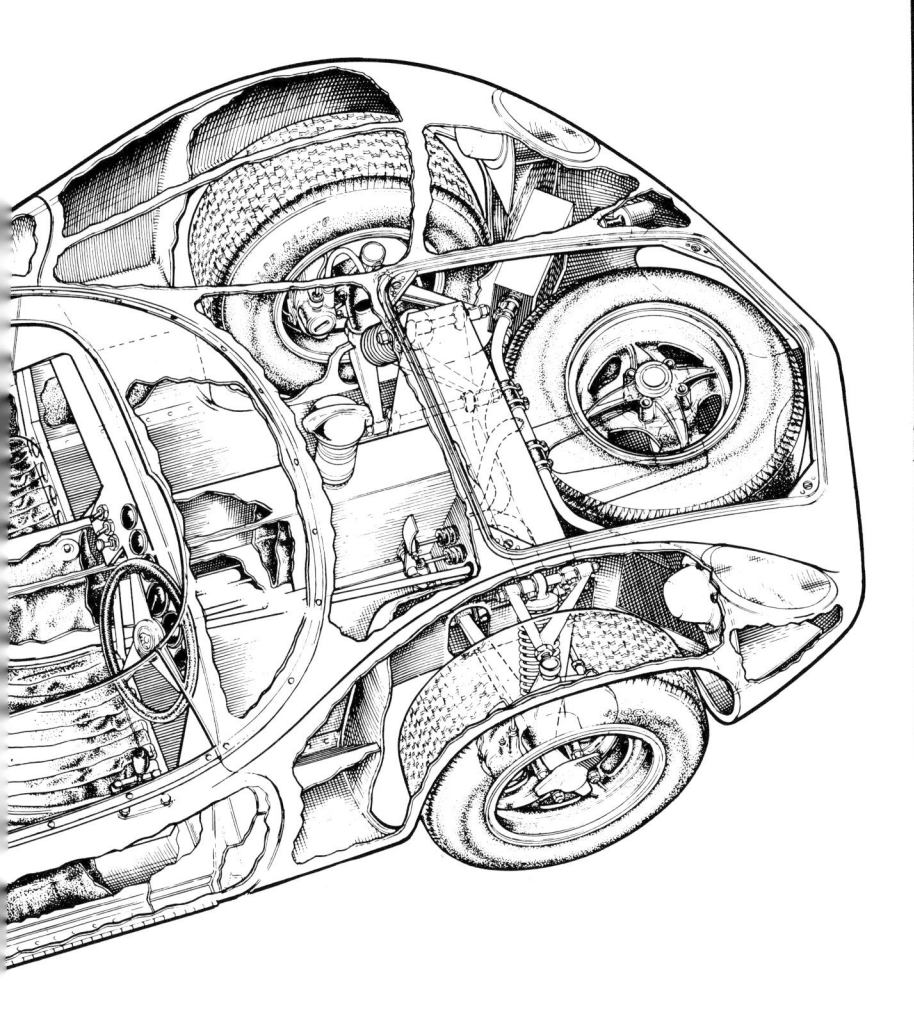

practice. The front wishbones are semi-trailing, and at the rear there is a narrow-based upper wishbone and a wide-based lower wishbone. The inboard pick-ups are laid out to eliminate roll-steer, but this could make the car a little twitchy, especially on high speed corners where most drivers would prefer a degree of roll-understeer. The springs are considerably stiffer, too, to minimize front end lift under acceleration. Roll centers are relatively low, and there is provision for anti-roll bars at both front and rear. Most of the wishbone links are made of folded sheet steel.

The hubs are of the center-lock type, and the cast magnesium wheels are vented to direct cooling air onto the brakes. The latter are 10 9/16-inch discs with Girling BR calipers; twin front calipers may be fitted if the normal set-up proves inadequate.

The standard power unit is the 289-cu-in Ford Fairlane, modified by Lotus to produce around 350 bhp, and transmission is by a new, heavy-duty 5-speed ZF gearbox/final drive unit, with a selection of ring and pinion gears ranging from 3.0 to one, to 4.0 to one. The drive shafts have large diameter Metalastik rubber couplings at their inboard ends.

To obtain the best possible degree of air penetration, the 30 has two small radiators (maybe too small, in view of the engine's cooling requirements) with separate intakes at either side of a slightly pointed nose; the radiators are carefully sealed to ensure that all the air goes through them.

The Mark 30 has not run yet. In fact, the prototype exhibited at the London Racing Car Show was little more than a chassis and body on wheels. However, things can move fast at Lotus, and it is quite possible that the car will be running before these words appear in print. It will probably make its debut at Sebring, driven by Jim Clark and Dan Gurney, and will subsequently be produced at a rate of up to five per week, the price being $8666 in England. A cheaper model with the Lotus-Ford 4-cyl. is also planned.

With 350+ bhp (it is not inconceivable that "works" cars will use aluminum or four-cam engines) the 30 should have a very competitive performance. However, it may not have things all its own way in U. S. racing, for there are likely to be several Chevy-engined cars about which will have more power and not much less handling. Riverside, Laguna Seca, Mosport, etc. should be very interesting this year. **C/D**

JB TRACK TEST
John Blunsden

JCB LOTUS

Above: The 'cow catcher' helps to keep the nose down and improves brake ventilation; speed after the start line was around 125 mph. **Left:** A bit tight above the knees, but bags of room for maintenance. **Right:** Two-in-one centre radiator, leaving ventilated brake discs in the air stream.

Right: Everything on view, including specially pinned top rear wishbones, and seven-row Dunlop R7s.

0

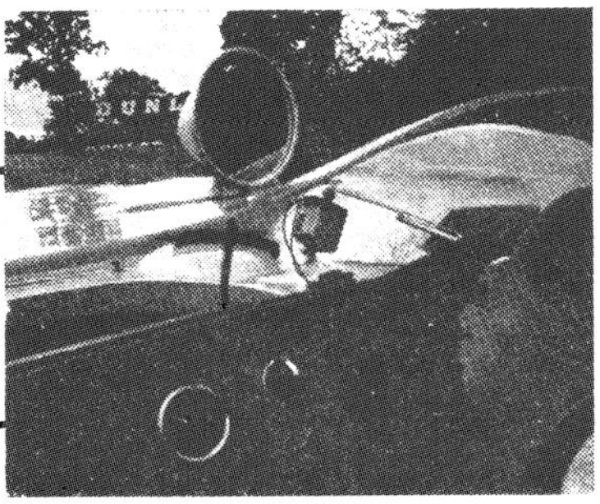

TREVOR Taylor didn't have much luck with it at Brands Hatch on August 30, but the trouble which put him out—local overheating of the rear brakes due to insufficient clearance—was soon rectified, and the JCB Lotus 30 was all ready for track testing on the Club circuit the following morning.

In its brilliant yellow finish this is the easiest of all the Lotus 30s to spot on a race circuit. It is also one of the most heavily modified, and after a somewhat chequered season (which included a fire 'sparked off' by a broken distributor just when the car was running better than ever before) it is now beginning to run very well indeed.

The most obvious modifications concern the bodywork. The 'cow catcher' on the front is a successful attempt to keep the nose down at high speed, while the rear spoiler is the usual Lotus 30 mod aimed at doing the same thing with the tail. But equally important is the splitting of the body horizontally, so that the front section lifts off completely. This is a great improvement over the 'trap door' arrangement of the standard body, and has been possible only because of a complete revision of the cooling system.

IMPROVED VENTILATION

The twin angled radiators have been replaced by a large single 'two-in-one' radiator right down in the central air intake, and the spare wheel has been remounted high up just in front of the instrument bulkhead. As a result, there is a greatly increased airflow to the front brakes, and an auxiliary transverse baffle along the air vent in the top of the body has helped to direct hot air away from the cockpit. The rear-hinged rear half of the body is liberally provided with large air vents.

The car has always been a bit of a tricky starter, and chief mechanic Geoff Payne has completely rewired the electrics, and to overcome the voltage drop from the front-mounted battery has put in a second battery at the back of the cockpit. Both batteries will ultimately be accommodated amidships. The oil cooler has been moved from the nose to the front of the engine bay, just behind the driver's shoulders, and there is provision for a second cooler on the passenger's side should this be necessary.

The deeper tail section of the body has called for some modification to the exhaust system, and the tail pipes and silencers have been cut off and remounted in the reverse position; they now clear the body, provide a different exhaust note, but appear to have had no effect on engine power.

J. C. Bamford's competitions manager, Michael Newton-Hugall, disliked the idea of having to refuel the car from a central filler (a full five-gallon drum takes a bit of hoisting), and so the Lotus 30 now has two separate fillers for each side tank, each of which drains into the central tank housed in the chassis backbone. This also allows only one side tank to be filled, to achieve a slight weight bias to the right, which is desirable on most British circuits. All the fuel lines have been double-armoured.

The production Lotus 30 has tended to suffer from a short brake life, and apart from the extra cooling the JCB car has now been fitted with the excellent new $10\frac{1}{4}$ inch Girling ventilated discs with three stirrup piston calipers.

Comparatively little has been done in the way of chassis alterations, although the rear top wishbones have been pinned right through at their inner ends; previously, there had been a tendency for the retaining circlips to fly off and for the wishbones to distort. To suit Trevor Taylor's driving technique, Armstrongs have provided a set of considerably uprated dampers, but the standard springs and roll bars have been retained, the only modification here being in the attachment of the rear bar on to the hub carrier instead of to the top wishbone. The steering Rose joints seem to wear fairly quickly, and the car is now to be fitted with larger joints to overcome this problem.

153 MPH AT 6,800 RPM

The 13 inch wheels have Dunlop R7 6.00M tyres on 7 inch rims at the front, and 7.00Ls on $8\frac{1}{2}$ inch rims at the back. Pressures were 40 psi front, 42 psi rear, for the test. The standard wheel settings are 1 degree of camber at the front and $1\frac{3}{4}$ degrees at the back at ride level, $\frac{1}{4}$ inch of toe-in at the rear, and 1/16 inch at the front, and the car is set up with 5 degrees of caster. Having been geared originally for Silverstone, the Lotus was running with a potential top speed of 153 mph at 6,800 rpm.

It is quite an electrifying experience climbing aboard one of these cars for the first time, conscious of the fact that even Jim Clark has been known to spin them! It's even more electrifying when you experience the kick in the back which even the 289 cubic inch (4.7 litre) Ford engine can give you in the low gears.

Let me say right away that this is a very difficult car to analyse—at least, I found it so! Initially, I couldn't get the feel of it at all. It went round the corners all right, and kept on the island, but I wasn't quite sure whether it was because I was doing the right thing, or whether it was sheer luck.

Then came stage two in the familiarisation process, when suddenly it all seemed to slot into place, and in fact it didn't seem to be such a difficult car to drive after all . . . until I progressed to stage three. When you start getting down to anything like a time, you suddenly realise that this is a car with a very strong will of its own, and you have to concentrate pretty damned hard to hold it on a tight rein.

A TIGHT FIT

In this case, there were two additional problems. The first was that, though I had more than enough seat and elbow room, and the pedals were just about the right distance away, I was a tight fit under the facia board and steering wheel, and in fact when I hit the brakes, my right leg was wedged quite firmly under the wheel. (Only when it was all over did I realise that I could have brought the wheel closer, which would have at least eased the problem.) This meant, of course, that I had to come off the brakes to double-declutch down, which in turn meant braking that much earlier in the first place.

The second problem was initial stickiness of the throttle. The first opening came as a jerk, although thereafter it was completely smooth, and it tended to make life a bit exciting up at the hairpin, and to a lesser extent, when reapplying the power at Paddock. A sudden burst of power, as might be expected, will bring the tail out in a flash, and you have to be on the ball to catch it.

THE HIGHER THE BETTER

During the test I tried many different combinations of gears for a lap, and notwithstanding the fairly high gearing I came to the conclusion that I was getting the best results from third, fourth and fifth. This was probably due to my limited experience of the car and because I could then go through some of the corners just below the critical engine speed of around 4,500 rpm, at which point it suddenly became a lot more difficult to maintain rear-end adhesion. I figured it was better to go through that much slower and come out smoothly than to scramble through faster and then get all crossed up and out of line. Anyway, the theory seemed to work out, because after it was all over the time sheet proved that the 'one gear up' technique had produced the better times—56.6 seconds.

The benefit was particularly noticeable at Clearways, where, possibly due to the firm dampers, there was a certain amount of lightness at the front end, and it only needed a small amount of power and steering wheel movement to make quite a big adjustment of the car's position on the road; with too much power under these conditions things could get very untidy.

4.7 SEEMED ENOUGH!

Although the 4.7 litre engine is to a certain extent outclassed by the really big power units, I never had the feeling that I could do with a few more horsepower! It really makes the car fly between 4,500 and the peak of 6,800 rpm, and it must have been doing all of 125 mph before the shut-off for Paddock. I thought the chassis rode the undulations of the top straight very well indeed, and despite the soft pedal, the brakes were extremely good, and showed no signs of fade. (The one occasion when I thought I was about to turn sharp left at the hairpin was not due to lack of braking on the nearside front, but because I was steering it with my right leg!)

The ZF gearbox has a bit of a truck feel about it, possibly because of the very robust linkage, but the shift is very quick, and apart from a slight hesitancy when going across the gate shifting down, very smooth. The clutch has quite a light action, and a reasonable length of travel.

Temperatures and pressures remained correct throughout the test, the engine proved 100 per cent oil- and water-tight, there were no rattles, squeaks or groans, and, in fact, it felt like a thoroughly well-prepared car. It was a pity that a minor fault should have eliminated it from the Guards Trophy race, because in other respects it has probably never before been as competitive. It is interesting to find that a number of the most important modifications carried out on this car are in line with the improvements incorporated in the new Lotus 40. In other words, they are really worthwhile, and based on good, sound reasoning. A Lotus 30 with a difference . . . and it's the difference that matters.

Nightmare come true

By reputation the Lotus 30 is the most lethal race car ever made. Tony Dron raced Brian Cocks' example on the Brands Hatch Grand Prix circuit and survived. Photography by Tim Wren

COLIN CHAPMAN had big plans for the 1964 Lotus 30. If it seems a little odd today in its design concept, with a big V8 motor fitted amidships in a chassis that was effectively a Lotus Elan backbone turned round to go the other way, you have to cast your mind back 20 years or more to understand it.

The highly successful road-going Elan had been going well for a couple of years, its fabricated steel backbone chassis proving easy to make, light, rigid and reliable. Meanwhile across the Atlantic Lotus had a very big and important deal going with the Ford Motor Company to race at Indianapolis. The logical extension of that deal would have been a Ford-powered Lotus race programme in the Can-Am series for big sports-racing cars.

In the back of his mind Chapman was also considering the production of a road car based on the Can-Am racer, according to Andrew Ferguson of Lotus. Put all these elements together and the concept of the Lotus 30 makes sense. Where did things go wrong?

Lotus and Jim Clark had made a sensational debut at Indy in 1963, only just being beaten by Parnelli Jones. The great Lotus victory at Indy did not come until 1965, and in 1964 things looked very bleak indeed after a disastrous tyre choice at the Brickyard. The famous affair of the summons to Detroit, at which Chapman and Ferguson faced a kind of boardroom inquisition over the poor showing at Indy, followed. Before the meeting, Chapman had had to find Andrew Ferguson, finally tracking him down at a party at about 3am. Full of confidence, he had said: 'Bring that file on the 30.' The discussions did not go too well, as we know, and they never got around to putting in a pitch for a deal on the 30 or even talking about the car at all. 'After that', says Ferguson, 'the Type 30 took a big dive.' Quite how Lotus achieved everything they did in the mid-Sixties is a mystery to me. The sheer work of building up a world-famous sports car factory and competing successfully in so many branches of motor racing was incredible. There had to be some element that did not come out on top and that was the Lotus 30.

Chapman designed the car and it was built in time for Jim Clark to make its debut at the Aintree 200 meeting in late April, 1964. That great sports-racing expert, the late Bruce McLaren, won the race from Clark, and Jack Sears was third in an AC Cobra roadster. The following month Clark did manage a win in the 30 in the Guards Trophy race at Mallory Park, when Roy Pierpoint was second in the perhaps more fearsome Attila.

Clark never liked the 30, saying he didn't feel safe when driving it. When asked to drive it, he always gave his best but not without little quips like: 'Not that again'. Considering that the spot welds on the main backbone of the chassis were always coming apart, necessitating re-welding after each driving session, Jim Clark's patience was truly saintly.

Fashionable revival

Those spot welds failed because of incorrect temperatures used in the welding of the first works car, but as far as I can tell the production cars were not affected in the same way. The 30 was intended as a production racer, and Lotus Components took it very seriously, investing in expensive sheet metal bending machines and special welding equipment to build the chassis. As many as 23 of the Series 1 and 10 of the slightly improved Series 2 model were made in all. Nobody ever managed to get one going properly and they were little loved at the time.

Today, however, the infamous 30 is enjoying something of a fashionable revival in historic racing circles, partly *because* of its evil reputation. 'I raced a Lotus 30 and lived' seems to be a good line. Certainly, when I told people that I was going to race Brian Cocks' car I was looked at in awe and wonder.

We know of two that are currently being rebuilt, plus Peter Denty's similar Lotus 40. Lotus themselves are giving all the help they can, as ever, but they are not releasing original drawings as they once did because of the proliferation of pirated copies of early Lotus models around these days. One can see their point, and it is unlikely that the new policy will hinder the restoration of genuine old cars in any significant way.

Brian Cocks, of course, is the chief executive of the Historic Sports Car Club and as such it is most appropriate that he should be seen to be racing such a challenging car as the 30, but he offered me the car to drive at the HSCC's International Weekend on the Brands Hatch GP circuit as his official duties took his every spare minute. I got in four laps at Silverstone in the car a couple of weeks before the Brands meeting. Knowing that a car set up for Brands feels awful at Silverstone I was not too dismayed if you see what I mean. The biggest worry was trying to find the right gear, though the linkage was improved somewhat for Brands Hatch. Brian warned me that the car feels *really* dangerous until the brakes are warmed up, adding that decent tyres are not available and care is needed at all times on the hard old rubber that has to be used. It was a bit like a hangman warning me not to slip on the steps.

With positive thinking I made sure we were at the front of the queue for the 15-minutes practice session and I set off on the first lap determined to master the machine and ignore all preconceived notions. After some warming of the brakes I used them a bit harder on the fast approach to Hawthorns Corner. The feeling as the car weaved all over the track was one of being shaken by a large wild animal. 'User friendly' is not a saying that springs to mind when one drives this car, even when the brakes have been warmed up and are working reasonably well. It felt unsafe because one could never be quite sure what it was going to do — quite unlike a typical Lotus. The driving position doesn't help. Although I was well down inside the car and not really uncomfortable the low body sides prevented that illusion of safety which I am accustomed to.

Seconds after taking all this in, a bright orange flash indicated that Tony Goodwin was coming through the field in his little Merlyn Mk 6A on his way to pole. At that moment I realised I was in real trouble: Steve Hitchins also passed me in his Lotus 23, and I ended up third on the grid, a hopeless 3.1sec down on Tony Goodwin's time. 'Maybe, using the five-litre V8's power I shall be able to make a good start and get in front in the race', I thought to myself. Even the anti-roll bars were non-adjustable so the little tweaks I wanted to try were not on. None of them in any case would make up three seconds, so it was just a matter of having to try hard and have a go.

When the lights went to green the car got off to a super start, approaching Paddock exactly level with the Goodwin Merlyn. Finding second is not easy however and though I managed it all right, the time taken changed the picture rather and I was about fourth equal into Paddock behind Goodwin, Hitchins and Tony Thompson's Elan 26R. I was surprised to find that the big car made little impression on the others on the long straight but managed to take third place by passing Tony Thompson on the exit from Stirlings.

Evil mental chuckle

There then followed a very interesting dice with Steve Hitchins' Lotus 23, a dice that did not go according to expectations in any way. Following Steve through what I still call South Bank, because I can never remember the new names for corners, the 30 was right on the 23's tail and I gave an evil mental chuckle thinking about how I would blast past him on the straight. Steve clearly had the same idea and was watching his mirrors closely as he lined up in the normal way for Hawthorns, but the fact was that the big V8-powered car was no faster than the 1600cc Twin Cam along the longest straight at Brands.

As this was Steve's first race on the GP circuit I managed to exploit this by moving up alongside on the exit from Hawthorns on the next lap, finally moving into second place overall as we went into Westfield. Tony Goodwin was well away in the lead and out of sight by this time. Steve followed me for another lap and finally picked me off with relative ease braking for Clearways. That was that, for despite the presence of many backmarkers whom we were lapping, some of whom produced a few exciting moments for us, I found there was no further opportunity to offer a serious challenge to Steve and had to settle for third quite close behind him. Brian had the car checked on a rolling road soon after the race and found it was well down on power with the ignition timing retarded 14 degrees from its correct position.

The race was fun, and satisfying as I don't think I could have made that car do any better, but at least I

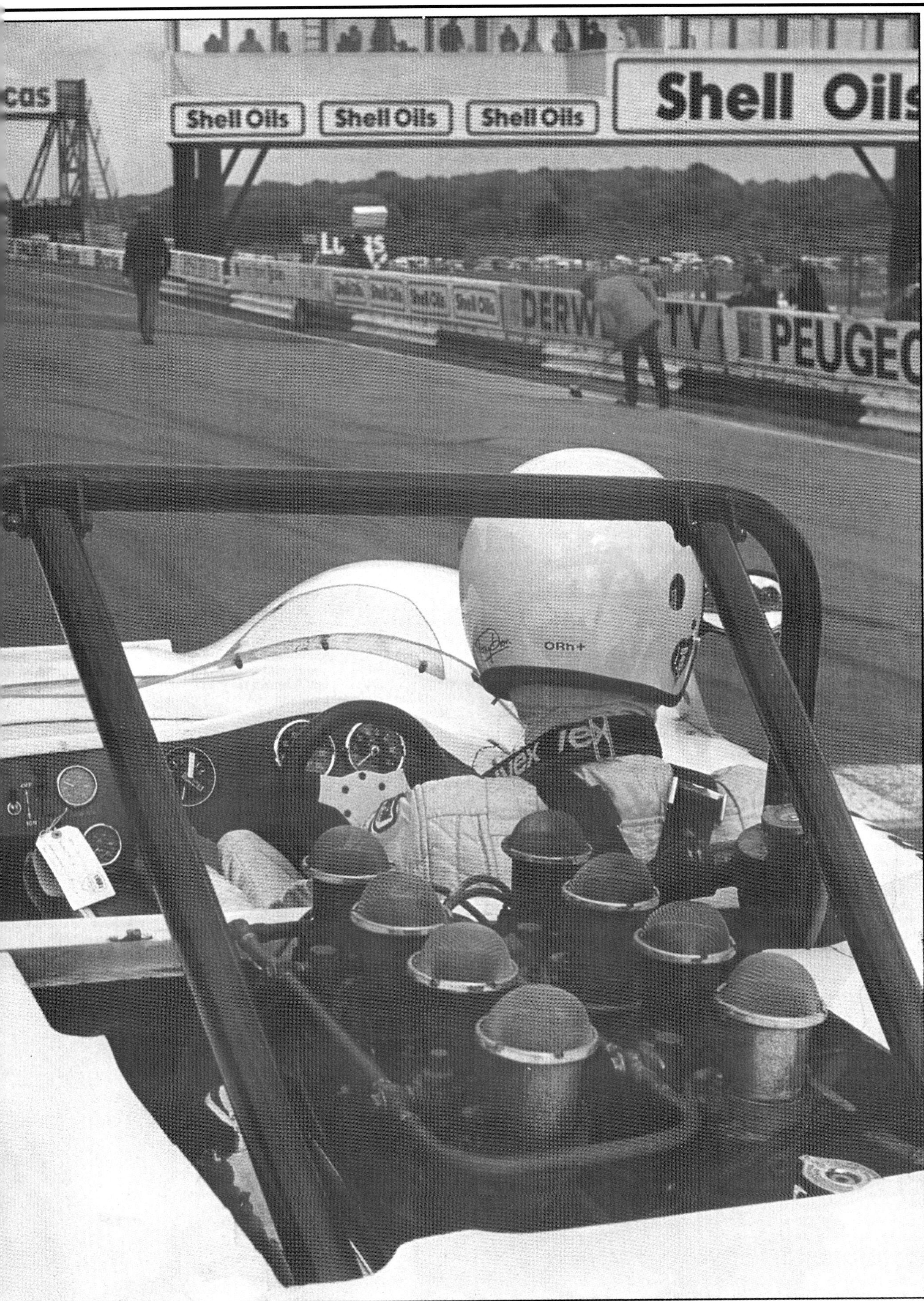
Shell Oils
Shell Oils
Shell Oils
Shell Oils
PEUGE
ORh+

Nightmare come true

know now why the Lotus 30 has such a terrible reputation. The car is nervous when pointed into a corner, and this manoeuvre invariably must be carried out with exaggerated precision. It is also necessary to brake disappointingly early to maintain the optimum exit speed from a corner. If a driver tries to push the car to its limit, like he would with any normal well-sorted race car, the 30 is sure to repay him unkindly. He will spin off regularly.

Late in the corners, with the power being fed in firmly, the car adopts a neutral to slightly oversteering attitude that is normally quite predictable, but the early part of the corners remained a very different matter for me, and once the car went very sideways at South Bank, needing full opposite lock and virtually no power to prevent it from turning round. Quite why it did that I still don't know. It was so far gone that I was thinking of banging the brake pedal hard with my left foot while opening the throttle with my right simultaneously, a desperate measure that has got me out of a spin in such dire straits in the past, but it came back under control on its own in the end.

Far be it from me to have a go at the designer of this car. The driver's function, and that is my training and discipline, is to report to his engineer on what the car is doing and contribute to its improvement in that way so that it can win races. While the driver may have some ideas of his own, it should be the engineer/designer who really knows what's going on, and who can interpret the subjective reports of the driver. Let it be said, therefore, that it would be absurd for me to correct Colin Chapman. Had it been necessary he would have sorted this car, a process that requires time and money, but as we have seen the money was not forthcoming for the 30: it remains thus an unsorted motor car.

As a driver I would like to go through some simple tests in the workshop. I'll bet the camber change in the suspension's normal working movement is horrific. But before getting to that I would like to do some torsional rigidity tests on the chassis itself. With the chassis stiff enough the suspension could be sorted to make the wheels point the right way, or near enough, at all times. Then the car would no longer be a Lotus 30, and it would lose its *macho* status.

In its early days this car was heavily modified by the very professional team which bought it: it was also heavily modified by its drivers, who quite understandably took the quick way of stopping from time to time, but that's another matter.

Chassis number 30-S2-04 dates back to an original purchase by JCB for Group 7 racing in 1964, and it was driven by Peter Sadler and Trevor Taylor in the top sports car races that year and in '65. Over those two years the car was altered so much as to be almost unrecognisable. Peter Sadler crashed it at Oulton Park in '64, while it was crashed and burnt with Trevor Taylor at the wheel in the '65 Martini Silverstone meeting. Each time it was updated and improved with the latest works mods and the capable JCB team's own ideas.

The flowing lines of the original car have been lost in the process but that is no bad thing: maybe it looked all right but that bodywork produced horrendous lift at the front, I am told. It was also difficult to get at the chassis in a hurry. JCB's men made their own improvements and then Peter Sadler, a glutton for punishment it seems, bought the car himself and the bodywork as we see it today is as he left it. It's an endearing feature of all keen race drivers that they feel they can overcome all odds. After that the car was shifted from dealer to dealer, probably as an unwanted condition to many otherwise super deals. In the process it lost its original engine and gearbox but in 1980 Brian Cocks reckoned that his Lotus 23B no longer offered a sufficiently frightening challenge to his driving skills and he was drawn to the great beast.

Captive nuts?

By 1982 he had it well enough sorted out to beat the best 23s in historic racing but it has proved unreliable over the years. He has spent some more money on ironing out the unreliability but is presently up against the aforementioned tyre problem. He knows that if he could lay his hands on some competitive tyres for the 30 it would be worth completely rebuilding the car. In time that is probably what will happen: he has already got the right 4727cc engine and Hewland LG600 gearbox so all the vital parts are there except proper tyres.

A rebuild on a car like this is not to be tackled lightly as the 30 was not an easy car to build when it was new. One mechanic I spoke to who used to build them at Lotus Components described the car as 'an absolute rat bag — nothing fitted. None of the wishbones cleared the chassis and it was covered in captive nuts — and we even had to cut *them* up to get them in.'

The appeal of running such a car today is of course its very difficulty. It's a hard job for the mechanics, I have no doubt, and take it from me it's a challenge to any driver. If you ever see Brian Cocks racing it, may your heart go out to him. If he ever asks me to race it again I would do so with enthusiasm, but I am mad. For the time being I am relieved to be able to cancel the funeral arrangements.

Since 1964 numerous modifications to the original car have changed the flowing lines of the Lotus 30's bodywork. Peter Sadler, one of the drivers for the JCB team which initially bought the car back in 1964, purchased it from JCB and the bodywork today is as he left it

Historic Lotus Register

The Register was formed in 1974 and caters for all Lotus cars built up to 1961 except for the Elite. Detailed records of original build lists and history of the cars are kept by the Marque Registrars plus information on the supply of spare parts. A newsletter keeps past and present owners in contact both technically and socially. The founder of HLR is:

Victor Thomas,
Badgers Farm,
Short Green,
Winfarthing,
Norfolk.
IP22 2EE
Phone: 01953 860508

The Lotus Forty

In mid-1965 Lotus produced their last sports racing car, the Lotus 40. This used a 5.8-litre, Ford V8 engine and incorporated a number of chassis and suspension modifications to improve the previous Lotus 30 that had developed a reputation as somewhat of a handful. American driver Ritchie Ginther dubbed it 'a 30 with 10 more mistakes', and unfortunately this was probably true.

The Lotus 40 was introduced to the press by *Motor Racing* magazine in October 1965 followed by a technical report by John Blunsden in *Sports Car Graphic* in November 1965.

The Lotus 40 first appeared at Zeltweg in August 1965 for the Austrian Sports Car Grand Prix where it retired. This was followed by retirement at the Guards Trophy at Brands Hatch. In the USA a second place was achieved at Riverside but by the end of 1965, and a production of just three cars, Lotus concentrated on Formula 1 and single-seaters. The Lotus 40 was the last sports racing car produced by Lotus.

Graham Capel

LOTUS 40

Intensive development programme planned for 5.8 litre successor to the 4.7 litre Lotus 30

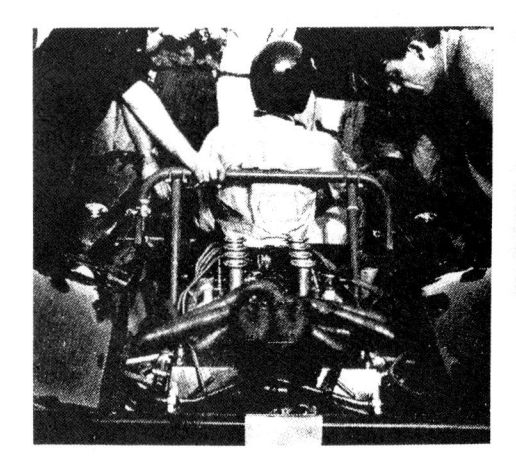

Right: The new 5.8 litre (351 cubic inch) Ford V8 engine fitted to the Lotus 40 has a cross-over exhaust system, and produces around 450 horsepower. Though rear-end maintenance is still through a 'trap door', there is considerably more working room behind the cockpit than on the Lotus 30.

THE Lotus 40 which Mike Spence drove in the Austrian Grand Prix on August 22, and which Jim Clark handled in the International Guards Trophy race at Brands Hatch, on August 30, is the first of a new series of sports cars to succeed the Lotus 30, production of which has now ceased.

A logical development of the earlier car, and fundamentally of the same design, the Lotus 40 is aimed at rival sports cars which, with their 5 to 6 litre engines, have been able to 'blow off' the 4.7 litre Lotus 30 with comparative ease. For this reason, the new Lotus has been designed around a new 351 cubic inch (5.8 litres) Ford V8 power unit, developing in the region of 450 horsepower, compared with approximately 350 horsepower turned out by the 289 cubic inch unit.

Although the body shape is not greatly altered, there is a longer nose to prevent lifting at high speed, and the rear spoiler, which has been found so essential on the Lotus 30, has been incorporated in the new design. There is also considerably improved underbody accessibility, the rear cockpit bulkhead being cut down deeply in the middle to expose the front end of the power unit. The facia shape has also been revised to give the driver more knee room.

The oil cooler has been moved back from the nose, and the intakes are fully ducted to the radiators. The spare wheel compartment has been considerably enlarged, and two batteries are housed beneath the wheel.

Compared with the Lotus 30, this is a considerably 'beefed up' sports car. All wishbones have been increased in size and strength, and new 11¼ inch diameter ventilated disc brakes are fitted alongside the 15 inch wheels, which have 7½J rims at the front and 8½J at the rear.

There is a revised fuel-filling system, individual fillers now being provided on each side of the car in place of the single central filler of the Lotus 30.

About three months of intensive development work has been put in on the new engine which, although developed from the 289, has a completely new block, an inch taller, and is mounted solid in the chassis (the smaller unit was rubber-mounted). The injection system has been modified, bigger inlet manifolds provided, and a revised water system incorporated to allow more water through the block. The exhaust manifolds work on the cross-over system, and the engine has new pistons, rods and crank.

The unit is coupled to the latest Hewland heavy-duty five-speed gearbox, and larger universal joints are used than on the Lotus 30.

The car's performance at Brands Hatch (this was its first appearance with the larger engine) could hardly be described as an unqualified success, but an intensive development programme has been started to get the car race-sorted. One of the problems revealed on August 30 was a lack of rubber on the ground, and so the body is now being drastically cut about in order to accommodate larger tyres. After the none-too-happy experience of the Lotus 30, which initially was beset with development problems, and subsequently suffered by being uncompetitive on engine power, a real effort is to be made to develop the Lotus 40 into a reliable race-winner.

It had been assumed that the new car would take part in the forthcoming Canadian sports car races, but the development programme will not allow this. However, Jim Clark should be in the cockpit of a Lotus 40 when the flag falls at Riverside, on October 30.

My nerves were fluttery and my jaw a jitter as I prepared to climb into Peter Denty's gleaming Lotus 40. Its infamous reputation will never die, thanks to one wag's comment at the Riverside *Los Angeles Times* GP in October '65: "Ten more mistakes than the 30," he quipped. Some say it was Lotus teamster Richie Ginther. Dig deeper in the history books and the message is even louder.

A fearful testing accident at Silverstone late in '66 ended 'Gentleman' Jack Sears' racing career. If major suspension componentry didn't snap, the nose had a habit of imitating a Top Fuel dragster. Said Bruce McLaren of maestro Jim Clark's struggle at Brands in the Guards Trophy: "Like a paper hanger in a storm." After two mighty spins at South Bend, Jimmy finally called it a day when the diff seized, causing another dramatic gyration at Clearways. Hence, you understand, a degree of tension at braving this hunky group 7 'pancake' racer, the biggest-engined Lotus ever built.

But sports-racing cars don't come more seductive than Chapman's rushed effort to catch the V8 pack of Lola T70 spiders and McLaren Elva Oldsmobiles in the class of '65.

Brands '65 – Clark drifts at Clearways

Forgotten forty

Some might say best forgotten, but was it simply rushed development that prevented the fearsome Lotus 40 from making the winner's circle? Mick Walsh braves the action seat of a rare survivor

His production Lotus 30s (all 33 of them), with back-breaking 289 Ford power, were being trounced by most, not to mention the giantkiller Brabham BT8s. And, after the Indy spoils had been claimed in June, attention was focused on beefing up the 'tuning fork' backbone and deploying 5.7-litres of Detroit iron to whip the 30 (now 40) up the grid. Only three were eventually built and within eight months the remains of the works cars were found in *Autosport*'s classifieds in a Lotus Components Ltd box ad – 'fresh' from America at £3750 each. For £100 less you could have purchased The Chequered Flag's Cobra 289 racer the very same week.

As the only 40 left this side of the Atlantic, Peter Denty's 10-year restoration project not surprisingly turned heads last April when it made its first public outing at Silverstone. Gleaming in ivy green with a demon yellow centre flash, and riding on mean black Lotus four-spoke wheels with three-eared spinners, it looked sensational. The Sperex-yellow exhaust manifold hugged the Mathwall-prepared 302cu in Ford V8, its army of Webers looking like a pair of lazy pythons. Tubular artistry.

Few sports racers match the aura of the mid-sixties big bangers. These swoopy open-cockpit muscle machines were a swansong before the wedge school, an era when artists like Michael Turner were called upon to style the new McLaren Elva Olds. The 40's bold, undulating form was the vision of Lotus' New Zealand stylist Jim Clarke, before Len Terry attempted to make the controversial one-piece body practical. Accessibility was never a strong consideration on any Lotus sports car, and the 30/40 was no exception – particularly with its closed underbody.

Despite the side door, which previously closed over a saddle gas tank, the wraparound screen is slung low enough to clamber over into the snug black plastic bucket seat. Once strapped up in the modern five-point Willans race harness, I took stock of the cockpit. The seat is flat on the body floor, the backbone box section of the chassis riding high in the centre. The dash is spread into a stressed body section – much like an aircraft fuselage brace. A large hoop is cut out for the footwell (as well as extensive holes for further lightness) and the metal edges are protected by thick foam padding. The pedal layout is typically offset, and outstretched legs are conveniently supported at the back of the knee by the body section. The flat, low driving position still puts your eye level over the screen, so buffeting is guaranteed. A small, thick leather-rimmed Moto-lita wheel is ideally positioned for a relaxed racing pose, while the stubby gear selector sits close on the right, its polished linkage running back to the protruding Hewland box.

Under your right foot the throttle cable runs back to the volume control. The crucial tacho hides behind the wheel redlined at 6500rpm with a cheeky 'Mooneyes' logo on the original Jones dial. To the left are scattered Smiths water temperature, oil temperature and oil pressure gauges complete with red warning light, fuel and ignition flick switches and action key.

The view forward is as voluptuous as a plastic form can get – tall, curvy wing forms with flat centre deck and offset bulge for extra pedal height. Centre and to the right are towering mirror stalks. In all, sparse and efficient, but oozing charisma from every rivet. Too new perhaps to feel heroes had once planted their famous butts here, but the fastidious finish is better than anything the works rushed to the grid.

There's nothing like cranking up a full-race V8 to get the adrenalin pumping. Flick on the ignition and fuel supply, prime the legion of Weber chokes and then churn the big four-bearing crank over on the key until it cracks into life behind. Flex the right

Walsh straps up

JOHN COLLEY

339

Left: 302 V8 powerhouse with hugging tubes. Above: big disc and four-spoke

The 40's steering is very, very light. And the harder you accelerate, the lighter it gets as the nose lifts. The lack of aerodynamics on what is left of the club straight is even more unnerving as the 40's dragster punch pushes you up to an easy 130mph before hauling back for the Brooklands left hook. Intoxicating it is, as I settle down and use the V8's pounding torque for a lazy last lap. With the Ford heavyweight yowling behind the shoulders it could be the '66 Martini Trophy as we sweep through Woodcote for the last time. For a V8 it feels cammy, with power (about 340bhp at the rear wheels) charging in at 4000rpm. An easy car to drive at six-tenths but full bore would be another situation, I suspect.

Historic racer Mike Littlewood, who is regularly entrusted with Peter Denty's testing, took over for a few quicker laps and came in frustrated with the brakes. But otherwise he felt enthusiastic about the infamous 40, having taken it as close as he dared to the limit: "Once you get over the initial lightness and drive harder the chassis feels right. Such cars have the confidence – it just takes longer for the driver to build up his. But with this, the harder you push it, the better it gets. Although there is lift on the straight, it doesn't wander and so far feels safe," Mike explained.

"I've raced 23s a great deal, and never really liked them. Chassis flex and an unpredictable rear end always tried to catch the driver out, but so far the 40 feels better balanced. If we could find the right group – mixing it with Piper's Ferraris and some GT40s – I'd relish the chance to find out what it can do."

Certainly the record books show the 40 was on the pace straight out of the box. Even on the bumpy Zeltweg airfield circuit for the Austrian GP in August '65 it broke the lap record (Gurney's F1 time) by 2secs. Still with the ZF gearbox, Mike Spence retired on lap 13 due to overheating.

But a combination of Chapman's weight-saving philosophy ('if it makes it out of the pit lane it's okay'), the back-breaking iron Ford block, and lack of serious development, made it a loser from the word go. Even Clark's genius couldn't counter its fragile makeup.

Thanks to the dedication of Peter Denty, this glorious loser has been reconstructed. Regarded as chassis No 1, it was the car Spence debuted at Zeltweg and which Clark later spun three times at Brands before a last works outing driven by Ginther at Riverside in the *LA Times* GP. The close-cropped LA racer claimed it, "the most evil thing I've ever driven." Privateer Bob Walters acquired the car from the works sale and after several seasons' club racing, used the engine, gearbox, exhaust and various other components

foot and that rumbustious idle clears to a carnivorous roar. Heady stuff, just sitting still in the pit lane. Peter Denty briefs me to take it easy for a couple of laps for the oil to warm up as I buckle up my ancient Bell open-face skid lid. The paint is still tacky on the peak – in honour of Clark, I sprayed it white just the night before. With a final adjustment of the goggles, Peter gives the all-clear in the pit lane, and I graunch the lever into first, haul up the clutch and we rumble on to the circuit.

First observations during the initial warm-up laps are the finger-light steering for such a brutish-looking machine, and unnerving brake pedal travel before the big discs grab. As we gain speed, this pumping-up becomes a real handicap, particularly for rapid down-changes. With the laboured Hewland LG500 'truck' box you really need to keep the cogs moving, so heel-and-toeing is essential. But the deep pumping up of the anchors means wasted time before stepping back on the gas. Since the first test at Snetterton the brakes have been a problem with this 40. Strong when they do haul, the problem seems to lie with the balance between master cylinder and calipers but on only its second shake-down run, the car's still in the sorting stage.

Although the brake problem unnerves me, the car's handling is quite the reverse: through the right-handers on the Luffield complex and charging round Woodcote, the 40 feels stable and confident. On the fast turn-in for Copse it changes direction superbly, particularly considering the weight of the car. Towards the end of the short session the lightness of the steering almost becomes irrelevant, and on tighter bends the throttle balances out slight understeer.

Chisel nose with essential air dam

for his Concord F5000 car – a dreadful project that even upstaged the 40, Walters recalls: it's an affair he'd rather forget.

Back in the early seventies Peter Denty was searching for a Hewland LG500 gearbox and tracked down the remains of the 40 in Maidstone. The engine had just been sold for a road-going Capri, but he eventually acquired the delapidated remains of the car which were delivered to Mallory Park where: "Everyone just fell about laughing. We dragged it home, pushed it to the back of the workshop and forgot about it."

But by 1984, Denty set to on restoring the project. The chassis reconstruction was the most time-consuming job. Using thicker gauge metal than standard, the sections were spot welded up as before but with nickel input to stop the dreaded splitting. During the 10-year project several Lotus 30s came to Denty's Norfolk shop for restoration, providing valuable reference. For the body moulds another 30 in Germany was used, while the No 2 Lotus 40 (Clark's second-place *Times* GP car) was tracked down to New Jersey and the owner Peter Regner generously allowed Denty to study it extensively.

The suspension was remade but again improvements were carefully considered, knowing how the big brakes snapped the original wishbones. Instead of Chapman's original Z-section design, a square profile was felt preferable: "In general the 40 is a very road-orientated design in the way it was hung together," Peter considers.

Mathwall Engineering prepared a Ford 302 (4.8-litre) to GT40 spec, as a 5.7-litre Cleveland proved difficult to find, and only one centre fuel tank was fitted. The project was finally finished last year but an engine failure caused withdrawal from the HSCC enduro at Snetterton last October. Hopefully we will see the car out in anger this summer.

Above: with inspiring turn in, the 40 lent Mick confidence at Silverstone's complex. Right: Walsh and Mike Littlewood discuss braking dilemma. Below: low seat and high backbone of cockpit

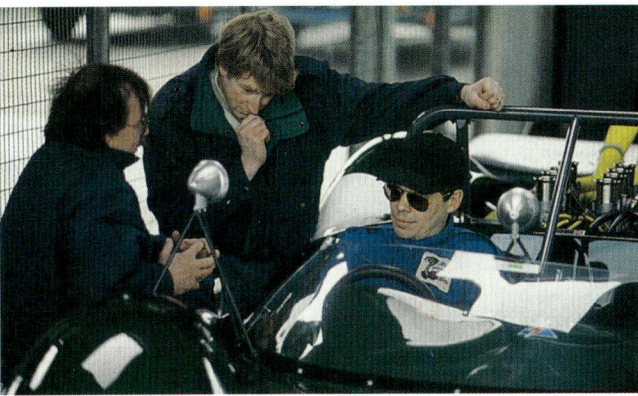

Did the Lotus 40 deserve its infamous reputation as a truly evil racer? Doug Nye discusses

For those with long memories I'll get it out of the way right here at the beginning. Yes, Richie Ginther really did describe the Lotus 40 as being "...the Lotus 30 with 10 more mistakes...".

Now Richie was able to make that point with feeling, as he had just driven one of the two works cars in the big *Los Angeles Times* GP at Riverside, California, in 1965.

There is a theory among some of Colin Chapman's former employees that the man really to blame for his celebratedly 'difficult' sports-racing cars – the front-engined Lotus 17, and the big Ford V8 mid-engined 30 and 40 – was Eric Broadley, of Lola Cars.

Team Lotus designer Len Terry told me: "Colin had been pretty miffed when Eric's new Lola 1100 replaced the Lotus 11 as the car to beat, so he responded with the 17 to outdo the Lola – but the strut-type suspension he insisted upon just couldn't work. It was a disaster.

"Then, while Lotus was running the Indy programme with Ford in '63, Colin angled for what would become the Ford GT contract, but Broadley got it instead thanks to his Lola GT. I think Colin set out to prove that Lotus could build a lighter, better, faster sports car using the Ford V8 than anything Lola could do. And the result was the backbone-chassied Lotus 30 which was structurally so frail its backbone chassis 'oil canned' and took on a set twist when they first ran – and then the 40 followed which looked even worse... and it was in effect all just to prove a point."

In fairness, the three Lotus 40s built were never properly developed to achieve their paper potential. In effect the design was prepared to put right what had been proved wrong with the 21 Lotus 30 Series 1 sports-racing cars built in 1964, and the 12 much-improved Series 2s which followed for '65.

While the basic Type 30 concept involved a grown-up version of the Elan's successful fabricated-sheet backbone chassis, it was reversed in layout to place an iron-block, initially 289cu in – 4.7-litre – Ford V8 engine behind the cockpit, driving via a ZF 5DS25 transaxle. An exceptionally low and rakish flat-roofed concept study had been prepared for a Lotus 30GT but the model emerged as an open Group 7 'big banger' sports-racing car which demanded Jim Clark's virtuosity to

Team Lotus clearout from Autosport

TEAM LOTUS offer for sale their LOTUS FORTY works cars

As raced by Jim Clark and Richie Ginther at Riverside in 1965, just returned to England. Fitted 5.8 litre (351 engine) Ford fuel injection engines 450 b.h.p., cross over exhaust systems, Hewland LG.500 gearboxes, 15" wheels, 11¼" ventilated disc brakes, option of tyres. Spares to customer's choice extra. **Price £3,750 each, fully race prepared.**

Contact: LOTUS COMPONENTS LTD.
DELAMARE ROAD, CHESHUNT, HERTS Tel: Waltham Cross 26181

make it a race winner. Its backbone frame flexed, its original brakes were far too small within their tiny 13-inch wheels and the iron-block engine was too heavy and under-powered against McLaren's 4.5-litre alloy-block Oldsmobiles.

For 1965 the 30 Series 2 was much improved with 15-inch wheels enclosing larger, ventilated brakes and with Tecalemit-Jackson-injected V8s delivering around 360bhp, but the engine's iron block remained a major disadvantage, since Lola was now running its T70 with 5.4 Chevy V8 power.

Consequently Chapman adopted enlarged 5.3-litre Ford V8s for the works 30 S2 in an attempt to offset the smaller Olds engine's weight advantage. And with development engineer John Joyce, a stronger backbone chassis was designed to carry an even larger 351cu in – 5754cc – unit on T-J fuel injection with a cross-over exhaust system feeding two upswept exhaust megaphones projecting through the tail deck. This 450bhp unit drove via a new Hewland LG500 transaxle, and the car now boasted meaty 11¼in ventilated disc brakes and an even more floridly curv-aceous 30-type body with air-pressure relief vents in its enormous wheel humps.

The prototype Lotus 40 made its debut in the Austrian GP sports car race at Zeltweg Aerodrome in August '65, with Team Lotus number two driver Mike Spence immediately qualifying on pole, 2.1secs faster than Dan Gurney's F1 record. He led for 13 laps on the bumpy concrete course until the 40's engine overheated.

Back in the Lotus plant at Delamare Road,

Cheshunt, the car was returned home and hurriedly prepared for the Guards Trophy at Brands Hatch on August Monday – where even Jim Clark spun it twice in heat one before stopping with the gear linkage adrift. In heat two its brakes gave out and the car subsided against the bank at Clearways.

Lotus-Cortina team driver Jack Sears had done much testing on the works 30 S2 and had raced it once at Silverstone when Colin Chapman invited him to carry out some tyre testing on Jimmy's 40, ready for shipping to Riverside, California, for the major *Los Angeles Times* GP. Jack liked the 30 S2: "Quite a pleasant and pretty car and the fastest thing I had ever driven up to that time..." and as harvest was over he agreed to test the 40 at Silverstone on September 24.

"We were running back-to-back tests between Dunlop and Firestone tyres. I remember we ran Dunlops in the morning and then Firestones after lunch. I found the Dunlops quite progressive, giving plenty of warning as they broke away but it was quite difficult to maintain the car in a slide or drift, it was certainly very twitchy – but *very* powerful and *very* fast. The Firestones then appeared to give more grip but much less warning as one approached breakaway.

"On one lap through the fast left-hander at Abbey it just let go and floated out to the right-hand verge. I got onto the grass there and then the tail came round and it spun back across the road to the left-hand side... the next thing I recall is waking up in the ambulance on the way to hospital..."

The 40 had careered into the left-side bank and rolled, injuring 'Gentleman' Jack's left arm and neck so badly he would spend 14 weeks in hospital and another nine months regaining fitness. He consequently missed the entire 1966 racing season, and early in '67 he decided against a comeback. His racing career was over...

The car that ended it was rebuilt at Cheshunt and shipped with two sisters to Riverside, the green-and-yellow works cars for Clark (race number 1) and Richie Ginther (race number 30) plus a pale-blue car for Holman & Moody, to be driven by AJ Foyt.

However, during Riverside testing, H&M mechanic/part-time driver Bob Tattersall shunted the Foyt car. In the race Ginther retired early with transmission problems. Hap Sharp's Chaparral won, while one report read: 'It was no secret that the three Lotus 40s that arrived at Riverside were anything but ready to race, their newness and undoubtedly accounting for the fact that they were not set up as well as they might... even Clark was heard muttering some very unkind things about the untested car...'

He still finished second – 9secs adrift of Sharp, 18secs ahead of Bruce McLaren.

Holman & Moody then rebuilt their car for Foyt's use in the Bahamas Speed Week at Nassau where it reputedly 'just fell to pieces', on lap three of the Governor's Trophy race.

In April 1966, Lotus Components offered its two works 40s for sale; 'Just returned to England' ex-Riverside, 'option of tyres and spares to customer's choice extra – £3,750 each, fully race prepared.'.

And off they went into obscurity. In truth the undeveloped Lotus 40 was never given a chance to demonstrate its potential – leaving it, as Jack Sears recalls: "Hard work – a very highly-strung and twitchy car..."

Left: maestro Clark in the 40 at Riverside. Above: rare sight of two 40s – Clark and Ginther chase Hap Sharp's Chaparral in *LA Times* GP. Right: Clark looks unconcerned about hub failure at Goodwood with Lotus 30. Below: first outing of 30, Aintree 1964

TECHNICAL REPORT:

LOTUS 40

There were many troubles with the Lotus 30 ... the Lotus 40 attempts to solve them all, and may just do it.

BY JOHN BLUNSDEN

AFTER NEARLY TWO SEASONS OF INDIFFERENT FORTUNE, the 4.7-liter Ford-powered Lotus 30 is being replaced by another car — a Lotus 40 — of similar basic design, but updated to accommodate the newer and more effective 5.8-liter (351 cubic inch) Ford powerplant.

The first public appearance of the new car was in the Austrian Grand Prix (held this year for sports and GT cars on the bumpy Zeltweg circuit on August 22), when Team Lotus driver Mike Spence drove it with a 289 Ford installed. It retired with minor engine trouble while leading.

A rush workshop program then took place at Cheshunt to re-equip the car with the larger unit, and have it ready in time for practice before the International Guards Trophy (see pages 34-35) at Brands Hatch, on August 30. But the team hit troubles, and after a panic session, the car was rushed down to the circuit to enable Jim Clark to qualify it during the final five minutes of practice.

The car was unsorted, and a handful. In the race (before which certain of the more obvious problems were dealt with) Clark had a busy time, and eventually retired. The Lotus 40 clearly needed what the Lotus 30 failed to get — an early development/test program by the factory — to make it fully competitive with its current rivals. This has now been put in hand.

Although a logical development of the Lotus 30, the new car has many detail differences. There is a longer nose section to prevent lifting at high speed, and the rear spoiler (fitted by so many private owners of '30s' to keep the back end stable) has been incorporated in the new design. Chassis accessibility is considerably improved, and although the power unit is still reached through a 'trap door' panel, there is a useful cutaway of the rear cockpit bulkhead to give extra working room. The dashboard has also been cut away at the bottom to give much needed extra knee room.

The oil cooler has been brought back amidships from in the nose, although the twin batteries are still up front, beneath the spare wheel, which now has a larger compartment, being a 15 instead of a 13 inch size. The air intakes are fully ducted to the radiators, and brand new 11¼-inch diameter ventilated disc brakes are fitted all around. The wheel rim widths are 7½ inch at the front and 8½ inch at the rear.

The fuel filling system is completely revised, two fillers now being provided on each side in place of the single central filler on the 'production' Lotus 30. The two side tanks each drain into the central tanks contained in the chassis backbone.

About three months of intensive development work has been put into the 351 powerplant, which has a block one inch taller than the 289. Apart from obvious changes, such as different pistons, rods, and crank, the newer unit has a modified injection system, a revised water system allowing more coolant through the block, bigger inlet manifolds and a cross-over exhaust system. Unlike the 289, which was rubber mounted, the 351 is solidly mounted in the chassis. It is mated to the latest heavy-duty Hewland gearbox.

One of the first results of the Brands Hatch experience has been the conclusion that insufficient rubber is getting on to the road, and the hacksaws have been busy on the body above the wheel wells, making room for larger tires. It may well be that by the time the car next appears in public, it will have lost some of its smoothness in profile, but Lotus campaigners will gladly trade a bit of style for added competitiveness. All the indications are that this newcomer from Cheshunt is unlikely to have the long and painful adolescence which was suffered by its immediate predecessor.

The new Lotus 40 first ran at the Austrian GP, then at the Guards International at Brands Hatch, above. It will be in the U.S. this Fall.

Feeling that the 4.7-liter (289 CI) Ford engine of the Lotus 30 was under-powered, Colin Chapman is using a 5.8 (351 CI) in the new 40!